IET HEALTHCARE TECHNOLOGIES SERIES 35

Blockchain for 5G Healthcare Applications

IET Book Series on e-Health Technologies – Call for Authors

Book Series Editor: Professor Joel P. C. Rodrigues, the National Institute of Telecommunications (Inatel), Brazil and Instituto de Telecomunicações, Portugal

While the demographic shifts in populations display significant socio-economic challenges, they trigger opportunities for innovations in e-Health, m-Health, precision and personalized medicine, robotics, sensing, the Internet of Things, cloud computing, Big Data, Software Defined Networks, and network function virtualization. Their integration is however associated with many technological, ethical, legal, social and security issues. This new Book Series aims to disseminate recent advances for e-Health Technologies to improve healthcare and people's wellbeing.

Topics considered include Intelligent e-Health systems, electronic health records, ICT-enabled personal health systems, mobile and cloud computing for eHealth, health monitoring, precision and personalized health, robotics for e-Health, security and privacy in e-Health, ambient assisted living, telemedicine, Big Data and IoT for e-Health, and more.

Proposals for coherently integrated International multi-authored edited or co-authored handbooks and research monographs will be considered for this Book Series. Each proposal will be reviewed by the Book Series Editor with additional external reviews from independent reviewers. Please email your book proposal for the IET Book Series on e-Health Technologies to: Professor Joel Rodrigues at joeljr@ieee.org or joeljr@inatel.br

Blockchain for 5G Healthcare Applications

Security and privacy solutions

Edited by
Sudeep Tanwar

The Institution of Engineering and Technology

Published by The Institution of Engineering and Technology, London, United Kingdom

The Institution of Engineering and Technology is registered as a Charity in England & Wales (no. 211014) and Scotland (no. SC038698).

The Institution of Engineering and Technology
Michael Faraday House
Six Hills Way, Stevenage
Herts, SG1 2AY, United Kingdom

www.theiet.org

British Library Cataloguing in Publication Data
A catalogue record for this product is available from the British Library

ISBN 978-1-83953-325-9 (hardback)
ISBN 978-1-83953-326-6 (PDF)

Typeset in India by Exeter Premedia Services Private Limited
Printed in the UK by CPI Group (UK) Ltd, Croydon

Contents

2   Ethical and legal aspects of using blockchain technology for 5G-based health-care systems   35
Shashank Srivastava, Richesh Gupta, Prateek Pandey,
and Ratnesh Litoriya

8   Architectural framework of 5G-based smart healthcare system using blockchain technology   **197**

M. Kiruthika, Vaishali Gupta, T. Poongodi, and B. Balamurugan

16 Detection of COVID-19 and its symptoms using chest X-rays for health care 451

Jayendra Kumar, Arvind R. Yadav, Anumeha, Shivam Kumar, and Anukul Gaurav

About the Editor

Dr. Sudeep Tanwar (M'15, SM'21) is currently working as a Professor of the Computer Science and Engineering Department at Institute of Technology, Nirma University, India. Dr Tanwar was a visiting Professor at Jan Wyzykowski University in Polkowice, Poland and the University of Pitesti in Pitesti, Romania. Dr Tanwar's research interests include Blockchain Technology, Wireless Sensor Networks, Fog Computing, Smart Grid, and IoT. He has authored 02 books and edited 13 books, more than 250 technical papers, including top journals and top conferences, such as IEEE TNSE, TVT, TII, WCM, Networks, ICC, GLOBECOM, and INFOCOM. Dr Tanwar initiated the research field of blockchain technology adoption in various verticals in 2017. His h-index is 43. Dr Tanwar actively serves his research communities in various roles. He is currently serving the editorial boards of Physical Communication, Computer Communications, International Journal of Communication System, and Security and Privacy. He has been awarded best research paper awards from IEEE IWCMC-2021, IEEE GLOBECOM 2018, IEEE ICC 2019, and Springer ICRIC-2019. He has served many international conferences as a member of the organizing committee, such as publication chair for FTNCT-2020, ICCIC 2020, WiMob2019, member of the advisory board for ICACCT-2021, ICACI 2020, workshop co-chair for CIS 2021, and general chair for IC4S 2019, 2020, ICCSDF 2020. Dr Tanwar is a final voting member for IEEE ComSoc Tactile Internet Committee in 2020. He is a Senior Member of IEEE, CSI, IAENG, ISTE, CSTA, and the member of Technical Committee on Tactile Internet of IEEE Communication Society. He is leading the ST research lab where group members are working on the latest cutting-edge technologies.

Preface

The healthcare industry has revolutionized from 1.0 to 4.0, where Healthcare 1.0 was more doctor-centric, and Healthcare 2.0 replaced manual records with electronic healthcare records (EHRs). Healthcare 3.0 was patient-centric, and Healthcare 4.0 uses cloud computing (CC), edge computing (EC), fog computing (FC), Internet of things (IoT), and telehealthcare technologies to share data between various stakeholders. However, framing a secure technique for Healthcare 4.0 has always been a challenging task. An in-secure technique for Healthcare 4.0 may lead to the healthcare data breach where hackers can gain full access to patients' email accounts, messages, and reports. On the contrary, a secured technique for Healthcare 4.0 can provide satisfaction to all stakeholders, including patients and caregivers?

Nowadays, most 5G Healthcare systems are built using centralized client-server, cloud servers, robust database, and the Internet. Two major limitations of the 5G Healthcare centralized infrastructure have been observed; (i) the single point failure, which can potentially topple the entire system, and (ii) the lack of trust between the entities involved in the system. To overcome the aforementioned limitations, decentralized architectures can be used for peer-to-peer (P2P) communications among the nodes. However, these systems have several privacy and security concerns, opening the doors for intruders to launch various attacks. Many applications are there using 5G Healthcare solutions to better the service, like Efficient prescription medication management, large image file transfers, virtual visits with doctors, augmented reality (AR) used in staff education and training, etc. The future is that 5G drive Healthcare deployment and maintain security, Healthcare devices will utilize blockchain technology. To secure a 5G Healthcare network, many blockchain solutions are available. Few operate on fast, trusted networks, and other work faster on unreliable networks. If new Blockchain operates efficiently and rapidly over unreliable networks, then 5G-enabled Healthcare devices can utilize the same in real-time. Security may not be the only task for utilizing blockchain and can take part in data distribution, as it works faster. However, as per the editor's knowledge, an independent mathematical proof for fast solutions is still unavailable. After the availability of the mathematical proof, a perfect environment is possible where fast and trusted nodes have been connected in the network and can take the benefit from 5G by using specific cloud or fog layers.

So, a blockchain-based decentralized system is one solution, which can store information in an immutable manner and requires no centralized database. In addition to this, it also provides a way to track and execute transactions among various participants in a trusted environment. With the usage of strong encryption with public-private key pairs, blockchain also provides high levels of security to its participants. Some decentralized applications (DApps) are available in the market, developed using healthcare devices and blockchain. Using 5G Healthcare infrastructure, the 'information sharing' of devices can be done using embedded sensors and sufficient network connectivity. The omnipresent network connectivity, which is very difficult to achieve in the modern era, can be achieved from 5G. These technologies decrease the latency by 100 times as compared to 4G. Moreover, integrating blockchain with 5G Healthcare enables the maintenance of an immutable ledger of information exchange transactions. By achieving this in a decentralized P2P manner, the 'middle-man-attack' can be eliminated, which allows the users to share without relying on a trusted third party.

This book is the first-ever "how-to" guide addressing one of the most overlooked practical, methodological, and moral questions in any nations' journeys to maintain Privacy and Security in the Healthcare sector: How reliable and real-time remote monitoring can be achieved? How hospitals and health systems can optimize their infrastructure and workflows to make the most of 5G promising use cases? Explore most promising aspects of 5G for healthcare industries? How can 5G help hospitals and health systems do better? What should I do if I think my information has been compromised? It differs from other published books. It includes a detailed framework to maintain security and privacy in 5G Healthcare Services using Blockchain Technologies and comparative case studies concerning various performance evaluation metrics, such as privacy preservation, scalability, and Healthcare legislation.

The book is organized into four sections; the first section is focused on 5G healthcare privacy and security concerns, which includes five chapters. The second section discussed the healthcare architecture and emerging technologies, which has four chapters. The third section discussed the role of Artificial Intelligence for data security and privacy in 5G healthcare services, which includes four chapters. Finally, the last part illustrates the adoption of blockchain in various applications of 5G healthcare with well-structured five chapters.

Section-1 Introduction to 5G Healthcare Privacy and Security Concerns

The chapter "Security and Privacy Requirements in 5G Healthcare" focused on various futures of 5G technology and compared with the traditional communication system. Moreover, it also focuses on the challenges that arise with the 5G network system when used in the healthcare sector. The technical challenges that arise in 5G technology and how to manage security and privacy when using 5G in the healthcare sector with IoT are also explored in this chapter.

The chapter "Ethical and Legal Aspects of Using Blockchain Technology for 5G-based Healthcare Systems" systematically presents the issues introduced by advanced technologies in healthcare systems. This chapter also discusses the possible solutions and their impact on the healthcare system in a broader context. Moreover, this chapter focused on the Ethical and Legal aspects of Blockchain and 5G with the amalgamation of healthcare. Various challenges are also discussed in this chapter, yet to be solved, such as executing complex cryptographic algorithms while using power as efficiently as possible.

The chapter "Blockchain-based 5G enabled Healthcare System: An analysis of Security & Privacy Issues" presents utilizations of blockchain in different fields, methodically dissects the security of each layer of the blockchain and conceivable digital assaults, explains the difficulties brought by the blockchain to organize management, and sums up research progress in the assurance innovation. This chapter is an audit of the current security of the blockchain and will successfully support the turn of events and improvement of security advances of the blockchain.

The chapter "Enhanced Blockchain Technology Associated with IoT for Secure and Privacy Communications in 5G" proposed a secure communication associated with blockchain technology, which will provide a secure automated communication based on IoT. The 5G networking is a new technology that can transmit the data at a higher pace than one gigabit in step with second and with reduced latency than the modern-day Long-Term Evolution (LTE) network. In this proposed framework, IoT offers various clever gadgets, ranging from all home equipment and televisions to every day and even aesthetic items, to connect independently to the network to alternate statistics, updates, and symptoms. Thus, the performance analysis shows that the framework with IoT automation requires low latency and excessive speed community, which the 5G community can provide.

The chapter "5G-driven Radio Framework for Proficient Smart Healthcare Institutions" expansively analyzed and compared the advanced waveforms such as filter bank multi-carrier (FBMC), Non-orthogonal multiple access (NOMA), Universal filter multi-carrier (UFMC) concerning the current waveform scheme known as orthogonal frequency division multiplexing (OFDM). Further, the requirements of the smart hospital are comprehensively studied. Further, the detection methods are analyzed. The simulation outcomes of the study reveal that the throughput, spectral efficiency, and data rate of the advanced waveform are better than the OFDM system, and the beamforming technique is suitable for advanced form.

Section-2: 5G Healthcare Architecture and Emerging Technologies

The chapter "Traditional Vs. Blockchain-based architecture of 5G Healthcare" aims to research traditional and blockchain-based architectures of 5G healthcare to identify the disadvantages of the individual and the merits of their integrations. Moreover, this chapter explored the blockchain-based architecture of 5G healthcare and have identified key advantages about traditional architecture and their future application. This chapter also presented the capabilities of blockchain technology and its importance to healthcare, analyzed the benefits of blockchain, implementation in healthcare. Decentralization, immutability, transparency, and security have been identified as the main advantages of the blockchain-based architecture of 5G healthcare about traditional architecture. As a result of the research, it was revealed that each of these technologies alone could not become a full-fledged network technology to ensure the capabilities of smart health care, and only their integration will help to use all the possibilities of modern medicine fully.

The chapter "Integrating Blockchain Technology in 5G enabled Smart Healthcare: A SWOT Analysis" provides a newfangled review and SWOT (Strengths, Weaknesses, Opportunities, and Threats) analysis of combining 5G and Blockchain technology to exemplify the building of a secured and proficient healthcare application platform. This chapter covers a holistic investigation of Blockchain over the real-time applications in healthcare and thus finds the possibilities of leveraging the 5G network over use-cases to make smart healthcare/medicare use cases. Finally, this chapter exemplifies SWOT Analysis to incorporate Blockchain and 5G technologies for simple, empathetic integration of both technologies in the smart healthcare sector.

The chapter "Architectural Framework of 5G based Smart Healthcare System using Blockchain technology" explored features of blockchain like immutability, distributed nature, and integrity, makes it appropriate for the healthcare industry. Blockchain can be applied in various grounds of the healthcare industry like remote patient monitoring, Tele-surgeries, maintaining Electronic health records, clinical trials, and medical research, pharmaceutical supply chain management, etc. Privacy and security of data are assured when blockchain is integrated with the healthcare system. When the number of users using smart devices expands, the network must handle huge amounts of data in various types and sizes. The prevailing communication technologies fail to fulfill the intricate and dynamic needs of the smart healthcare system. On the mission of developing communication technologies, 5G is expected to cater to the needs of smart healthcare applications with its broad set of salient features and advanced design. The future smart healthcare systems are expected to be a mixture of the 5G, smart IoT devices, and blockchain technology.

The chapter "Application of Millimeter Wave (mm-Wave) based Device to Device (D2D) Communication in 5G Healthcare" proposes an application of mm-Wave based D2D communication for the implementation of efficient and secure Wireless Body Area Network. This chapter aims to elucidate the application of D2D communication in the implementation of a 5G-based real-time health monitoring system. Special emphasis is given to the exploitation of the mmWave band for D2D communication. This chapter covers the major features of 5G that make it a frontier of innovation in the entire wireless communication industry and make it different from currently available technologies. This chapter includes the Internet of Medical Things (IoMT) applications in remote health monitoring of various common diseases. The last section of this chapter deals with the technical challenges encountered while implementing 5G bases healthcare systems.

Section-3: AI for Data Security and Privacy in 5G Healthcare Services

The chapter "Security and Privacy in Health Data Storage and its Analytics" aims to develop an understanding of various Data analytic tools. Then, it discusses the various storage methods of healthcare data, new technologies used for the security of health care data, and various privacy-preserving methods for healthcare data. Moreover, this chapter presents the security of healthcare-related data with the introduction of the Healthcare data security life cycle and various technologies used to secure healthcare data. Further, it describes the various models such as the 5GHealthNet and the Health chain for health care data security. The Health chain uses blockchain technology for securing healthcare data. Finally, it discusses the privacy of healthcare data with laws developed by various countries.

The chapter "Artificial Intelligence and Machine Learning Techniques for Diabetes Healthcare" explores the Artificial Intelligence and Machine Learning methods with virtually endless applications in the healthcare industry. With the help of FastAI librariies, anyone can create a design model using fewer programming codes. This CNN model is effective for the image processing model trained with the GPU system provided by Google Colab. The pre-compiled neural network will help in getting a timely and accurate result. This proposed model classifies images of diabetic retinopathy images with the normal retina. This CNN can assist ophthalmologists in clinical diagnosis. Regular and good research in health care has always been in demand, which helps for more accurate prediction for diagnosis and prognosis of many diseases.

The chapter "Analytics for Data Security and Privacy in 5G Healthcare Services" discusses security risks and privacy worries at each level of the IoMT architecture design. The security of every level on the internet of things architecture needs to be used simultaneously. Significant additional analysis is necessary to develop a detailed protection mechanism for the whole IoT architecture. Conversion on a taxonomic framework of market cap internet of thing-based sensors enhances sensor-centric knowledge plus usability understanding. It offered threat analysis to help law-making by assisting owners in understanding and quantifying shelter on the internet of healthcare issues and discusses privacy and security issues regarding sensor info and methods to eliminate them.

The chapter "Contactless Attendance System: A Healthcare Approach to prevent Spreading of Covid-19" proposed a framework that uses a powerful class participation method utilizing face acknowledgment strategies. The proposed framework will have an option to stamp the participation through face Id. It will identify faces using a webcam and afterward perceive the appearances. After the acknowledgment, it will check the participation of the perceived understudy and update the participation record.

Section-4: Applications of Blockchain for 5G Healthcare

The chapter "Blockchain-based Smart Contracts for E-Healthcare Management 4.0" facilitates the stakeholders involved in the medical system to deliver better healthcare services. Moreover, this chapter discusses the adoption of blockchain technology in the E-healthcare sectors. The proposed system is a mix of secure record storage alongside the granular access rules for those records. It makes such a system much simpler for clients to utilize and comprehend. Additionally, the system proposes measures to guarantee the system handles information storage as it uses the off-chain storage system of IPFS. What's more, the job-based access likewise benefits the system as the clinical records are just accessible to the trusted and related people. This likewise takes care of the issue of data asymmetry of an EHR system.

The chapter "An Amalgamation of Blockchain, Internet of Medical Things and 5G Technologies for Healthcare 4.0" performed an extensive study of IoMT, 5G, blockchain literature. The taxonomy of concepts and the highlights from each paper are tabulated. The number of papers reviewed technology-wise is depicted as a pie chart. Then, a comparative analysis of curated papers with specific parameters is presented. The research issues, implementation challenges, and future directions are illustrated. Finally, a case study of a healthcare solution implementation has been discussed.

The chapter "Detection of Covid-19 and its Symptoms using Chest X-Rays for Healthcare" discusses computer vision applications and a deep learning approach to detect an outbreak of the influenza virus "2019-nCov", caused by the novel coronavirus. Moreover, Chest X-ray modality has been investigated in this chapter to detect CoVID-19 infected person(s) and understand its impact on a human chest and respiratory system. Further, convolutional neural networks (CNN), a deep learning technique, have been used to comprehend the correlation of coronavirus on the human respiratory system using the Chest X-ray data of human patients. The proposed model has reported CoVID-19 detection accuracy of 99.59% with attention and 99.92% without attention.

The chapter "Security and Privacy control in 5G -enabled Healthcare using Blockchain" focuses on the issues and challenges of 5G enabled smart healthcare are discussed. Also, the security and privacy concerns of 5G-enabled smart healthcare are analyzed, and the existing solutions are compared. Moreover, comparative analysis with various blockchain-enabled healthcare solutions with 5G is covered with open challenges and issues.

The chapter "M2M for Healthcare with Blockchain Security Aspects" provides a brief outline of the M2M+-based heterogeneous connection, technology, its impact on healthcare industries, and the challenges they face concerning security. This chapter also discusses the evolution of the M2M applications. These M2M architectures are concentrating more to dominate non-cellular technologies, which are purely recommended for future M2M services. Finally, for efficient, optimized, and reliable communication, all the above-stated challenges need to be worked upon, including the challenges for complete the end-users right from the regulation of organizations, companies of network tools and consumer devices, network operatives, to the application sources.

The editor is very thankful to all the members of IET Publication, especially Prof. Joel J P C Rodrigues, Series Editor, and Ms. Nicki Dennis, Books Commissioning Editor, for the given opportunity to edit this book.

Dr. Sudeep Tanwar, Ahmadabad, Gujarat, India

Chapter 1

Security and privacy requirements in 5G healthcare

Nagendra Singh[1] and Yogendra Kumar[2]

Technologies are predominantly meant to give solutions to critical problems related to the well-being of human life. Whenever, a new technology comes into existence, it affects human life, directly or indirectly. Cellular communication technology is one of the most life-changing technologies to have come into existence and has soon got acknowledged worldwide. After the invention of 4G technology, people have started to move into the digital world. The fourth generation of wireless communications is also used in many industrial, business, and personal applications. Many countries are using this technology in health-care services very effectively. But the fourth generation of wireless communications has a major issue, of lagging of high-speed bandwidth Internet connectivity. The health-care sector is very essential and important for each and every country. But due to the nonavailability of health-care resources and low-speed Internet, many countries are finding it difficult or next to impossible to accomplish the smart hospital dream. Even in rural areas, the different health-care systems are using the conventional system, because of which they are facing lots of problems in the monitoring of the health-care system and it is getting more difficult day by day. The fifth-generation mobile network is a new global wireless standard after 1G, 2G, 3G, and 4G networks. The 5G enables a new kind of network that is designed to connect virtually everyone and everything together including machines, objects, and devices. As 5G technology provides a very high Internet connection speed and requires less time to receive or send big data, it is largely suitable for the health-care sector. The fifth-generation mobile network provides a very high bandwidth of Internet connectivity access and is very tranquil to maintain. Therefore, it can be used effectively and efficiently to maintain the data of all patients, and the medical team can easily monitor it online 24×7 from any place and there would be no need for them to visit the hospital again and again for routine check-ups. This technology also overcomes the problems associated with voice- and video-calling communications. So it becomes easy for the medical staff to monitor

[1]Department of Electrical Engineering, Trinity College of Engineering & Technology, Karimnagar, India
[2]Electrical Engineering, MANIT, Bhopal, India

all the systems from one place and this enables them to take action quickly as per the requirement of the patients. In this paper, we emphasize on various future uses of 5G technology and try to compare it with the fourth generation of wireless communications. Second, we also tried to compile the challenges that arise with the use of the 5G network system in the health-care sector. The third section deals with technical challenges associated with the 5G technology itself. Our fourth objective is to explain about the security and privacy in healthcare sector when using 5G technology and the last part, the fifth one aim on to how cover the various application of 5G with Internet of things (IoT) in the health-care sector.

1.1   Introduction

Health-care services are a very important and essential need of humanity. Most hospitals are operating with the old system and are waiting to be upgraded in our country. In metro cities, most private health-care centers try to maintain the new generation health-care system, but their services are very costly and out of reach for citizens.

Some government health-care centers also have advanced techniques, but the uses are limited only to a few diseases. If seen in the rural areas, the situation is also not good. Even the rural areas do not have any good and established health-care centers. Only some government hospitals are working in rural areas. Most private centers are available in the city area only because they want to earn money by providing the service.

With the advent of new technologies in the health-care sector, it has become easier to heal patients suffering from critical diseases. Hospitals have many types of patients, and their records are generally managed on paper. So if any expert away from the city or country wants to see the report and the treatments given to the patients, it becomes very difficult. Also, patients living in the rural areas are unable to reach the city health-care centers, so it is challenging to take care of such people. This example shows that without changing the technology, it is difficult to provide health services to all around the country without any interruption [1].

The conventional health-care management system is very complicated and needs to be upgraded so that proper care can be taken of all patients as per their requirements. The latest technology helps to provide treatment facilities using a wireless system, and if the number of patients increases, there is no problem for a doctor. He can manage his time from home because there is no need to go anywhere, and so it also saves time.

With the invention of the latest technology used in the health-care sector, living standards have improved and people live more comfortably. A recent report given by the World Health Organization shows the average life of the people is now increasing, and it is approximately 71 years at present. Globally, it is possible because of advanced technology used in the health-care sector. In earlier times, the death rate of children during childbirth was very high, and the risk to the mother was also very high, but nowadays, the death rate of newborn babies is less. Still, medical services have not spread to all the countries due to unbalanced distribution and a lack of resources. It is a big issue for any country to manage medical services for smooth treatment of patients [2].

The main challenge is how to supply sufficient medical resources at all health-care centers in time so that the expert uses them properly and people get benefitted from these available facilities. For resolving the problems discussed above, tele-medicine is the best choice. Telemedicine helps high-speed communication, such as audio calls, video-conferencing, messages to remote locations, and the urban areas, to supply and deliver medical resources from a centralized location to big hospitals and other hospitals situated in rural and remote areas. A telemedicine system can be used to send available resources for treatment of existing patients. However, it can-not help detect or diagnose psychological and other critical diseases [3].

Over the past decade in the 4G environment, computing, control, storage, and networking using the Internet, a centralized unit provided all services as per the requirements. With the increasing number of IoT devices, the traditional 4G wire-less technology cannot meet the efficiency, speed, and latency for IoT requirements. Therefore, 5G has been designed to satisfy the demands of future IoT devices and connect a more significant number of devices than 4G. 5G stands for fifth-generation cellular wireless, which will be a standard change to provide very high carrier fre-quencies with massive bandwidths [4].

Innovation developments and financing are driven by business rules, for exam-ple, benefit, proficiency, and quantifiable profit. It is critical to investigate how these will impact advancement, assessment, and execution of 5G medicinal services. The development of 5G innovations will perhaps improve the patient's health through applications, work processes, and continuous distribution of the health-care material in all the hospitals without delay. When connecting with a 5G network, the main difficulty of maintaining accurate data with privacy protection depends on the use of the network in medical services or in any other applications. If used in other applica-tions, it will be difficult to maintain privacy and security in medical services, so it is better to use only the medically regulated 5G network for health-care services [5].

When applied in the clinical field, 5G technology with IoT shows incredible potential to empower distant medical procedures. In the present situation, remote surgery is very effective for patients who are far away from the city or stay in a remote location and also for patients with mental ailments, depression problems, children with autism, sleep-deprived patients, and so on. A difficult issue is how to apply the best approach to distantly organize effective mental therapy for the patients [6].

The development of versatile systems will fulfill the new requests for improved execution, transportability, flexibility, and effective vitality of novel system admin-istrations. 5G versatile systems also have new systems administration ideas to improve above-mentioned highlights [7] additionally.

Security has become an essential worry in numerous media communication enterprises today as the danger associated with breach of security can have the worst results. Primarily, as central and vigorous progress will be related to the 5G system, personal data will move at all levels in the remote infrastructure of the future. In the

Table 1.1   A comparative analysis of state-of-the-art approaches

Reference number	Contributions
1	Explain the computer tools used in health-care services for providing support to the patients.
2	The authors of this article proposed radio frequency identification techniques that help manage the relationship of health-care industries. This technique will help to handle patients' data efficiently.
3	This article explains 5G technology and how it is different from the other old communication technologies used in recent years.
4	This article aims to encourage the development of effective cloud computing, data on smart clouds that can support the IoT operation, and help to operate in a machine learning system, and is useful in analytics systems.
5	This work proposed the intersection of larger Tactile Internet and the concept of 5G technologies. They also suggested the requirement of a technical key and the architecture of the Tactile Internet system.
6	A CPSS domain is recommended for the activity conducted in the group. This technique improves the accuracy of the data and supports a multi-model system.
7	Discuss the security system of the 5G network. They focused on the many security policies and provided solutions to handle such policies.
8, 9	How the use of IoT, big data, artificial intelligence, and 5G improves patient treatment and service quality of the health-care service proposed in this work.
10	What is the necessary architecture required for 5G suggested using potential technologies like SDN and NFV?
12	This work explains the potential and opportunities of the blockchain system when using 5G. Also discussed are the many challenges that arise during the use of blockchain with 5G.
14	Provide an overview of long-term evolution (LTE) and worldwide interoperability for microwave access for 5G technology.
19, 20, 21	These articles focus on the use of the mobile networking system in the health-care monitoring system. It is a very efficient system that can interconnect health-care services to patients directly.
23	This article evaluates how all people get the same benefit of health-care services at the same cost.
27	The m-Health technology converted from an academic concept to a practical contest all over the word very rapidly is discussed in this article. M-Health services mainly depend on sensor units, computational units, and communication units.
28	How mobile communication versions change with time and the role of this technology in our daily lives. How the use of IoT changes the effect of mobile broadband is discussed in this article.
30	The authors of this article discussed the side effects of using 5G technology in the health-care sector.

(Continues)

Table 1.1   Continued

Reference number	Contributions
32	It proposes how to control the security aspects using a control panel based on the LTE network system.
34	Suggests the legacy security mechanism which protects LTE architecture.
36	This article suggests how to enhance the use of energy-efficient and environmentally friendly technology for video-conferencing. Also proposes a lazy algorithm which is suitable for a green energy system and also improves the battery back-up time.
37	The proposed design of smart clothing is used to diagnose various physiological indications of the human body, for example, collecting blood pressure. How to use smart clothing with mobile communication is also discussed in this article.
38	Proposes the techniques which use less storage systems for managing the security key while following communication protocols.
40	Suggests the use of 5G technology using IoT in various applications. Various technological aspects are considered, and following of many standards are also discussed.
41	For 4G technology, the challenges faced when using indoor and outdoor communications are discussed in this article.
42	IoT advance applications in various sectors are discussed along with the safety model, which protects the data store in the cloud system.

CPSS, computerised pilot selection system; NFV, network function virtualization; SDN, software-defined networking.

wireless system, most of the time-hanging problem arises which is sensitive matter for security and protection. Due to such issues, many complex and serious problems arise in a wireless network system. In the past few years, attacks on security and privacy have increased, posing a challenge for 5G network systems when using IoT [8].

1.1.1   How will 5G affect health-care system?

As already discussed above, 5G technology is the latest innovation, which is very useful and effective in the health-care system. Some of the important applications of 5G technology are described as follows.

1.1.1.1   Telemedicine

To work in an effective manner, the health-care system requires a strong network that supports the telemedicine system in real time and its server cannot slow down, especially when video calling is on. Telemedicine is effectively used in the health-care sector. When 5G techniques are added to any system, then they provides a very high-speed of operation help to process data in high-speed. Also, 5G will help the health-care IoT network system so that experts can handle the cases in remote areas and of hospitalized patients well in time, therefore there will not be any need to move in all areas, and surely, this is going to save time [9].

1.1.1.2   Monitoring of patients living in remote areas

5G technology helps to maintain the real-time data of all patients, so video-conferencing experts can handle patients living in rural and remote areas. 5G with IoT connection provides monitoring of patients, tracking the medicine given, helping the staff to transfer big data at great speed, and so the experts can take action and decisions well in time. 5G also provides high connectivity with mobile devices, so details of patients can be sent from anywhere, and details of medicine can be read anytime. There is no necessity to be present at the health center to take care of the patients. The health worker is free to move anywhere anytime and manage the system. In the remote areas, there is the problem of network connectivity faced by the patients' when they tried to fetch their healthcare data. Most of the rural areas are not connected with mobile networks. With the connection of the 5G network, these problems will be resolved and will help in quick operation and fast access of data, and high-quality video calling. This will affect medical services like unobtrusive monitoring, helping in the living of individuals with ceaseless conditions, dynamic maturing, and that would be just a beginning.

1.1.1.3   Augmented and virtual reality

For providing online training to the clinical staff and monitoring the patients, 5G supports the application of augmented reality and virtual reality (AR/VR). It is already used in many developing countries. The main aim of the investigation is to reduce torment and tension for certain hospice patients by giving quiet, diverting substance through 5G empowered by AR/VR. 5G operated augmented reality, and virtual reality helps to facilitate the specialist, attendants, assistants, and staff member to visualize the impact of haptic devices and learn the system how to take care of the patients and provide relief to them.

1.1.1.4   Analysis of data

5G technology will help to secure important data more prominently, so there is no risk of exchanging data from one office to another. Information on medical services can be harnessed to bring down operational expenses and to improve efficiencies. Prescient examination, prescriptive investigation, and AI information are presently being utilized to perform key functions like deciding diagnoses and choosing treatment plans for patients. For all these, transferring information at a good speed is a colossal job. The ultra-low latency features characterize 5G. This feature will permit multi-access edge computing which helps to send information most quickly. 5G will help the association of mobile and portable applications, cloud administrations, gadgets, sensors, machines, and frameworks that can be utilized to control large information related to investigation. With the assistance of 5G, information can be disseminated for different purposes related to the care of patients. This will help to enable advancements in remote locations, rural location medical procedures, brilliant hospitalization co-ordinations, intercession arranging, more noteworthy transparencies, and improved patient commitment [10].

1.1.1.5   Decentralization of the ideal health-care model

The invention of 5G help the health-care centers to provide care in the hospital at the time of admission and provides emergency center outside of the hospital. For example, a walk-in health center, special arrangements for the outstation patients. They provide health-care services at patients' home directly at a low cost. Generally, the cost of medicine and medical services increases as new technology is involved because medical centers want to recover the money that they have invested in their setup. 5G will help this decentralized medical services environment by assisting with making activities more dependable and open. 5G can upgrade live-transfer video-conferencing with low latency and give significantly quicker remote control access to the electronic health data of patients. It improves online interaction with patients and provides very high speed to transfer bulk data within seconds. It also stores the history of the patients, so robotic surgeries can be controlled very easily.

1.1.1.6   Transfer of large files

5G will have the option to help improve a medical clinic's capacity to transfer huge picture records. If system bandwidth is low as in 3G and 4G, the transfer speed will be very slow, sometimes even resulting in failure of data transfer. This kind of a problem will not arise in the 5G network system. If the internet system is slowing, the waiting time for a patient will belong, and he has to stand longer for treatment, and health experts are just ready to see a couple of patients in a similar measure of time. 5G can empower quicker exchanges of colossal clinical pictures with uncommon network system execution.

In the health-care sector both suppliers and distributors will be affected by 5G with IoT. The supplier can supply health-care-related machinery to the distributor easily and so effectively both will be benefitted. 5G will largely affect the nature of medical services received by countless patients and will bring about noteworthy changes in how social insurance is conveyed.

5G will also help to set up many business models so that people who are interested can be set their business as a supplier and a distributor and supply of the health-care instruments very easy worldwide. So the involvement of 5G technology provides benefits to the patients and the people who are connected with this business.

The monetary results of the personalization of social insurance are considerable. State-of-the-art methods are more prominent to help the suppliers based on real-time results which are not dependent on the volume of the supplied material but also on the insights from the data. These methods help to curtail the cost of the complete eco system.

New technology like 5G helps to gather patients' data, so experts can easily analyze their problems. It also helps to manage the care of patients from any location. There is no need to move patients, who are in a critical condition, from one place to another. The personalization of medical services likewise implies that doctors and other health-care experts, when they are needed to do the care of the patients, have an option to make "first time right" analyses and cures as per the specific patient's needs.

1.1.2   Integration of blockchain, 5G and healthcare

The dream of smart hospitals can be achieved after the invention of 5G because it can provide high Internet bandwidth. To be more specific, 5G will open new possibilities for patient care while using machine learning and AI after blockchain is included. With 5G, the potential of the use of the Internet with security will increase. When using smart hospitals, the main problem is maintaining the data of all patients and providing security. Many private agencies provide services to maintain hospital records and data, but they do not guarantee data security. One of the MIT scientist teams observed this situation and invented the blockchain system that is mainly used to secure health-care data of smart hospitals. So data handling is easy when implementing blockchain [11].

The blockchain system is designed with Ethereum software, which can help integrate and perform many contracts, whereas Bitcoin cannot be used for big data. A blockchain system with 5G support can connect the health-care providers and provide reliable data sharing. It is also suitable for patients for managing their health history and if required, for sharing their medical data with health-care professionals. Since data security is very high, the health-care provider can get accurate and correct patient data. In that case, the patient can get proper treatment in time.

The main advantage for the health-care sector and patients in uploading their data on the blockchain is that they can access their data anytime, control it, and manage it as per their needs. Patients want to sell their data to research scholars or any medical research agency and earn money. Furthermore, blockchain can make sure that the data of the health-care system is fully secured in the health-care system with the utmost transparency.

1.1.2.1   Challenges for the blockchain system

Here we discuss the challenges arising when a blockchain system is used with 5G [11].

1.1.2.1.1   Scalability

The latency of 5G networks is about 1 ms for sending data. This shows the required high-speed transaction architecture of the networking system. Blockchain networks can handle only 10–14 transactions per second. Some private blockchain implementations can reach 3 000–20 000 transactions per second. Therefore, novel blockchain architectures are required, which can support the 5G networking system.

1.1.2.1.2 Smart contracts

There are so many public blockchain contracts available in the market. The main issue is to interconnect all contracts at the same time using 5G. When using high-speed IoT devices with 5G, it is challenging to synchronize all blockchain contracts. The second problem is legally developed for various contracts. And the third problem is the security of data for all smart contracts. The smart contract code may contain bugs and susceptibility, which hackers can use to explore the smart contract data [12].

1.1.2.1.3 Standardization and regulations

At the national and international levels, blockchains and contracts are following particular standards and regulations. When using blockchain with 5G, it is required to set some standards and regulations on local, national, and international levels. These standards and regulations help to use blockchain with 5G in a secure manner.

1.1.2.1.4 Transaction and cloud infrastructure costs

For the use of a blockchain network, it is required to set up an optimized cloud infra-structure in such a manner that the cost for the blockchain node user is low. When people use any transaction they have to pay some amount. The amount paid by the smart contractor depends on the use of the function code. If the smart contractor function and respective codes require less computation and are arranged adequately, they have to pay less.

1.1.2.1.5 Data privacy

Privacy of data for any sector like industrial, government, healthcare, and personal is a major issue when using the blockchain network. It is also challenging for the 5G operator to manage personal data such as email details, debit/credit card details, contact numbers, user id/password, and much more very essential information. It requires some specific regulation, a policy which protects personal information of the people [13]. Once personal details of the users are stored on the blockchain then no one have the right to modify the already stored data (which makes the complete process as tamperproof).

If considering blockchain privacy design, personal data cannot be stored in blockchain, only has pointers.

1.1.2.2 Naming, registration, and reputation

Blockchain with the 5G network system manages a huge number of participants and units simultaneously, so it requires a decentralized system to register the number of participants and units effectively and efficiently for good performance. The registration center can be designed by using a smart contract and decentralized storage system. A unique registration center is also required, which manages the blockchain with 5G network addresses, public keys, and the legal identities of the user [14].

1.1.3   Contributions of this chapter

This chapter has the following contributions:

- Focus on various features of 5G technology that are compared with the old communication system
- Focus on the challenges that arise with the 5G network system when used in the health-care sector
- Consideration of the technical challenges that arise in 5G technology
- How to manage security and privacy when using 5G
- The various applications of 5G in the health-care sector.

1.1.4   Motivation

"Health is wealth" is the motive of humanity. But due to the lack of medical facilities people spend a significant amount of their savings on healthcare. People are faced with the problem of traveling long distances, because treatment facilities with new machinery systems are not available in all the cities. Overall, people require good medical facilities within their surrounding areas with the latest technological machinery. The digital medical care system can help people overcome these problems and get medical treatment in time. The tremendous and attractive features of 5G technology help to operate health-care services very easily with good efficiency [15].

1.2   Related work

This section provides an in-depth review of the articles related to the proposed work. Table 1.1 presents the comparative analysis of different works.

1.2.1   Research gap

After a deep analysis of the reference articles the following research gaps were found:

- Since 5G has many disadvantages when used in the health-care sector, how many types of challenges arise when using 5G technology in the health-care sector.
- Which type of technical challenge arises when using 5G communication technology in countries like India that are already facing lots of problems using 4G. Security and privacy are critical when using 5G technology, and it is a big challenge for the operator.
- Health experts are happy with the old system because they do not know how to operate the new machinery, so it is a big challenge to provide suitable training to handle the new upcoming machinery.

- When using 5G with IoT, it requires various security features for use in medical services.

1.3   Challenges associated with the present health-care system

Many challenges are associated with the present health-care system, like the aging of the devices, increase in the number of diseases like sugar and blood pressure, which increases the burden on the system. Due to this, maintaining all patients' data and following routine check-up reports is a difficult task in modern systems. Providing health-care services at a low cost is also very difficult because the private sector wants to earn more profit, so they use the new technology system in their hospital [16]. Worldwide health-care challenges are examined as given below.

1.3.1   Challenges with health records

In a modern health-care system, data of all patients are maintained electronically, and it is shared with the other authorities as per requirement. Security and privacy of this data are significant challenges for the management. It stores review, planned, and simultaneous health-care data with the reason to help producers, proceeding, and quality services in incorporating well-being. The absence of interoperability is a significant issue since medical clinics and doctors are generally not associated. Records of patients can be stored and used by the clinical staff as well as research laboratories [17].

1.3.2   Universal access limitations

If the health-care services are available for everyone, there is no economic limitation, people may belong to any specific place in the country and still be able to avail health-care services, and there is no discrimination on the basis of gender. Generally, it is seen that rich people get the benefits of health-care services quickly whereas the poor people, and the people belonging to remote areas face problems in getting health-care services.

Health-care services are also restricted in a nation because of untrained experts, limited services, and outdated equipment, high cost of medication and treatment, and lack of resources. Widespread social health administrations are especially trying in developed and undeveloped nations, where well-being assets and specialists are hard to come by, especially in rural regions. If we can remove the old system problems then it is better to avail the health-care services [18].

1.3.3   Long-term constant care burden

If seen in the current scenario, most people are suffering from many diseases and the rate of infected people is increasing continuously; this is a severe problem in present times, because in the health-care sector, very less number of experts, nurses, and resources are available. Even in rural and remote areas, very few hospitals are available. Emergency services are not available in rural areas. So monitoring the patients and providing continuous treatment is a big challenge in underdeveloped countries. In some places, health-care services are available with good technology and latest equipment, but their service cost is very high, so all people cannot afford such high-cost services. Due to the lack of experts in the health-care centers, people face long waiting times [19].

1.3.4   Challenges for aging populations

In society, the number of old people is increasing very rapidly; of late the rate of growth of older people is also increasing by 8–10 per cent. People aged 65 years or more will increase by 16 per cent in the upcoming years. As the age increases the risk of death rate also increases. These segments show health-care services facing various challenges. Since health-care services are available in a limited area and in limited cities, so taking care of a huge number of older persons is not possible with the limited resources. So handling the age factor is a big challenge in any country [20].

1.3.5   Limitation of the resources

In the health-care sector services have improved but the administration is not good till date. Patients need to go to far-off places to visit their primary care physicians. If they miss a bus or train, they miss their appointment, and again, they have to reschedule a meeting with the doctor. This way, his/her treatment will be delayed and may be his/her infection will increase to critical limits [21].

Globally, many countries are faced with a shortage of health-care workers and resources. People do not get treatment on time, and many old people have lost their lives. India has 22.8 skilled health workers per 10 000 population, and as per the

Table 1.2   *Ratio of health workers against the population (data taken from WHO)*

Name of country	No. of health workers available per 1 000 population (2018)
India	0.8
South Africa	0.8
Korea	2.3
Japan	2.4
Canada	2.8
Ireland	3.2
France	3.4
Australia	3.7
Spain	3.9
Russia	4.0
Norway	4.8

WHO, this does not meet the minimum limit. Table 1.2 shows the ratio of health workers from different countries [22].

1.3.6 Problems associated with health-care information systems

The patient's health-related data generated from the internet-operated medical devices sometimes heterogeneous in nature. It provides automatic transactions of the amount from the patient's account for hospital management without any error, so it develops reliabilities between them. The health-care system is very complicated because they maintained the patient's data, data related to medicine. Resources available in the hospital: they maintain communication in audio and video system and the transaction of the amount given by the patients, so required optimal operation of the system unless so many privacy and security problems arise [20].

The traditional wireless systems like 3G and 4G provide protection and security for limited data. If the size of the data increases, its services fail. So 3G and 4G technologies are used for small data monitoring, monitoring, smart health devices, and social interactions. But for large data, the health-care system requires advanced wireless technology, which supports multiple devices at a time and its frequency range is also very wide [23].

1.3.7 Lack of data driven

In the present scenario, the health-care services are used worldwide but some times these services evaluate patients based upon population-wise rather than as per their actual need. If anyone wants to take random information on any particular patient, it's challenging. We can't get the complete information. Even they have not maintained the history of the patient treatment, so if anyone wants to know which medicine is effective for patients and the new treatment required, it is not possible. So poor management of data cannot help experts and underestimate the health worker. Also, decrease the efficiency of the worker. Here it shows we are missing the various opportunities and unable to develop an evidence-based health-care system. So it's difficult to provide safety and security to the patient [24].

1.3.8 Health-care disparities

Due to the shortage of health-care resources, most organizations are working to generate a huge amount, which means systems are not developed to fulfill the people's basic needs fully but are set up to earn money. The people require health services but poor people cannot expend lots of money so they cannot get any medical services, whereas the rich people have sufficient amount to pay, but they need very fewer services. The Indian government announced the Ayushman Bharat policy to provide health-care services to poor people in any hospital at any place of India. This policy is game-changing for the people who cannot pay lots of money for medical treatment. Similarly, developed countries such as the United States provide health insurance for all the people [25].

1.3.9   Standardization and interoperability

When many devices operated simultaneously need specific network which provide security and reduce the complexity of the network. Keeping up information-sharing systems and exchanging personal information are crucial for 5G and IoT. When a large number of devices is operating at the same time in the complex network, these technologies ensure the information is shared smoothly without any error and in a highly secure manner [26].

1.3.10   Effective regulation

When new technology has come then it is important to set the rules and regulations so the people can use the system without any problem. they can use new technology without any doubt and hesitation for security. The regulation is designed in such a manner so that protects the consumer information and should be user-friendly. Every country has its' own rules and regulations to operate the 5G technology [25].

1.3.11   Data privacy and research needs

For security and protection of health-care information, the government stabilized the act of 1996. This act has lots of rules and regulations which are to be followed by the users. The data used in telemedicine are sensitive, so there cannot be any compromise with the basic security and privacy of data.

1.4   5G technology

5G is the fifth-era mobile wi-fi system that used the stepped forward availability. It is based on a cloud system assisting multiple gadgets and assisting the quick switch of big data. It helps the quick computing functionality of the data, very clean to AR and VR, presents fact connectivity with the cell phone the use of the IoT. 5G is a superior virtual method in which many gadgets and sensors may be operated at a time. The use of ultra-reliable low latency communication, high reliability, and 99.9% of availability of existing communication infrastructure such as 5G and beyond 5G makes the services more efficient, such as on line teaching, control of transportation system, robotic automation, precision agriculture, and plenty of other automation operations [26].

Presently, cutting-edge innovations and remote communication systems are being pushed as far as possible by the massive development in remote information administrations. The new age wireless 5G system required many characterized for efficient and fast operation of the system, which include the advanced capability of the network system, minimal latency, nonstop connectivity, power productivity, and excessive dependability. Wireless cell era changed into commenced round 1970 with the formation of the cell community, updating the traditional machine, and growing new generation structures, as shown in Figure 1.1.

Since the early 1970s, mobile wireless technology has commenced its formation, revolution, and evolution. The first generation, second generation, third generation,

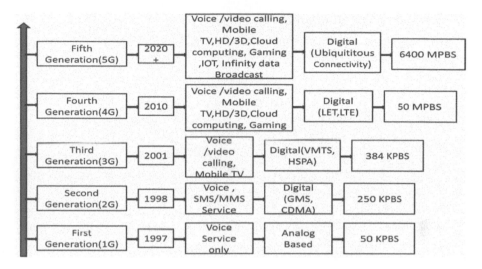

Figure 1.1   The evolution from 1G to 5G [4]

fourth generation, and novel, fifth generation (5G) are coming under wireless mobile networks and are updated continuously. As shown in Figure 1.1, the growth of the 1G started in approximately 1980. After 40 years, new generation 5G has been developed. Traditional systems like 2G, and 3G had so many obstacles, like high-speed connectivity not being available, information switch capacity, and the quality of video calling became very poor. When 4G technology had arrived, most of the disadvantages of 2G and 3G were eliminated; however, it required greater updates in the system. The 5G technology is very advanced and almost reduces the disadvantages of the traditional systems.

Fifth-generation technology is not only the improved model of traditional communication systems. It is an extraordinary transformation of the biometric system. It is the combination of diverse advanced technology like fourth-generation wireless technology, millimeter wave, sensors, and a high-capacity wireless operating system. It is a cloud-based system that stores all types of information of patients. An excessive protection system is used which protects the information of the users. It has a high capacity to compute the data very fast which helps distribute and control the flow of data by the huge number of connected mobiles and different networks.

The Smartphone recently using the fourth-generation long-term evolution (4G LTE) techniques that provides uninterrupted transmission, excessive connectivity, and use of excessive bandwidth. The latest 5G innovation further improves the bandwidth and data transfer limits using low latency techniques and concerned numerous technologies. 5G techniques are looking to offer very high Internet connectivity (around 40–50 times faster than the 4G system) compared to 4G [25].

The wireless network system could be very complicated due to the massive variety of devices connected and operated simultaneously. This complexity of community structures faced many problems, and 5G will overcome these problems. Due

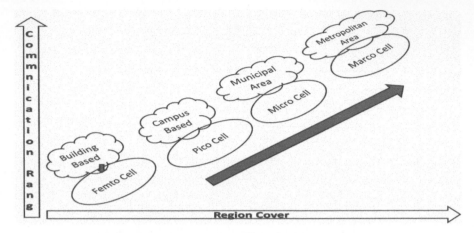

Figure 1.2   Connectivity of 5G network [28]

to the newness of 5G, it is far appropriate for diverse programs such as health-care services, education, production in industries, and on online operations [26]. Since 5G has many applications connected with billions of wireless systems, security and protection is a brutal issue [27].

5G technology supports high frequency and spectrum compared to a 4G system. That is why the connectivity and transfer capacity of 5G is better than the 4G system. Connectivity of the signal, proper management of data, and security process makes the 5G technology an incredible wireless network [4]. It is user friendly for long-range as well as short-range devices. Figure 1.2 shows the different connectivities of the 5G network, while Figure 1.3 suggests the utility of 5G technology in numerous sectors.

Technologies used in the 5G network system are as follows.

1.4.1   Millimeter waves

In the 4G communication technology used, electromagnetic waves have frequency limits of 30–300 GHz. In the 4G technology, microwave band and its frequency limit are below the millimeter-wave frequency band and the range of frequency limit for microwave technology used is 3–30 GHz. In the 5G wireless technology, very huge records may be transmitted through millimeter waves only for short distances. Millimeter waves also allow using the unauthorized frequencies with 5G network using Wi-Fi connection without any conflict of interest with the small mobile and other conventional communication networks [29].

1.4.2   Small cells

Small cells are used in the capacity of the network system when demand increases. It is operating on small gadgets of base stations which might be related with a couple of gadgets of microcells. Since it transfers the signal for short distances loss of power is very less [30]. Small cell technology is mainly used in areas where the population

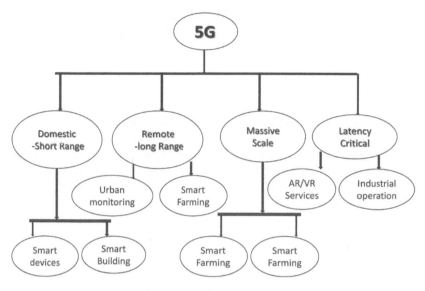

Figure 1.3   Applications of 5G [28]

density is high, for example, stadiums and indoor auditoriums. Thus 5G systems will depend on a multi-faceted foundation comprising large-scale and little ultra-dense cells.

1.4.3   Big multiple input/output system

Multiple inputs and multiple output systems are extended applications of MIMO. Multiple input/output systems have a large number of groups of antennas and transmitters. They are used for large-scale transmission of a high range of spectrum frequencies. In general, about 128 antenna units are connected with the 64 units of transmitters and 64 units of receivers in a MIMO system. It helps to enhance the transmission of the spectrum frequency range by connecting with multiples devices using base communication [30].

1.4.4   Beamforming

This technology is especially centered on the wi-fi alerts that are receiving in any unique receiving station. It cannot focus to spread the signals in all directions. This technology is used to change most of the signals generated by a large number of transmitter antennas. Beamforming facilitates in the delivery of a good quality signal to the receiver station. The beamforming facilitates the data transfer capacity and reduces the errors in the system [30].

1.4.5   Full duplex

Today cell phones depend on handsets that must alternate when sending and getting data over a similar frequency limit or work in various frequencies if a gadget requires communication and getting data simultaneously. With full-duplex innovation, a gadget will have the option to send and get information simultaneously on a similar frequency. Such innovations can double the limit of remote systems [30].

1.4.6   Software-defined networks

Software-defined networks enhance the flexibility of the network. They provide separate controls for the various transmission networks. They are used to make the plan for the operation of the network and then forward the plan for the control units to control the programmed data. Many numbered hierarchies are developed by the 5G software-defined networks integrated with virtualization technologies used to create the network topology [30].

1.5   Technical challenges and the path to 5G

Transmission of private customers' information to the utility company and service providers requires a strong data security system. This information can be used to infer customers' behavior, and the house occupied by them. Since in an intelligent grid, several devices can manage the electricity supply and network demand simultaneously, some attacks can enter the devices through the network. Most smart grid devices focus on a specific functionality only; it results in the devices lacking enough memory space or capability to deal with security threats [31].

An M2M control system additionally has numerous security issues. At the point when one device is assaulted, it might send the fake state to another device in an undesirable manner. Numerous devices in the smart grid need a controller. It requests the equipment remotely has a long life cycle and effective security software with update ability. Otherwise, when the disk operating system (DOS) attack accesses the equipment, the equipment will stop working.

Smart Logistics in the supply chain IoT mainly considers three types of security and protection issues. The first is data corruption, that the attacker accesses the system, sends a fake request, and causes the device to make a wrong decision. The second threat is the maintenance of the equipment. The DoS attack can damage the equipment or facility if it lacks a security protection update or maintenance. Data privacy is a common threat in smart logistics. The supply chain consistently contains the clients' private data that should be carefully protected.

Identity and authentication efficiency and privacy validation scheme are required in the 5G-enabled IoT environment. Previously, the verification protocols are planned dependent on the single worker conditions, which are not appropriate for the new design of the 5G-enabled IoT distributed services environment. Back in 2009, cloud computing as new technology came into our life [32]. With the numerous growths of clients and the solicitation to share the service, numerous scientists started to focus harder toward planning the trust and security validations between cloud clients and the service. Additionally, they tracked down that past validation like SSL Authentication Protocol (SAP) is very complicated to use for most clients [33].

Therefore, many researchers construct more effective confirmation plans to secure the E-health-care database. After finding the disadvantage of the single server validation schemes, some pursue the creation of inter-cloud identity management systems, such as open ID, SAML to provide Single Sign-On (SSO) authentication. However, these authentication schemas rely on the third party, which may bring some new security threats. Be that as it may, these confirmation mappings depend on the outsider, which may bring some new security dangers. Hence health-care administration used plans for productivity, and protection confirmation [34].

1.5.1   Trust management

In 5G-enabled IoT systems, the user does not feel secure especially for the different IoT devices, service providers, and remote servers. Developing the trust relationship between device-device, device-user, and user-server is a challenge. How to efficiently create the trust management framework is the most attractive research field for many researchers. Previously, trust management was developed for cloud computing environments to solve the trust issues between IoT users and the cloud server. At the beginning of trust management in cloud computing, Service Level Agreements are the foundation technique but not consistent among cloud providers. This will lead to the user being unable to identify a trustworthy cloud provider. Therefore, many trust management frameworks are proposed [33].

1.5.2   Encryption method

Encryption has been the research interest of many researchers for many years. The traditional encryption methods such as Triple DSE (3DSE), Triple Data Encryption Algorithm (TDEA) have drawbacks that the devices must need to know the identities of the information recipients and share credentials with them in advance [35].

1.5.3   Access control

Access control is used to ensure that unauthorized entities cannot access the IoT devices and collect data. Previously, most research focused on designing the access control system for cloud computing. Article [36], proposed how to create the access control system by advanced techniques for many procedures and develop a control system to access the efficient finer access data. They also proposed another novel framework for access control to the health-care domain within a cloud computing environment.

1.5.4   Privacy

When using IoT with 5G its architecture will be complicated and distributed. The information of the IoT devices collected is sensitive and personal. More complex privacy mechanisms are required now. In the past, many privacy protection mechanisms such as k-anonymity, differential privacy, quasi-identifier, and pseudonymization, and so on were used. At the beginning of IoT privacy research, there were many privacy protection mechanisms focused on cloud computing.

Table 1.3   Difference between privacy and security

Privacy	Security
Provides protection against personal information	Provides security to unauthorized access of personal data
It provides security only for personal data	It provides protection for all types of data
It provides protection against the name, address, and other personal details of the people	It provides protection for all types of data or program of any organization or company
Without security it is not possible to achieve privacy	Without privacy it is possible to achieve security

1.6   Security and privacy

While working on 5G innovation with an IoT framework, the main difficulties are the security of the framework and individual information protection. Anyhow required to provide security and privacy of the network system. If it is found that any firm or person tries to disturb security and steal the private data must have some punishment and have to pay the penalty. Security indicates against the unauthorized access of data. Privacy refers to protect personal identification information. Table 1.3 shows the primary difference between security and privacy [36].

Providing security of the 5G mobile networks is a challenging task for a management system. The 5G network system has many protocol stacks, which consist of multiple layers as follows:

- Physical layer
- Radio resource control layer
- Nonaccess stratum layer.

Every layer consists of protocols which are implemented during the procedures. When it is required to connect or disconnect the devices, they have to follow some protocol. Similarly, if any device wants to send or receive calls or SMS, some protocols have to be followed [33]. Some of the essential security systems are as follows.

1.6.1   Authentication

The 5G wireless communication system uses two types of authentication: entity authentication and message authentication. These authentications are used in the 5G network to protect against any cyber attacks when two people communicate with each other using audio calls. User equipment and mobility management entities work together and provide security to the users.

In the traditional communication system, authentications between the user equipment and mobility management are very important because it secures the system and protects leakage of personal information. In the 4G network system, authentications collaborate with key agreement systems for smooth communication between the users.

When using the 5G network, users require authentication to each other (user and mobile management) and with the service provider. When they are using any network, the trust of any user is crucial, and the traditional network system uses different types of trust models. Still, the 5G system requires flexible and integrated authentication management for protection and security. Since the operation of the 5G system is high-speed which provides fast data transfer compared with traditional methods, faster authentication is required [37].

1.6.2   Confidentiality

Everyone has some confidential aspects, and when they are using mobile communication, they don't want to share their documents. When using a mobile network, it is required to protect the user's data and provide him privacy. When data are being transferred, there is a need to protect it from passive attacks by another user; it cannot be disclosed to unauthorized users without permission. Privacy is used to prevent information that hackers can misuse.

5G technologies are used in many applications such as healthcare, education, safety department, transportation, and many more, so they required very high security to protect the data. Inscriptive and descriptive data are protected by using an encryption key management system. In this method, they have sent a security key to the users before sharing the information. In the conventional networking system, it was not used, and they assume that hackers may be having very little knowledge about our system.

1.6.3   Availability

Availability is characterized by how much help is available and usable to any authorized clients at whatever point and place mentioned. An availability attack is a typical active attack. One of the significant attacks on accessibility is DoS. In this attack, the network cannot allow the legal user to access the system [28].

The communication link can be disrupted using jamming by radio signals. In this case, legal users are also not allowed to access the service. This system is implemented, sometimes for the purpose of security of any particular area or for protection of an important VIP. 5G network is implemented with the IoT; it provides many nodes for the users out of which some nodes are unprotected due to technical issues. These unprotected nodes easily used jam or DoS attacks and theft of personal data.

1.6.4   Integrity

Security management provides message authentication to legal users using their sources, but they cannot protect against duplicate or modified messages. The 5G network system requires very high security to protect the users' personal and important data. Key security management systems are required for the protection of integrated data. This security system alerts the authorized users if any illegal user tries to modify their SMS information. If the inside user wants to attack integrated data saved in the network system or if they're going to change or inject the information in such case, it is tough to identify the hackers [38].

1.7 5G and health-care opportunities

A 5G communication system plays an important role in implementing and operating health-care services. 5G technology has many important characteristics which can have an important impact on health-care services. 5G can be operated with very high reliability and low latency. It can connect a large number of devices at a time. It supports the sensor and other devices for transfer of the information.

It can transfer big images in a short period. It supports very high quality video calling, which the health expert can utilize to examine the patients living in remote locations. The 5G technology has many advantages, as listed below [38–44].

1.7.1 Fast and intelligent networks

5G technologies provide a very high speed of data transmission and fast downloading. 5G can support many integrated devices, and all users get high connectivity, so 5G also characterizes the intelligent networking modern system. As people are already using a conventional system like 3G and 4G, transferring large data and downloading speed is also not good. Video quality provided by conventional systems is also not good. 5G technology has many advanced characteristics which make it suitable and user friendly for the people in terms of high speed and high quality of communication [45].

People can enjoy online gaming, video calling, and watching videos, operate robotic-operated equipment, watch and download high-quality videos within seconds and, much more. In the metro cities, 5G is used in traffic control systems. It is also used in the health-care sector for robotic surgery, online monitoring of the patients, and communicating with patients living in remote and rural areas. In the industries, it is used to control the production process and to develop a high-quality product with zero error [46].

1.7.2 Back-end services

One of the key components in allowing 5G to address the data throughput concerns is edge computing. It is a distributed computing model which brings computation and data storage closer to the source (i.e., client). This allows for faster processing of data, reducing latency, saving bandwidth, and improving customer experiences. Figure 1.4 shows the edge computing and network functions connected to a 5G system [48].

Using this technique, computation of the data will be economical and efficient, thus reducing storage costs. Since the 5G infrastructure is a very complex and integrated system, using optimization techniques will improve the performance of the

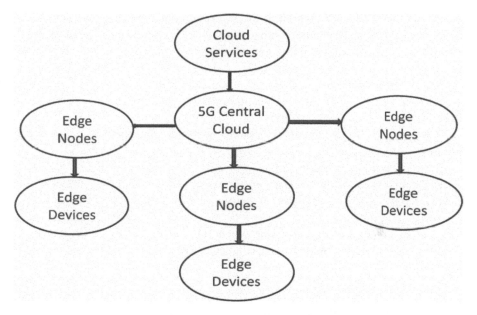

Figure 1.4   Edge computing and network functions [47]

physical system connected to the network system. This provides rapid connectivity to legal users.

1.7.3   Low latency

The time required to transfer the data between the two users is known as the latency of the people's network to share the information. If any network system has high latency, then the data transfer speed will be slow, and user Internet speed will also be reduced. 5G technology has very low latency. That's why the communication speed is very high as compared to the previous generation of communication technology [47].

The latency of any network system depends on the network's speed, the bandwidth available for transferring the data, and the size of the data which we want to transfer. Usually, the latency of 5G technology is faster than the blink of an eye. 5G services provide high-speed services to send and download large data and videos almost in real time. So we can say that operating a network system on a high-speed system has to maintain low latency, which helps to use massive IoT to handle a significant data transfer rate. Mobile users get quick connectivity to transfer or download large video files.

1.7.4   Applications of 5G in healthcare

The new 5G network technology has many advanced features. It has many applications in various fields like mobile-operated robotics, automatic traffic control systems, and the most important area where it is widely used is the health-care sector.

IoT-integrated 5G technology is used in many applications of health-care efficiently. IoT systems used in the medical system are connected with various sensors and bio-medical equipment used for online robotic surgery of critical diseases. The sensors are used to record various information, like blood report, sugar level, blood pressure reports, electroencephalogram (EEG) reports, and so forth, which help monitor and take care of patients. High-quality video transmission helps the efficiency of the sensor to operate the health-care equipment [27].

Advantages of the 5G networking system with the application of IoT are listed as follows:

- It provides high quality of performance.
- It provides connectivity to a large number of devices efficiently.
- It improves the system's operating efficiency and supports high-quality videos used in online health-care services.
- It supports high bandwidth for communications.

1.7.4.1   Smart clothing

5G technologies have a very important feature in the health-care sector called smart clothing, used to collect physiological data of various micro-physiological data systems. The diagnosis of some diseases in the patient's body requires bioelectrical signals generated by the human body. Experts collect the human body electrode signal for continuous tracking and collecting the bioelectric signal. Scientists design a textile structure of electrodes using acquisition technology. This structure can be used for a long time and, as per retirement, can easily provide cleaning because it is very soft [32]. This structure easily collects the bioelectric signal of the patient's body. Smart clothing is used to identify the ECG signal of patients by using electrodes placed in specific body parts. It also helps to measure the blood pressure of the patients. It has also helped to identify various types of diseases and is not required to be worn at all times by the patients.

1.7.4.2   Diagnosis services in rural areas

Health-care services are not available in rural areas with advanced technology. If available, suitable experts are not available to operate such advanced equipment. So most people living in rural areas do not get the benefits of smart health-care services. In India, most people are working in rural and remote areas, so developing a smart health and diagnosis service center [11] is necessary.

If the health-care center is developed in rural areas, farmers easily get advantages of health services without traveling long distances. Also, they can use these health-care services at any time and diagnose their diseases. It is also required to connect all rural area medical services to the urban medical centers. Hence, if they have any health issues, they can immediately connect with the experts in the urban hospital and get consultancy [41].

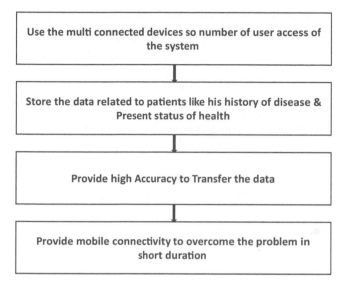

Figure 1.5   Hospital management systems [14]

The advanced telemedicine system is managed in such a way that it can work as an integrated system and be utilized by urban and rural people easily. Required strong management systems which monitor the whole system and diagnose the patients suffering from critical diseases that why they can get health service in time and cure the problem Required strong management systems which monitor the whole system and diagnose the patient's critical diseases, so that they can get health service in time and cure the problem.

1.7.4.3   Management in hospitals

The performance of the hospital depends on the management and proper operation of the system. If the system is managed correctly and in a suitable manner, not only do the patients get easy services but also health-care workers' working efficiency [14] is improved. Figure 1.5 shows the services which can improve hospital performance.

1.7.4.4   Use of robots

Robotics is used in many applications in healthcare. It can help to collect the sample as well as transmit the patient report data to the expert. It also helps to operate the surgery online. Robotics system performance depends on the connected network system. 5G has many advanced characteristics to support efficient robotic applications in the health-care sector. 5G technologies have a very low value of latency, so sending and receiving information very quickly, is essential for robotics in health-care services [49].

1.7.4.5   Monitoring of health-care data

For smooth and efficient operation of any health-care services, it is required to store and monitor all patients taking services from the same center to maintain the

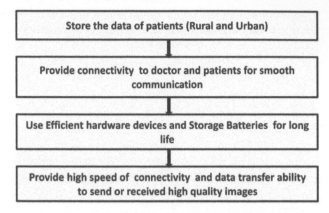

Figure 1.6   Monitoring of health record [50]

necessary data on the cloud system. These data need very high security and privacy. Figure 1.6 shows the basic requirements to monitor health-care data [50].

The 5G networking system helps set up the smart medical system, which includes high-level health-care facilities with longer life equipment, which consume less power during the operation. IoT-based 5G networks can provide a secure and reliable system, so the only legal person or authorized person accesses the system to handle the data management of the healthcare center.

1.7.4.6   Imaging

In the health-care system, digital medicine plays a vital role. A 5G networking system supports the transfer of high-quality images in a concise period. This means it reduces the computing time and is able to send big data rapidly. If any person living in a rural area is unable to come to the urban hospital, they can send their health report to the doctor for analysis immediately. The doctor also, without traveling anywhere, can check the report and suggest the treatment required. So it is comfortable for both the patient and the doctor. Similarly, if expert doctors are not available in our country, it is possible to consult the expert in another country if patients send their report in terms of high-quality image and video-conferencing to get treatment [16].

1.7.4.7   Diagnostics

It is a dangerous situation for patients if the doctor cannot diagnose the actual problem. In some health issues, patients have many signs, and experts easily understand his problem. But some cases, patients do not show symptoms for a long time, and the symptoms only come at the critical situation like cancer. In the critical stage of diagnosis of the diseases, there are very few chances to save the patients. So the diagnosis of the problem is the key factor for treatment. 5G technology is now being used in the health-care sector and it supports health-care equipment. This equipment works very accurately and helps diagnose the diseases very easily. These are very attractive features of the 5G technology in the medical system [41, 42].

1.7.4.8 Data analytics and treatment

In the digital health-care system, the patients' data play an important role in diagnosing the problem. The first thing is to collect the correct details of the patients (past and present health history). In the new medical system, people also get the various reports immediately online. If sufficient data of any patient are available, the doctor can easily analyze that data and identify the patient's actual problem and accordingly provide the correct treatment. The doctor also follows the progress of the patients in real time [43].

1.7.5 Impact of 5G on medical access, quality, and cost

Enough health resources and workers are not available compared to the population ratio. As already mentioned in Table 1.1, only 28–30 medical experts are available for every 10 000 people. Patients suffering from critical diseases cannot survive for a long time, therefore a long waiting period for such a patient could be a dangerous scenario [20].

After the invention of 4G technology people started digital medicine services. But they face slow-speed connectivity of the Internet that does not support transferring long data. Now, 5G technologies are available with high-speed connectivity, helping to share big data and high-definition video calling, which is very appropriate for the digital medicine system.

Now people are beginning to take appointments online and additionally getting an online treatment system. Most of the medical experts feel more comfortable giving treatment through online video-conferencing. In the present time, people are facing the problem of Covid-19, and the medical experts do not feel safe meeting the patients face to face. In this situation, they are able to use video-conferencing and offer appropriate remedies.

Patients dwelling in rural areas and coming to urban areas for treatment have to take a long journey. Traveling and consulting are very expensive. If they use digital medical services, they can save time and transportation charges.

Nowadays most of the medical practitioners using 5G-enabled smart devices. These smart devices helps the doctors to get accurate reports on time, accesses the patient details simultaneously, and gives a suitable solution. So there is no risk of wrong diagnosis of diseases, and patients get correct information about the progress of their health [49].

1.7.6 The impact of 5G on healthcare

5G techniques play a vital role in telemedicine services and can be more effective using the following steps

1.7.6.1   Continuous monitoring

People are suffering from many kinds of diseases. In some instances required the most effective regular remedy however, a few instances required prolonged remedy and non-stop tracking of patients. If patients are hospitalized, the doctor monitors their health regularly and gives treatment, but it is very costly for the patients, and they have to pay a big amount for a longer time. As we know that 5G supports sensor-operated devices and robotics systems, so using such sensor-operated devices can easily monitor the health of the patients who are not hospitalized and are living in rural areas [45–48].

1.7.6.2   Predictive analytics

Health-care centers preserve the statistics of patients, which helps the medical experts provide better treatment. Continuous data monitoring is also required to be store in the health-care cloud, which guides the doctor to determine whether they are doing the treatment in the right direction or not. Sometimes the expert takes predictive analysis using the patient's data when he wants to give some medicine, which is not directly related to current diseases. Generally, experts use some optimization techniques for predictive analysis in real time. This technique is used to optimize the big data of the patient, and as per the optimized results, experts make decisions. The upgradation in technology helps the health-care systems to process large amount of data in real time, security to electronic health record systems, cure the patients' health, and also reduces the overall cost of health services. However, this opportunity raises a series of policy, ethical, and legal challenges. The improvement of the health of the people's predictive analytic models is considered. It recommends the best design of health-care services in real time of the situation. 5G technology helps to analyze big data using optimization techniques and provides suitable results quickly. So without delay, an expert can take a decision [26].

1.7.6.3   Impact on business models

After the invention of the 5G wireless networking system, many fields have undergone tremendous changes in their system. The health-care system also changed and developed many new equipment to support the 5G network. After the invention of 5G, many companies are starting to manufacture new equipment in bulk. But the delivery of such equipment requires efficient services especially in rural areas, transportation systems, and local distributors to deliver the equipment as per the need of health-care centers. So 5G helps to set up the new business model and helps to enhance the profits of commercial enterprises [44].

1.7.6.4   Remote diagnosis and imaging

5G supports high-definition video calling, sensors, and robotics applications in real time. This helps to diagnose the diseases of patients who are away from the urban area. There is no need for the patient to travel from a rural area to a hospital situated in the city area. With the help of a remote sensor system, the expert can easily identify the patient's problem and advise the treatments. Imaging is the process of sending the reports and another diagnosis record in terms of high-quality pictures. 5G supports the health-care services in transferring or receiving the big picture data with high speed. It takes a few minutes to transfer the entire data. An expert can receive the data in terms of high-quality images and examine the reports [51].

1.7.6.5 Improved state of art

5G is an advanced communication technology and has many important features. It provides high-speed Internet connectivity for wireless users. It helps to improve the connectivity with a Smartphone, so users can access fast data computing. It allows operating the robotics system accurately, so it is used in health-care services such as online surgery, taking care of admitted patients, and diagnosing diseases. 5G with IoT supports the sensor and actuators used in online surgery [23].

1.8 Conclusions

Health-care services are very poor in many countries. Most of the service centers are using classical equipment and methods for the treatment of patients. Some places have advanced technology, but people cannot handle such machines due to a lack of knowledge. After the launching of 4G technology, many private-sector health service centers started advanced techniques in the metro cities. Still, they are very costly, and far away from the rural areas; it is out of reach for poor people. These are very common problems all over the world. The health-care sectors using 4G technologies are also facing so many problems such as low bandwidth speed of connectivity, required large data storage devices, interrupted Internet connectivity, slow speed of data transfer and download, and much more. After the invention of 5G, some of the problems as mentioned above can be tackled. Moreover, 5G provides a very high Internet connectivity speed for the users, operates robotics in real-time, transfers big data with high speed, and has many applications used in health-care sectors. 5G supports the mobile system, which improves health-care resources in a wide range. The 5G wireless networking system with its application will transform healthcare by enhancing human capacity, transport, and health-care equipment in rural and remote areas in real time. It allows operating virtualization, a high-quality telemedicine system that provides high performance and reliability. It cannot allow illegal users to access the networking system using high security and privacy. Operating such a high-speed system requires a high-security system to protect the patients' important hospital data and personal records. 5G-operated mobile systems enable the personalization of health-care services. The personalization of medical services helps to give more precaution, more care, proper monitoring, and provides less time to improve patients' health, and most significantly reduces the cost of treatment.

References

[1]   Röcker C., Maeder A., Gupta R., *et al.* 'User centered design of smart health-care applications'. *Electronic Journal of Health Informatics*. 2011;**6**(2):1–3.

[2]   Alzahrani A., Qureshi M.S., Thayananthan V. 'RFID of next generation network for enhancing customer relationship management in healthcare industries'. *Technology and Health Care: Official Journal of the European Society for Engineering and Medicine*. 2017;**25**(5):903–16.

[3]   Andrews J.G., Buzzi S., Choi W. 'What will 5G be?' *IEEE Transaction on Selected Areas in Communications*. 2014;**32**(6):1065–82.

[4]   Hwang K., Min C. *'Big data analytics for cloud, IoT and cognitive computing'*. John Wiley & Sons: New York; 2017. pp. 234–67.

[5]   Meryem S., Adnan A., Mischa D., Joachim S., Gerhard F. '5G enabled tactile Internet'. *IEEE Journal on Selected Areas in Communications*. 2016;**34**(3):460–73.

[6]   Zhang Y. 'GroRec: a group-centric intelligent recommender system integrating social, mobile and big data technologies'. *IEEE Transactions on Services Computing*. 2016;**9**(5):786–95.

[7]   Jayakody D.N.K. *'5G enabled secure wireless networks'*. Springer; 2019. pp. 1–456.

[8]   Li D. '5G and intelligence medicine – how the next generation of wireless technology will reconstruct healthcare?' *Precision Clinical Medicine*. 2019;**2**(5):205–8.

[9]   Brito J.M.C. 'Technological trends for 5G networks influence of e-health and IoT applications'. *International Journal of E-Health and Medical Communications*. 2018;**9**(1):1–22.

[10]   Zhang J. 'An architecture for 5G mobile network based on SDN and NFV'. *International Conference on Wireless mobile & Multimedia*; 2015. pp. 87–93.

[11]   Chaer A., Salah K., Lima C., Pratha P.P., Tarek S. 'Blockchain for 5G: opportunities and challenges'. *IEEE Transaction*. 2019;**31**(4):12–19.

[12]   Panwar N., Sharma S., Singh A.K. 'A survey on 5G: the next generation of mobile communication'. *Physical Communication*. 2016;**18**(2):64–84.

[13]   Salih A.A., ZeebareeSubhi R.M., Abdulraheem A.S., Rizagr R., Zebari R.R. 'Evolution of mobile wireless communication to 5G revolution'. *CRRU*. 2020;**62**(5):2121–38.

[14]   Horn G., Schneider P. 'Towards 5G security'. *14th IEEE International Conference on Trust, Security and Privacy in Computing and Communications*; 2015. pp. 1165–70.

[15]   Sánchez J.D.V., Urquiza-Aguiar L., Paredes. 'Survey on physical layer security for 5G wireless networks'. *Annals of Telecommunications*. 2020:37–45.

[16]   Silva B.M.C., Rodrigues J.J.P.C., Lopes I.M.C., Machado T.M.F., Zhou L. 'A novel cooperation strategy for mobile health applications'. *IEEE Journal on Selected Areas in Communications*. 2013;**31**(9):28–36.

[17] Taylor D.N., David T.N. 'A literature review of electronic health records in chiropractic practice: common challenges and solutions'. *Journal of Chiropractic Humanities*. 2017;**24**(1):31–40.

[18] Agarwal D. 'Universal access to health care for all: exploring road map'. *Indian Journal of Community Medicine*. 2012;**37**(2):69–69.

[19] Rodrigues J.J.P.C., Pedro L.M.C.C., Vardasca T., de la Torre-Díez I., Martins H.M.G. 'Mobile health platform for pressure ulcer monitoring with electronic health record integration'. *Health Informatics Journal*. 2013;**19**(4):300–11.

[20] Shin Y.W., Green A. 'Projection of chronic illness prevalence and cost inflation'. *Rand Health*. 2000;**18**:121–32.

[21] Harous S., El Menshawy M., Serhani M.A., Benharref A. 'Mobile health architecture for obesity management using sensory and social data'. *Informatics in Medicine Unlocked*. 2018;**10**(10):27–44.

[22] Ahad A., Tahir M., Aman Sheikh M., Ahmed K.I., Mughees A., Numani A. 'Technologies trend towards 5G network for smart health-care using IoT: a review'. *Sensors*. 2020;**20**(4):40–7.

[23] Saraladevi N., Jacob P., Roger C.T., John B.E. 'Shortage of healthcare workers in developing countries – Africa'. *Journal of Ethnicity and disease*. 2009;**19**(1):60–9.

[24] Robert S.H I., Woodward I. *M-health: fundamentals and applications*. John Wiley & Sons; 2016. pp. 1–424.

[25] Andre N.B., Bruno F., Erika A., *et al.* '5G: vision and requirements for mobile communication system towards year 2020'. *Journal of Communication and Information Systems*. 2016;**31**(1):146–63.

[26] Dickman S.L., Woolhandler S., Bor J., McCormick D., Bor D.H., Himmelstein D.U. 'Health spending for low-, middle-, and high-income Americans, 1963–2012'. *Health Affairs*. 2016;**35**(7):1189–96.

[27] Kostoff R.N., Heroux P., Aschner M., Tsatsakis A. 'Adverse health effects of 5G mobile networking technology under real-life conditions'. *Toxicology Letters*. 2020;**323**:35–40.

[28] Palattella M.R., Dohler M., Grieco A., *et al.* 'Internet of things in the 5G era: enablers, architecture, and business models'. *IEEE Journal on Selected Areas in Communications*. 2016;**34**(3):510–27.

[29] NIS Cooperation Group. EU coordinated risk assessment of the cyber security of 5G networks. 2019. Available from https://ec.europa.eu/commission/presscorner/detail/en/IP_19_6049.

[30] Hongil K., Jiho L., Eunkyu L., Yongdae K. 'Touching the untouchables: dynamic security analysis of the lte control plane'. *IEEE Proceedings on Security & Privacy*; 2019. pp. 273–82.

[31] Busari S.A., Huq K.M.S., Mumtaz S., Dai L., Rodriguez J. 'Millimeter-wave massive mimo communication for future wireless systems: a survey'. *IEEE Communications Surveys & Tutorials*. 2018;**20**(2):836–69.

[32] Liyanage M., Ahmad I., Ylianttila M., Gurtov A., Ahmed B.A. 'Leveraging lte security with SDN and NFV'. *IEEE International Conference on Industrial and Information Systems*; 2015. pp. 220–5.

[33] Jing L., Yang X., Shuhui L., Wei L C.L., Philip C.L. 'Cyber security and privacy issues in smart grids'. *IEEE Communications Surveys & Tutorials.* 2012;**14**(4):981–97.

[34] Ali Hassan A.S., Ye L., Madad A.S. 'Green and friendly media transmission algorithms for wireless body sensor networks'. *Journal of Multimedia Tools and Applications.* 2017;**76**(19):20001–25.

[35] Chen M., Ma Y., Song J., Lai C.-F., Hu B. 'Smart clothing: connecting human with clouds and big data for sustainable health monitoring'. *Mobile Networks and Applications.* 2016;**21**(5):825–45.

[36] Ali H.S., Ye L., Madad A.S. 'Novel key storage and management solution for the security of wireless sensor networks'. *Indonesian Journal of Electrical Engineering.* 2013;**11**(6):3383–90.

[37] Sophia C. Difference between security and privacy. 2018. Available from http://www.differencebetween.net/technology/internet/difference-between-security-and-privacy/.

[38] Tanwar S., Parekh K., Evans R. 'Blockchain-based electronic healthcare record system for healthcare 4.0 applications'. *Journal of Information Security and Applications.* 2019;**50**:1–14.

[39] Tanwar S. '*Fog Computing for Healthcare 4.0 Environments: Technical, Societal, and Future Implications, Signals and Communication Technology*'. Springer International Publishing; 2020. pp. 1–430.

[40] Hathaliya J.J., Tanwar S. 'An exhaustive survey on security and privacy issues in healthcare 4.0'. *Computer Communications.* 2020;**153**(6):311–35.

[41] Hathaliya J.J., Tanwar S., Evans R. 'Securing electronic healthcare records: a mobile-based biometric authentication approach'. *Journal of Information Security and Applications.* 2020;**53**(3):102528–14.

[42] Hathaliya J.J., Tanwar S., Tyagi S., Kumar N. 'Securing electronics healthcare records in healthcare 4.0: a biometric-based approach'. *Computers & Electrical Engineering.* 2019;**76**(4):398–410.

[43] Kumari A., Tanwar S., Tyagi S., Kumar N. 'Fog computing for healthcare 4.0 environment: opportunities and challenges'. *Computers & Electrical Engineering.* 2018;**72**(5):1–13.

[44] Hathaliya J., Sharma P., Tanwar S., Gupta R. 'Blockchain-based remote patient monitoring in healthcare 4.0'. *9th IEEE International Conference on Advanced Computing (IACC)*; Tiruchirappalli, India; 13–14th December, 2019. pp. 87–91.

[45] Gupta R., Tanwar S., Tyagi S., Kumar N., Obaidat M.S., Sadoun HaBiTs B. 'Blockchain-based telesurgery framework for healthcare 4.0'. *International Conference on Computer*; August 28–31, 2019. pp. 6–10.

[46] Vora J., Devmurari P., Tanwar S., Tyagi S., Kumar N., Obaidat M.S. 'Blind signatures based secured e-healthcare system'. *International Conference on Computer*; 11–13 July 2018. pp. 177–81.

[47] Vohra J., Kaneriya S., Tanwar S., Tyagi S. 'Standardising the use of duplex channels in 5G-wifi networking for ambient assisted living'. *IEEE Conference on Communications (IEEE ICC-2019)*; Shanghai, China; 20–24th May, 2019. pp. 1–6.

[48] Gupta R., Tanwar S., Tyagi S., Kumar N. 'Tactile Internet and its applications in 5G era: a comprehensive review'. *International Journal of Communication Systems*. 2019;**32**(14):e3981–49.

[49] Olabode I., Kennedy O., Ryan H., Michael A. '5G wireless communication network architecture and its key enabling technologies'. *International Review of Aerospace Engineering*. 2019;**12**(2):32–9.

[50] Bloch M., Barros J., Rodrigues M.R.D., McLaughlin S.W., João B., Miguel R.D. 'Wireless information-theoretic security'. *IEEE Transactions on Information Theory*. 2008;54(6):2515–34.

[51] Laxmi E.L., Shankar K., Ilayaraja M., Sathesh K.K. 'Technological solutions for health care protection and services through Internet of things'. *International Journal of Pure and Applied Mathematics*. 2018;**118**(7):277–83.

Chapter 2

Ethical and legal aspects of using blockchain technology for 5G-based health-care systems

Shashank Srivastava[1], Richesh Gupta[1], Prateek Pandey[1], and Ratnesh Litoriya[2]

Abstract

The fifth generation of cell-based mobile communication architecture is commonly called 5G. Due to the growing speed of internet services and Device-to-Device communication (D2D), the role of Internet of Things (IoT) has become prominent. IoT on a 5G-enabled environment ensures readiness and round-the-clock availability of essential services such as healthcare. Due to the health-care data's sensitivity, blockchain architecture can be used with 5G to provide secure exchange and interoperability of data. Blockchain keeps the integrity of the health-care data intact, and it prevents unauthorized access using state-of-the-art cryptographic techniques. Keeping multiple copies of the health-care data on various nodes and practical consistency algorithms ensures that if the data at any node are compromised, the network will not allow this change to permeate through it. In this new internet era, healthcare with 5G and blockchain comes up with many new techno-legal challenges that need to be understood well before implementing or investing in this domain. Though 5G with blockchain will bring the ability to set up an environment by keeping patients at the core, accountability in case of medical neglect is hard to establish. Legal frameworks to deal with such IoT and blockchain-based network issues are practically nonexistent. This chapter systematically presents the issues introduced by the use of advanced technologies in health-care systems. The chapter also discusses the possible solutions and their impact on the health-care system in a broader context.

Keywords: IoT, Blockchain, Healthcare, 5G, Ethical grounds, Security in 5G

[1]Jaypee University of Engineering & Technology, Guna, India
[2]Medi-caps University, Indore, India

2.1   Introduction

One department where innovation has never been seen is the health-care system, but if we talk about the current scenario, it requires upgradation from top to bottom while preserving the sanctity of the health-care system [1–3]. With the inception of technologies such as 5G, IoT, and blockchain it is easy to inspire such changes but the process has various challenges to implement the same [4–6].

A health-care system needs privacy and security but it also demands a mechanism through which we can access information instantly everywhere, at all times [7–9]. Blockchain provides privacy and security but to implement instant access, 5G will play a crucial role.

According to securitytoday.com, 26.6 billion IoT devices are connected to the internet [10]. It is only natural to leverage IoT to cease the hurdle of the geological boundary of network access.

First let us understand what each technology is, to understand the cause and effect of their amalgamation.

Blockchain is essentially a decentralized network of nodes that processes all transactions securely and according to its own rules [11]. Blockchain does not allow editing of the stored data and it also shares copy of the data with all the nodes participating in the blockchain network. Moreover, it allows no user to have special access and there is no central node exist in the blockchain network [9, 12–14].

5G is the fifth generation of cellular technology, and it increases data transfer rate to a great degree in the wireless device using its hood components such as advanced antenna system and its bandwidth [15, 16]. Also, it is designed to support a large number of people, all of which 4G did not have.

5G opens up new financially viable possibilities in a variety of markets. 5G has dramatically enhanced our ability to obtain real time data which opens up momentous opportunities concerning how we use data to inform and improve decision-making at all levels [17–22]. IoT is a network of interconnected devices that supports the network by generally acting as an intermediary between the end user and network [23–25]. It has been a well-known technology and it is on the boom.

In this chapter, we are trying to understand these technologies within the technological aspect and their integration within themselves and the health-care system along with the challenges that we will face while doing the same.

2.1.1   Research contribution

Currently, there are 4.66 billion active internet users, but the existing health-care systems are in adequate to handle this ever increasing demand of the users. Amalgamation of IoT with blockchain and 5G would support the health-care sector to handle the massive number of users.

According to Statista, in the USA alone around 16.9 percent of their GDP spent on healthcare, which is approximately 347 billion USD (2018), whereas the deployment of 5G and blockchain in the USA overall costs around 18 billion USD, which is 5.18% of the yearly budget of the health-care system in the USA; therefore, with one-time spending of the minuscule percentage of expenditure, we can turn up the entire system for better [26].

2.1.2 Motivation

In this chapter, we address the ethical and legal aspects of blockchain. The central focus of this chapter is to boost 5G and health-care systems. 5G is going to play a vital role in upcoming years which is useful in telecommunication industries and the health-care sector, and many more industries will get benefited. This will improve the internet speed, help huge data handling, and process the data fast. 5G technology has the potential to transform health-care delivery by boosting speed and capacity while reducing computation. In the 5G health-care ecosystem, patients will become less idle consumers of healthcare and more engaged in driving their outcomes.

2.1.3 Organization

This chapter is organized in a way that the reader gets the idea of the technologies (i.e., blockchain, IoT, 5G) before discussing them deeply. First, we have defined technologies briefly along with some statistic showing the need for this chapter.

Then, we have described each technology and described the under-the-hood technologies such as blockchain, 5G, and IoT we are using. After that, we have discussed the potential applications and future challenges. Finally, we have concluded the chapter.

2.2 Blockchain technology and 5G in healthcare

It is essential to understand the meaning of these terms. A blockchain is originally a collection of records that stores the information of some transaction in a cryptography form. Blockchain can provide us the security of a high level so that our transactions are safe, and we can prevent ourselves from malicious attacks [21].

Each block is associated with different tasks and stored with some digital piece of information. Blockchain mainly includes three parts:

1. Each block is associated with some information in it.
2. Blocks store the address of who is involved in the particular transaction.
3. Blocks store different information so that we can easily differentiate.

Blockchain provides us an excellent level of security to secure the health-care information such as hospital details and patient transaction details, and stores their reports in a much secure way that can prevent hackers to break our system [27, 28].

Due to the increase in internet services and D2D, 5G will give an extreme speed in the future, which will be helpful in many sectors. Some reports state that by the end of 2021, we all are ready to enter the fifth-generation era [29, 30]. 5G will bring great benefits for the users who need high-speed internet, and also it is good for industries, e.g. medical services, to download a huge amount of data, smart devices.

The role of 5G in healthcare is crucial; it can bring new possibilities to overcome these upcoming challenges in the health-care sector. We will discuss more of these technologies.

5G provides high-speed connectivity so that machines can work efficiently on different platforms. Reports predicted that by the end of 2022, there would be high increase in the existing medical market, which means we need new technologies, upgraded tools, high-speed internet so that patients can also be treated remotely.

Web development is also going to be affected with 5G inclusions, by encouraging web developers to prepare their existing web applications to win the 5G race and launch enhanced and more dynamic web applications with 5G possibilities in mind [31–33].

5G technology has the potential to have a transformative upshot on the global market through various verticals; for example, agriculture, smart cities, mobile app development, and artificial intelligence certainly are the most prominent areas that consider 5G will bring a lot of opportunities to the students that will help them to do augmented and virtual reality (AR-VR) surgery, and the students will become expert doctors in the future [34–39]. After the launch of 5G, the exchange of data, reports between two persons, is very easy and fast, and it is secured and patients can be easily monitored in the home from anywhere and any time [40].

There is no need to visit the hospital every time. Technology is already used to do secure patients' information. Estonia is using blockchain technology from 2012 to secure health-care data, reports, number of visits, and transaction details. With the way this country is moving toward blockchain and 5G healthcare, in the coming years, their health-care sector will become very efficient and fast and everyone should follow the path of this country so that every country can take advantage of the technology provided by the 5G healthcare [41, 42].

Some technologies that use 5G are edge computing, virtual reality, augmented reality, and mobile app.

2.2.1   Edge computing

Edge computing is also known as "fog computing." in which we store the data on the cloud and it provides, the fast computation and easy data storage closer to the location where it is needed. In this way, one can save bandwidth and reduce time. The massive increase in the amount of data may lead to system problems and lower the speed of the computation. Edge computing brings analytical computational methods close to the end users and therefore helps them to speed up the communication.

For example, face recognition takes very few seconds to identify the person, and in a similar way edge computing is able to process data in a very short duration of time.

2.2.2   Augmented and virtual reality

AR is an experience of a real-world using objects but these objects are computer vision-based and with the help of graphical work it makes them look real. It is used to augment graphics, videos, sounds, and other sensors. Generally, it is used to get a real view of the world without any problem [43, 44].

VR takes you out of the physical world and lets you enjoy virtual environment related to the application where you want to deploy these haptic devices. Many gaming companies are using this technology to move forward in the gaming world. If we take a look toward healthcare, then in the future AR-VR will give a great advantage to this industry. New interns can do virtual surgery; it will allow medical professionals to help patients understand surgical procedures and the way medicines work.

2.2.3   Ambulance drones

Ambulance drones are compact flying toolboxes containing essential supplies for a suffering person [45]. The portability of these drones is anywhere, even indoors. An ambulance may take some time to reach the destination but with the help of a drone, one can easily reach and supply needed medicines to the suffering person. It is very helpful for the patients in critical condition as brain death and permanent death start to happen in just some minutes. Drones can detect the GPS location of the person and reach there for certain kinds of emergency and, hence, ambulance drone could be the future of emergency responses.

A conclusion can be drawn that 5G in healthcare could bring change in the future, which is needed. Moreover, the adoption of 5G in the coming years provides high data security through blockchain, or any decentralized systems.

2.2.4   5G on mobile app development

5G has the power to impact mobile app development and that too with the full potential to transform the mobile users' experience. Mobile users are demanding technology that offers seamless connectivity, full accessibility, convenience, and very high speed, while using it [46–48]. Although 4G has all these features, people desire something even better. 5G is a game-changing technology that is presenting extremely high-speed and stable mobile internet connectivity, which has eliminated various issues of mobile app development and allows quicker downloads and supports the transfer of vast amounts of data in real-time from scores of connected devices.

2.3   Issues of privacy and security

Privacy issues are those involving the access of private information. Some examples are tracking, hacking, trading, spying and snooping.

Security issues occur when a hacker gains unauthorized access. There are many ways through which one gets attacked, and an example of an open wireless network is Wi-Fi. When someone is using open Wi-Fi, then there are a lot of chances that the details get stolen; it may be login id (passwords), some text messages, transaction details, and many more. So, these are some security issues associated with using internet [49].

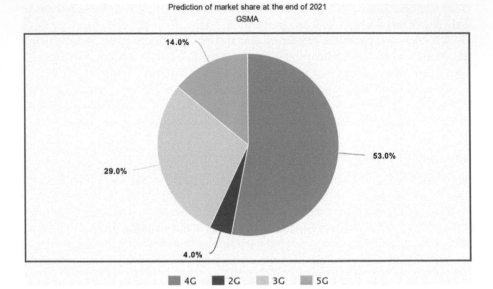

Prediction of market share at the end of 2021
GSMA

Figure 2.1   Prediction of Market share by the end of 2021 (Source: GSMA) [51]

The expansion of 5G in the coming years will create a boom in the industry. More and more devices get connected for a single person and this will require a huge amount of data. 5G networks will change the market view, medical proce-dures, financial transactions, remote industrial automation, military operations, or delivery of local emergency services [50]. To enable this in future, countries should level up to take advantage of these technologies.

Some privacy issues are tracking location, identity, reports, transactions, and other personal data. The future concern of many tech giants will be to save their data in a secured way, because with updated technologies, hackers and crackers are also updating.

Figure 2.1 shows some information about how 5G will grow and 4G is run-ning. Reports state that at the end of 2021, we are ready to start with 5G, and in 2025 everyone will have 5G network at their fingertips and that is how the generation changes.

The following table explains the characteristics of blockchain [52], the description of the particular characteristic, and its potential use in the current health-care system.

Characteristics	Description	Potential
Decentralized network	Blockchain is made up of decentralized nodes; it is not governed by a single entity. Instead, groups of nodes verify the transactions happening on the network.	There is no single point of failure, and there is almost no effect of nodes entering and leaving the network. This makes the system effective at all times, which is essential in the health-care industry.
Distributed ledger	In the blockchain, every node has a copy of the ledger that a network is generating; the network syncs all the entries to all nodes and verifies the legitimacy of the transaction.	With the distribution of this level, data loss never occurs. Also, one bad actor cannot corrupt the entries, because of the syncing of entries to all nodes.
Fast transaction resolving	With many nodes dividing transactions within themselves, waiting time decreases to a great degree.	In the industry where time taken to make a decision is crucial for the lives, which depends on the system, this feature is a must and blockchain fulfills it.
Consensus	It is the most interesting feature of blockchain: blockchain architecture is designed to include every node to help decision-making while following a particular protocol.	It helps in faster processing of the transaction and makes sure that no party is special. The total fair decision is taken within this feature.
Immutability	Nothing is ever altered or deleted without getting noticed. This means history is preserved in the blocks and if there is any change then another block is added to represent the change.	In healthcare, stakeholders will have patients' full report within a click and there is always a guarantee that all the information provided is legitimate.

2.4 Security spectrum of 5G-enabled devices

Security is always judged on the fact that how many vulnerabilities exist in the system—fewer vulnerabilities means the system is more secure. Therefore, discussing possible vulnerabilities that can occur in the system is a better way to understand its security status.

5G technology relies on numerous other technologies and one of them is IoT; Ultra-reliable low-latency communication technology is used with IoT to provide 5G [53]. But as we all know IoTs are prone to many types of vulnerabilities, which can lead to massive damage.

With every company working to make the 5G dream a reality, they are also realizing that taking care of security and privacy is a challenge task. With the huge potential of 5G-enabled devices, there is going to be a massive scale integration of various categories of devices, e.g., smart vehicles, medical equipment, and smart bands, which create points of vulnerability and if a hacker gets a successful exploit then not only financial destruction would happen but lives would be lost too.

Integrating 5G and blockchain into the health-care system is revolutionary, and it removes many hindrances that people face on a day-to-day basis [54, 55].

Blockchain, when incorporated with 5G with deployment in the health-care sector, has many advantages, and they are discussed in Sections 2.4.1 to 2.4.3.

2.4.1   Privacy

Maintaining privacy in the health-care sector has always been an important but difficult task. Blockchain's integral principle promises privacy right from the start to the end. Patients have the confidence to share whatever they want with their doctors and the information would be secured and cannot be traced back to the patients' physical social identity.

2.4.2   Transparency

Designing a system that is both transparent and privacy-centric is one of the most difficult tasks, which blockchain has done successfully. Blockchain provides the flexibility to all the users to know that what is going on in the network. Also, no bogus entry can happen because of the proof-of-work concept, which also increases the trust in the network [56].

2.4.3   No single point of failure

Security of data for any healthcare system is a prime concern and blockchain (being a Peer-to-Peer network) ensures that once the data is stored on the blockchain then no one have the rights to modify the data. Because of ledger distribution to every node on the network, data are not only secured but also irresistible to corrupt changes, as the changes are verified with all the nodes.

However, blockchain alone cannot make this system foolproof, but every element of this system has to contribute. Also, blockchain networks have some vulnerabilities that are very serious and can destroy the entire essence of security.

According to the BPI Network report, 94% of telecom operators and industry experts feel that 5G will escalate the security challenges with the advent of 5G networks as given in Figure 2.2.

2.5   Key issues and stakeholders

Let us try to understand why experts think that 5G-enabled devices will escalate security challenges.

2.5.1   Tweaking of IoT devices

2.5.1.1   Stakeholder profile: Individuals and industries

IoT is effective because of its vast coverage and this requires a lot of devices planted, sometimes even in locations that have virtually no scrutiny, which leads people with

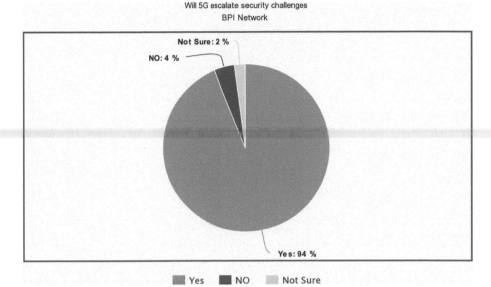

Figure 2.2   5G security scenario (Source: BPI Network) [57]

bad intentions to tweak hardware or software that compromises the particular device or, worse, the whole network.

With IoT devices in the health-care network, this can be very fatal.

2.5.2   No protocol right now to govern them all

2.5.2.1   Stakeholder profile: Individuals and government

Being a new technology, many government bodies are either not interested in adopting this new technology, or unaware about the benefits of adopting this technology in their services. Industrialists and lobbyists might always try that the situation to stay the same, which can continue the exploitation of people and would degrade the trust in the technology and later the industry.

2.5.3   Blockchain owning

2.5.3.1   Stakeholder profile: individuals

Blockchain has many advantages and straightforward security is one of them, but blockchain has a theoretical (till now) vulnerability that might become very serious in the future.

Blockchain has a feature called census, meaning that blockchain adds a block if at least 51% of its node provides and verifies it. Hence, if one industry/group of industries/individual/group of individuals gets hold of 51% of its nodes of the network (owning 51% of the proof-of-work entities), they will virtually own the integrity of the network, which eliminates the entire point of having blockchain in the first place.

2.5.4   Energy inefficiency

2.5.4.1   Stakeholder profile: industries

IoT has the fundamental design that requires an energy efficient with internal or external supply ranging from millivolts to a few volts.

With this much power, high complexity algorithms are not supported, which makes it extremely hard to integrate 5G and blockchain with the same hardware having the same quantity of power. Blockchain requires many complex cryptographic algorithms, which are hard to implement with this computation power. If we switch to simpler algorithms, this can create vulnerabilities in the system.

2.5.5   High-altitude limitations

2.5.5.1   Stakeholder profile: industries

A successful 5G service needs to support all types of terrain; however, 5G implementation in high remote terrain is very hard. High-altitude platform systems (HAPSs) are deployed there to cover for the connection, but 5G integration with HAPS still has to improve a lot to be effective and reliable. Because of this constraint, the entire dependency on the 5G network is not possible in the current scenario.

2.5.6   Man-in-the-middle attack

2.5.6.1   Stakeholder profile: individuals

A man-in-the-middle (MiTM) attack is very common with this type of technology, which has nodes placed publicly. If no proper security measures are taken, it can cause a huge cybersecurity mess [58]. This involves identity theft, packet sniffing, etc. To prevent MiTM attacks or similar attacks, authentication and tamper-detection are used, which again requires complex algorithms and protocols, which require IoT devices to be computationally powerful.

2.6   Trust and regulations

Trust is built with accountability and reliability.

Trust determines the acceptance of the technology, and for the success of the product, its technology must convince the mass that it is reliable.

Currently, regulations for 5G and blockchain are still in formation individually, let alone their combination [59]. No government body or any authority has decided their rules and regulations related to 5G. The USA's Federal Communications Commission (FCC) tried but a trial was held against them.

Late regulation formed by authorities may result in the industry exploiting the situation and also this gives them time to lobby their opinions with the politicians and affect the laws.

According to Cisco's white paper on 5G, technology is made by its infrastructure, and technology is trustable if its infrastructure is trustable.

With IoT underlying 5G, 5G becomes vulnerable with all the vulnerability that IoT has. The MiTM attack is one of them, which is a very high-risk security lapse.

To gain trust in technology and to make sure that there is minimum risk of security lapses, we need to have strict regulations in place. Recent regulation marvel is the General Data Protection Regulation (GDPR), which is formed by the EU and has jurisdiction in the EU countries [60].

The EU's model on data regulations (GDPR) is followed by the entire world because it is most privacy-centric, and its strict implementation makes it dynamic according to the requirements of companies.

GDPR is the most comprehensive compliance and it values personal data. Companies with power cannot just harvest the data and use it to manipulate the consumers; they have to now take consent from the users.

2.7   Regulatory bodies and the role of the government

According to Telenor, regulation in the field of 5G will decide the success of 5G. Although Telenor wants the regulation to be in favor of them, as "the rule of law" by Aristotle states that rules should be made with consideration of the general public.

In the United States, about 82% of the surveyed people are saying that they worry about online privacy and security. But within the current framework, very few countries are taking steps to ensure that the data of the public are safe and at least are used with their consent.

Governments are not competitive enough to research and update laws according to the cybercrimes. There should be a global authority such as the World Wide Web consortium, which should define regulations for 5G developments to ensure that there are standardizations and are implemented right from the genesis of this great technology.

This is just starting, more technologies will evolve based on the current fundamentals, and strict laws implemented today will play a crucial role in the formation of guidelines for other technologies based on the current one.

2.8   Future challenges

Challenges are a common part of any new technology. Making 5G a reality comes with some challenges [61]. Easy access to technology and also ease of use are the biggest challenges we face to instantiate the use. Enabling remote monitoring for patients will be a challenging task in the future. There are a lot of challenges including cost, infrastructure, security and privacy, frequency bands in the current scenario. With 5G in existence, there will be an explosion of information handling it, and using it securely is also a difficult task.

We will discuss each topic in detail to understand the clear meaning of each challenge.

2.8.1   Cost

It is a major challenge to discuss as many countries may face a problem in installing 5G services. Some countries do not have enough funds to install the 5G network connectivity because maintaining a 5G network requires a huge amount of investment.

With the increase in computing, network becomes a more complex structure than that was in the past generations. Instead of installing large cell towers, operators will be ready to launch small antennas.

Installing small antennas would require quite a much capital and also technical expertise. Also, there are too many endpoint dependencies to maintain, which increases maintenance cost.

2.8.2   Infrastructure

5G will use a spectrum that covers the frequency range of 600 Mega Hz–6 Giga Hz combined with the new millimeter-wave bands (24–86 Giga Hz) to enclose new features such as low latency, high output, high mobility, and high connection [62].

This will require small antennas to set up in a huge amount. 5G network infrastructure is a combination of macro- and small-cell base stations with edge computing capabilities. In health-care infrastructure, existing buildings may require an update to promote efficient healthcare, with specific services in specific sites, integrated therapy, and social services.

2.8.3   Security and privacy

5G promotes security threat partly because there are more vectors through which the opponent can attack. The technology is set to enable a huge number of connected devices, collectively known as the IoT.

The cybersecurity threat is a malevolent act that seeks to damage data, steal data, cause damage to a person or organization. Some of them are listed below.

Distributed denial-of-service (DDoS): A DDoS attack occurs when multiple systems flood the bandwidth or resources of a targeted system, usually one or more web servers, and make the network or system offline.

MiTM: In a MiTM attack, the attacker snoops the packets by posing as the intermediate device between packet relays, capturing packets and then extracting or corrupting the data as per the purpose of the attacker. Lack of proper encryption makes it easy to perform MiTM.

Botnet attacks: these are the devices infected by malware and are in control of hackers. Hackers can use these botnets to perform various malicious activities while the hacker being anonymous, and only the bot gets revealed.

2.8.4   Frequency bands

5G requires a high-band frequency to run and this could be a challenge for 5G network connectivity. In 5G, more spectrum is needed to maintain its Quality-of-Service

(QoS) and growing demand. High bands are needed to meet the expected speeds of 5G.

2.8.5 Training and education challenges

The health-care sector should improve so that it can pop up with the need of the citizens. The new technologies come up with an upgraded level of tools. In these technologies, change is not easy, and during this transformation phase, many organizations are struggling to sustain and also they are facing competition from various organizations that have already upgraded their businesses with the current technologies [62]. The sector requires trained professionals now, more than ever, and they are scarce. To leverage the opportunity and sieging it would require training and education about the market.

2.9 Conclusion

This chapter focused on the ethical and legal aspects of blockchain and 5G with the amalgamation of healthcare.

We have found that there can be immense possibilities that can be achieved with the intersection of blockchain and 5G in healthcare. But this integration has some challenges also like heterogeneity of devices, network connectivity issues, and interfacing problems.

However, we still have not achieved the methods to spread the technology to a sufficiently large population to make it more mainstream than the privileged use. Various challenges are yet to be resolved, for example, executing complex cryptographic algorithms while using power as efficiently as possible. Security lapses, providing sufficient bandwidth, and stable connection are some of the challenges too.

Adequate infrastructure and cost are the key challenges and these challenges can be solved when there is some central authority that will supervise the resources that are required to research and develop the technologies and to define guidelines to make sure there is no exploitation of the people with the help of these technologies.

References

[1] Tanwar S., Tyagi S., Kumar N. 'Security and privacy of electronics health-care records'. *IET Book Series on e-Health Technologies*; 2019. pp. 1–433. Available from https://digital-library.theiet.org/content/books/he/pbhe020e.

[2] Prateek P., Ratnesh L. 'Securing and authenticating healthcare records through blockchain technology'. *Cryptologia*. 2020;**44**(4):341–56.

[3] Zhang J., Xue N., Huang X. 'A secure system for pervasive social network-based healthcare'. *IEEE Access*. 2016;**4**:9239–50.

[4] Mistry I., Tanwar S., Tyagi S., Kumar N. 'Blockchain for 5G-enabled IoT for industrial automation: a systematic review, solutions, and challenges'. *Mechanical Systems and Signal Processing*. 2020;**135**(5):106382.

[5]   Pandey P., Litoriya R. 'An IoT assisted system for generating emergency alerts using routine analysis'. *Wireless Personal Communications*. 2020;**112**(1):607–30.

[6]   Pandey P., Litoriya R, Prateek P., Ratnesh L. 'Promoting trustless computation through blockchain technology'. *National Academy Science Letters*. 2020:1–7.

[7]   Pandey P., Litoriya R. 'Legal/regulatory issues for MMBD in IOT BT – multimedia big data computing for IOT applications: Concepts, paradigms and solutions' in Tanwar S., Tyagi S., Kumar N. (eds.). Singapore: Springer Singapore; 2020. pp. 367–88.

[8]   Litoriya R., Gulati A., Yadav M., Ghosh R.S., Pandey P. 'Social, ethical, and regulatory issues of fog computing in healthcare 4.0 applications'. *Fog Computing for Healthcare 4.0 Environments*. Cham: Springer; 2021. pp. 593–609.

[9]   Vora J., Tanwar S., Nayyar A., *et al.* 'BHEEM: a blockchain-based framework for securing electronic health records'. *2018 IEEE Globecom Workshops (GC Wkshps)*; 2018. pp. 1–6.

[10] Davin G.M. The IOT rundown for 2020: Stats, risks, and solutions [online]. 2020. Available from https://securitytoday.com/articles/2020/01/13/the-iot-rundown-for-2020.aspx [Accessed 01 Dec 2020].

[11] Satoshi N. 'Bitcoin: a peer-to-peer electronic cash system'. 2008:1–9.

[12] Pandey P., Litoriya R. 'Securing e-health networks from counterfeit medicine penetration using blockchain'. *Wireless Personal Communications*. 2021;**117**(1):7–25.

[13] Kabra N., Bhattacharya P., Tanwar S., Tyagi S. 'Mudrachain: blockchain-based framework for automated cheque clearance in financial institutions'. *Future Generation Computer Systems*. 2020;**102**(4):574–87.

[14] Toyoda K., Mathiopoulos P.T., Sasase I., Ohtsuki T. 'A novel blockchain-based product ownership management system (POMS) for anti-counterfeits in the post supply chain'. *IEEE Access*. 2017;**5**:17465–77.

[15] Qualcomm. With 5G here, what's next for the Internet of Things? [online]. Available from https://www.qualcomm.com/news/onq/2020/05/12/5g-here-whats-next-internet-things [Accessed May 2020].

[16] Kumari A., Tanwar S., Tyagi S., Kumar N., Obaidat M.S., Rodrigues J.J.P.C. 'Fog computing for smart grid systems in the 5G environment: challenges and solutions'. *IEEE Wireless Communications*. 2019;**26**(3):47–53.

[17] Sharma N., Litoriya R., Sharma D., Singh H.P. 'Designing a decision support framework for municipal solid waste management'. *International Journal on Emerging Technologies*. 2019;**10**(4):374–9.

[18] Sharma N., Litoriya R., Sharma A. 'Application and analysis of k-means algorithms on a decision support framework for municipal solid waste management' in Hassanien A., Bhatnagar R., Darwish A. (eds.). *Advanced Machine Learning Technologies and Applications. Amlta 2020, Advances in Intelligent Systems and Computing*. Singapore: Springer; 2021. pp. 267–76.

[19] Pandey P., Kumar S., Shrivastava S. 'An efficient time series forecasting method exploiting fuzziness and turbulences in data'. *International Journal of Fuzzy System Applications.* 2017;**6**(4):83–98.

[20] Sharma N., Litoriya R., Sharma D. 'An analytical study on the importance of data mining for designing a decision support system'. *Journal of Harmonized Research in Applied Science.* 2019;**7**(2):44–8.

[21] Pandey P., Litoriya R. 'Software process selection system based on multicriteria decision making'. *Journal of Software: Evolution and Process.* 2021;**33**(2):e2305.

[22] Pandey M., Litoriya R., Pandey P. 'Novel approach for mobile based APP development incorporating MAAF'. *Wireless Personal Communications.* 2019;**107**(4):1687–708.

[23] Pandey P., Litoriya R. 'Ensuring elderly well being during COVID-19 by using IoT'. *Disaster Medicine and Public Health Preparedness.* 2020:1–10.

[24] Rao R.N., Sridhar B. 'IoT based smart crop-field monitoring and automation irrigation system'. *2018 2nd International Conference on Inventive Systems and Control (ICISC)*; 2018. pp. 478–83.

[25] Pandey P., Litoriya R. 'An activity vigilance system for elderly based on fuzzy probability transformations'. *Journal of Intelligent & Fuzzy Systems.* 2019;**36**(3):2481–94.

[26] Aditya R. Is blockchain the solution for healthcare? *Dataconomy [online].* 2017. Available from https://dataconomy.com/2017/03/blockchain-solution-healthcare/.

[27] Esmaeilzadeh P., Mirzaei T. 'The potential of blockchain technology for health information exchange: experimental study from patients' perspectives'. *Journal of Medical Internet Research.* 2019;**21**(6):e14184.

[28] Abhijit M. 'Reimagining health information exchange in India using blockchain'. 2019:1–28.

[29] Gupta A., Jha R.K. 'A survey of 5G network: architecture and emerging technologies'. *IEEE Access.* 2015;**3**:1206–32.

[30] Xiang W., Zheng K., Shen X.S. '5G mobile communications'. 2016:1–691.

[31] Prateek P., Ratnesh L. 'Fuzzy cognitive mapping analysis to recommend machine learning based effort estimation technique for web applications'. *International Journal of Fuzzy Systems.* 2020;**22**(4):1212–23.

[32] Litoriya R. '*Existing Software Estimation Models Validation and Improvements for Web Based Projects*'. Shri Jagdishprasad Jhabarmal Tibarewala University; 2015.

[33] Qiao X., Ren P., Nan G., Liu L., Dustdar S., Chen J. 'Mobile web augmented reality in 5G and beyond: challenges, opportunities, and future directions'. *China Communications.* 2019;**16**(9):141–54.

[34] Pandey P., Litoriya R. 'A predictive fuzzy expert system for crop disease diagnostic and decision support'. *Fuzzy Expert Systems and Applications in Agricultural Diagnosis.* IGI Global; 2019. pp. 175–94.

[35] Phan A., Qureshi S.T. 5G impact on smart cities. 2017. Available from https://www.researchgate.net/publication/315804922_5G_impact_On_Smart_Cities/citations.

[36] Pandey M., Litoriya R., Pandey P. 'An ISM approach for modeling the issues and factors of mobile APP development'. *International Journal of Software Engineering and Knowledge Engineering*. 2018;**28**(07):937–53.

[37] Pandey M., Litoriya R., Pandey P. 'Application of fuzzy dematel approach in analyzing mobile APP issues'. *Programming and Computer Software*. 2019;**45**(5):268–87.

[38] Building your visions, creating reality [online]. Paladin. 2019. Available from https://paladinsoftwares.com/ar-vr/ [Accessed 23 Sep 2020].

[39] Pandey P., Litoriya R. 'Elderly care through unusual behavior detection: a disaster management approach using IoT and intelligence'. *IBM Journal of Research and Development*. 2019;**64**(1):15:1–15:11.

[40] Ahad A., Tahir M., Yau K.-L.A. '5G-based smart healthcare network: architecture, taxonomy, challenges and future research directions'. *IEEE Access*. 2019;**7**:100747–62.

[41] Soldani D. '5G mobile systems for healthcare'. *IEEE Vehicular Technology Conference*; 2017.

[42] Prasad V.K., Bhavsar M.D., Tanwar S. 'Influence of monitoring: fog and edge computing'. *Scalable Computing: Practice and Experience*. 2019;**20**(2):365–76.

[43] Li X., Yi W., Chi H.-L., Wang X., Chan A.P.C. 'A critical review of virtual and augmented reality (VR/AR) applications in construction safety'. *Automation in Construction*. 2018;**86**(1):150–62.

[44] Dhivya A.J.A., Premkumar J. 'Quadcopter based technology for an emergency healthcare'. *Proceedings of the 3rd International Conference on Biosignals, Images and Instrumentation, ICBSII 2017*; 2017.

[45] Pandey M., Litoriya R., Pandey P. 'Validation of existing software effort estimation techniques in context with mobile software applications'. *Wireless Personal Communications*. 2020;**110**(4):1659–77.

[46] Pandey M., Litoriya R., Pandey P. 'Empirical analysis of defects in handheld device applications'. *Advances in Computing and Data Sciences*; 2019. pp. 103–13.

[47] Pandey M., Litoriya R., Pandey P., *et al.* 'Perception-based classification of mobile apps: a critical review' in Luhach A.K., Hawari K.B.G., Mihai I.C., Hsiung P.-A., Mishra R.B. (eds.). *Smart Computational Strategies: Theoretical and Practical Aspects*. Singapore: Springer Singapore; 2019. pp. 121–33.

[48] Vora J., Italiya P., Tanwar S., *et al.* 'Ensuring privacy and security in e-health records'. *2018 International Conference on Computer, Information and Telecommunication Systems (CITS)*; 2018. pp. 1–5.

[49] Skouby K.E., Lynggaard P. 'Smart home and smart city solutions enabled by 5G, IoT, AAI and CoT services'. *2014 International Conference on Contemporary Computing and Informatics (IC3I)*; 2014. pp. 874–8.

[50] GSMA. *GSMA: 5G moves from hype to reality – but 4G still king. GSMA*. March 2021. Available from https://www.gsma.com/newsroom/press-release/gsma-5g-moves-from-hype-to-reality-but-4g-still-king/.

[51]   Gupta R., Tanwar S., Tyagi S., Kumar N., Obaidat M.S., Sadoun B. 'HaBiTs: blockchain-based telesurgery framework for healthcare 4.0'. *2019 International Conference on Computer, Information and Telecommunication Systems (CITS)*; 2019. pp. 1–5.

[52]   Sachs J., Wikstrom G., Dudda T., Baldemair R., Kittichokechai K. '5G radio network design for ultra-reliable low-latency communication ultra-reliable low-Latency communication'. *IEEE Network*. 2018;**32**(2):24–31.

[53]   Nguyen D.C., Pathirana P.N., Ding M., Seneviratne A. 'Blockchain for 5G and beyond networks: a state of the art survey'. *Journal of Network and Computer Applications*. 2020;**166**(4):102693.

[54]   Gupta R., Shukla A., Tanwar S. 'AaYusH: a smart contract-based telesurgery system for healthcare 4.0'. *2020 IEEE International Conference on Communications Workshops, ICC Workshops 2020 – Proceedings*; 2020.

[55]   Olazabal M., Neumann M.B., Foudi S., Chiabai A. 'Transparency and reproducibility in participatory systems modelling: the case of fuzzy cognitive mapping'. *Systems Research and Behavioral Science*. 2018;**35**(6):791–810.

[56]   Foukas X., Patounas G., Elmokashfi A., Marina M.K. 'Network slicing in 5G: survey and challenges'. *IEEE Communications Magazine*. 2017;**55**(5):94–100.

[57]   Callegati F., Cerroni W., Ramilli M. 'Man-in-the-middle attack to the https protocol'. *IEEE Security & Privacy Magazine*. 2009;**7**(1):78–81.

[58]   Suryanegara M. '5G as disruptive innovation: standard and regulatory challenges at a country level'. *International Journal of Technology*. 2016;**7**(4):635.

[59]   Murphy J.F.A. 'The general data protection regulation (GDPR)'. *Irish Medical Journal*. 2021.

[60]   O'Connell E., Moore D., Newe T. 'Challenges associated with implementing 5G in manufacturing'. *Telecom*. 2020;**1**(1):48–67.

[61]   Foukas X., Patounas G., Elmokashfi A., Marina M.K. 'Network slicing in 5G: survey and challenges'. *IEEE Communications Magazine*. 2017;**55**(5):94–100.

[62]   Sarre S., Maben J., Aldus C., *et al.* 'The challenges of training, support and assessment of healthcare support workers: a qualitative study of experiences in three English acute hospitals'. *International Journal of Nursing Studies*. 2018;**79**:145–53.

Chapter 3

Blockchain-based 5G-enabled health-care system: an analysis of security and privacy issues

Shweta Kaushik[1]

Abstract

Blockchain offers an imaginative method to manage information, executing trades, setting limits, and setting up trust in an open area. Numerous associations consider blockchain as an advanced forward jump for cryptography and network safety, with use cases from globally used computerized money systems such as Bitcoin, insight contracts, and sharp grids over the Internet of Things. Regardless of the way that blockchain has gotten creating interests in both insightful world and industry starting late, the security and insurance of blockchains continue to be the point of convergence of the conversation while sending blockchain in different applications. This chapter presents an exhaustive outline of the security and protection of blockchain. To encourage the conversation, we initially present the idea of blockchains and their utility with regard to Bitcoin-like applications on the web exchanges. At that point, we also portray the fundamental security properties that are upheld as the basic necessities, building obstructs for Bitcoin-like digital money frameworks, trailed by introducing the extra security, and furthermore, security properties that are required in numerous blockchain applications. Finally, we survey the security and protection procedures for accomplishing these security properties in blockchain-based frameworks, including delegate agreement calculations, hash fastened capacity, blending conventions, unknown marks and non-intelligent zero-information verification. We believe that this study can assist perusers with gaining an inside and out comprehension of the security and protection of blockchain concerning ideas, traits, methods, and systems. This chapter presents the utilizations of blockchain in different fields, methodically dissects the security of each layer of the blockchain and conceivable digital assaults, explains the difficulties brought by the blockchain to organize management, and sums up research progress in the assurance innovation. This chapter is an audit of the current security of the blockchain and will successfully support the turn of events and improvement of security advances of the blockchain.

[1]ABES Engineering College, Ghaziabad, India

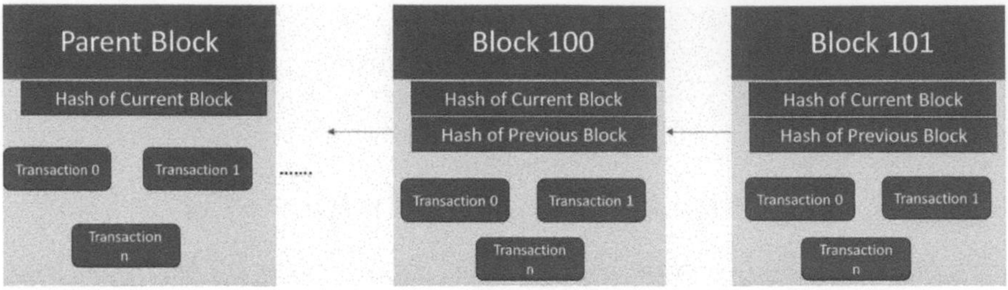

Figure 3.1   Blockchain working

Keywords: 5G, Blockchain, Healthcare, Privacy, Security

3.1   Introduction

3.1.1   Blockchain

Blockchain is generally known as the innovation fundamental of the cryptographic money Bitcoin [1]. The center thought of a blockchain is decentralization. This infers blockchain does not store any of its information bases in a central territory. Or maybe, the blockchain is imitated and spread over an arrangement of individuals. At whatever point another block is added to the blockchain, every Personal Computer (PC) on the framework invigorates its blockchain to reflect the change. This dispersed engineering guarantees hearty and secure procedure on the blockchain with the upsides of alter obstruction and no single-point disappointment weaknesses. Specifically, blockchain can be available for everybody and is not constrained by any system element. This is empowered by an instrument called accord, which has a lot of rules to guarantee the understanding among all members on the status of the blockchain record. The overall idea on how blockchain works is presented in Figure 3.1. Blockchain, a circulated record innovation, empowers clients to connect and execute (store and recover information) with guaranteed information legitimacy, changelessness, and non-disavowal. The appropriated idea of blockchain permits the mechanical elements and different 5G/Internet of Things (IoT) gadgets to trade information, to and from their friends, taking out the concentrated operational necessity.

The blockchain-based 5G biological system is fit for building up responsibility, information provenance, and non-denial for each client. The principal hinderance in a blockchain is alluded to as the beginning square, which does not contain any exchange. Each square from that point contains various approved exchanges and is cryptographically connected with the past square. When all is said and done, blockchains can be named either an open (authorization-less) or a private (permissioned) blockchain [2]. An open blockchain is available for everybody and anybody can join and cause exchanges just as to take an interest in the agreement procedure. The most popular open blockchain applications incorporate Bitcoin and Ethereum.

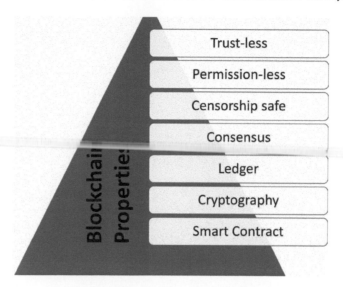

Figure 3.2   Blockchain properties

Private blockchains then again are a greeting just system oversaw by a focal element. A member must be permissioned utilizing an approval component. So, to understand the capability of blockchain with 5G systems, it is important to comprehend the activity idea, principle belongings of blockchain, and see how it can carry chances to 5G applications. Moreover, blockchain is unique in relation to other disseminated frameworks dependent on agreement and following properties [3], as depicted in Figure 3.2.

1. **Trust-less:** The elements associated with the system are obscure to one another. Be that as it may, they can convey, coordinate, and work together with one another without realizing each other, which implies there is no prerequisite of guaranteed advanced character to play out any exchange between the substances.
2. **Permission-less:** There is no limitation of who can or cannot work inside the system, i.e., there are no sort of consents.
3. **Censorship safe:** Being a system without controllers, anybody can communicate or execute on the blockchain. Additionally, any affirmed exchange cannot be altered or blue-penciled. Notwithstanding the previously mentioned legitimacies, blockchain innovation has four fundamental segments [4], which are talked about as follows
4. **Consensus:** The Proof of Work (PoW) convention is mindful to check each activity in the system, which is basic to keep a solitary excavator hub from commanding the whole blockchain system and, furthermore, to control the exchanges history.
5. **Ledger:** It is a common and conveyed database that contains data of pretty much all exchanges performed inside the system. It is changeless commonly, where data once put away cannot be erased using any and all means. It ensures

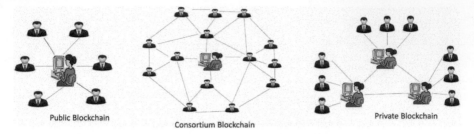

Figure 3.3   Types of blockchains

that each exchange is checked and afterward acknowledged as a legitimate one, by greater part of the customers required at a specific moment of time [5].

6. **Cryptography:** It guarantees that all information of the system is made sure about with solid cryptographic encryption. It permits just approved clients to unscramble the data.

7. **Smart contract:** It is utilized to approve and confirm the members of the system.

3.1.2   Types of blockchain

There are a few kinds of blockchains, the most absolute significant are Public, Private, and Consortium blockchain (crossbreed blockchain). Each type has its preferences and drawbacks, permitting them to address the issues of different applications. Figure 3.3 delineates the types of blockchain technologies. In particular, utilizing (a) Public blockchain, anybody can execute on the system exchanges that are straightforward and are mysterious. A Public blockchain, for example, Bitcoin, is totally decentralized. The framework works are dependent on clients' accord; there is no essential issue of disappointment. In any case, Public blockchain is defenseless against framework assaults. For example, an assailant could reproduce and appropriately change all the obstructs that had been altered, without being identified by the members; (b) In Private blockchain, the exchanges are mystery, the information isn't accessible for general visibility, however, the individuals are known. In a Private blockchain organize, a member cannot peruse or compose the blockchain except if the member has a consent or an encouragement to join the system. Private blockchain is generally utilized by enormous organizations with consents characterized between different partners of the venture blockchain. For example, a bank can have its own blockchain organize for its private use with confined access to its different partners, for example, clients, representatives, and providers; (c) Consortium blockchain is a half-and-half model of both Public and Private blockchains. Picking this model, undertakings or foundations can have their own Private blockchain system to share the information among the consortium members (e.g., banks, establishments, and different ventures or firms). The correlation between the three sorts of blockchains is recorded in Table 3.1.

Table 3.1   *Correlation between three types of blockchains*

Belongings	Public blockchain	Private blockchain	Consortium blockchain
Agreement assurance	All drillers	Only one organization	Selected nodes
Browse authorization	Public	Either public or restricted	Either public or restricted
Immutability	Possible to modify	Could be modified	Could be modified
Efficiency	Very less	Very high	Moderate
Centralized	No	Yes	Partially
Agreement process	Allowed	Allowed	Allowed

1. **Agreement assurance:** In open or public blockchain, each hub might participate within the agreement method. Additionally, on the grounds it was partner demonstrated arrangement of centres are responsible for thoughtful the hamper in connected blockchain. Regarding personal chain, it is fully affected by one association and also the association solely might decide the last agreement.
2. **Browse authorization:** Any info interactions in an exceedingly public blockchain are perceptible to general society whether or not it is contingent with respect to a personal blockchain or an association blockchain.
3. **Immutability:** Since info is placed far-off on a colossal variety of members, it is virtually troublesome to change or update associate exchanges in an open blockchain. On the other hand, exchanges in an exceedingly personal or an association blockchain might be reworked with success and a lot of expeditiously as there are simply planned variety of members.
4. **Efficiency:** It needs some savings to stimulate exchanges what's a lot of, hinders as there are a huge variety of hubs on open blockchain prepare. Consequently, exchange outturn is affected and also the dormancy is very high. With less validators, association and personal blockchain might be more and more effective.
5. **Centralized:** The principle distinction among the various forms of blockchains is that public blockchain is localized in nature, association blockchain is part brought along, and personal blockchain is totally centralized because it is controlled by a sole gathering.
6. **Agreement process:** Anybody might be a part of the accord procedure of public blockchain. However, public blockchain, each association blockchain, and personal blockchain are permissioned.

3.1.3   5G technology

In the course of recent periods, the world has perceived a consistent improvement of correspondence systems, introducing from the original and moving toward the fourth era [2, 6]. The worldwide correspondence circulation has demonstrated an extraordinary increment of late and is normal to proceed, which triggers the presence of the prospective age of media transmission systems, to be specific 5G, pointing to address the constraints of past cell guidelines and scope with such ever-expanding system limit. The 5G system can beat before adaptations of remote correspondence innovation and offer assorted assistance capacities as well as support full systems administration among nations, all inclusive. Blockchain innovation would be a promising possibility for 5G systems and administrations by giving various specialized advantages. We sum up the potential requests given to 5G by blockchain in Table 3.2.

The 5G organize engineering must help the organization of security systems and capacities (for example, virtual security firewalls) at whatever point required in any system border. The most conspicuous innovation for streamlining the board is software defined networking (SDN). SDN isolates the system control from the information sending plane. The control plane is intelligently brought together to administer the entire system underneath, what's more, and to control organize assets through programmable application programming interfaces. System functions virtualization executes network functions for all intents by decoupling equipment machines (for example, firewalls, entryways) from the capacities that are running on them to give virtualized entryways, virtualized firewalls. Moreover, the virtualized segments of the system, prompting the arrangements of adaptable system capacities. In the meantime, cloud processing/cloud RAN underpins boundless information stockpiling and information preparing to adapt to the developing IoT information traffic in 5G. The mixes of 5G empowering innovations guarantee to encourage portable systems with recently rising administrations such as wise information investigation and huge information handling. Uncommonly, not the same as past system ages (for example, 3G/4G), 5G is promising to offer portable types of assistance with incredibly low inertness, vitality investment funds because of adaptability (for example, arrange cutting what's more, closeness of edge processing), all of which will improve the QoS of the system and guarantee high Quality of Experience (QoE) for clients.

3.1.4   Healthcare

There are four kinds of health-care frameworks that are most well-known to created nations and the three types of medical services frameworks are single-payer, as given in Figure 3.4. The framework supported by the USA relies on the age, salary and, in general, on favorable luck of the citizens.

1. **The Beveridge model:** The essential public single-payer clinical consideration structure is the Beveridge model. In this system, the vast majority of the crisis facilities and experts work for the organization, though private specialists do exist. The people who live in a nation with such a structure never notice an expert's bill, as all clinical consideration is paid by the assembly through obligations. Additionally, considering the way that the organization controls what drug associations and experts can charge, this system saves a gigantic sum of money. While rivals of single-payer care guarantee that this causes longer hold

Table 3.2   *Blockchain characteristics and their possibilities in 5G*

Blockchain characteristics	Description	Application for 5G
Security and privacy	Blockchain pays uneven cryptoanalysis for protection with excessive verification, truthfulness, and nonrepudiation. Smart contracts to be had at the blockchain can aid records auditability, get entry to manage, and records provenance for confidentiality.	Deliver excessive protection for 5G grids concerned in dispersed registers. Blockchain enables stable 5G networks with the aid of using supplying dishursed believe fashions with excessive get right of entry to authentication, in flip allowing 5G structures to shield themselves and make sure facts privacy. By storing facts statistics (i.e., IoT metadata) throughout a community of processers, the project of cooperating facts will become tons extra tough for hackers. Besides, clever contracts, as trust-less 1/3 parties, probably assist 5G services, which include facts authentication, person verification, and upkeep of 5G useful resource in opposition to attacks.
Immutability	It could be very hard to regulate or alternate the records recorded withinside the blockchain.	Empower unreasonable changelessness for 5G administrations. Range sharing, realities sharing, virtualized network-valuable asset arrangements, helpful asset purchasing, and selling might be recorded permanently into the best attached blockchain. Also, D2D interchanges, omnipresent IoT organizing, and enormous scope of human-driven interconnections might be refined through distributed organizations of universal blockchain hubs without being changed or changed. The unnecessary unchanging nature might be useful for 5G organizations to acting bookkeeping assignments, for example logging of counsel records and usage measurements for charging, helpful asset use, and style examination.

(Continues)

Table 3.2   Continued

Blockchain characteristics	Description	Application for 5G
Transparency	All data on communications on blockchain may be available to all communal participants.	Deliver better-localized perceptibility into 5G carrier utilization. The identical replica of information of blockchain spreads throughout a massive community for public verifiability. This permits carrier companies and customers to completely get rid of entry to, verify, and music transaction sports over the community with identical rights. Also, blockchains probably provide obvious ledger answers for certainly open 5G architectures. Blockchain ledgers additionally assist truthful carrier buying and selling applications (i.e., useful resource buying and selling, payment) beneath the manipulation of all community entities.
Decentralization	No principal authority or dependency on 1/3 celebration is necessary to carry out transactions. Users have complete access on their personal records.	Eliminate the want for dependency on outside government in 5G ecosystems, i.e. spectrum licenses, band managers, and database managers in spectrum management; principal cloud/area carrier supervisor in cellular computing and D2D networks; UAV manipulate middle in 5G UAV networks; and complicated cryptographic primitives in 5G IoT structures. Decentralizing 5G networks probably dispose of single-factor failures, guarantees facts availability, and beautify carrier transport efficiency.

UAV, unmanned aerial vehicle.

up times because of the absence of doctors, the information does not prove this. Britain, for instance, utilizes this model, and their nature of care is not undermined, and most medical clinic holdups are still under four hours in length.

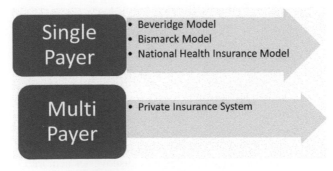

Figure 3.4   Health-care models

2. **The Bismarck model:** The second sort of a public single-payer clinical consideration structure is the Bismarck model. From the beginning, the Bismarck system has all the earmarks of resembling the US structure, as clinical consideration is given through protection organizations that are paid by business and specialist money deductions. Nonetheless, under Bismarck, everybody must be secured, and nobody is left with no admittance to mind. Moreover, medical clinics and specialists may not work for benefit, so, by and large, expenses are again significantly more reasonable than they are under the present US model. While the facts demonstrate that specialists in Germany will short of what they do in the USA, they additionally leave clinical school with practically zero obligation.

3. **The National Health Insurance model:** It offers a third kind of public single-payer medical services framework. These kinds of medical services frameworks are generally famous in Asian nations, and this model joins parts of both Beveridge and Bismarck. Medical services are paid through higher tax assessment; nonetheless, patients are allowed to pick any specialist or emergency clinic they wish. What's more, once more, similarly as with Beveridge and Bismarck, there is no benefit motivator, so costs will in general remain lower. Also, they have better well-being results. For instance, Japan utilizes this framework with a substantial accentuation on deterrent consideration and, in that capacity, has the absolute most noteworthy futures on the planet.

4. **The Private Insurance system:** The last of the four kinds of medical care frameworks is the one that most of the US residents are secured by—the private protection framework. In this framework, people are either secured by their managers, secured by a private approach the policyholder buys themselves or they abandon inclusion by any means. This is at present the medical services framework in the USA, and this combined with contracting compensation, ever-expanding costs, and an ever increasing number of bosses changing to a "gig" model of work that leaves a great many Americans with no place to go for care other than the trauma center.

3.2 Blockchain integration with 5G

Coordinating blockchain in the 5G versatile organizations is a hot exploration point now. Many examination endeavors have been given to the advancement of blockchain innovation for 5G portable organizations. The study has covered and featured the advantages of blockchain to enable the central 5G administrations, for example, range the board, information sharing, network virtualization, asset the executives, impedance the executives, protection and security administrations. We additionally break down the coordination of blockchain in a wide scope of 5G IoT applications, going from savvy medical care, shrewd city, brilliant transportation to keen network and UAVs. In light of the flow of the extraordinary examination endeavors in the writing, in this segment, we will sum up the key discoveries acquired from the joining of blockchain in 5G organizations and administrations.

3.2.1   Blockchain for 5G advancements

It can propose a numerous talented specialized possessions, for example, region-alization, security, permanence, detectability, and straightforwardness to enable 5G advances. Assessing the writing works, we find that blockchain can uphold well 5G advances principally from three key angles, including security, frame-work execution, and asset the executives. The current 5G innovation framework is basically empowered by the brought together organization settings, for example, edge/distributed computing and SDN, which clearly show security weaknesses because of the dependence on outsiders. Blockchain can show up to manufacture decentralized organization structures for 5G innovation stages. For instance, the idea of blockchain-based distributed computing empowers decentralization of cloud/edge 5G networks, which disposes of centralized control at the organization and offers a decentralized control with blockchain. In any event, when an element is undermined by malignant assaults or dangers, the general activity of the elaborate organization is as yet kept up through agreement on appropriated records. Moreover, blockchain can help to set up a secure distributed eco system among clients (for example, in D2D communication) utilizing the processing intensity. This would conceivably lessen correspondence inertness, lessen exchange costs, and give the worldwide openness to all clients, all of which will upgrade the general framework execution. Moreover, blockchain is required to improve the asset the board for network work virtualization and organization cutting. From one perspective, blockchain can sup-port the trust and straightforwardness among members and partners and empower more consistent and dynamic trade of figuring assets in the helpful. The protected range asset arrangement can be accomplished by means of blockchain that gives a decentralized sharing foundation of the organization for organization workers, spe-cialist co-ops, and clients. Besides, the organization work asset can be shared at a quicker speed, contrasted with traditional incorporated plans, which consequently encourages administration conveyance. At present, the plan of organization depends on the open cloud-based designs, and aggressors may mishandle the limit flexibility to burn through the assets of another objective, which makes the objective unavail-able. Blockchain can be misused to assemble solid start to finish network cuts and permit network slide suppliers to deal with their assets, giving the dynamic control of asset dependability.

3.3   Need of blockchain in healthcare

With the ongoing progressions in Internet innovations, the world is confronting an advanced change regarding procuring an improved and better nature of everyday-life administrations. Advances, for example, the IoT, detecting innovations, and 5G, are giving various helpful commitments in different parts of medical care admin-istrations [7]. The current medical service frameworks are generally founded on concentrated workers where different substances inside the organization expect con-sent to get to clinical data. This can cause a deferment in offering clinical admin-istrations and furthermore expected spillage of the data. In such sort of health-care

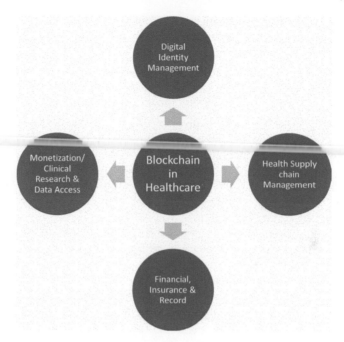

Figure 3.5   Blockchain use case in healthcare

frameworks, patients are generally uninformed of which substances are putting away and utilizing their clinical information without their assent. One of the difficulties with the current medical service frameworks is the safe openness of the clinical information by different substances inside the framework or organization. Blockchain can be used in such cases to accomplish the safe availability and honesty of the medical services information. Hence, the fundamental focal point of this part is to propose a safe and effective system for information availability.

To strengthen clinical administrations, the middle man (third party) should be eliminated. Blockchain development can be used to help drug arrangements and effortlessly chain the heads, pregnancy, and any risk data on the board similarly to help access control, data sharing, and directing of a survey trail of clinical activities. Other clinical consideration domains that can benefit by blockchain advancement are provider affirmations, clinical charging, contracting, clinical record exchange, clinical starters, and against distorting drugs. Clinical consideration organizations are changing to enable a patient-driven technique, as portrayed in Figure 3.5. Blockchain-based clinical consideration structures could redesign the security and privacy of patient's data since patients would have authority over their clinical consideration records. Those systems help in exchanging the clinical records across different clinical administrations associations.

Taking care of the clinical data of patients is critical in clinical administrations. These data are incredibly sensitive and moreover a common goal for computerized attacks. It is basic to ensure the security of pretty much all delicate data. Another perspective is order over data, which would ideally be managed by the patient. Thus, sharing and overseeing patient's clinical consideration data is another usage case that can benefit by forefront present-day progressions. Blockchain development is good against attacks and dissatisfactions and gives different techniques for access control. In like manner, the blockchain gives a respectable structure to clinical administrations data. For individual clinical information, the most satisfactory kind of a blockchain would be a private blockchain. As indicated by the Würst and Gervais choice model, a blockchain can be utilized in a situation where various gatherings who do not confide in one another need to collaborate and trade normal information, however, might not want to include a Trusted Third Party (TTP) [8]. Their model presents a few factors that should be viewed to determine, while examining, whether a particular situation requires blockchain. With this respect, there are a few elements (questions) that should be considered [8–11]:

- Is there a requirement for putting away information (concerning the creators of a particular state)?
- Do you need numerous compose access?
- Is a TTP accessible and can one that is consistently online be utilized?

Right off the bat, we need to decide the requirement for information putting away (in a commonplace situation this is an information base). Consequently, it should be resolved if there is a requirement for composing access for various gatherings. On the other side, if single leader exist in the system to take decisions then no blockchain is required . It must be noticed that conventional information bases offer preferred execution over a blockchain. In the event that a TTP is accessible, is consistently on the web, and can be completely trusted, at that point there is no requirement for blockchain. The Würst and Gervais choice model additionally figures out what kind of blockchain ought to be utilized. If the scholars are not known, the main evident decision would be a public permission-less blockchain. Assuming that the TTP is disconnected, it could work likewise to an affirmation authority and the included gatherings do not commonly confide in one another, and a permissioned blockchain could be utilized. Notwithstanding, in case that all the gatherings commonly trust one another, at that point an information base with shared admittance could be utilized rather than a blockchain. Then again, if authors are known and can be trusted, the decision falls between a public permissioned and private blockchain. The first is for the situation where you need public unquestionable status and the second for the situation when it is not required. If it is not too much trouble, note that these pieces of the model infer that the initial three inquiries expressed before are addressed decidedly—in any case conveying a blockchain is pointless. The current clinical information framework generally relies upon outsiders. In a few cases, these cannot be completely trusted. The blockchain, which depends on agreement and need not bother with a focal power, is a potential answer for this issue.

The current online medical care administrations, for example, EHR or electronic medical record, assume a key part for putting away, sharing and keeping up close to home clinical records of the patients. Nonetheless, there are various inadequacies that may prompt spillage of the patient's touchy clinical data. Blockchain innovation can be fundamental in such cases since it gives information record-based highlights, which is appropriated to all elements inside the organization. Patients have access to the screen which help them to give their consent regarding the access of their stored data by medical practitioners. Subsequently, the center inspiration driving this work is to use blockchains for medical services frameworks and to address the possible deficiencies in the current medical services frameworks.

Li *et al.* [12] overviewed the security dangers of famous blockchain frameworks, evaluated the assault cases endured by blockchain, and broke down the weaknesses abused in these cases. Most security and protection research concentrate on blockchain have been engaged along two strings: (1) revealing a few assaults endured by blockchain-based frameworks to date, and (2) advancing explicit proposition of utilizing some best-in-class countermeasures against a subset of such assaults. Be that as it may, very few efforts have been made to give a top to bottom investigation of the security and protection properties of blockchain and diverse blockchain usage strategies. This section is planned with double objectives. To begin with, it will give a section highlight no security specialists to increase better comprehension of security and protection properties of blockchain innovation. Second, it will support pros and specialists to investigate the forefront security and protection strategies of blockchain. Moreover, we distinguish essential security ascribes of blockchain and extra security and protection properties, examine some security answers for accomplishing these security objectives, and suggest open challenges. We foresee that this review will likewise manage area researchers and architects to reveal appropriate blockchain models and strategies for some space explicit application situations.

3.4   Blockchain-based health-care system

For the most part, EHRs predominantly contain persistent clinical history, individual insights (for example, age and weight), research center test outcomes, etc. Consequently, it is significant to guarantee the security and protection of these information. Furthermore, clinics in nations, for example, USA, are liable to demanding administrative oversight. There are likewise various difficulties in conveying and actualizing medical services frameworks by-and-by. For instance, concentrated worker models are powerless against the single-point assault impediments and vindictive insider assaults, as recently examined. Clients (for example, patients) whose information is stored in EHR framework have no scope to know that who is viewing their information and for purposes (for example, infringement of individual protection). Such data may be in danger of being spilled by malevolent insiders to another association, for instance, an insurance agency may deny protection inclusion to the specific patient based on the released clinical history.

In the interim, information sharing is progressively significant especially as our general public and populace become more portable. By utilizing the interconnectivity between various medical care substances, mutual information can improve clinical assistance conveyance, etc. Defeating the "Data and Resource Island"

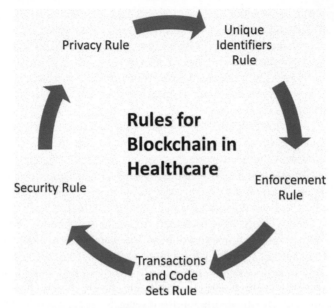

Figure 3.6   Rules for blockchain in healthcare

(data storehouse) will be trying, for instance, because of protection concerns and guidelines. The data storehouse likewise adds to pointless information excess and formality. For this situation, the Health Insurance Portability and Accountability Act (HIPAA) was recognized by the US Congress and marked in 1996. It built up arrangements for keeping up the protection and security of individual well-being data and made a few projects to control misrepresentation and maltreatment inside the medical services frameworks, remembering five standards as portrayed in Figure 3.6.

1. **Privacy Rule:** Guidelines for the utilization and divulgence of patient well-being data in medical care therapy and activities.
2. **Transactions and Code Sets Rule:** Necessities for all well-being intends to take part in the medical care exchanges in a normalized approach to disentangle medical care exchanges.
3. **Security Rule:** The security rule supplements the protection rule, including controlling admittance to PC frameworks and making sure about the inter-changes over open organizations from being blocked.
4. **Unique Identifiers Rule:** Just the National Provider Identifier distinguishes canvassed substances in the standard exchanges to secure the patient personal-ity data.
5. **Enforcement Rule:** Examination and punishments for abusing HIPAA rules. So as to fulfill the above objectives, existing blockchain-based exploration in the medical care space incorporates the accompanying fundamental angles, as appeared in Figure 3.7.

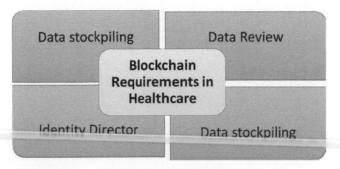

Figure 3.7   Blockchain requirements in healthcare

6. **Data stockpiling:** Blockchain fills in as a believed record information base to store a wide scope of private medical care information. Information protection ought to be ensured when secure capacity is accomplished. In any case, medical services information volume will in general be huge and complex by-and-by. Subsequently, a comparing challenge is the way to manage large information stockpiling without adversely affecting the exhibition of blockchain network.
7. **Data sharing:** In most existing medical care frameworks, specialist co-ops, as a rule, keep up essential stewardship of information. With the idea of self-sway, it is a pattern to restore the responsibility for information back to the client who is equipped for sharing (or not sharing) his own information freely. It is additionally important to accomplish secure information sharing across various associations and areas.
8. **Data review:** Review logs can fill in as evidences to consider requestors responsible for their collaborations with EHRs when debates emerge. A few frameworks use blockchain and common agreement for auditability reason. Any activity will be recorded in the blockchain ledger and can be recovered whenever there is need.
9. **Identity director:** The authenticity of every client's personality should be ensured in the framework. As it were, just real clients can make the pertinent solicitations to guarantee framework security and keep away from pernicious assaults.

3.5   Security and privacy properties requirements in healthcare

The fundamental safety possessions of blockchain originate from both cryptography advances and Bitcoin plan and execution. Hypothetically, the principal secure chain of squares was figured utilizing cryptography in 1991 [13]. The blockchain is built to guarantee various intrinsic security ascribes, for example, consistency, alter safe, protection from a distributed denial of service (DDoS) assault, pseudonymity, and protection from twofold expenditure assault, as described in Figures 3.8 and 3.9. Be

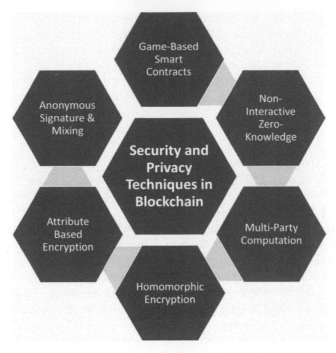

Figure 3.8   Security and privacy in blockchain

that as it may, to utilize blockchain for secure disseminated capacity, extra security and protection properties are required.

1. **Consistency:** The idea of consistency with regard to blockchain as a dissemi-nated worldwide record alludes to the property that all hubs have a similar record at the equivalent time. Bitcoin frameworks just give possible consistency, which

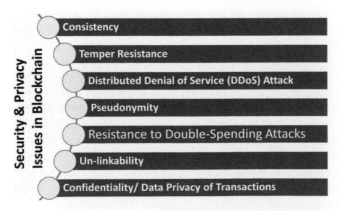

Figure 3.9   Security and privacy issues in blockchain

is powerless. Eventual consistency is a model proposed for dispersed processing frameworks by looking for a trade-off among accessibility and consistency. It ensures that information of every section is reliable inevitably to accomplishes high accessibility. With inevitable consistency, time taken by the hubs of the framework to get steady may not be characterized. Accordingly, information getting predictable in the long run implies that (1) it will take effort for updates to be engendered to different imitations; and (2) on the off chance that somebody peruses from a copy that is not refreshed at this point (since reproductions are refreshed in the end), there is some danger of returning old information [14]. Within a blockchain network framework, the solid consistency model implies that all hubs have a similar record simultaneously, and when the circulated record is being refreshed with new information, any resulting read or compose solicitations should hold up until the responsibility of this update. Interestingly, the inevitable consistency model implies that the blockchain at every hub of the framework becomes predictable in the end, despite the fact that some read or compose solicitations to the blockchain may restore flat information. The key test for solid consistency is that the presentation cost is too high to possibly be moderate for all cases. The key test for inevitable consistency is the means by which to eliminate the irregularity that might be brought about by flat information. The blockchain in Bitcoin receives a consistency model that looks for a superior trade-off between solid consistency furthermore, possible consistency for accomplishing segment resilience, and consistency with conceded accessibility.

2. **Temper Resistance:** Alter opposition alludes to the protection from a purposeful altering of a substance by either the clients or the foes with admittance to the element, be it a framework, an item, or other coherent or physical article. Alter opposition of blockchain implies that any exchange data put away in the blockchain cannot be altered during and after the cycle of square age. In particular, in a Bitcoin framework, new squares are created by mining hubs. There are two potential ways that the exchange data might be altered: (1) diggers may endeavor to mess with the data that got exchanged; (2) an enemy may endeavor to mess with the data put away on the blockchain. We examine why such altering endeavors are carefully forestalled by the blockchain conventions in Bitcoin. For the primary sort of altering, a digger may endeavor to change the payee address of the exchange to his address. Be that as it may, such endeavor cannot be succeeded, since every exchange is compacted by a protected hash work, for example, SHA-256, at the point marked by the payer utilizing a safe mark calculation, for example, ECDSA, in a Bitcoin organization. Finally, the exchange is sent to the whole organization for check and endorsement through mining. Hence, different diggers may get the exchange to mine, which is done in a non-deterministic design. On the off chance that a digger adjusts any data of the exchange, it will be identified by others when they check the mark with the payer's public key, since the digger cannot create a substantial mark on the altered data without the payer's private key. This is ensured by the unforgeability of the safe mark calculation. For the second sort of altering, a foe will bomb

its endeavors to modify any verifiable information put away on the blockchain. This is a result of the two insurance methods utilized in the circulated capacity of blockchain in Bitcoin: the hash pointer, a cryptographic strategy, and the organization-wide help for both capacity and confirmation of the blockchain. In particular, if an enemy needs to alter the information on some square (say k), the principal trouble experienced by the foe is the befuddle issue, to be specific, the altered square k has a conflicting hash esteem contrasted with the hash of the previous square k kept up in the $k + 1$ square. This is on the grounds that utilizing a hash work with impact opposition, the yields of the crash-resistant hash work with two distinct data sources will be totally conflicting with a staggering likelihood, and such irregularity can be handily distinguished by others on the organization. . Besides, in the blockchain of the Bitcoin organization, everybody has a duplicate of blockchain. It is exceptionally difficult for an enemy to change all duplicates in the whole organization.

3. **DDoS Attack:** It assault on a multitude is the kind of cyberattack that disturbs the facilitated Net administrations by construction the host mechanism or the organization asset on the host inaccessible to its expected clients. DoS assaults endeavor to overburden the host framework or the host network asset by flooding with unnecessary solicitations, thus slowing down the satisfaction of genuine administrations [15]. A DDoS assault alludes to a "dispersed" DoS assault, specifically, the approaching traffic flooding assault on a casualty is begun from numerous different sources disseminated over the Internet. A DDoS aggressor may bargain and utilize some person's PC to assault another PC by exploiting security weaknesses or shortcomings. By utilizing a lot of such undermined PCs, a DDoS assailant may send colossal measures of information to a facilitating site or send spam to specific email addresses [15]. This successfully makes it difficult to forestall the assault by just sticking individual sources individually. The arm-race relies upon the fixing pace of such undermined hubs against the achievement pace of trading off PC hubs in the organization. The genuine worry in a DDoS assault is on the accessibility of blockchain and is identified with the topic of whether a DDoS aggressor can make the blockchain inaccessible by taking out a fractional or the entire organization. The response to this inquiry is no, on account of the completely decentralized development and support of the blockchain and Bitcoin framework, and the agreement convention for new square age and expansion to the blockchain, which guarantees that the handling of blockchain exchanges can proceed regardless of whether a few blockchain hubs go disconnected. All together for a digital assailant to prevail with regard to making blockchain disconnected, the attacker would need to gather adequate computational assets that can bargain overwhelmingly enormous bits of the blockchain hubs over the whole Bitcoin. The bigger the Bitcoin network turns into, the stiffer it is to prevail in such enormous scope DDoS assault.

4. **Pseudonymity**: It alludes to a condition of camouflaged character. In Bitcoin, discourses in blockchain are confusions of public keys of a hub (client) in the organization. Clients can interface with the framework by utilizing their public key hash as their pseudo-character without uncovering their genuine name. In

this way, the location that a client uses can be seen as a pseudo-character. We can reflect the pseudonymity of a framework as a security property to ensure a client's genuine name. What's more, clients can create the same number of key matches (numerous locations) as they need, along these lines as an individual can make numerous financial balances as she wishes. In spite of the fact that pseudonymity can accomplish a feeble type of namelessness by methods for the public keys, there are still dangers of uncovering character data of clients.

5. **Resistance to Double Spending Attacks:** The twofold spending assault with regard to Bitcoin blockchain alludes to a particular issue especially to computerized cash exchanges. Note that the twofold spending assault can be considered as an overall security worry because of the way the advanced data can be recreated generally without any problem. In particular, with exchanges trading advanced tokens, for example, electronic money, there is a danger that the holder could copy the computerized token and send various indistinguishable tokens to different beneficiaries. In the event that an irregularity can be caused because of the exchanges of computerized copy tokens, the twofold spending issue turns into a genuine security danger. To forestall twofold spending, Bitcoin assesses and confirms the realness of every exchange utilizing the exchange signs in its blockchain with an agreement convention. By guaranteeing all exchanges are remembered for the blockchain, the agreement convention permits everybody to freely check the exchanges in a square before submitting the square into the worldwide blockchain, guaranteeing that the sender of every exchange just spends the bitcoins that he has really. Moreover, every exchange is marked by its sender utilizing a protected advanced mark calculation. It guarantees that in the event that somebody adulterates the exchange, the verifier can without much of a stress distinguish it. The blend of exchanges marked with advanced marks and public confirmation of exchanges with a larger part agreement ensures that Bitcoin blockchain can be impervious to the twofold spending assault.

6. **Unlinkability:** Unlinkability alludes to the powerlessness of expressing the connection between two perceptions or two watched elements of the framework with high certainty. Obscurity alludes to the condition of being mysterious and unidentified. Despite the fact that the blockchain in Bitcoin guarantees pseudonymity by offering pseudo-way of life as the help for the obscurity of a client's personality, it neglects to give clients the insurance of unlinkability for their exchanges. Instinctively, the full obscurity of a client must be secured by guaranteeing both pseudonymity and unlinkability if the client consistently utilizes her pseudo-personality to collaborate with the framework. This is on the grounds that unlinkability makes it difficult to dispatch de-anonymization surmising assaults, which connect the exchanges of a client together to reveal the genuine personality of the client within the sight of foundation information [16]. Solidly, in Bitcoin-like frameworks, a client can have numerous pseudonymous addresses. However, this does not give ideal obscurity to clients of blockchain on the grounds that each exchange is recorded on the record with the addresses of sender and recipient and is detectable uninhibitedly by anybody utilizing the related locations of its sender and beneficiary. Subsequently, anybody can relate

a client's exchange to different exchanges including her records by a straightforward factual investigation of the addresses utilized in Bitcoin exchanges. For instance, by examination, for a sender, one can without much of a stress get familiar with the number and aggregate the sum of bitcoins coming out or going into this record. On the other hand, one can connect numerous records that send or get exchanges from one IP address. All the more truly, a client may lose her secrecy and consequently security for all the exchanges related with her bitcoin address if the linkage of her bitcoin address to the client's certifiable character is uncovered.

7. **Confidentiality/Data Privacy of Transactions:** Information security of blockchain alludes to the stuff that blockchain can give privacy to all information or certain delicate information put away on it. In spite of the fact that the blockchain was initially contrived as a dispersed worldwide record for the computerized money framework Bitcoin, its possible extent of utilizations is a lot more extensive than virtual monetary standards. For instance, blockchain can be utilized for overseeing savvy contract, copyrighted works, and digitization of business or authoritative vaults. As anyone might expect, an attractive security property basic in all the blockchain applications is the classification of exchange data, for example, exchange content (e.g., exchange sums in Bitcoin), and addresses. Tragically, this security property is not upheld in Bitcoin frameworks. In Bitcoin, the exchange substance and addresses are openly distinguishable, despite the fact that the alias utilized as the location of sender and collector of an exchange rather than the genuine personality. The capacity of keeping exchange content hidden will assist to secure the data. This is basic for elevating the need-to-know-based sharing rather than freely perceptible of the whole blockchain. Additionally, blockchain frameworks utilize keen agreements to actualize complex exchanges, for example, Ethereum, which require (1) the information of each agreement and the code it runs on the information to be free and (2) each excavator to copy executing each agreement. This will prompt the spillage of client data.

3.6   Security and privacy techniques

In this segment, we give a nitty-gritty conversation of a choice of procedures that can be utilized to improve the security and protection of current and upcoming blockchain frameworks, as described in Figure 3.10.

- **Anonymous Signature:** Advanced mark innovation was created by a few variations. Some signature plans themselves have the capacity of giving secrecy to the signer. We call this sort of mark plans unknown mark. Among the mysterious mark plans, bunch mark and ring mark were proposed before and they are the two generally significant and regular unknown mark schemes. Group signature [17] has a gathering chief who oversees bunch individuals dealing with the

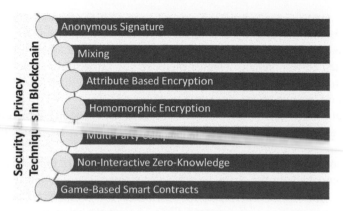

Figure 3.10   Security and privacy techniques in blockchain

occasion of debates, including uncovering the first underwriter. In blockchain framework, we additionally need a power element to make and disavow the gathering and progressively add new individuals to the gathering and erase/ disavow enrollment of certain members from the gathering. Since the gathering mark requires a gathering supervisor to arrange the gathering, the gathering mark is appropriate for consortium blockchain. Ring mark [18], likewise, can accomplish obscurity through marking by any individual from a gathering of clients. The term ring mark starts from the mark calculation that utilizes the ring-like structure. The ring mark is unknown in the event that it is hard to decide which individual from the gathering utilizes his or her key to sign the message. Ring marks contrast from bunch marks in two head ways: First, in a ring mark plot, the genuine character of the underwriter cannot be uncovered in case of contest, as there is no gathering administrator in the ring mark. Second, any clients can aggregate a "ring" without anyone else's extra arrangement. Along these lines, ring mark is relevant to public blockchain. One of the average utilizations of ring mark is CryptoNote [19].

- **Mixing:** Mixing administrations (or tumblers) was intended to keep clients' locations from being connected. Blending, truly, is an arbitrary trade of client's coins with other clients' coins. Thus, for the spectator, their responsibility are jumbled. Nonetheless, these blending administrations do not give security from coin robbery. In this segment, we portray two such blending administrations and dissect their security and protection properties. It can be acted regarding CoinJoin or mixcoin. CoinJoin [20] necessitates that clients arrange exchanges with whom they wish to join installment. The original of the mixing administrations to offer this usefulness (for example, SharedCoin [21]) has utilized unified workers and expected clients to confide in the administrator not to take or permit others to take the bitcoins. Nonetheless, notwithstanding the single purpose of disappointment, unified administrations may have danger of spillage of clients' security since they will keep logs of the exchanges and record all members of joint installment. MixJoin gives unknown installment in Bitcoin and bitcoin-like cryptographic forms of money. To safeguard against latent foes, Mixcoin stretches out the obscurity set to permit all clients to blend coins all the while. To safeguard against dynamic foes, Mixcoin gives obscurity like customary correspondence blends. Moreover, Mixcoin utilizes a responsibility system to identify taking, and it shows that clients will utilize Mixcoin soundly without taking bitcoins by adjusting motivators [22].

- **Attribute-based Encryption:** Attribute-based encryption (ABE) is a cryptographic strategy where ascribes are the characterizing, what's more, managing factors for the ciphertext scrambled utilizing the mystery key of a client. One can decode the encoded information utilizing the client's mystery key if her credits concur with the characteristics of the ciphertext. The intrigue obstruction is a significant security property of ABE. It guarantees that when a malignant client connives with different clients, he cannot get to other information aside from the information that he can unscramble with his private key. In 2011, a decentralized ABE plot was proposed [23] to utilize ABE on a blockchain. For instance, on a blockchain, authorizations can also be achieved through tokens. All hubs in the organization, which have a specific token given to them, will be conceded admittance to the unique rights and benefits related with the token. The token gives a method for following who has certain credits and such following ought to be done in an algorithmic and predictable manner by the power substance that disperses the token. Tokens can be seen as identifications that speak to traits or capabilities, what's more, ought to be utilized as non-adaptable quantifiers of notoriety or qualities.

- **Homomorphic Encryption:** It is an incredible steganography. It can play out particular kind of calculations legitimately on ciphertext and guarantee that the activities performed on the scrambled information, while decoding the processed outcomes, will produce indistinguishable outcomes to those performed by similar procedure on the plaintext. There are a few halfway homomorphic crypto-frameworks [24] just as complete homomorphic frameworks [25]. One can utilize homomorphic encryption (HE) procedures to store information over the blockchain with no huge changes in the blockchain properties. This guarantees that the information on the blockchain will be encoded, tending to the security concerns related with public blockchains. The utilization of HE strategy offers security assurance and permits prepared admittance to encoded information over open blockchain for evaluating and different purposes, for example, overseeing representative costs. Ethereum savvy contracts give HE on information put away in blockchain for more noteworthy control and protection.

- **Multi-Party Computation:** The multi-party calculation (MPC) model characterizes a multi-party convention to permit them to convey out some calculations mutually over their private information contributions without disregarding their info security, with the end goal that an enemy adapts nothing about the contribution of a valid gathering yet the yield of the joint calculation as of late, MPC has been utilized in blockchain frameworks to ensure clients' protection. Andrychowicz *et al.* planned and actualized secure MPC conventions on Bitcoin framework in 2014 [14]. They built conventions for secure multi-party lotteries with no confided power. Their conventions can ensure reasonableness for the legit clients paying little mind to how deceptive one acts. In the event that a client abuses or meddles with the convention, she turns into a failure and her bitcoins are moved to the legitimate clients. A decentralized SMP calculation stage, called Enigma, was proposed in 2015 by Zyskind *et al.* [26]. By utilizing a serious variant of SMP calculation, Enigma utilizes a certain secret sharing plan to ensure protection of its computational model. Additionally, Enigma information utilizing an altered circulated hash table for productive capacity. Additionally, it uses an defilement safe chronicle of occasions and the controller of the friend to peer network for characterizing the board and access control.

- **Non-Interactive Zero-Knowledge:** The fundamental thought is that a conventional verification container is planned to check that a sequencer performed with some info secretly known by the client can produce some freely open yield with no divulgence of some other data. As it were, a certifier can demonstrate to a verifier that some declaration is precise without giving any valuable data to the verifier. It is appeared in [23] that, with the non-intelligent variation of zero-information evidences, instituted as non-interactive zero-knowledge, one can accomplish computational zero-information deprived of needful certifier and verifier to communicate by any stretch of the imagination, given that the certifier and the verifier share a typical reference string. In its application, all record adjusts are scrambled and, also, put away in the chain. At the point when a client moves cash to another client, without much of a stress, he can demonstrate that he has adequate offset for the exchange with zero-information confirmations, without uncovering the record balance.

- **Game-Based Smart Contracts:** Arbitrum [27] hosts planned a motivator system for gatherings to concur chain on the conduct of cybernetic machineries, so it just needs the vouchers to confirm computerized marks of the contracts. For untrustworthy gatherings who attempt to lie about the conduct of virtual machines, Arbitrum has planned a proficient-test-based convention to distinguish and punish the untrustworthy gatherings. The impetus instrument of off-chain confirmation of virtual machine's conduct has fundamentally improved the versatility and the security of brilliant contracts. TrueBit [28] utilizes an intelligent "confirmation game" to choose whether a computational undertaking was effectively performed or not. TrueBit offers compensations to urge players to check calculation assignments and discover bugs, with the end goal that a keen agreement can safely play out a calculation task with evident properties. Also, in each round of "confirmation game," the verifier recursively checks a littler and littler subset of the calculation, which permits TrueBit to extraordinarily decrease the computational weight on its hubs.

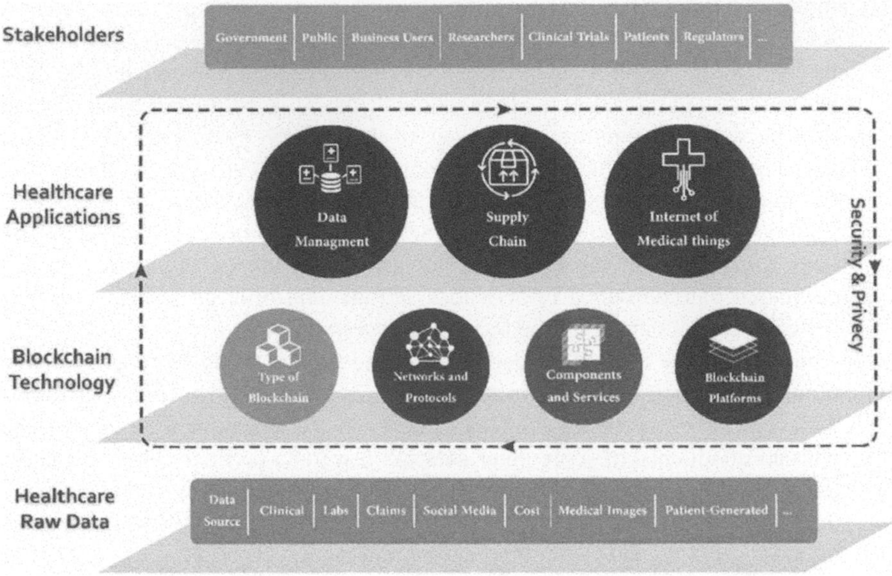

Figure 3.11   Blockchain workflow in healthcare [29]

3.7   Healthcare-based application in blockchain

Blockchain innovation is rethinking the information displayed and the administration sent in numerous medical care applications. This is predominantly because of its versatility and capacities to fragment, secure, and share clinical information and administrations in an exceptional manner. Blockchain innovation is at the focal point of numerous current improvements in the medical care industry. Rising blockchain-based medical care innovations are adroitly composed into four layers, including information sources, blockchain innovation, medical care applications, and partners. Figure 3.11 shows a portrayal of blockchain-based work process for medical services applications.

At first, all the information from clinical gadgets, labs, web-based media, and numerous different sources are combined and make crude information that in this way developed in scale to enormous information. This information is the basic element of the entire blockchain-based medical services, and it is the chief segment that makes the primary layer of the stack. Blockchain innovation sits on the head of the crude information layer that is viewed as the center structure in the interest to make sure about medical care engineering, which is partitioned into four segments. Each blockchain stage has various highlights, for example, agreement calculations and conventions [30]. Blockchain stages encourage clients to make and deal with their exchanges. A few blockchain stages were made and are at present used, for example, Ethereum [31] and Hyperledger Fabric [32]. The essential segments of the blockchain are shrewd contracts, marks, wallet, occasions, participation, and advanced resources. For speaking with other projects and structures, or even across various

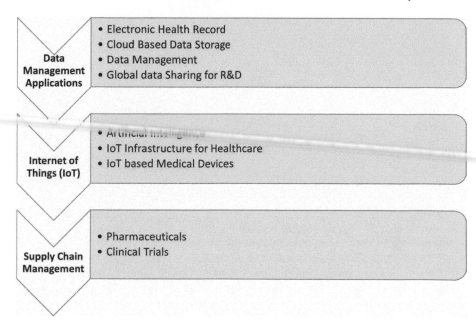

Figure 3.12   Health-care applications in blockchain

organizations, a wide scope of conventions could be utilized. This may incorporate, for example, P2P, unified, decentralized, and circulated. Policymakers could settle on a decision that is either open, private or even combined dependent on the scope of the necessities they have to satisfy. When the stage is made by actualizing blockchain innovation, the following stage is to guarantee that the applications are coordinated with the entire framework. Blockchain-based medical care applications can be grouped into three wide classes. First thing, data the chiefs, including overall intelligent data sharing for imaginative work, data leaders, data storing (e.g., cloud-based applications) and EHRs. The below average speaks to Supply Chain Management (SCM) applications, including clinical preliminaries and drugs. The second rate class covers the Internet of Medical Things (IoMT), including an intersection of medical services IoT and clinical gadgets, medical care IoT foundation and information security, and AI. Figure 3.12 shows health-care applications in the blockchain. At last, at the head of the progression comes the partner layer, which comprises gatherings who are profiting by blockchain-based medical care applications, for example, business clients, scientists, and patients. The fundamental worries of clients at this layer are to successfully share, measure, and also, oversee information without endangering its security and protection.

With the headway in electronic prosperity-related data, cloud clinical consideration data accumulation, and understanding data security confirmation rules, new open entryways are opening for prosperity data, in chief, similarly concerning patients' advantage to access and offer their prosperity data [33]. Making sure about information, stockpiling, exchange, and also, dealing with their smooth mix

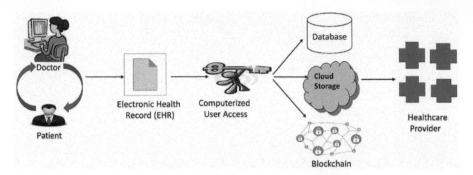

Figure 3.13   Security and privacy

are hugely significant to any information-driven association, particularly in medical services where blockchain innovation can possibly resolve these basic issues in a vigorous and successful manner. Figure 3.13 shows seven stages of medical services information that the board work processes in blockchain, which are talked about beneath. Blockchain-based applications in this classification incorporate information sharing, information the executives, information stockpiling (e.g., cloud-based applications), and EHR, which are talked about in subtleties beneath.

- **Step 1**: Primary information is produced by the collaboration between the patients and their Pre-Commercial Procurement (PCPs), what's more, experts. This information comprises clinical history, current issues, and other physiological data.
- **Step 2:** An EHR is made for every patient utilizing the essential information gathered in the initial step. Other clinical data, for example, those produced from nursing care, clinical imaging, and medication history, are likewise remembered for EHR.
- **Step 3:** Individual patient has the responsibility for EHR, and tweaked admittance control is offered distinctly to the proprietor of this property. Gatherings who need to access such significant data must demand consent which is sent to the EHR proprietor, and the proprietor will choose to whom access will be allowed.
- **Steps 4, 5, and 6:** These three stages are essential for the center of the entire cycle including information base, the blockchain, and distributed storage. Information base and distributed storage store the records in a conveyed way and a blockchain gives extraordinary protection to guarantee tweaked genuine client access.
- **Step 7:** Health-care suppliers, for example, specially appointed facility, network care focus, and clinics are the end clients who need to get access for a free from any danger-care conveyance, which will be approved by the proprietor. For instance, regardless of where you are treated in the globe, your well-being record will be accessible and open on your telephone and approved through an

appropriated record, for example, blockchain, to which medical care suppliers would keep on adding after some time [34].

3.8 Conclusion

The blockchain innovation is increasingly receiving noteworthy consideration from people, just as associations of practically numerous sorts and measurements. The blockchain takes into account well-being records are time-stepped so nobody can alter them in the wake of it turning out to be essential for the wholesaler record. The patients have the rights to know that who can, or cannot access their information and for what reason. In any case, there are as yet a few open difficulties that require further examination. For instance, cross-outskirt sharing of wellbeing information where unique, frequently clashing locales exist may prevent the advantage of blockchain's information sharing. In fact, the desire for person's security fluctuates starting with one nation and then onto the next dependent on the administration guidelines. Subsequently, future exploration on guidelines, normalization, and cross-outskirt wellbeing information recovering strategies including maintenance and use expectation are appropriately dire. Another likely issue that is under-investigated is the capacity of the blockchain to store and cycle monstrous information access exchanges in an ideal way.

References

[1] Nakamoto S. 'Bitcoin: aA peer-to-peer electronic cash system'. *Manubot*. 2019:1–9.

[2] Kumari A., Tanwar S., Tyagi S., Kumar N., Parizi R.M., Choo K.-K.R. 'Fog data analytics: a taxonomy and process model'. *Journal of Network and Computer Applications*. 2019;**128**(3):90–104.

[3] Panarello A., Tapas N., Merlino G., Longo F., Puliafito A. 'Blockchain and IOT integration: a systematic survey'. *Sensors*. 2018;**18**(8):2575.

[4] Singh M., Singh A., Kim S. 'Blockchain: a game changer for securing IoT data'. *2018 IEEE 4th World Forum on Internet of Things (WF-IoT)*; 2018. pp. 51–5.

[5] Bhushan B., Sahoo C., Sinha P., Khamparia A. 'Unification of blockchain and internet of things (BIoT): requirements, working model, challenges and future directions'. *Wireless Networks*. 2020;**6**:1–36.

[6] Tanwar S. *Fog computing for healthcare 4.0 environments technical, societal, and future implications, springer nature*; 2021. pp. 1–622.

[7] Baker S.B., Xiang W., Atkinson I. 'Internet of things for smart healthcare: technologies, challenges, and opportunities'. *IEEE Access*. 2017;**5**:26521–44.

[8] Wüst K., Gervais A. 'Do you need a blockchain?'. *2018 Crypto Valley Conference on Blockchain Technology (CVCBT)*; 2018. pp. 45–54.

[9]   Kumari A., Gupta R., Tanwar S., Kumar N. 'Blockchain and AI amalgamation for energy cloud management: challenges, solutions, and future directions'. *Journal of Parallel and Distributed Computing.* 2020;**143**(11):148–66.

[10] Hathaliya J.J., Tanwar S., Tyagi S., Kumar N. 'Securing electronics healthcare records in healthcare 4.0 : A biometric-based approach'. *Computers & Electrical Engineering.* 2019;**76**(4):398–410.

[11] Hathaliya J.J., Tanwar S., Evans R. 'Securing electronic healthcare records: a mobile-based biometric authentication approach'. *Journal of Information Security and Applications.* 2020;**53**(3):102528.

[12] Li X., Jiang P., Chen T., Luo X., Wen Q. 'A survey on the security of blockchain systems'. *Future Generation Computer Systems.* 2020;**107**:841–53.

[13] Haber S., Stornetta W.S. 'How to time-stamp a digital document'. *Conference on the Theory and Application of Cryptography*; Berlin, Heidelberg; 1990. pp. 437–55.

[14] Vogels W. 'Eventually consistent'. *Communications of the ACM.* 2009;**52**(1):40–4.

[15] Miller A., Xia Y., Croman K., Shi E., Song D. 'The honey badger of BFT protocols'. *Proceedings of the 2016 ACM SIGSAC Conference on Computer and Communications Security*; 2016. pp. 31–42.

[16] Narayanan A., Bonneau J., Felten E., Miller A., Goldfeder S. *Bitcoin and Cryptocurrency Technologies: a Comprehensive Introduction.* Princeton University Press; 2016.

[17] Chaum D., Heyst Evan [n.d.]. 'Group Signatures':257–65.

[18] Rivest R.L., Shamir A., Tauman Y. 'How to leak a secret'. *International Conference on the Theory and Application of Cryptology and Information Security*; Berlin, Heidelberg; 2001. pp. 552–65.

[19] Saberhagen Nvan., Meier J., Juarez A.M., Jameson M. 'CryptoNote signatures'. 2012:1–20.

[20] Maxwell G. 'Coinjoin: Bitcoin privacy for the real world. Post on Bitcoin forum'. 2013. Available from https://bitcointalk.org/index.php?topic=279249.0.

[21] Moniz H., Neves N.F., Correia M., Verissimo P. 'Experimental comparison of local and shared coin randomized consensus protocols'. *2006 25th IEEE Symposium on Reliable Distributed Systems (SRDS'06)*; 2006. pp. 235–44.

[22] Bonneau J., Narayanan A., Miller A., Clark J., Kroll J.A., Felten E.W. *Anonymity for Bitcoin with Accountable Mixes.* Preprint; 2014.

[23] Lewko A., Waters B. 'Decentralizing attribute-based encryption'. *Annual International Conference on the Theory and Applications of Cryptographic Techniques*; Berlin, Heidelberg, Springer; 2011. pp. 568–88.

[24] Rivest R.L., Shamir A., Adleman L. 'A method for obtaining digital signatures and public-key cryptosystems'. *Communications of the ACM.* 1978;**21**(2):120–6.

[25] Van Dijk M., Gentry C., Halevi S., Vaikuntanathan V. 'Fully homomorphic encryption over the integers'. *Annual International Conference on the Theory and Applications of Cryptographic Techniques*; Berlin, Heidelberg; 2010. pp. 24–43.

[26] Zyskind G., Nathan O., Pentland A. 'Enigma: decentralized computation platform with guaranteed privacy'. *arXiv*. 2015.

[27] Kalodner H., Goldfeder S., Chen X., Weinberg S.M., Felten E.W. 'Arbitrum: scalable, private smart contracts'. *27th USENIX Security Symposium 18*; 2018. pp. 1353–70.

[28] Teutsch J., Reitwießner C. 'Truebit: a scalable verification solution for blockchains'.

[29] Khezr S., Moniruzzaman M., Yassine A., Benlamri R. 'Blockchain technology in healthcare: a comprehensive review and directions for future research'. *Applied Sciences*. 2019;**9**(9):1736.

[30] Saraf C., Sabadra S. 'Blockchain platforms: a compendium'. *2018 IEEE International Conference on Innovative Research and Development (ICIRD)*; 2018. pp. 1–6.

[31] Ethereum. *[online]*. Available from https://www.ethereum.org/ [Accessed 20 Mar 2019].

[32] Hyperledger. *[online]*. Available from https://www.hyperledger.org/ [Accessed 20 Mar 2019].

[33] Dimitrov D.V. 'Blockchain applications for healthcare data management'. *Healthcare Informatics Research*. 2019;**25**(1):51–6.

[34] Panesar A. *Machine Learning and AI for Healthcare*. Apress; 2019.

Chapter 4

Enhanced blockchain technology associated with IoT for secure and privacy communications in 5G

Arulananth T S[1], Baskar M[2], Ramkumar J[2], and Koppula Srinivas Rao[3]

As there is cutting-edge technology in 5G, blockchain gambling is a critical function of human life in the present era. COVID-19 has made many modifications inside the human being, and has also modified the human lifestyle. However, research aspects have created many new possibilities for humans to interact with fast and secure communication. The feasibility can be attained by transformation alternate within the everyday existence of humans via interaction with the so-called Internet of Things (IoT). Providing the requirement of faster and safe conversation methodologies with a verbal exchange of devices is unavoidable in this situation. Here we propose secure communication associated with blockchain technology, which will secure automated communication based on IoT. The 5G networking is a new technology community that can transmit data faster than one gigabit in step with second and decreases latency than the modern-day Long-Term Evolution (LTE) network. In this proposed framework, IoT offers various clever gadgets, ranging from all home equipment and televisions to everyday and even aesthetic items, to connect independently to the network to alternate statistics, updates, and symptoms. Thus, performance analysis shows that the framework with IoT automation requires low latency and excessive speed community, which the 5G community can provide.

[1]Department of Electronics and Communication and Engineering, MLR Institute of Technology, Telangana, India

[2]Department of Computer Science and Engineering, College of Engineering and Technology, SRM Institute of Science and Technology, Kattankulathur, Chennai, India

[3]Department of Computer Science and Engineering, MLR Institute of Technology, Telangana, India

4.1 Introduction

In Recent days, Blockchain and 5G are the two technologies that may anchor the digital future, associate government at China telecommunication believe. The Digital Economic Joint Laboratory expressed that blockchain will accelerate the expansion of 5G, particularly with charge and payments, network sharing, and so on [1, 2].

As so much as rising technologies go, blockchain technology has arguably generated a lot of buzz than any of the others. In its short time underpinning many crypto currencies and suburbanized applications, this information platform has garnered the eye of varied trade leaders, policymakers, and enormous organizations willing to take a position in its development. A blockchain may be a style of peer-to-peer arrangement for storing transactional information in containers referred to as blocks. Because the name suggests, these blocks square measure coupled during a chain and secure exploitation cryptography [3, 4]. They largely operate as a supporting technology for systems within which a token is changed between many parties or information regarding a selected object is entered and kept. 5G can revolutionize the planet, particularly IoT and quality. However, there are a variety of challenges in setting it up. He remarked, "The readying of trillions of nodes, the interconnection of all things, and therefore the provision of services to every different cause new challenge to information security, data value, and exchange dealing models." Blockchain technology will solve most of those challenges. Therefore, the 5G antennas have a brief difference, roughly one mile, a smaller amount than a tenth of their 4G counterparts. This necessitates the application of ten times more antennas within the 5G network, a pricey enterprise. Blockchain will facilitate the telecommunication company's crowd fund for the installation of those antennas. The revenue generated would be shared through a transparent platform, enabled by blockchain [5]. Blockchain would conjointly make it simple to share 5G infrastructure between the mobile network operators. 5G technology can accelerate the increase of the IoT. When multiple interconnected devices are sharing information autonomously, security is a key challenge, which blockchain can take care of. "Blockchain is wont to solve information security and price exchange issues in IoT applications and has become a crucial underlying technology to push the event of IoT applications."

China telecommunication is the largest in the country with fixed-line service and therefore the third largest mobile telecommunications supplier. Besides the opposite two major telecoms, they need to be endowed greatly in the 5G rollout. With the company's estimate, China can have over a 170 million mobile subscribers on the 5G network. The use of blockchain in telecommunications in China is anticipated to soar within the next five years. Allen Li, the founding father of the QLC (QLink Token) Chain, a startup that develops suburbanized mobile network protocols, expressed, "In following 3 to 5 years, we can expect to ascertain quite sixty percent of telecoms services use blockchain technology [6, 7]. Blockchain won't solely facilitate telos lower operational prices for user identification, charge, and content delivery. However, it'll function the simplest resolution to enhance network security." 5G and blockchain square measure two technologies which might

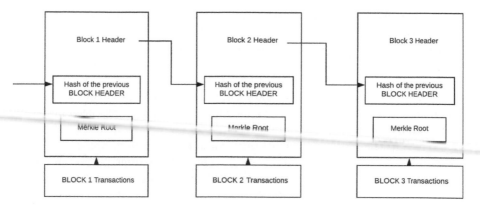

Figure 4.1   Basic structure of blockchain

have an amazing impact on the world of telecommunications and mobile technology. The rollout of 5G has already started in selected cities. The world coverage with a gradual rollout is anticipated by the year 2020. With the mixture of Web of Things, 5G and Blockchain would add a significant quantity to society. These technologies bring many benefits and provide many potentialities. The block is that basic item of a blockchain that usually includes a block header and a group of transactions, as shown in Figure 4.1. Therefore, a block is generally outlined as an instrumentation style of arrangement in sensible applications. The basic structure of blockchain has to be seriously designed in step with the requirements of systems [5].

The blockchain provides several components like a bitcoin public ledger. It uses the timestamp to record the transaction while transferring the amount in the blockchain environment in an ordered manner. Here in the blockchain scenario, the double-spending attack problem should be protected while doing the transaction in the blockchain, and modification in the previous transaction has to be monitored and recorded. Apart from the above components, for each node, the blockchain gets an independent network, which has certain blocks validated by the node that is specified. The consensus plays a role when several nodes have accessed the same block in the blockchain. The consensus rules have certain validated rules when a certain node has to maintain the consensus rules.

As the blockchain plays a significant role, which establishes secure communication for a particular network. IoT will generate a lot of information based on certain devices enabled with IoT as the data are generated as the raw data and get processed into structured data and are used for a particular purpose. In this chapter, we have discussed the characteristics of blockchain and its services, and how it will be associated with real-time applications. Then we have extended the discussion with Healthcare 4.0 as it paves the way to combine the IoT with blockchain as it helps to provide secure communication while transferring the data from IoT devices. Here we have discussed the integration of 5G with blockchain technology for real-time applications via crypto assets. The above concepts and significance to applications help the blockchain to establish secure communication with IoT. Finally, a proposed secure framework has been designed, displayed as a secure representation, and a case study of an IoT-based system related to health-care has been discussed. This chapter contributes to establishing secure communication using blockchain technology for the IoT framework. We have initially discussed the general structure of blockchain and how transactions can be performed using blockchain. Further, the discussion has moved with the integration of IoT with blockchain to establish secure communication. Finally, a secure communication framework has been designed, and a real-time case study has been discussed.

The blockchain structure and its mechanism is discussed in Section 4.2. Then integration of 5G with IoT with the help of blockchain technology is discussed in Section 4.3. 5G technology associated with blockchain is further discussed in Section 4.4. The discussion on 5G technology has moved to the next extend with distributed ledger technology in section 4.5. Blockchain technology with respect to smart contracts and secure communication for the banking sector is discussed in Sections 4.6–4.8. Key issues, challenges, and future opportunities of the blockchain technology are discussed in Sections 4.9–4.11. The working mechanism of secure communication is discussed in Section 4.12. The proposed secure mechanism layout is discussed in Section 4.13, and a real-time case study is discussed in Section 4.14. Finally, the overall conclusion states that the blockchain plays a phenomenal role in developing a secure communication network.

4.2   Design process of blockchain-based systems

The accompanying flowchart in Figure 4.2 depicts the different advances associated with the blockchain-based framework plan. The significant advance in the configuration process is identifying the issue and objective, identifying the reasonable blockchain stage, and blockchain ideation developing a proof of work (PoW) [8].

The significant advantages of the blockchain procedure are recorded as follows:

1. Transparency: by making it workable for each individual from the system to get to the information simultaneously.
2. Decentralization: to expel the single purposes of disappointment from the framework.
3. Trust: through mass accord.
4. Security: through changeless records of exchanges.

There is a transaction part in the blockchain structure in the block, which contains one or more transactions and transfers the amount between the nodes (or participating users). Then, for these transactions has are generated using double SHA 256, and they are paired with the next transactions with the link previous transaction. This process will continue till the transaction remains in the network and finally the Merkle tree as the root in the blockchain is constructed, which is to be used to verify all transactions. Then the block header present in the single block transaction is referred to as the Merkle root. During the block transaction, each block stores the

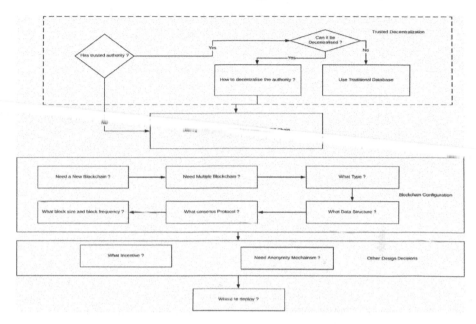

Figure 4.2   Design process of blockchain-based systems

hash of the previous transaction associated with the combined block. The transaction modifications can be reflected with every node in the particular blockchain as it is hashed with the previous node as a chain network.

4.3   IoT–with 5G and blockchain

The technological specialists of the world have referred to that IoT has a lot of manageable to fulfill [9]. However, there are two predominant stumbling blocks in its way safety and ordinary capacity. With the inception of 5G, IoT gadgets have higher flexibility and wider software in their deployment phases. The various processes involved in IoT are shown Figure 4.3.

Here, the blockchain emphasizes the PoW, which the third-party user in the network can associatively monitor. As the block in the blockchain plays a significant role where work can get created by the third-party users, they will work on the past transaction. As the third-party users can modify the past work transaction, it may be much harder as the user who is working on the new set of blocks is added on the blockchain. In blockchain, the blocks cannot be modified and if the transactions inside the blocks will be modified then the entire blockchain network is in security breach level. The PoW gets expanded as the cost of the PoW gets increased whenever the new blocks get added into the blockchain. The PoW gets expanded as hash cryptography plays a significant role in random nature as the normal subjective data is converted into random numbers. The random number gets generated while the

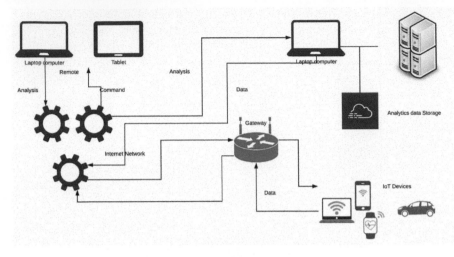

Figure 4.3   The process of IoT

modification is done on the blocks in the blockchain and whenever the hash gets run again.

Figure 4.4 shows the IoT and blockchain elements. IoT, 5G, and blockchain like and impact on another to flourish in the future world [10, 11]. There is no quitting and IoT today. Therefore we have to expect that engineers and programmers will find a way to fix or move around the expected blockchain scalability problem. Hence these three technologies can attain their unified possibility.

4.3.1   Requirements of IoT

The term inertness alludes to the delay between a solitary sign send/get to the following. Low idleness is a necessity for IoT gadgets to impart easily without confronting

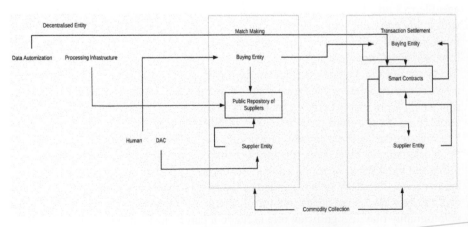

Figure 4.4   Blockchain with IoT elements

a lot of slack. This is one of the issues IoT gadgets may look at in the course of their lifecycle. This opens up the utilization of another bleeding-edge innovation called the Internet of Skills. To open the capability of this innovation, the inertness of a system must be decreased [12]. The five versatile systems can convey information at a much higher speed and lower dormancy than the 4G systems. This will permit the IoT gadgets to work with their full burden-bearing ability.

4.3.2 Benefits of 5G

The intensity of the 5G systems will empower even the smallest of the IoT gadgets to work completely inside the structure of the associated organizes without any problem. Till 2025, 5G organized communication would empower roughly 100 billion IoT associations. With 5G profoundly affecting the IoT showcase, there are a couple of reasons of concern that must be tended to by the system itself. The low inertness of the 5G organizes likewise brings expected issues for the IoT gadgets with the associated gadget space being attacked by maverick components [13, 14]. These maverick gadgets can upset a given system setup. Budgetary infrastructure can be taken over by blockchain with a wealth of IoT gadgets. They can exploit the blockchain innovation's one-of-a-kind capacity to make sure about, decentralize, and bestow an unchanging nature to a given system.

4.3.3 Impact of blockchain technology on digital commerce

The decentralized blockchain can discover utilization as a basic convention layer with built-up security exchanges and savvy contracts among the system of inter-connected IoT gadgets without much of a stretch. In the future, rather than entirely dependent on the systems, a secure hashing calculations and blockchain technology can be used to make the interaction between IoT gadgets to be more secured. The versatility of blockchain innovation is a significant deterrent to be worked upon later on for better organization of IoT [15].

Computerized record innovation can assume a significant job in changing the scene of exchanges. The conveyed record can deal with an enormous number of exchanges in a solitary second. It is conceivable in genuine practice to defer the vast majority of the exchanges to a level 2 blockchain that sudden spikes in demand for the head of the essential one as the Lightning Network ideally on LTC (LiTe Coin) or BTC (Bite Coin).

All gadgets ought to have distinct locations. Along these lines, adaptability and on-chain exchanges ought to enhance both layers. The gigantic increment in the transmission capacity of blockchain because of the lessening in the dormancy of systems given by 5G has a significant advantage for blockchain systems. The whole worldview of blockchain reception can be improved through the merger of 5G portable communication systems [16, 17].

4.3.4 Impact of blockchain on IoT

For IoT-enabled devices, privacy and security always plays an important role, for example, in the healthcare application, as a patient I do not want to disclose my personal healthcare data, my identity, etc. So there is always a need to use a secure platform while exchanging the data between the multiple stakeholders [18].

This total blend of 5G, blockchain, and IoT will smoothen the advancement of the ascent of brilliant homes, driverless vehicles, and savvy urban areas. In the coming times, a few standard businesses, including mining, horticulture, and boring, will see the usage of mechanization through an IoT arrangement of a great many keen machines and sensors interfacing over fast 5G [19]. 5G innovation has been at the bleeding edge of incalculable conversations [20, 21].

4.4   5G technology for greater connectivity

With the rise in population and high usage of electronic gadgets, the entire eco system is now shifted to more heterogeneous in nature (in terms of devices, in terms of users, etc.). This advancement is like a mad world wonder as countries like Indonesia, China, Malaysia are making significant PDA (Personal Digital Assistant) penetration.

There's an open door rising inside these developing markets, in any case. More individuals, for instance, approach a telephone or cell phone as their essential method for getting to the internet: which is quickly turning into the mainstream methods. Acquainting 5G innovation with the creating scene as a market implies that cell phones can be made far less expensive while allowing more noteworthy independence to people than at any time in recent memory.

4.4.1   Mobile payment networks to worldwide communication

Portable reimbursements are the distinguished style in rising markets as the blockchain and crypto-forex assignments are tentative. Coin Telegraph, for instance, recommended the expedient upward push of M-Pesa.

M-Pesa is a cell value answer similar to an enormous cluster of intelligent and more seasoned cell phone models. Since its dispatch 13 years prior, more than 96 Kenyan family units have articulated that they have at any rate one individual in their family that utilizes it. This fact is a distinct advantage for those that would have lived in need in any other case, giving them remarkable financial self-rule. M-Pesa has been widely used in the Kenyans in their administrations, which increases their profit over 30% compared to traditional systems [22, 23].

This is the spot 5G science to make the quality with Kenya and allow this equivalent person to incorporate the indistinguishable upgrades globally I have had for ten years at this point. For the world's unbanked populace, this is an amazing victory.

4.4.2   How blockchain and 5G help secure versatile banking

5G and blockchain mechanical expertise mixed with the entirety of the substances and universe of counts ablaze with unmatched inclusion, net openness, and insurance in one association. In the future, the financial institutions can use DLT, or Blockchain technologies in their routine work.

Dispersed Ledger Tech allows for easy and quite invulnerable approval for exchanges on an excessive scale other than any need for a brought together, all-encompassing position to permit it. DLT decentralization has presented advantage as well and the bank's focal workers have been using it to block a malicious user,without affecting the genuine end-client. This happened because the DLT would keep the record of all transactions, which can be referred in the case of any ~~~~~ [24].

A blend of 5G Innovative skin and blockchain would control to make a previously amazing contraption much more prominent dumbfounding for the end cli ent. "Blockchain can be resistant cell banking systems that should insusceptible exchanges on a granular level, while 5G itself will make positive these confounded systems don't worry beneath the heaviness of blockchains." "If cryptosystems can change reimbursements choices flexibly to these populaces, it will be a most significant step ahead for each the unbanked and underneath banked."

4.4.3   *How will 5G WiFi enhance blockchain-based crypto assets?*

Portable makers, correspondences, and supplier organizations are justifiably certain about the ramifications of 5G innovation, and it is trying to accuse them. Altogether, organizations in this venture accept and those clients:

- Condensed interchanges and net inertness
- Enhanced insights cities (lower feasible expenses)
- Reduced expenses on vitality
- Broader limits in cost
- Enhanced structures limit
- Altogether quickened availability.

Every one of these focal points can improve specifications for the utilization of blockchain, DLT innovative skill as efficiently as digital currencies around the world. In the coming time, 5G technologies would plays an important role in the development of seamless applications, which uses the innovative skill of blockchain . These technologies also extend the scope of blockchain attributes, such as neglecting the third party security, delegation, invulnerability with ambush and intruder as appropriately as structures of accord appearance and mediation inside the central layers [25]. There is a dynamic between upgrades, which makes the possibilities of automated vehicles, smart homes, development, and the urban areas are noteworthy with great possibility—every last bit of building the dynamic 5G-fueled blockchain structure.

The necessities to utilizing blockchain as reality require a broad quantity of network volume to work strongly. 5G technologies already demonstrated their adoption in decentralised applications to make them fast and more responsive in the case of failure also [26].

Advantageousness of 5G applied sciences moreover lays in the truth that more prominent system volume and transfer limit that square cases can be diminish dejected fundamentally, allowing for these the utilization of blockchain to scale without any problem. [4].

4.4.4   Scaling of blockchain functionality by 5G

Many redesigns are done to the blockchain because 5G innovation is utilized with definite adaptability. What's more, contemplating the determined difficulties that blockchain has stood up to by scale, this is a tremendous forward leap. Until now, there is some original issue dumbfounding the sustained utility of blockchain. As it manages unbelievable insurance and unwavering quality, the measure is the thing that hamstrings it.

As few are recognized instances of the endeavor that measure speaks to originate by the exchange speeds. As Bitcoin and Ethereum have progressed, intending to measure, their exchange rapidity (4.6 and 15, separately) really can't analyze such a scale that virtual money-related elements are accustomed to managing. Master Card and Visa are two models that help manage 45 000 and 1 700 exchanges for every second [14].

As diverse cryptographic forms of money and blockchain go faster than any other options, they remain on the earth with essential fiscal elements. The execution of 5G makes the computerized B12 shot, with 5G conferring paces of more than 10 GB every second. To measure the response, a response has certain volume bottlenecks. 5G should give a quick response highly required for the mission critical applications. Acquainting 5G mechanical skill with blockchain's environment will explain its inactivity and versatility issues while upgrading hub support and diminishing low on time taken to framework squares. In rundown, 5G innovative expertise would give the potential to set up a blockchain hubs network.

4.4.5   5G for boosting keen agreements credibility

Keen contracts have won notoriety among clients because of the favorable circumstances it can concede for clients from people to global business. 5G mechanical skill moreover conceivable to made smart agreements for extra working to enterprise's global than any time in recent memory [17]. With the development of 5G mechanical skills worldwide, the usage of prophets and wise agreements would be made some separation simpler by expanding, even in faraway regions.

4.4.6   How 5G will increase network volume for blockchain improvement?

The 5G services like ultra-high network reliability of more than 99.999% availability of data and very low latency (of 1 millisecond) for transmission are the backbone for any decentralised applications (like healthcare). The volume is that open blockchain shows the host some separation more prominent assortment of hubs, consequently upgrading its speed. Finally, 5G services are also plays a crucial role in larger network based applications.

Improved investment expected more prominent hubs dynamic and additional hubs possible drastically unrivaled security and some separation bigger degrees of decentralization. Bitcoin has stood up to its honest portion of analysis by its circulation of hubs. These reactions come from the reality that a mammoth level of its removal ponds and dominant part of its hubs abide in China [27].

The potential to vote to project a larger part of Bitcoin's people group lives in China, which ~~~~ ~~~~~~~~ively a decent arrangement danger for a few. As the presentation of 5G advancements, this ~~~~~~~~ ~~ ~~~~ would be settled and annihilated with an expected issue. It makes it less hard to exclusively ~~~~~~ blockchain, anyway democratize them overall [20].

4.4.7 Will 5G bargain blockchain innovation's latent capacities?

Here recorded a scope of intentions why 5G science should, without trouble, gain blockchain innovation. The question should be whether there is any confirmation to show that 5G science should harm blockchain in all actuality harm blockchain? There are some likely drawbacks with this sort of coordinated effort. There is consistently the open door that noxious units and elements should enter the network and reason turmoil. This is an inescapable subordinate of extended interconnectivity, in any case.

One of the potential difficulties, as threatening to drawbacks, is the possibility that, even with the presentation of 5G, interest for cryptographic forms of money and blockchain may furthermore territory a lopsided amount of interest on these systems, leaving these systems with an absence of scale with which to keep up [23].

At long last finished up here, Mobile telecoms and gatherings in cell phones are naturally excited for the entirety of the achievable and potential outcomes that accompany 5G innovation. The total of 5G with blockchain science has the entirety of the conceivable to be an unprecedented take-off ahead for organizations and individuals everywhere throughout the world.

4.5   5G-based blockchain distributed ledger technology

5G plays a vital role in the growth of various industries, ought the blockchain has made a large impact. End-users can take fast delivery of their requests after amalgamation of blockchain and 5G. As 5G will make interaction with science greater value effective and quicker for the developing international. 5G have to gasoline with the micro-bills era, like cryptocurrencies, as extra people undertake smartphones. Meanwhile, within the evolved international, 5G has an upward push of AI, improved fact, and clever strategies, making extra global superior to ever.

Qualcomm President Cristiano Amon expects 5G to spread for the duration of foremost metropolitan regions in 2020, after which boom into growing global places in 2021. Amon moreover assumes cell phone groups to ship over two hundred million 5G smartphones as the way of the subsequent year. As 5G conversation sciences develop international as it wants to additionally gasoline the upward thrust of disbursed ledger applied sciences (DLTs) and blockchain. In truth, 5G may need to be the most important difficulty while it moves to occur to cryptocurrencies and dispensed register generation [25, 28]. By the way of larger communication establishment and a feasible 100× quicker net expectancy capacity, 5G is projected that the modern-day lag impact of 100 ms.

In 2020, blockchain led to a profound era. Among worldwide ambiguity of the present economic systems, prosperity understands, and booms are in unpredicted bets. In an international, the place frugality can reputedly modification as soon as a person notion can alternate; period needs to deliver all dimensions. If cash had been the measurement branch, it needs to be based on time [29].

4.6   Secure mobile banking using 5G and blockchain

A blend of 5G and blockchain needs to help banks impenetrable their applications. Banks are now the use of blockchain for assurance. Administered record innovative information can approve exchanges other than the need for an administration. Regardless of how the essential position, much the same as the money-related foundation's worker, is undermined, the gatherings can, in any case, gadget transactions. 5G and Blockchain may need to join to make this gadget significantly more remarkable. Blockchain can be adopted in banking systems to exchange the currencies with trust. 5G itself will make positive impact, as these perplexing systems don't worry under the heap of blockchain. Figure 4.5 shows a decentralized model of a blockchain. It's far separating the real model of the unified and decentralized blockchain model.

4.7   5G benefits to blockchain and crypto users

5G mobile communication providers provide various benefits as mentioned below:

- Decreased latency
- Improved data rates
- Energy efficiency

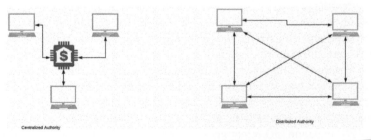

Figure 4.5   A basic blockchain model

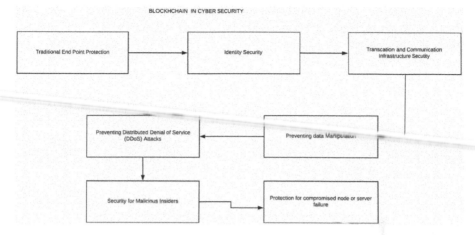

Figure 4.6   Blockchain in cybersecurity for the digital future

- Reduced cost
- Increase in the system capacity
- Numerous device connectivity.

Figure 4.6 illustrates the involvement and interconnection in cybersecurity. All of those edges may benefit blockchain and cryptocurrency. In a single day, cellular communiqué turns into cheaper and less complicated by 5G. 5G is additionally projected to excellent gasoline devices. Using a decrease in the latency and rising rapidity, 5G takes IoT gadgets additional on hand. IoT devices would possibly raise blockchain even extra. These gadgets will influence the blockchain capabilities such as protection, devolution, and agreement intercession as initial layers. Thus, the best towns, automated vehicles, and good homes for the longer term would consider 5G-fuelled blockchain. Blockchain technology needs immeasurable community functionality. 5G and Blockchain technologies can be excessively used across the world in the times to come. That developed network capability would possibly abbreviate chunk times, developing with blockchains to measure. 5G might also contribute blockchains to boost node participation and decentralization [26, 30].

4.7.1   5G affect on revolutionizing blockchain

Measurability lots of 5G's blockchain enhancements return all of the manners with measurability. The massive: up to now, blockchain's largest trouble during measurability. Blockchain is more secure and data reliability; as of now, there is no continuously climbable. Bitcoin takes 3.8 transactions in step with second (tps) and cannot contend as the 5 000 tps of credit card and Visa. Alternative cryptocurrencies provide quicker answers; however, bitcoin stays the head of the crypto. 5G gives increase speed to 10 gigabits in step with 2nd. It'll expand the rate of cellular networks and residential broadband. 5G might get rid of bottlenecks [29]. It might enhance functionality and speeds whereas lowering latency. It makes blockchain extra climbable

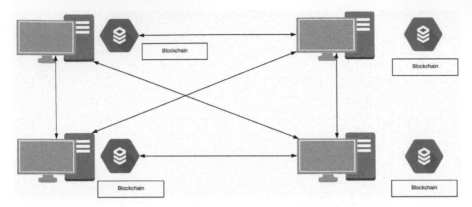

Figure 4.7   First 5G-embedded network

night long with the aid of growing node participation and marginal block instances. In short, 5G would possibly create easy to prepare a suburbanized, worldwide community of blockchain nodes. Figure 4.7 illustrates the first 5G-embedded networks.

4.7.2   How 5G authorizes smart contracts

5G makes smart contracts to make them usable forever. Smart contracts count number on visions as exterior statistics provide the relay data towards the smart contract. As oracles need web get entry toward ship statistics. In worldwide, 5G will provide easier oracles to ship the record, particularly in way flung parts of the region. This would, in any other case, now not be viable.

5G will deliver big growth as bandwidth with additionally dropping expectancy. The capacity greater node should be part of public blockchains. There may also be elevated system contribution using extending coverage in some distance of areas and enhancing connectivity for cells and tablets. Additional contribution potential increased nodes. Extra nodes mean more protection and higher reorganization. Numerous disparage bitcoin from most of the people of nodes based totally in China. As the miners in China give a few have an effect over the community. 5G can also remove this difficulty, making it less complicated for blockchain networks to diversify networks globally [31].

Malicious gadgets need to cause chaos inside networks, as an instance. They are fueled by way of interconnectivity, a malicious unit with unsecured networks. Or, 5G results in a disutility from the people using cryptocurrencies and blockchains. It has to be a rolling call for the identical growing older organization and moving clients even. Mobile conversation groups already suppose 5G to be a significant ahead. The integration of Blockchain and 5G can give a boost up not only to the financial institutions but to other verticals of industry 4.0.

4.8 Blockchain in defense to secure communications

The Department of Defense investigates blockchain science as an approach to modernize its technique to cryptography and cybersecurity, in agreement with a report propelled for the current month. Employment of blockchain might need to include making sure about interchanges between naval force gadgets in the region and their central station, and allowing mind officials to securely communicate delicate insights to the Pentagon, in agreement to the DoD Information Resource Management Strategic Plan FY19-23, propelled on July 12 [32]. The endeavor is a segment of the DoD's Digital Modernization Strategy, which is fixated on four regions: distributed computing, manufactured insight, cybersecurity, and C3: order, control, and interchanges. In particular, the record notes that the Defense Advanced Research Projects Agency (DARPA) has started to test with blockchain to make an insusceptible specialized gadget in which messages can be tried through a decentralized record the innovative ability blockchain is developed on.

DARPA is pulled into three components of blockchain innovation, in agreement with the report. First, they are "trustless," which potential they "expect bargain of the network through every insider and untouchable." .Second, blockchains are straightforwardly secure: they do no longer make a difference on disappointment inclined privileged insights, anyway on the other hand on the shape of a cryptographic record that makes altering each generally extreme and straight away self-evident. Finally, blockchain systems are issue open-minded: they adjust the endeavors of clear hubs to dismiss these that are deceptive. Taken together, the final product is that blockchain mechanical ability no longer exclusively makes it substantially less potentially correspondences will be undermined; it makes the system of bargaining them parts harder and more noteworthy expensive, the record notes. DARPA is engaged with zero-information evidence, which can be utilized to affirm a fact other than uncovering any significant purposes of the fundamental measurements used to affirm it.

"A zero-information evidence incorporates an announcement of the real world and the basic confirmation of its exactness," expressed Dr. Josh Baron, an application-tion manager in DARPA's Information Innovation Office (I2O), in a July 18 delivery. "The holder of the truth does now not want to uncover the hidden insights to convince its intended interest group that the fact of the matter is precise. Take, for instance, money-related establishment withdrawal. Likewise, you may pick a gadget that licenses you to make a withdrawal excepting also sharing your budgetary organization balance. The device would need some method of checking that there is sufficient money to attract from except perceiving the particular amount of money sitting inside your record." While noticing that the crypto forex advertise been the gracefully of "a checked make greater in the effective and genuine utilization of zero-information evidence," DARPA expressed that its cryptology wants are scarcely extraordinary from these required by the method of Bitcoin and various tokens.

Digital currencies "organize discussion and confirmation affectivity anyway do no longer consistently scale for exchanges that are additional complex," expressed the delivery. "For exceptionally entangled verification articulations like these that the DoD can likewise need to utilize, novel and additional condition amicable strategies are required." DARPA has made the Securing Information for Encrypted Verification and Evaluation (SIEVE) program to encourage this. Its aspirations to "create PC science standard and programming program that can produce scientifically unquestionable explanations that can be shared freely aside from parting with tricky insights."

Regardless, the DoD's exemplify of blockchain science remains exploratory. While DARPA's credit comprises of developing the internet, its order is to test with and increment surely useful new advancements routinely pleasantly sooner than the big business would make speculations intently in them. As indicated by the DoD key arrangement, DARPA has moreover been "attempting to expand an unshakable code which blockchain might need to encourage, because of the reality the innovative expertise presents Genius on programmers who endeavor to harm into immune databases."

4.9   Key issues in blockchain in communications

There are many core issues in blockchain communication based on the present scenario. Every important issue is discussed below with suggested remedial actions [33–41].

a. Companywide collaboration

When team patrons are in the indistinguishable working environment or division, there is a work in recognition and have confidence that makes coordinated effort consistent. Individuals see each other, so distinguishing proof approval isn't required, and venture-related reality is reachable to all. Numerous associations, be that as it may, tend to be a progression of storehouses where information is eagerly watched, even inside.

More progressive partnerships are endeavoring to develop societies of straightforwardness, specifically when trying to develop to be client-driven. In these situations, storehouses exist a transcendent obstruction for achieving companywide targets, which is by and large envelopes joint effort and expertise sharing. Contingent upon the way of life, now it cannot be likewise reasonable to remove storehouses; anyway, separating them a piece can go a long way to helping cross-useful groups.

Here, blockchain would be a high use case for a coordinated effort. Consider projections in which sensitive information inside a branch should be suggested for a companywide joint effort activity, such as shopper records, charge chronicles, financial realities, and programming program code. Utilizing blockchain, divisions may need to safely share their most-watched information, notwithstanding destroying storehouses or uncover any data for abuse.

b. Voice security as a communications channel

Since voice correspondences are a foundation of UC, on the off chance that Information Technologies (IT) organizations' impenetrable voice works firmly, the UC sending will be extra powerful. As cloud science advances and discourse consideration makes Artificial Intelligence (AI) voice science undefined from the human voice, voice structures will develop as an expanding number of inclined to malignant movement.

While pastimes that utilize voice are rather amiable, circumstances do exist to spot the guest's distinguishing proof wishes to be perceived with entire sureness. This applies similarly to one-on-one correspondence, for example, two chiefs examining a merger, as it does to team cooperation, for example, a scope of offices defining a way to deal with counter another contender. With basically a little social building, it tends to be strikingly easy for awful entertainers to bargain these situations.

As of not long ago, Direct Inward Dialing (DID)—these pervasive 10-digit cell phone numbers—has been our prevailing identifier for ongoing correspondence. Considering how we use DID for voice and informing, our personality, private privateness, and data security are in danger. Presently, consider the prevailing voice applied studies of people, in general, exchanged telephone arrange, voice over IP (VoIP) and portable and how everyone has superb well-being inadequacies that make them beneficial interests for programmers. Additionally, consider the truth that VoIP is denied or perilous for non-open discussions in numerous nations. Blockchain wasn't structured considering voice; anyway, basically use examples exist for coordinated and group-based interchanges. With DID, approving recognizable proof is transforming into extra troublesome, as calls can be without issues mock or listened in, and guests can be mimicked the utilization of AI.

These darkish consequences are interest's parts of the cybercrime toolbox. For example, the spot privateness and guest ID should have supreme sureness; Blockchain in correspondences is extra firmly shut than the DIDs we have depended on sooner than the web arrived along. It is likely an appropriate idea to set up these hyperlinks to the blockchain in that specific situation.

4.10   5G challenges facing deployment

Conveying 5G will never again be simple. While there is a ton of promising potential, CSPs should choose out methods to manage the accompanying 5G challenges:

a. Building mind-boggling and thick systems

5G systems will be more mind-boggling than fresh out of the plastic new systems. One thing of this developing multifaceted nature is the decision for denser systems. New 5G receiving wires and RAN equipment, even regardless of the amazing, spread altogether masses significantly less home in qualification with existing 4G macrocells. This capacity-related protection plan calls for higher 5G equipment and helping programming application—a range that duplicates along these lines as vacationer's strikes inside.

b. Maintaining running and security costs low

Including the basic equipment required for 5G systems can altogether expand working costs (OpEx). These costs cross past the equipment itself. Systems should be designed, analyzed, controlled, and for the most part, forward-thinking all issues that exponentially draw out OpEx.

c. Meeting low-inactivity necessities

5G systems require ultra-low- deterministic idleness to the top component. While not as crucial for telecom bundles, it's far favored for a developing commercial center of devices that could thoroughly allow a solitary millisecond extends for one path interchanges throughout the whole framework. Heritage systems, except uncertainty, can't deal with this pace and amount of insights.

d. Managing new well-being inconveniences

Each new mechanical information accompanies new dangers, and 5G isn't any special case. Given the fairly dispensed, related, and now and again far-off nature of 5G systems, new thought needs to get to capacity digital security gives that ascent up.

e. Recurrence groups

Even though 4G LTE now works on set up recurrence groups less than 6 GHz, 5G calls for frequencies the entirety of the path up to 300 GHz. Some are more referenced as mmWave. Those groups can raise a procedure's enormous potential and give ultra-expedient speeds that offer a 20-overlap make greater over LTE's quickest theoretical throughput. WI-FI merchants paying little heed to the reality that longing to offer for the all-encompassing range groups as they unite and reveal their particular 5G systems. In Canada, as a case, the government held a range closeout for 600 MHz in 2019, with 3 500 MHz progressing for 2020 and 1 GHz at present got ready for 2021. In the United States, millimeter wave (mmWave) range barters got 4$. Forty-seven billion (US), the biggest single entire inside the universal areas, reports the spring in 2020 [32].

f. Deployment and protection

Despite 5G providing an enormous increment in pace and data transfer capacity, its bigger constrained range will also require a framework. Better frequencies permit particularly directional radio waves that embrace they might be focused or meant to practice is referenced as shaft framing. The endeavor is that 5G receiving wires, while in an element to adapt to more customers and insights, shaft out over shorter separations.

Notwithstanding reception apparatuses and base stations getting littler on this situation, increased of them could presumably be snared on structures or homes.

Table 4.1   *Forecast annual global mobile operators*

S. No	Years	Capex (Billions)
1	2018	$0.6
2	2019	$8.6
3	2020	$16.0
4	2021	$34.2
5	2022	$58.5
6	2023	$87.9

Urban communities will pick to set up expanded repeaters to spread out the waves for broadened assortment while keeping typical paces in denser populace territories. Its imaginable transporters will apply lower-recurrence groups to cowl more extensive regions until the 5G people group develops. In the predetermination, it might moreover recommend that modems and wi-fi switches are changed with 5G little cells or exact equipment to flexibly 5G associations into homes and organizations, for that cause pushing off worried web associations as we remember them today. Spreading out get right of access to provincial zones will be an endeavor since it used to be as fast as LTE.

g. *Cost to assemble price to adopt 5G in smart applications*

Building a community is steeply priced, and companies will increase the money to grow consumer revenue. Similar to LTE plans incurred a higher preliminary cost, 5G will in all possibility comply with an equal route. And it's no longer surely establishing a layer on top of a modern-day community. It's laying the basis for something new altogether. Table 4.1 shows the forecast as much as 2023 of annual worldwide mobile customer growth. In keeping with Heavy analyzing cell Operator 5G Capex, whole global spending on 5G is about to achieve $88 billion with the useful resource of 2023. As soon as it comes to be feasible, first-class computing device segments can be related in certain new ways, mainly cars, home equipment, robots, and town infrastructure.

Currently, that 5G-empowered mobile telephones and various gadgets rectangular measure movement into the marketplace arranges square measure growing in various international locations worldwide. The notion behind the net of factors (IoT) relies upon a speedy machine that can tie devices and administrations alongsideside. This is one of all the guarantee professionals have anticipated for 5G's latent ability. Citizens of any smart country have to learn themselves that how to make the optimum utilization of available technologies (like 5G, IoT, etc).

h. *Laws and principles*

Government controllers can consider 5G preparing, eminently with the other foundation expected to open up the system. Providers can be constrained to put in new reception apparatuses, base stations, and repeaters. In the past, controllers must be constrained to handle 5G administrations in waves over numerous vertical divisions. These will grasp range accessibility, voltage radiation laws, foundation sharing, and digital security. An inquiry and markets report plunges into the varying viewpoints and difficulties worried about getting there. Canada's biggest media agencies have focused on their strict rulings defined by Innovation, Science and Economic Development North American nation (ISED), the Canadian Radio-TV and Telecommunications Commission (CRTC), and Health North American nation.

i. Modernizing rules to make 5G a reality

In the United States, every one of the four significant transporters square measure running 5G systems with confined property to pick markets. The Federal Communications Commission (FCC) selected recommended the required modifications in the RF to be used in 5G. Those will also open entryways for littler players and new participants to flexibly provincial and local administrations. In Europe, transporters inside the UK have just followed up on their few intends to extend in 2020, despite pushback and assaults on media transmission representatives and pinnacles. The nation's interchanges controller has regarded 5G signs to be at spans globally endorsed pointers. For its a large portion of, the ECU Union has effectively advanced 5G improvements as a piece of its financial procedure designs and released subtleties on any way part nations can move toward examination and guidelines. Range barters that were deferred because of the pandemic could result before the tip of 2020. In the interim, China has 50 million 5G telephone endorsers, with the nation heading the correct way to prevail in 70 per cent of 5G cell phone shrinks by the tip of 2020. The Republic of Korea lingers behind anyway is steadfast in expanding its system, though the Asian nation is poised to control the methods for nations in a geographic region.

j. Security and protection

This would look at any facts that pushed innovation; anyway, the 5G rollout can get the danger to persuade every normal and entangled cybersecurity danger. Despite the reality that 5G falls under the Authentication and Key settlement (AKA), a framework intended to determine among structures, it would be potential to observe human beings' close exploitation of their telephones. They may even be cognizant of stay calls. Similar to it's as of now, the heap is on the transporters and web work consortiums to flexibly a complicated well-being net for benefactors, aside from client self-smugness can be similarly dangerous. With information speeds predicted to be extents faster than new tiers, thus too might assets be able to increment. It's going to constrain cloud-based and records virtualization administrations to be as hermetically sealed as the capability to observe client data and protection. On a proportional token, their clients can get the hazard to be extra cautious and alert as stewards in their perception.

4.11 New opportunities for 5G applications

The potential for 5G goes on the far side of antiquated media transmission applications. New ventures can use 5G innovation because of the spine to control astute edge gadgets. 5G brought new opportunities for the researchers, which open the ~~nnur~~ for wide variety of applications like transportation, smart city, government services, etc [42–55].

A. Industrial and artificial consciousness

The most recent mechanical and artificial brainpower advancements can utilize 5G at the sting for self-governing tasks. Associated robots that may "see" need low inertness to respond to visual data sources.

B. Automotive 5G with self-ruling vehicles

Inside the future, the car exchange imagines level four (L4) autonomous vehicles that heft people around as though they were an item – with no human driver. This needs a huge amount of figuring force and property to work securely.

C. Part and resistance

For the most part, this exchange sees 5G as some approach to help universal protection correspondences and drive Urban Air Quality (UAM) innovation.

4.12 Blockchain works to secure communications

As decentralization unfurls, it's an ideal opportunity to modernize our way of dealing with secure, steady, and self-sovereign interchanges by utilizing shared systems. By moving up to a suburbanized system layer, we will, in a general square measure prepared to digest away the fundamental geologically detectable web transport layer, secure information substance, and flexibly an extra steady foundation for the net to flourish. A blockchain could be a developing rundown of records, packaged along in structures known as obstructs that square measure joined exploitation cryptography. Each square contains a logical order hash of the past square, a timestamp, various headers, and dealings information. Complete duplicates of blockchains square measure joined across hubs that work along to make AN open, unchanging record of truth exploitation refined understanding algorithms. Designed as some approach to adequately share non-open information on an open foundation, blockchain innovation gives a new substrate to correspondences that decentralizes the board and wipes out single purposes of disappointment while also giving bigger information security.

4.12.1 Centralized, distributed, and decentralization networking

By putting away copy duplicates of data across distributed systems, an appropriately structured blockchain disposes of an assortment of dangers that escort information being control halfway along with police work, the board, and inside and out framework disappointment. Here investigate anyway appropriated, suburbanized systems encourage improve correspondences framework accessibility, while significantly rising information protection.

4.12.2   Coding modern technologies

A necessary piece of blockchain's vehicle conventions making certain information security and disposing of dangers of police work as a matter of course. Blockchain gives conventions to coordinate and one-to-many coding exploitation lopsided key sets identified with each hub. Keys interpret information bundles implied for explicit hubs. When one hub sends a bundle to an alternate, it encodes the parcel exploitation of the overall population or pre-organized shared key of the implied beneficiary hub. Here referenced, an approach to collected degrees of coding improves information protection and limits the intensity of difficult entertainers to block or control correspondences.

4.12.3   Vulnerabilities in existing communications protocols

The net conference (IP) suite gives a start to complete data correspondence indicating how facts need to be packetized, tended to, dispatched, and directed. The IP suite is the standard machine version and correspondence convention stack applied across laptop systems. It is likewise in the main alluded to as TCP/IP when you consider that the primary conventions inside the suite are the Transmission Control Protocol (TCP) and the net Protocol (IP). The IP Suite is also separated into seven sections in greater specialized discussions, known as the Open structures Interconnection model (OSI model). Right here investigated the four precept areas that classify internet Protocol suite: Packets, Addresses, Transmission, and Routing. We can take a gander at every successively to clarify the weaknesses that range various gadget layers and how blockchain addresses those shortcomings.

4.12.4   Weaknesses in packetization

The ability to supplant huge content material as URLs with IP arranges addresses is fundamental for pragmatic net interchanges. Currently, the net depends on the domain name system (DNS) that was created in 1985. It is essentially a unified database that defends IP addresses with their comprehensible reciprocals. Recollect it the internet's place eBook in which each host is recorded and can be followed utilizing the WHOIS management.

Area name enlistment is overseen midway with the aid of the net organization for Assigned Names and Numbers (ICANN), a non-benefit affiliation centered in California. Administrations that depend on DNS are based upon disturbance and manage through influential people and institutions. It is a commonly unimportant task to utilize DNS and take down notification to make content hard to reach via planning with a couple of superb associations that control the internet's place.

Moreover, an introduced DNS vault collectively represents a solitary reason for sadness for the web. The handiest 13 legitimate workers serve the DNS root zone, typically known as the "root employees." This dependence upon a gaggle of believed entertainers makes few functions of sadness. Simultaneously, as these root workers are bunched with a device of around 1 000 employees in several countries around the world, the organizations are prone to disbursed Denial-of-carrier (DDoS) assaults. On the off threat that anyone or the entirety of the believed CAs falls flat, URLs might be irresolvable all around. This has occurred and could continue to occur as more gadgets are arranged on the internet.

4.12.5   Securing community packets with blockchain

The blockchain and web three networks are taking a shot at non-compulsory call intention conventions, such as the Handshake Protocol. Handshake is a non-stop project drawing near open dispatch to accumulate a decentralized DNS system that uses crypto monetary motivations to facilitate settlement on the connection among names and declarations.

The goal of the Handshake assignment is not to supplant all of DNS, however, to supplant the foundation area document and the basis employees with extra open and democratized picks. This can viably commoditize DNS below an open supply ethos, permitting root zones to get censorable, permissionless, and liberated from unified guards, such as ICANN. This opportunity will permit the internet to emerge unhindered by uncalled-for, integrated control while bringing down the economic obstructions that limit net omnipresence.

4.12.6   Weaknesses in net protocol addresses

An Internet Protocol cope with (IP deal with) is a numerical name allotted to each gadget associated with a laptop set up. All interchanges sent via the net are prompt, making use of available IP addresses. An IP address is a customary postal letter. Contained a header and a payload, the header calls for open tending to intelligible by using all and sundry to help with directing like place facts on an envelope. The substance, or payload, is darkened within the envelope itself. Any extra wrapping, for instance, encryption, may be included as desired for well-being.

The parcel header consists of brazenly discernible information, as an example, source and purpose prepare addresses, blunder discovery codes, and sequencing statistics. The open concept of the header records implies it's far viable to music down statistics dispatched between two endpoints and to remake messages contained numerous bundles.

To entangle matters also, in normal interchanges, bundles are seldom encoded as indicated by the Breach degree Index, of the enormously wide variety of information taken because 2013, just 4% became encoded and delivered unusable through aggressors. Due to the fact each net service company (ISP) is accountable for diverse scopes of IP addresses, and enlisting the owners doled out for each IP addresses, it's far surely simple to call for records from them to locate the areas and personalities related with a selected endpoint, at the back of which as a minimum one bodily and virtual gadgets can also exist. Regularly, net crawlers can find this record without a proper or valid solicitation. The geographic vicinity of an IP address can most commonly be pinpointed interior squares of the physical location, and owner touch subtleties inclusive of smartphone numbers and postage data go together with the enlistment.

Anyhow, its miles likewise achievable to control those IP addresses tends to utilize intermediaries, onion steering, or VPNs, essentially satirizing the beginning reason of a message. That is proper now the main strategies for assurance to cloud a message endpoint and shield it from being certainly focused on or distantly got to via corrupt methods.

This would take a look at any fact-pushed innovation; anyway, the 5G rollout can be given a chance to steer every common and entangled cybersecurity danger. Despite the truth that 5Gprovide uninterrupted services to the community, there are many issues in the 5G also that needs to be tackled by the researchers across the globe. Such as the heap is on the transporters and webwork consortiums to flexibly a complicated well-being net for benefactors, except purchaser self-smugness can be similarly dangerous. The speed of executing the tasks in cloud-based systems will be improved with the adoption of 5G. It'll constrain cloud-based totally and information-tion virtualization administrations to be as hermetically sealed as the ability to look at client statistics and safety. On a proportional token, their customers can get the risk to be more cautious and alert as stewards of their perception.

4.12.7   *Protecting IP addresses with decentralized communications*

A superior method to ensure the personality and area of a message endpoint is to decentralize tending to. Decentralization combines the bundles over many hubs and can be intended to darken explicit tending to by utilizing the blockchain as a message transport, making extra boundaries against reconnaissance and altering. Replication of the parcel over different hubs likewise includes repetition of the message for included deliverability and adaptation to non-critical failure [32].

Utilizing distributed systems, blockchain innovation can make a layer of deliberation that makes the geological areas and personalities of hubs hard to decide, keeping them from being focused on. Encoded messages are distributed comprehensively on a blockchain. Figure 4.8 shows the usage of blockchain in smart cities developments.

These shortcomings produce an asylum for hazardous entertainers and hamper the general utility and security of the web. By Cybersecurity Ventures, wrongdoing can value the globe in route over $6 trillion every year by 2021, up from $3 trillion out of 2015. For firms like JP Morgan Chase, these costs reach over $600 M per year. What's extra, 70% of data is made by individuals and 80% of data is overseen by organizations—and individuals zone unit pitiful with their prosperity record. This can be why it's an ideal opportunity to modernize web correspondences to be secure as a matter of course [30].

4.13   Propose framework along with blockchain technology

In the standard structure of the blockchain, the block segment will have the transaction IDx, Merkle tree, and hash block, which is used to hash with the next transaction

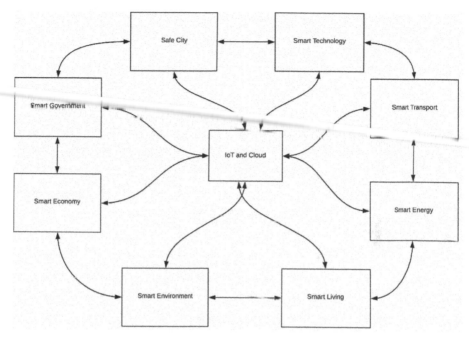

Figure 4.8   Blockchain in secure smart city systems

and previous transaction block in the network. Here, blockchain technology is well deployed in the distributed environment, which helps avoid double-spending attacks while performing the transaction. In the modified structure of the blockchain, the header, which is used for each block, contains certain components to be added as represented in Figure 4.9 and mentioned below:

1. Block Version
2. Timestamp
3. Merkle tree Block Hash
4. N Bits
5. Nonce
6. Parent Block Hash.

Figure 4.10 is added to the IoT device, which helps establish secure communication with the help of blockchain technology, as represented in Figure 4.10.

4.14   Case study

Here we have discussed the application related to healthcare where pill dispenser is considered, and it is represented diagrammatically in Figure 4.11.

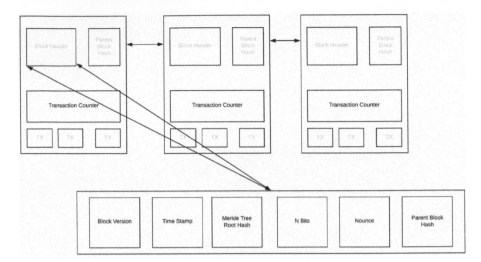

Figure 4.9   Modified Blockchain Structure

4.15   Chapter summary and conclusions

Here discussion states that how blockchain technology helps IoT to provide security and privacy communications. Various issues and challenges are described in order and corrective measures are suggested. The scalability is difficult inside the blockchain technology at better data feed is to be decreasing remarkably to reliable and speedy communications. As a result of the above, at the same time as 5G IoT provides the speed for IoT devices, integration with blockchain may surely result in slower processing of records and transactions. The integration of 5G and IoT with blockchain will provide better perspectives to mobile technologies to boost up their processing capabilities. The aggregate of IoT and 5G has a boundless latent that may best be found out by infusing the blockchain technology. 5G offers a connectivity cowl for the IoT gadgets and transactions; blockchain grips protection and guarantees the defense of person and transaction statistics. The discussion of secure communication works well, and it helps the blockchain play a significant role. Then

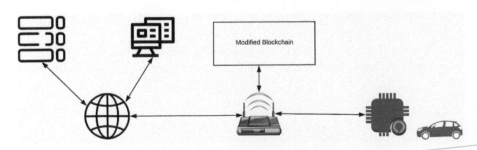

Figure 4.10   Proposed secure IoT communication design

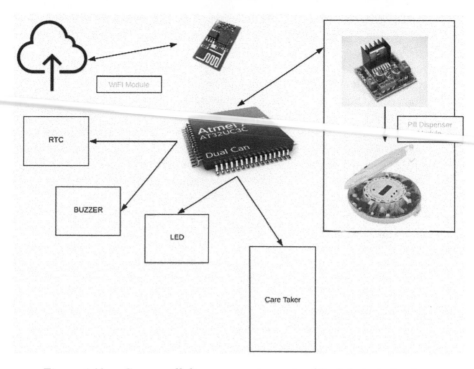

Figure 4.11   Secure pill dispenser system using blockchain technology

the modified blockchain is designed integrated with IoT networks. That communication becomes secure as it adds up with nonce, timestamps and hashing concepts as it helps build the cryptography-based secure communication. Finally, a real-time case study has been designed as a pill dispenser as it integrates IoT devices to manage and monitor with the help of blockchain technology.

References

[1] Hewa T., Gür G., Kalla A., Ylianttila M., Braeken A., Liyanage M. 'The role of blockchain in 6G: challenges, opportunities and research directions'. *2020 2nd 6G Wireless Summit*. 2020:1–5.

[2] Zheng Z., Xie S., Dai H.-N., Chen X., Wang H. 'An overview of blockchain technology: architecture, consensus and future'. *2017 IEEE International Congress on Big Data*. 2017:557–64.

[3] Chaer A., Salah K., Lima C., Ray P., Sheltami T. 'Blockchain for 5G: opportunities and challenges'. *2019 IEEE Globecom Workshops*. 2019:1–6.

[4] Eyal I., Sirer E.G. 'Majority is not enough: bitcoin mining is vulnerable'. *Proceedings of International Conference on Financial Cryptography and Data Security*; Berlin, Heidelberg; 2014. pp. 436–54.

[5]   Yu T., Wang X., Zhu Y. 'Blockchain technology for the 5G-enabled internet of things systems: principle, applications and challenges'. *CRC Press.* 2019:1–21.

[6]   Joshi A., Han M., Wang Y. 'A survey on security and privacy issues of blockchain technology'. *Mathematical foundations of computing.* 2018;**1**:121–47.

[7]   Dorri A., Kanhere S., Jurdak R., Gauravaram P. 'Blockchain for IoT security and privacy: the case study of a smarthome'. 2017.

[8]   Markets and Markets,Statista Estimates. *Market for blockchain technology worldwide* [online]. 2018. Available from https://www.statista.com/statistics/647231/worldwideblockchaintechnology- market-size/ [Accessed Apr 2021].

[9]   Crosby M., Pattanayak P., Verma S., Kalyanaraman V. 'Blockchain technology: beyond bitcoin'. *Applied innovation.* 2016;**2**:6–10.

[10]   Panikkar S., Nair S., Brody P., Pureswaran V. 'Adept: an IoT practitioner perspective'. *IBM Institute for Business Value.* 2015.

[11]   Siddiqi M., All S.T., Sivaraman V. 'Secure lightweight context-driven data logging for body worn sensing devices'. *Proceedings of the IEEE 5th International Symposium on Digital Forensic and Security (ISDFS)*; 2017. pp. 1–6.

[12]   Han D., Kim H., Jang J. 'Blockchain based smart door lock system'. *Proceedings of International Conference on Information and Communication Technology Convergence (ICTC)*; 2017. pp. 1165–7.

[13]   Tanas C., Delgado-Segura S., Herrera-Joancomarti J. 'An integrated reward and reputation mechanism for mcs preserving users privacy'. *Data Privacy Management, and Security Assurance. Springer*; 2015. pp. 83–99.

[14]   Biryukov A., Khovratovich D., Pustogarov I. 'Deanonymisation of clients in bitcoin P2P network'. *Proceedings of the 2014 ACM SIGSAC Conference on Computer and Communications Security*; New York, NY, USA; 2014. pp. 15–29.

[15]   Bruce J. *The mini-blockchain scheme* [online]. 2014. Available from http://cryptonite.info/files/mbc-scheme-rev3.pdf [Accessed Jun 2020].

[16]   Yang Y., Wu L., Yin G., Li L., Zhao H. 'A survey on security and privacy issues in internet-of-things'. *IEEE Internet of Things Journal.* 2017;**4**(5):1250–8.

[17]   Tschorsch F., Scheuermann B. 'Bitcoin and beyond: a technical survey on decentralized digital currencies'. *IEEE Communications Surveys & Tutorials.* 2016;**18**(3):2084–123.

[18]   Wang J., Li M., He Y., Li H., Xiao K., Wang C. 'A blockchain based privacy-preserving incentive mechanism in crowdsensing applications'. *IEEE Access.* 2018;**6**:17545–56.

[19]   Bonneau J., Miller A., Clark J., Narayanan A., Kroll J.A., Felten E.W. 'SoK: research perspectives and challenges for bitcoin and cryptocurrencies'. *Proceedings of IEEE Symposium on Security and Privacy (SP). IEEE*; 2015. pp. 104–21.

[20]   *Blockchain with 5G Technology: The Future Catalyst of Cryptocurrencies Adoption.* Available from https://gainbitcoin.com/blockchain-5g-technology/ [Accessed April 2020].

[21] *Blockchain And 5G Technologies: Combining The Two.* Available from https:// www.thattechguru.com/2019/05/29/blockchain-and-5g-combination/ [Accessed May 2020].

[22] Zhou Z., Xie M., Zhu T. 'EEP2P: an energy-efficient and economy-efficient p2p network protocol'. *Proceedings of International Green Computing Conference (IGCC)*; 2014. pp. 1–6.

[23] NRI. *Survey on blockchain technologies and related services, Technical Report*. 2015. Available from http://www.meti.go.jp/english/press/2016/pdf/ 0531 01f.pdf.

[24] Dorri A., Kanhere S.S., Jurdak R., Gauravaram P. 'LSB: a lightweight scalable blockchain for IoT security and privacy'. *CoRR, abs/1712.02969.* 2017.

[25] Lee Kuo Chuen D. *Handbook of Digital Currency*, 1st edn. *Elsevier*. 2015. Available from http://EconPapers.repec.org/RePEc:eee:monogr: 9780128021170.

[26] Noyes C. 'Bitav: fast anti-malware by distributed blockchain consensus and feed forward scanning'. *arXiv preprint arXiv:1601.01405.* 2016.

[27] *5G for Blockchain Technology: Will Fifth Generation Internet Boost Distributed Ledgers?* Available from https://bitcoinexchangeguide.com/5g-blockchain-technology/ [Accessed Apr 2020].

[28] *Key use cases of blockchain in communications.* Available from https://searchun ifiedcommunications.techtarget.com/tip/2-key-use-cases-of-blockchain-in-communications [Accessed Mar 2021].

[29] Buterin V. 'A next-generation smart contract and decentralized application platform'. *White paper.* 2014.

[30] *5G Challenges: Exploring the Biggest Challenges for 5G Deployment.* Available from https://blogs.windriver.com/wind_river_blog/2020/03/5g-challenges/ [Accessed May 2020].

[31] *Blockchain and Cryptocurrency: People, Culture and Tech.* Available from https:// modernconsensus.com/technology/defense-department-turns-to-blockchain-to-secure-communications/ [Accessed Sep 2021].

[32] *Whitepaper: Secure Communications Using Blockchain.* Available from https:// provide.services/secure-communications-using-blockchain/ [Accessed Sep 2021].

[33] Tanwar S. *Fog Computing for Healthcare 4.0 Environments: Technical, Societal and Future Implications Signals and Communication Technology.* Springer International Publishing; 2020. pp. 1–430.

[34] Tanwar S. *Fog Data Analytics for IoT Applications – Next Generation Process Model with state-of-the-art Technologies, Studies in Big Data.* Springer International Publishing; 2020. pp. 1–550.

[35] Tanwar S., Tyagi S., Kumar N. '*Security and Privacy of Electronics Healthcare Records : Concepts, Paradigms and Solutions*'. Stevenage, United Kingdom; 2019. pp. 1–450.

[36] Mehta P., Gupta R., Tanwar S. 'Blockchain envisioned UAV networks: challenges, solutions, and comparisons'. *Computer Communications.* 2020;**151**(14):518–38.

[37] Tanwar S., Bhatia Q., Patel P., Kumari A., Singh P.K., Hong W.-C. 'Machine learning adoption in blockchain-based smart applications: the challenges, and a way forward'. *IEEE Access*. 2020;**8**:474–88.

[38] Mistry I., Tanwar S., Tyagi S., Kumar N. 'Blockchain for 5G-enabled IoT for industrial automation: a systematic review, solutions, and challenges'. *Mechanical Systems and Signal Processing*. 2020;**135**(5):106382–19.

[39] Kabra N., Bhattacharya P., Tanwar S., Tyagi S. 'MudraChain: blockchain-based framework for automated cheque clearance in financial institutions'. *Future Generation Computer Systems*. 2020;**102**(4):574–87.

[40] Bodkhe U., Tanwar S., Parekh K., *et al.* 'Blockchain for industry 4.0: a comprehensive review'. *IEEE Access*. 2020;**8**:79764–800.

[41] Tanwar S., Parekh K., Evans R. 'Blockchain-based electronic healthcare record system for healthcare 4.0 applications'. *Journal of Information Security and Applications*. 2019;**50**:1–14.

[42] Kumari A., Gupta R., Tanwar S., Kumar N. 'A taxonomy of blockchain-enabled softwarization for secure UAV network'. *Computer Communications*. 2020;**161**(12):304–23.

[43] Bodkhe U., Tanwar S. 'Taxonomy of secure data dissemination techniques for IoT environment'. *IET Software*. 2020;**14**(6):563–71.

[44] Gupta R., Kumari A., Tanwar S., Kumar N. 'Blockchain-envisioned softwarized multi-swarming UAVs to tackle COVID-19 situations'. *IEEE Network*. 2020:1–7.

[45] Kumari A., Tanwar S., Tyagi S., Kumar N. 'Blockchain-based massive data dissemination handling in IIoT environment'. *IEEE Network*. 2020;**35**(1):318–25.

[46] Gupta R., Kumari A., Tanwar S. 'A taxonomy of blockchain envisioned edge-as-a-connected autonomous vehicles: risk assessment and framework'. *Transactions on Emerging Telecommunications Technologies*. 2020:1–23.

[47] Kanisha B., Mahalakshmi V., Baskar M., Vijaya K.,Kalyanasundaram P . 'Smart communication using tri-spectral sign recognition for hearing-impaired people'. *The Journal of Supercomputing*. 2021;**4**(1)1–17.

[48] Bodkhe U., Tanwar S., Bhattacharyaa P., Kumar N. 'Blockchain for precision irrigation: a systematic review'. *Transactions on Emerging Telecommunications Technologies*. 2020:1–33.

[49] Kumari A., Gupta R., Tanwar S., Tyagi S., Kumari N. 'When blockchain meets smart grid: exploring demand response management for secure energy trading'. *IEEE Network*. 2020:1–7.

[50] Kumari A., Gupta R., Tanwar S., Kumar N. 'Blockchain and AI amalgamation for energy cloud management: challenges, solutions, and future directions'. *Journal of Parallel and Distributed Computing*. 2020;**143**(11):148–66.

[51] Gupta R., Tanwar S., Kumar N., Tyagi S. 'Blockchain-based security attack resilience schemes for autonomous vehicles in industry 4.0: a systematic review'. *Computers & Electrical Engineering*. 2020;**86**(106717):106717–15.

[52] Aggarwal S., Kumar N., Tanwar S. 'Blockchain-envisioned UAV commu-
     nication using 6G networks: open issues, use cases, *and future* directions'.
     IEEE Internet of Things Journal. 2020;**8**(7):5416–41.

[53] Akram S.V., Malik P.K., Singh R., Anita G., Tanwar S. 'Adoption of block-
     chain technology in various realms: opportunities and challenges'. *Security
     and Privacy Journal, Wiley.* 2020:1–17.

[54] Bhattacharya P., Tanwar S., Bodke U., Tyagi S., Kumar N. 'BinDaaS:
     blockchain-based deep-learning as-a-service in healthcare 4.0 applications'.
     IEEE Transactions on Network Science and Engineering. 2019:1–14.

[55] Singh R., Tanwar S., Sharma T.P. 'Utilization of blockchain for mitigating the
     distributed denial of service attacks'. *Security and Privacy Journal, Wiley.*
     2019;**1**(5):1–13.

Chapter 5

5G-driven radio framework for proficient smart health-care institutions

Himanshu Sharma[1], Mahmoud A M Albreem[2], and Arun Kumar[1]

A smart hospital is seen as one of the most important requirements in the present scenario. The use of technologies for health monitoring in remote areas will change the life and standard of people. The smart remote care is experiencing a fast change from customary medical clinic and the authority centered way to deal with a dispersed patient-driven methodology. During recent years, the 4G radio system is playing a substantial role in smart health-care. However, its contribution was not effective in smart health care due to several constraints such as poor network connectivity, low data-rate, ineffective utilization of bandwidth, high detection delay, and so on. Currently, the implementation of fifth era (5G) and blockchain is taking place all around the world, and it is expected that the 5G radio system will fulfill all the demands of smart health care. High bandwidth utilization, high data rate, excellent network coverage, and low latency are the requirements of digital hospitals. The choice of an efficient waveform will be critical for the standardization of smart health care with 5G. Hence, it has become necessary to investigate advance waveform schemes for the 5G network. In this correspondence, we have expansively analyzed and compared the advanced waveforms such as filter bank multi-carrier (FBMC), non-orthogonal multiple access (NOMA), universal filter multi-carrier (UFMC) with respect to current waveform scheme known as orthogonal frequency division multiplexing (OFDM). Further, the requirements of the smart hospital are comprehensively studied. Additionally, the detection methods are analyzed. The simulation outcomes of the study reveal that the throughput, spectral efficiency, and data rate of the advanced waveform are better than the OFDM system and beamforming (BF) technique is suitable for advanced form.

[1]Department of Electronics and Communication Engineering, JECRC University, Jaipur, India
[2]Electrical Engineering, College of Engineering, University of Sharjah, Sharjah, UAE

5.1   Introduction

The therapeutic administrations is a great idea to go for a perspective change with an extending appointment of contraptions with distinguishing equipment, advancement, and telemedicine improvement. In this chapter, we take a gander at the diverse natural framework needs, propelling advancement, and gathering of a part of the basic use cases driving toward 5G [1]. We will in like manner address a bit of the key motivation factors, for instance, information transmission, progressing response, fundamental organizations, and wearable that will affect the advancement improvement [2]. As this arcade progresses, the network necessities for the unstable development of gadgets and apparatuses with sensor-centered solicitations in bigger emergency clinics drive the development of device–device message. Moreover, the use cases, for example, Tactile Internet and mechanically inaccessible medical procedures resolve the spike requirement for precarious device broadcasting and low latency communications [3]. Today, the human services environment is confronted with various difficulties running from the framework, availability, ideal asset, the requirement for specialists, exactness, information the board, and continuous checking [4]. A nearby assessment of the overall insights with accessible information for 2005–15 additionally demonstrates that around 40% of nations have short of what one doctor for every 1 000 populace and under 18 clinic beds for every 10 000 populace [5]. This plainly makes way for different innovation models in medicinal services to meet this tremendous hole and prerequisite.

1.   Availability: Depending on use prerequisites, ultimate link can be taken care of by Wi-Fi: aimed at device functions, 4G, 100 Mbps variety of utilizations. Requests and criticality of the consumption circumstance is pivotal to elect the obtainability conveyor [6].
2.   Spectrum: Depending on the consumption, data transfer capacity necessity may change from Mbps to the demand for Gbps. These might in altogether probability be assisted by wireless radio. This is again a focus to the organic system, solicitation and the operation circumstance running after a vital social insurance community, a connected clinic, a structure of linked medical hospitals, outside to emergency clinic obtainability, and telemedicine [7].
3.   Low detection delay: Devices utilized might brand some reaction memories of few moments to barely any milliseconds. The crucial point is recognizing those lookouts with worthy degrees of inertness [8].
4.   Blockchain: Medical consideration might be a diverse upright that possesses a structure failure. The organize spiteful resolve drive around as a sanctioning agent aimed at pioneering human facilities by managing fundamental dimensions since a gigantic sum of connected devices, giving fortification and safety to clinical and analyzing data. The innovation possibly will give device-2-device (D2D) backing to leading explicit errands, for example, essential data communication [9, 10].

There is surely not a single development or game plan that will be utilized absolutely by the human administration partition. This backbone is a deliberate, stepwise, and requirement-centered headway from surviving advances to whatever exactly to originate. Human administration prototypes are rapidly fluctuating a direct result of the fragment and monetary fluctuations from a facility-centered, master-connected approach to manage an open-minded-driven model. At the point when patients are checked distantly by wearable sensors and correspondence supplies, the consequently noted data is significant for the ~~~~~~ ~ ~~~~ ~~ ~~~~~ analysis of the sufferers' real ailment, and it is a significant piece of the customized well-being care idea [11]. In a review and assessment of various radio answers for remote heart patients, it is proposed that cutting-edge telecardiology organize design should consolidate a sign-preparing module for nearby investigation of chronicled biological estimations and just convey distinguished occasions that are obtainable for characterized limits esteems. The frameworks ought to have the option to utilize different remote interfaces and incorporate area mindful administrations [12]. It has been proposed to utilize a nearby sign-handling arrangement and broadcast of intermittent information with distinguished cautions to a focal network as a section used for the expert operators to screen the chronicled information [13]. As of late, 5G remote systems have pulled in broad examination intrigue. 5G systems should bolster three significant groups of uses, including upgraded portable broadband [14], huge machine-type correspondences, and ultra-dependable and low-inactivity interchanges. On this, upgraded vehicle-to-everything correspondences are additionally considered as a significant assistance that ought to be upheld by 5G systems. These situations require gigantic networks with high framework throughput and improved unearthly proficiency, and force huge difficulties to the plan of general 5G systems. So as to meet these new prerequisites, new balance and numerous entrance plans are being investigated [15].

5.2 Motivation and contribution

New 5G arrangements can give prospects of totally better approaches for tolerant-observing, information examines, and activity control. For instance, the predominance of cardiovascular sickness will later on have a critical illness. To handle it, patient development and prescription treatment can be regulated in new manners as a result of the novel prospects in a forthcoming 5G technologies [16]. It backbone be conceivable to have a persistently broadcast of detailed biomedical information to a medical authority focus, which drive have preparing limit with respect to cutting edge design acknowledgment and master frameworks recognizing basic circumstances and advanced identifications of heart arrhythmias. The framework can consequently control the instrument on the persistent by isolated regulator to record various boundaries and fix up a quicker transmission construction, so as to immediately follow-up the recognized circumstance [17]. Remote observing of patients will require high transfer speed and high caliber of administration in the versatile correspondence frameworks. Today, there are a few snags that may forestall wide sending of cutting-edge observing arrangements [18]. Impediments in a standard General Packet Radio Service (GPRS) framework will typically forestall ongoing transmission of clinical waveforms from an account framework on a patient uninhibitedly moving around during physical exercises such as outside running; in this manner, the clinical indicative methods should be completed inside a medical clinics condition with the patient running on a treadmill. Wearable observing arrangements inside a clinic's structures utilize antiquated radio frameworks, with devoted reception apparatus frameworks and impediments on the secured zone [19]. In this work, we have studied the different needs of smart hospital and analyzed multiple advanced spectral efficient waveforms for transmission of huge data at high data rate.

5.3   Waveform techniques for 5G

The decision of a reasonable waveform is a key factor in the plan of the 5G physical layer. New waveform/s must be equipped for supporting a more noteworthy thickness of clients, higher information throughput, and ought to give increasingly effective use of accessible range to help 5G vision of "everything all over the place and consistently associated" with the impression of endless limit [20]. Albeit symmetrical recurrence division multiplexing (OFDM) has been embraced as the transmission waveform in wired and remote frameworks for quite a long time, it has a few impediments that make it inadmissible for use in future 5G air interfaces [21]. In this part, we explore and dissect elective waveforms that are promising competitor answers to address the difficulties of various applications and situations in 5G.

5.3.1   OFDM

OFDM, which utilizes a square window in time space permitting an extremely productive usage, has been received as the air interface in a few remote correspondence guidelines, including third-age organization (3GPP) and IEEE 802.11 standard families because of the related preferences, for example,

a.   strength against multipath blurring
b.   simplicity of execution
c.   effective one-tap recurrence space balance empowered by the utilization of cyclic prefix (CP).

Regardless of its preferences, OFDM experiences various downsides including high top-to-average force proportion (PAPR) and high side projections in recurrence. OFDM requires rigid time synchronization to keep up the symmetry between various client (sorts of hardware). Every one of these have an appropriation of OFDM in the 5G air interface [22] . The schematic diagram of OFDM is given in Figure 5.1.

The OFDM signal is given as

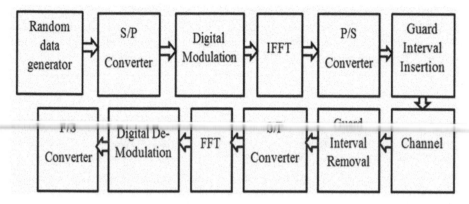

Figure 5.1   OFDM [23]

$$z(t) = \frac{1}{\sqrt{N}} \sum_{l=0}^{N-1} Y_l exp^{i2\pi \frac{kt}{T}} \tag{5.1}$$

$$z(t) = \frac{1}{\sqrt{N}} \sum_{l\in\alpha}^{N-1} Y_l exp^{i2\pi \frac{lt}{T}} \tag{5.2}$$

Considering the oversampling, the multi-carrier signal is given as

$$y(n) = \frac{1}{\sqrt{N}} \sum_{l=0}^{N-1} Y_l exp^{i2\pi \frac{kn}{LN}} \tag{5.3}$$

$$y(n) = \frac{1}{\sqrt{N}} \sum_{l\in\alpha}^{N-1} Y_l e^{j2\pi \frac{ln}{LN}} \tag{5.4}$$

5.3.2   FBMC

FBMC is a type of multi-bearer regulation that has its foundation inside OFDM. It is an advancement of OFDM and plans to defeat a portion of the concerns, in spite of the fact that this comes at the expense of expanded sign preparation [24]. FBMC has a greatly improved use of the accessible channel limit and can offer higher information rates inside a given radio range transmission capacity, for example, it has a more elevated level of range productivity. The schematic diagram of FBMC is given in Figure 5.2.

Let us consider a FBMC signal with N subcarriers given as

$$y(n) = \sum_{l=0}^{N-1} \sum_{n\in y}^{l} b_{l,n} f\left[m - \frac{nN}{2}\right] exp^{\frac{2\pi}{N}} 1\left(m - \frac{D}{2}\right) exp^{i\Psi_{l,n}} \tag{5.5}$$

The complex FBMC with the function of phase $\varphi_{l,n}$ is

$$\Psi_{l,n} = \Psi_0 + \frac{\pi}{2}(n+l) - nl \tag{5.6}$$

$$y(m) = \sum_{l=0}^{N-1} \sum_{n\in y} b_{l,n} f_{l,n}[m] \tag{5.7}$$

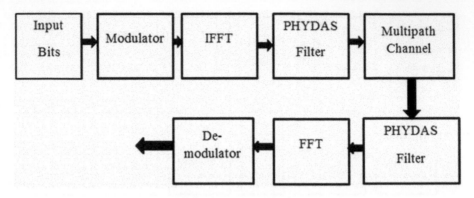

Figure 5.2   FBMC [25]

The detected signal of N^t is expressed as

$$h_{l,n'} = \langle f_{l,n'} \rangle = \sum_{m=-\infty}^{+\infty} x[m] f^*_{l\,n'}[m] \tag{5.8}$$

The characteristics of antenna are

$$h_{l\,n'} = \sum_{m=-\infty}^{+\infty} f_{l0,\,m0}[m] f^*_{l\,n'}[m] \tag{5.9}$$

Considering $n = m + n_0 N/2$ we get

$$h_{l\,n'} = \sum_{m=-\infty}^{+\infty} f[m] f\left[m - \frac{\Delta nN}{2}\right] exp^{j\frac{6.28}{N}} \Delta l\left(\frac{D}{2} - m\right) \tag{5.10}$$

5.3.3   NOMA

It is one of the supreme encouraging radio access procedures in cutting-edge remote correspondences. Contrasted with symmetrical recurrence division numerous entrances, which is the current true standard symmetrical various access procedure, NOMA offers a lot of attractive likely advantages, for example, upgraded range productivity, diminished inactivity with high dependability, and gigantic network. The gauge thought of NOMA is to serve numerous clients utilizing a similar asset as far as time, recurrence, and space [26]. The schematic diagram of NOMA is given in Figure 5.3.

The NOMA signal is given by

$$y_m = \frac{1}{\sqrt{M}} \sum_{m=0}^{M-1} z(m) \, exp^{\frac{j2\pi lm}{M}} \tag{5.11}$$

The characteristics of PHYDAS filter are given

$$r(t) = \delta(t - nT) \tag{5.12}$$

$$y(l) = exp^{j3.26 F_c t} \sum_{m=0}^{M-1} z_m * r(t) \tag{5.13}$$

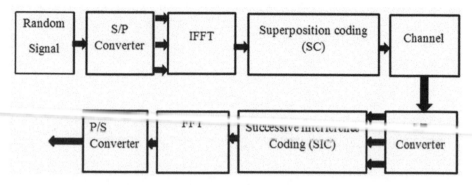

Figure 5.3   NOMA [27]

$$y\left(l\right) = exp^{j3.26F_c t} \sum_{m=0}^{M-1} z_m * \delta(t - nT) \tag{5.14}$$

5.3.4   UFMC

It is a low-multifaceted nature promising waveform that gives semi-symmetrical properties among subcarriers. Also, it can accomplish much better out-of-band emanation execution than the OFDM framework [28]. The schematic diagram of NOMA is given in Figure 5.4.

The UFMC signal for number of sub-bands is

$$w^S = \begin{pmatrix} w + \frac{W}{2}, & 1 \le w \le \frac{W}{2} \\ w - \frac{W}{2}, & \frac{V}{2} + 1 \le v \le V \end{pmatrix} \tag{5.15}$$

Further it is expressed as

$$z_w = r_w * \left(\frac{1}{\sqrt{m}} \sum_{k \in O_w} \sqrt{\alpha P_w}\left(l\right) e^{\frac{i\omega L}{NF}} \right) \tag{5.16}$$

P_w is the UFMC signals in frequency domain and r_w is the filter characteristics. The detected signal is

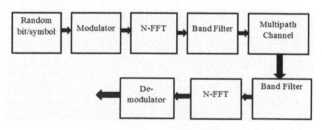

Figure 5.4   UFMC [29]

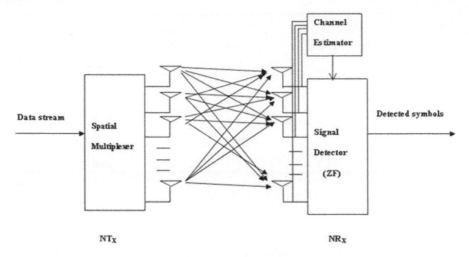

Figure 5.5   ZF [31]

$$y(t) = \sum_{w=1}^{W} z_w \, r(t) + n \tag{5.17}$$

The channel coefficient h (t) is represented by

$$r(t) = \sum_{j=0}^{P-1} b_i \, \delta(t - \tau_j) \tag{5.18}$$

5.4   Detection systems

In light of re-creation results, a bit blunder pace of all the signal location strategies is analyzed [30].

5.4.1   ZF

ZF is a straight symbol location method and is given in Figure 5.5. All the communicated signals, with the exception of the ideal information stream from the objective, transmit radio wire, are treated as impedances in a straight sign recognition plot [32].

To distinguish the ideal sign from every reception apparatus, the impact of the channel is upset by a reasonable weight network M_{ZF}, where

$$M_{ZF} = (h^h h)^{-1} h^h \tag{5.19}$$

It alters the impact of the channel as

$$\acute{X}_{ZF} = M_{ZF} \acute{Z} f \tag{5.20}$$

$$= \acute{X} + (h^h h)^{-1} h^h . \acute{N} \tag{5.21}$$

$$= \acute{X} + \acute{N}_{ZF} \left\| \acute{N}_{ZF} \right\|_{2.}^{2} \tag{5.22}$$

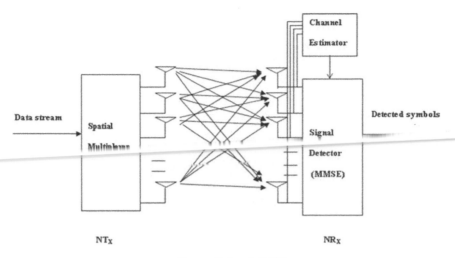

Figure 5.6   MMSE

Noise power is estimated as

$$\acute{N}_{ZF} = M_{ZF}N\acute{n} = (h^h h)^{-1}h^h.\acute{N} \tag{5.23}$$

$$E\left\{\left\|\acute{N}_{ZF}\right\|^2_{2.}\right\} = \sum_{i=1}^{N_s} \frac{\sigma_n^2}{\sigma_i^2} \tag{5.24}$$

5.4.2   MMSE scheme

MMSE is a detection framework shown in Figure 5.6 [33]. To identify the ideal sign from the independent transfer receiving wire at the accepting side, the impedance symbols are limited utilizing some reasonable methods [34].

The received signal is

$$M_{MMSE} = (h^h H + \sigma_N^2 I)^{-1}h^h \tag{5.25}$$

It condenses the intrusion through withdrawing the network effect as

$$\acute{X}_{MMSE} = M_{MMSE}\acute{Y} \tag{5.26}$$

$$= (h^h H + \sigma_N^2 I)^{-1}h^h\acute{Y} \tag{5.26.a}$$

$$= \acute{X} + (h^h h + \sigma_N^2 I)^{-1}h^h\acute{N} \tag{5.27}$$

$$= \acute{X} + \acute{N}_{MMSE} \tag{5.27.a}$$

$$\acute{N}_{MMSE} = (h^h h + \sigma_N^2 I)^{-1}h^h N\acute{n}$$

The signal distortion is estimated as $\left\|\acute{N}_{MMSE}\right\|^2_2$.

The average of signal distortion is

$$Avg\left\{\left\|\acute{N}_{MMSE}\right\|^2_2\right\} = \sum_{i=1}^{N_T} \frac{\sigma_N^2.\sigma_j^2}{\left(\sigma_j^2+\sigma_N^2\right)^2} \tag{5.28}$$

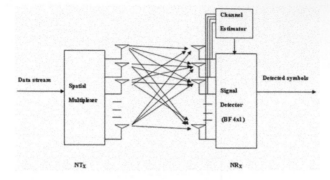

Figure 5.7   BF [35]

5.4.3   Beamforming

In BF as shown in Figure 5.7, we have a transmit decent variety plot. In this technique, the beneficiary conveys input channel data to the objective spreader [36].

The received signal is

$$\acute{y} = hx + \acute{N} \tag{5.29}$$

$$= \acute{H}_1 x_1 + \acute{H}_2 x_2 + \ldots + H_{N_T} x_{N_T} + \acute{n} \tag{5.30}$$

$$\text{In matrix form } y = \left[H_1 H_2, \ldots, h_{N_T} \right] \begin{bmatrix} x_1 \\ x_2 \\ x_3 \\ . \\ . \\ . \\ x_{N_T} \end{bmatrix} + n \tag{5.31}$$

$$y = \left[H_1 H_2, \ldots, H_{N_T} \right] \begin{bmatrix} exp^{-i\theta 1} \\ exp^{-i\theta 2} \\ exp^{-i\theta 3} \\ . \\ . \\ . \\ exp^{-i\theta N_T} \end{bmatrix} \begin{bmatrix} x_1 \\ x_2 \\ x_3 \\ . \\ . \\ . \\ x_{N_T} \end{bmatrix} + n \tag{5.32}$$

where $Hi = |H_i| exp^{i\theta j}$

The detected signal is

$$y = \left(|H_1| + |H_2| + \ldots + |H_{N_T}| \right) x + N \tag{5.33}$$

Table 5.1 Parameters

S.No	Parameters
1	256-QAM transmission scheme
2	N = 64 subcarriers
3	N-FFT = 64
4	PHYDAS filter
5	Bandwidth = 16 MHz

N-FFT, N-fast Fourier transform.

5.5 Simulation results

In this chapter, we have investigated and explored the different advanced waveforms and detection techniques using MATLAB® 2014. The constraints used in this simulation are given in Table 5.1.

The power spectral density performance of the waveforms for overlapping factor (L = 4) is given in Figure 5.8. From the simulation graph, it is noted that the spectrum leakage characteristics of the FBMC, NOMA, and UFMC are better than the OFDM system. The Bit Error Rate (BER) of modulation schemes are estimated and analyzed in Figure 5.9. The BER of 10^{-5} is obtained at the Signal to Noise Ratio (SNR) of 12 dB for OFDM, 10.6 dB for UFMC, 9.8 dB for FBMC, and 9.6 dB for NOMA. Hence, it is concluded that the optimal result is achieved by NOMA system. The Peak to Average Power Ratio (PAAPR) of the waveform schemes are observed in Figure 5.10. From the graph, it is clear that UFMC achieved a gain of 0.8 dB, 1.2 dB, and 2.8 dB as compared to NOMA, FBMC, and OFDM. However, it is noted that the advanced waveforms outperform the current OFDM waveform technique. The BER of detection schemes are analyzed in Figure 5.11. It is noted that the performance of BF is better than

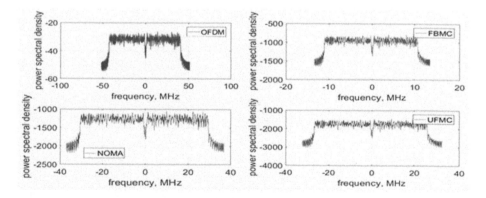

Figure 5.8 PSD

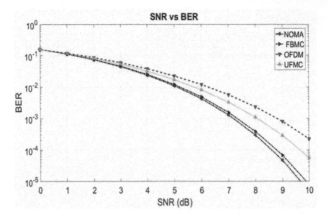

Figure 5.9   BER of advanced waveforms

the ZF and MMSE. The BF achieved a gain of 1.2 dB and 2 dB as compared to the MMSE and ZF methods. The PAAPR of the detection schemes is observed in Figure 5.12. From the graph, it is clear that BF achieved a gain of 0.4 dB and 1.7 dB as compared to MMSE and ZF.

5.6   Case studies

In the current scenario when the whole world is globally facing common pandemic Covid-19, the demand of communication-based health-care scheme is on the priority list of all researchers and scientists. It promises to use a profound influence on patient that helps to reduce the overall cost of the health-care systems. For instance, permitting the recurrently sick and aged to take care from household diminishes the routine of clinic charges and organization appointments, which are perforated with payment. Additionally, by devouring systematic apprises on

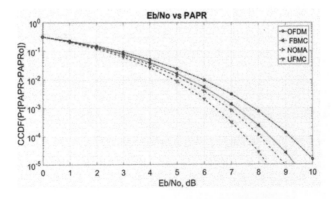

Figure 5.10   PAPR of advanced waveforms

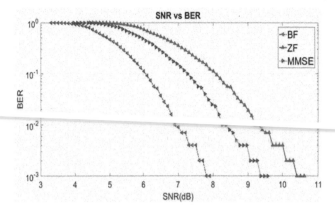

Figure 5.11   BER of detection techniques

a patient's information from smart fitness gadgets, medics can be instantaneously alarmed to a prospective curative delinquent that requires treatment. Deprived of these advanced mechanisms such as blockchain, 5G, and Cr, the patient might just call the clinician after the indications have developed to a serious level, which could call for robust cure and longer hospital halts. Last, many research and studies advise that elderly patients cared for in their own homes live longer, healthier, and more productive lives. With 5G health-care machinery, the remote peculiar attention can be provided to the patients.

5.7   Conclusion

The presented work outlines the requirements and obstacles of smart hospital-based 5G radio system. In this chapter, we have investigated the best waveform technique for 5G radio. The outcome of the study reveals that the spectral

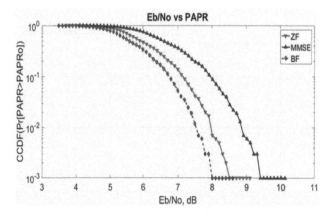

Figure 5.12   PAPR of detection techniques

efficiency of the advanced waveform is superior to the OFDM. In addition, the advanced waveforms do not the use the CP, which will further boost the spectrum performance of new waveform schemes. The 13% of spectrum is wasted due to the use of CP, which can be utilizing by advanced waveforms. From the simulation curve, it is observed that the NOMA and UFMC will play a key role in enhancing the throughput of the system. Low latency is also seen as one of the concerns in 5G radio network. It is estimated that the latency should be lesser than 1 ms for an efficient system. The current detection techniques are studied in this work, and it is concluded that BF is the best available technique but it may not support the requirement of 5G. Hence, a hybrid detection technique based on BF and MMSE can be the future of 5G radio. However, it is concluded that the emergency of accessibility of blockchain, good clinical specialists, medical caretakers, facilities, or emergency clinics also, exorbitant expenses acquired during clinical treatment enhanced the performance of smart health-care.

References

[1]   Kumari A., Gupta R., Tanwar S., Kumar N. 'A taxonomy of blockchain-enabled softwarization for secure UAV network'. *Computer Communications*. 2020;**161**(12):304–23.

[2]   Gupta R., Tanwar S., Tyagi S., Kumar N. 'Tactile internet and its applications in 5G era: a comprehensive review'. *International Journal of Communication System*. 2020;**3 2**(14):1–49.

[3]   Ahad A., Tahir M., Yau K.-L.A. '5G-based smart healthcare network: architecture, taxonomy, challenges and future research directions'. *IEEE Access*. 2019;**7**:100747–62.

[4]   Gupta R., Tanwar S., Tyagi S., Kumar N. 'Tactile-internet-based tele-surgery system for healthcare 4.0: an architecture, research challenges, and future directions'. *IEEE Networks*. 2019;**3**(6):22 9.

[5]   Kumari A., Tanwar S., Tyagi S., Kumar N. 'Fog computing for healthcare 4.0 environment: opportunities and challenges'. *Computers & Electrical Engineering*. 2018;**72**(5):1–13.

[6]   Budhiraja I., Tyagi S., Tanwar S., Kumar N., Rodrigues J.J.P.C. 'Tactile internet for smart communities in 5G: an insight for NOMA-based solutions'. *IEEE Transactions on Industrial Informatics*. 2019;**15**(5):3104–12.

[7]   Santos J., Rodrigues J.J.P.C., Silva B.M.C., Casal J., Saleem K., Denisov V. 'An IoT-based mobile gateway for intelligent personal assistants on mobile health environments'. *Journal of Network and Computer Applications*. 2016;**71**(2):194–204.

[8]   Brito J.M.C. 'Trends in wireless communications towards 5G networks—the influence of e-health and IoT applications'. *2016 International Multidisciplinary Conference on Computer and Energy Science (SpliTech)*; Split, Croatia; 2016. pp. 1–7.

[9] Shi X., Hu Y., Zhang Y., *et al.* Multiple disease risk assessment with uniform model based on medical clinical notes'. *IEEE Access*. 2016;**4**:7074–83.

[10] Li Y., Jin D., Yuan J., Han Z. 'Coalitional games for resource allocation in the device-to-device uplink underlaying cellular networks'. *IEEE Transactions on Wireless Communications*. 2014;**13**(7):3965–77.

[11] Sun J., Reddy C.K. 'Big data analytics for healthcare'. *19th International Conference on Knowledge Discovery and Data Mining*; 2013. p. 1525.

[12] Vallati C., Virdis A., Mingozzi E., Stea G. 'Mobile edge computing come home connecting things in future smart homes using LTE device-to-device communications'. *IEEE Consumer Electronics Magazine*. 2016;**5**(4):77–83.

[13] Ni J., Lin X., Shen X.S. 'Efficient and secure service-oriented authentication supporting network slicing for 5G-enabled IoT'. *IEEE Journal on Selected Areas in Communications*. 2018;**36**(3):644–57.

[14] Al-khafajiy M., Kolivand H., Baker T., *et al.*. 'Smart hospital emergency system'. *Multimedia tools and applications*. 2019;**78**(14):20087–111.

[15] Gupta R., Shukla A., Tanwar S. 'A smart contract-based tele-surgery system for healthcare 4.0'. *IEEE Conference on Communications (IEEE ICC-2020)*; Dublin, Ireland, 07–11th June, 2020; 2020. pp. 1–6.

[16] Gupta R., Shukla A., Mehta P., Bhattacharya P., Tanwar S., Tyagi S. 'A block chain-based outdoor delivery scheme using UAV for healthcare 4.0 services'. *IEEE International Conference on Computer Communications (IEEE INFOCOM 2020)*; Beijing, China, 27–30th April, 2020; 2020. pp. 1–8.

[17] Tanwar S. 'Fog Computing for Healthcare 4.0 Environments: Technical, Societal, and Future Implications'. *Signals and Communication Technology*. Springer International Publishing; 2020. pp. 1–430.

[18] Liu J., Zhang S., Kato N., Ujikawa H., Suzuki K. 'Device-to-device communications for enhancing quality of experience in software defined multi-tier LTE-A networks'. *IEEE Network*. 2015;**29**(4):46–52.

[19] Chen Y., Liu H., Liu L., Gao L. Intelligent liquid drip rate monitoring and early warning systems. *2011 International Conference on Electric Information and Control Engineering*; 2011. pp. 3320–3.

[20] Kumar A. 'A novel hybrid PAPR reduction technique for NOMA and FBMC system and its impact in power amplifiers'. *IETE Journal of Research*. 2019;**5**(1):1–17.

[21] Kumar A., Gupta M., Manisha M. 'A comprehensive study of PAPR reduction techniques: design of DSLM-CT joint reduction technique for advanced waveform'. *Soft Computing*. 2020;**24**(16):11893–907.

[22] Tanwar S. '*Fog Data Analytics for Iot Applications – Next Generation Process Model with State-Of-The-Art Technologies*'. *Studies in Big Data*. Springer International Publishing; 2020. pp. 1–550.

[23] Kongara G., He C., Yang L., Armstrong J. 'A comparison of CP-OFDM, PCC-OFDM and UFMC for 5G uplink communications'. *IEEE Access*. 2019;**7**:157574–94.

[24]   Kumar A., Rathore H. 'Modified DSLM technique for PAPR reduction in FBMC system'. *Radioelectronics and Communications Systems*. 2019;**62**(8):416–21.

[25]   Kumar A., Bharti S., Gupta M. 'FBMC vs. OFDM: 5G mobile communication system'. *International Journal of Systems, Control and Communications*. 2019;**10**(3):250.

[26]   Wei Z., Yuan J., Ng D., Elkashlan M., Ding Z. 'A survey of downlink non-orthogonal multiple access for 5G wireless communication networks'. *ZTE Communication*. 2016;**14**(4):17–23.

[27]   Ding Z., Lei X., Karagiannidis G.K., Schober R., Yuan J., Bhargava V.K. 'A survey on non-orthogonal multiple access for 5G networks: research challenges and future trends'. *IEEE Journal on Selected Areas in Communications*. 2017;**35**(10):2181–95.

[28]   Baig I., Farooq U., Hasan N.U., Zghaibeh M., Sajid A., Rana U.M. 'A low PAPR DHT precoding based UFMC scheme for 5G communication systems'. *2019 6th International Conference on Control, Decision and Information Technologies (CoDIT)*; Paris, France; 2019. pp. 425–8.

[29]   Kamurthi R.T., Chopra S.R. 'Review of UFMC technique in 5G'. *2018 International Conference on Intelligent Circuits and Systems (ICICS)*; 2018. pp. 115–20.

[30]   Daly M.P., Bernhard J.T. 'Directional modulation technique for phased arrays'. *IEEE Transactions on Antennas and Propagation*. 2009;**57**(9):2633–40.

[31]   Hafez M., Arslan H. 'On directional modulation: an analysis of transmission scheme with multiple directions'. *Proceedings of IEEE International Conference on Communications Workshops*; 2015. pp. 459–63.

[32]   Xie T., Zhu J., Li Y. 'Artificial-noise-aided zero-forcing synthesis approach for secure multi-beam directional modulation'. *IEEE Communications Letters*. 2018;**22**(2):276–9.

[33]   Sarestoniemi M., Matsumoto T., Kansanen K., Iinatti J. 'Turbo diversity based on SC/MMSE equalization'. *IEEE Transactions on Vehicular Technology*. 2005;**54**(2):749–52.

[34]   Tuchler M., Koetter R., Singer A.C. 'Turbo equalization: principles and new results'. *IEEE Transactions on Communications*. 2002;**50**(5):754–67.

[35]   Arun K. 'Design, simulation & concept verification of 4×4, 8×8 MIMO with ZF, MMSE and BF detection schemes'. *Electrical, Control and Communication Engineering*. 2017;**13**:69–74.

[36]   Arun K. 'Design and simulation of MIMO and massive MIMO for 5G mobile communication system'. *International Journal of Wireless and Mobile Computing*. 2007;**14**(2):197–207.

Chapter 6

Traditional vs. the blockchain-based architecture of 5G healthcare

Khalimjon Khujamatov[1], Nurshod Akhmedov[1], Ernazar Reypnazarov[1], and Doston Khasanov[1]

The development of information technology contributes to creating more innovative technologies that can change the face of any industry. Thus, the introduction and application of emerging technologies elevate the healthcare system to a new stage of development called Healthcare 4.0. The capabilities of 5G technologies and its applications, such as Device-to-Device (D2D) communication, Millimeter Waves (mmWaves) communication, Software-Defined Network (SDN), Network Function Virtualization (NFV), and Edge computing, have made it possible to improve the quality of the existing ones and offer new services, such as telemedicine, remote monitoring, and diagnostics. On the other hand, blockchain technologies open up new opportunities to improve the quality and security of medical data management services. However, the integration of these technologies to eliminate the shortcomings of the individual is poorly studied. We aim to research traditional and blockchain-based architectures of 5G healthcare to identify the disadvantages of the individual and the merits of their integrations. In this chapter, we have studied the blockchain-based architecture of 5G healthcare and have identified critical advantages with traditional architecture and their future applications.

6.1 Introduction

Thanks to the development of the healthcare system and the introduction of modern technologies. Many new applications are connecting to the network and exchanging information in various formats and volumes. This requires network improvements and solving several issues, including data rate, bandwidth, and latency issues [1]. Also, many Internet of Things (IoT) devices and sensor-based devices in healthcare systems require revolutionizing the network because the available technologies

[1]Tashkent University of Information Technologies, named after Muxammad al-Xorazmiy, Uzbekistan

cannot meet the dynamic and complex requirements imposed on the network by healthcare applications.

The introduction of emerging 5G technology can meet healthcare application requirements, such as high-energy efficiency, high reliability, high bandwidth, low latency, and high density. There are three main characteristics of 5G, which include provisioning ultra-reliable low-latency communication services to support enhanced mobile broadband and massive machine-type communication [2]. 5G is expected to connect all aspects of human life in the future, solve problems associated with increased traffic, and introduce emerging services [3].

One of the main challenges of 5G is security management. Many security methods have been used in previous-generation technologies, such as 2G, 3G, and 4G [4]. However, the introduction of modern technologies, such as Software Defined Networking (SDN), Network Function Virtualization (NFV), and Device-to-Device (D2D) communication, makes security challenges for 5G more complicated. The 5G healthcare network requires features, such as decentralization, immutability, and transparency. On the other hand, blockchain could be a technology that can meet these requirements and reshape the 5G healthcare communication system [5, 6].

The integration of blockchain into 5G healthcare provides numerous benefits for the system, such as better security and privacy [7], transparency and immutability of heterogeneous healthcare data [8, 9], low operational costs, and service efficiency [10]. Blockchain is the only technology available today to completely meet the 5G healthcare requirements with minimal management overhead.

6.1.1 Motivations

The versatility and practicality of 5G technologies and blockchain have made these areas relevant and actively studied topics in the scientific environment. Despite this, application of blockchain and 5G in the same architecture to provide emerging healthcare technologies is an open question. Also, there are no researches on the traditional and blockchain-based architecture of healthcare. Motivated by this, we analyzed the existing use of 5G and blockchain in the healthcare system to identify the advantages and disadvantages. We felt it was necessary to compare the two architectures to identify new directions for future work.

6.1.2 Structure of the chapter

This chapter provides a comparative analysis of traditional and blockchain-based 5G healthcare architectures. The structure of the chapter is given in Figure 6.1. The first section describes 5G and blockchain, motivation, and the chapter's structure. The second section discusses 5G technology, its challenges, benefits, and use cases. The third section discusses the architecture of 5G healthcare, its generalized architecture, infrastructure building architecture, radio access architecture, and core network architecture. The next section of the chapter is devoted to blockchain-based 5G healthcare architecture, where the components and functions of the blockchain are studied. Also, it discusses the architecture of the blockchain and its integration into the functions and applications

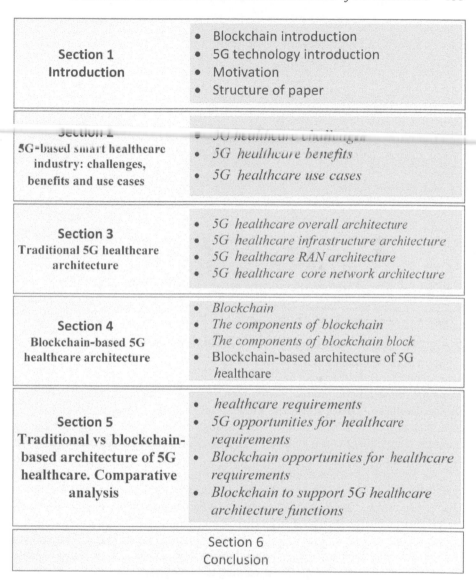

Figure 6.1   Structure of the chapter

of 5G healthcare, the integration of the blockchain into the SDN, NFV, D2D communications, and edge/cloud computing. The final section of the chapter provides a comparative analysis of traditional vs. blockchain-based architecture of 5G healthcare.

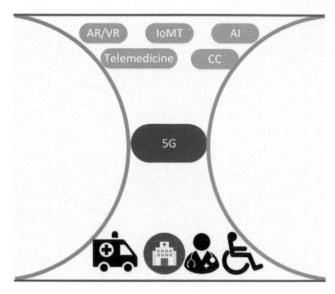

Figure 6.2   5G as a narrow band for a wide range of services

6.2   5G-based smart healthcare industry: challenges, benefits, and use cases

5G is the fifth generation of mobile network, specially designed to meet the modern needs of vertical industries in various fields. Unlike its predecessors, 5G specializes in connecting everything possible, from various smart devices to supercomputing machines, providing them with broadband communications, high data transfer rates, and ultra-high reliability.

As the level of violence increases, so does the pressure on modern infrastructure. The healthcare system is affected significantly, and its technical needs are also overgrowing. The lack of the usage of various emerging technologies, such as IoT, Artificial Intelligence (AI), telemedicine, augmented reality/virtual reality (AR/VR), Internet of Medical Things (IoMT), Cloud Computing (CC), and others requires a revolution in healthcare network technologies. 5G is a technology capable of revolutionizing the concept of networking technologies.

The volume and complexity of traffic in the healthcare system are growing rapidly. Unlike the previous mobile technologies, the 5G network can eliminate technological limitations, give a huge bandwidth and a variety of service methods, thereby opening the way to providing a variety of medical services, such as shown in Figure 6.2.

Following the concept of 3GPP and IMT-2020, 5G has capabilities [11] to provide:

- high data transfer rates upto 20 Gbps;
- high mobility upto 500 km/h;

Table 6.1   Challenges and their importance in healthcare

Challenges	Challenge features	Importance
Hidden cost	Infrastructure upgrades and maintenance schedules are expected to be very expensive, and it is still not clear who will pay for the network upgrade.	High
Security	Characteristics and small sizes of IoT devices used in the network do not allow complex security protocols.	High
Small range	5G implies dividing the network into small cells, installing many portable cellular antennas at close distances.	High
Inter-operability	A lot of different types of devices in healthcare require to be connected via different communication technologies.	High
Equal access	The use of small cell architecture in rural areas is not very effective.	Low
Low power communication	Power usage of 5G technology is high, which reduces the battery life of medical sensors.	Low

- ultra-high bandwidth;
- low energy usage;
- connect 100× number of devices and achieve 10 years of battery life for medical devices.

To provide such capabilities, 5G requires using several modern technologies, such as D2D, NFV, mmWaves communication, Edge computing, Cloud computing, network slicing, blockchain, and so on.

6.2.1   5G healthcare challenges

Despite the obvious advantages, 5G has several challenges of introducing technology into the healthcare system. Table 6.1 shows the challenges of introducing 5G in the healthcare system and the importance of solving these challenges [12].

The hidden cost in 5G requires a rethinking of the network architecture and other technologies, the costs of which are unaffordable for many operators. Also, in the case of healthcare, the return on such costs is not guaranteed.

Security is a critical issue in healthcare as different devices connect to the Internet. Thus, 70% of smart health devices can be attacked because of the weak characteristics and limited battery life. Such limitations do not allow complex protection systems. Attacks can be of different types, varying from theft of personal data to changes in data and parameters of medical devices, which have serious consequences.

In 5G healthcare, small cellular antennas of low range are installed every few tens of meters. This antenna density can be detrimental to human health as the medical effect on the health of people of such small cells is explored poorly. However, the psychological impact is already manifesting itself in discontent on the part of the population. Besides, such density can interfere with the operation of ultra-sensitive medical devices.

Inter-operability is an important issue as smart healthcare is based on different IoT devices, sensors, and biochips belonging to other domains. The lack of common standards complicates the exchange of data between disparate devices from different domains.

Small cells aim to serve densely populated areas, but the populations are scattered over a large area in a locality. In such conditions, the use of 5G is not economically effective, making the technology inaccessible to many people.

Healthcare devices are small in size and have a large number of sensors. Under such conditions, these devices should spend as little energy as possible for data transmission since the primary energy is spent on operating the sensors. Providing communications with low energy consumption is a significant challenge.

6.2.2   5G healthcare benefits

The adaptation of 5G to the healthcare system will undoubtedly increase its quality for patients and service operators. This will provide reliable and high-quality medical services at a low price, a higher level of labor, and low costs of technical processes. The main key health benefits are:

- Fast data transfer
- Personalized care
- Futuristic application enabling.

6.2.2.1   Fast data transfer

Equipments, such as MRI and PET, produce huge files with gigabytes of data. Very often, such data have to be sent to specialists for viewing. With current technologies, this process takes a very long time, and there is a risk of data loss, which causes inconvenience to patients, forcing them to wait for the results for hours. By introducing the elements of the 5G network into the existing network, it is possible to ensure fast and reliable transportation of huge medical imagery, thereby improving access to medical care and its quality. The files will be delivered to their destination as soon as the patient leaves the scanner.

The high speed of data transmission makes telemedicine more accessible. The remote examination by a doctor and visual inspection of problem areas without visiting special rooms can become a common procedure. Patients will get prompt medical help from the doctor while being in any part of the world.

6.2.2.2   Personalized care

5G can provide more personalized services to patients. Wearable devices, biosensors can generate, transmit, and process personal medical data in real-time, performing various tasks, including timely notification of doctors and patients about changes in health. 5G, in turn, when integrated with additional components (blockchain), provides less energy consumption, increasing the autonomy of devices that control the health of patients in the background.

6.2.2.3 Futuristic application enabling

5G .... of futuristic technologies and applications. As an example, remote surgery, although it has great opportunities, most patients are apprehensive and distrustful due to the low speed of the Internet and possible network failures.

Thanks to 5G, AR, and VR, which are no longer distant technologies. Doctors can participate virtually in procedures and enhance their experience. Medical students will have the opportunity to gain practical knowledge without straying for the patient's life. Also, AR/VR technologies will provide psychological support to patients and more easily endure painful periods.

6.2.3   5G healthcare use cases

The dependence of the healthcare system on network is growing every year. That is, the number of medical services and applications is growing, the work of which directly depends on the speed, bandwidth, and network delay. 5G technologies can completely transform the healthcare system and turn old hospitals into smart healthcare facilities where services are provided without restrictions, including remote service around the world.

There are many options for using 5G in healthcare. The main ones are listed as follows.

6.2.3.1   Telemedicine

Telemedicine is remote examination by a doctor via video communication or virtual reality.

According to statistics, 70% of a patient's time is spent while commuting to the hospital or waiting for an appointment. 5G-enhanced Mobile Broadband (eMBB) technology will save patients from regular visits to the doctor. 5G will allow medical personnel to remotely examine their patients using telepresence systems.

The following telemedicine formats are distinguished:

- consultations (councils) for remote interaction of medical workers with each other;
- remote interaction of medical workers with each other to make an opinion on the results of diagnostic studies;
- remote interaction of medical workers with patients and (or) their legal representatives;
- remote monitoring of the patient's health (including obtaining data on the patient's health in automatic mode when using medical devices with data transmission functions).

6.2.3.2   Large data transfer

The daily volume of data generated by the healthcare system exceeds hundreds of gigabytes. One patient a day can generate a huge amount of data from MRI or PET images for conventional electronic health records (HER). Usually, in practice, the transfer of such data from one point of the city to another is carried out outside working hours when the load on the network is minimal. Adding 5G to the existing network can solve this problem and reduce transmission times from hours to minutes. This means timely diagnosis, timely and sometimes emergency treatment as doctors receive data and the ability to analyze it much faster than ever.

5G can solve the ever-increasing bandwidth needs, as it has bandwidths over 10 Gbps.

6.2.3.3   Real-time remote monitoring

Today, technical limitations related to network bandwidth do not allow full use of remote monitoring capabilities. Inconsistent network speeds and unstable connections in the presence of slightest disruption can prevent critical data from being received, especially at crucial times. This fact greatly reduces the trust in remote monitoring systems, both on the part of service providers and patients.

5G technology increases network reliability and reduces the likelihood of outages, allowing service providers to implement and expand remote monitoring services. Wearable devices that collect important health data are especially well-proven. Such devices provide real-time monitoring for both doctors and patients themselves. Thus, patients, especially those with chronic diseases, are more conscious about their health, positively affecting it.

6.2.3.4   Sensors

In modern society, sensors are gaining huge popularity, including healthcare. In 2017, Qualcomm presented a sensor device that fits on the palm and checks the state of health. Such sensors and devices from the IoMT family help doctors get a complete understanding of the patient's condition and apply individualized treatments. Unlike 3G and 4G technologies, 5G fully meets the requirements for networks from sensor devices.

6.3   Traditional 5G healthcare architecture

The main objective of 5G is to meet the ever-growing needs of a highly mobile, flexible, and rapidly developing healthcare system. In the 5G NFV, the service architectures of End-to-End (E2E), Network Slicing (NS), Software Defined Networking (SDN), and D2D communications are considered as the fundamental foundation of 5G healthcare architecture for the provision of new services with a high-efficiency factor to meet the requirements of healthcare.

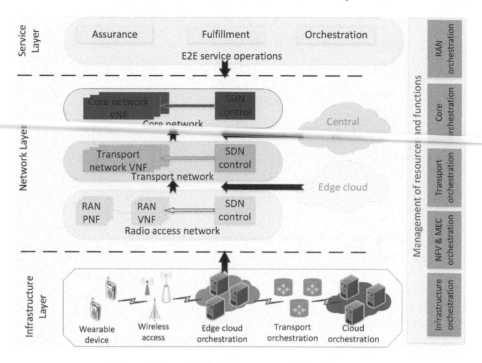

Figure 6.3   5G healthcare overall architecture

6.3.1   5G healthcare overall architecture

Healthcare is a system where it is required to serve various logical network instances to support a wide range of services. The range of medical services is expanding rapidly, and service providers request the creation of communication services with different service requirements. The network slicing capability allows the distribution of the infrastructure for different services but requires continued compliance with the Service Level Agreement (SLA) at the network level [13]. The increase in the number of such requests requires automation of network slice instances throughout the service life cycle, which consists of preparing, creating, configuring, and loading the service.

E2E service operation functions interact with Radio Area Network (RAN), transport network, core network, NFV, Mobile Edge Cloud (MEC), and central cloud management functions while creating services. This interaction is based on fundamental technologies, such as programmable software-defined networking and virtualization of network functions, making it possible to automate control with the capabilities of service assurance, service fulfillment, and service orchestration. This process can be seen in Figure 6.3.

Despite the variety of services provided by healthcare, they are based on the essential services, such as high-definition multimedia and high-speed data exchange. This property makes it possible to improve the scalability of services as it allows

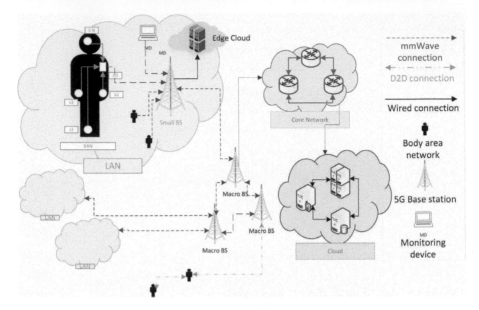

Figure 6.4   5G healthcare infrastructure architecture

creating new services based on the existing ones. The 5G architecture has a recursive architecture. That is, the 5G architecture allows to reapply procedures or rules when deploying new services. The recursive architecture allows entire service categories to be deployed concurrently at different locations. Also, parts of the service can be distributed by instances of one technological unit while unloading the overall load of individual parts.

Network virtualization and 5G architecture provide slice instances to function on a common infrastructure, enabling each service provider to deploy its Management and Orchestration System (MANO). This requires supporting the recursive structure using API of the slice control and virtual resources. The APIs allow service providers to customize the slice characteristics, control plane, and management plane.

6.3.2   5G healthcare infrastructure architecture

The construction of 5G networks is based on dividing networks into small subnetworks—small cells, especially when building a healthcare network. Small cells allow you to maximize the data transfer rate in individual cells and maintain high, uninterrupted communication quality within the cell. This capability is one of the core requirements of healthcare applications. For example, to carry out remote-surgical procedures, the data transfer rate should be around 1 Gbps, and the latency should be less than 10 ms. Figure 6.4 shows the divided infrastructure architecture.

Small cells are radio access nodes with coverage ranging from several meters to several kilometers, emitting low-power signals. In contrast, large cells–macro cells cover about 30 km in diameter. Several small cells can use the same high

Table 6.2   Small cells characteristics

Cell types	Cell radius (km)	Users	Users locations
Macro cell	8 to 30	More than 2000	Outdoor
Micro cell	0.2 to 2.0	100 to 2000	Indoor/Outdoor
Pico cell	0.25 to 1.0	30 to 100	Indoor/Outdoor
Femto cell	0.010 to 0.1	1 to 30	Indoor

frequencies, which increases the spectral efficiency of the network. Furthermore, user plane and control planes work separately from each other by distributing functions. The control plane works for connectivity and mobility. User plane works for data transportation. Small cells are of three types: (1) micro cell; (2) pico cell; (3) femto cell [14]. Their characteristics are given in Table 6.2.

Unlike macro, micro, and pico cells, femto cells maintain communication in a home or hospital territory. Macro cells cover wide areas and support over 2 000 users. Despite this, the power of the antenna does not exceed 10 watts. This distributed architecture makes the network flexible and spectrally efficient.

Body Area Network (BAN) is a network of wearable devices, smart gadgets, and biochips. The main purpose of BAN is to collect information about the state of human health, monitor, and sometimes perform certain actions such as calling a doctor [15].

Device to Device (D2D) communication is a direct communication technology between devices without exchanging traffic with infrastructure nodes. D2D is an integral part of the 5G architecture and was not previously envisioned in 4G or 3G. D2D allows IoMT devices, mobile gadgets, and smartphones to directly connect to exchange traffic without the participation of a base station. Thus, the device can act as an infrastructure node or a normal user terminal [16]. D2D can solve high network density where heterogeneous healthcare data can be transmitted over close distances in an end-to-end manner that reduces latency. D2D can increase spectral efficiency, reduce network response time, and optimize power consumption as it eliminates the need for base stations and allows to share own radio access frequency resources [17]. D2D in 5G, although it has a great potential, problems with interference in radio communications and security issues require consideration and application of additional infrastructure. The use of a single spectrum of a D2D node (i.e. a mobile device) by many devices contributes to the appearance of interference, and direct communication between devices is not protected from attacks by any means.

Millimeter Waves (mmWaves) communication is a high-frequency communication with a spectrum bandwidth ranging from 20 to 90 GHz. This technology allows the use of a huge spectrum since untouched frequencies are found at high frequencies. mmWaves communication has several advantages to meet the bandwidth needs of an exploding number of healthcare applications and gadgets, such as high transmission quality, high bandwidth, and heterogeneity of services [18].

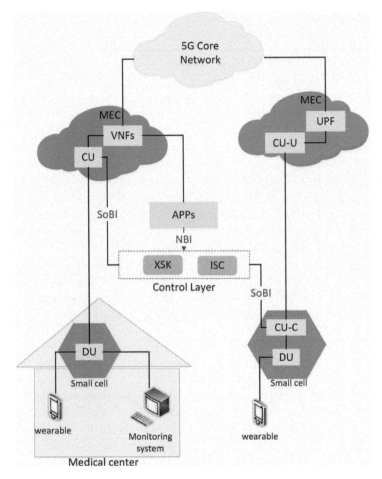

Figure 6.5   5G healthcare RAN architecture

Also, mmWaves in small 5G cells reduce data loss at high data rates, especially for healthcare applications, such as tele surgery and telemedicine [19].

Edge computing involves serving servers close to data sources. Edge computing was introduced to optimize the management of the network and its resources by allowing computations to be performed at the network's edge. This technology allows us to reduce processing latency, timely access, fast application response, and real-time computation, which is critical for healthcare [20].

6.3.3   5G healthcare RAN architecture

The RAN architecture is a two-tier architecture. The first tier provides low latency services, and the second tier provides high processing power for network applications. The two-tier architecture enables the distribution and provision of small cells as a service. The RAN architecture is given in Figure 6.5.

The RAN architecture can organize lightweight virtual resources, which makes it possible to have effective virtualization of network functions. Improved virtualization methods are used to provide NFV, which allows efficient use of resources and reduces latency. Also, the RAN architecture supports edge cloud computing providing the network with enhanced services.

One of the main features of RAN architecture is the possibility of programming RAN control functions as a separate application (APP), which is provided by an extension of the control level. APP can interact with RAN through the Southbound Interface (SoBI) and access the Northbound Interface through the Cross-Slice Controller (XSC), and Intra-Slice Controller (ISC).

In RAN network, the Service Data Adaptation Protocol (SDAP) is used, which allows the communication devices to be divided into Centralized Unit (CU) and Distributed Unit (DU) layers. This separation provides a two-tier architecture. In future, to ensure even greater flexibility of the network, the CU can be divided into CU-C and CU-U, which will allow distributing the CU-C and the CU-U to different locations.

Another feature of the architecture is the ability to treat many small cells as one. This feature is achieved by deploying the NFV technology. In this scenario, Virtual Network Functions (VNF) are deployed in the cloud as a Multi-Access Edge Computing (MEC).

6.3.4   5G healthcare core network architecture

The 5G healthcare core network is the heart of the entire network and serves to sustain multiple access technologies. The 5G core provides services over fixed, wireless, and heterogeneous networks. The 5G core has a Service-Based Architecture (SBA) capable of providing flexible connectivity, flexible services, and reusability.

The elements of the 5G core, commonly referred to as Network Functions (NF), are software-based, facilitating the formation of new services and adaptability to different needs. The architecture of the 5G core consists of the functions shown in Table 6.3.

Of course, 5G can become a technology to support smart health infrastructure. However, there are still many open issues, such as security, privacy, data safety, interoperability, and resource sharing, which the 5G technology cannot solve on its own. These problems require new tactics of accounting and monitoring, developing transparency, and deploying new technical solutions.

6.4   Blockchain-based 5G healthcare architecture

Modern healthcare relies on intelligent applications that meet high-quality service demands, high density, and ultra-high reliability. New technologies can support smart applications, but blockchain integration with 5G ensures decentralization, security, privacy, and high performance, thereby improving the existing system [21]. Also, blockchain contributes to simplifying the system, which improves service efficiency and reduces operating costs [22]. Blockchain's versatility allows it

Table 6.3   Core network functions

Network Functions	Abbreviations	Function supports
Authentication Server Function	AUSF	Authentication server
Policy Control Function	PCF	Unified policy framework, providing policy rules to CP functions, access subscription information for policy decisions in UDR
Access and Mobility Management Function	AMF	Termination of NAS signaling, NAS ciphering and integrity protection, registration management, connection management, mobility management, access authentication and authorization, security context management
Session Management Function	SMSF	Session management (session establishment, modification, and release), UE IP address allocation and management, DHCP functions, termination of NAS signaling related to session management, DL data notification, traffic steering configuration for UPF for proper traffic routing
User Plane Function	UPF	Packet routing and forwarding, packet inspection, QoS handling acts as external PDU session point of interconnecting to Data Network (DN) and is an anchor point for intra- and inter-RAT mobility
Application Function	AF	Application influence on traffic routing, accessing NEF, and interaction with a policy framework for policy control
Network Exposure Function	NEF	Exposure of capabilities and events, secure provision of information from an external application to 3GPP network, and translation of internal/external information
Unified Data Management	UDM	Generation of Authentication and Key Agreement (AKA) credentials, user identification handling, access authorization, and subscription management
NF Repository Function	NRF	Service discovery function maintains NF profile and available NF instances
Network Slice Selection Function	NSSF	Selecting of the Network Slice instances to serve the UE, determining the AMF set to be used to serve the UE

to integrate with major 5G technologies, such as edge/cloud computing and softwar-ization. Softwarization opens the way to exchanging data with IoT devices based on the network functions of the NFV. Although, cloud and edge computing will enable quickly rollout services and organize timely healthcare. The main role of blockchain in 5G healthcare is to implement Peer-to-Peer (P2P) database to record and control all passing transactions. At the same time, the blockchain provides transparency of services. Every transaction is visible and available to all members of the network, from patients to doctors.

6.4.1   Blockchain

Blockchain is a distributed system, which is based on a chain of blocks connected with the help of cryptographic hashes. Each block has a time stamp. These chains allow creating P2P networks between untrusted participants without the need for a trusted intermediary. Blockchain has the following distinguishing properties from other distributed systems [23]:

- Permission-less: All network participants have the same access rights. That is, there are no restrictions on access to the network.
- Trust-less: Network participants can exchange data and cooperate without having any information about the participant. Transaction performing does not require identification.
- Censorship resistant: Each block contains metadata of the previous blocks. Also, any transaction cannot be changed, which guarantees that the data are not censored.

Blockchain is a general-purpose technology, and its characteristics can improve certain scenarios of 5G architecture in one way or another. The key characteristics of blockchain useful for architecture have the following aspects:

- Decentralization: Network participants perform transaction management. That is, it does not require the participation of a central management node. Transactions are validated based on consensus protocols to ensure incorruptibility and network reliability. The lack of central control simplifies network operations and eliminates the problem of single-point failure. Also, decentralization ensures data availability and efficient service deployment.
- Immutability: It is the ability of the blockchain to protect transaction data from modifications and corrections. This property allows data to be securely stored in shared environments, efficient spectrum allocation, virtualization, and more. This property is achieved because each transaction has a timeline; blocks are cryptographically cached and have the hash function data of the previous block, which creates a chronological chain.
- Security: It is one of the most important benefits of blockchain. It is achieved by using asymmetric cryptography and public and private keys. Also, smart contracts allow checking access levels and protecting against unauthorized access.
- Transparency: It is a property related to the availability of all information about transactions. Information about transactions is distributed over the network, where each participant has access to verify the information. This property helps preserve the integrity of the 5G network and protect against unauthorized

access. Also, each participant can trace the source of the transaction, which contributes to detecting counterfeit products in healthcare.

6.4.2 The components of a blockchain

The main components of a blockchain are:

- Ledger: It is a database that is distributed across multiple sources. It consists of information about transactions ever committed on the network. Once the information is stored, it is no longer possible to delete it by any means. The reason is that all transactions are verified and accepted by many network participants.
- Consensus: It is a collection of rules that ensure the consent of network participants on the status of the blockchain ledger. Owing to consensus, the blockchain is available to all participants and does not require controlling nodes. Consensus is a protocol for matching ledgers of different nodes. Blockchain is a decentralized network where every new transaction must be written to a specific node. The choice of a node cannot be random since random selection algorithms are vulnerable to attacks. Therefore, to assign a new block to a particular node, calculations are performed using algorithms, such as Proof of Work (PoW) or Proof of Stake (PoS) algorithms. The PoS algorithm is based on the choice of a node with more powerful equipment to determine the block, while in the PoS algorithm, the probability of block formation depends on the stake of chain belonging to the node. PoW and PoS are the most common consensus algorithms.
- Smart contract: It refers to a smart application of the blockchain network that identifies and verifies network participants. A smart contract provides a guaranteed transaction between unknown network participants and information stored in the blockchain as an immutable ledger.
- Cryptography: Encrypting data guarantees the privacy of data and only an authorized user will decrypt that data. A digital signature is used for cryptography purposes and to verify the reliability of a node in the blockchain. A digital signature consists of a private and a public key which are based on asymmetric cryptography. The private key is required to sign transactions and is not published anywhere. The public key is required to verify the value of the transaction. Thus, a transaction signed with a private key is broadcasted over the network where anyone with a public key can find out its source and history.
- Blockchain applications: These are the applications that perform a variety of blockchain tasks. The application should not be confused with functions since, unlike functions, they are not part of the blockchain and expand the capabilities of the blockchain. In healthcare, applications such as fraud detection, identity verification, and smart contracts are essential. Fraud detection is a process used to detect tampering, alteration, forwarding, or other malicious behavior. Identity verification is the process of identifying a user through a distributed

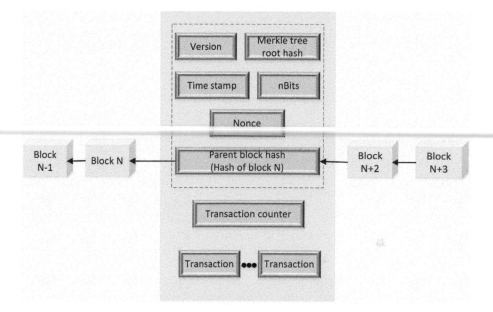

Figure 6.6   Blockchain block components

ledger where the user is required to prove the existence in a specific place and time.

6.4.3   The components of blockchain block

The blockchain consists of a chain of sequential blocks that contain information about transactions in the public ledger. Each block consists of a header, body, and hash belonging to the parent block, as given in Figure 6.6.

Each block can have a hash of one parent block, in contrast to the genesis block. The genesis block is the first block in the chain.

The header contains general information about the block and consists of the following parts:

- A version of block: It contains the set of block validation rules that must be followed.
- Merkle tree root hash: It contains a total hash value of transactions of a block.
- Time stamp: It contains information about actual time.
- nBits: It contains the valid block hash's target threshold.
- Nonce: It contains a field of 4 bytes starting at zero and incrementing for each hash.
- Parent block hash: It contains a hash of 256 bits, which is the hash of the previous block.

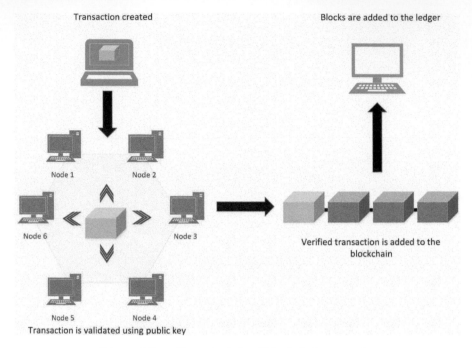

Figure 6.7   The principle of blockchain operation

The body of the blockchain contains transactions, the number of which depends on the block size. In addition, the body contains a transaction counter.

The created transaction is broadcasted over the network to the P2P network of nodes. The network of nodes validates and verifies the transaction, which is then added to the ledger block. The PoW and PoS algorithms are used to determine the node to which the block will be added. The principle of blockchain operation is given in Figure 6.7.

6.4.4   The blockchain-based architecture of 5G healthcare

The blockchain architecture itself is universal and can collaborate with most systems. The integration of blockchain into 5G healthcare systems will improve the system and provide a number of performance benefits in security, privacy, and decentralization. Also, the integration will contribute to the simplification of the system and, as a result, will reduce the operating costs and increase the efficiency of the system maintenance. The architecture of blockchain-based 5G healthcare is given in Figure 6.8. The main feature of the architecture is that the blockchain integrates with 5G components as NFV, SDN, D2D communication, edge, and cloud computing to create a combined system.

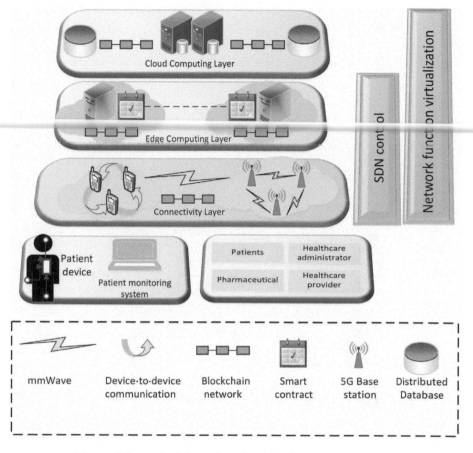

Figure 6.8   Blockchain-based 5G healthcare architecture

6.4.4.1   Blockchain for network function virtualization

NFV is a technology that allows separating network functions from network equipment and providing virtualized network components. NFV allows saving on equipment, operation, and maintenance. Also, the automation of network operations is simplified, making network functions flexible. NFV consists of the following components:

- Network Functions Virtualization Infrastructure (NFVI): Infrastructure serving to provide VNF
- VNF: Functions performed in NFVI
- Management and Network Orchestration (MANO): management service for both hardware and software network resources.

The NFV architecture is vulnerable to internal and external attacks. Network services provided to virtual machines can cause data leakage. Also, the point of

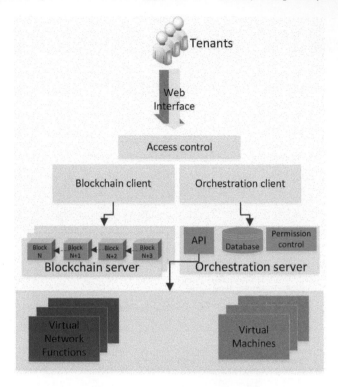

Figure 6.9   Blockchain for NFV

contact between the physical machine and the orchestra is highly vulnerable. Such shortcomings make NFV unreliable and require additional measures to ensure security.

In this case, the blockchain is seen as a solution to security and privacy, as given in Figure 6.9. Blockchain can perform the following functions for VNF:

- Ensure system integrity and secure delivery of network functions, that is, protection against modifications to virtual machines.
- Provide secure and flexible orchestration of VNF services, and increase system reliability.
- Monitor the network to detect malicious components.

6.4.4.2   Blockchain for software-defined networking

SDN: A logical controller carries out technology, the concept of which is to separate the data plane from the control plane and the control level. SDN allows for programmability and dynamic control over services. SDN simplifies the specifications of healthcare services, thereby providing flexible, heterogeneous services for the state of health management.

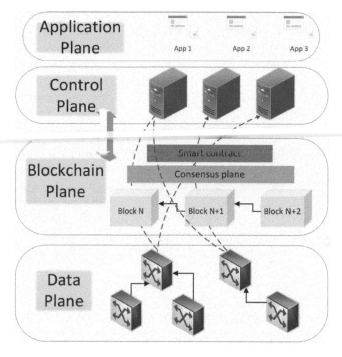

Figure 6.10   Blockchain for SDN

Despite all the advantages, the SDN has several disadvantages and open problems require additional components. Disadvantages of SDN:

- This technology is based on the concept of a centralized design, which means there is a single point of failure in the network, which can disrupt the entire network.
- The scalability of the SDN network assumes the interconnection of many controllers with each other. The communication channel between the controllers and the exchange of information between them is a weak point of SDN since no security protocols meet the requirements.
- In the environment of multi-SDN, it is difficult to ensure reliable network cooperation, effective joint use of common resources due to conflict of interest of service providers.
- The most painful point of SDN is security, as it has a larger attack surface compared to traditional architecture. Also, the control plane is another point for potential attacks.

A lot of work is being done to eliminate the shortcomings of the SDN, and most of them agree that the use of blockchain, as given in Figure 6.10, can improve the situation. In this regard, blockchain can ensure communication efficiency between patients and healthcare providers using encrypted authorization algorithms to solve compatibility and storage security problems and secure delivery of medical data. Also, smart contract technology ensures the security of the healthcare database.

In the multi-SDN controller environment, blockchain provides a secured communication channel between controllers where transactions can be shared using transfer keys assigned by blockchain. Blockchain can solve the scalability problem since the consensus between the blockchain layers can quickly transfer the functions of a failed controller [24].

6.4.4.3   Blockchain for D2D communications

The D2D technologies noticeably improve the mobility of the network response, which is very important in healthcare. D2D is an end-to-end communication technology used between mobile devices that do not require an access point or core network. This technology uses network resources efficiently, reducing data latency between devices, using network bandwidth, and reducing network load and energy consumption [25]. This technology is very important for healthcare since most participants in the system exchange data within one cell.

D2D technologies have several weak points, mainly in security, as there is no reliable authentication system. Authentication occurs through external sources, which increases the latency of authentication requests. Since D2D is an untrusted environment, there is a threat of data leakage and unauthorized access to the network.

The use of blockchain significantly improves the situation with D2D since users, based on consensus, can check the security of data sources and share data only in a trusted environment. Smart contracts guarantee protection against privacy leaks in various healthcare applications. Essential medical data such as Electronic Health Records (EHR) can be stored in decentralized ledgers.

6.4.4.4   Blockchain for edge computing

Edge computing is a low-power service server system located at the edge of the network, near medical devices. Edge computing or MEC performs a range of fast response services, which includes storing and processing of data, performing previously loaded tasks, and so on. MEC can also provide various applications for medical services with minimal delays and even with artificial intelligence. The distributed structure of the MEC can offer services to support IoT devices as they meet their requirements and has the ability of optimal resource allocation.

A distributed and open architecture is highly vulnerable in a dynamic edge network. One of the reasons for this is that it is not secure and may have untrustworthy data from the edge server provider (ESP). Confidentiality and immutability of data from external heterogeneous networks is also an important issue.

Blockchain essentially has similar characteristics and principles of decentralization and MEC, so their integration is natural in storage, communications, networking, and computation. The integration of blockchain and edge computing can be seen in the following aspects:

- Blockchain integration into edge network for optimization of networking capabilities: In this scenario, the role of blockchain is to create a trusted environment and build a distributed authentication system that will allow IoT platforms to use encrypted and reliable authentication. User access information and authentication data are stored on the blockchain, which will allow tracking the actions of mobile users.
- Integration of blockchain to ensure secure storage of resources, including resource allocation, sharing, and resource management. The blockchain creates a distributed data store for storing and sharing data, a united storage capacity of network nodes.
- Integration to support computational processes where the main task of the blockchain is to monitor and verify computational tasks loaded on the MEC server to detect and prevent external attacks: Thus, the properties of the blockchain as the ability to detect unauthorized access, consistency, and decentralized architecture, allow creating a reliable level of authentication between IoT devices and edge servers.

In general, the main task of the blockchain is the safe transmission and storage of data on the health status of patients, support of telemedicine applications in edge servers. Blockchain offers an agreed protocol for prioritizing and determining the patient's access level for computing resources. This approach optimizes resource allocation. Also, the availability and transparency of the blockchain protocols can provide an offline storage solution [26] for storing hashes of healthcare data, which allows patients to control their data.

6.4.4.5   Blockchain for cloud computing

Cloud technology is one of the key technologies providing a variety of healthcare services. It is in great need of a reliable authorization system, data protection, and confidentiality of data exchange since a large amount of data and many connections are often processed.

Blockchain consensus provides reliable storage and management of medical data between IoT devices [27]. The blockchain also supports a decentralized big data storage platform, such as Internet Planetary File System (IPFS) that improves the storage environment in the cloud, providing low latency and fast response times. This platform has service data stored outside the chain, provides a chain identifier, which, complete with a hash function, serves as an additional means for monitoring [28]. In the end, blockchain integration with cloud computing, as in Figure 6.11, can provide solutions to many challenges in 5G healthcare, such as lack of immutability, lack of transparency, data availability, data integrity, and privacy management.

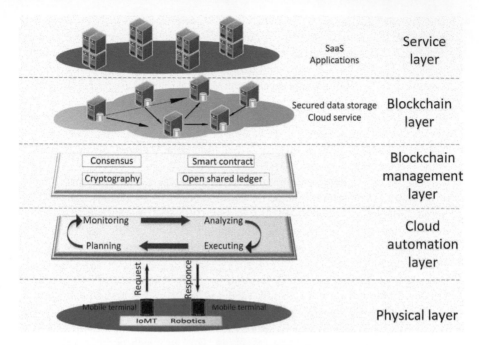

Figure 6.11   Blockchain for cloud computing

6.5   Comparative analysis: traditional vs. blockchain-based architecture of 5G healthcare.

The healthcare system has very strict requirements for network security and data privacy. The importance of the safety and privacy of information about patients is crucial. It is also very important to protect medical equipment connected to the network from external interference from a legal and social point of view.

It is no secret that the development of network technologies makes traditional methods of protecting networks vulnerable, and data stored on the cloud can easily be attacked. As a patient usually consults several doctors, more and more patients' data are leaked onto the web, affecting the patient's reputation or finances. The healthcare system is forced to place stringent requirements on network components, such as system security, authentication, data sharing, interoperability, EHR transmission, and mobile healthcare.

6.5.1   Healthcare requirements

6.5.1.1   Security system

The main requirements for the security of medical data are authentication, access control, and non-repudiation. Medical data refer not only to medical records but also to live information from wearable sensors and medical applications. The modern medical database and requests for accessing must be monitored continuously, access

Table 6.4   Security requirements

Requirements	Description
Access control	The system must provide control and authorized access to medical records.
Anonymity	The system must guarantee the confidentiality of the patient's identity.
Auditing	The transaction registration process must be provided to ensure trust in applications.
Authenticity	Only an authentic party should have an access to health data.
Availability	Medical data have to be accessible, if necessary. In any situation, the physician should have an access to the data immediately.
Data freshness	Medical data must be received in real-time. Delays are unacceptable.
Integrity	Medical records must be correct, uncensored, and unmodified.
Non-repudiation	The data must be encrypted by digital signature so that no one can deny it.
Ownership	The source of the received data must be accurate and guaranteed.

should be controlled strictly. The securing methods used today show their ineffectiveness, and the use of complex encryption algorithms leads to problems associated with the diversity of standards in different systems. General security requirements are given in Table 6.4.

6.5.1.2   Interoperability

Usually, in medical centers, all data are stored in centralized databases. Every day, the records of different patients are recorded in the databases of different hospitals. The records of one patient can be scattered across many hospitals, some of which are sometimes lost. Such storage does not allow obtaining complete data and leads to lack of interoperability, fragmentation of medical records, slow access, and lack of quantity and quality of medical data. Therefore, the system architecture of the network serving healthcare must ensure the interconnection of scattered data, the interoperability of different databases, and prevent fragmentation and data loss.

6.5.1.3   Data sharing

The exchange of data and access to them in medicine is a very important task. However, since patients can visit different hospitals and their records are stored in separate hospitals in a scattered form without any identifiers that may allow them to combine, this task is a problem. Thus, there is a gap between the data, making it difficult for service providers to obtain up-to-date records.

A healthcare network can share terabytes of data every day. Such a volume of information requires a huge bandwidth, high data transfer rate, and, most importantly, high reliability.

6.5.1.4   Mobility

The demand for healthcare mobility is associated with patient mobility since patients do not want to be tied to one point. Also, IoMT devices and wireless technologies allow them to move at ease without interrupting the treatment process. Besides, the rapid development of vital infrastructure requires healthcare to be in touch with patients from different countries. The fact that the healthcare database must be accessed by any device from anywhere in the world complicates the task of protecting and ensuring data security.

Mobility is due to the use of wireless wearable sensors that make Wireless Body Area Network (WBAN) and smart gadgets from several IoMT devices capable of processing, transmitting, and receiving signals from wearable sensors, which we will consider as follows:

- **WBAN** is a network of wearable sensors and biochips to control and monitor health in real-time. Requirements for WBAN include network availability, secure management, flexibility, accountability, data integrity, and reliable authentication. Also, WBAN is usually not controlled by anyone. There are probable failures in sensors, incorrect data received from sensors, connection failures, authentication problems, data corruption during transmission, or special manipulations in the transmitted data. Also, changing the parameters of devices for the administration of any drugs can have serious consequences. Such shortcomings make wireless health monitoring technologies unreliable, and it is too early to consider them as large-scale services.
- **IoMT** includes IoT devices that consist of smart devices and sensors capable of recording, sending, in more advanced versions making their own decisions about the state of health. The most common of these devices are smart fitness bracelets, smart watches, wireless sensors, and so on. The biggest problem with these devices is the presence of many vulnerabilities. The main vulnerability is the lack of protection of the data transmission channel. This allows listening, intercepting, redirecting data from sensors, modifying or stealing data about users, impersonation attacks, and others. Generally, for large-scale application of IoMT, the tasks of confidentiality of personal data, the owner's location, and control of access to data in the cloud and devices must be solved. The user should strictly control access, but at the same time, in emergencies, doctors should have access to devices. These issues require further work on the development of security technologies.

6.5.2   5G opportunities for healthcare requirements

The 5G mobile networks of next generation have great possibilities. The 5G architecture provides healthcare applications with mobility, exchanging large files with low latency, high bandwidth, high data transfer rates, and reliability. Also, many additional schemes are used in 5G to meet healthcare requirements. The main opportunities of 5G healthcare architecture to meet healthcare requirements are given as follows:

- **Reliability**: 5G is a network that is capable of performing various network functions with less loss. It can support the connection of a large number of devices and the transmission of a huge amount of traffic, ensuring network reliability [29]. Also, 5G allows increasing or decreasing the number of small cell nodes without affecting the work of others, which shows its good scalability and flexibility. This property of 5G complies with the requirement of data sharing.

- **Low latency**: Real-time healthcare applications are extremely sensitive to latency. For example, signal delays of more than 200 ms can lead to irreparable consequences in tele surgery [30], or delays in signals of the heart sensors that can lead to a wrong diagnosis by the examining physician. 5G can provide a network of healthcare applications with less than 1 ms latency. 5G integration with SDN and NFV technologies makes it possible to distribute network functions into multiple layers using network slicing. Data storage and computation can be performed on the software layer, which helps to reduce latency [31]. The low latency property of 5G meets the healthcare requirements for mobility and data sharing.

- **High bandwidth:** 5G is the generation of mobile networks where mmWaves—waves with a higher—frequency are used. High frequencies allow the use of a large spectrum that provides high data transfer rates up to 20 Gbps. Sharing data at these speeds provide physicians with a flexible workflow and the ability to transfer huge medical files. Applying schemes for optimizing resources and machine learning elements makes it possible to increase throughput and increase bandwidth [32]. Another property of 5G is the ability to allocate bandwidth, which allows D2D communications to be used. D2D provides the ability to reuse frequencies, which helps to provide high bandwidth for an individual cell. These 5G capabilities provide data sharing and network mobility by healthcare requirements.

- **Efficient energy consumption**: The healthcare network is a high-density network where thousands of devices with the ability to transmit data can be used on the territory of one cell, from mobile phones and wearable devices to MRI and PET. Also, most devices have small sizes and batteries of small capacity. Therefore, the network must provide efficient power consumption for both network devices and connected ones. The use of femto cells in combination with cloud computing allows optimizing resource consumption. Optimization leads to high data transfer rates and reduces power consumption. This property allows 5G to meet healthcare requirements for data sharing and mobility.

- **Enhancing QoS**: Healthcare is in contrast to other areas of heterogeneity of the network. Diverse applications have different data formats and prioritize data to optimize the network, since optimization is the key to ensuring QoS. A lot of research has been done to provide 5G QoS. QoS can be achieved through prioritization by giving high priority to individual applications using the Congestion Control based on Reliable Transmission (CCRT) algorithm when congestion is detected [33]. QoS can be achieved by managing congestion according to Congestion Control and Energy Balance based on the Hierarchy (CcEbH) scheme. It is proposed to divide the network into hierarchies as upstream, similar, and downstream to optimize the network. QoS can be ensured using SDN and NFV technologies [34]. The division of networks into femto, micro, and pico cells also provides a high data rate, thereby supporting QoS. Thus, there are many possibilities for using QoS in 5G that meets the security requirements of the healthcare system.

6.5.3   Blockchain opportunities for healthcare requirements

Blockchain has many properties capable of providing 5G healthcare with innovative solutions to improve performance, ensure privacy, security, decentralization, improve network manageability, and support QoS. Leveraging blockchain in 5G healthcare can assist great opportunities, including simplifying networks, security improvement, and system performance enhancement.

6.5.3.1   Simplification of the network

The properties of blockchain can justify the simplification of network as equal access rights, decentralization, and the ability to manage internal resources of the network. All transactions are managed and controlled by network participants, where everyone has equal rights, due to which the network does not need a management infrastructure. The ability to use the internal resources of the blockchain network participants also helps to reduce the dependence on additional facilities [35]. Using the blockchain, operators do not need additional centralized databases and control servers. The reason is the decentralized architecture of the blockchain, which allows the deployment of services, user access, and some other functions that can be performed in decentralized ledgers, that is, on the user's equipment. This eliminates the need for additional control devices.

6.5.3.2   Security improvement

Blockchain is a good system that can improve the security system of 5G healthcare. Decentralized blockchain architecture removes the need for central management by building a P2P network. For example, based on consensus, cloud computing functions are decentralized across blockchain nodes, central control is replaced by collision control based on fair agreements. D2D communication based on the decentralized blockchain architecture allows each D2D device to become part of the management, storage, and monitoring system. That is, the device has access to all transactions and can track and verify transactions, which improves the transparency of the network.

Smart contracts allow building a decentralized security architecture where authentication, access control, and access security are performed on the computing capabilities of the network nodes. Smart contracts are used to access and encryption rules to detect threats, provide authentication and access level, block and protect the network from unauthorized access, which simplifies the security system and does not require external verification nodes. These properties increase the resilience of services and eliminate single points of vulnerabilities.

As known, each transaction added to a block is assigned a hash function, which allows controlling user data and maintaining reliable protection. Users get the ability to track their data, which would be impossible without the use of a blockchain.

6.5.3.3   System performance enhancement

The blockchain provides flexible and efficient data transfer to provide direct communication between the service provider and the user while meeting the health security requirements. Unlike traditional SQL databases, decentralized databases provide more reliable and efficient data storage and low latency in data exchange. This is because transaction requests are verified at decentralized nodes through smart contacts, not at a central control point, which reduces latency in the public network.

The D2D based on blockchain potentially reduces latency and ensures data availability by managing the network across node devices without the need for third-party intermediaries. This approach solves the problem of a single point of failure. If one of the nodes fails, the node functions are distributed among the participants based on consensus without affecting the process of network functioning.

6.5.4   Blockchain to support 5G healthcare architecture functions

The architecture of blockchain-based 5G healthcare has several advantages concerning the traditional architecture due to the advantages offered by the blockchain and support of the functions of the 5G architecture. Blockchain supports the performed functions, such as data sharing, security, privacy, resource management, spectrum management, and interference management.

6.5.4.1   5G Healthcare architecture performance enhancement

5G is an excellent solution for data sharing, but fast delivery of large files requires reliable security in unreliable environments [36]. Typically in healthcare, data are transferred over corporate networks, but data sharing is a vulnerability in 5G.

Blockchain and its characteristics can provide data sharing in healthcare networks with security, privacy, transparency, and traceability. Blockchain can be used as reliable storage consisting of a decentralized storage cloud for sharing data. Also, since 5G healthcare is based on IoMT devices that have several vulnerabilities, such as low security, high cost, and complexity of data center control, the authors of [37] proposed the use of blockchain to ensure flexible data sharing by security requirements of healthcare.

Blockchain smart contracts help build a trusted environment for exchanging data between mobile devices, even in cases of movement in ambulances, which demonstrates the effectiveness of blockchain. Blockchain can be used as a "function as a service," as shown in [38], where blockchain is viewed as a platform for providing secure data exchange to identify threats to data from IoMT applications.

6.5.4.2   Security

As we said, healthcare has strict safety requirements. The 5G architecture is not capable of providing a sufficiently reliable security system that meets healthcare requirements. The 5G architecture can provide security in three dimensions, including authentication, access control, and data integrity.

- **Authentication**: Authentication in the blockchain is done through smart contracts that identify and control user access. Only an authorized user has the right to receive the service. Also, authentication can be provided by evaluating personal information retrieved from requests. Another authentication method is through credentials or a certificate that allows the server and user to authenticate each other [39].
- **Access control**: Access control is supported through smart contracts that scan the level of access to the network. All rights are recorded in the contract and verified directly between the requesting party and the service provider, eliminating external intermediaries and improving security [40]. To simplify access control, the authors of [41] applied an attribute system that allows access control through a blockchain ledger to control and protect resources effectively.
- **Data integrity**: Integrity date is very important for 5G healthcare as it guarantees the safety of data during delivery. Each blockchain transaction has a hash function that stores the metadata of the previous blocks, which guarantees the tracking and integrity of the blocks. Applying consensus mechanisms to validate blocks for integrity provides transparency and efficiency.

6.5.4.3   Privacy

Privacy is primarily based on the fact that control and monitoring in the blockchain is a common function performed by all participants It allows the user to follow and control personal data. Privacy in the blockchain is achieved in three steps. First, the blockchain collects data on the genesis of the blocks; second, the data on the genesis of the blocks are stored; and third, the data on the genesis are validated. These records are sent to the network for the block to be confirmed by the consensus participants, mobile users, and service providers.

Authors of [42] propose an automated control and audit mechanism in which the role of blockchain is to maintain confidentiality and comply with security policies. Blockchain can provide an open, decentralized network with data protection in IoMT networks through cryptographic encryption combined with consensus. The authors of [43] propose ensuring privacy by combining hash and encryption algorithms with blockchain architecture. A distinctive feature of this method is that the data are stored offline, and records of storage, management, and reading transactions are stored in a block for tracking. This approach allows controlling each operation using blocks.

6.5.4.4 Resource management

Mobile resources such as memory, storage, computing, and others are among the most common services used in healthcare applications. Each NFV slice requires different resources for a specific category of applications depending on requirements and functions. Also, the resource requirements of different applications can be heterogeneous, even applications performing similar functions may have different resource requirements due to the number of available users. Thus, the variety of applications and the variety of requirements of these applications make resource management a very important issue in 5G healthcare.

The 5G healthcare architecture addresses resource management through a central authority that oversees this process and ensures security and access control. Central management has disadvantages such as poor traceability of shared resources and a single point of failure that can affect all healthcare applications and services, which is not acceptable.

Blockchain capabilities can be applied in resource sharing due to its transparency and the use of smart contracts. The use of smart contracts provides transparent and efficient distribution of user requests according to the auction scheme in dynamic networks. Another property of the blockchain is decentralization, which can solve latency issue in the resource sharing process [44]. Also, the blockchain can provide a reliable exchange of resources between nodes to support low-performance nodes, if necessary, providing these nodes with additional resources [45]. The authors of [46] raised a very important issue where they proposed a Blockchain RAN (B-RAN) model. The B-RAN network is capable of providing optimal spectrum distribution. When a resource is requested, the smart contract implements the access level and authentication, and the blockchain provides resources.

6.5.4.5 Spectrum management

The limited spectrum and growing needs of network users and the number of users make it difficult for service providers to offer reliable services. The 5G architecture can offer a wide spectrum, but it does not cope with the optimization of the used spectrum. Since the spectrum is fragmented between services according to a fixed allocation policy, the unused spectrum of certain services remains unavailable. This approach is contrary to the requirements for network scalability. The problem can be solved by using a spectrum monitoring node that monitors the vacant spectrum and shares it [47]. Still, this approach does not provide spectrum protection and therefore is not effective.

Blockchain architecture has several advantages. It is capable of providing reliable and secure spectrum management. The decentralized architecture improves integrity and confidentiality, which protects against data leakage during spectrum sharing. All shared spectrum information is published on the open network, making the free network resources available to the nodes in need. Also, the absence of a central authority allows new applications to be added to the shared network. They automatically get the ability to share resources that comply with the network scalability policy. Spectrum data are visible to all users as all transactions are recorded on the blockchain. This allows monitoring and control of spectrum use and enforcement of spectrum security policies.

6.5.4.6　Interference management

The architecture of 5G healthcare is based on small cells and involves using a large number of mobile devices and IoMT sharing one large spectrum. This small network density can lead to cross-layer interference. Blockchain offers a consensus architecture for determining access levels and priorities that will allow optimal allocation of resources to prevent application conflicts of interest and interference [48]. Also, the authors of [49] applied blockchain to power management, which allowed QoS to be provided. Although blockchain has interference control capabilities, developments in this area are at an early stage.

6.5.5　*Blockchain-based 5G healthcare architecture use cases*

Blockchain-based 5G healthcare technology is an emerging technology, and real developments and technical solutions fully reveal the weight of its potential. As we know, it does not exist. However, in some areas, we can see the intersection of blockchain and 5G; research in this area is actively gaining popularity. The use of 5G and blockchain has proven very well in the storage of medical data, fight against counterfeit medicines, and ensuring the reliable transfer of medical experience.

6.5.5.1　Secured and distributed medical database

Blockchain provides the ability to track and control access to data, such as EHR and PHR. The data of each patient have different parameters, and the storage of different data requires an adaptive database, which is what a blockchain is. The 5G technologies, in turn, can provide a reliable and uninterrupted access to these data. The current developments in this direction are the MedRec, SimplyVital, MTBC, and Medical chain (see Table 6.5).

6.5.5.2　Trace medical products to detect counterfeit products.

According to the World Healthcare Organization information, 16% of counterfeit drugs have the wrong composition, and 17% have the wrong dosage. In many developing countries, at least 10% of the drugs are counterfeit. Technologies based on 5G and blockchain help ensure traceability of drugs from manufacturer to consumer by assigning hashes to them and then adding them to the blockchain. Active developments in this direction are FarmaTrust and MediLedger (see Table 6.5).

Table 6.5   Blockchain-based 5G healthcare use cases

Technology	Description
MedRec	Provides reliable storage of data based on the blockchain with the POA mechanism. In testing mode.
SimplyVital	Provides medical service coordination and centralized data storage
PharmaTrust	Provides traceability of medical products to protect against counterfeiting.
MTBC	Provides storage and control over EXP. Allows patients to control their data transfers.
Hashed Health	Provides storage of data of medical personnel, thereby allowing the tracking of their credentials and career.
Medical chain	Provides complete control over patient data, allows medical staff to access patient data quickly, and has telemedicine support.
MediLedger	Protects counterfeit drugs. Builds a blockchain-based supply chain, allowing you to trace the entire path of drugs from manufacturer to consumer.

6.5.5.3   Telemedicine and medical experience.

Medical experience usually accumulates over the years. The availability and reliability of these data are not always monitored. Blockchain, in turn, reduces the risk of falsification of bottom-up experiences and improves credibility. The 5G combined with blockchain solves several obstacles for telemedicine. The current technologies in this direction are Hashed Health and Medical chain (see Table 6.5).

6.6   Conclusion

Like all industries today, the healthcare system is undergoing tremendous changes. The introduction of new technologies, smart devices, and applications in the healthcare system requires solution to the existing problem in the system. In this article, we have analyzed issues related to introducing new technologies, including 5G and blockchain.

Healthcare 4.0 imposes many demands on networking and networking functionality. The main requirements are related to security, mobility, distribution, and storage of medical data.

The traditional architecture is based on small cells and has several properties to meet healthcare requirements, such as reliability, low latency, high bandwidth, and effective energy consumption. We have presented the capabilities and importance of the 5G technology for healthcare system and analyzed the benefits of introducing 5G in healthcare. Owing to its key advantages, such as high data rate, low latency, high mobility, and energy efficiency; and supporting technologies, such as D2D communication, SDN/NFV, and Edge networking, 5G opens the door to modern healthcare solutions. However, security, interoperability, and accessibility issues cannot be solved without third-party services.

Our research shows that blockchain is an ideal tool to compensate for these shortcomings. This chapter presented the capabilities of blockchain technology, and its importance to healthcare analyzed the benefits of blockchain and implementation in healthcare. Decentralization, immutability, transparency, and security have been identified as the main advantages of the blockchain-based architecture of 5G healthcare concerning traditional architecture. As a result of the research, it was revealed that each of these technologies alone could not become a full-fledged network technology to ensure the capabilities of smart healthcare, and only their integration will help to use all the possibilities of modern medicine fully.

References

[1]   Khujamatov K., Kh A., Reypnazarov E., Khasanov D. 'Markov chain based modeling bandwith states of the wireless sensor networks of monitoring system'. *International Journal of Advanced Science and Technology*. 2020;7(4):4889–903.

[2]   Agiwal M., Roy A., Saxena N. 'Next generation 5G wireless networks: a comprehensive survey'. *IEEE Communications Surveys & Tutorials*. 2016;18(3):1617–55.

[3]   Panwar N., Sharma S., Singh A.K. 'A survey on 5G: the next generation of mobile communication'. *Physical Communication*. 2016;18(1):64–84.

[4]   Ahmad I., Shahabuddin S., Kumar T., Okwuibe J., Gurtov A., Ylianttila M. 'Security for 5G and beyond'. *IEEE Communications Surveys & Tutorials*. 2019;21(4):3682–722.

[5]   Christidis K., Devetsikiotis M., Devetsik M. 'Blockchains and smart contracts for the internet of things'. *IEEE Access*. 2016;4:2292–303.

[6]   Zheng Z., Xie S., Dai H., Chen X., Wang H. 'An overview of blockchain technology: architecture, consensus, and future trends'. *IEEE International Congress on Big Data*. 2017:557–64.

[7]   Thuemmler C., Rolffs C., Bollmann A., Hindricks G., Buchanan W. 'Requirements for 5G based telemetric cardiac monitoring'. *14th International Conference on Wireless and Mobile Computing, Networking and Communications*; 2018. pp. 1–4.

[8]   Mistry I., Tanwar S., Tyagi S., Kumar N. 'Blockchain for 5G-enabled IoT for industrial automation: a systematic review, solutions, and challenges'. *Mechanical Systems and Signal Processing*. 2020;135(5):106382–19.

[9]   Kumari A., Gupta R., Tanwar S., Tyagi S., Kumari N. 'When blockchain meets smart grid: exploring demand response management for secure energy trading'. *IEEE Network*. 2020:1–7.

[10] Cech H., Grobmann M., Krieger U. 'A fog computing architecture to share sensor data by means of blockchain functionality'. *IEEE International Conference on Fog Computing (ICFC)*; 2019. pp. 31–40.

[11] Tanwar S., Tyagi S., Kumar N. 'Security and privacy of electronics healthcare records'. *The IET Book Series on e-Health Technologies, Institution of Engineering and Technology*. Stevenage, United Kingdom; 2019. pp. 1–450.

[12] Ahad A., Tahir M., Yau K.-L.A. '5G-based smart healthcare network: architecture, taxonomy, challenges and future research directions'. *IEEE Access*. 2019;**7**:100747–62.

[13] Kapassa E. 'Slas in 5g: a complete framework facilitating vnf- and ns- tailored slas management'. *International Conference on Advanced Information Networking and Applications Workshop*; 2018. pp. 469–74.

[14] Agiwal M., Saxena N., Roy A. 'Towards connected living: 5G enabled Internet of things (IoT)'. *IETE Technical Review*. 2019;**36**(2):190–202.

[15] Jovanov E., Milenkovic A. 'Body area networks for ubiquitous healthcare applications: opportunities and challenges'. *Journal of Medical Systems*. 2011;**35**(5):1245–54.

[16] Jameel F., Hamid Z., Jabeen F., Zeadally S., Javed M.A. 'A survey of device-to-device communications: research issues and challenges'. *IEEE Communications Surveys & Tutorials*. 2018;**20**(3):2133–68.

[17] Kar U.N., Sanyal D.K. 'An overview of device-to-device communication in cellular networks'. *ICT Express*. 2018;**4**(4):203–8.

[18] Wang X., Kong L., Kong F., *et al.* 'Millimeter wave communication: a comprehensive survey'. *IEEE Communications Surveys & Tutorials*. 2018;**20**(3):1616–53.

[19] Al-Falahy N., Alani O.Y.K. 'Millimetre wave frequency band as a candidate spectrum for 5G network architecture: a survey'. *Physical Communication*. 2019;**32**(2):120–44.

[20] Hassan N., Gillani S., Ahmed E., Yaqoob I., Imran M. 'The role of edge computing in internet of things'. *IEEE Communications Magazine*. 2018;**56**(11):110–5.

[21] Thuemmler C., Rolffs C., Bollmann A., Hindricks G., Buchanan W. 'Requirements for 5G based telemetric cardiac monitoring'. *14th International Conference on Wireless and Mobile Computing, Networking and Communications*; 2018. pp. 1–4.

[22] Kumari A., Tanwar S., Tyagi S., Kumar N. 'Fog computing for healthcare 4.0 environment: opportunities and challenges'. *Computers & Electrical Engineering*. 2018;**72**(5):1–13.

[23] Mistry I., Tanwar S., Tyagi S., Kumar N. 'Blockchain for 5G-enabled IoT for industrial automation: a systematic review, solutions, and challenges'. *Mechanical Systems and Signal Processing*. 2020;**135**(5):106382–82.

[24] Yazdinejad A., Parizi R., Dehghantanha A., Choo R. 'Blockchain-enabled authentication handover with efficient privacy protection in SDN-based 5G networks'. *arXiv preprint arXiv*. 2019;**1905**(03193).

[25] Ansari R.I., Chrysostomou C., Hassan S.A., *et al.* '5G D2D networks: techniques, challenges, and future prospects'. *IEEE Systems Journal*. 2017;**12**(4):3970–84.

[26] Rahman M.A., Hassanain E., Rashid M.M., Barnes S.J., Hossain M.S. 'Spatial blockchain-based secure mass screening framework for children with dyslexia'. *IEEE Access*. 2018;**6**:61876–85.

[27] Talukder A., Chaitanya M., Arnold D., Sakurai K. 'Proof of disease: a blockchain consensus protocol for accurate medical decisions and reducing the disease burden'. *IEEE SmartWorld, Ubiquitous Intelligence & Computing, Advanced & Trusted Computing, Scalable Computing & Communications, Cloud & Big Data Computing, Internet of People and Smart City Innovation*. 2018:257–62.

[28] Confais B., Lebre A., Parrein B. 'An object store service for a fog/edge computing infrastructure based on IPFS and a scale-out NAS'. *IEEE 1st International Conference on Fog and Edge Computing*; 2017. pp. 41–50.

[29] Chen M., Yang J., Hao Y., Mao S., Hwang K. 'A 5G cognitive system for healthcare'. *Big Data and Cognitive Computing*. 2017;**1**(1):2.

[30] Han Q., Liang S., Zhang H. 'Mobile cloud sensing, big data, and 5G networks make an intelligent and smart world'. *IEEE Network*. 2015;**29**(2):40–5.

[31] Hao Y., Tian D., Fortino G., Zhang J., Humar I. 'Network slicing technology in a 5G wearable network'. *IEEE Communications Standards Magazine*. 2018;**2**(1):66–71.

[32] Lloret J., Parra L., Taha M., Tomás J. 'An architecture and protocol for smart continuous eHealth monitoring using 5G'. *Computer Networks*. 2017;**129**(2):340–51.

[33] Hua S. 'Congestion control based on reliable transmission in wireless sensor networks'. *Journal of Networks*. 2014;**9**(3):762–8.

[34] Chaudhary R., Kumar N., Zeadally S. 'Network service chaining in FOG and cloud computing for the 5G environment: data management and security challenges'. *IEEE Communications Magazine*. 2017;**55**(11):114–22.

[35] Xiao F., Miao Q., Xie X., Sun L., Wang R. 'Indoor anti-collision alarm system based on wearable internet of things for smart healthcare'. *IEEE Communications Magazine*. 2018;**56**(4):53–9.

[36] Mollah M.B., Azad M.A.K., Vasilakos A. 'Secure data sharing and searching at the edge of cloud-assisted internet of things'. *IEEE Cloud Computing*. 2017;**4**(1):34–42.

[37] Liu C., Lin Q., Wen S. 'Blockchain-enabled data collection and sharing for industrial IoT with deep reinforcement learning'. *IEEE Transactions on Industrial Informatics*. 2018.

[38] Kumari A., Gupta R., Tanwar S., Kumar N. 'Blockchain and AI amalgamation for energy cloud management: challenges, solutions, and future directions'. *Journal of Parallel and Distributed Computing*. 2020;**143**(11):148–66.

[39] Kumari A., Tanwar S., Tyagi S., Kumar N. 'Blockchain-based massive data dissemination handling in IIoT environment'. *IEEE Network*. 2020;**35**(1):318–25.

[40] Zhang Y., Kasahara S., Shen Y., Jiang X., Wan J. 'Smart contract based access control for the internet of things'. *IEEE Internet of Things Journal*. 2018;**6**(2):1594–605.

[41] Ding S., Cao J., Li C., Fan K., Li H. 'A novel attribute-based access control scheme using blockchain for IoT'. *IEEE Access*. 2019;**7**:38431–41.

[42] Butt T.A., Iqbal R., Salah K., Aloqaily M., Jararweh Y. 'Privacy management in social internet of vehicles: review, challenges and blockchain based solutions'. *IEEE Access*. 2019;**7**:79694–713.

[43] Wan J., Li J., Imran M., Li D., Fazal-e-Amin. 'A blockchain-based solution for enhancing security and privacy in smart factory'. *IEEE Transactions on Industrial Information*. 2019;15(6):3652–58.

[44] Kitindi E.J., Fu S., Jia Y., Kabir A., Wang Y. 'Wireless network virtualization with SDN and C-RAN for 5G networks: requirements, opportunities, and challenges'. *IEEE Access*. 2017;**5**:19099–115.

[45] Liu Y., Yu F.R., Li X., Ji H., Leung V.C.M. 'Decentralized resource allocation for video transcoding and delivery in blockchain-based system with mobile edge computing'. *IEEE Transactions on Vehicular Technology*. 2019;**68**(11):11169–85.

[46] Le Y., Ling X., Wang J., Ding Z. 'Prototype design and test of blockchain radio access network'. *IEEE International Conference on Communications Workshops*; 2019. pp. 1–6.

[47] Zhang L., Xiao M., Wu G., Alam M., Liang Y.-C., Li S. 'A survey of advanced techniques for spectrum sharing in 5G networks'. *IEEE Wireless Communications*. 2017;**24**(5):44–51.

[48] Lin D., Tang Y. 'Blockchain consensus based user access strategies in D2D networks for data-intensive applications'. *IEEE Access*. 2018;**6**:72683–90.

[49] Liu Z., Gao L., Liu Y., Guan X., Ma K., Wang Y. 'Efficient QOS support for robust resource allocation in blockchain-based femtocell networks'. *IEEE Transactions on Industrial Informatics*. 2019.

Chapter 7

Integrating blockchain technology in 5G-enabled smart healthcare: a SWOT analysis

S Sridevi[1], G R Karpagam[2], B Vinoth Kumar[3], and J Uma Maheswari[4]

Healthcare is undergoing a dramatic transition to a dispersed patient-centered approach from a conventional hospital to a physician-based process. Advances in many developments are enabling this accelerated development of the vertical healthcare sector. Communication innovations have made it possible for diverse innovations to provide customized and remote healthcare facilities. Healthcare has now made a vast use of the current 4G network and other connectivity systems for innovative healthcare applications. It is continuously evolving to address the demands of emerging intelligent healthcare applications. As the intelligent healthcare business distributor increases network-connected applications, the generated data will differ in size and format. It would put dynamic demands on the network concerning bandwidth, data rate, network transmission, and latency. The emergence of 5G technology will be expected to enable ultra-reliable connectivity with less energy consumption. However, healthcare applications would have a chance to expose privacy and security problems. It imposes demands of characteristics, such as immutability, trustworthiness, and distributed framework for exchanging healthcare/medicare data. These paucities will be achieved with the advent of blockchain technologies. The chapter's objective is to provide a newfangled review and Strengths, Weaknesses, Opportunities, and Threats (SWOT) analysis of combining 5G and blockchain technology to exemplify the building of a secured and proficient healthcare application platform.

[1]Research Scholar, Computer science and Engineering, PSG College of Technology, Coimbatore, India
[2]Professor, Department of Computer Science and Engineering, PSG College of Technology, Coimbatore, India
[3]Associate Professor, Department of Information Technology, PSG College of Technology, Coimbatore, India
[4]Assistant Professor (Sr.Gr), Department of Computer Science and Engineering, PSG College of Technology, Coimbatore, India

Keywords: Healthcare, Web service, 5G technology, Blockchain.

7.1 Introduction

The fifth generation of 5G technology, called communications networks on the far side 2020, represents a significant consequent step in evolving the worldwide telecommunications system, with recent active implementations in several areas across nearly all continents. The three main features of 5G cellular networks are categorized as enabling the massive machine style communication, improved mobile broadband, and intensively reliable networking services. The concept of 5G networks here applies to the 5G cellular networks, which have been urged from the long-standing growth of 1G to 4G cellular networks [1]. The explosive development of intelligent mobile devices and the rapid growth of networking technology allows seamless communication across domains by interconnecting billions of devices. Thus, the 5G cellular network via intelligent machines will be a technical enabler for many new innovative business opportunities, communication engineering, and industrial applications. The 5G wireless networks aim to modernize global markets and have immediate impacts on consumers and company stakeholders. A personalized and advanced user-centered value is the key vision of future 5G networks, allowing human interconnection to meet the ever-increasing demands of user traffic and evolving networks. At present, many wireless technologies are proposed to allow 5G technology to enable over cellular networks, together with network communication, edge computing, cloud computing, etc. Though for the new security challenges, such as network reliability, immutability, and privacy issues over the wide deployments, there is a hope to solve these before the rapid expansion of 5G wireless services. New service delivery models will be supported by 5G cellular technology, thereby further exacerbating these security challenges. The 5G networks will act as open, widespread, and universal service-based applications, unlike existing cellular networks, with a particular focus on protection and privacy standards from the service perspective.

Specifically, 5G protection management is highly complicated for its several categories of immersive connected devices. For example, it is critical to have an open data infrastructure for data sharing, versatile spectrum sharing, multi-user access to execute ubiquitous 5G amenities while maintaining a high data transmission rate, immutability, security, and transparency. Concisely, the security system layouts of the existing telecommunication's peer groups lack the complexity that required extending to protect the 5G networks. Immutability, transparency, decentralization, and openness are the key security factors in the 5G era that ensure the fruitful roll out of innovative services, particularly driverless cars, IoT data collection, Federated Learning (FL), and Unmanned Aircraft Vehicle (UAV) systems. However, owing to the evolution of blockchain, the technology promises an entire range of latest technologies to combat the security challenges and also to redesign 5G connectivity environment in order to safeguard the communication network [2]. Hence, the 5G network desires blockchain for its intrinsic wide-embracing 5G service implementations. Blockchain is a distributed ledger that is primarily utilized for economic transactions for Bitcoin digital cryptocurrency transactions [3].

The perception of blockchain is emanated from a P2P network system layout in which all network members flexibly handle the transaction information and are not governed by any single centralized authority. Specifically, blockchain technology has some attractive features of decentralization, distributed, immutability, transparency, and fully trustless storage of databases that greatly enhance network privacy and security, and economize operational cost charges [4]. It paves an effective way for the exponential growth of the upcoming generation's financial, commercial, and industrial services. Blockchain was researched and incorporated in real-time in various applications, such as edge computing, energy-saving, Internet of Things (IoT), law and enhancement, vehicular networks, smart cities, smart irrigation, etc. [5]. Blockchain can incorporate the 5G environment to enable secure mobile wireless networks and services for its intrinsic loftier characteristic. Owing to the advanced technological competencies to provision future potential network services, Mobile World Congress considered blockchain to be one of the key technology factors for 5G [6].

Blockchain has been expected as an essential technology to reap legitimate facilities from 5G telecommunication networks, which would give birth to a new technology as self-governing, self-determined, self-sufficient resource sharing pervasive computing service to maintain intelligent data management system. It is also predicted that incorporating 5G and blockchain technologies would lay a foundation for new-age mobile networks (blockchain + 5G). In reality, by 2030, 5G will entirely be concerned about connecting many heterogeneous devices and complex networks, and it will be expected to interconnect beyond 500 billion smart mobile gadgets [7].

By 2021, Massive Machine Communications (MMC) and the IoT are expected to build over 80 billion connections. In this sense, ultra-thick microcellular networks, a vital component of the 5G services, would have fast data speeds and low latencies for radio link communications and energy efficiency. Yet, it exhibits security, reliability, compatibility, and interoperability issues between complicated subnets. Thus, it is a vital prominence for 5G services to provide stable cooperation between heterogeneous devices. In this respect, blockchain will build massive P2P distributed network architecture and preserve reliability and high security by its immutable and trustworthy ledgers.

Besides, network slicing is also a crucial enabler for the upcoming 5G generation's telecommunication networks connected to various emanant technologies, such as Network Functions Virtualization (NFV), edge computing, and P2P networks. The significant challenge in the present 5G platform is instigated while maintaining an open, clear, transparent, and stable infrastructure enabled between the weird resources and intelligent users. Thus, blockchain technology is anticipated as an invaluable method to meet the efficiency demands of 5G networks by reduced costs and management overheads.

7.1.1 Motivation of the chapter

Presently, various research conceptions are currently employed across the deployment of 5G + blockchain in the healthcare sector. Yet, in the meantime, there is no existing investigation offering an in-depth discussion about the incorporation of 5G + blockchain technology in this sector. Inspired by this constraint, the chapter summarizes the incorporation of 5G and blockchain technology along with a detailed investigation of different aspects of 5G and blockchain technology.

7.1.2 Contribution of the chapter

The key contributions of the chapter are emphasized as follows:

1. A survey over the convergence of blockchain and 5G is being conducted, beginning with a context analysis, definitions, and highlighting the reasons for the incorporation of two new technologies in the healthcare sector.
2. The chapter provides a summary of the implementation of 5G technologies over blockchain in addition to a specific emphasis on fog computing, data transferring, virtualization, and P2P communication.
3. The chapter exemplifies a holistic investigation over the possibilities of bringing blockchain technology to 5G wireless networks, including data distribution, virtualization, spectrum governance, resource regulation, federalized learning, intrusion management, privacy, and security networks.

7.1.3 Organization of the chapter

The rest of this chapter is organized as follows. Section 7.2 exemplifies the overview of blockchain technology. Section 7.3 explains the overview of 5G technology. Section 4 labels the potentials of incorporating blockchain and 5G technology. Section 7.5 depicts the incorporation of blockchain technology and 5G technology in the healthcare sector. Section 7.6 illustrates use-case scenario of the implementation of blockchain and 5G technology for online innovative healthcare application. Section 7.7 describes a SWOT analysis for the incorporation of blockchain technology and 5G technology in healthcare sector. Finally, Section 7.8 concludes the chapter.

7.2 Overview of blockchain technology

The blockchain is a public ledger, which is decentralized, distributed, persistent, suitable, anonymity immutable, and tamper-proof that has profligate attention over current years. According to Melanie Swan *et al.* [8], the evolution of blockchain technology has three generations. The application of cryptography-based digital currency is considered Blockchain 1.0. Development of Distributed Applications (DApps) and smart contracts (SCs) for business are considered Blockchain 2.0. Finally, applications beyond economics and cryptocurrency are considered

Blockchain 3.0. Blockchain is integrated by several core technologies: digital signature (using asymmetric cryptography), cryptography hash generation, and distributed consensus technique. Blockchain is a public ledger where data miners verify and add the transaction as blocks into the blockchain using consensus mechanisms (such as Proof of Work, Proof of Stack, Proof of Burn, Proof of Byzantine Fault Tolerant, etc.) in a distributed decentralized fashion.

As a consequence, blockchain technology improves the efficiency significantly. The chain of blocks is enlarged when a list of transactions is appended continuously. At present, cryptocurrency has been glowing as a buzzword in both academia and industries. In 2016, Bitcoin cryptocurrency enjoyed great fruition by reaching the financial assets of 10 billion dollars [9]. Bitcoin network transaction and data storage structures were designed in 2008 and implemented in 2009. These mainly focused on secure transactions without the intervention of third parties. Though Bitcoin is an eminent cryptocurrency for blockchain application, it has also been applied in diverse financial fields beyond cryptocurrency, such as remittance, online payments, and digital assets. Moreover, blockchain technology is becoming a standard and promising for the next-generation digital era of an internet interaction system by using smart contracts, reputation systems, security services, healthcare, IoT, public services, education, financial services, land registry, cybersecurity, royalty, e-voting, government, business, and industrial applications [10, 11], etc. The synergy between blockchain and these fields exists appropriately in multiple ways for its properties. For example, business requires the blockchain to ensure high trust, honesty, and reliability. As for the concept of smart contracts, once the contract has been designed and deployed, it could be executed automatically by miners without any intervention. Besides, blockchain, as a decentralized distributed ledger, it avoids a single point of failure. Blockchain attains a much-glorified effect where a lot of literature and experimented technology are established in content put on as patents on proprietary forums, such as web articles, company websites, etc., and also in blogs, research papers, journals, conference proceedings, etc., which made a surge over applications of blockchain.

As communities are very active, multitudinous blockchain has emerged day-by-day for its features. A consortium blockchain is soundly applied for business applications that ensure centrally secured, transparent, and permissioned environments. For its properties, blockchain is incorporated in various applications, such as business, government applications, medical and healthcare, education, royalty, IoT, cybersecurity, human resources, wills and inheritance, etc. However, the papers focus on the incorporation of blockchain in a real-time environment.

7.2.1 Blockchain structure

Generally, blockchain has a chain of blocks that maintain a list of transactions, such as a formal public ledger. Each block is connected with previous and subsequent blocks using hash values. The genesis block is the first block that acts as a parent block created as soon as the blockchain originates. Each block consists of two parts: (i) block header and (ii) body parts where header parts include block version

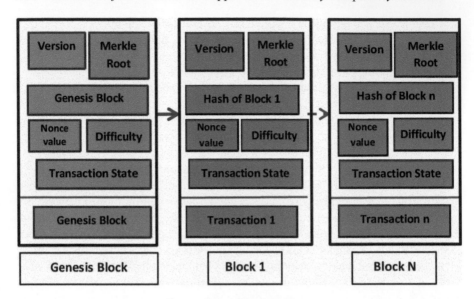

Figure 7.1   Block structure

number: validation of rules to be followed, a hash value that points towards the preceding block. Timestamp: shows the time of block creation as seconds, e.g., 2018-01-04 T10:00 UTC. Nonce value: it is a four-byte value field that commonly instigates by "0," and the value would be increased for each forthcoming block hash calculation. Merkle tree: a root hash of integrating all blocks. The body part consists of a transaction counter wherever transactions may be saved as plain text or as a hashed value. The maximum number of blocks pivots over the size of the blockchain. Currently, the size of the block is fixed as 1 MB. The asymmetric cryptography algorithm is used to verify and validate the transactions. An Elliptical Curve Digital Cryptography Algorithm (ECDCA) is used to validate the transaction in an untrustworthy environment. The block structure is illustrated in Figure 7.1.

7.2.2   Key characteristics of blockchain

- Decentralization: In a conventional system, each transaction is verified and validated by a centralized trusted third party, e.g., banks. This results in increased costs, control of users, and reduced performance bottlenecks. However, in blockchain, a transaction between peers (P2P) is accomplished without the intervention of a third party and achieves the cons lead by the centralized system.
- Distributed: All generated transactions are broadcasted to all peers who have participated in blockchain networks.
- Immutability: No changes are made once the transactions are updated. The hash value updates each block. Even a single value change leads to an avalanche effect over networks. It ensures tamper-proof property.
- Auditability: Each transaction is recorded with a timestamp. Any participating user can easily trace the previous records based on their privacy limit by

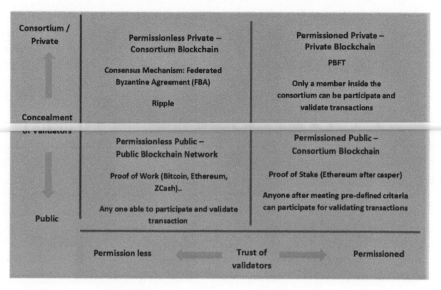

Figure 7.2   Illustration between types of public and private blockchain

accessing any participated nodes. It improves the transparency of transactions and reduces the falsification of documents.

- Anonymity: Each peer (user) participates with the generated address. Further, multiple addresses can be caused by the user to avoid identity revelation. It preserves a certain level of privacy of experienced users in the network.
- Persistence: Each block is broadcasted to all networks. Thus, each node could validate the transaction, which reduces the falsification of transactions and preserves from tampering.

Formerly, the blockchain network is characterized into three types. They are the public blockchain network, private blockchain network, and consortium blockchain network. In public blockchain, any participating peer can view and validate the transactions. Anyone can participate in the mining mechanism, add blocks in the blockchain, and gain rewards for adding the blocks. In consortium networks, only a selected set of nodes can participate in the consensus mechanism since a fully controlled organization can participate in mining the blocks. The differentiation between private and public blockchain is exemplified in Figure 7.2.

7.2.3   Applications of blockchain in healthcare

The incorporation of blockchain within the healthcare sector is given as follows.

Blockchain application in electronic Health Information Exchange (HIE): HIE aims to provide the efficient and secure delivery of healthcare data beyond institutional and geographical boundaries. A lot of aspects that are considered for sharing data are infrastructure, security, and interoperability. All medical documents, such as lab reports, physicians, medicines, records, etc., are encrypted by a private key and only a few traditional centralized paper-based transformation of drugs supply chain system. It has overcome using blockchain via an open, transparent, and tracking supply chain system. Using distributed ledger, all participants, such as raw material suppliers, manufacturers, transporters, retail shoppers, government, retail shops, and patients can easily track the drugs' current status quo and location using timestamps. A permanent record has been maintained from the raw material collection for drug preparation in the pharmacy. The records entered are immutable, decentralized, permanent, and distributed. This results in easy tracking of malicious intent nodes in the supply chain, which controls vulnerability due to fraud or human errors. Counterfeit drugs are significantly reduced by maintaining logs at each level of the supply [12].

Blockchain in claim and billing management: One of the main challenges in the claiming and billing process is preventing fraudulent billing. Some of the most common frauds in healthcare are claiming bills for providing unnecessary services unrelated to patients' medical condition, overcharging of essential services, claiming for non-performed services, claiming uncovered medical benefits. Many mediators are involved in adding, verifying, and adjudicating the billing and claim procedure, making a trustless administrative system. However, blockchain reduces mediators by executing smart contracts automatically from admission time of the patient to the discharge date, and achieves transparency in billing and claim process [12].

Blockchain for Personal Health Record (PHR) and National Health Record (NHR): Owing to the recent abundance of Artificial Intelligence (AI) growth entrenched in IoT devices in the healthcare system, more wearable devices, such as sensors, have been developed to predict human health conditions. Real-time AI healthcare analytic sensors monitor and feed information to the related participants, including patients, doctors, physicians, pharmacists, and relatives, etc. It also maintains the personal data management system about the patient's health condition called Personal Health Records (PHR). Decentralized Distributed Applications (DApps) are developed using ethereum blockchain under development, enabling easy participation of patients, doctors, pharmacists, and physicians in telemedicine without any mediators. This process reduces the cost and time taken for the mediators' services. NHS states to the government-subsidized medical and healthcare service center in the UK. People in the UK can utilize this service without paying for the cost. The service includes consulting doctors, surgery, treatments at the hospital until getting well, pregnancy period, and ambulance service. All information is securely maintained and managed via blockchain [13].

Blockchains in neuroscience: The modern neuroscience system seeks a new system paradigm to manage equipment and data over human mental feedback. These systems can comprehend and read the brain signal's activity patterns and convert the signals as commands. This process can facilitate detecting the person's current mental state and control external devices regarding data patterns received from their brain activity. This special task of understanding and annotating brain signals can be obtained via neural interface devices fortified via computing chips, perceptive sensors, and wireless communication devices. The equipped fortified device should be wearable on the head. In this way, the device can easily read and interpret, decipher, and store the brain electricity signals in storage equipment. Big data and complex algorithms in neural activities will utilize the philosophy of blockchain to keep brain signals secure.

For instance, one of the firms, registered in Geneva, in 2017, conforms to use blockchain technology for Neurogress. The firm's primary focus is to create neural-control systems, which enable consumers to handle smart applicants, virtual reality devices, drones, and robotic arms with their thoughts. Machine learning techniques are used for the Neurogress control system to enhance brain-reading legibility. For this purpose, the AI system requires 90% of brain data to train the model. According to the firm's white paper, big data needed for understanding the human brain's neural activity project is estimated as 1 exabyte (1 EB = 1 billion GB) of storage memory. At this point, the firm intends to use blockchain to preserve data storage security and privacy. It guarantees data resistance against hackers and proposes a neuro system to be open for all potential executives working in the Neuroscience platform. Breaches are easily traceable, and the entire system assures privacy and security of peculiar personal data [14].

Blockchain for Genomics screening: Per Timi Inc, the worth of patients' medical record data is estimated as 7 000 $ per year. At present, many medical enterprises are mounting blockchain-based systems by intending the potential patients to buy and sell their electronic PHRs, wellness routine monitored details gathered by wearable sensors and personal genome data. Currently, many enterprises are proposing to store DNA sequencing for a particular timespan. The 23andMe firm, which was founded in 2006, provides a direct communication between DNA testing services and significant peers.

However, the primary concern of the healthcare firm is data privacy. The 23andMe enterprise proclaimed that the company had sold $ 300 million stakes to pharmaceutical giant GlaxoSmithKline by efficiently handling access to exome data of approximately 5 million customers.

Blockchain startups are now developing projects in medical and healthcare claims to propose a solution for data ownership. For example, a blockchain-based startup named Nebula Genomics provides a free genome sequence to improve their genetic stock market business strategy. If the registered users have their account, then they could charge a remuneration in tokens from a person who needs to access the data. Genemes.io is another alternative genome enterprise that allows humans to stockpile their genome sequence and consequently provides access grants for the owner. The company aims to prevent getting genome information into the wrong hands and gives an opportunity to owners to vend the genomics data if they wish [15]. The real-time implementation of blockchain in healthcare is represented in Table 7.1.

7.3 Overview of 5G networks

Mankind is seeing a stable growth in communication networks over the past few decades, starting from the 1st generation and going towards the 4th generation. In

Table 7.1   Real-time implementation of blockchain in healthcare

---

Real-Time Implementation of Blockchain in Healthcare

- **MedRec 2.0:** Ethereum blockchain is developed for enhanced access to a medical record by the joined contribution of Robert Wood Johnson Foundation and MIT Media Lab. Currently, MedRec 2.0 is being tested and hosted at Israel Deaconess Medical Hub. The code is an open source [16].
- Digital Treasury Corporation (DTCO) and Taipei Medical University. PhrOS aims to increase transparency among patient records by placing various medical centers' patient records on a blockchain. The project is already completed and can access via the phrOS website [17].
- **Coral's Health discovery and research:** Blockchain stimulates patient caution, self-governing management practices and integrates smart contracts among doctors, technicians, and patients to ensure accurate lab data and treatments [18].
- **FarmaTrust** is developed by ICO, which intends to end counterfeit drugs. It monitors manufacturers and regulatory compliance aids for following government guidelines. Inventory is traced and tracked easily via blockchain. Using supply chain visibility management anyone can track easily if any alteration is made on the product [19].
- **MTBC** intends to enhance the traditional Electronic Health Record (EHR) system by changing the Application Program Interface (API). Blockchain is entrenched on API, which puts the medical records in the control of patients. Using MTBC, a patient can transfer his/her reports from one doctor to another. Currently, the Hyperledger blockchain platform is available. MTBC project can be accessed via MTBC's website [20].
- **Hashed Health product** intends to make a transparency of medical sector professional credentials. It enables that the credentials are easily tracked and verified by the authorized members of the chain. It streamlines the unalterable history of medical professional's education and career [21].
- **"Change Healthcare"** streamlined the regulators and security involved in a healthcare transaction. The product is available on the Change Healthcare website. It simplifies the health system's remittances, claims, minimizes denials, evades high and down payments, manages the business operation, and manages daily revenue cycles effectively using blockchain. As stated by the website, 92% of the topmost US health centers plan to utilize their services [22].

Some other real-time applications of blockchain in healthcare are [23]:

- Factom: secure storing of Digital Health Records.
- MedicalChain, Simplyvital Health, Robomed: to maintain the integrity of patient records from an outside source.
- Guardtime: to maintain data privacy of cyber systems including healthcare.
- A blockchain-based chatbot app developed by Opet Foundation helps students for preparing tests by recommending resources and answering the questions whereas it keeps track of the progress of the students in blockchain [79].
- Airbnb is a blockchain-grounded file storing platform. In Airbnb, Filecoin has great potential for storing information of students of educational institutions in a safe way [21].

---

recent years, the overall communication transmission has increased dramatically, and it is estimated to continue in the future as well. It ascends an issue in terms of providing Quality-of-Service (QoS) and Quality-of-Experience (QoE) to various applications [24]. This would be overcome with the advent of the next-generation telecommunications networks, called the 5G, which has a goal of overcoming the constraints of previous cellular standards and the reach of increasing network capability. The developments in 5G connectivity are intended to open new applications in different fields. These may significantly affect almost every area of our lives, such as smart grid, innovative healthcare, smart city, IoT, and vehicular networks.

7.3.1 Relevance of 5G in the healthcare sector

To protect patient data privacy and quality of operation for mission-critical applications, reliability and security gains are essential; efficiency improvements enable new applications to be delivered; greater network capacity brings size and coverage. Patients have increased awareness, insight, and control on their treatment. Therefore, in their approach to healthcare options, they can be selective regarding particular treatment methods, facilities, and goods, and thus become a more demanding customer. Thus, the 5G advantages can be consolidated into an improvement in the end-user's experience (often the patient/consumer), helping implement use cases and reach the scale required for the technology to extract value from the industry.

7.3.2 Performance driving with 5G

Through the capabilities mentioned earlier, three of the main technological pillars required to drive productivity in the healthcare industry can be impacted (both directly and indirectly) by 5G. To manipulate this real-time and preventive steps would be incorporated into patient care. In addition to the direct effect on connectivity, 5G will positively influence both the data and management pillars by providing the industry with a more trustworthy communications solution:

1. Data management platform: To address the number of data sources and higher data volumes, data management systems with a more consistent interface across localities.
2. In terms of management, because of its potential to push general digital transformation in the industry, we have previously noted that 5G has created a buzz. It involves creating local data management systems with a more reliable interface to accommodate the rising number of data sources and higher volumes of data.

The 5G networks exploit a range of underlying technologies to achieve such exciting performance objectives: edge computing, network virtualization, network slicing, P2P communications, millimeter-wave communication, etc.

NFV: Using NFV, various network functions can be performed by single software. It requires the network functions to be decoupled from patented hardware devices. Thus, they could activate expanding generic hardware.

The significant aim of NFV is to enhance the network design and distribution of services efficiently. Through NFV, a wide variety of network features can be streamlined by any 5G service provider and maximizes proficiency and new

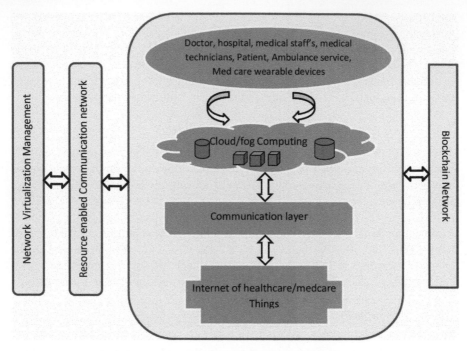

Figure 7.3   Functional flow of 5G network and blockchain technology for the healthcare sector

remuneration-gaining services that can deliver quicker and simpler than ever [25]. The functional flow of integrating 5G and blockchain technology in the healthcare sector is illustrated in Figure 7.3.

P2P communication: It enables the proximity IoT appliances to interconnect via conventional base stations by utilizing a direct link instead of consuming long-signal transmissions. Through D2D networking, heterogeneous 5G data can be easily transmitted between short-range mobile devices, offering ultra-low latency for user-to-user networking. Also, D2D communication would make 5G operators more versatile in improving spectral performance, discharging core network traffic, and removing excessive loss of energy caused by stretched data transmissions [26].

Cloud/fog computing: In the 5G era, cloud computing was deployed to meet the growing requirements for data storage, resource management, and mobile sensing. Specifically, 5G services, such as resource offloading, mobility/network management, and sensing services in different application domains can be supported by cloud computing paradigms with resourceful virtual computation centers. Meanwhile, edge computing has been seen as a promising technology to enable 5G ecosystems as an expanded form of cloud computing. It offers computing services at the edge of the mobile network, allowing far lower transmission delays for computing and storage services.

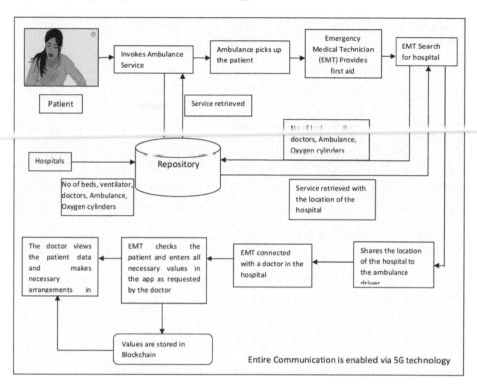

Figure 7.4   Use case diagram for mobile application interactions between 5G and blockchain technology for serving the patient requirement

Mobile connectivity: The 5G mobile communication networks having modern facilities with a massive spectrum meet the need for mobile data requirements. It has a range of advantages, including enormous bandwidth, narrow beam, and strong capacity to access data to address vulnerabilities caused by the exponential increase in volumes of unparalleled connected devices, mobile traffic, and diversified use cases [27]. The functional flow of the 5G network and blockchain technology in the healthcare sector is illustrated in Figure 7.4.

The above-mentioned innovations will be used in 5G networks to meet the demands of numerous applications resulting from the current traffic explosion of connected devices. The combination of software-defined networking, cloud/edge computing, and NFV is considered potential facilitators for scalable deployment and network operation. Also, network slicing and D2D connectivity would allow ultra-reliable, affordable broadband access and smart network data usage to enable the efficient use of extremely low latency and high-speed device link network resources [28].

7.3.3   Advance features of 5G technology

• Lower latency and higher bandwidth

- Enhanced capacity
- Lower battery consumption
- Enable larger coverage area
- High data rates
- Infrastructure development at a lower cost
- Larger number of supporting devices
- Support abundant amount of device connectivity
- 5G infrastructure will be distributed, decentralized, programmable, and device-centric.

7.3.4   Potential applications of 5G technologies

- Smart city, smart grid, and smart homes
- eHealth
- Smart medical examination
- Data analytics
- Factories of the future
- Autonomous driving vehicles
- Cloud-based video conferencing
- Virtual reality
- 3D and ultra HD videos
- Power electronics.

7.4   Potentials of integrating blockchain and 5G technology

Let us illustrate the most important features of both integration technologies. Blockchain will provide secured 5G data services via its secure distributed ledger. Some interesting features, such as immutability, decentralization, openness, and privacy, make this possible. Thus, the key points of the blockchain are its features for 5G networks and applications to support encryption and network management. On the other hand, 5G in this chapter refers to the new generation of wireless networks that are expected to provide higher capacity, higher data rate, lower latency, massive convergence of devices, increased quality-of-experience (QoE) for end-users, decreased operating costs, and reliable provisioning of services. Therefore, the key points of 5G are its benefits of delivering fast and high-quality services and the need for enhancement of security and networking.

Then, the impetus behind the combination of blockchain and 5G stems mainly from the promising advantages of blockchain in terms of encryption, privacy, networking, and service management to solve problems in 5G networks. 5G is expected to solve the current barriers and open up new possibilities to empower blockchain 5G-based services and applications with the help of creative blockchain designs. In the following text, we address the impetus for adoption arising from existing 5G problems and then present opportunities arising from the introduction of blockchain-5G.

Security issues in 5G networks: Security related to 5G technology has been considered as one of the main criteria for 5G systems and beyond. Owing to its centralized architecture, the current 5G technology infrastructure has remained unresolved, including networking and computing efficiency degradation. For instance, current cloud computing models depend on centralized service providers, which expose different bottlenecks in security. This configuration is also vulnerable to single-point failures, which pose threats to the availability of on-demand user access to cloud/edge services.

In 5G networks, NFV and service function chaining also generate new security problems. Subsequently, end-to-end service function chains can deploy NFVs in an environment involving multiple cloud providers; curious cloud entities can compromise such data exchanges, leading to concerns about data leakage. Moreover, tenants also share the same cloud infrastructure in a virtualized scenario. In this context, the likelihood of cloud-based attacks could increase, thus harming the transparency and accountability of service providers. Virtualization servers can run on Virtual Machines (VMs) in NFVs and provide unique functions for running different operating systems, such as migrating VMs or allocating resources using orchestration protocols. However, the security of communication between the orchestrator and the VM manager of the physical machine is a real challenge.

The rapid explosion of mobile data traffic and the rising demands of 5G infrastructure users also pose new security and performance degradation challenges. For example, the growing demand for 5G services, such as big data processing, mobile video streaming for bandwidth-hungry applications requires a proper 5G spectrum resource management plan to avoid resource shortage issues to ensure continuous service functionality. Spectrum sharing is therefore important between operators of mobile networks (MNOs) and mobile users. However, spectrum sharing in such cases also poses security issues and provides malicious users with a central point of attack. A potential solution would be to use the certification authorities to have cognitive radio certificates within each cell. Also, greater computational complexity is required, increasing overheads for spectrum sharing and decreasing the system's Quality of Service (QoS). Significantly, when the authority is assaulted or out of service, the use of such centralized architectures often adds single-of-failure bottlenecks, contributing to the interruption of the entire spectrum-sharing network.

Generally, smart cities where mobile environments are highly diverse with the combination of IoT devices, complex networks, and ubiquitous services that pose high security and privacy problems then go for more complex 5G IoT scenarios, such as smart healthcare. In reality, from ubiquitous IoT sensor devices, a prohibitively large amount of IoT data will continuously be produced. It is very hard to recognize the objects of interest instantly or detect malicious behavior on a wide scale from thousands of data transactions. Owing to long latency, privacy threats due to interested third parties, and network congestion, the solution of using centralized management may be infeasible for such use cases [29].

1. Security enhancement: By offering many promising technical features, such as decentralization, privacy, immutability, traceability, and transparency, blockchain promises to improve the safety and privacy of 5G ecosystems. By decentralizing the network infrastructure where there is no need for third-party authority, blockchain will remove the principle of a centralized network management system. The concept of blockchain-based cloud computing, for example, allows cloud 5G networks to be decentralized, eliminating centralized control over the core network and providing a decentralized, eliminating single-point failure bottlenecks, fair agreement with the blockchain consensus platform, and significantly improving system confidence. Besides, the protection of D2D communication can be accomplished by creating a blockchain P2P network, which transforms each D2D computer as a blockchain node to hold a ledger copy for better system of transparency and efficiency to verify and track transactions.

    Precisely, blockchain with smart contracts can enforce decentralized user access validation by using the computational capacity of all legitimate network members, unlike traditional database management systems that mainly use a centralized server to conduct access authentication and protection mechanisms. It makes the 5G networks highly immune to data changes (i.e., data sharing, spectrum sharing, and resource allocation). Many studies on blockchain indicate that the implementation of blockchain is advantageous to the management of spectrum 5G in terms of better verification of spectrum access through blockchain contracts, increased connectivity via blockchain transparency. Also, the use of blockchain encourages scalable spectrum exchange over the peer-to-peer ledger network, where high trustworthiness excludes spectrum license holders and band managers. Ledger services also support a high degree of security and better device defense capabilities against Distributed Denial-of-Service (DDoS) attacks and threats with clear immutability from blockchain [30]. Blockchain may implement new authentication solutions for 5G cellular networks, powered by smart contracts, which provide highly flexible, efficient user access control mechanisms through access rules and smart coding logic. Contracts will automatically authenticate user access, identify threats, and discard malicious access from the networks independently without exposing user information instead of depending on external public key infrastructure. Also, blockchain systems maintain robust data security by publishing user data to ledgers where data are signed by hash functions and immutably appended to blocks. When sharing over an untrusted network, blockchain can provide complete personal data control, which is unique from all conventional methods that prohibit users from monitoring their data.

2. System efficiency enhancement: The incorporation of blockchain would further enhance the efficiency of 5G networks. The blockchain facilitated the improvement of the reliability of data storage and administration services with minimal response time in contrast to conventional database platforms, such as SQL. In reality, a data request is validated via decentralized nodes without going through a centralized authority that promises to minimize network latency with the help

of intellectual, smart contracts. Besides, blockchain will create direct connections between 5G consumers and providers, as inspired by the elimination of decentralization, for that the management cost might be reduced dramatically. It will enable 5G ecosystems with a much more versatile and effective data distribution model but still satisfy stringent safety criteria. For instance, blockchain would help to inaugurate secure P2P connectivity between consumers and providers by leveraging the computational resources to all members instead of going to a third-party mediator to manage the network. It will theoretically reduce communication delays, transaction costs, and provide all users with global connectivity, all of which would increase overall device efficiency.

3. Network simplification: Blockchain is claimed to simplify 5G network implementations through its decentralized architectures. Indeed, owing to the blockchain, at present, mobile operators would not have a necessity to have concern regarding the establishment of centralized management servers. Suppose the distribution of 5G services can be accomplished via a blockchain network. In that case, user access, communication transmission, and service trading might be achieved without the need for additional management infrastructure over the decentralized ledger participants, including service providers and consumers. The use of the blockchain thus theoretically decreases the complexity of the network and therefore dramatically saves operating costs. Besides, data and resource transactions for 5G services are governed by the blockchain network itself. The decentralized network is operated and maintained by all individuals with equal rights. The great advantage of blockchain is that it could establish simple network management to improve user experience by leveraging internal resources from users, especially in future 5G diverse mobile environments.

4. Blockchain over 5G services: By endorsing 5G technology, blockchains provide enormous promise for enhancing current 5G networks and software. It could accomplish this perception by attaining the exciting advantage of blockchain: privacy, decentralization, traceability, and immutability. Blockchain would be considered as a prevalent alternative to expedite the next-prosperous and effective digital generation telecommunication networks to provide enhanced 5G services.

A blockchain is a form of distributed decentralized database by which no individual organization has a right to control, by which it is withstanding with high security and superior performance, i.e., low response time with high throughput. Specifically, blockchain has the following benefits for achieving efficient data management [29].

- Decentralization: The incorporation of a blockchain removes the necessity of trustworthy peripheral administrators, such as band managers, spectrum licenses, and database managers. There are two inherent advantages. First, it reduces the excessive network overhead that arises owing to data sharing.

Second, it enhances device integrity, and security by managing data leakage pitfalls created by exotic third-party intermediaries.

- Transparency: As all transactions are represented and registered on distributed blockchain ledgers between consumers and service providers, the blockchain-grounded approach can offer greater regional perceptibility of data usage. Also, despite pre-determined distribution strategies, blockchain may use smart contract to inspect data sharing activities.
- Immutability: Data services, i.e., data tracking, distribution, or user reimbursement, are registered in an immutable way on the only appended blockchain. Blockchain ledgers afford immutability to changes caused by malevolent users and attacks using consensus. This also guarantees the stability of data services and increases the quality of deployment of the network.
- Availability: For data sharing and payment, all network participants, such as smartphone consumers, could access middle-party administrators operated by service providers. As the blockchain transmits entire service information to all peers, the databases for data sharing are also to be evaluated by anyone who participated in the network. Also, there is no central administration for the verification and recording of transactions, which would implicitly allow high transparent system without compromising security assets.
- Permissionless: As no solitary administration is acting as the dominant network control authority, it is possible to add novel users to the network without requiring other middle-party approval, which creates a versatile sharing environment.
- Protection: Blockchains allow efficient communication with highly reliable security competencies against threats and DDoS attacks between users and service providers.

5G is the newest iteration of mobile technology, independent from previous iterations and, in terms of speeds, it is not only a step up from 4G; but is built to consolidate specifications from several different use cases and drivers:

- Reliability and security: 5G promises ultra-reliable and secure communication, with some claiming that 5G would offer 99.999% network reliability. Through new capabilities, such as data in motion encryption, network slicing technology, and secure radio/network node handover. Furthermore, the shift of 5G towards virtualized and software-defined networks ensures that it can significantly minimize network failures. It is a primary advantage of 5G over other (e.g., 4G, Wi-Fi, bluetooth) networking solutions.
- Efficiency: 5G would bring significant changes in network efficiency. It will reduce latency by 90% as compared to 4G. It will require substantial bandwidth increase for data to travel on an average at 100 Mb/s (compared with 10 Mb) and reach up to 20 Gb/s at peak speeds (while 4G is limited to 1 Gb/s).
- Capacity: It is anticipated that by 2022, the number of connected devices would increase worldwide, with several connected devices as about 29 billion. This increase in device density is not expected to manage current communication solutions, such as Bluetooth, Zigbee, LPWAN, and NB-IoT, particularly as use

cases begin to rely on not one or two elements being controlled but hundreds of different factors. 5G offers up to 1 million connected devices per square kilometer of capacity (as opposed to just 100 000 on 4G).

7.5 Perceptual overview of integrating blockchain and 5G technology in the healthcare sector

Healthcare is an industrial field in which companies and medical institutions support healthcare facilities, medical devices, and health insurance to promote healthcare delivery. The current Healthcare/medicare 4.0 era has achieved extraordinary improvement with the emergence of AI. This technology promotes the advent of healthcare devices, such as smart wearable devices, smart patient monitoring systems, which drastically enhance the way of providing services to patients [31]. In this way, the new generation evolving 5G technologies can support smart healthcare applications that meet modern healthcare criteria, such as enhanced proficient connectivity, QoS, and frequency and reliability. However, security and privacy are significant issues that arise in the current healthcare industry. The malevolent peers who participate in the network could access the lab reports, EHR, PHR, medical notes, and medical images; thus, damage the reputation of the organization [32–36]. The incorporation of blockchain with 5G technology will enhance the existing healthcare networks and afford high-performance welfares for enhanced quality, safety, decentralization, and lower operating costs for system simplification. With 5G innovations, such as fog/cloud computing for new-fangled smart healthcare systems, blockchain will integrate via NFVs that facilitate IoT connectivity, where the software infrastructure can perform network functions. In contrast, fog computing would help rapid healthcare provisioning systems to reveal the patient's health condition. Blockchain is incorporated in such a 5G medicare scenario towards creating a P2P blockchain system that could verify and archive all transactions (i.e., medicare requests, medicare reports, patient data, etc.) and stockpile the transactions in an immutable decentralized ledger. To improve data transmission at the moments of drug supplement and treatment procedures, all transactions have been available to physicians, medicare staff, patients, and healthcare network participants. For safe data sharing through user authentication, a consensus mechanism empowered by smart contracts is incorporated to prevent unauthorized peers from protecting healthcare data resources.

A P2P communications-based medicare architecture would be an effective solution for successful knowledge exchange and large-scale data exchange; however, there arise significant privacy problems owing to critical sharing circumstances. For instance, in healthcare, image characteristics derived from the processing of health data contain valuable information of the patient and thus need to be protected. By transferring the information to decentralized ledgers that all members manage, blockchain ensures secure data storage. All stored blockchain data is digitally signed along with appropriate hash values, which safeguard the system from privacy leaks, tampering, or counterfeiting issues.

Blockchain is recently considered in Mobile Edge Computing (MEC) research intended for empowered medicare applications. For telemedicine applications, edge blockchain is considered, with the primary objective of providing safe health data sharing and computation. A base terminal station and a group of mobile consumers are included in the MEC-based cellular health network. Here, consumers might be connected to the Internet through a mobile network and share the computing resources of the MEC server via a small cell attached to the base station. To verify and validate the priority of patients, blockchain affords a consensus mechanism that uses wireless resources for their computation. Thus, the optimum provisioning of resources would be achieved to assure the reliability of data transmission and blockchain storage.

Meanwhile, fog computing and cloud computing are considered noteworthy 5G network enabling technology, providing numerous prominent healthcare service solutions. Several academic reports exemplify the significance of using blockchain for fog-based medicare networks. Blockchain has proved its efficacy in this work to improve the protection of exchanging EHRs in fog-assisted healthcare. Fog/cloud storage is used to stockpile the ciphertext of EHR, whereas the blockchain holds keyword ciphertext records for data discovery and sharing. Moreover, a blockchain-assisted telecommunication protocol precisely achieves safe record sharing among IoT medicare devices and fog/cloud servers. The blockchain might store and manage the entire sensitive data and medical test results of the patient. In contrast, a consensus technique is designed for peer verification during the depiction of medical examinations.

Blockchain for fog-based medicare administration network has also been investigated and designed very recently [37]. We have developed a fog platform to develop a reliable record sharing system between medicare patients and medicare providers using blockchain. Whole EHR documents are stockpiled in fog/cloud IPFS decentralized storage systems, where smart contracts are entrenched to offer trustworthy data-sharing services. The user should not have any rights to retrieve cloud data without passing through the authentication process. The problem faced by the traditional system and rectified by blockchain and 5G technologies is exemplified in Table 7.2.

7.5.1   Challenges of incorporating 5G and blockchain in the healthcare sector

- **Smart Contracts**: The primary concern is to transmit smart contracts in a 5G environment. The legal status and legitimacy of SC to transfer healthcare data are not verified technically. Even small bugs pave the way for exploitation of the entire healthcare network.
- **Transaction:** The computational fee may be high during the deployment of smart contracts for accessing healthcare records or financial transactions. By incorporating the 5G network and blockchain, there are chances of high computational cost and network overhead.

Table 7.2   Problem faced by traditional system and rectified by blockchain
system in healthcare

Healthcare and Medical Applications	Problems Faced by Traditional System	Problems Rectified by Blockchain and 5G System
	The origin of medicines, ownership details, and its components are identified.	Origin of raw materials, ownerships, manufacturer of pharmaceuticals at each stage are easily tracked and identified. It avoids the stealing and forging of pharmaceutical goods with higher network reliability and efficiency.
	At present, for the shipment of medical drugs, shipment details are tracked from information given by the shipping sectors. Crucial issues are raised to compromise fraud during shipment. Any compromise can affect the well-being of the patient and even lead to bereavement.	**Medical Fraud Detection:** To reduce the occurrence of fraudulent complexity, 5G provides immediate traceability of shipment and a blockchain-based supply chain platform provides drug transparency and traceability throughout shipment.
	The traditional system has a range of issues including data integrity, data confidentiality, data sharing, data privacy, patient registering and record-keeping, and so on. At this juncture, cyber offenders can have a chance to extract and tamper the data in their favor. No secure storage of medical documents.	**Clinical Research:** Blockchain platform along with 5G fortifies a framework for any information collaboration by manipulating medical records that grandly assures data integrity, data confidentiality, secure data sharing, and data privacy. Offenders are impotent to access data on a blockchain.
	No data integrity preserved in conventional Electronic Health Record (EHR)	The data integrity of EHR is well-preserved and transferred through the blockchain and 5G platform.

(Continues)

Table 7.2 Continued

Healthcare and Medical Applications	Problems Faced by Traditional System	Problems Rectified by Blockchain and 5G System
	Neuroscience research in the conventional system raises a crucial computational complexity owing to the insecure storing of data, able to be tampered, and inefficiency to execute automation of integrated system consists of several sensors, integrated chips, and wireless communication systems.	Blockchain, along with 5G, automates the incorporated system comprising several sensors, integrated chips, and wireless communication systems. The digitalization of neuro activity of the brain requires some prevailing medium to store brain activity. An anticipated system can handle big data and complex algorithms intricate in neural activities that will utilize the concept of blockchain to store brain signals and use 5G networks to securely transfer over the communications system.
	The current system has more manual mediators for storing, billing, verifying, etc., at high cost.	**Cost-efficient:** A smart contract automates billing, storing, and verifying of healthcare and medical records, which are less costly. 5G also helps in transmitting those details at the lowest cost.

- **Interoperability:** The 5G network has advanced technical formats, such as cloud/fog, mmWave, beamforming, etc. Thus, adapting to blockchain communication via 5G still remains a major challenge.
- **Scalability:** The latency speed of a 5G network is lesser than one millisecond. However, the latency speed of blockchain must be varied from 11 to 14 transactions per second (TPS) to 4 000 to 20 000 TPS based on its platform. It slows down communication transmission between systems via the 5G network.

7.6 Use case scenario

Consider the pandemic situation where a patient was in critical condition and was suffering from severe breathing problems. In this situation, we can take that patient to the hospital in an ambulance. Owing to the Covid crisis, the patient is in a situation where he may not get admission in the hospital. The hospitals may be overloaded, or due to the protocol also, the hospital may refuse the patient with breathing problems. We need a solution to this type of problem. While traveling in the ambulance itself, we should be able to locate the hospitals with all facilities required by the patient, and the hospital also should have free beds for the admission of the new patient. Using emerging technologies, such as blockchains and 5G, provides the best pathway for solving these problems. We aim to develop a mobile application where we can use all these technologies in serving the patient. This is elucidated in Figure 7.4.

All hospitals should register their facilities, such as the number of beds, ventilators, oxygen cylinders and their ambulances, etc., in the centralized repository. Consider 'patient 1' having a severe breathing problem. The attendant of that patient is using our mobile app to call an ambulance. Our application will get the patient's location and call the ambulance service near the patient's location. The ambulance will pick up the patient with complete ~~, ...lom. ~~ ~~.... emergency~~ medical technician who is serving the patient in the ambulance can give first aid to the patient, including the supply of oxygen. In the meantime, he/she can log in to his/her mobile application and choose the search option to find a hospital where the patient with breathing problem can be treated. Also, it will check all necessary parameters, such as the number of available doctors, beds, oxygen cylinders and the distance of the hospital from the ambulance, etc. According to the parameters, our app will get the hospital service to the attendant. Now, the hospital's name and location will also be shared with the attendant. Now the attendant can instruct the ambulance driver to go to the particular hospital. In the meantime, directly, the attendant can be connected to a specific doctor in the hospital. The doctor can now request the attendant to check the necessary parameters, such as BP, sugar level, heartbeat, oxygen level, etc. The attendant has to measure all parameters and has to enter all these parameters along with the patient's details in the app. All patient-related information should be confidential. Therefore, all patient-related information is stored in a blockchain where nobody can change the value. Even the doctor can only view the values. Based on the values of the patient parameters, the doctor can instruct the emergency medical attendant to take the necessary action, and in the meantime the doctor can make arrangements required in the hospital with all communications through the use of 5G technology. Therefore, we will achieve a high speed of communication with low latency. Because of the 5G technology, communication in vehicles, such as ambulance is also possible without interruption. Using blockchain technology, the integrity, and confidentiality, and immutability of the patient record are also preserved.

7.6.1 Characteristics of mobile application interactions between 5G and blockchain technology for serving the patient requirement

- **Decentralization:** There will be no need to carry medical reports, lab test records, or medical images. The patients can easily access the records from blockchain.
- **Immutability:** Patient records cannot be changed by malicious peers for money. No one can modify even a single data from the blockchain.
- **Confidentiality:** No one can access the patient records unless the user gives permission.
- **Ultra-reliable service:** 5G enables the ultra-speed data transmission of data, records, or documents, which allow earlier treatment for patients.

7.6.2 Challenges arise in mobile application interactions between 5G and blockchain technology for serving the patient requirement

- **Deployment of smart contracts:** As the emergence of blockchain is at the beginning stage, accessing medical data or records via smart contracts from blockchain via 5G mobile network, even minor bugs might exploit the entire network.
- **Transaction:** There exists two computational fees, one for smart contract execution to access the medical data and the other for data transmission, which would be high for social adaption.
- **Interoperability:** As the data transmission in blockchain is different at different platforms, developing a technology that integrates a particular blockchain platform with 5G networks will not support another blockchain platform.
- **Scalability:** The latency speed of data processing over the 5G network is very low as compared to the latency speed of blockchain. Thus, processing of the request can generate bottlenecks over a network.

7.7 SWOT analysis of incorporating blockchain and 5G technologies in the healthcare sector

The SWOT analysis for incorporating blockchain and 5G technologies in the healthcare sector is illustrated in Table 7.3.

7.8 Conclusion

Blockchain is observed as an emerging technology that has recently gained considerable attention for its unique role in security, which provokes the technology as a key enabler for incorporating with 5G networks. The chapter provided a systematic review and elucidated the possibilities of integrating the 5G network and blockchain technology for building effective healthcare applications. Our study also covered a holistic investigation of blockchain over the real-time applications in healthcare and thus found the possibilities of leveraging the 5G network over use cases to make smart healthcare/medicare use cases. Finally, the chapter exemplified SWOT analysis for the incorporation of blockchain and 5G technologies for simple empathetic integration of both technologies in the smart healthcare sector.

The key lessons learned from the study of incorporating 5G + blockchain are emphasized as follows:

- Primarily, by providing many exciting technological characteristics, namely immutability, distribution, and decentralization, etc., blockchain aims to strengthen the reliability and security of 5G networks.

Table 7.3   SWOT analysis for incorporating blockchain and 5G technologies in the healthcare sector

SWOT Analysis of Blockchain + 5G

Strengths	Weaknesses	Opportunities	Threats
Cost-efficient	Lesser number of devices to be managed	Fraud risk becomes lesser when incorporating over medical supply chains	The technology incorporation is doubtful for social adoption
Faster access and sharing of autonomous data	Low scalability	Beneficiaries get more control over data	Non-standardization
Tamper-proof sharing of information	Have less storage space. Difficult to handle a large volume of information	Potential technology for industrial start-ups and trustworthy networks	Issues related to inter-operability
Privacy enhanced secure transactions	Private money with no legal tender	Business revolutions by smart contracts	Government's heavy regulations
Protection of rights	Absent leadership and oversight bodies	Efficient cross-border payments	Government current papers and digital currency
No reliance on third-party with greater transparency	Non-scalability	True sharing economy	Systemic contagion risk
Instant settlement	Irrevocable smart contracts	Supply chain revolutions	Instant jobs loss for lots of people
Distributed ledger database	Indelible records	Inclusion of the unbanked population	Risk of bubble collapse
Audibility trail	Energy consumption	Programmable control mechanism	Not-suitable for a existing processes
Higher efficiency	Reduced users privacy	Speed up financial transactions	Uncertainty about the impact
No data loss/ modifications/ falsification	Volatility of cryptocurrency	KYC database	Time-consuming negotiations

- Secondly, the usage of blockchain will correspondingly enhance the efficiency of 5G networks. In contrast to conventional database frameworks, blockchain would afford an efficient document storage network and administration services within a minimal response time.
- Finally, incorporating a 5G network provides a secure way of accessing and transferring medical data without worrying about theft or malicious acts created by hackers.

However, incorporating 5G + blockchain technology remains in its beginning stage. Blockchain and 5G technology will greatly enhance the form and experience of future networks and applications. Though, the chapter provides timely research on the study of the integration of blockchain and 5G technologies ,which inspires the fascinated researchers and medical practitioners to put further efforts into this promising sector.

References

[1]   Panwar N., Sharma S., Singh A.K. 'A survey on 5G: the next generation of mobile communication'. *Physical Communication*. 2016;**18**(1):64–84.

[2]   Zheng Z., Xie S., Dai H., Chen X., Wang H. 'An overview of blockchain technology: architecture, consensus, and future trends'. *IEEE International Congress on Big Data (BigData Congress)*; 2017. pp. 557–64.

[3]   Nakamoto S. *Bitcoin: a peer-to-peer electronic cash system [online]*. 2017. Available from https://bitcoin.org/bitcoin.pdf [Accessed 12 Sep 2020].

[4]   Tschorsch F., Scheuermann B. 'Bitcoin and beyond: a technical survey on decentralized digital currencies'. *IEEE Communications Surveys & Tutorials*. 2016;**18**(3):2084–123.

[5]   Bodkhe U., Tanwar S., Bhattacharyaa P., Kumar N. 'Blockchain for precision irrigation: a systematic review'. *Transactions on Emerging Telecommunications Technologies*. 2020:1–33.

[6]   *MWC Barcelona* [online]. 2020. Available from https://www.mwcbarcelona.com/ [Accessed 10 Sep 2020].

[7]   *Internet of things* [online]. 2016. Available from https://www.cisco.com/c/dam/en/us/*products/collateral/se/internetof-things/at-a-glance-c45-731471*.pdf [Accessed 12 Sep 2020].

[8]   Melanie Swan. *Blockchain – blueprint for a new economy* [online]. 2017. Available from *https://epdf.pub/queue/Blockchain-blueprint-for-a-new-economy.html* [Accessed 12 Sep 2020.].

[9]   Hileman G. *State of blockchain q1 2016: blockchain funding overtakes bitcoin* [online]. 2016. Available from http://www.coindesk.com/state-of-Blockchain-q1-2016 [Accessed 12 Sep 2020].

[10]   Bodkhe U., Tanwar S., Parekh K., *et al.* 'Blockchain for industry 4.0: a comprehensive review'. *IEEE Access*. 2020;**8**:79764–800.

[11] Akram S.V., Malik P.K., Singh R., Anita G., Tanwar S. 'Adoption of block-chain technology in various realms: opportunities and challenges'. *Security and Privacy Journal, Wiley.* 2020:1–17.

[12] Rawal V., Mascarenhas P., Shah M., Kondaka S.S. *Blockchain for health-care* [online]. 2018. Available from https://www.citiustech.com /up-loads/knowledge hub/pdf/Blockchain-for-healthcare - 341/ Citiustech [Accessed 20 Sep 2020].

[13] Dimiter V Dimitrov *Blockchain Applications for Healthcare Data Management, HIR-Healthcare Informatics Research* [online]. 2018. Available from https://ehir.org/DOIx.php ?id=10. 4258 /hir.2019.25.1.51, 2020 [Accessed 12 Sep 2020].

[14] Siyal A.A., Junejo A.Z., Zawish M., Ahmed K., Khalil A., Soursou G. Applications of Blockchain Technology in Medicine and Healthcare: Challenges and Future perspectives [online]. 2018. Available from https://www.mdpi.com/2410-387X/3/1/3,2020 [Accessed 12 Sep 2020].

[15] Herper M. *23 and Me Gets 300 Million Boost From GlaxoSmithKline To Develop New Drugs* [online]. 2018. Available from https://www.forbes.com/sites/matthewherper/2018/07/25/23andme-gets-300-million-boost-from-glaxo-to-develop-new-drugs/ [Accessed 12 Sep 2020].

[16] *MedRec 1.0 [online].* 2017. Available from https://medrec.media.mit.edu/technical/,2020 [Accessed 12 Sep 2020].

[17] DTCO. *DTCO and TMU Hospital Reveal Joint Blockchain Project to Improve Patient Record Security* [online]. 2017. Available from https://medium.com/dtco/dtco-and-tmu-hospital-reveal-joint-Blockchain-project-to-improve-pa-tient-record-security-bee98520413c, 2020 [Accessed 15 Sep 2020].

[18] Coral Health Research Discovery. Examples of How Blockchain is Reviving Healthcare [online]. 2017. Available from https:/builtin.comBlockchain-Blockchainhealthcare-applications companies,2020 [Accessed 14 Sep 2020].

[19] Farmatrust. *Blockchain and AI Solutions for the Pharmaceutical and Healthcare Sector* [online]. 2017. Available from https://www.farmatrust.com/ [Accessed 12 Sep 2020].

[20] MTBC. *MTBC Takes Electronic Health Records to the Next Level with Blockchain Technology* [online]. 2017. Available from https://ir.mtbc.com/node/10676/pdf", 2020 [Accessed 12 Sep 2020].

[21] Hashed Health. *A Platform for Blockchain Innovation in Healthcare* [online]. 2017. Available from https://hashedhealth.com/,2020 [Accessed 12 Sep 2020].

[22] Sam Daley. *15 Examples of How Blockchain is Reviving Healthcare* [online]. 2016. Available from *https://builtin.com/Blockchain/Blockchain-healthcare-applications-companies 2019* [Accessed 12 Sep 2020].

[23] Maersk. *Shipping and Cargo Services* [online]. 2017. Available from https://www.maersk.com/Solutions/Shipping, 2020 [Accessed 20 Sep 2020].

[24] Gupta R., Tanwar S., Tyagi S., Kumar N. 'Tactile internet and its applications in 5G era: a comprehensive review'. *International Journal of Communication Systems.* 2019;**32**(14):e3981–49.

[25]   Gupta A., Jha R.K. 'A survey of 5G network: architecture and emerging technologies'. *IEEE Access*. 2015;**3**:1206–32.

[26]   Kar U.N., Sanyal D.K. 'An overview of device-to-device communication in cellular networks'. *ICT Express*. 2018;**4**:203–8.

[27]   Wang X., Kong L., Kong F., *et al.* 'Millimeter wave communication: a comprehensive survey'. *IEEE Communications Surveys & Tutorials*. 2018;**20**(3):1616–53.

[28]   Christidis K., Devetsikiotis M. 'Blockchains and smart contracts for the internet of things'. *IEEE Access*. 2016;**4**:2292–303.

[29]   Dinh C., Nguyen., Pubudu N., Pathirana., Ding M., Seneviratne A. 'Blockchain for 5G and beyond networks: A state of the art survey'. Journal of Network and Computer Applications. Elsevier. 2020. Available from https:// doi.org/ 10.1016/j.jnca.2020.102693 [Accessed Aug 2020].

[30]   Singh R., Tanwar S., Sharma T.P. 'Utilization of blockchain for mitigating the distributed denial of service attacks'. *Security and Privacy Journal Wiley*. 2019;**1**(5):1–13.

[31]   Hathaliya J.J., Tanwar S., Evans R. 'Securing electronic healthcare records: a mobile-based biometric authentication approach'. *Journal of Information Security and Applications*. 2020;**53**(3):102528–14.

[32]   Tanwar S., Tyagi S., Kumar N. 'Security and privacy of electronic healthcare records'. *The IET Book Series on e-Health Technologies, Institution of Engineering and Technology*; Stevenage, United Kingdom; 2019. pp. 1–450.

[33]   Tanwar S., Parekh K., Evans R. 'Blockchain-based electronic healthcare record system for healthcare 4.0 applications'. *Journal of Information Security and Applications*. 2019;**50**:1–14.

[34]   Vora J., Tanwar S., Verma J.P. 'BHEEM: a blockchain-based framework for securing electronic health records'. *IEEE Global Communications Conference (IEEE GLOBECOM-2018)*; Abu Dhabi. UAE, 09-13th; 2018. pp. 1–6.

[35]   Hathaliya J.J., Tanwar S. 'An exhaustive survey on security and privacy issues in healthcare 4.0'. *Computer Communications*. 2020;**153**(6):311–35.

[36]   Hathaliya J., Sharma P., Tanwar S., Gupta R. 'Blockchain-based remote patient monitoring in healthcare 4.0'. *9th IEEE International Conference on Advanced Computing (IACC)*; Tiruchirappalli. India, 13-14th; 2019. pp. 87–91.

[37]   Nguyen D.C., Pathirana P.N., Ding M., Seneviratne A. 'Blockchain for secure EHRS sharing of mobile cloud-based e-health systems'. *IEEE Access*, [online]. 2019. Available from https://ieeexplore.ieee.org/document/8717579 [Accessed Aug 2020].

Chapter 8

Architectural framework of 5G-based smart healthcare system using blockchain technology

M. Kiruthika[1], Vaishali Gupta[2], T. Poongodi[2], and B. Balamurugan[2]

Today's healthcare industry uses various technologies such as internet of things (IoT), blockchain and machine learning (ML) for its efficient and secure operation. With the advancements and increased research in IoT, many wearable devices (WD) are being used by the people to track the health issues. Large amount of data is collected by these devices and there has to be a suitable technology to securely store this information. Blockchain is an emerging technology that can be used for secured storage of healthcare records. Many features of blockchain such as immutability, distributed nature and integrity make it appropriate for healthcare industry. Blockchain can be applied in various grounds of healthcare industry such as remote patient monitoring, tele-surgeries, maintaining electronic health records (EHRs), clinical trials and medical research and pharmaceutical supply chain management. Privacy and security of data are assured when blockchain is integrated with healthcare system. When the number of users using smart devices expands, the network must be capable to handle huge amount of data in various types and sizes. The prevailing communication technologies fail to fulfil the intricate and dynamic needs of smart healthcare system (SHS). On the mission of developing communication technologies, 5G is expected to cater the needs of smart healthcare applications with its broad set of salient features and advanced design. The future smart healthcare systems are expected to be a mixture of the 5G, smart IoT devices and blockchain technology.

8.1 Introduction

Today, many pandemic diseases are spreading across the world that demands more attention towards the healthcare industry. It is one of the most intensive industry that is evolving continuously from doctor-centric approach to patient-centric approach. Many new technologies such as IoT, blockchain and artificial intelligence (AI) have

[1]Department of Computer Science and Engineering, Jansons Institute of Technology, India
[2]School of Computing Science and Engineering, Galgotias University, India

to be integrated with healthcare industry to save the lives of millions of people. According to the report from Gartner, there will be 1.37 billion IoT endpoints at the end of year 2020 and 86% of these IoT projects will incorporate blockchain technology to achieve more productivity. So, there is no doubt that blockchain technology will be readily adopted in healthcare industry. With the advancements and increased research in IoT, many WD are being used by the people to track and monitor the health issues. These devices have in-built sensors to monitor people's heartbeat, pulse, physical activity, etc.

IoT-based healthcare devices are widely used by people as they can easily monitor and store their health-related information at their comfort. Now, the focus has to be given to the communication technologies that enables the IoT devices to effectively communicate with the backend storage devices. Eventually these data are unceasingly monitored by healthcare professionals for further directions.

This chapter gives the overview of SHS and 5G networking. It describes the architecture of smart healthcare system with blockchain technology. The features of 5G networking that supports smart healthcare applications are discussed. Blockchain architecture can support 5G in terms of communication and networking. The architecture for the integration of SHSs using blockchain based on 5G is presented. A comparative study is performed between the traditional healthcare architecture without 5G and the advanced healthcare architecture with 5G. Major challenges arise when converging smart healthcare with blockchain and 5G related to resource utilization, quality of Service (QOS), etc. These are discussed in brief along with further directions for research.

8.1.1   *Overview of blockchain for healthcare*

WD have in-built sensors and these can be effectively used in healthcare industry for monitoring the health and tracking the fitness of the user [1]. Many popular WD that are used in healthcare are iWatch, Fitbit, Samsung Gear, etc. The invention of these WD has opened up new paces in healthcare industry. These WD aid in remote healthcare services to patients by monitoring them and by providing medical help whenever needed. For instance, patients residing in remote villages need not travel to hospitals for checking blood pressure, heart rate, etc. Instead they can be at their home and with the help of these WD, they can be monitored remotely by healthcare professionals anytime and anywhere. If there is a suspicion in the patients' health condition, they can be taken to the hospital without further delay and this can be a boon to them, as it saves their life. The WD continuously monitor the patients using sensors and the sensors generate and store these data [2]. Healthcare professionals access the data stored in healthcare networks. The vital challenge lies in securing this huge amount of data. If the data are accessed by intruders, it may lead to drastic effects and may even question the life of oneself. Hence utmost care should be taken in securing the medical data.

When blockchains are incorporated in medical network, there is a likelihood to overcome the security-related concerns. Blockchain provides and controls the way the digital data is accessed. Incorporating blockchain can help in deciding who can access what data under what condition. There are various areas in healthcare where blockchain can be used. Blockchain can be used for preserving medical records, clinical trials and supply chain management in pharmaceutical industry, insurance claim, etc. [3]. Smart contracts in blockchain are contracts that are executed automatically and these contract conditions can be fixed up by the patients in a patient-centric healthcare network. The smart contracts can be used to accumulate and transfer the medical data collected by sensors. When patients are using WD it is easy to track their health. In case of contagious diseases such as Corona, this traceability may even lead to safeguarding other people in nearby locality.

The key characteristics of blockchain that make it suitable for healthcare industry are distributed nature, data immutability, accountability, traceability and transparency. The medical data of the patients and their lab reports can be stored in a distributed way. This helps the doctors to easily access the data from anywhere. Since there is no central management, it reduces the risk of performance bottleneck, saves cost and eventually becomes more fault-tolerant. Data stored in blockchain are immutable, that is, the data cannot be altered in blockchain. This property is very much helpful in healthcare industry as the data of the patients are more sensitive and even a small modification may lead to loss of one's life. The owners/patients can decide who can access their data and the data are preserved using private keys. The data can be tested by others using their public/private key pair. Therefore, the parties cannot deny later that they haven't accessed the data and the participating entities (patients and healthcare professionals) are accountable for the data. Wearing WD makes it easier to trace the location of the patients. Blockchain provides additional supports such as traceability by timestamps. Each data stored by the sensors in a blockchain holds the timestamp, making the transaction traceable. The healthcare data stored in blockchain are transparent to the users who are all allowed to access the data. All these characteristics make the blockchain technology more reliable and usable in healthcare industry.

8.1.2 Need for 5G

Mobile phone users are increasing day-by-day and almost every household uses a smart phone to connect to internet. The usage of mobile phone network for data access is increasing and every user expects a very faster and a reliable data service. The most promising next generation wireless networking is 5G that assures faster data service [4]. It is said that a task that takes 10 min in 4G network, can be completed in a second in 5G. This improvement in networking leads to drastic improvement in fields such as IoT, unmanned vehicles, ML, robotics and virtual reality (VR). The challenge that will be faced by 5G networking is that it needs to handle a greater number of mobile users that obviously leads to more data traffic.

The future networks are indebted to provide more connectivity to many devices and smart gadgets [5]. The future mobile networks are required to provide massive data rates and must be able to support real-time applications in a pervasive environment. To satisfy these requirements, it is essential to restructure the architecture of wireless networking. These requirements have paved way for 5G networks that is gaining more attention from various industries including healthcare industry. The studies show that 5G networking will highly support user and machine centric communications over the network. 5G connectivity has drawn major expectations that can be listed as follows:

- Should be capable to support huge number of devices
- Should provide flawless coverage and connectivity
- Should consume less battery power
- Should incur less cost related to deployment and service
- Should provide data transfer with high throughput with very less delay
- Should support IoT devices and compatible to other new technologies.

5G must be capable to support those functionalities that are not provided by 4G. 5G should support more applications that work along with AI and ML [6]. Another important area of research is that the radiations produced in 5G should not harm humans and animals. That is, it should produce harmless radiations. The possible applications of 5G can be enlisted as follows:

- Students can attend e-classes from any institution world-wide
- Doctors can give telemedicines to patients
- Wireless charging of devices
- Security surveillance from anywhere
- Home automation
- Predict catastrophic changes, etc.

8.1.3   Implication of 5G in healthcare

The current healthcare system is supposed to interoperate with many trending technologies such as IoT, big data, wireless access and ML [7], as shown in Figure 8.1. These technologies work efficiently using the 5G networking and this can be explained as follows. IoT consists of smart devices that are capable to seize, sense, monitor and transmit data to a network to which it is connected. IoT helps in automation of many entities such as energy management, smart cities, home automation, emergency services, industrial operations, healthcare industry and security surveillance. IoT is considered as a cutting-edge technology in healthcare networks. Use of IoT devices in healthcare can help in remote monitoring of patients, teleconsultations, patient tracking, monitor pharma supplies, etc. The patients can wear any WD such as smart watches that sense the health status of patients and generate reports of the patients in a period of time. More data are generated frequently by these devices and they are stored in healthcare networks. It is inevitable to have a proper internet connection that will allow these WD to communicate with the cloud/server for storing data any number of times in a day.

Big data is the massive volume of data generated by the smart devices. As seen before, the WD and the sensors collect huge amount of data related to patients'

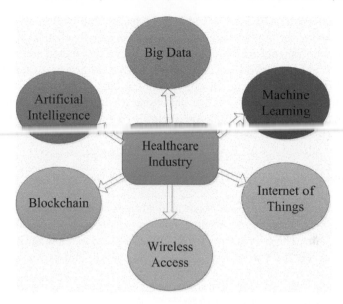

Figure 8.1   Integration of technologies with healthcare

health. These devices may record huge volume of data including the patients' body temperature, glucose level, pulse rate, blood pressure, number of steps walked, etc. These data will be very much helpful in assessing the health condition and behavioural pattern of the patients. Data are analysed to gain deep insights regarding the diseases and their impacts. Recent analysis of the novel Corona virus has given a conclusion that people with diabetes or organ failure are more prone to get affected. This analysis occurs by deeply analysing the data of the patients affected by the Corona virus. So, there is no reservation that big data is very useful in healthcare industry. But to store and transmit the huge volume of data, one needs to depend on the high-speed data transfer facilities such as 5G.

Most of the prominent e-health applications rely on wireless connectivity. Wireless technology is used by smart devices to transmit data. It is also used by expert healthcare professionals for tele-consultation and telemedicine. Telemedicine works as a blessing to the patients who live in far-off places and have difficulty in going to hospitals. When a high-speed wireless technology such as 5G is used, the patients and doctors can even share high quality images and medical records over a long distance.

AI and ML can pave way to diagnosing diseases using image processing and recognition [8]. Various diseases such as lung cancer, eye defects and skin allergies can be identified accurately and diagnosed using ML techniques. Using these advanced technologies in healthcare industry can help in reducing many numbers of errors and thereby saving many lives. The decisions taken by the ML must be robust, secure and be on time. AI and ML algorithms need to optimize with 5G networks to handle the healthcare-related problems.

Blockchain is yet another advanced technology that can be used extensively in healthcare industry for guaranteeing security and privacy to medical records. The healthcare data of patients are stored in blocks across a distributed architecture and the deployed wireless networking must be supportive' for accessing the data from anywhere. The healthcare professionals access the data through wireless devices and similarly the IoT devices store the data using a wireless transmission. So, the wireless technology should assure fast and reliable delivery of data. 5G can actively play a role in ensuring fast data delivery.

8.2   Traditional architecture – SHS using blockchain

Three architectural structures are discussed in this part of the chapter. First architecture gives the basic structure of e-healthcare systems. The second gives the architecture of blockchain. These two architectures are combined to show how blockchain interoperates successfully with SHS and assures security and privacy of medical data.

8.2.1   Basic architecture of SHS

The SHS is designed to have three parts/layers and they are user interface (UI) layer, communication layer and backend supporting layer [9]. The simplified architecture can be shown as in Figure 8.2 that is followed by the explanation of each of these layers.

8.2.1.1   UI layer

This layer consists of a wide range of devices used by the patients and healthcare providers to monitor the health condition. These devices may include WD, medical devices, IoT sensor devise, etc. These devices check the health condition of the patients periodically and generate data that are used as reports. These reports are stored in cloud/server platform that can be accessed by the doctors to monitor the health condition of patients. The data collected by these devices are real-time information that are to be processed further to gain a fruitful information. Various communication protocols are used by these devices to transmit the gathered data to the network/cloud server. Secure authentication protocol [9], yoking-proof-based authentication protocol for WD [10], a light weight authentication-based protocol [11], a three-factor authentication protocol for WD that works in a user-centric manner [12] are few of the protocols that enable communication between WD and cloud platform. The medical devices can make use of two types of sensors – physical and virtual sensors – to observe the patients' health and to perform remote diagnostics.

8.2.1.2   Communication layer

This layer is liable for handling data that comes from the front-end UI devices and for safely sending these data to the backend gateways. This layer acts as an intermediary

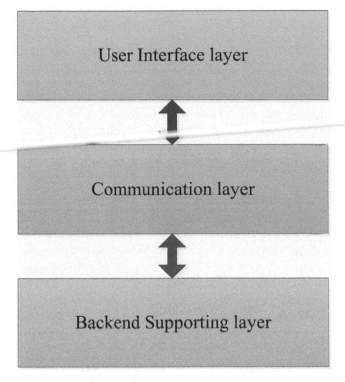

Figure 8.2   SHS architecture

between the UI layer and backend supporting layer. This layer categorizes the data as normal data and emergency data. Cloud gateway is used for forwarding the normal data and fog gateway is used for forwarding the emergency data. Fog computing is a prolonged form of cloud computing through which it provides a set of new services and applications [13]. Few low-power fog nodes (FN) can be deployed in this layer, and they can be connected with the medical devices for processing the data accurately. The time taken by the FN are much lesser compared with cloud servers. FNs perform various tasks on the data sent by the WD such as filtering, compressing, formatting and accumulation. All these processes ensure accuracy of collected healthcare data. This layer also uses encryption-based communication protocols to protect the data from intruders.

8.2.1.3   Backend supporting layer
This layer handles the secure storage of data that is collected from the previous layer. This layer handles the data centres and cloud servers to store the patient's information. The data stored here can be used for analysis of a particular disease or a patient. The medical records of patients are secured by permitting only the authenticated users to access the data store. The authenticated persons can be doctors, patients, lab technicians or pharmacists. These data of patients are termed as EHR of patients

and this can accessed anytime from anywhere. The patients do not want to carry and maintain physical files. Many improvements can be added to this EHR. For instance, a rule can be enforced as when an unauthorized person tries to access the EHR, a notification can be sent automatically to the owner of the data/patient.

Each layer of the SHS architecture makes use of more than one technology to enable a chaos free service to healthcare professionals and patients. Since wireless connectivity is used for transmitting data, the data are exposed to security issues. Though many secure communication protocols are used, still the data are vulnerable to attacks by intruders. Proper mechanism should be built-in to ensure security and privacy of medical record.

8.2.2   Architectural structure of blockchain

Blockchain can be simply defined as the chain of blocks and these blocks hold the data in a secure way. The implementation of blockchain is similar to that of a linked list implementation. There is no central authority/server and they are implemented in a distributed manner. Each block will hold the value of hash function that is generated by the previous block header and the hash value of itself. There are three types of blockchain as public blockchain, private blockchain and consortium blockchain. The working of the blockchain can be explained in the following steps:

- A block is created when a transaction is initiated. Any particular combination of events can be termed as a transaction. For instance, in banking, when an amount has to be transferred to one's account, it has to follow many steps as: the amount has to be debited from the sender's account and the sender's balance has to be updated. Similarly, the amount has to be credited to the receiver's account and the receiver's bank balance has to be updated. These steps should be collectively successful. If one step gets failed, then the entire transaction gets failed.
- The created block is sent to all users or nodes connected within the blockchain.
- The users or the nodes validate the transaction.
- After validation by all the nodes, the block is appended to the chain of blocks marking the transaction to be completed.

A blockchain architecture can be defined to carry these processes in an effective manner. The layers of the blockchain architecture [14] can be given as in Figure 8.3. The blockchain architecture defines five layers for its working.

8.2.2.1   Hardware/infrastructure layer

This layer is responsible for physically connecting the data centres that are distributed across the world. Blockchain networks store the transactions in a shared distributed ledger. All the entities that are connected to the blockchain network are termed as nodes and these nodes are distributed. When a transaction is successful, the nodes save the transaction and update its entry in the distributed ledger. This layer includes virtual resources used for storage. The infrastructure layer supports

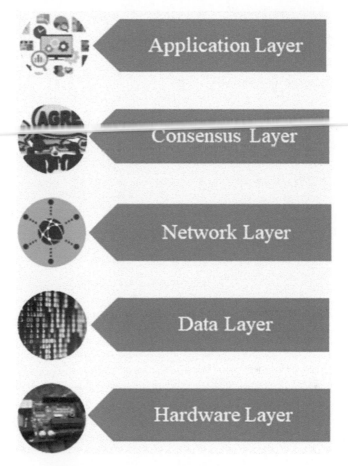

Figure 8.3   Layers in blockchain architecture

Ethereum and Hyperledger. Ethereum is the platform to control digital currencies in a distributed way that features the smart contract functionality. Hyperledger is a distributed ledger where entries are made regarding a transaction and they are modular and secure.

8.2.2.2   Data layer

This layer is dedicated and answerable for storing the data in blocks in a decentralized environment. The data later ensures the data are immutable based on a consensus. The two important components of a blockchain data structure are linked list and pointers to the list. Linked list is the chain of blocks that holds the data. Pointer is a variable that points to the address of another block. Each block has three components as block header, hash value of previous block header and a Merkle tree. The tree is a tree of hashes that stores the timestamp, block number, nonce value, etc. The data block can be shown as in Figure 8.4.

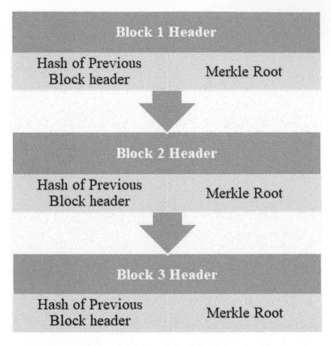

Figure 8.4   Data in blockchain architecture

A hash is a message digest of the data that is capable to generate a hash value of fixed length. Every hash value is different for different data. A slight modification to the data will yield an entirely different hash value. So, hash functions and digital signatures can easily ensure integrity and security of the data.

8.2.2.3   Network layer

This layer is also referred to as point-to-point layer or propagation layer as it is responsible for delivering/transmitting the data among the nodes. Nodes can discover other nodes in the network using this layer. The main challenge in network layer is that the nodes are completely distributed, and it has to feature some protocols that can make the communication reliable. Also, the network layer is responsible for maintaining balance in terms of workload. The network layer supports two types of nodes in the blockchain network. They are light nodes and full nodes. Light nodes just have the blockchain header. Full nodes are completely responsible for transaction validation, consensus rule enforcement, etc.

8.2.2.4   Consensus layer

This layer is the most important layer in blockchain that enforces all the functionalities of blockchain. Consensus rules are set up by this layer to which the participating nodes adhere to. Consensus is responsible for synchronization of nodes and it is real challenge as the nodes are distributed. The transactions are validated only when the consensus rules are followed strictly. This layer ensures the truthfulness and reliability of the blocks. Many consensus algorithms are proposed [15], some of which includes proof of work (PoW) algorithm, proof of stake (PoS) algorithm, delegated proof of stake (DPoS) algorithm, Practical Byzantine fault tolerance (PBFT) algorithm and raft algorithm.

8.2.2.5   Application layer

Application layer includes all the applications that interact with the end users directly. They hold the UIs, IoT applications, WD, etc. Blockchain networks are often backend networks and they use application programming interface (API) to interact. The applications are executed based on smart contracts that have rules that are executed automatically when a specific condition is met.

8.2.3   *SHS architecture using blockchain*

Having seen the architectures of SHS and blockchain, now an integrated architecture can be proposed that can turn out to be more helpful in healthcare industry. The architecture can be shown as in Figure 8.5. The layers used in SHS are discussed earlier and the only modification is that the blockchain network is added next to the backend support layer of SHS.

Integrating SHS architecture with blockchain network imposes many advantages. The healthcare data transactions can be more secure and free form attacks that occur on IoT devices. SHS architecture can operate in a distributed and decentralized manner as blockchain is used at the backend. Only the verified transactions are added to the blocks of data and they are entered in the distributed ledger. Healthcare data can be even more secured as hash functions are used. Even when one hash value varies, the node cannot access the entire block as each block carries the hash value of the previous block header. So, the entire chain of blocks cannot be accessed.

This architecture can serve as a base for multiple use-cases in the healthcare industry. There are numerous use-cases in healthcare industry where blockchain can be employed efficiently. Few of those use-cases where blockchain technology can be applied are enlisted as:

- As seen before, employing blockchain can protect the medical records of patients from attackers. Medical records are collected using smart IoT devices that are viable to numerous threats.
- Patient-centric approach can be used for medical data handling and monitoring.
- Data generated in clinical trials and medical research are very important, and they can serve as the input of any analysis function. These data can be secured with blockchain.
- Smart contracts can be executed when patients need to claim insurance that will help the hospitals, insurance companies and the also the patients.
- Drug supply management can be monitored with the help of blockchain and it can ensure that counterfeit drugs are not delivered to patients.

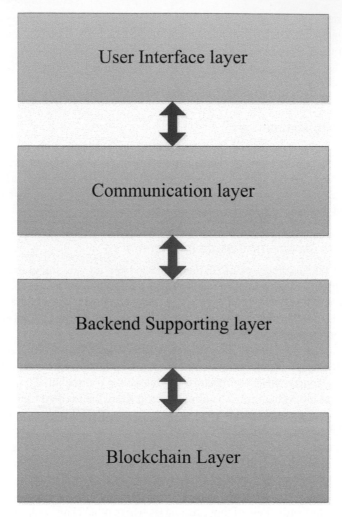

Figure 8.5   Modified SHS architecture using blockchain

- Using blockchain can resolve the problems that occur due to medical errors. A small mistake in medical data can lead to drastic consequence and may question the lives of individuals.

8.3   5G-based smart healthcare architecture using blockchain

8.3.1   Introduction

IoT technology has brought a revolutionary concept 'Smart' in each and every urban sector including healthcare system. However, IoT technology is essentially

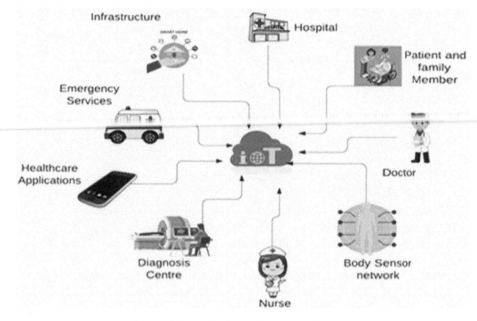

Figure 8.6   IoT-based smart healthcare

linked with two major concerns – security and capacity. 5G and blockchain are the two emerging technologies that can address these issues strategically. Therefore, a merger of IoT, 5G and blockchain technologies has a great potential to shape the future of 'smart' concept in urban settings.

In smart healthcare scenario, the trends are largely boosted by the requirement of better patient care, quick and more accurate data analysis, and on-demand access to health data. This is when the synergistic role of 5G and blockchain is considered important in SHS as 5G will help to improve the main barrier of internet bandwidth in terms of connectivity and blockchain will address the security issue of medical data. Therefore, to redefine and rethink smart healthcare, integration of 5G wireless networks and blockchain is essential.

8.3.2   Smart healthcare

SHS is technology-driven system where technology leads to better and smarter medical services that enhance the quality of life for individual. Smart healthcare connects patients and health practitioners, hospitals, pharmacist, etc., without any geographical barriers using technologies such as IoT, implantable devices, WD and smartphone applications. Smart healthcare aids in remote health monitoring of patients by recording day-to-day activities and it also makes medical services and resources approachable and affordable to patients. Figure 8.6 shows a general idea about SHS using IoT technology.

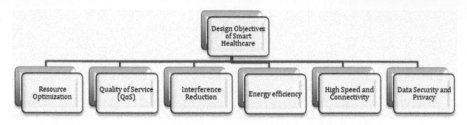

Figure 8.7   Design objectives of SHS

8.3.3   Design objectives of SHS

The design objectives of a SHS are the functional and non-functional requirements of the system. Functional requirements deal with specific demands of the healthcare system design while non-functional requirements are not very particular. Functional requirements are the properties that determine the quality of the system. There are large numbers of verticals that are needed to be considered in designing an efficient SHS. Figure 8.7 shows the main design objectives of the SHS.

- **Optimizing Resources:** Resource optimization techniques are important in 5G-based SHSs where a large number of IoT devices are connected and produce immense data and absorb more network bandwidth. Resource optimization techniques are used to minimize energy consumption and maximize lifetime of network [16].
- **Enhancing QoS:** QoS refers to the network ability to achieve network performance measures such as high bandwidth, low error rate and low latency. QoS also ensures data security in the network.
- **Reducing Interference:** Co-channel inference acts as a threat to SHS. This co-channel interference arises problems such as load increase and network density in the system [17]. Hence there is a need of efficient interference schemes to reduce co-channel interference.
- **Enhancing Energy Efficiency:** The main designing criterion in SHS is energy efficiency. The participation of large number of IoT devices with more number of access points leads to increased energy consumption in the network.
- **Improving Speed and Connectivity:** One of the main design objectives of healthcare system is assuring timely and quickly medical services. By enhancing mobile broadband in 5G-based SHSs, data rate and network capacity can be improved.
- **Enhancing Security:** In designing of SHS, security and privacy of all health related data is also a main concern. The amount of data handled by IoT devices in SHS grows exponentially which leads to higher exposure of sensitive medical data.

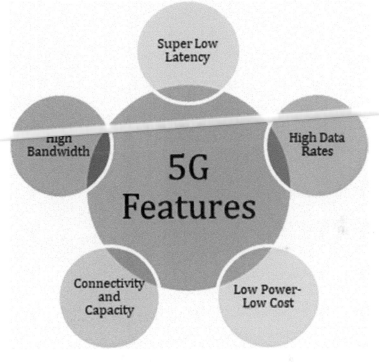

Figure 8.8   Features of 5G

8.3.4   5G for SHS

8.3.4.1   5G

5G is the fifth generation of mobile wireless communication network after 4G wireless networks that are designed to enable prompt connectivity to large number of devices and the IoT to make a truly connected world. The major goals for 5G include massive IoT and critical communications, broadband enhancement, boundless connectivity for all, ultra-low-latency communication and vertical or industrial enhancement.

8.3.4.2   5G features that support SHS

The 5G wireless technology has a great impact on future smart healthcare services. The 5G networks could be considered as an essential technology in designing of highly dynamic, diversified and time sensitive healthcare applications. The highly dynamic smart healthcare services are expected to generate a massive amount of diverse data that needs attention in terms of factors such as end-to-end delay, energy efficiency, network bandwidth and latency. The 5G-based SHSs are designed to tackle such various communication needs of future smart healthcare applications. Figure 8.8 shows the unique features of 5G technology that added value to the future SHSs.

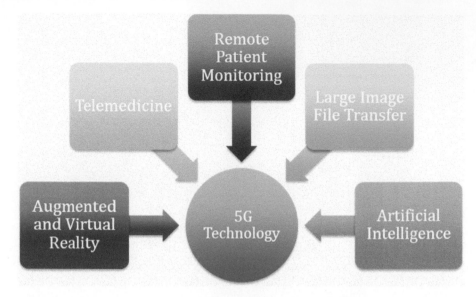

Figure 8.9   Applications of 5G in SHS

- **Low Latency:** Latency refers to the delay between the time of the sending and receiving the data. 5G offers super low latency <1 ms which is almost zero data response time in real-world. This data response is critical to the success of many new healthcare applications.
- **High Data Rates:** 5G technology offers great increase in data transmission speed that is up to 10 Gbps which is 100 times faster than 4G.
- **High Bandwidth:** 5G provides high bandwidth that allows greater optimization of network traffic and smooth usage of resources.
- **Low Power-Low Cost:** Low power consumption feature of 5G allows connected devices to operate for months or years without the need for human assistance.
- **Connectivity and Capacity:** To expand IoT, 5G has the ability to connect up to 1 million devices per unit at once.

These 5G features lead to an intelligent and SHS that can serve real-time interaction among the medical services and patients.

8.3.4.3   How 5G affects SHS

5G communication technology has the ability to resolve the issues that arises due to continuous growth of the amount of data on networks in the use of IoT to build the smart and intelligent healthcare system. Figure 8.9 shows main applications of 5G technology in SHS.

- **Reliable Real-Time Remote Patient Monitoring:** Remote patient monitoring includes monitoring of patients and gathering real-time data using IoT devices to improve personalized and preventive care. The limitation of network capacity to handle large amount of data leads to slow speed networks and unreliable connections. This gives rise to problem of timely unavailability of data in making quick healthcare decisions by the doctors. With the lower latency and high capacity features, 5G technology enables more reliable connections to facilitate the health practitioners in real-time data transfer.
- **Expansion of Telemedicine:** Telemedicine refers to the service where all the health services are provided to patients remotely using telecommunication technology when patients and health providers are at a distance. With 5G, SHSs are enabling to have a network that supports real-time high-quality video-based consultations to improve access of healthcare services.
- **Improving Augmented Reality (AR), VR and Spatial Computing:** 5G-enabled AR and VR enhances a doctor's ability such as to deliver innovative as well as less invasive treatments and simulating complex medical scenarios to find alternative treatments in case of critical health conditions of any patient.
- **Quick Transmission of Large Imaging Files:** A high-speed 5G network helps to transport large data file of medical images quickly and reliably.
- **Use of AI/Predictive Analysis:** Nowadays, AI and Predictive analysis are playing an important role in SHS to perform the key functions such as determining diagnoses and deciding treatment plans for patients [18]. 5G with its high-speed feature allows smartphones, devices, sensors and mobile applications to power the big data analytics.

8.3.4.4   5G-based SHS architecture

The main components of 5G-based SHS network are D2D (device-to-device) links, small cell access points (base stations), macro-cell base stations, network cloud and IoT. These are depicted in Figure 8.10. Small cells are one of the major features of 5G networks. Small cells are small base stations in radio access network that make use of new millimetre wave (mmWave) frequencies for the short-range connection. They are capable to handle high data rates for IoT where low-powered devices are connected in high density.

This is when small cells play a key role in smart healthcare network architecture where most of the applications such as remote surgery require high data rates. Based on the coverage capability, small cells are divided in to three categories – femtocells (coverage radius is 10–50 m), picocells (coverage radius is 100–250 m) and micro-cells (coverage radius is 500–2 500 m). These small cells provide limited area coverage compared to macrocell that provide wide area coverage. 5G macrocells use MIMO (multi input-multi output) antennas that are capable to send and receive more data simultaneously [19]. 5G macrocells enable more people such as patients,

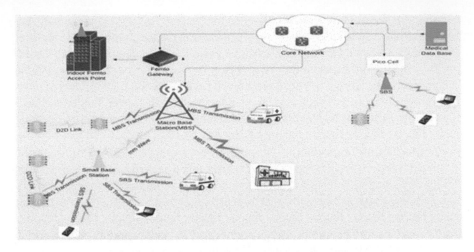

Figure 8.10   5G network architecture for SHS

doctors, nurses, technicians, etc. to connect19 network simultaneously to maintain high throughput.

8.3.4.5   Communication technologies in 5G architecture

There are number of key communication technologies that tremendously increase 5G network capacity by making all the resources efficiently utilized.

8.3.4.5.1   Massive MIMO technology

Massive MIMO is a key technology in developing 5G network. In MIMO technology, radio access points (base stations) use arrays of many service antennas over active channels simultaneously, without requiring more frequency spectrum. In massive MIMO, the term "massive" refers to the number of antennas. By increasing the number of antennas in the network, the high data transmission rate can be achieved [19].

The formation of antenna arrays is very attractive. It is a rectangular half wavelength-spaced array about 1.5 × 0.75 m large in the 2 GHz band with 200 dual-polarized elements [20]. According to study [21], using the massive MIMO, the network capacity can be increased approximately up to 10 times and the radiated energy efficiency can be increased up to 100 times.

8.3.4.5.2   mmWaves communication technology

5G mmWaves communication technology is developed to fulfil the incredible demand for wireless data bandwidth. To increase the channel bandwidth, high operating frequency bands are required. The 'mmWaves' are the short wavelengths high frequency bands that are measured in millimetres. To achieve higher data throughput, the mmWave bands up to 100 GHz are capable of supporting bandwidths up to 2 GHz.

8.3.4.5.3 D2D communication technology

D2D is a communication technology that allows direct communication between two user equipment such as mobile phones, vehicles, etc. without involvement of the base stations in the core network. D2D communication makes ultra-low latency communication possible in 5G networks. D2D communication technology helps to increase network capacity in 5G networks as it involves device-centric communication where no direct communication is required with the network infrastructure

8.3.4.5.4 Cognitive radio

Cognitive radio is another innovative communication system to improve congested Radio Frequency (RF) spectrum utilization while minimizing interference to others. Cognitive Radio (CR) intelligently detects the status of surrounding communication channels and regulates the transmission accordingly. The main advantages of CR technology include delivery of high spectral efficiency, support to large number of users and achieve higher coverage and throughput.

8.3.5 Blockchain in smart healthcare

Blockchain is a distributed ledger technology that ensures authenticated, immutable and permanent transactions related to different parties. The blockchain technology uses consensus mechanism to verify each transaction before recording in the ledger.

The blockchain technology has already gained massive attention in smart healthcare. There are many areas in healthcare where blockchain technology is being used. The main applications of blockchain include facilitating the secure transfer of patient medical data, managing the secure medicine supply, managing the outbreak of harmful diseases and helping health researchers to unlock genetic code. The decentralized nature of the blockchain also allows sharing of information among the patients, doctors and healthcare providers quickly and safely. Blockchain technology serves as a catalyst to efficient smart healthcare record systems, WD and medical examination system in smart hospitals.

8.3.6 5G-based architecture for SHS using blockchain

The aim of 5G technology is to support various applications such as connecting massive ubiquitous devices in heterogeneous networks with enhanced QoS, increasing network capacity, providing ultra-low latency and enhancing system throughput in an IoT system. As 5G is deployed in heterogeneous networks with large number of IoT devices, network security and data interoperability, decentralization remains a challenge in 5G networks.

The distributed nature of blockchain allows exchange of data among various 5G-based IoT devices without any centralization. This decentralization concept of blockchain can be utilized in 5G heterogeneous network for storage of massive data with high level of data privacy and security. Blockchain potentially empowers all key technologies of 5G networks that include D2D communication, network function virtualization (NFV), network slicing and edge computing. Thus, blockchain is expected to be a crucial technology to enhance the 5G systems performance.

In the 5G-based SHS where the environment is highly dynamic with the co-occurrence of massive IoT devices, security and privacy of medical data are the major issues to be solved. Due to the involvement of massive IoT WD in smart healthcare, large amount of health service data is expected to be generated continuously. The high degree of data security is required in 5G networks in case of third-party involvement and network congestion. Therefore, blockchain is an innovative solution to overcome the limitations of security and network performance in 5G-based architecture of SHS.

Blockchain is able to provide secure and trusted automated system for all the major smart healthcare applications such as remote patient monitoring to early diagnosis, accessing patient medical history, sharing health related data, etc. that demand high level security and protection of medical data.

Blockchain can integrate with 5G technologies such as NFVs, network slicing, edge or cloud computing for advancing SHS [22], as shown in Figure 8.11. The 5G-technology supports IoT communication while cloud computing provides uninterrupted medical delivery services such as early detection of disease so that timely medical service can be provided to the needy patient. In a 5G-based SHS, blockchain is deployed to build a site-to-site- distributed database system which can validate and store all transactions in decentralized ledgers. All of the stored transactions in ledgers are immutable. To accelerate secure data sharing, all transaction blocks in blockchain are also visible to all healthcare network users, including doctors, clinicians, patients and their family members, and ambulances in case of emergency service.

8.3.7   Smart health devices and their significance

Smart health devices are electronic devices that are designed to collect user's personal health data. These devices are at-home diagnostic testing and examination devices that play a key role in SHS. These internet-connected health devices collect invaluable additional massive data, which give extra insight into symptoms and trends that help health researchers. The health devices enable remote care and give users more control over their health and treatments. In healthcare services, medical diagnosis is one of the most expensive services in terms of money and time. With the growth of IoT-enabled smart health devices, diagnosis services can move from hospital to a patient's home. With the use of smart health and medical devices, the quality and efficiency of treatment can be improved. Some of the health devices are:

1. Wearable fitness trackers are sensor-enabled wristbands to keep track of the user's physical activity and heart beat rate. These fitness trackers are synchronized with the smartphone healthcare applications to provide health and fitness recommendations.
2. Smart health watches are the smart watches with all the functionalities similar to a smart phone from messaging and calling to receiving notifications. They also have fitness and health benefits associated with fitness tracker.

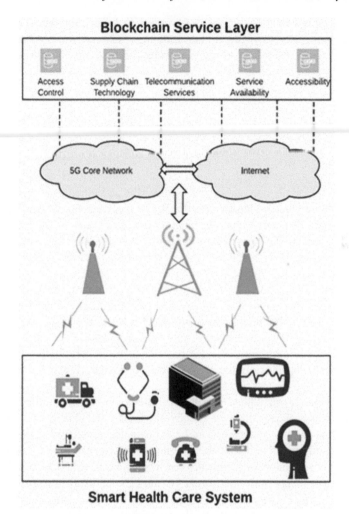

Figure 8.11   5G-based SHS using blockchain

3. Wearable blood pressure monitors are the innovative form of wristwatch to measure wearer's blood pressure and daily routine activity such as distance travelled, calories burned, etc. They hold up all the readings in memory and can transfer to syncing smartphone applications.
4. Wearable electrocardiogram (ECG) monitors are able to measure ECGs and detect atrial fibrillation.
5. Wearable smart asthma monitoring is used to identify an oncoming asthma attack. Even wearer can identify the attack before noticing the symptoms.
6. Wearable biosensors are self-adhesive patches that allow wearer to move around while collecting data on heart rate, temperature, movement and respiratory rate.

7. A smart drill is a medical device that can be helpful in surgeries to recommend surgeons where and how to drill based on the resistance and bone density. The drill makes its own calculations. Surgeons can also see the chosen depth to screw on screen in real-time.

8.4   Privacy and security in 5G-based SHS

Privacy and security issues are analysed in the context of confidentiality, integrity and availability (CIA) properties aspect. Confidentiality refers that the healthcare data are allowed to be accessed by the authorized entities. The communication process among those entities is encrypted which ensures that the medical data is safeguarded from the unauthorized users. The blockchain is inherently more resistive on the modification of the stored health information without proper permission. The distributed ledgers in blockchain are immutable, hence the stored medical data cannot be modified easily. Availability of data is guaranteed due to the distribution property of blockchain, since the data are maintained locally with all active participants rather than storing it in a centralized server. Users cannot create fake blocks and the transactions are verified only by the miners. Unauthorized removal or modification of stored hash values of patient data is hard because of immutable ledger exploitation. A false ledger can be advertised by the attacker, the miners from outside organization is not permitted to generate and advertise the malicious block in the private blockchain network which is significantly followed in the health centres and hospitals.

Digital identity is maintained for all transactions by adopting public key cryptographic mechanisms. Hence, the real identity of patient's sensitive data can be hidden using this digital identity approach. The health data are transferred through multiple organizations, and it is required to be monitored persistently to prevent tampering information and to enhance the healthcare services. The convention supply chain management relies on a centralized approach, whereas the blockchain increases trust on transferring the sensitive data through diverse stakeholders by maintaining the distributed ledgers. By considering 51% attack, the probability of modifying data that is available in the health centres is likely less, and even 51% of miners try to compromise consensus protocols by creating a fake block [23].

8.5   Advantages of 5G-based architecture in SHS

Low-speed internet connectivity causes difficulty in downloading large size files and consumes more time for completing a task. Hence, there is a great impact among medical practitioners in providing healthcare services. It also limits several functionalities such as doctor-to-doctor communication, doctor-to-patient communication or suggesting telemedicine. 5G network reinforces healthcare services by enhancing the speed of internet connectivity in the digital platform. The American Medical Association (AMA) defines policies and regulations which supports rapid internet access and broadband extension. The patients in the rural region face numerous problems due to the absence of wireless and broadband connectivity. However, 5G technologies could be easily deployed in any kind of environment such as remote or rural areas. It brings huge benefits in the healthcare system including continuous remote monitoring, providing medicine on time, rapid data transmission and seamless downloading capability. 5G facilitates robot-based telesurgery by managing the data traffic in the network. 5G infrastructure allows medical practitioners to transfer the data instantaneously with the patients. Moreover, the patients are monitored in homes similar to taking ... intensive care units (ICUs).

The blockchain technologies potentially overcome the challenges faced regarding security- and privacy-related issues in SHS. Data infringement is the major concern in several digital services including smart healthcare services. For instance, suppose the patient is visiting a doctor for the first time and the doctor requires some knowledge regarding the medical history of the patient. And for sending medical prescription after treatment to a pharmacy requires access to the medical data which is already maintained in the electronic system. The exponential growth of patients' everyday results in huge volume of medical data. Moreover, it is highly difficult to store, manage, and process the medical information with the available healthcare facilities. The solution for this problem is fragmenting and managing the data by various agencies, however it is hard to have a control over the personal data access. MedRec enables secured data exchange with the Ethereum software which is considered as a more reliable platform when compared to bitcoin. Smart contract developed using Ethereum platform connects the healthcare professionals to share the data in a secured manner.

The security issues in the smart devices can be solved with the inherent features of blockchain technology include smart contract, decentralization, Peer-to-Peer (P2P) network, distributed ledger, consensus mechanisms and enhanced security. The major benefits of 5G network are lower latency, high bandwidth, high-speed data transmission, wide coverage and supporting virtual private network (VPN). The potential advantages of these technologies are described below:

- Manages and monitors clinical trial records efficiently with 5G-based blockchain system [24].
- Precision medicine is well affordable with the medical records maintained using 5G-based blockchain technology [25].
- Smart contracts in the Ethereum platform significantly improve the transparency of complete clinical trial records [26].
- Traceability of transaction records to identify the falsified drugs is pertinent with the Hyperledger and Ethereum platform, PBFT and delegated proof-of-stake (DPoS) in the public blockchain network [27].
- Improves medical data processing, transparency and traceability of clinical trial records using proof-of-concept mechanism [28].
- Regulates compliances for the government audit on the drug delivery transaction records using Gcoin (Consortium) platform and proof-of-work concept in the private blockchain network [29].

- Anti-counterfeits in the supply chain management system are stalked by adopting Radio Frequency Identification technology with proof-of-concept mechanism and Ethereum platform [30].
- Wireless body area network (WBAN) can be integrated with smart contract to secure the data in remote patient monitoring using proof-of-concept in the public blockchain network [31].
- Diagnosed (multimedia) data can be shared among medical practitioners in a secured way using Hyperledger and Ethereum platform in the private blockchain network [32].
- Data gathered from the sensor devices are secured using PoW consensus mechanism in the private blockchain network [33].
- Immutability and anonymity of sensor data is ensured in the public blockchain network [34].
- Mining overhead in Electronic Health Record (EHR), Electronic Medical Record (EMR) and Personal Health Record (PHR) is minimized [35–47].
- Privacy in health prediction model of medical records is enhanced using proof-of-information in the private blockchain network [48, 49].

8.6   Open research issues and challenges

There are several issues and challenges in adopting 5G-based blockchain technology in SHS [50–57]. The below-mentioned points support the new researchers by suggesting few research directions:

- Ensuring connectivity among several devices located far apart that covers a wide range and providing connectivity for high-mobility devices in the 5G network.
- Interoperability is a major concern among different devices due to the unavailability of common standardization [58] and communication among healthcare devices using distributed ledger is also difficult.
- Tamperproof medical data transmission is substantial.
- Devices to be exploited in SHS should consume less energy with low cost.
- Data produced by smart devices should be analysed by adopting efficient big data algorithms and techniques.
- Data secrecy and user privacy are the essential factors to be considered during data analysis.
- A secure communication between the cloud server and healthcare devices is significant to ensure authenticity and data integrity.
- Robust risk assessment policy should be defined to defend against various threats and vulnerabilities.
- Block mining in the blockchain technology is computationally intensive and requires more energy, processing time.
- Data sharing in PHR and EHR is limited in the private blockchain network.

- Data management in the Ethereum platform is practically not feasible.
- No exhaustive authorization and access control are considered in managing e-health personal data in the hyperledger platform.
- Interoperability is not examined among various healthcare parties in EMR and PHR which maintains the patient's personal clinical data.
- Scalability is a major concern in clinical records maintained using Ethereum platform.
- C.l........ l... .....l... .... .l..... .l.. .. achieved properly for provisioning better precision medicine.
- Patient identity in the physical and digital platform is imprecise in clinical records that limit traceability to some extent.
- Electronic product codes in RFID are assigned with a fixed value, which are exposed to attacks in copying the original product tag.
- Devices that are involved in 5G network should be compatible with high-speed connectivity and appropriate upgradation.
- It is highly challenging for manufacturers and service providers to adopt blockchain in healthcare sector by following legal compliances.

References

[1] Marakhimov A., Joo J. 'Consumer adaptation and infusion of wearable devices for healthcare'. *Computers in Human Behavior.* 2017;**76**(3):135–48.

[2] Dai H.-N., Zheng Z., Zhang Y. 'Blockchain for internet of things: a survey'. *IEEE Internet of Things Journal.* 2019;**6**(5):8076–94.

[3] Mettler M. Blockchain technology in healthcare: the revolution starts here. *2016 IEEE 18th International Conference on e-Health Networking, Applications and Services*; 2016 September. pp. 1–3.

[4] Nordrum A., Clark K. 'Everything you need to know about 5G'. *IEEE Spectrum.* 2017;**27**.

[5] Dat P.T., Kanno A., Yamamoto N., Kawanishi T. '5G transport networks: the need for new technologies and standards'. *IEEE Communications Magazine.* 2016;**54**(9):18–26.

[6] Hossain S. '5G wireless communication systems'. *American Journal of Engineering Research.* 2013;**2**(10):344–53.

[7] Latif S., Qadir J., Farooq S., Imran M. 'How 5G wireless (and concomitant technologies) will revolutionize healthcare?' *Future Internet.* 2017;**9**(4):93.

[8] Morocho-Cayamcela M.E., Lee H., Lim W. 'Machine learning for 5G/B5G mobile and wireless communications: potential, limitations, and future directions'. *IEEE Access.* 2019;**7**:137184–206.

[9] Das A.K., Wazid M., Kumar N., *et al.* Design of secure and lightweight authentication protocol for wearable devices environment'. *IEEE Journal of Biomedical and Health Informatics.* 2018;**22**(4):1310–22.

[10] Liu W., Liu H., Wan Y., Kong H., Ning H. 'The yoking-proof-based authentication protocol for cloud-assisted wearable devices'. *Personal and Ubiquitous Computing*. 2016;**20**(3):469–79.

[11] Das A.K., Wazid M., Kumar N., *et al.* Design of secure and lightweight authentication protocol for wearable devices environment'. *IEEE Journal of Biomedical and Health Informatics*. 2018;**22**(4):1310–22.

[12] Jiang Q., Qian Y., Ma J., Ma X., Cheng Q., Wei F. 'User centric three-factor authentication protocol for cloud-assisted wearable devices'. *International Journal of Communication Systems*. 2019;**32**(6):e3900.

[13] Bonomi F., Milito R., Zhu J., Addepalli S. Fog computing and its role in the internet of things. *Proceedings of the First Edition of the MCC Workshop on Mobile Cloud Computing*; 2012. pp. 13–16.

[14] Acharya V., Yerrapati A.E., Prakash N. 'Oracle blockchain quick start guide'. *A Practical Approach to Implementing Blockchain In Your Enterprise*. Packt Publishing Ltd; 2019.

[15] Mingxiao D., Xiaofeng M., Zhe Z., Xiangwei W., Qijun C. 'A review on consensus algorithm of blockchain'. *2017 IEEE International Conference on Systems, Man, and Cybernetics (SMC)*, October; 2017. pp. 2567–72.

[16] Jan M.A., Jan S.R.U., Alam M., Akhunzada A., Rahman I.U. 'A comprehensive analysis of congestion control protocols in wireless sensor networks'. *Mobile Networks and Applications*. 2018;**23**(3):456–68.

[17] Mwashita W., Odhiambo M.O. Interference management techniques for device-to-device communications. *Predictive Intelligence Using Big Data and the Internet of Things. IGI Global*; 2019. pp. 219–45.

[18] Li E.-L., Wang W.-J. '5G will drive the development of health care'. *Chinese Medical Journal*. 2019;**132**(23):2895.

[19] 5G explained - how 5g works. Available from http://www.emfexplained. info/?ID=25916 [Accessed Jan 2021].

[20] Larsson E.G. *Wireless Future: News, and Commentary*. Available from https://ma-mimo.ellintech.se/what-is-massive-mimo/ [Accessed Jun 201].

[21] Prasad K.N.R.S.V., Hossain E., Bhargava V.K. 'Energy efficiency in massive MIMO-based 5G networks: opportunities and challenges'. *IEEE Wireless Communications*. 2017;**24**(3):86–94.

[22] Salahuddin M.A., Al-Fuqaha A., Guizani M., Shuaib K., Sallabi F. 'Softwarization of internet of things infrastructure for secure and smart healthcare'. *arXiv preprint arXiv:1805*. 2018;**11011**.

[23] Ali M.S., Vecchio M., Pincheira M., Dolui K., Antonelli F., Rehmani M.H. 'Applications of blockchains in the internet of things: a comprehensive survey'. *IEEE Communications Society*. 2018.

[24] Choudhury O., Fairoza N., Sylla I., Das A. 'A blockchain framework for managing and monitoring data in multi-site clinical trials'. *arXiv*. 2019.

[25] Shae Z., Tsai J.J. 'On the design of a blockchain platform for clinical trial and precision medicine'. *Proceedings of the 2017 IEEE 37th International Conference on Distributed Computing Systems (ICDCS)*; Atlanta, GA, USA, 5–8 June; 2017. pp. 1972–80.

[26]   Nugent T., Upton D., Cimpoesu M. 'Improving data transparency in clinical trials using blockchain smart contracts'. *F1000Research*. 2016;**5**:2541.

[27]   Sylim P., Liu F., Marcelo A., Fontelo P. 'Blockchain technology for detecting falsified and substandard drugs in distribution: pharmaceutical supply chain intervention'. *JMIR Research Protocols*. 2018;**7**(9):e10163.

[28]   Benchoufi M., Porcher R., Ravaud P. 'Blockchain protocols in clinical trials: transparency and traceability of consent'. *F1000Research*. 2017;6:66.

[29]   Tseng J.-H., Liao Y.-C., Chong B., Liao S.-W. 'Governance on the drug supply chain via Gcoin blockchain'. *International Journal of Environmental Research and Public Health*. 2018;**15**(6):1055.

[30]   Toyoda K., Mathiopoulos P.T., Sasase I., Ohtsuki T. 'A novel blockchain-based product ownership management system (POMS) for anti-counterfeits in the post supply chain'. *IEEE Access*. 2017;**5**:17465–77.

[31]   Griggs K.N., Ossipova O., Kohlios C.P., Baccarini A.N., Howson E.A., Hayajneh T. 'Healthcare blockchain system using smart contracts for secure automated remote patient monitoring'. *Journal of Medical Systems*. 2018;**42**(7):130.

[32]   Rahman M.A., Hassanain E., Rashid M.M., Barnes S.J., Hossain M.S. 'Spatial blockchain-based secure mass screening framework for children with dyslexia'. *IEEE Access*. 2018;**6**:61876–85.

[33]   Jo B.W., Khan R.M.A., Lee Y.-S., Blockchain H. 'Hybrid blockchain and internet-of-things network for underground structure health monitoring'. *Sensors*. 2018;**18**(12):4268.

[34]   Saia R. 'Internet of entities (IoE): a blockchain-based distributed paradigm to security. arXiv 2018'. *ArXiv*. 1808;**08809**.

[35]   Esposito C., De Santis A., Tortora G., Chang H., Choo K.-K.R. 'Blockchain: a panacea for healthcare cloud-based data security and privacy?' *IEEE Cloud Computing*. 2018;**5**(1):31–7.

[36]   Tanwar S. *Fog Computing for Healthcare 4.0 Environments: Technical, Societal and Future Implications, Signals and Communication Technology*. Springer International Publishing; 2020. pp. 1–430.

[37]   Tanwar S. *Fog Data Analytics for IoT Applications – Next Generation Process Model with State-of-the-Art Technologies, Studies in Big Data*. Springer International Publishing; 2020. pp. 1–550.

[38]   Tanwar S., Tyagi S., Kumar N. *Security and Privacy of Electronics Healthcare Records the IET Book Series on e-Health Technologies, Institution of Engineering and Technology*. United Kingdom: Stevenage; 2019. pp. 1–450.

[39]   Mehta P., Gupta R., Tanwar S. 'Blockchain envisioned UAV networks: challenges, solutions, and comparisons'. *Computer Communications*. 2020;**151**(14):518–38.

[40]   Tanwar S., Bhatia Q., Patel P., Kumari A., Singh P.K., Hong W.-C. 'Machine learning adoption in blockchain-based smart applications: the challenges, and a way forward'. *IEEE Access*. 2020;**8**:474–88.

[41] Mistry I., Tanwar S., Tyagi S., Kumar N. 'Blockchain for 5G-enabled IoT for industrial automation: a systematic review, solutions, and challenges'. *Mechanical Systems and Signal Processing*. 2020;**135**(5):106382–19.

[42] Kabra N., Bhattacharya P., Tanwar S., Tyagi S. 'Mudrachain: blockchain-based framework for automated cheque clearance in financial institutions'. *Future Generation Computer Systems*. 2020;**102**(4):574–87.

[43] Bodkhe U., Tanwar S., Parekh K., *et al.* 'Blockchain for industry 4.0: a comprehensive review'. *IEEE Access*. 2020;**8**:79764–800.

[44] Tanwar S., Parekh K., Evans R. 'Blockchain-based electronic healthcare record system for healthcare 4.0 applications'. *Journal of Information Security and Applications*. 2019;**50**:1–14.

[45] Kumari A., Gupta R., Tanwar S., Kumar N. 'A taxonomy of blockchain-enabled softwarization for secure UAV network'. *Computer Communications*. 2020;**161**(12):304–23.

[46] Bodkhe U., Tanwar S. A taxonomy of secure data dissemination techniques in IoT environment. IET Software; 2020. pp. 1–10.

[47] Gupta R., Kumari A., Tanwar S., Kumar N. Blockchain-envisioned softwarized multi-swarming UAVs to tackle COVID-19 situations. *IEEE Network*; 2020. pp. 1–7.

[48] Kumari A., Tanwar S., Tyagi S., Kumar N. 'Blockchain-based massive data dissemination handling in IIoT environment'. *IEEE Network*. 2020;**35**(1):318–25.

[49] Kuo T.T., Ohno-Machado L. 'ModelChain: decentralized privacy-preserving healthcare predictive modeling framework on private blockchain networks. arXiv 2018'. *ArXiv*. 1802;**01746**.

[50] Gupta R., Kumari A., Tanwar S. A taxonomy of blockchain envisioned edge-as-a-connected autonomous vehicles: risk assessment and framework. *Transactions on Emerging Telecommunications Technologies*; 2020. pp. 1–23.

[51] Bodkhe U., Tanwar S., Bhattacharyaa P., Kumar N. Blockchain for precision irrigation: a systematic review. *Transactions on Emerging Telecommunications Technologies*; 2020. pp. 1–33.

[52] Kumari A., Gupta R., Tanwar S., Tyagi S., Kumari N. When blockchain meets smart grid: exploring demand response management for secure energy trading. *IEEE Network*; 2020. pp. 1–7.

[53] Kumari A., Gupta R., Tanwar S., Kumar N. 'Blockchain and AI amalgamation for energy cloud management: challenges, solutions, and future directions'. *Journal of Parallel and Distributed Computing*. 2020;**143**(11):148–66.

[54] Gupta R., Tanwar S., Kumar N., Tyagi S. 'Blockchain-based security attack resilience schemes for autonomous vehicles in industry 4.0: a systematic review'. *Computers & Electrical Engineering*. 2020;**86**(106717):1–15.

[55] Aggarwal S., Kumar N., Tanwar S. 'Blockchain envisioned UAV communication using 6G networks: open issues, use cases, and future directions'. *IEEE Internet of Things Journal*. 2020:1–26; In press.

[56] Akram S.V., Malik P.K., Singh R., Anita G., Tanwar S. 'Adoption of block-chain technology in various realms: opportunities and challenges'. *Security and Privacy Journal, Wiley.* 2020:1–17.

[57] Bhattacharya P., Tanwar S., Bodkhe U., Tyagi S., Kumar N. 'BinDaaS: block-chain integrated deep-learning as-a-service in healthcare 4.0 applications'. *IEEE Transactions on Network Science and Engineering.* 2019;**8**(2):1242–55.

[58] Akpakwu G.A., Silva B.J., Hancke G.P., Abu-Mahfouz A.M, 'A survey on 5G networks for the internet of things: communication technologies and chal-lenges'. *IEEE Access.* 2017;**6**:3619–47.

Chapter 9

Application of millimeter wave (mmWave)-based device-to-device (D2D) communication in 5G healthcare

Anant Sinha[1], Sachin Kumar[1], and Pooja Khanna[1]

According to the recent statistics provided by Global Health Observatory (GHO), approximately 40% member states of WHO have ten or less doctors available per 10 000 persons in a population, statistics depict uneven distribution of health workers across the globe. On the world map, African region faces 22% of the global disease hit but has access to only 3% of health workers. Indian economic survey 2018--19 reveals that health facilities are still inaccessible in rural areas of India. The digital healthcare system can bridge this gap between health-care services and consumers, but it has its own limitations in terms of connectivity of infrastructure. To enhance reachability and to virtualize the health-care system, industries across the globe are heading towards the deployment of 5G. The 5G facilitates the exchange of highly secure data in real-time required for health services and to support decision-making. Device-to-Device (D2D) communication is one of the key technologies that enhances the 5G performance. D2D often refers to the technology that allows User Equipment (UE) to communicate with or without network infrastructures, such as an access point or base stations. The direct communication mode requires half of the resources compared to the cellular communication mode, thus offering double spectral efficiency per connection. To enhance the network performance and meet the bandwidth requirements, D2D can be integrated with millimeter wave (mmWave) technology. mmWave provides high throughput and allows the efficient use of spectrum as frequencies can be reused over relatively small distances. Wireless Body Area Network (WBAN) is emerging as a rapidly growing wireless technology. The role of WBANs in digital healthcare and telemedicine is highly crucial and sensitive. Thus, it requires to ensure high data speed and uninterrupted communication. The chapter proposes mmWave-based D2D communication for the implementation of an efficient and secure WBAN.

Keywords: Millimeter Wave, Device to Device, Digital healthcare, 5G, Wireless Body Area Network (WBAN), Telemedicine

[1]Amity University, Lucknow Campus, Lucknow, India

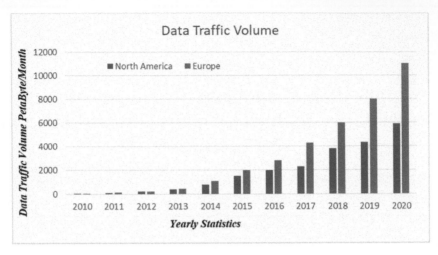

Figure 9.1   Traffic in the cellular system from 2010 to 2020 [1]

9.1   Introduction

The increased usage of multimedia services has driven the necessity of wireless communication technologies and has led to an exponential rise in wireless traffic and volume, as depicted in Figure 9.1 [1]. Over the years 2010–20, the traffic in cellular system in the highly developed communication societies (Western Europe and North America) has increased by a factor of 84. With its innovative technologies, 5G communication system is capable of fulfilling the demands of the users far beyond the currently available technologies. The 5G networks are heterogeneous (Het Nets), i.e., different networks all integrated into a unified system enable the aggregation of existing Radio Access technologies (RATs) [2]. The 5G architecture provides a suitable, programmable, and flexible infrastructure for networking, storage resources, and computing. This allows for more dynamic, efficient, and optimized utilization of resources. 5G is designed to be a viable, robust, and scalable technology and involves vertical markets, such as healthcare, manufacturing, food, and agriculture, etc.

Dominating application classes of 5G technology are massive Machine Type Communication (mMTC), enhanced Mobile Broadband (eMBB), and Ultra-Reliable and Low Latency Communication (URLLC). These classes facilitate the scenarios associated with applications that demand the realization of industry 4.0 and the Internet of Things (IoT) [3].

9.1.1   5G: features

1. **Network Slicing:** The process in which the network architecture enables the multiplexing of independent networks on the same physical infrastructure is known as network slicing. Each slice is an end-to-end network that is configured

to fulfill the requirements of a particular application. Network slicing is an emerging technique to maintain the Quality of Service (QoS) [4].

2. **Mobile Edge Computing:** Also known as Multi-access Edge Computing (MEC), it is a network architecture concept defined by ETSI that enables the IT services and cloud computing capabilities at the edge of the network. The basic idea of MEC is to reduce network congestion and enhance the performance of the application. MEC facilitates the rapid deployment of new services for non carriers. MEC is implemented at the cellular base station [4, 5].

3. **Network Function Virtualization (NFV):** NFV is based on Software-Defined Networking (SDN). It is utilized to minimize service deployment time and increases the overall network flexibility [5].

4. **Novel Multiple Access Schemes** Non-Orthogonal Multiple Access (NOMA) is one of the Novel Multiple Access Scheme. NOMA uses cancellation techniques to remove the more powerful signals [5].

9.2   Introduction to D2D communication technology

The primary objective behind the evolution of the 5G cellular wireless network is to provide high throughput, low end-to-end latency, efficient utilization of spectrum, and less energy consumption. One of the key technologies required to enhance 5G performance is D2D. It establishes a direct communication link between User Equipment (UEs) that are in proximity. D2D does not require a signal to travel through a core network or Base Station (BS) [5, 6]. Owing to the short signal transverse path, D2D offers ultra-low latency in communication. As compared to cellular communication infrastructure, only half of the resources are required in D2D communication; hence, double spectral efficiency per connection can also be achieved. The transmission power level will be lower, which will ultimately lead to battery saving in the device [6]. There are three ways in which users can communicate in D2D. Based on the licensed and unlicensed spectrum resources utilization, D2D communication can be divided into outband D2D and inband D2D [6].

1. **Outband D2D:** Unlicensed spectrum is utilized by D2D communication, due to which the interference between D2D link and cellular link can be avoided. Outband D2D can be further subdivided into controlled and autonomous communication. In controlled outband D2D, cellular networks control the coordination between radio interfaces. In autonomous outband D2D, cellular network does not control D2D communication [7].

2. **Inband D2D:** Licensed spectrum is utilized by D2D communication, which is also allotted to the cellular communication network. Inband D2D can be further subdivided into overlay and underlay inband D2D. A comparison between outband and inband D2D is illustrated in Figure 9.2.

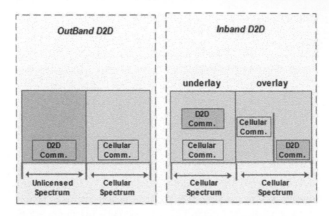

Figure 9.2   Outband vs. inband D2D communication [6]

9.2.1   D2D-assisted cellular communication

D2D communication in cellular networks facilitates multiple performance benefits. As depicted in Figure 9.3 [9], the communication between two devices U-1 and U-2 is more efficient when there is a direct link between the two as compared to routing the communication between the two through BS-1. As compared to the traditional cellular communication network, which exploits both uplink and downlink resources, D2D communication utilizes less energy and offers higher spectral efficiency [8, 9].

Another significant benefit of D2D communication is an extension of the coverage. U-6 can transmit data via U-5 by establishing a D2D communication link even though it is out of the coverage area for base stations [8].

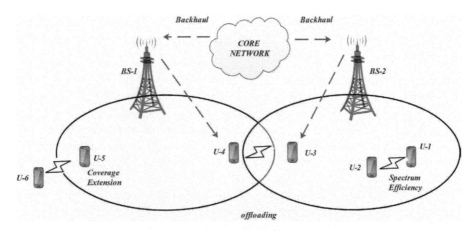

Figure 9.3   Benefits of D2D communication [8]

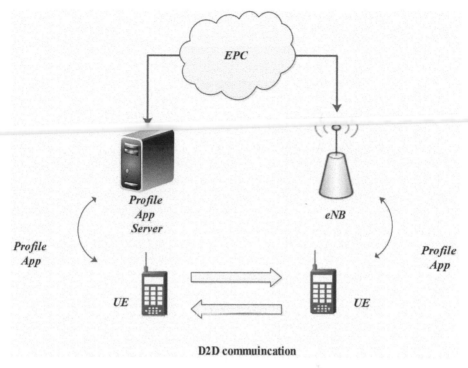

D2D commuincation

Figure 9.4   *D2D communication model based on ProSe architecture [10]*

9.2.2   D2D communication in LTE advanced

The Third Generation Partnership Project (3GPP) introduces the general concept of Proximity-based Services (ProSe). ProSe utilizes a global LTE structure to support direct communication link between devices; hence, it is also known as LTE direct. The ProSe architecture-based simplified model for D2D communication is depicted in Figure 9.4 [10].

In *ProSe*, base station is known as Evolved Node B (eNB) in 3GPP, which is connected to the Evolved Packet Core (EPC), can directly communicate with UE through cellular communication. In addition, there can be a direct communication between UEs via the D2D link. The direct link between the two UEs is known as a sidelink in terms of the channel structure. For the synchronization of UE with eNB or other UEs, several signals are defined in 3GPP. Various ProSe applications can be installed in UEs, and those applications can exchange data from a remote ProSe APP server. When a UE tries to initiate communication with peer UEs, then its ProSe APP requests an expression code for itself and for the UE with which it has to establish communication. After the allocation of expression codes, the discovery procedure is initiated by the UE in which it inquires regarding the presence of target UE. The direct communication link is established once the target device is discovered [10].

9.2.3   Technical aspects of D2D communication

1. **Synchronization:** This is an important aspect in D2D communication, as it enables UEs to choose appropriate slots of time and frequency to communicate with peers, thus facilitating more energy-efficient communication. In cellular communication networks, a periodic broadcast from the base station is utilized for the time and frequency synchronization of UEs. Still, synchronization can be challenging when UEs belong to different base stations when some UEs are not in the network coverage area. In a D2D communication network, there is no need for global synchronization between UEs. Rather local synchronization between peers is required. Complex algorithms are involved in achieving accurate synchronization in D2D communication [10, 11].
2. **Peer Discovery:** This is used when UEs can quickly navigate their nearby peers to establish a communication link. There are two types of techniques to discover peers: restricted and open. In the restricted technique, the end-user cannot find the device without its permission. On the other hand, the available device permission is not required in open technique, it automatically gets discovered when it is in proximity [12].
3. **Resource Allocation:** To establish a direct link between D2D communication pairs (more specifically, in inband mode), resource allocation is a necessary procedure. In inband architecture, two orthogonal portions of the uplink spectrum are created. The fraction η is allocated to D2D communication, and $(1-\eta)$ is allocated to cellular communication. The underlay spectrum is divided into B bands. UEs can randomly choose βB ($\beta \in [0, 1]$) of them. The η and β can be determined by assuming that UEs are distributed according to a random process. The selection of the model depends on the distance between UE and its target user [12].
4. **Interference Management:** D2D cellular links may interfere with each other in inband communication depending on their spectrum sharing. In outband communication, D2D links interfere with each other and with other devices operating in the same frequency range. Although UEs may transmit signals at lower power, there is a possibility that interference may be reduced, but this may lead to the degradation of the QoS of the receiver [12].

9.2.4   mmWave for D2D communication

Despite potential advantages of D2D communication, several challenges are encountered in the large-scale implementation, such as interference and insufficient bandwidth in the microwave band [13]. A feasible solution to address this challenge is, utilization of the millimeter-wave (mmWave) band for D2D communications. Since the unlicensed spectrum is abundant in mmWave, the scarcity of spectrum will no longer remain a significant issue. The mmWave communication occupies a frequency range of 30 to 300 GHz. The propagation characteristics of mmWave are not the same as those of microwave frequencies, in general, the overall loss in mmWave is much more significant as compared to microwave. The comparison of mmWave and microwave is illustrated in Table 9.1 [14].

Owing to small wavelength of mmWave, large number of smaller aperture antenna elements can be deployed, which improves spatial diversity and minimize path loss. Deployment of multiple antennas, facilitates Multiple-Inputs Multiple-Output (MIMO) communication in mmWave [15]. MIMO is one of the effective techniques to improve link-level channel performance. This system facilitates spatial multiplexing, i.e., different antenna elements are used to transmit independent information signals. The outgoing stream of a signal is divided into multiple pieces. Each piece will be transmitted simultaneously over the same RF channel but through different antennas. There should be sufficient decorrelation between closely located antenna elements [15, 16].

9.2.5 *mmWave communication features*

1. **Beamforming:** It is defined as a process used to control the amplitude and phase of the transmitted and received signals as per the specific application and channel environment. Installation of multiple antennas at the transmitter and the receiver end improves the overall performance of the communication system. This enhanced performance is achieved by using beamforming, which is realized through Channel State Information (CSI). In wireless communication, CSI defines the properties of a channel in a communication link [16]. CSI conveys information regarding how the signal propagates through a channel and represents the combined effect of scattering, power loss, fading, etc. The maximum benefits from the performance of the beamformer can be achieved only when each pair of transmitting and receiving antenna experiences fading independently. This can be achieved by maintaining $\lambda/2$ distance between the two consecutive antenna elements, here λ represents the wavelength [17].

2. **Spatial Multiplexing:** This is also known as space-division multiplexing, and is a multiplexing technique that is used in MIMO wireless communication. Spatial multiplexing facilitates multiple transmission simultaneously. Each spatial channel contains independent information, this increases the throughput of the communication system without manipulating the frequency and transmitting power. Figure 9.5 [17] shows a spatial multiplexing system. A matrix of channels is formed, where each transmitting antenna transmits different data streams while all the receiving antenna receives all the transmitted data streams.

   In Figure 9.5, Nt and Nr represent the number of transmitting and receiving antennas, respectively. The rank of the matrix $\{Nt, Nr\}$ will give the minimum number of data streams that can be transmitted or received over the MIMO system [17].

3. **Atmospheric Absorption:** The size of a rain drop is approximately equal to the wavelength of mmWave, which causes scattering. Scattering causes the signal to deviate from its original path. If the cell size is 200 m, then rain attenuation and atmospheric absorption will not introduce additional path loss. mmWave characteristics at different frequencies are depicted in Table 9.2 [17].

Table 9.1   *mm-Wave vs. microwave [14]*

	mmwave frequency	Microwave frequency
Frequency band	30–300 GHz	300 MHz–30 GHz
Wavelength	10–1 mm	1–0.1 m
Bandwidth	Ultra high	High
Antenna size/weight	Smaller due to very short wavelength	Large especially at the lower part of the band
Coverage	Suitable for short distance	Long distance application especially at 4–13 GHz band
System gain	Very high gain	High gain
Attenuation	High during rainfall	Good resistance to rain at lower frequencies
Peak rate	10–100 Gbps	1–5 Gbps
Frequency reuse option	Suitable for frequency reuse	Frequency reuse is likely to cause interference
Application	Radar, mmWave imaging, medicine, mmWave scanning	Radio and TV broadcasting,cellular telephony, satellite and terrestrial comm, radar navigation

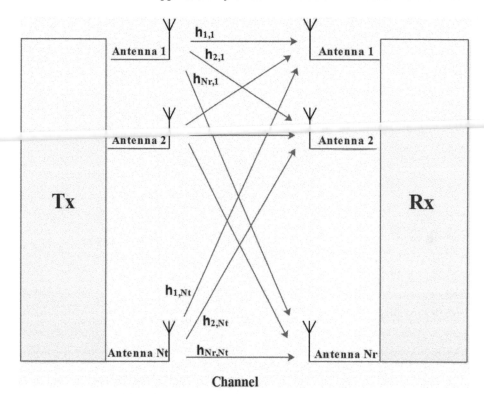

Figure 9.5   Spatial multiplexing scheme [17]

9.3   Introduction to WBAN

For applications, such as e-healthcare and telemedicine, WBAN is emerging as an exponentially growing wireless technology. The applications of WBAN have gained tremendous interest for researchers in recent years.

According to Allied Business Intelligence (ABI), a research organization, "the market for the health-care monitoring electronics devices will attain a

Table 9.2   mmWave characteristics at different frequencies [17]

		28 GHz	38 GHz	60 GHz	73 GHz
Path loss exponent	LOS scenario	1.8–1.9	1.9–2.0	2.23	2
	NLOS scenario	4.5–4.6	2.7–3.8	4.19	2.45–2.69
Rain attenuation at 200 m	5 mm/h	0.18 db	0.26 db	0.44 db	0.6 db
	25 mm/h	0.9 db	1.4 db	2 db	2.4 db
Oxygen absorption at 200 m		0.04 db	0.03 db	3.2 db	0.09 db

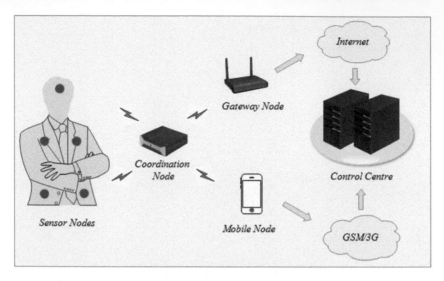

Figure 9.6   WBAN architecture [19]

compound annual growth rate of 77% in the next few years." The body area net-work market is projected to grow from USD 9.1 billion in 2019 to USD 15.8 billion by 2024 [18]. WBANs are highly efficient in real-time monitoring of human health. These are capable of transferring biological signals generated in the human body to the doctor and facilitate instant medical diagnosis. A WBAN typically consists of miniature and lightweight biological sensor components. Sensors that are used for real-time health monitoring can be either a physiological sensor or a biokinetic sen-sor. Physiological sensors are used to determine vital parameters of the human body (internal or external), such as body temperature, blood pressure, Electrocardiogram (ECG), etc. In contrast, biokinetic sensors are used to detect movements of the body.

In addition, ambient sensors can sense the surrounding environment parameters, such as humidity, temperature, etc. The sensors can be implanted directly into the human body or integrated into smart patches or clothing [18, 19]. A simple WBAM architecture is depicted in Figure 9.6 [19]. As shown in the Figure 9.6, the architec-ture is divided into four sections.

The first section consists of sensor nodes deployed on the human body to mea-sure vital health parameters. Sensors chosen for the deployment on a human body should satisfy the following conditions: wearability, interoperability, security, and reliability. The second section is known as the coordination node. It consists of the Central Control Unit (CCU). All sensor nodes are directly connected to CCU. A CCU is responsible for extracting data from the sensors and transferring it to the next section. The third section acts as a gateway node for transmitting the extracted data to the destination [19]. The last section is the control center, responsible for the storage and analysis of data. The WBAN scheme is depicted in Figure 9.7 [19].

Telemedicine is one of the most popular applications of WBAN. Telemedicine network is responsible for delivering health-care services to patients residing in

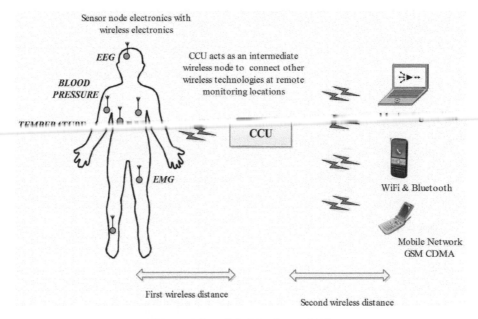

Figure 9.7   WBAN scheme [19]

remote areas where the healthcare services are inaccessible. Telemedicine can provide medical assistance, diagnosis, and prescription from a doctor or a healthcare professional sitting thousands of kilometers away. The chances of recovery improve significantly when the diagnosis is right and timely treatment is given. WBANs are also applicable in the performance monitoring of athletes. A trainer can keep track of the performance data of his trainee. The applications of WBAN can be further extended to the military and space. The wearable sensors can be used to monitor the status and condition of soldiers and astronauts. Deployment of WBAN for helping physically disabled people is another important application [19, 20].

9.3.1   Wireless personal area network (WPAN)/wireless local area network (WLAN)

WLAN/WPAN are low power and short-range networks used to construct a small network for data exchange. These technologies can be utilized to build low-cost wireless sensor networks, such as WBAN. Some of the currently available technologies used to build small-scale wireless sensor networks are shown in Table 9.3 [21].

Bluetooth and Zigbee are used for short-range applications, whereas WiFi is generally used for long-range applications and thus consumes more power. WBAN generally utilizes WPAN platform, which is available commercially. The required distance between the sensor and the control unit in WBAN is very small. In most of the applications based on WBAN, sensor nodes are required to send data at a lesser rate, about one physiological signal at a time. Generally, small frequency

Table 9.3   Current technologies to build wireless sensor network [21]

		Date rate	Range	Standard	Transmission power
Bluetooth	2.4 GHz	Upto 1 Mbps	1-100 m	IEEE 802.15.1, WPAN	1–100 mW
Zigbee	2.4 GHz Worldwide 868/915 Europe/ US	Upto 250 Kbps	0-10 m	IEEE 802.15.4, WPAN	1–10 mW
WiFi	2.4 GHz 5GHz	Upto 400 Mbps	300 m	IEEE 802.11 (b/g/n)	250–1000 mW
6 LoWPAN	2.4 GHz	250 Kbps	30 m	IEEE 802.15.4/ IETF	~10 mW

components are occupied by a physiological signal [21, 22]. The most commonly used biological signals in WBAN applications are shown in Table 9.4 [22].

In addition to wearable sensors, implanted sensors are also used in WBAN applications; capsule endoscopy is one of the examples. All the sensors depicted in Table 9.4 require low data transmission rate except retina implant and electronic pills. The sensor requires a high data rate of around 10 Mbps for the delivery of good quality video from inside the body.

9.3.2   WBAN design requirements

The nature of application and customer requirement, decide the QoS that WBAN as a technology can offer. In health-care applications, low latency and high reliability are expected from a WBAN. The coordination of data transmission from sensors can be controlled by appropriate medium access control protocols [23]. Routers or

Table 9.4   Commonly used biological signals [22]

	Implantable
Electrocardiogram (ECG)	Pacemaker
Heart rate	Cochlear implants
Electromyography (EMG)	Implantable defibrillator
Temperature	Wireless capsule endoscope
Pulse oximeter	Electronic pill (for drug delivery)
Blood pressure	Deep brain stimulator
Oxygen, pH value	Retina implants
Glucose sensor	
Movement (accelerometer)	

multi-hop networks can extend the WBAN range, thus connecting WBAN to external networks and allowing data transmission to a longer distance[24]. A modular design approach is adopted in the development of WBAN set-up for long-distance applications. Common design attributes of a WBAN system are as follows:

- Sensors in a WBAN should transfer data over a short distance by using a single-hop connection.
- The dimensions of sensor   should be as minimum as possible so that they   be wearable.
- To avoid interference with nearby networks, appropriate frequency bands should be used.
- To ensure longer battery life, sensor nodes should consume less power.
- WBAN system should be designed in such a way that the failure or malfunctioning of any sensor can be detected easily, and it should not affect the overall network operation.

In order to meet these specifications, following points should be taken into consideration.

1. **Reliable Data Transmission:** For accurate medical diagnosis, the data provided by sensors must be error-free and reliable. To achieve maximum accuracy, efficient error detection and correction mechanisms should be adopted.
2. **Security and Privacy:** Protocols should be developed so that the data are inaccessible to intruders. Robust encryption methodologies should be developed.
3. **Gateway Devices:** These devices should be utilized to interfere with sensor nodes with existing wireless communication networks used in medical applications.

9.3.3   mmWave in WBAN

Currently, the available WBAN systems operate on a 2.4-GHz frequency band, but this frequency band is now occupied by other technologies also, such as WiFi, Bluetooth, etc. WBANs are becoming increasingly popular, and resources available in 2.4-GHz band are limited. Hence, the most feasible solution is to switch from a 2.4-GHz band to a higher frequency band, such as 60 GHz [25]. There have been some studies to compare the 2.4 and 60 GHz bands. Carrier Interference Ratio (CIR) is one of the significant parameters used for comparison. CIR computes the ratio of the amount of information transmitted successfully to information loss during transmission through the network[26]. Figure 9.8 shows the interference between two WBANs in the same area operating under the 2.4-GHz band.

Although, the 60-GHz band has many advantages, the strength of the 60-GHz signal is significantly affected by environmental factors by interrupting the line of sight, thus causing blocking [25, 27].

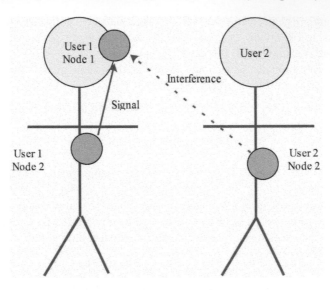

Figure 9.8   Interference in WBAN [25]

9.4   5G-based internet of medical things

Internet of medical things (IoMT) facilitate efficient data transfer over the wireless network without involving human to machine or human to human interaction. According to Gartner Research and Advisory Company, 20.4 billion devices will be connected to the Internet by 2020 [28]. An IoMT mainly comprises electronic circuits and sensors capable of acquiring biomedical signals from the human body, processing of signals, and transmitting them over the network. As per application requirement, IoMT may also consist of an Artificial Intelligence module for real-time decision-making. The bulky size of the conventionally available remote health monitoring systems attached to the body cause discomfort to the patient. This issue was resolved by the revolution that IoMT brought, as devices developed here are ultra-small and have low-power sensors. The remote health monitoring system comprises a Portable Patient Monitoring Unit (PPMU) installed at the patient's place or in a medical service vehicle and a real-time monitoring system at the hospital [29, 30]. The diagrammatic representation of PPMU is shown in Figure 9.9 [29].

The remote monitoring systems for general diseases can be summarized as:

1. **Remote monitoring system for heart-related diseases:** Diseases, such as arrhythmia, which are hidden and do not surface until later, can be revealed from the signals received from the heart. Generally, ECG electrodes are attached to the chest to receive physiological signals. After digitizing, conditioning, and processing, the signals will be sent to the central server (remote server or a cloud-based server). There is a web page that acts as a graphical user interface

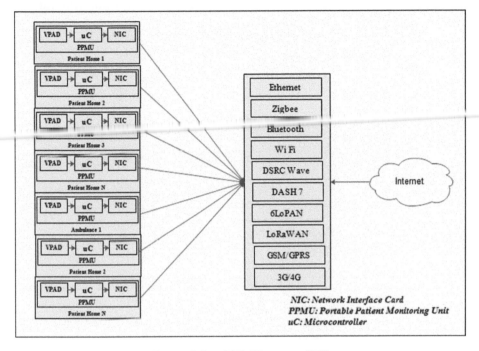

Figure 9.9   PPMU system [29]

for the doctor. Based on the received signals, the doctor can make real-time decisions according to the data displayed on the GUI [30, 31].

2. **Remote monitoring system for neurological diseases:** Remote monitoring system for brain-related disorders serves as a great comfort for the patients suffering from Alzheimer's, stroke, or Parkinson. The sensors employed for data acquisition are either contact-based or contact-less. The most commonly used sensors in the signal acquisition node [31] are EEG sensors, galvanic skin response sensors, wristwatches with integrated multi-sensors, Salivary Alpha-Amylase bio-sensors, etc.

3. **Remote monitoring system for diabetes patients**: The sugar levels of diabetic patients need to be monitored periodically in order to ensure controlled glucose levels. Although many devices are available in the market for measuring sugar levels at home, such devices cannot provide real-time monitoring taking physician into loop simultaneous. IoMT makes this task possible by measuring sugar levels with smart nodes and making data available to the doctor for real-time consultancy through the web or mobile application [31].

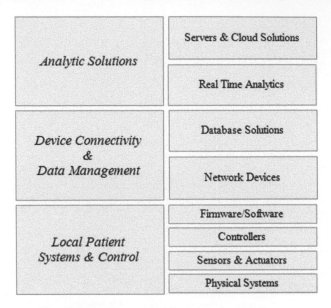

Figure 9.10   IoMT architecture [32]

9.4.1   IoMT architecture

There are three layers in the macro-level IoMT architecture—local devices, connectivity, and data analytics. The architectural block diagram is depicted in Figure 9.10 [32].

1. **Local system and control layer:** The fundamental attribute of an IoMT system is its decentralized intelligence, i.e., designing and developing medical devices with intelligent control capabilities. This will help in the local level processing of operational data. These devices usually consist of sensors to acquire operational parameters, analog to digital converter to produce digital inputs, and a network interface for sharing data with central servers and other machines. Encrypting devices, encoders, and actuators perform transformations in data and transmit it to the next layer for further analysis [32].
2. **Device connectivity and data layer:** This layer is responsible for acquiring data from sensors and other devices in the network and storing it in predefined data servers. Throughout the process, the quality is ensured by the secured medical data transfer technologies. Networking firms, such as Cisco and Oracle are pretty active in providing such advanced technologies [32].
3. **Analytic solution layer:** The central or remote server collects data from multiple devices in a network irrespective of the type of health-care solution. The server is equipped with an in-built algorithm that provides insight and conclusion from the data. This helps in diagnosing diseases and implementing preventive measures [32].

9.5 Open issues

9.5.1 Security issues in 5G-D2D-based WBAN

The mechanism of pre-shared keys cannot be applied in WBAN as it involves many devices. To define security policies and for the distribution of pre-shared keys, there is no central administration in WBAN. Here the keys are generated dynamically by IoT nodes when the network is formed. The process of dynamic key generation is not feasible in group based communication where either all the devices are provided with an identical key, or each pair may have different keys [33]. Secure D2D communication should satisfy the following conditions:

1. **Identity management, authentication, and authorization of medical devices:** Owing to direct communication between WBAN node and authentication process, management of identity is a significant issue. Any malicious device can create multiple fake identities and pretend to be a legitimate device. Hence, there is a need for mutual authentication between devices [34].
2. **Availability and dependability:** Wireless network must be accessible to any authorized D2D user anytime and anywhere, even when there is a DDoS or DoS attack. Since there is no centralized infrastructure, it is more challenging to identify DoS attacks in a D2D network. For example, a simple jamming attack can hamper the communication between two D2D users [34].
3. **Secure routing and transmission:** Information should be exchanged in a secure environment between D2D users when adversaries are present. Moreover, the transmission of the message from sender to receiver and modification in the information must be prohibited [34].
4. **Integrity:** It prevents modification and falsification, and provides reliable and accurate information exchange among D2D users. However, if an attacker compromises a node and launches a malicious attack, the integrity gets violated [34]. The possible attacks in D2D networks are summarized in Table 9.5 [35].

9.5.2 Propagation losses in mmWave communication

Environmental factors contribute largely at higher frequencies. In the GHz band, atmosphere is a medium of propagation with constituents, such as suspended droplets of water, oxygen molecules, fog, etc. These constituents absorb the mmWave signal and cause attenuation. Also, GHz range signals are susceptible to attenuation due to rain [36, 37].

It is observed that in e-band at 75 GHz, the signal suffered 0.4 dB loss due to drizzling, and tropical rain causes a loss of about 30 dB [38, 39]. Thus, attenuation increases with an increase in the intensity of rain. In addition to rain attenuation, atmospheric absorption is also an impediment challenge in mmWave communication [40].

9.5.3 Impact of mmWave radiations on human health

Earlier, we have discussed the potential benefits of transmitting data in the frequency range of 30 to 300 GHz. However, it is essential to analyze the effects, that exposure

Table 9.5   Possible attacks in D2D networks [35]

No.	Attack	Description
1	Denial of service	The attacker attempts to disrupt the communication by flooding the messages in the channel.
2	Man-in-the-middle attack	The attacker sniffs the information exchanged between sender and receiver.
3	Masquerading	The attacker uses a false identity and pretends to be an authenticated user.
4	Impersonation	The attack is launched by using the identity of another mobile user.
5	IP spoofing	IP information, especially the header, is manipulated by the attacker.
6	Bandwidth spoofing	Unauthorized access to the bandwidth.
7	Jamming	Transmitted messages are lost or corrupted.
8	Malware attack	A malicious virus is introduced in the network, which can target operating systems and user applications.

to mmWave communication may have on environment and people. mmWave radiations are non-ionizing, unlike other higher frequencies, such as X-rays, gamma rays, etc. This signifies that the smallest unit of mmWave does not have enough energy to pull out the electron from its orbit. Being non-ionizing is the phenomenon associated with development of cancer. Thus, the primary concern is the heating effect on human skin and eyes caused due to the absorption of mmWave. The government has set up different standards and guidelines that specify the amount of power to be transmitted at different frequencies keeping the heating effect minimum.

Owing to the short wavelength, the penetration of mmWave radiations in the human body is less as compared to microwaves. The penetration of mmWave is limited to the outer layer of human body, i.e., skin and eyes. The two significant standards used to control the thermal effect of mmWave radiation are Power Density (PD) and Specific Absorption Rate (SAR). A 24-GHz system operating at the maximum allowed radiated power just 5 cm away from a human body will have a PD value of 0.3 mW/cm^2 below the maximum limit [37]. Moist and aqueous tissues absorb more energy. Hence, the two primary layers of skin (epidermis and dermis) absorbs about 80% of energy. Several studies suggest that the conductivity of skin increases with increasing frequency.

On the other hand, some theories state that skin conductivity varies with the level of water content. For example, the level of water is less in the human palm and wrist and thus offers lower conductivity. The heat in the skin is related to the blood flow, and as per the available literature, the blood flow in the eyes is comparatively low, the eyes are therefore more vulnerable to thermal effects [41, 42].

9.6   Conclusion

Existing communication techniques are not able to meet the required QoS for addressing complex and dynamic requirements of smart health-care services; however, 5G network with features, such as reliability, high bandwidth, low latency, and increased energy efficiency can be the potential solution. Solutions proposed for smart health-care services are expected to be a functional mixture of 5G network and 5G communication techniques. These services are supposed to be equipped with enhanced cellular coverage, improved performance, and well-secured network. This chapter aims to elucidate on the applications of D2D communication in the implementation of a 5G-based real-time health monitoring systems. Detailed emphasis has been given to the exploitation of a mmWave band for D2D communication. The work presented here covers significant features of 5G, that makes it a frontier of innovation and gives it an edge over the other available technologies. An extensive overview of D2D architecture, applications, advantages, and challenges has been presented. The concept of a WBAN has been addressed, and the construction of a body area network by deploying D2D communication technology has been illustrated. Advantages of mmWave over microwave are also discussed extensively along with the summary of key technologies that enable mmWave-based 5G communication systems, such as spatial multiplexing and MIMO beamforming. The chapter further covers the IoMT for applications in remote health monitoring of various common diseases, finally open issues and technical challenges encountered while implementing 5G-based health-care systems have been addressed.

References

[1]   Ezhirpavai R. *The four key factors to focus on for successful 5G deployments*. 2019. Available from https://www.rcrwireless.com/20190214/opinion/readerforum/successful-5g-deployments-reader-forum [Accessed Feb 14].

[2]   Oladejo S.O., Falowo O.E. '5G network slicing: a multi-tenancy scenario'. *Proceedings of 2017 Global Wireless Summit*. 2017.

[3]   Wei H., Zhang Z.F., Fan B. 'Network slice access selection scheme in 5G'. *Proceedings of IEEE 2nd Information Technology Networking Electronic and Automation Control Conf. (ITNEC)*; 2018. pp. 52406–20.

[4]   Chio Y., Park N. 'Support for edge computing in 5G network'. *Proceedings of Tenth International Conference on Ubiquitous and Future Networks (ICUFN)*; 2018.

[5]   Tanwar S., Kumar N., Niu J.-W. 'EEMHR: energy-efficient multilevel heterogeneous routing protocol for wireless sensor networks'. *International Journal of Communication Systems*. 2014;**27**(9):1289–318.

[6]   Ordonez-Lucena J., Ameigeiras P., Lopez D., Ramos-Munoz J.J., Lorca J., Folgueira J. 'Network slicing for 5G with SDN/NFV: concepts, architectures, and challenges'. *IEEE Communications Magazine*. 2017;**55**(5):80–7.

[7]   Fan Q., Ansari N. 'Application aware workload allocation for edge computing-based IoT'. *IEEE Internet of Things Journal*. 2018;**5**(3):2146–53.

[8]   Sun X., Ansari N. 'Edgeiot: mobile edge computing for the internet of things'. *IEEE Communications Magazine*. 2016;**54**(12):22–9.

[9]   Li X., Li D., Wan J., Liu C., Imran M. 'Adaptive transmission optimization in SDN-based industrial internet of things with edge computing'. *IEEE Internet of Things Journal*. 2018;**5**(3):1351–60.

[10]   Sigwele T., Hu Y.F., Susanto M., *et al.* 'Intelligent and energy efficient mobile smartphone gateway for healthcare smart devices based on 5G'. *IEEE Proceedings of the Global Communications Conference*; 2018.

[11]   Kiss P., Reale A., Ferrari C., *et al.* 'Deployment of IoT applications on 5G edge'. *Proceedings of 2018 IEEE International Conference on Future IoT Technologies (Future IoT)*; 2018.

[12]   Karvonen H., Hämäläinen M., Iinatti J., *et al.* 'Coexistence of wireless technologies in medical scenarios'. *Proceedings of 2017 European Conference on Networks and Communications (EuCNC)*; 2017.

[13]   AbdElnapi N., Omran N. 'A survey of the internet of things technologies and projects for healthcare services'. *Proceedings of International Conference on Innovation Trends in Computer Engineering (ITCE2018)*; 2018.

[14]   Chen M., Yang J., Zhou J., Hao Y., Zhang J., Youn C.-H. '5G-smart diabetes: toward personalized diabetes diagnosis with healthcare big data clouds'. *IEEE Communications Magazine*. 2018;**56**(4):16–23.

[15]   Rehman M., Nasralla A.A. 'Small cell-based ambulance scenario for medical video streaming: A 5G-health use case'. *Proceedings of 15th International Conference on Smart Cities: Improving Quality of Life Using ICT & IoT (HONET-ICT)*; 2018.

[16]   Hossain M.S., Muhammad G. 'Emotion-aware connected healthcare big data towards 5G'. *IEEE Internet of Things Journal*. 2018;**5**(4):2399–406.

[17]   Soldani D., Fadini F., Rasanen H. '5G mobile systems for healthcare'. *Proceedings of IEEE 85th Vehicular Technology Conference VTC*; 2017.

[18]   Voigtländer F., Ramadan A., Eichinger J., *et al.* '5G for robotics: ultra-low latency control of distributed robotic systems'. *Proceedings of 2017 International Symposium of on Computer Science and Intelligent Controls*; 2017.

[19]   Yamada S., Nomura T., Takayuki Kanda T. 'Healthcare support by a humanoid robot'. *Proceedings of 14th ACM/IEEE International Conference on Human-Robot Interaction (HRI)*; 2019.

[20]   Sachs J., Andersson L.A.A., Araujo J., *et al.* 'Adaptive 5G low-latency communication for tactile Internet services'. *Proceedings of the IEEE*. 2019;**107**(2):325–49.

[21]   Sukhmani S., Sadeghi M., Erol-Kantarci M., El Saddik A., *et al.* 'Edge caching and computing in 5G for mobile AR/VR and tactile internet'. *IEEE MultiMedia*. 2018;**26**(1):21–30.

[22]   Schmoll R., Pandi S., Patrik J., *et al.* 'Demonstration of VR/AR offloading to mobile edge cloud for low latency 5G gaming application'. *Proceedings*

of 15th IEEE Annual Consumer Communications & Networking Conference (CCNC); 2018.

[23]   Tanwar S. *Fog Computing for Healthcare 4.0 Environments: Technical, Societal and Future Implications, Signals and Communication Technology.* Springer International Publishing; 2020. pp. 1–430.

[24]   Tanwar S., Tyagi S., Kumar N. *Security and Privacy of Electronics Healthcare Records the Iet Book Series on E Health T...... Institution of Engineering and Technology.* Stevenage, United Kingdom; 2019 pp. 1–450.

[25]   Healy M., Walsh P. 'Detecting demeanor for healthcare with machine learning'. *Proceedings of IEEE International Conference on Bioinformatics and Biomedicine*; 2017.

[26]   Sheth K., Patel K., Shah H., Tanwar S., Gupta R., Kumar N. 'A taxonomy of AI techniques for 6G communication networks'. *Computer Communications.* 2020;**161**(5):279–303.

[27]   Tanwar S., Parekh K., Evans R. 'Blockchain-based electronic healthcare record system for healthcare 4.0 applications'. *Journal of Information Security and Applications.* 2019;**50**:1–14.

[28]   Hathaliya J.J., Tanwar S. 'An exhaustive survey on security and privacy issues in healthcare 4.0'. *Computer Communications.* 2020;**153**(6):311–35.

[29]   Brumm J.-C., Strohm H., Bauch G. 'A stochastic channel model for ultra wideband in-body communication'. *Proceedings of the 41st Annual International Conference of the IEEE Engineering in Medicine and Biology Society*; 2019. pp. 4032–5.

[30]   Hathaliya J.J., Tanwar S., Evans R. 'Securing electronic healthcare records: a mobile-based biometric authentication approach'. *Journal of Information Security and Applications.* 2020;**53**(3):102528–14.

[31]   Bodkhe U., Tanwar S., Bhattacharyaa P., Kumar N. 'Blockchain for precision irrigation: a systematic review'. *Transactions on Emerging Telecommunications Technologies.* 2020:1–33.

[32]   Rawlinson K. *HP Study Reveals Smartwatches Vulnerable to Attack* [online]. 2015. Available from https://www8.hp.com/us/en/hp-news/press-release.html?id=2037386 [Accessed 17 Jun 2019].

[33]   Gupta R., Tanwar S., Tyagi S., Kumar N. 'Tactile-Internet-based Telesurgery system for healthcare 4.0: an architecture, research challenges, and Future Directions'. *IEEE Network.* 2019;**33**(6):22–9.

[34]   Bhudiraja I., Kumar N., Tyagi S., Tanwar S., Obaidat M.S. 'URJA: usage jammer as a resource allocation for secure transmission in CR-NOMA based 5G femtocells'. *IEEE Systems Journal.* 2020:1–10.

[35]   Turner J. *Security for connected medical devices* [online]. 2018. Available from https://www.medtechintelligence.com/feature_article/security-for-connected-medical-devicesq [Accessed 19 Apr 2019].

[36]   Gupta R., Tanwar S., Tyagi S., Kumar N. 'Tactile-internet-based telesurgery system for healthcare 4.0: an architecture, research challenges, and future directions'. *IEEE Network.* 2019;**33**(6):22–9.

[37] Budhiraja I., Kumar N., Tyagi S., Tanwar S., Obaidat M.S. 'URJA: usage jammer as a resource allocation for secure transmission in a CR-NOMA-based 5G femtocell system'. *IEEE Systems Journal*. 2020;**15**(2):1776–85.

[38] Budhiraja I., Tyagi S., Tanwar S., Kumar N., Rodrigues J.J.P.C. 'DIYA: tactile internet driven delay assessment NOMA-based scheme for D2D communication'. *IEEE Transactions on Industrial Informatics*. 2019;**15**(:12):6354–66.

[39] Budhiraja I., Tyagi S., Tanwar S., Kumar N., Rodrigues J.J.P.C. 'Tactile internet for smart communities in 5G: an insight for NOMA-based solutions'. *IEEE Transactions on Industrial Informatics*. 2019;**15**(5):3104–12.

[40] Shah K., Obaidat M.S., Modi P., Bhatia J., Tanwar S., Sadoun B. Amalgamation of fog computing and software defined networking in healthcare 4.0: The challenges, and away forward. *17th International Conference on e-Business and Telecommunications (ICETE-2020)*; Setubal, Portugal; 2020. pp. 1–8.

[41] Sinha A., Kumar S., Mishra S., Asthana P. 'Impact and remedy of EM radiation from cell phone towers'. *JCA, Journal of Analysis and Computation*. 2019.

[42] Tanwar S., Tyagi S., Kumar S. 'The role of internet of things and smart grid for the development of a smart city'. *Intelligent Communication and Computational Technologies (Lecture Notes in Networks and Systems): Proceedings of Internet of Things for Technological Development, IoT4TD*. **19**. Springer International Publishing; 2017. pp. 23–3.

Chapter 10

Security and privacy in health data storage and its analytics

Lucky Kumar Agrawal[1], Deepika Agrawal[1], and Srinivasa K G[2]

The 5th generation (5G) wireless network has enabled various features, such as low-latency, high bandwidth, and mobile edge computing, which help to ensure fast data communication. Data analytic tools play an essential role in healthcare. This includes analyzing data and integrating big volumes of semi-structured, structured, and unstructured essential data produced by the various hospitals and clinics. The 5G wireless networks will connect billions of devices to billions of people. It will lead to new security threats and more focus on the privacy of users. The transformation of healthcare technology from offline to online method and more capacity of healthcare data create many privacy and security issues. These issues include authentication, authorization, inference control, data confidentiality, access control, integrity, and abusive use of cloud-based healthcare data, making the data more vulnerable. The healthcare industry cannot take full advantage of its current resources due to these security and privacy issues. In this chapter, we aim to develop an understanding of various data analytic tools. We discuss the various storage methods of healthcare data, new technologies used for healthcare data security, and different privacy-preserving healthcare data methods.

10.1 Introduction

5G is the upcoming mobile generation that is anticipated to lead a huge volume of new services and many new user experiences. A dual role is played by data analytic in the context of 5G. A huge amount of stored data will be in various forms, which includes Medical Imaging (MI), Electronic Health Records (EHRs), Pharmaceutical Research (PR), Genomic Sequencing (GS), Clinical Records (CR), Medical Devices (MD), and wearables. This chapter aims to evolve understanding about various data analytic tools, such as Hadoop Distributed File System, Hive,

[1]Department of Information Technology, Government Polytechnic, Gondia, Maharashtra, India
[2]Department of computer science and Engineering, NITTTR, India

Jaql, Text Mining, Pig, HBase, and key performance indicators. Various methods for storing large-scale healthcare data are available. The data that the various hospitals and clinics produce need to be stored. Most organizations store data on-premise with control over security, but it is expensive and difficult to maintain. Cloud storage is becoming an increasingly popular option for most healthcare organizations. Some organizations use hybrid approach to store data as per their storage needs. Many organizations use Relational Database Control Structures (RDBMS) and Not only Structured Query Language (NoSQL) to store their information data. Wireless communication systems have been prone to security vulnerabilities from the very beginning. New technologies with new architecture and network services in 5G create new challenges to security and privacy protection. Earlier, the records of the patients were stored in the form of papers consisting of medical records and diagnostic reports. It means that the patient carried his/her reports, and he/she was responsible for preserving those records and presenting them to the medical practitioners when needed. This created many problems and improper diagnosis of patients due to the non-availability of reports with patients. Hence, digitization of health records has been introduced. Data security is one of the major concerns for healthcare organizations, mainly in critical condition, including a sequence of prominent breaches, hacking, and ransomware events. Another important concern for healthcare organizations is that the personal healthcare data generated and shared by people are highly sensitive. Healthcare organizations and industries cannot benefit from their current resources due to these security and privacy issues. Healthcare laws, such as Health Insurance Portability and Accountability Act (HIPAA), Personal Information Protection, and Electronic Document Act (PIPEDA), save the health information and govern their dissemination. We have discussed the various technologies, such as authentication, encryption, data masking, access control, 5GHealthNet, HealthChain enhanced RSA, and blockchain, used to secure healthcare data. We have also discussed the various privacy-preserving methods, such as de-identification, HybrEx, and identity-based anonymization, for healthcare data. Finally, we have given the key points discussed in this chapter. In future, more models and technologies based on the 5G network and blockchain will help secure a large amount of healthcare data and privacy of healthcare data.

Keywords: Data analytics in healthcare, Cloud storage, Relational Database Control Structures (RDBMS), Not only Structured Query Language (NoSQL), Electronic Health Records (EHRs), Data security and privacy, Denial of Service (DOS), E2E security, Healthcare data security life cycle, HybrEx, Encryption, 5GHealthNet, Health chain, Data masking, Health Insurance Portability and Accountability Act (HIPAA).

10.1.1   Contribution

The main contributions of the chapter are described as follows. First, we evolve the understanding about various data analytic tools. Then we have explained various data methods for storing large-scale healthcare data. We have described the security

Table 10.1   Summary of main acronyms

Acronym	Description
5G	Fifth generation wireless network
DoS	Denial of service
IoT	Internet of things
MEC	Mobile edge computing
CAE	Context aware engine
ERR	Error code
ACID	Atomicity, consistency, isolation, and durability
CSMA	Carrier sense multiple access
E2E	End to end
HMAC	Hash-based message authentication code
EHR	Electronic health records
SEMS	Security and edge management system
QoS	Quality of service
DIP	Data integration and processing
PC	Persistence and concurrency
DTB	Data transport broker
IPFS	Interplanetary file system
USA	United States of America
DTB	Data transport broker

and privacy with different wireless networks. Finally, we have presented various ways of securing and maintaining the confidentiality of healthcare data.

10.1.2   Organization

Table 10.1 provides the summary of main acronyms. The rest of the chapter is organized as follows. Section 10.2 explains the data analytic in 5G. Section 10.3 gives the various tools for analysis. Section 10.4 describes the various methods of data storage. Section 10.5 introduces the concept of security and privacy. Section 10.6 describes the security threats in wireless communication. Section 10.7 gives an overview of the E2E security solution for 5G. Section 10.8 lists the privacy challenges in 5G networks. Section 10.9 gives the privacy solutions for the 5G network. Section 10.10 describes the privacy and security concerns in healthcare data. Section 10.11 explains the security of healthcare data. Section 10.12 explains the privacy of healthcare data. Finally, Section 1.13 provides the conclusion and suggestions.

10.2   Data analytic in 5G

The 5G network provides connectivity to remote sensors with low-latency data transmissions that enable intelligent network and application services. Data analytics play an essential role in developing the 5G network, enabling intelligence across the network, business, and applications. These take all the advantage of 5G network

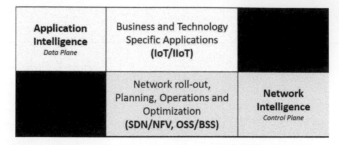

Figure 10.1   Dual-faceted role of data analytics in 5G [1]

characteristics, such as low-latency, high-bandwidth, and MEC. Data analytics play a dual role in 5G. Various business applications and use-cases are supported by the analytic as the first role. The roll-out of 5G and network operations is done by the analytic as the second role (as shown in Figure 10.1).

10.2.1   Application intelligence

The 5G network application use-case spectrum is too large and broad, including industrial automation, wearables, autonomous cars, smart cities, and smart homes. Industry 4.0 and IoT are going to be the main drivers for 5G network applications. Individual subscribers will get smart experiences since CAE will become an essential part of 5G, making networks cognizant of the underlying context.

10.2.2   Network intelligence

To build a flexible 5G network in which operational complexity and roll-out are simplified, network analytics become very critical and are hence required. Various machine learning algorithms are used to analyze network utilization and traffic data patterns to decide where to scale application services and specific network functions. Operations and business support systems will have analytics embedded and integrated into their toolset while in the conventional systems analytics has been a second thought until today.

10.2.3   Phases in data analytic

There are five phases of data analytics that play an important role in the evolution of healthcare applications and research [2].

10.2.3.1   Phase 1

Data collection, storage, and accumulation: This phase is used for the collection of various healthcare data from different hospitals and clinics. The stored data will be in different formats and types. After this, the data are either transferred for analysis or stored in the data warehouse. Owing to privacy and security issues and lack of data protocols, there are many challenges in handling healthcare data. Also, we cannot find the correct metadata that shows which kind of health data are stored and how we can measure them. Also, it will increase the extra load of analyzing the metadata. One more problem is the cleaning of data. If the stored information is not useful, then it will pass through the whole analysis phase and increase the processing error.

10.2.3.2 Phase 2

Data classification, cleaning, and extraction: This phase is used to pull and the healthcare information and store it onto a particular single database. Data cleaning is a process in which the inaccurate health records are identified and removed. During this phase, the main challenge is to add or remove the missing values. The data received from various hospitals and clinics may contain medical images (i.e., MRI, CT, PET/CT, and Ultrasound, etc.). In this case, retrieving data depends on the application and is hard to filter based on their structure. The classification of these data can be done in structured, semi-structured, and unstructured format to perform the meaningful analysis.

10.2.3.3 Phase 3

Data aggregation, integration, and representation: This phase uses different varieties of healthcare data for aggregation, which can be further used for data analysis. The main motive is to get descriptive information of health data based on some distinct variables, such as the similarity between other records, patients' names, critical status, history of past record readings, and date on which the record was created. After this, all aggregated information is transferred to researchers, data scientists, clinics, hospitals, and other government healthcare organizations. Healthcare data information is very sensitive. In a real-time environment, dynamic medical information with currently available static information is a challenging task. Also, at the same time, to treat diseases properly, the healthcare organizations want accurate and up-to-date information. Even after noise removal and data reduction, the representation of meaningful data must be manageable in size, and the original information of health data should not be changed.

10.2.3.4 Phase 4

Data analysis, modeling, and query processing: In this phase, complex healthcare information is processed into a form that is easy to understand using symbols, text, and diagrams. Different types of data modeling approaches, which include physical, logical, and conceptual levels, are used. These ensure data consistency in original values, semantics, and security while guaranteeing the quality of the data [2]. Data mining algorithms are used for analyzing the data so that meaningful information can be obtained from the healthcare data. Once the analysis and integration of data are done, the next level is query processing. User-level queries are responded to by the query-processing method. It may be simple or complex from the families of the patient and physicians regarding the status of their health. The analyst must select suitable tools based on the type of query.

10.2.3.5 Phase 5

Data feedback, interpretation, and delivery: This is the final phase. It is a very important phase as the interpretation of data is done in this phase after completing all the processing steps. The interpretation of healthcare data results should be clear enough to understand. Otherwise, it will be challenging for the healthcare professionals, patients, and others to recognize the results of the interpretation given by the decision-maker, data analyst, and computer system. However, in various phases of analysis, a decision-maker already inspects the difficulties. Health reports are generated based on the previous data model in the data delivery phase. To improve the patient's care standard, feedback is taken from the decision-makers and the patient.

10.3 Tools for analysis

Owing to the huge capacity of healthcare data, it is not easy to process it manually. There are various data analysis tools available. These tools help to examine, clean, transform, and model the data so that meaningful information can be obtained, recommended the finest possible solutions, and supported with correct decision-making in critical situations.

10.3.1 Hadoop distributed file system

Hadoop mainly uses distributed file system to store a huge capacity of real-time, not structured data and flow at a high velocity [3]. The primary data storage file system controls storage for health data applications running in clustered healthcare systems. In Hadoop distributed file system, voluminous healthcare data are divided into small groups distributed across various medical servers.

10.3.2 Text mining

It is the procedure of taking out important information, patterns, or knowledge from the existing unstructured text documents related to healthcare [4]. It is a tool used in various ways to analyze the patients' records and responses from various hospitals and clinics so that a better treatment plan for the patient can be carried out.

10.3.3 Complex event processing

It is the method of analyzing past events and obtaining a conclusion. This tool has been started recently in healthcare to identify the latest pattern of the patients from ongoing changing event and also to forecast the related events in real-time.

10.3.4 Hive

This tool is mainly used to process, manage, and arrange the large healthcare data set in the Hadoop distributed file system. It uses Hive query language to analyze, review, and queries the large set of fixed data. It resides on top of the Hadoop.

10.3.5 Jaql

It simplifies parallel processing and converts the high-level queries into low-level ones. It easily manages and analyzes the large volume of semi-structured data. It is a functional query language and is mainly used for conversion-based analysis on very large healthcare data sets. It uses the Hadoop MapReduce framework.

10.3.6 Zookeeper

It is a tool that provides a centralized infrastructure and can coordinate between different nodes in the cluster and send configuration attributes to all nodes or a particular node in the cluster. It will then select the head of all nodes among different nodes and give authenticated communication.

10.3.7 Apache solr

It is used with Hadoop. It helps to find the required information from voluminous information that Hadoop contains. It is a NoSQL database used for providing centralized configuration, distributed indexing, highly reliable, fault-tolerant, and self-respond to failure and more.

10.3.8 Lucene

Lucene is an open-source and fast search library based on Java. It is mainly used for indexing, searching work, and analyzing. It supports information retrieval and high-performance multi-index search.

10.3.9 Presto

It is a distributed, structured query engine that has high speed and interactive analytic query for any size of data. It can analyze data on different distributed medical servers and combined health-related data.

10.4 Data storage

The healthcare information, including unstructured or semi-structured information, photographs, reports, etc., is increasing daily. Storing and processing such large amount of data is a difficult task. Health information is characterized by the following characteristics [5].

10.4.1 Value

Meaningful and valuable information is obtained from the stored health information by using different analytical tools. We have healthcare information with us, but it is useless unless there is some value in it. It is essential to extract the value which is not visible from the combination of different isolated sources.

10.4.2   Variety

The healthcare information is collected from various sources, which can be changed at various intervals. If the information is changing during the processing phase, it will increase inconsistency in giving valuable information.

10.4.3   Velocity

The amount of healthcare information generated is increasing and will continue to increase in the future. Meeting this increased demand requires quick processing and analysis.

10.4.4   Veracity

Veracity is a method to promise trustworthiness and use healthcare information crucially. The way a patient expresses himself/herself, may affect different types of devices to show poor quality, performance, or correctness. It is essential to consider these issues and deal with them accordingly. There are two ways in which a large amount of healthcare information can be stored on-premise data storage and cloud storage.

10.4.5   On-premise data storage

On-premise data storage means storing data on local servers and computers. The whole infrastructure is located on the premises of the organization itself, as illustrated in Figure 10.2.

One of the major advantages of on-premise data storage is that the users do not require internet access to data [6] [7]. Most of the organizations run their business on the internet. There is always a fear in mind that if the internet connectivity is lost, it will affect productivity and hamper the access of important data. An internal network is available in on-premise data storage in which we can access data all the time without an internet connection. Since a high-speed internet connection is not required, it saves the cost involved. It provides more security and privacy since data are not available to the third party as they are not online. Security and privacy of the data are the responsibility of the organization itself. Also, the infrastructure purchased is a one-time investment for the organization. The storage is mainly dedicated to the organization itself. The organization can upgrade the infrastructure, if required. There is no need to depend on the third party. Also, there are some disadvantages of using on-premise data storage. It requires extra IT support, high maintenance cost, increased risk of data loss, and the limited company ability to scale. To overcome all these disadvantages, a cloud-based storage is used.

10.4.6   Cloud storage

Data storage is done on remote servers, which is maintained by a third-party organization. These organizations are entrusted with users' data, and for security and privacy purposes, the exact storage location of these data is not known to most people [8]. While storing data, the users see a virtual server, which shows that the data are

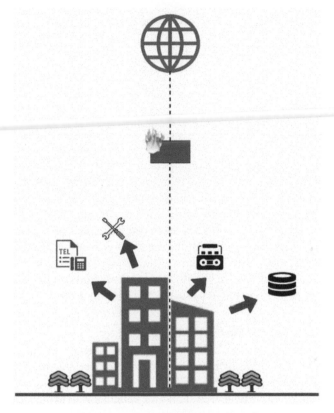

Figure 10.2   On-premise data storage [6]

stored on some particular location; however, that location does not exist in reality. Data can be stored in any geographical location. Classic cloud storage architecture is shown in Figure 10.3.

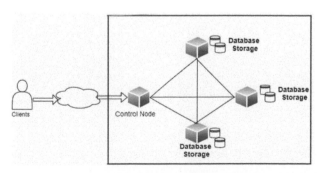

Figure 10.3   Cloud storage system architecture [8]

Table 10.2   Data storage format in relational database MySQL

visit_id	date	complaint	diagnosis_id	d_ssn	prescription_id
v001	2019-14-02	High temperature	diag_001	999003	psc002
v002	2019-20-03	High fever	diag_006	999006	psc004
v003	2019-29-04	Headache	diag_007	999008	psc005
v004	2020-14-07	Acidity	diag_009	999010	psc007

Cloud storage resources can be procured on a pre-paid or pay-as-you-go basis. It is a good option for an organization as it gives a cost-saving advantage and the regular backup of its data. It also reduces the number of IT staff and third-party organizations that manage cloud storage. It does not require one large time investment for the infrastructure as cloud storage is taken care of externally. Organizations pay monthly for the services they use from third-party organizations. Cloud-based storage is built to scale. Also, there are some disadvantages of using the cloud storage service. These include the facts that data access is based on an internet connection, the internet determines user experience and security of the data.

10.4.6.1   Relational database MySQL

It is a widely used data storage model for storing healthcare information [9]. It is a simple data storage approach in which Healthcare data are stored in relational database MySQL as shown in Table 10.2, where each field or cell is identified by a column and a row. A simple table that shows the patient's visit to the hospital and the treatment given is shown in Table 10.2.

Relational database technology scales vertically, but the modern approach to application architecture must scale horizontally [10]. In the relational database MySQL, we have added compulsory schema before adding records to the database. Irrespective of what record we have added, it should strictly comply with the database schema and its data types and fixed column names. The database acknowledges this model normalization process in which large tables are broken down into smaller tables that are linked together. This is shown in Figure 10.4.

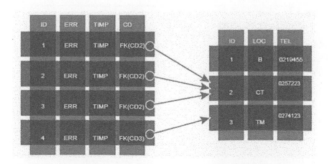

Figure 10.4   Relational data model [10]

In the example shown in Figure 10.4, error log is used to store database information. Every error log is made up of an ERR, the Time It Took Place (TIMP), and the Data Center (CD) in which it has occurred. Many records share a few attributes. Records are distributed across multiple tables. The advantage is that this eliminates the chances of duplicating data in the database. The disadvantage is that if a single record is modified, it will lock down multiple tables simultaneously. Transactions in relational database MySQL are complex even for a single record. Now the prices of data storage system have reduced a lot as compared to earlier. Using a more storage space model in exchange for increased system application performance and the capability to distribute the workload in multiple machines easily is now the best option in many situations. In MySQL, memory space must be reserved for the attribute values [11], irrespective of the fact whether the attribute values are available or not. Owing to these drawbacks, relational database MySQL is not an efficient storage for large health database.

10.4.6.2 NoSQL database

Organizations that gather a huge volume of unstructured data are mainly moving to non-relational databases called NoSQL databases [12]. Here, the database is not designed on tables, and also it does not use SQL to manipulate data. NoSQL database is a schema-less approach to the management of data. It is document-oriented, with key-value implementation, and column-oriented, which scales horizontally. It does not require the schema before inserting data into the database. It does not require modification of schema. Figure 10.5 shows the document data model. Processing of facts in NoSQL databases is faster than that in the relational database [13]. The features of NoSQL are as follows:

1. Easy horizontal escalation.
2. Distribution of data among different servers and capability to replicate.
3. Interaction with data is through simple call level protocols or interference.
4. Distributed indexes are used for storage.
5. Data are not structured and add new attributes any time.
6. It contains Basically Available, Soft state, Eventually consistent (BASE) instead of ACID properties.

NoSQL performs parallel processing across multiple servers. NoSQL databases are classified into the following categories.

10.4.6.3 Key value store

Data formats can vary from easy text strings to complex formats. Data are arranged as an array of entries that contains key-value pair. Each key is unique while value represents the real data. No secondary keys are available. It gives transactions, replication, persistence, locking sorting, versioning, and interfaces for index look-ups, deletes, and inserts. Here queries depend only on a single attribute. Amazon makes

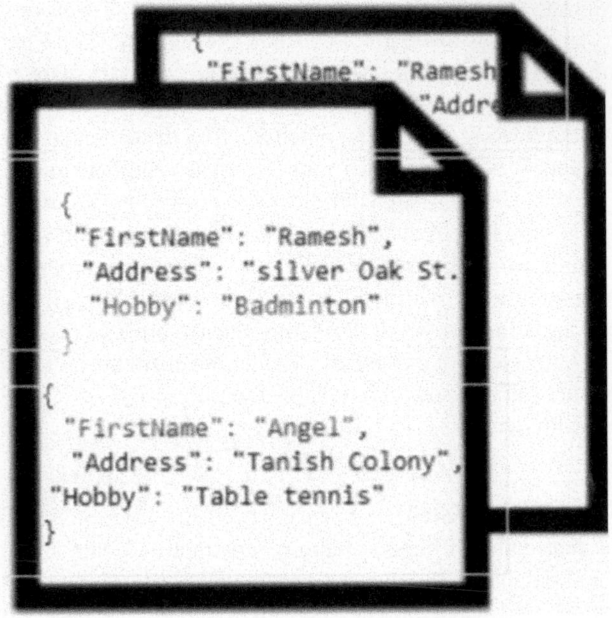

Figure 10.5   Document data model [10]

an extensive use of the key-value store. An example data storage format is given in Table 10.3.

10.4.6.4   Document store

Every document is identified with a special unique key. It is used to manage and save documents, a file in different formats, such as PDF, DOC, XML, and JSON. It uses many indexes that are defined on collections and support different types of

Table 10.3   Data storage format in relational database MySQL [13]

Car	
Key	**Attributes**
1	Make: Maruti Suzuki
	Model: Swift
	Color: white Year: 2017
2	Make: Nissan
	Model: Pathfinder
	Color: green Year: 2007
3	Make: Hyundai
	Model: i10
	Color: gray Year: 2019

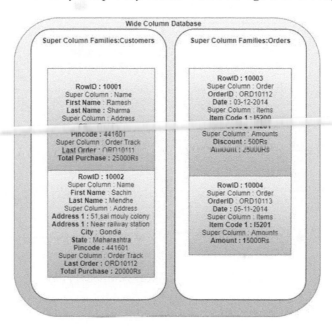

Figure 10.6   Extensible record stores or wide column/column family stores [12]

documents. Queries are allowed based on multiple attribute value constraints. It is generally a good solution to look at objects based on numerous fields.

10.4.6.5   Extensible record stores or wide column/column family stores

It can be divided horizontally and vertically across nodes, which permits having a pliable structure related to the key. Column groups are used to distribute the columns of a table across multiple nodes. Shading on the primary key is used to split the rows over nodes. The row key is used to access data that are based on easy read and write operations based on a table. Access to the entire row or a particular row is provided. It is the most desirable solution when queries are based on field and its necessary stronger concurrency guarantees a higher throughput. It provides a sharp data partitioning which is based on column families. An example database is provided in Figure 10.6.

10.4.6.6   Graph database

Here, data are represented using nodes that define entities, edges, and properties that define information. It is helpful in representing networks and relations, a largely interconnected huge volume of data that can be simply represented like a graph, as shown in Figure 10.7. In common, graph databases are helpful when we focus more on the association between data than on the data themselves.

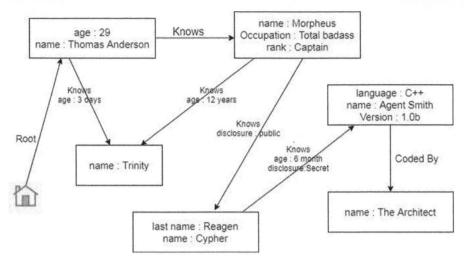

Figure 10.7   Graph NoSQL database [12]

10.4.7   Hybrid approach

This is one of the widely adapted options for storing healthcare information, which is a combination of both on-premise storage and cloud storage. It provides the best option by using both storage solutions. Here, the local resources of the company are combined with the remote resources provided by the third-party organization [14]. This helps the company host the sensitive information locally and the goal of data processing, which is critical. Figure 10.8 provides a pictorial illustration of the scenario.

10.5   Introduction to security and privacy

Security is generally defined as "the protection against access which is not authorized, with some including explicit mention of availability and integrity" [15]. Its main aim is to save data from harmful attacks and to steal health information data for profit. Although security is important for protecting data, it is not sufficient for addressing privacy.

Privacy can be defined as "the capability to prevent sensitive information about personally identifiable healthcare information." Its main focus is on the use and governance of individuals' personal data, such as establishing authorization requirements and making policies to ensure that an individual's personal information is being shared, collected, and utilized in the right way, as shown in Figure 10.9.

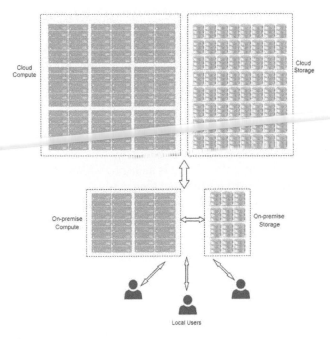

Figure 10.8   Generic setup of a hybrid cloud system [14]

10.6   Security threats in a wireless communication system

Communication through wireless mobile networks has increased widely in the last few years. With more wireless mobile networks and communications in our day-to-day life, the community has become tremendously exposed to threats and cyber security attacks [17]. Radio propagation in a wireless network is broadcast and has an open wireless interface that is open and accessible to all [18]. This open communication makes wireless mobile communication more vulnerable to malicious

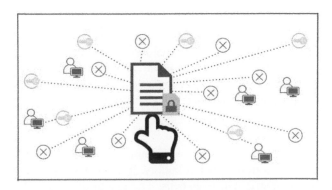

Figure 10.9   Security and privacy [16]

attacks. Sniffing can be done easily in a wireless communication network. Attacks on the wireless communication network are divided based on availability, confidentiality, access control, authentication, and integrity. There are several security threats in a wireless communication network. Some of the security threats are given as follows.

10.6.1   Rogue access points

It is the method that generates a back door in the trusted network by installing an access point that is not secure inside the firewall. It is a wireless access point that has been installed on a company network and is authentic without getting a license from the local authority. It is created to carry out the man-in-the-middle attack. There are two categories of rogue access points. In the first category, an employee having full access of the company premises can install local cheap wireless routers and permit the access of secure network of company premises to unauthorized third parties. In the second category, he/she selects that network which does not employ server-client authentication and client-server.

10.6.2   Denial of service (DoS)

This kind of attack is carried out using the CSMA method by making the channel seem busy. This could be done intentionally or accidentally. Wireless mobile communication networks use the bandwidth of 2.4 GHz, usual for all wireless and radio services, such as microwave oven, bluetooth, and a cordless phone. Therefore, interference can occur to a limited range. This is the reason it can be done accidentally, but the interference can be done through flooding attacks by some attackers.

10.6.3   Configuration problems

Many vulnerabilities may cause simple configuration problems. This is because numerous consumers/SOHO grade access points ship with no security configuration [19]. A trainee user can gain access by making the setup of one of these devices very fast.

10.6.4   Passive capturing

Passive capturing can be done easily by acquiring the inside range of a selected wireless LAN and then capturing and listening to data. These details can be used for many things, including an attempt to analyze non-secured traffic and to break current security settings. It is impossible to prevent this type of attack because of the wireless mobile communication network environment.

10.6.5   1G networks

It is the first generation network that was launched in the early 1980s [20]. 1G provides only a voice communication facility. It is an analog-based network. The geographical area is distributed over cells. The length of each cell is 10–25 km, where each cell has its own base station. As 1G is based on analog technology, it is extremely insecure because any unknown receiver with all-band radio can listen to the conversation. There are a lot of such incidents that have occurred. Theft of airtime is also a big issue.

10.6.6   2G networks

This is based on digital transmission technology. There are many security threats, such as obscurity, which means that all security algorithms that GSM generally uses, are available to the public. The facility of accessing services and updating cryptographic mechanisms is very difficult. Mobile subscriber visibility and authentication of the individual user to the network is missing.

10.6.7   3G networks

The 3G network for cellular communication focuses on providing high transmission bandwidths, worldwide roaming for mobile users, and preservation of advanced services, such as multimedia on the demand of mobile users and the global positioning systems. There are many security issues, such as interception in which the attacker could read signaling messages or intercept information, though he\she cannot remove or change it. There are data-based attacks in which attackers cause destruction by inserting, dropping, or altering the data stored in the system. Fabrication, modification of resources, and interruption are some other security issues in the 3G network.

10.6.8   4G networks

The 4G network is the generation of wireless communication technology, which leads to improvement in data rates over the earlier wireless communication technologies. The 4G wireless communication technology increases security issues as it works entirely on the IP architecture and suite of protocols. There are many security issues, such as scrambling in which interference of attackers is activated for short intervals.

10.6.9   5G networks

The 5G network technology is the new stage of wireless mobile communication where the objective is to have a fully connected mobile community that features high transmission speeds. There are some security threats, such as user confidentiality and identity, in which security methods are almost the same as in 4G. The users are protected against private attacks but not from active attacks. Security for the latest service delivery models in which 5G network uses virtualization and cloud computing to achieve maximum efficiency in the service, resulting in the rise of a new security threat level. The third-party organization operates its applications in clouds operating on the same hardware in which their services are executing, increasing demand for virtualization with more security. Threat landscape will develop as other technologies link; mass surveillance privacy concerns are already an issue;

the destruction may be even more critical and could influence public safety. Bigger threat space and low-cost new technology lead to more attacks on the radio network.

10.7   E2E security solution for 5G

E2E data safety gives more security, avoids duplication of security functions, such as encryption and decryption, and gives differentiated security based on the services. E2E security mainly deals with integrity, key management, authentication, and confidentiality. As 5G focuses on a diverse-networked society, the attack surface of a 5G technology is huge. The benefits of E2E security [21] include:

1. Differentiated security for various discrete services.
2. Security architecture is flexible, which supports attributes of security within a network slice.
3. Unique security management regardless of proprietary security.

The main issue to ensure E2E security in the 5G network is to acquire secure quantum approaches. This task aims to create and assess the framework of E2E security for 5G applications. The security functionality includes authentication in which devices and users are given authenticated 3D passwords. Session key generation is used to prevent quantum attacks. Secret key is generated with the support of quantum key generators to give good quality key generation to ensure unpredictability, randomness, and higher security. Confidentiality of data is provided by generating key with the help of quantum cryptography used for validation of message using HMAC. Secure communication is guaranteed by E2E security in a 5G network technology. Two phases of secure communication are suggested as follows:

1. Authentication in which communication is ensured from a specific party to stop man-in-the-middle attack. A 3D password is used to authenticate the device and key exchange protocol to validate the communicating parties. Key agreement is done between two parties to ensure a secure and shared private key.
2. Key usage in which a secure key is used when it is established for quantum-safe message exchange. Quantum key distribution enables secure disposition of secret keys that may be used with hash-based encryption algorithms, such as HMAC.

10.8   Privacy challenges in 5G networks

The growth of new technologies, new architecture and data network services in 5G will expose new challenges to privacy preservation and meeting privacy objectives [22]. Today, many users save their personal information on mobile, so mobile phones have a huge amount of personal information and this should be prevented in the upcoming generation. The privacy of users in the 5G network is divided into three main categories: location privacy, data privacy, and identity privacy. Location privacy is important as new 5G technology is coming, and users access services based on location. For example, various mobile applications give the location of railway stations, hotels, and shopping malls. Also, various social networking sites have introduced new features that specify the location of the users very easily. Different actors can constantly trace users through their personal gadgets, which are embedded in the environment and could lead to significant concerns to the users' privacy. Data privacy represents the privacy and confidentiality of data that are stored. Identity privacy refers to saving the identity information of the subscriber and the user equipment. Since in the 5G network, a lot of devices are going to be connected, some specific identity is required to identify a particular device and deliver a service. For example, healthcare online application requires identity to access the information of the patient. There are various privacy challenges in 5G network. Some of these challenges are given below.

10.8.1 Loss of data ownership

The 5G network will involve various entities, such as third-party application developers, mobile network operators, and cloud service providers. However, the confusion of roles of various users and corresponding responsibilities may generate legal dissension or business. Also, loss of data ownership has the same confusion about who is going to take responsibility. The ownership of user data should be defined clearly between the various entities and network operators, and utilize strong set up, and privacy-enabled service agreements.

10.8.2 Location of legal disputes

Data projection of the usage is dependent on the law of that country as per the various relevant jurisdictions. There are a minimum of three feasible locations to select from. These may include those of the service provider, or the victim, or the offender.

10.8.3 Shared environment

Resources of the network are virtualized, and various network service users share similar infrastructure. In this type of shared information, unauthorized access to data will compromise the user's privacy.

10.8.4 Hacking

The 5G network also is an IP-based open architecture. This is unsafe to a whole range of web-based attacks, including hacking and IP-based attacks. More dependency of the 5G network on cloud technologies will add vulnerabilities to hacking attacks, leading to important privacy issues.

10.8.5   Providing information for third party

The 5G network has created a new environment for third-party application developers to utilize the communication network. This third-party developer can sell the private information of individual users to other third-party organizations.

10.9   Privacy solutions for 5G

To achieve the possible privacy solutions for 5G, some privacy protection objectives are identified. These include promoting the single digital market, balancing the interests, having a privacy legislation in a worldwide context, fostering interoperability and data portability, defining an easily applicable law, including the right to erasure and correction, increasing the responsibility, and accountability. Some possible privacy solutions for 5G are given as follows. Regulatory approach to promotion of objectives of privacy between different entities requires regulation.

Regulation can be classified into three main types.

1.   Industry self-regulation: To protect privacy, different industrial groups and industries are developing principles and practices.
2.   Consumer or market regulation: Consumers are the main end-users of the network, and these are the ones who require protection of privacy. They can impose conditions to acquire the desired level of privacy.
3.   Government regulation: Each government has responsible bodies for enforcing and writing regulations that are specific to each country.

10.9.1   Privacy-aware routing mechanisms by using SDN

The utilization of SDNs on the internet and 5G networks will authorize the creation of privacy-aware routing mechanisms. It should be recognized that the data packets of users containing privacy information in the SDN network should not cross borders of the country.

10.9.2   Hybrid cloud approach

A hybrid cloud method permits the mobile operators to save more sensitive data on the on-premise cloud and process on-premise private clouds while data that are not much sensitive are saved.

Privacy by design

In this, privacy is integrated from the design process itself. The concept is based on seven primary principles, which include full functionality, proactive and not reactive, privacy embedded into the design, privacy as the default setting, respect for user privacy, end-to-end security, visibility, and transparency. The main aim of this design is to prevent privacy risks from occurring.

Figure 10.10   Healthcare data concerns and challenges [24]

10.9.3   Service-oriented privacy preserving, mechanism

It plays an important role in 5G. This is mainly due to the privacy needs in the 5G network that differs from one service to another. For example, privacy required for healthcare-related applications should be more than the information search-based applications.

10.10   Privacy and security concerns in healthcare data

This is a very important issue for healthcare data. Privacy is generally defined as "having the capability to protect sensitive and critical information about personally distinguishable healthcare information" [23]. Its main aim is the administration and use of personal data of individuals like establishing authorization requirements and making policies to ensure that the patient's private information is being aggregated, utilized, and shared incorrectly. Security is generally defined as "the shielding against access which is unauthorized, with few including explicit mention of availability and integrity." Its main focus is to protect data from various attacks and use for profit. Figure 10.10 shows the various concerns and challenges that the healthcare data are facing.

10.10.1   Importance of security and privacy in healthcare data

Smart healthcare system has made healthcare technologies more dependent on smart technologies [25]. The robustness of the data stored on EHR systems is important for healthcare service providers. Thus data should not be affected by the virus and must always be secured. Otherwise, the technologies used will not work correctly. Nowadays, many healthcare data are stored electronically, and many records are also duplicated. If some unauthorized users gain access to patient data, then personal information, such as name, mobile number, address, etc., can be sold in the market which can harm the patient in future. Therefore, security and privacy of healthcare data are increasingly becoming important for data safety.

10.10.2   Sharing data in cloud

Cloud technologies can support sharing of healthcare data information. Healthcare information from different sources is collected and combined to analyze the insights into diagnosis and medical treatment. Sharing healthcare data information through cloud technology creates a disturbance in environment where healthcare security practices are not in place.

10.10.3   Data administration and laws

Healthcare data information requires to follow guidelines, certification, and rules defined by the HIPAA. It does not mean that patient records are safe because HIPAA does not give any rules for the execution of data safety. However, it is concerned with assuring that security procedures and policies are in place. Large healthcare data information is collected from different resources, resulting in an overburden for processing power, high-speed networking, and storage.

10.10.4   Malware attacks

Healthcare company and organization have faced a range of attacks, such as malware treatment plan attacks, DDoS, external attacks, and medical identity theft by insiders.

10.10.5   Medical identity theft

It is the most usual form of privacy violation in healthcare where an individual's personal information is exposed and then later impersonated for financial gain.

10.10.6   Social issues

The exposed state of health of an individual may lead him/her to an undesirable social situations.

10.10.7   Incorrect diagnosis and treatment

Modification of medical information in an unwanted way may lead to wrong treatment of the patient. If the medical information is not correct, it may lead to a wrong diagnosis or inappropriate treatment plan, which can possibly harm the patient's health.

10.10.8   Denial of valid insurance claims

A patient may be unable to claim additional insurance after his/her health insurance treatment amount gets over. Fake medical bills can be acquired based on insurance and stolen identity for financial gain.

10.10.9   Employment issues

Employers do ask for the medical history of potential employees and later destroy medical information that has the potential of causing employment issues [24].

10.11   Security of healthcare data

Huge amounts of healthcare information data are maintained, transmitted and stored in healthcare organizations and industries. Delivery in healthcare data is efficient with proper care, but with a lack of minimal security and technical support. Health organizations are considered to be most vulnerable to reveal data publicly. Attackers use various techniques and procedures to find the healthcare information sensitive data and disclose it to the public. Implementation of security measures is a very difficult process. The old patient records of paper-based format are transformed into electronic format, which are saved in centralized databases in the form of EHR, and are accessible through the internet. EHR management provides advantages related to easy access of healthcare information data and the use of patient information, without any constraint in space, time, and human resources for monitoring patients. More security measures are needed to ensure protection for data communication [26] and information, which is in electronic form. To ensure access management and secure storage of EHR, various security needs must be considered with corresponding QoS measures. These include the following.

10.11.1   EHR storage

The patient's information can be saved electronically on the local computer, on devoted storage servers using cloud computing technology, and on the company network storage facilities. The main issue is to find an appropriate understanding between the security of access to resources and speed because the security needs are growing as the usage of IT infrastructures is becoming extra difficult.

10.11.2   Malicious code

Computer viruses, malicious software, and unpatched applications can create interference of standard operation in healthcare services resulting in the damage of EHR. Protection from anti-virus applications, intrusive attack, software updates, and firewalls are some of the ways to protect the healthcare system.

10.11.3   Mobile devices

Advanced healthcare methods, such as remote surgery systems or remote medical diagnosis, have to involve the mobile IT equipment in the access, decision, and acquisition process over the medical information. Communication channels should be secured over a devoted communication link, secure VPN technologies while accessing the internet, and some secure protection rules for smartphones and laptops should be defined to allow efficient and secure access to medical facilities.

10.11.4   Online systems protection

EHR content contains critical and confidential information. The latest trend is to systematize the information from medical terms to networking protocols so that

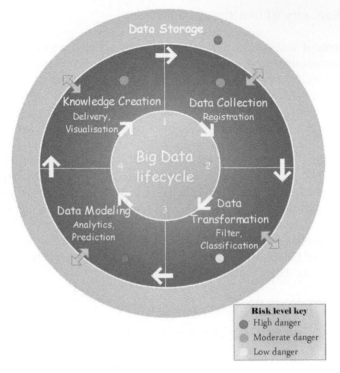

Figure 10.11   Healthcare data security life cycle [23]

medical documents can be saved electronically and accessed instantly and sent in any part of the world.

10.11.5   Protected access

As healthcare data hold personal information, EHR should be protected, processed, or accessed only by the authorized person.

10.11.6   Healthcare data security life cycle

Security in healthcare data mainly refers to three events: information security, data security, and access control. In this consideration, healthcare industries and organizations should apply security approaches and measures to protect their healthcare data, associated software and hardware, and both administrative and clinical information from external and internal risks. The security life cycle of data during the establishment of the project should ensure that proper decisions are made about reuse, retention, audit of historical data, cost-effectiveness, and/or new data. Figure 10.11 shows a healthcare data security life cycle model containing the various phases to give mechanisms and policies that ensure addressing attacks and threats in each step of the healthcare data security life cycle.

10.11.6.1   Data collection phase

It is the first step in the healthcare data security life cycle, and here collection of healthcare information is completed from various sources. There is a requirement to secure the first phase of the healthcare data security life cycle. It is very important to collect healthcare information data from the authorized and trusted sources, protect patient privacy, and ensure that this phase is protected and secured.

10.11.6.2   Data transformation phase

After the data are collected and sorted based on their form, the meaningful data are obtained after completing the required transformations and analysis. More commonly, sorting, transformation and enrichment are needed to improve the data quality ahead of the modeling or analytics phase and remove or suitably deal with outliers, noise, duplicate data instances, missing values, etc. Since the healthcare data collected are sensitive, it is very important to take necessary precautions during storage and transformation. The collected healthcare data can be protected by maintaining access control and access level security. It should remain isolated and define few security measures, such as data partitioning, data anonymization, and permutation.

10.11.6.3   Data modeling phase

After the healthcare data have been aggregated, transformed, and saved in secured storage solutions, healthcare data processing is carried out to generate meaningful knowledge. This phase consists of the implementation of data mining techniques, such as association, clustering, and classification. Also, there are several learning techniques to improve the robustness and accuracy of the final model. A secure processing environment should also be provided. The main focus here is to use different data mining algorithms to extract sensitive and critical healthcare information.

10.11.6.4   Knowledge creation phase

Decision-makers use valued knowledge and new information in the modeling phase. This knowledge is examined as sensitive data, particularly in a competitive environment. Healthcare organizations and industries are aware that their sensitive and private data should not be released publicly. Accordingly, verification and security observation are the primary objectives in this phase.

10.11.7   Technologies used for security of healthcare data

There are various technologies used for the security of healthcare data. Some of these are given below.

10.11.7.1   Authentication

It is the function of establishing or validating claims created by or about the subject that are authentic and true. It provides several important pieces of information within any organization, such as protecting the identity of users, securing access to organization networks, and ensuring that the end-user is actually who he/she is pretending to be. The information authentication can create specific issues, mainly man-in-the-middle attacks. Endpoint authentication is done by much cryptographic protocol to prevent man-in-the-middle attacks. Secure sockets layer, transport layer security, and its predecessors are the protocols that use cryptography to secure communication between the networks. Secure sockets layer and transport layer security perform encryption of the segments of network connections at the transport layer, which are end-to-end. Applications, such as instant messaging, electronic mail, and web browsing, use various protocols. Transport layer security or secure sockets layer may be used to validate the server using trusted certification authority. Kerberos mechanism and Hashing techniques, such as SHA-256, can also be used for achieving authentication. Sensitive health information can be monitored by using the Bull Eye algorithm. Relation between the actual and replicated data is maintained by this algorithm and it assures data security [27]. Only the authorized person is permitted to write or read critical data [28]. Communication between the servers is done without passwords in this model. At the entry of each access, the healthcare data information which is given by both identities of consumer and providers should be verified in a healthcare system.

10.11.7.2 Data masking

In this method, sensitive data are replaced by unidentifiable values. The original value is lost in this method as it is not completely an encryption technique. It uses an approach of de-identifying data sets or masking personal identifiers, such as social security numbers, names and generalizing quasi-identifiers, such as zipcodes and date-of-birth. It is the most desirable method to have data anonymization. K-anonymity fails to protect against attribute disclosure but protects against identity disclosure. P-sensitive anonymity secures from both attribute and identity disclosures. The remaining anonymization techniques fall into the classes of swapping cells within columns, replacing groups of k records with k copies of a single representative, and adding noise to the data. The main advantage of this method is that the cost of securing healthcare-related information data deployment is reduced.

10.11.7.3 Encryption

Unauthorized access to critical and sensitive healthcare data is prevented by an efficient data encryption method. Maintenance and protection of data ownership over its life cycle is done by the data encryption method. Encryption is helpful to keep away from exposure to breaches, such as theft of storage devices and packet sniffing. Healthcare industry or organizations should make sure that the encryption scheme is well organized, feasible for both healthcare professionals and patients, and simply expandable to include new electronic health records. Various encryption algorithms, such as RSA, AES, etc., have already developed. However, it is difficult to select algorithm to impose secure storage.

10.11.7.4 Auditing and monitoring

Auditing is a method which involves recording user activities, such as modifying data and keeping a log of each access of the healthcare system in sequential order. These are two elective security metrics to evaluate and ensure the protection of a healthcare system. Precaution methods and intrusion detection on the complete network traffic are absolutely difficult. A security monitoring architecture has been created by analyzing IP flow records, DNS traffic, honeypot data, ~~~~~~ ~~ ~~~~~~c. The suggested solution contain~ ~ ~~~~~~g and storing data in distributed sources ~~~ ~~~ ~~~~~~ation schemes. Up to this stage, calculation of three likelihood metrics has been done to identify whether packet, flow, or domain name is malicious. An alert takes place in the detection system or process stop by prevention system based on the score obtained by this calculation.

10.11.8 Access control

After the user has been authenticated, he/she can make an entry in the information system. However, their access will still be controlled by an access control policy which is usually based on the rights and privileges of each practitioner allowed by an authenticated third party or patient. It is a flexible and strong mechanism to allow permission to users. It gives advanced authorization controls to ensure that users can perform only those activities for which they have approval, such as job submission, data access, and cluster administration, etc. To address the access control and security concerns, various solutions have been proposed. Attribute-based access control and role-based access control are the most suitable models for electronic health records.

10.11.9 5GHealthNet

It is a cloud-based framework for rapid and authorized access to personal healthcare-related records through the 5G network [29]. Healthcare data in cloud are secured by the double key encryption algorithm. The main aim of 5GHealthNet is to save personal records and intensify the authorized access to cloud through the 5G wireless communication network. The functionalities of the 5GHealthNet framework are given as follows:

1. Multi-user access,
2. 5G wireless communication networks provide remote and fast access to data,
3. Easy usage and user-friendly interface,
4. Double encryption secure access.

Figure 10.12 shows the 5GHealthNet architecture. A load balancer starts the data stream transfer; SEMS is applied using a double encryption algorithm to ensure safe access of data. DIP, PC and DTB, and modules ensure data flow within the cloud. When the data access request is made, a copy of the data back up is taken each time with the access request. The controlled movement of the whole working is monitored in API management and API library, which have the functionalities to

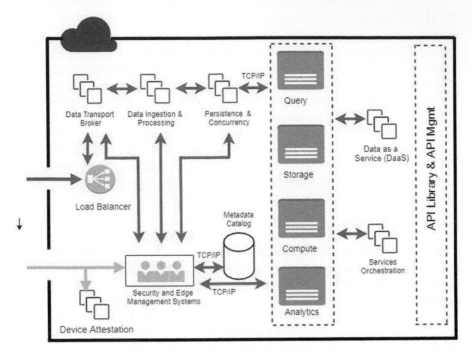

Figure 10.12   5GHealthNet architecture [29]

ensure access to private data. The connectivity of the user individual is an important part of this system. The application has to assist the inbuilt 5G connectivity through which safe access of healthcare data in the cloud can be done with less uncertainty. The framework of the double encryption algorithm is built by considering a dynamic key-value irrespective of the number of users. Each time the user logs in, a new value of the key is generated. After successful encryption of the new key-value, a new decryption key is generated. The final goal of this 5GHealthNet system is to implement the 5GHealthNet application in smartphones, and data in the cloud are accessed with some inbuilt security functions included within the application through the internet connection. The smartphones using 5GHealthNet do not need a wireless connection; internet connectivity is inbuilt for accessing the data in the cloud. 5GHealthNet connects to the data end, and the user end encourages mutual communication and improves access. The main problem in 5GHealthNet is in the connectivity of data end and user end and depends on the wireless connection provided by 5G networks.

10.11.10   Healthchain

It is a blockchain-based privacy-preserving scheme for a large amount of healthcare data. This encryption is done on healthcare data to conduct fine-grained access control. The technology of blockchain gives a digitized, public, and distributed ledger. In the health chain, the healthcare data collected by IoT devices are regularly

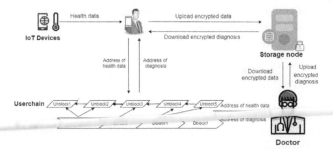

Figure 10.13   System model of health chain [30]

uploaded by users and published as a transaction. Artificial Intelligence (AI) health analyzers or doctors can diagnose anywhere and anytime based on the IoT data and publish the diagnosis as a transaction [30]. The blockchain node storage capacity is limited and cannot store many healthcare data. Therefore, the HealthNet system uses IPFS, a distributed file system and a content-addressable system, in which data are stored with resiliency and high integrity. There is no central server in IPFS. It can distribute a huge volume of data efficiently without replication. To improve the security of healthcare data, the health chain permits users to modify encryption keys, add authorized professional healthcare providers at any time and revoke. Figure 10.13 shows the system model of the health chain. Health chain can be classified into several different components, which are given as follows.

10.11.10.1   IoT devices

IoT devices monitor patients' health parameters, such as heart rate, weight, sleep patterns, calories burned, blood glucose levels, and others. Every IoT device has only a single user node as its management node. This node sends different healthcare data collected at the user node regularly. IoT devices have low power with limited storage and computing capabilities. Hence, they are indirectly involved in the blockchain.

10.11.10.2   User nodes

Every user node manages IoT devices that can collect and encrypt data from IoT devices, and forward them to the storage node. Some nodes are lightweight user nodes and save the block headers of the user chain and can only publish and generate a transaction. Some nodes are core nodes that have strong computing power and have a larger capacity. Core user nodes can publish, create, verify, and support lightweight user nodes to find transactions.

10.11.10.3   Doctor nodes

Every doctor node represents the AI health analyzer from healthcare organizations and real doctors from the hospital and clinic. They provide a diagnosis based on healthcare data collected from IoT devices. All hospitals and healthcare organizations form an association, and the rules of the association restrict the behavior of all the doctor nodes. Authorized doctor nodes can read the information on the user chain and create transactions for Docchain.

10.11.10.4   Accounting node

Association deploys this node as a special node in the system. This node verifies whether transactions from the doctor node are correct or not. After some time, accounting node selects the leader. The leader collects the authorized transactions from the doctor nodes in the association and creates a new Dblock, and adds this new Dblock to Docchain.

10.11.10.5   Storage nodes

These nodes collaboratively store all encrypted IoT data of users and encrypted doctors' diagnoses in a distributed manner. In the health chain system, every storage node is IPFS-based. Association of healthcare organizations manages and maintains the IPFS system. The content addressing method is used by the IPFS, in which the address is derived from the content of every file. Anybody can search the complete file stored in IPFS through the hash string of the file on Docchain or Userchain. The large volume of data with high efficiency can be distributed using IPFS.

10.11.10.6   Userchain

It is a blockchain that is public and is used to publish the data of users. It consists of a sequence of Unblocks that grow over time. Every Unblocks holds the hash of earlier Unblocks and transactions which the user generates.

10.11.10.7   Docchain

Docchain is an association blockchain, which is used to publish doctors' diagnoses. Only those doctor nodes that the association authorizes could create diagnosis transactions. These can be appended to Docchain by the accounting nodes. Information, however, can be read by anybody on Docchain. Docchain contains a sequence of Dblocks that grows over time. Every Dblocks holds the hash of earlier Dblocks and transactions that doctors create. In the health chain system, IoT devices forward healthcare data to the user node regularly or when some event occurs. The user node performs encryption of healthcare data and forwards it to the IPFS storage node. Hash of the encrypted data as a transaction to Userchain is added by the user node. The doctor node decrypts the healthcare data of users and provides an online real-time diagnosis. After this, the doctor sends the diagnosis in the encryption form to the storage node and generates a transaction for diagnosis, which contains the address of the encrypted diagnosis. Users read the information on Docchain for their health status.

10.12   Privacy of healthcare data

Nowadays, exposure of advanced targeted attacks against information systems and persistent threats are seen whose principal aim is to smuggle recoverable data by the attacker. Hence appropriation privacy of patients is observed as an increasing problem in healthcare data, making the healthcare industry and organization address these various critical and complementary problems. Data security controls access to data all over the data life cycle. In contrast, data privacy coordinates this access depending on the laws and privacy policies that decide, for example, who can see financial, private data, confidential, or healthcare information. Privacy of healthcare information data is very important and must be considered seriously.

10.12.1   Data protection laws

Healthcare organizations and industries must control and safeguard patients' personal information and address their threat and legal responsibilities concerning the refinement of personal data to address the growing thicket of applicable data protection legislation. Different countries have different laws and policies for the privacy of data. Some of the data protection laws and regulations in different countries are given as follows.

10.12.2   HIPAA Act, Patient Safety and Quality Improvement Act (PSQIA), and HITECH Act

This is the law of the United States. It needs the formation of national standards for electronic healthcare transactions. It provides the right to privacy to users, which ranges from age 12 to 18. The concerned user signs a disclosure before providing any healthcare information to anyone, including parents. Disclosure of patient safety work product should not be done. There is a civil penalty for those who violate the confidentiality provisions. It protects the privacy and security of electronic health information.

10.12.3   IT Act and IT (Amendment) Act

This is the law of India. It provides reasonable security practices for critical and sensitive personal information or data. There is a provision of compensation for an affected person by wrongful gain or wrongful loss. It provides for imprisonment and a fine for an individual who causes wrongful gain or wrongful loss by leaking personal information of another person while giving services under the terms of a lawful contract.

10.12.4   Constitution

This is the law of Brazil. The private life, intimacy, image of the people, and honor are inviolable, with assured right to compensate by moral or material damage resulting from its violation.

Russian Federal Law on personal data

This is the law of Russia. It requires data operators to take all the compulsory technical and organizational measures needed for saving private data against accidental or unlawful access.

10.12.5   Data Protection Act (DPA)

This is the law of the UK. It provides a method for users to manage themselves.

10.12.6   Data protection directive

This is the law of the European Union. It protects the fundamental rights and freedom of a person and, in specific, their right to privacy concerning the processing of personal data.

10.12.7   The 09-08 Act, dated 18 February 2009

This is the law of Morocco. It protects the privacy of individuals via the establishment of the CNDP authority by restricting the use of sensitive and personal data by data controllers in any operation of data processing.

10.12.8   Methods of privacy preservation for healthcare data

Some conventional methods for privacy preservation of healthcare data are given as follows.

10.12.8.1   De-identification

In this method, similar information from the healthcare data is removed to protect the disclosure of confidential information. The safe harbor method, used for de-identification, is a statistical method in which similar personal information is removed from healthcare data. This personal information can be address, name, telephone number, e-mail address, fax number, healthcare record number, social security number, full-face photographic image, finger and voice print, certificate/license number, health plan beneficiary number, account number, etc. A code is allocated to the de-identified information to de-identify information with the covered entity to later re-identify it. The code may not be obtained from information associated with the individual. The covered entity is not permitted to reveal the key to the code to anyone else. In the statistical method, a person or statistician has verified with suitable training that sufficient identifiers have been discarded, so the risk of identifying the individual user is very small.

10.12.8.2   HybrEx

It is a model for privacy and confidentiality in cloud computing. The nonsensitive healthcare data of an organization are stored on a public cloud, that is, when the industry and healthcare organization announce that there is no confidentiality and privacy risk in performing computation and exporting the data on it using public clouds. The organization's critical and sensitive, private data are stored on the private cloud, and computation is also performed on the private cloud. When an application needs access to both the public and private data, the application itself gets divided and runs in both the public and private clouds. It examines the sensitivity of data before the execution of the job and provides integration with safety.

10.12.8.3 Notice and consent

In this model, patients can manage their data, and a notice is given to them before the release of healthcare data for secondary use. Before collecting any private information from patients, a notice of an entity's information practices is provided to them, which includes recognition of the usage to which the data will be put to and identification of any potential recipients of the data [31]. The majority of current records-based research cannot obtain individual informed consent for each particular secondary use. Most of the studies depend on the previous information collected in years or decades when there was no secondary use expected.

10.12.8.4 Micro aggregation

It is the process of collecting the records into groups. The observation of the group is recorded and revealed instead of the information that is sensitive to an individual. This process includes different subprocesses, such as frequencies for all variables, including emergency services, hospital utilization, survival estimates for days to first medication visit post-discharge by patients enrolled in healthcare medication management and outpatient services. It is a critical process to reduce the loss of information by grouping the same records.

10.12.9 A privacy framework for healthcare data in cloud computing

This maintains the reliability and privacy of the healthcare data. It also ensures that only the authorized third-party will access the corresponding healthcare data. This privacy framework uses the data perturbation method, which safeguards the healthcare data from inference attacks. This privacy framework performs two main functions. In the first one, the hybrid data perturbation method is used to randomize the query result so that the individual user's privacy does not break. This method limits the inference attack in the cloud database. In the second one, a new rule-set has been suggested to manage the complete view of healthcare data for authorized users. We will first see the concept of data perturbation. Data perturbation is a method that is mostly used to control the privacy of electronic health records from inference attacks. Noise is added to the released query result in this method. It gives approximate results to all passing queries. There are various data perturbation methods, such as random projection-based perturbation, tree-based perturbation, data output, micro-aggregation perturbation swapping, orthogonal transformation-based perturbation, rounding perturbation, etc. Privacy framework for healthcare data in cloud computing consists of two concepts: rule-set and data perturbation. Figure 10.14 shows the various components, such as data perturbation module, EHR manager,

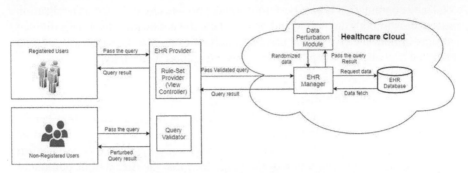

Figure 10.14   Privacy framework for healthcare data in cloud computing [32]

EHR provider (rule-set provider and query validator), healthcare database storage, and users (registered users and unregistered users), which are included in the framework.

Registered users have to give their credentials to log in, while without any credentials, unregistered users can log in as guest users. Any user can access the healthcare cloud by implementing the following steps:

1. EHR provider (middle tier) authenticates the user first.
2. User can forward the query to the EHR provider after successful authentication.
3. Query validator validates the querying user and forwards it to the EHR manager.
4. EHR manager extracts the data from the database of EHR concerning the given query and transfers it to the data perturbation module.
5. Data perturbation module randomizes the extracted results.
6. The result of the query is shown to the user concerning the rule-set given by the rule-set manager.

In this way, a privacy framework works for healthcare data in cloud computing.

10.13   Conclusion

At the start, we saw the various phases of data analytics. We have discussed various tools for the analysis of data. We looked at the storage options of large healthcare data. These storage options include on-premise data storage, cloud storage, hybrid approach, relational database storage MySQL, and NoSQL database. Special importance was given to how security and privacy can be preserved in the healthcare data system. Various security threats in wireless communication networks, including the 5G network, are described. The subsequent section focused on presenting E2E security solutions for 5G with privacy challenges and solutions for those challenges in the 5G communication network. This was followed by a discussion on various privacy and security concerns in the healthcare data. Finally, we presented the security of healthcare-related data with the introduction of the healthcare data security life cycle and various technologies used to secure healthcare data. We have described the various models, such as the 5GHealthNet and the health chain for healthcare data security. The health chain uses blockchain technology for securing healthcare data. We discussed healthcare data privacy with laws developed by various countries, methods of privacy preservation of healthcare data, and privacy framework for healthcare data in cloud computing. We have mainly focused on different new technologies and methods for securing and maintaining health ~~~~~ ~~~ privacy. In future ~~ ~~~~~ ~~~~ and technologies based on the 5G network and blockchain will help ensure a large amount of healthcare data and privacy of healthcare data.

References

[1] Somisetty M. Big data analytics in 5G. *IEEE 5G*; 2020. pp. 1–5.

[2] Ambigavathi M., Sridharan D. 'Big data analytics in healthcare'. *IEEE 2018 Tenth International Conference on Advanced Computing (ICoAC)*; 13–15 Dec 2018. pp. 269–76.

[3] Suganya S., Selvamuthukumaran S. 'Hadoop distributed file system security – a review'. *Proceeding of 2018 IEEE International Conference on Current Trends toward Converging Technologies*; Coimbatore, India; Mar 2018. pp. 1–5.

[4] Uma Maheswari M., Uma Maheswari M. 'Text mining: survey on techniques and applications'. *International Journal of Science and Research*. June 2017;6(6):1660–4.

[5] Cordeiro JoÃ£o Rala., Postolache O. 'Big data storage for a health predictive system'. *Proceeding of 2018 IEEE International Symposium in Sensing and Instrumentation in IoT Era (ISSI)*; 6–7 Sept 2018. pp. 1–6.

[6] *Enterprisestorageforum* [online]. Available from https://www.enterprisestorageforum. com/cloud-storage/on-premise-vs-cloud-storage.html [Accessed May 2020].

[7] *Morefield Communications* [online]. Available from https://www.morefield. com/blog/on-premises-vs-cloud [Accessed Apr 2021].

[8] Odun-Ayo I., Ajayi O., Akanle B., Ahuja R. 'An overview of data storage in cloud computing'. *2017 IEEE International Conference on Next Generation Computing and Information Systems (ICNGCIS)*; 11–12 Dec 2017. pp. 29–34.

[9] Singh M., Kaur K. 'SQL2neo : Moving health-care data from relational to graph databases'. *2015 IEEE International Advance Computing Conference (IACC)*; 12–13 Jun 2015. pp. 721–5.

[10] BÃ£ÆfZÃ£ÆfR C., Sebastian C. 'The transition from RDBMS to NoSQL. A comparative analysis of three popular non-relational solutions: cassandra, mongoDB and couchbase'. *Database Systems Journal*. 2/2014:49–59.

[11] Grover P., Johari R. 'Review of big data tools for healthcare system with case study on patient database storage methodology'. *2016 IEEE 6th International*

Conference – *Cloud System and Big Data Engineering (Confluence)*; 14–15 Jan 2016. pp. 698–700.

[12]   Moniruzzaman A.B.M., Hossain S.A. 'NoSQL database: New era of databases for big data analytics – classification, characteristics and comparison'. *International Journal of Database Theory and Application*. 2013;**6**(4):1–14.

[13]   Yalini M., Sridevi S. 'An approach for storing and retrieving health informatics big data'. *Proceedings of the 2nd International Conference on Inventive Communication and Computational Technologies (ICICCT 2018)*; 20–21 Apr 2018. pp. 1017–21.

[14]   Samy I., Koyluoglu O., Rawat A.S. 'Efficient data access in hybrid cloud storage'. *Fifty-Fifth Annual Allerton Conference Allerton House*, UIUC; Illinois, USA; October 3–6 2017. pp. 1–8.

[15]   Samy I., Ozan Koyluoglu O., Rawat A.S. 'Efficient data access in hybrid cloud storage'. *Journal of big data*. 2018:1–18.

[16]   *United States Cuber Security magazine* [online]. Available from https://www.uscybersecurity.net/csmag/data-security -privacy [Accessed Aug 2021].

[17]   Barakovi S., Kurtovi E., Bo˘zanovi O., *et al.* 'Security issues in wireless networks: an overview'. *2016 IEEE XI International Symposium on Telecommunications (BIHTEL)*; October 24–26 2016. pp. 1–6.

[18]   Gupta A., Jha R.K. 'Security threats of wireless networks: a survey'. *IEEE International Conference on Computing, Communication and Automation (ICCCA2015)*; 15–16 May 2015. pp. 389–95.

[19]   *Pluralsight* [online]. Available from https://www.pluralsight.com/blog/it-ops/wire less-lan-security-threats [Accessed 17 July 2019].

[20]   Bhandari N., Devra S., Singh K. 'Evolution of cellular network: from 1G to 5G'. *International Journal of Engineering and Techniques*. Sep–Oct 2017;**3**(5):98–105.

[21]   AnithaKumari K., Sudha Sadasivam G., Shymala Gowri S., Akash S.A., Radhika E.G. 'An approach for end-to-end (E2E) security of 5G applications'. *2018 4th IEEE International Conference on Big Data Security on Cloud, Communication and Automation (ICCCA2015)*; 3–5 May 2018. pp. 133–8.

[22]   Liyanage M., Salo J., Braeken A., Kumar T., Seneviratne S., Ylianttila M. '5G privacy: scenarios and solutions'. *2018 IEEE 5G World Forum*; 9–11 July 2018. pp. 197–203.

[23]   Abouelmehdi K., Beni-Hessane A., Khaloufi H. 'Big healthcare data: preserving security and privacy'. *Journal of Big Data*. 2018;**5**(1):1–18.

[24]   Chandra S., Ray S., Goswami R.T. 'Big data security in healthcare survey on frameworks and algorithms'. *2017 IEEE 7th International Advance Computing Conference (IACC)*; 5–7 Jan 2017. pp. 89–94.

[25]   Tanwar S., Parekh K., Evans R. 'Blockchain-based electronic healthcare record system for healthcare 4.0 applications'. *Journal of Information Security and Applications*. 2020;**50**(10):102407–13.

[26]   Chiuchisan I., Balan D.-G., Geman O., Chiuchisan I., Gordin I. 'A security approach for health care information systems'. *The 6th IEEE International*

Conference on E-Health and Bioengineering – EHB 2017; Grigore T. Popa University of Medicine and Pharmacy, Sinaia, Romania; June 22–24 2017. pp. 721–4.

[27] Karim A., Abderrahim B.-H., Hayat K., Mostafa S. 'Big data security and privacy in healthcare: a review'. *The 8th International Conference on Emerging Ubiquitous Systems and Pervasive Networks (EUSPN 2017)*; Elsevier; 2017. pp. 73–80.

[28] Yang C., Lin W., Liu M. 'A novel tri... ...ryption scheme for hadoop-based cloud d... ...urity'. *2013 Fourth International Conference on Emerging Intelligent Data and Web Technologies*; 9–11 Sept. 2013. pp. 437–42.

[29] Ardi N.K., Joshi N. 'Poster abstract: 5Ghealthnet –a cloud based framework for faster and authorized access to private medical records through 5G wireless network'. *2016 IEEE/ACM Symposium on Edge Computing (SEC)*; 27–28 Oct. 2016. pp. 89–90.

[30] Xu J., Xue K., Li S., *et al.* 'Healthchain: a blockchain-based privacy preserving scheme for large-scale health data'. *IEEE Internet of Things Journal*. Oct 2019;**6**(5):8770–81.

[31] Lawand V., Sargar P., Bhalerao A., Jadhav P. 'Analytical approach for privacy preserving of medical data'. *International Journal of Engineering Research and Technology*. 2015;**4**(10):430–3.

[32] Kundalwal M.K., Singh A., Chatterjee K. 'A privacy framework in cloud computing for healthcare data'. *IEEE International Conference on Advances in Computing, Communication Control and Networking (ICACCCN2018)*; 12–13 Oct.2018. pp. 58–63.

Chapter 11

Artificial intelligence and machine learning techniques for diabetes health-care

Manjiri M. Mastoli[1], Urmila R. Pol[2], R.V. Kulkarni[3], and Rahul Patil[4]

In today's world, an endocrine disease diabetes mellitus, which is also known as diabetes, is influencing our lives considerably. We need a viable model that can precisely anticipate diabetes and its types in the beginning phase. To improve the precision and effectiveness, machine learning model (MLM) has been proposed. This can diagnose diabetes and its types as type 1, type 2, and gestational diabetes that the patient is experiencing. The proposed MLM can determine diabetes precisely compared with other existing methodologies. During data collection, the researchers observed that diabetes is a disease that affects the eyes. Moreover, the majority of diabetic patients have been found to have an eye complication called diabetic retinopathy. This research aims to model a convolutional neural network (CNN) to predict diabetic retinopathy using deep learning techniques. These have been tested with data samples. The CNN model classifies the dataset of diabetic retinopathy. Also, it helps in combining the command of AI with the ML platform. Health-care 4.0 application has a huge impact on patients and caregivers where machine learning and deep learning technologies change the forecasting accuracy in health-care. However, the necessity for enhancements, multi-disciplinary research, strong protocols, inventories related to the impact of novel methods in health-care, and the level of automating majority health-care are indubitable.

Keywords

Data science, Diabetes mellitus, Artificial intelligent, Machine learning, Deep learning, Diabetes complication, Diabetes retinopathy, Decision tree algorithm, CNN

[1]Research Scholar, Department of Computer Science, Shivaji University, India
[2]Assistant Professor, Department of Computer Science, Shivaji University, India
[3]Head, Department of Computer Studies, CSIBER, Shivaji University, India
[4]Quality Engineer, Menon Bearing Ltd, Kolhapur, Maharashtra, India

The world has now moved into the era of data science. Therefore, the tools applied traditionally in other domains are now being considered in health-care. These data sources comprise regular, systematic data entry reports, data claims, data surveys, and data derived from biometric monitoring. Given the capital wealth of data that is being made available, the researcher needs to find the best data science approach, deep learning, and machine learning techniques available for applying to these datasets. Diabetes is a metabolic sickness characterized by an excessive degree of sugar, which is glucose in the blood, either due to insulin resistance or insulin deficiency. According to International Diabetes Federation (IDF), approximately 350+ million people had diabetes in 2011, which could possibly mean 550+ million people by 2030 [1]. Out of 180 per cent, diabetes-associated deaths occur in developing countries, such as India. Numerous researches have proven that diabetes is becoming an epidemic in developing as well as advanced countries worldwide. This demands a reliable, speedy, dependable, and sturdy method that can use science and technology to deal with diabetes [2].

11.1 Introduction

The field of medicine faces new difficulties, such as new diseases, high costs, new therapeutics, fast decisions, and so on. Since medical decision-making demands the utmost accuracy in diagnosis, it is a tedious, demanding, and challenging task for physicians. An automated system that helps in disease diagnosis is the prognosis of the disease. Thus, researchers focus on designing medical decision support systems with utmost accuracy.

Diabetes mellitus puts a huge financial burden on the health-care organizations and requires a big budget across the world. This burden can be calculated through clinical charges. These are direct and indirect charges connected to the loss of efficiency, early mortality, and the adverse effect of diabetes on the country's GDP. On the basis of a recent cost evaluation, the direct yearly expected budget of diabetes in the whole world is approximately US$ 830 billion [3, 4]. As per the IDF, the expenditure of global health-care system on the treatment of diabetes has increased during 2004 to 2014. The increase in the number of diabetic patients has resulted in an increment in the per capita diabetes spending [5]. In the present scenario of medical services, the administration is adequately furnished to observe, gather, and store information. In the process of assembling information, databases require specific instruments to access, store, and load data pertaining to investigations and operational utilization [6].

The expansion of information volume causes incredible troubles in mining relevant data for investigation. To adapt to this requirement, health-care informatics may utilize innovations in the new interdisciplinary field of information revealed in databases, that is, in KDD. This comprises statistical study, ML, AI, and pattern recognition technique to help the examination of data and reveal regularities encoded inside the information [7].

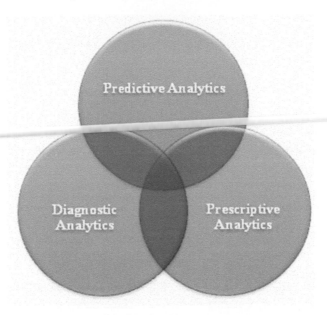

Figure 11.1   Data science health-care applications

11.1.1   Research contribution

Health-care uses data science solutions to recognize shortcomings and drive them out of managerial cycles in the medical care framework. Therefore, it helps reduce costs and supports payers, suppliers, and patients in a secure way. This research is based on data science concepts, such as AI, ML, data mining (DM), and deep learning. It presents ways to deal with it, which can be utilized to remove clinical information for analysis, forecast, checking, and understanding administration for diabetes mellitus.

11.2   Data science health-care applications overview

As per the recent research studies, the majority of data science analytic researches use cases. Also, they use various clinical data mining methods. These are of the following types, as shown in Figure 11.1:

Predictive

In predictive analytics, the companies, businesses, and health-care professionals apply AI, ML, and data mining to look at quiet records and decide possible results of the patient's health, for example, the chance of an exacerbating or improving health or odds of acquiring an ailment.

Diagnostic

Diagnostic analytics is characterized by advanced examination, which analyzes information to study the result that has occurred.

Prescriptive

In prescriptive analytics, the research firms use AI for calculations in order to complete investigation of the patient and to improve patient administration, for example, taking care of patient's belongings and planning the progression of errands employments, such as requesting tests.

11.3 Data science

Data science deals with the study of huge quantity of data, which includes mining significant information from raw, unstructured, and structured data that is treated using latest tools, technologies, algorithms, and scientific methods.

Data science is termed as a multi-disciplinary approach that utilizes many latest techniques and tools for operating the records. These databases discover the novel and meaningful usable or forecasting type of information.

Data science extensively uses AI and computer applications in variety of domains. It uses the leading hardware, programming systems, and best algorithms to resolve any difficulties. Data science is the future of AI. Therefore, machine learning and its algorithms have a significant role in modeling the data science models. There are many machine learning algorithms, but some are being broadly used to construct many of the data science models. Following are the significant algorithms used by data scientists:

- Naïve Bayes algorithm
- Decision tree algorithm
- Support vector algorithm
- A priori algorithm
- Regression algorithm
- Clustering algorithm
- Principal component analysis algorithm
- Artificial neural network algorithm.

11.3.1 Health-care management and health informatics

Data science applications help in clinically related regions, for example, the medical gadget industry, hospital management, and pharmaceutical industry. In social insurance industry, data science plays a vital role in distinguishing proofs and examining diseases. Individual assessment finds the most supportive and disguised data from the dataset and structures the judicious model. This is the reason behind the use of data science. Thus, data science has tremendous application in the domain of human service. Data science can be utilized for analysis, for example, pattern identification, testing of hypothesis, and risk evaluation. Also, it can be used to forecast, for example, AI models that help in calculating the probability of the occurrence of an event, in the light of known information factors.

A medicinal service covers itemized procedures to identify, prognose or diagnose, treat, and avoid ailment [8]. The clinical business and health-care service are advancing at a quick pace in many countries. The medical and clinical domains use the available information to create electronic clinical records, managerial reports, and different databases [9]. However, sometimes this information remains unutilized in databases. Data mining can scan for new and significant data from these databases. Medicinal services and information mining are mostly used by specialists to anticipate disorders and lead to conclusion about the choice of identifying their clinical and medical method.

Health informatics is presently turning into a research-intensive field and the biggest customer of public funds. With innovations and new calculations, the field of medical service has seen an upsurge in the use of computer devices and can no longer avoid their usage. This is coming about into joining of human service parts and registering to shape health-care informatics. This enables adequate and proficient health-care system while simultaneously improving the nature of medical services and reducing cost [10].

11.3.2 *Machine learning*

Machine learning is becoming increasingly important because the models can independently adapt to the situation when exposed to newer information. Learning from previous computations is used to produce reliable outputs. This method is a subset of AI, which utilizes measurable techniques to encourage machine to improve with understanding. This kind of programming gives the system the capacity to gain from information without being expressly customized naturally. This implies that these projects change their presentation and conduct by gaining from information [11, 12].

Machine learning is related to the theory of computational learning. Machine learning provides computer with the capability to acquire knowledge without being coded openly. The main objective of studying with machines is to design algorithms and develop a thorough analysis of the data. The use of computers and a proper machine learning strategy eases the process of construction of computer models and algorithms for analysis and prediction in data analytics. This, in turn, allows researchers and data analysts to provide reliable results and uncover hidden knowledge.

Machine learning has attained a very critical role in handling high-dimensional data. The machine should train rapidly, and the ability to train and learn should scale readily with volume and dimension. In health-care research, conventional machine learning approaches work efficiently with traditional datasets. However, usually, their performance deteriorates when applied to high-dimensional datasets. Therefore, there is a need to work with high-dimensional data. Machine learning can acclimate to different situations and discover and

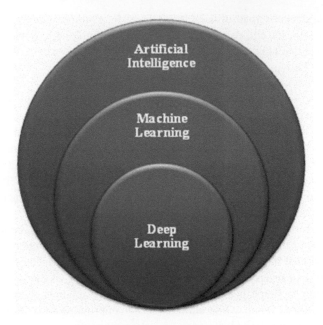

Figure 11.2   Artificial intelligence, machine learning, and deep learning

generalize arrangements. This machine learning can be categorized into three categories.

Machine learning algorithms are structured into different categories based on the anticipated output of an algorithm. In supervised learning, the algorithm produces a task that is mapped to inputs or an input that is mapped to anticipated outputs. The classification task problem was the ordinary creation of supervised learning. In unsupervised learning, the framework of fixed inputs is considered unavailable. There is a combination of both labeled and unlabeled instances for generating an applicable, suitable class or function in semi-supervised learning. In reinforcement learning, this algorithm studies an approach or strategy, or policy that acts on the observation. Transduction is similar to supervised learning; change is this. It does not openly build a method in its place, efforts to predict novel outputs depending on training inputs or new inputs and training outputs. These algorithms studies works earlier knowledge, which is to be considered as an input to them while taking any future action. The relation ship between the Artificial Intelligence, Deep Learning and Machine Learning is shown in Figure 11.2..

11.3.3   Deep learning

Deep learning refers to learning various stages of representations. The deliberation helps to understand information, for example, content, sound, and pictures. Deep learning approach is a part of machine learning and is portrayal based learning. A system takes in and builds intrinsic highlights from each progressive concealed layer of neurons. The word "deep" refers to various concealed layers in the Artificial

Neural Network (ANN). These ANN algorithms are similar to the functionality of a human brain. This model is based on input, hidden, and output layers. Each neuron or hub is associated with every neuron-like cerebrum neuron in the following layer through an association interface.

11.4 Diabetes mellitus and its complication

Diabetes mellitus is a chronic disease that occurs either when the pancreas does not produce enough insulin or when the body cannot effectively use the insulin it produces.

Insulin is a hormone that directs blood glucose. It is likewise called hyperglycemia or raised glucose. It is a typical impact of uncontrolled diabetes and, after some time, prompts genuine harm to our body's framework, particularly the nerves and veins (WHO). Diabetes can be classified into four types: type 1 diabetes, type 2 diabetes, Prediabetes, and gestational diabetes. In type 1 diabetes, the body is unable to create insulin. The body needs this hormone for consuming glucose from food as a source of energy. This type mostly affects young adults and children. An autoimmune response when the body's autoimmune system destroys the insulin-producing cells, called beta cells from islets of Langerhans, is termed as type 1 diabetes. As a result, the body is unable to yield insulin. This is an absolute deficiency of insulin hormone. The reasons for this destructive condition are not known. However, some of the reasons for this could be a mix of hereditary defenselessness or natural triggers, such as viral contamination, poisons, or some dietary components [13].

Type 2 is the most common kind of diabetes. It is the most widely recognized sort of diabetes, representing approximately 90% of all instances of diabetes. Type 2 diabetes causes hyperglycemia, which is the after effect resulting from the lack of insulin and body's inability to react to insulin, characterized as insulin opposition. During insulin obstruction, insulin becomes ineffectual and subsequently prompts an expansion in insulin creation to diminish the rising glucose levels. However, after some time, a condition of a relatively deficient product of insulin can create. Type 2 diabetes is observed more commonly in older adults. Yet, it is found more in youngsters, teenagers, and more older grown-ups because of the rising stoutness, physical latency, and undisciplined eating routine [14–16].

Gestational diabetes occurs during pregnancy. Therefore, this kind of diabetes may put the mother in danger of getting diabetes later. Likewise, such babies may suffer from overweight and inherit diabetes.

It is a transitory condition that happens in pregnancy and leads to a long-term risk of type 2 diabetes. The condition occurs when blood glucose rises higher than the average but remains below the analytic of diabetes. Women with gestational diabetes are at a high risk of various complexities during pregnancy and transmits it to the child. Gestational diabetes is analyzed through pre-birth screening. Hyperglycemia that is first recognized during pregnancy is termed as gestational diabetes mellitus or hyperglycemia in pregnancy. It has been assessed that most (75–90%) of the instances of high blood glucose during pregnancy are gestational diabetes [17, 18].

According to the International Diabetes Federation report, currently there are 240+ million people worldwide living with diabetes mellitus, and this number is expected to rise to 380+ million by 2030.

Diabetes is possibly reaching the predominant extents in India, where 62 million diabetic people are supposed to be suffering from the illness [19, 20]. In 2000, India broke the world record by having 31.7 million diabetic cases followed by 20.8 million in China. The United States with 17.7 million individuals in the second and third spots separately. India presently faces a questionable future than the potential weight that diabetes may force upon the nation [21].

Artificial intelligence and machine learning have a remarkable impact on many domains, and health-care is no exception. As tools and technology have become more developed and common, it is expected that AI and ML will help diagnose the disease in a wider range of population. Early detection of diabetes mellitus is a key task. Data science is an important asset and has played a vital role in the diabetes-related study. There are various tools and techniques, such as machine learning, deep learning, and other methods, that aid the study of diabetes. These eventually develop the quality of health-care in diabetes. For achieving correct treatment, there is a need for systematic diagnosis in medical science. The progress in information technology and data science has invigorated the investigators to design software to help physicians and patients make proper judgment.

This chapter has reviewed many research papers on diagnostic and predictive applications of artificial intelligence and machine learning for diabetic health-care. The researcher has targeted designing and developing a predictive model for diabetic health-care using machine learning and AI techniques.

Eye complication is one of the major symptoms of diabetes. Out of the total number of diabetic people, 30% of them have signs of retinopathy [22] and this statistic is growing continuously. These numbers are expected to increase significantly by 2040. Diabetes mellitus increases the risk for many serious health problems. These are classified as macro- and microvascular disorders. It is called a macro disorder if the injury occurs in larger blood vessels, while it is called a micro disorder if small blood vessels are injured. This type of vessel injury leads to incapability of kidneys (nephropathy), and eyes (retinopathy). It causes impaired vision and damage of nerves called neuropathy, leading to improper working (Figure 11.3). AI has played a very significant role in many health-care domains. The most common application in health-care has been in the field of ophthalmology for image diagnosis. The advantages of artificial intelligence in medicine are vast. Artificial intelligence is mainly appropriate for an ophthalmologist for handling difficulties. If practitioners are essential to hold control of professional upcoming, they must have intelligent algorithms and teach themselves and become well-informed for using, assessing, and applying deep learning positively [23]. This aids the practitioner and helps them reduce investigation and human errors with the help of proficient algorithms from image datasets by simple notice and forecast structures of images.

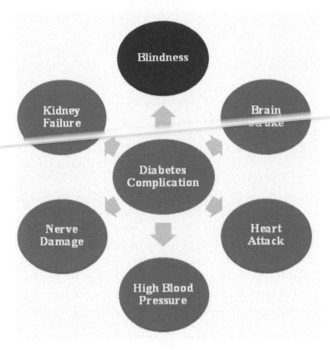

Figure 11.3   Major complications in diabetes

AI, ML, and profound learning ability to distinguish disease patterns and original associate structures to improve original scientific insight. Hyperglycemia is termed as the main pathophysiological condition in diabetes. To prevent the complications because of increasing sugar level is of great apprehension. Macro- and micro-vascular disorders are damaging effects of diabetes. Figure 11.3 shows the major complications of diabetes.

11.5   Deep learning model for prediction of diabetes retinopathy

The retinal disease, diabetic retinopathy (DR), is recognized as a worldwide epidemic. One-third of an estimated 285 million people with diabetes have signs of DR, and one-third of them have vision-threatening DR. In addition, these numbers are increasing. It is anticipated that 288 million people will have AMD by 2040, and those with DR will triple by 2050.

Diabetes mellitus increases your risk for many serious health complications. These complications are divided into microvascular, which is due to damage to small blood vessels, and macrovascular, due to damage to larger blood vessels (WHO). Micro-vascular complications include damage to eyes called retinopathy leading to blindness, to kidneys called nephropathy leading to renal failure, and to nerves called neuropathy leading to impotence.

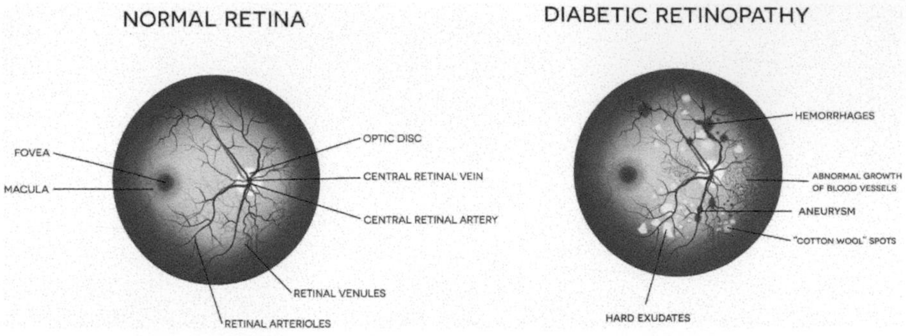

NORMAL RETINA　　　　　　　　　DIABETIC RETINOPATHY

FOVEA
MACULA

OPTIC DISC
CENTRAL RETINAL VEIN
CENTRAL RETINAL ARTERY

RETINAL VENULES
RETINAL ARTERIOLES

HEMORRHAGES
ABNORMAL GROWTH OF BLOOD VESSELS
ANEURYSM
"COTTON WOOL" SPOTS
HARD EXUDATES

Figure 11.4　　Diabetic retina and normal retina (Gadsden Eye Associates)

Data science solutions have just demonstrated ideas in numerous clinical fields that have striking similitude to ophthalmology. They are mind-boggling in indicative imaging, the most noticeable use of AI in medical care. The benefits of man-made reasoning in medication are tremendous. The computerized reason is especially appropriate for dealing with the multifaceted nature of 21st-century ophthalmology. It can help clinical practice by utilizing productive calculations to identify and foresee highlights from imaging information. It assists with lessening symptomatic and remedial mistakes. Furthermore, ML and profound learning can perceive infection explicit examples and relate novel highlights to pick up creative, logical understanding. On the off chance that ophthalmologists need to control their expert future, they should grasp shrewd calculations and teach themselves to assess and helpfully apply AI.

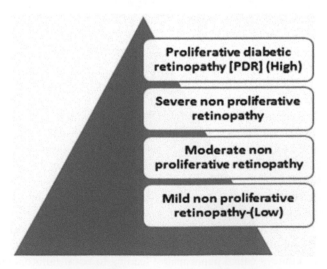

Proliferative diabetic retinopathy [PDR] (High)

Severe non proliferative retinopathy

Moderate non proliferative retinopathy

Mild non proliferative retinopathy-(Low)

Figure 11.5　　Phases of retinopathy

11.5.1 Diabetic retinopathy

When the body is unable to store and use glucose (sugar) properly, the disease is referred to as diabetes mellitus, commonly known as diabetes. When blood sugar levels increase, this high blood sugar of the patient damages the nerve cells. This condition is called diabetic neuropathy while the damage caused to the minute blood vessels in the retina is called DR. The function of retina is to detect light; this light is converted to signal sent through the optic nerve to the brain. DR can cause blood vessels in the retina to leak fluid or result in hemorrhage or bleeding, leading to distorted vision. In the most advanced stage of DR, new abnormal blood vessels proliferate on the retina's wall, leading to scars and cell loss. DR can progress through four stages: mild non-proliferative retinopathy, moderate non-proliferative retinopathy, severe non-proliferative retinopathy, and proliferative DR. Constantly extra glucose content in the blood of humans directly connected to injury of minute arteries and veins from human eyes, leading to DR [24, 25]. The function of the human retina is to sense light emissions. This light then translates these signs by optic nerve fiber to the human intelligence. This diabetes complication may lead to distorted visualization and leak eye liquid or bleed the blood vessels in the retina (Figure 11.4.). In the extreme stage where this damage number increases, the irregular blood arteries and veins increase on the superficial side of the retina leading to cell damage and a blurred vision of the eyes (American Academy of Ophthalmology) (NEI).

The four progressive phases of retinopathy have been shown in Figure 11.5..

After studying the diagnostic and predictive applications of artificial intelligence, expert systems, fuzzy expert systems, and machine learning in diabetic health-care, data science model plays an important role in solving complications caused due to diabetes.

11.5.2 Methodology for deep learning model

The following steps are performed while creating deep learning models using FastAI libraries.

11.5.2.1 Image classification using FastAI library

The FastAI library permits us to assemble models by using codes. The FastAI is an examination objective of creation AI available by giving a simple to use library expand on PyTorch. It is an elevated level library developed on the basis of PyTorch, which follows simple prototyping method and gives you admittance to a ton of present-day strategies or methods. The researcher of this paper used "Diabetic Retinopathy Detection" kaggle dataset and trained the machine to judge images as per normal retina as well as retina with DR.

11.5.2.2 Google Colaboratory

A Jupyter notebook works either on a cloud or locally. This Jupyter is an open source and browser-based tool that interprets and integrates languages, libraries, and tools for visualization. Google Colaboratory is a technology used for the execution of a program.

11.5.2.3   CNN using FastAI

The proposed deep learning classification model consists of convolution with pooling layers that are fully connected and give a binary classification of DR and normal retina, that is, no diabetic retinopathy (NODR). The author has used a convolutional neural network backbone and a fully connected head with hidden layers as a classifier. In the last step, the final model is applied to find out if the patient has DR or normal retina. In this model, the authors have used a dataset of fundus images of human retina having pixels over $2\,000 \times 3\,000$. The Kaggle dataset is freely available for download and has over 800 images for training and 200 for testing. The dataset proposed by its resolution fluctuates for different images. For this study, $1\,000$ images were chosen in a 8:2 training to testing ratio. This model needs to differentiate between normal and diabetic retina. The model with FastAI library simplifies training. FastAI performance is better because it has a fast and accurate image processing ability.

For creating the image classification model, the author used FastAI with cloud GPU provider Google Colaboratory. The steps performed for image classification are as follows:

1. Downloading dataset (image)
2. Loading/viewing data
3. Create and train a model
4. Clean the data
5. Interpret the results.

Step 1: Downloading image data

The FastAI library can download different datasets. It can also download images from files containing the image URLs. To get the URLs, file the dataset stored on your server.

Step 2: Load and view data

Data objects of FastAI, called data bunches, are required for training a model. These data bunches are formed by ImageDataBunch (Figures 11.6.–11.7).

```
[ ]  data.classes

[>  ['diabretina', 'normalretina']
```

Figure 11.6   Data classes

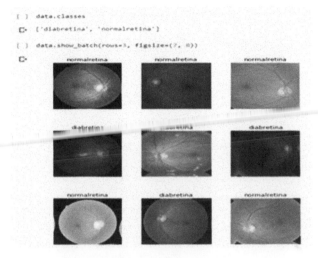

Figure 11.7   Data classes

Step 3: Create and train a model

The FastAI library helps to design and create models. In FastAI, these models are called learners with fewer lines of code.

These models give a technique called create_cnn, which is used to make a CNN. These models use the architecture resnet34 design and loads pre_trained data. Just the completely associated layers at the top can be prepared. To prepare the layers creator utilized the fit_one_cycle strategy. The suitable technique is a method of preparing a neural net with a consistent learning rate. The fit_one_cycle (Figure 11.8.) technique uses one cycle strategy, which essentially changes the learning rate over the long run to accomplish better outcomes.

Step 4: Cleaning the data

Using Jupyter widgets, the FastAI provides functionality for cleaning data. The ImageCleaner class displays images for the deletion or relabeling. For ImageCleaner, the author used DatasetFormatter () from_toplosses to get misclassified images as top losses (Figure 11.9).

epoch	train_loss	valid_loss	error_rate	accuracy	time
0	0.240868	0.621682	0.210526	0.789474	00:01
1	0.196123	0.644820	0.157895	0.842105	00:01
2	0.203185	0.662209	0.157895	0.842105	00:01
3	0.185842	0.667164	0.157895	0.842105	00:01
4	0.199340	0.659575	0.157895	0.842105	00:01

Figure 11.8   The fit_one_cycle

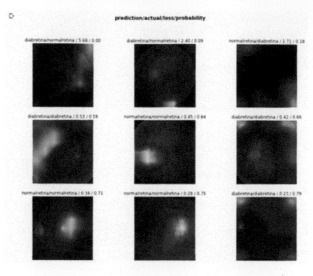

Figure 11.9   Top losses

Step 5: Interpretation

In the last step, the Classification_Interpretation class is used to interpret the results. To create an interpretation object, researchers need to call the from_learner method and pass it to the learner model (Figure 11.10).

11.6 Results and discussion

In DR, much work has been done by researchers. The related work in medical sciences and machine learning shows that researchers have proposed and implemented various machine learning methods. As deep learning libraries are available, this can become the main attribute to the model's performance. Hence, the work done proves to be a new approach while considering the results and findings of various machine learning algorithms for DR. The increasing use of digital information provides opportunities to create deep and rich datasets for health-care analysis. This study demonstrates that a deep learning neural network effectively distinguished DR fundus images from standard retina images with reasonable accuracy. This deep learning algorithm using FastAI libraries and the Google Colaboratory GPU is a novel application to retinopathy classification in ophthalmology to our best knowledge.

Researchers define specificity as the number of images correctly identified the diabetic retina (diabretina) and normal retina (normalretina) for this two-class problem. Researchers define accuracy in terms of several test images with a correct classification. The final trained network achieved 85.5% accuracy. The potential benefit of FastAI CNN is that it can categorize thousands of retinal images. The professional convolutional neural network makes quick diagnosis and instant response to a patient possible. Accuracy rate can be increased because it is dependent on the

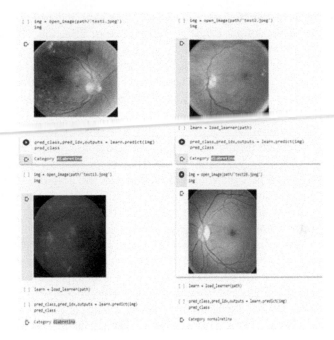

Figure 11.10   Prediction of categories by convolution model (normal retina vs. diabretina)

training dataset; therefore, the beauty of innovation is the use of FastAI libraries, which will reduce the time for neural network compilation. This proposed model focuses on verifying how the deep learning algorithm categorized the images as diabetic retina and normal retina. The researcher performed testing in which the location of the test images, which had already been classified by the dataset source, were systematically uploaded. The deep learning neural network successfully identified the test images with great accuracy. The application of testing provides an insight into the trained deep learning model, where features were most important in distinguishing diabetic retina images from normal retina images. In Figure 11.6, testing shows an accurate classifier, which was an important feature. Finally, deep learning models can identify diabetic retina images and efficiently display them to the clinician to aid in diagnosing and treating ophthalmology [26].

11.7   Machine learning model for prediction of diabetes mellitus

The effect of AI is outstanding in the domain of medical care. Information science and AI can be utilized for investigation and forecast in medical care. Medical services are a progressive and promising industry for actualizing the information science answers for predictive medicine, genetics research, medical images analysis, and drug discovery. As the innovation turns out to be more regular, if there should arise an occurrence of medical services space, it is expected that man-made reasoning will help visualization, analyze a wide zone of infection. This copies the dynamic capacity of the human brain. As per the IDF, it has been estimated that 415 million individuals live with diabetes globally, and India is the second biggest nation with 69 million diabetic individuals. These numbers are an inspiration for this particular study, where there is a need for a mechanized framework that will diagnose diabetes in the beginning phases.

Diabetes is an issue of sugar digestion. This is described by a debilitated capacity of the body to create insulin or react insulin and consequently keep up legitimate degrees of glucose (sugar) in the blood. Diabetes is extensively classified into three primary sorts as type 1 diabetes, type 2 diabetes, and gestational diabetes. On account of type 1 diabetes, the decimation of the islets of Langerhans of the pancreas happened due to immune system frameworks. This pancreas is a wellspring of insulin. From the complete populace of diabetes individuals, it accounts for just 5–10%. Type 2 diabetes is exceptionally normal and records 90–95% of the absolute diabetes populace; it's firmly connected with weight and is a consequence of opposition and inadequacy of insulin. Gestational diabetes is an impermanent condition in which blood glucose (sugar) levels increment during pregnancy state, and it will be getting back to ordinary conditions after conveyance. The ladies, who are experiencing gestational diabetes, have a future danger of being diabetic.

The researchers have proposed a novel strategy for predicting diabetes disease and its sorts of eye complications. This prescient examination will help a person know their own risk of being diabetic and the individual activity should be accomplished for staying away from such medical issues. The reason for this examination is to plan a machine leaning model (MLM) for diabetes determination. Procuring the right side effects of the patient is a significant factor in the use of rules. This information help the doctors to decide whether the patient is diabetic or not, for example, type 1 diabetes, type 2 diabetes, and gestational diabetes. An MLM was tried on 150 patients. It has accomplished precise outcomes as specialists. An MLM that analyses have planned can be utilized adequately and proficiently to analyze diabetes types. It helps patients in lacking nations where the quantity of specialists isn't sufficient. This MLM means to diminish the reliance on specialists. It will help the two specialists and patients to settle on more precise and speedier choices.

11.7.1   Description of the dataset

The dataset contains information about symptoms related to the type of diabetes where values are provided. This dataset contains 65 columns where the prediction value as PredictionOfDiabetes is given in one column and values of type 1, type 2, and gestational diabetes in three columns, while the remaining columns show symptoms. The authors have considered the dataset, with each row in the dataset representing one test case for each diabetes type. A total of 500 test cases are entered into the dataset. These are the rules for the model. Selecting and designing of rules for the model needs expert knowledge for increasing prediction accuracy.

11.7.2   Knowledge base designing

Table 11.1 lists the significant symptoms of diabetic patients. These are arranged based on their types and qualities. These qualities are "0" and "1" of the case side effects, which will take parallel rates and numbers when indications are changed from multiple qualities. In side effects with two classifications, either True OR False, doled out double qualities 0 and 1 (Table 11.2). For instance, FamilyHistory is termed by the parallel worth 0 and 1. On account of multi-valve symptoms, it will take the arrangement of numbers. Age with three classifications Young, Adult, Old termed to by the number with values 11, 12, and 13: Obesity with three classifications Low_Normal_Obese termed to by the number with values 21, 22, and 23; Hypertension with four classifications Normal, Elevated, High, and very high termed to by the number with values 3, 4, 5, and 6; HDL Cholesterol with three classes Low_Medium_High termed to by the number with values 1, 2, and 3; and Triglyceride with four classifications such as Normal, BoarderLine, High, and very high are known by the number with values 2, 3, 4, and 5. Table 11.1 is set up based on essential information assortment and auxiliary information assortment, for example, doctors information, books, Internet, clinical diaries, diabetes patients, and so forth. Table 11.1 is considered as one of the three contributions for the framework. Similarly, various side effects for each type of diabetes are thought of while planning rules in the CSV record.

11.7.3   Knowledge base as a dataset

Table 11.1 contains a rundown of the significant indications of diabetic patients. Those are characterized based on their sorts, now planned with the assistance of qualities. These qualities are zero, and one of the case side effects will take parallel rates and the arrangement of numbers when indications differ from multiple attributes. Segments termed to X-Type1Diabetes, Y-Type2Diabetes, Z- and Gestational Diabetes.

Table 11.2 shows the analysis of the dataset. It contains the number representation for the symptoms.

11.7.3.1   Methodology

The secondary data for this research have been gathered from WHO, IDF reports, reference books, Internet, and clinical diaries. The essential information assortment about the symptoms influencing diabetes mellitus is done through surveys from doctors. The principle for this MLM was planned, followed by proposal information investigation. The rules are entered into the CSV file. This file is a dataset for the proposed model. A cloud service of Jupyter Notebook known as Google Colaboratory is used to execute an AI-based MLM. This dataset contains the information or knowledge base for a model as symptoms represented by numbers referred from Tables 11.1 and 11.2. This MLM predicts the types of diabetes which patients are experiencing. Here dataset with values which are rules and the information base

Table 11.1   Knowledge base as dataset

Symptoms	X	Y	Z
1. FamilyHistory	0	1	0
2. Age	11	12	12
3. Obesity	22	23	21
4. PreviousIFG/IGT	0	1	0
5. Hypertension	0	5	5
6. HDLCholesterol	0	3	0
7. Triglyceride	0	5	0
8. IncreasedThirst	1	1	0
9. IncreasedUrinate	1	1	0
10. IncreasedAppetite	1	1	0
11. WeightVariation	0	1	0
12. ImpairedVision	0	1	0
13. Tiredness	1	1	0
14. Impatience	0	1	0
15. Infection	0	1	0
16. ItchySkin	0	0	0
17. DepressionStress	0	0	0
18. TinglingSensation	0	0	0
19. FruityBreathOdour	1	0	0
20. BedWetting	1	0	0
21. SlowHealingWound	0	1	0
22. FamilyHisPregnancy	0	0	1
23. PreviousPregnancy	0	0	1
24. BabyOver9PdPrePreg	0	0	1
25. Sleeplessness	1	1	0
26. Trembling	1	1	0
27. Sweating	1	1	0
28. Anxiety	1	1	0
29. Confusion	1	1	0
30. Weakness	1	0	0
31. MoodSwings	1	0	0
32. Nausea	1	0	0
33. Vomiting	1	0	0
34. DrySkin	0	1	0
35. Aches/Pains	0	1	0
36. RecurrentFungalInfectn	0	1	0
37. Nightmares	1	1	0
38. Seizures	1	1	0
39. Sadness	1	1	0
40. Unconsciousness	1	1	0
41. Numbness	1	1	0
42. Vaginal_Mycotic_Infectn	1	1	1
43. RapidHeartBeat	0	1	0
44. RecurringGumInfe	0	0	0
45. Impotency	1	1	0
46. High_blood_Pressure	0	0	1
47. SleepWalking	1	1	0

(Continues)

Table 11.1 Continued

Symptoms	X	Y	Z
48. MakeGunusualNoises	1	1	0
49. LegCramps	1	1	0
50. SlurredSpeech	1	1	0
51. FlushedFace	1	1	0
52. PaleSkin	1	0	0
53. Loss_Of_Menstruation	1	1	0
54. StomachPain	1	1	0
55. DeepBreathing	1	1	0
56. AreasDarkedSkin	0	1	0
57. DifficultConcentrating	1	1	0
58. Dehydration	1	1	0
59. Lack_Of_Coordination	1	1	0
60. HistHeartStroke	0	0	0
61. PolyOvarySyndrome	0	0	0
62. Low_blood_Sugar_Newborn_Baby	0	0	1
63. Waist_Size_02cmM88cmF	0	0	0
64. Waist_Hip_Ratio.9M.85F	0	0	0

of the MLM. A portion of the standards for including one of the classes of diabetes analysis that can be deciphered is as per the following.

Family_History 0, Age 12, Obesity 23, PreviousIFG/IGT 1, Hypertension 1, HDLCholesterol 0, Triglyceride 1, IncreasedThirst 1, IncreasedUrinate 1, IncreasedAppetite 1, WeightVariation 0, ImpairedVision 0, Tiredness 1, Impatience 0, Infection 0, ItchySkin 1, DepressionStress 1, TinglingSensation 1, FruityBreathOdour 1, BedWetting 0, SlowHealingWound 1, FamilyHisPregnancy 1, PreviousPregnancy 1, BabyOver9PdPrePreg 1, Sleeplessness 0, Trembling 0, Sweating 0, Anxiety 0, Confusion 0, Weakness 0, MoodSwings 0, Nausea 0, Vomiting 0, DrySkin 1, Aches_Pains 1, Recurrentfungalinfectn 0, Nightmares 1, Seizures 1, Sadness 1, Unconsciousness 1, Numbness 1, Vaginal_Mycotic_Infectn 1, RapidHeartBeatm 0, RecurringGumInfe 0, Impotency 1, high blood Pressure 0, SleepWalking 1, MakeGunusualNoises 0, LegCramps 0, SlurredSpeech 0, Flushedface 1, PaleSkin 1, Loss_of_Menstruation 1, StomachPain 1, DeepBreathing 1, AreasDarkedSkin 0, DifficultConcentrating 1, Dehydration 1, LackOfCoordination 0, HistHeartStroke 0, PolyOvarySyndrome 1, LowbloodSugarNewbornBaby 1, WaistSize02cmM88cmF 1, WaistHipRatio.9M.85F 1.

11.7.3.2 Machine learning model

Classifier decision tree is the most suitable methodology used for multiclass classification of the dataset. The calculations in such decision tree can be considered as a paired tree. The study from root node to inner hubs is presented, where the information on the hub is also a part of discrete records with various attributes. The dataset are the leaves of the tree that imply the classes. In Scikit_learn accompanying the

Table 11.2 Symptoms with number representation

Symptoms (Boolean value)			Symptoms (multi-value)		
Family_History	True	1	**Age**	Old	13
	False	0		Adult	12
				Young	11
Obesity	Obese	23	**Triglyceride**	Normal	2
	Normal	22		Boarder Line	3
Hypertension	Low	21	**HDL_**	High	4
	Normal	3		very high	5
	Elevate	4	**Cholesterol**	Low	1
	High	5		Medium	2
	Very High	6		High	3

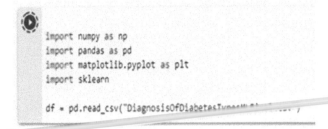

```
import numpy as np
import pandas as pd
import matplotlib.pyplot as plt
import sklearn

df = pd.read_csv("DiagnosisOfDiabetesT...
```

Figure 11.11   Libraries and dataset

code bit, the analysts train a decision tree classifier. The classifier decision tree is a class fit for performing multiclass classification of a dataset.

11.7.3.3   Libraries and dataset

The researcher used Panda's read_csv method by importing libraries and datasets for associated content; while the respective dataset was in CSV design (Figure 11.11). Getting data frame in the dataset and saving the marks into a variable. The received information is executed using the df.head() and df.shape() methods to make them segmented in respective dataset. Set up the data for additional activity. The isolated information into traits, names, and partition the resultant information preparing and test sets. After testing, there is the preparation of needful calculation. This gives a much precise perspective on how respective calculations will perform the tasks. The partition information into preparing and test sets is completed in reprocessing step. The model_selection library of Scikit-Learn contains the train_test_split method, which haphazardly parts the data into testing sets and preparing sets. The data need to be isolated into the preparation and testing sets. To prepare the decision tree classification on this information and make forecasts considered the last step. The strategy for the DecisionTreeClassifier class is utilized for making decisions.

11.7.4   Results and discussion

An extensive survey of certain models and frameworks for diagnosing diabetes was done [27–40] to recognize fundamental correlations between the proposed model and the generally existing models. Onuiri *et al.* designed an electronic system to analyze diabetes by determining side effects and different boundaries intended to re-enact a specialist framework. The application uses input boundaries to decide the type of diabetes [41]. Though planned standard-based framework which is healthcare choice sensitively network, that is, decision support system for facilitating analysis of diabetes, respective decision support system can create categories diabetes into type 1, type 2, gestational, and prediabetes, dependent on the symptoms selected by patients, this system designed by Dilip Kumar Choubey and team [42]. Tawfik Saeed Zeki *et al.* utilized VP Expert_Primer used for designing the diabetes predictor framework. THis framework uses a choice table to find and represent different factors of the patient like age, manifestations, tests, and other important factors which help the doctors to do proper diagnosis [43].

Similarly, Pratama *et al.* designed an android application, which is a portable application used to determine the complications of diabetes in an individual. For this, the model uses an apparatus for early counteraction [44]. Fuzzy expert system/ FIS with improved the exactness and to accomplish better ability. For diabetes diagnosis, Hanslal Prajapati *et al.* designed and executed expert system with the help of the Pima Indian diabetic dataset [45].

There is tremendous innovation in medical care and its related domains. The AI applications have an immense scope for treating disorders identified in diabetes, such as diabetic neuropathy and retinopathy. Future investigations for discovering more exact manifestations and utilizing the intensity of new innovation upgrade the exactness of forecast with a higher rate along these lines. Bypassing the values of symptoms for the patient referred from Tables 11.1 and 11.2 predicting diabetes types of a patient by utilizing the respective model author gave five distinctive test cases out of 150 patients. It has accomplished accurate outcomes as a physician.

11.7.5   Prediction tests

TEST 1:

```
[ ] My_Pred=dtree_model.predict([[0,13,23,1,6,3,5,1,1,1,1,1,1,1,1,0,0,0,0,0,1,0,0,0,1,1,1,1,1,0,0,0,0,1,1,1,1,1,1,1,1,1,0,1,0
```
↑ ↓ ⊝ ▤ ✿ 🗑 ⋮

```
▶ My_Pred
```

```
[→ array(['Type2Diabetes'], dtype=object)
```

Test 1 result as Type2Diabetes

TEST 2:

```
[ ] My_Pred=dtree_model.predict([[1,12,23,1,6,3,5,1,1,1,1,1,1,1,1,0,0,0,0,0,1,0,0,0,1,1,1,1,1,0,0,0,0,1,1,1,1,1,1,1,1,1,0,1,0
```
↑ ↓ ⊝ ▤ ✿ 🗑 ⋮

```
▶ My_Pred
```

```
[→ array(['Type2Diabetes'], dtype=object)
```

Test 2 result as Type2Diabetes

TEST 3:

```
[ ] My_Pred=dtree_model.predict([[0,11,23,1,5,3,5,1,1,1,1,1,1,1,1,0,0,0,0,0,1,0,0,0,1,1,1,1,1,0,0,0,0,1,1,1,1,1,1,1,1,1,0,1,0
```
↑ ↓ ⊝ ▤ ✿ 🗑 ⋮

```
▶ My_Pred
```

```
[→ array(['Type2Diabetes'], dtype=object)
```

Test 3 result as Type2Diabetes

TEST 4:

```
[ ]  My_Pred=dtree_model.predict([[1,12,23,1,5,3,5,1,1,1,1,1,1,1,1,0,0,0,0,0,1,0,0,0,1,1,1,1,1,0,0,0,0,1,1,1,1,1,1,1,1,1,1,0,1,0
```

```
  My_Pred
```

```
  array(['Type2Diabetes'], dtype=object)
```

Test 4 result as Type2Diabetes

TEST 5:

```
[ ]  My_Pred=dtree_model.predict([[0,11,22,0,0,0,0,1,1,1,0,0,1,0,0,0,0,0,0,0,0,0,0,0,0,0,0,1,1,1,1,1,1,1,1,1,1,1,1,1,1,1,1,1,1
```

```
  My_Pred
```

```
  array(['Type1Diabetes'], dtype=object)
```

Test 5 result as Type1Diabetes

A wide assortment of energizing and future-looking utilizations of AI/ML procedures and stages in the space of medical services are conceivable. The proposed MLM is creative for a finding of diabetes is more precise when contrasted with other existing methodologies. The majority of people with diabetes have an eye complication called DR. The CNN can classify the retinal images, which is an aid to ophthalmologists. As technologists and AI professionals, one ought to take a stab at a splendid future where the intensity of AI benefits billions of ordinary citizens to improve their essential well-being and prosperity.

11.8 Conclusion

AI reasoning in medical care is an all-encompassing term used to depict the usage of all calculations and programming, or AI, to copy human cognizance in the investigation, translation, and appreciation of convoluted clinical and medical care information. This study suggests that AI and ML methods have virtually endless applications in the health-care industry. Today AI and ML are helping to simplify administrative processes in hospitals, personalized medical treatment, and treatment of infectious diseases. Data science research has a remarkable potential to improve the diagnosis of diabetes mellitus and identify the type of diabetes, which is helpful for medical practitioners and patients. ML method saves time while diagnosing diabetes. The scope of AI and ML application in analytical research is expected to increase in the up coming years. The MLM uses a simple decision tree classification algorithm that is a supervised learning process and is non-parametric and applicable for forecasting diabetes and grouping the different types of diabetes. This modelMLM diagnoses diabetes and its kind on the basis of symptoms. This is a universal method from which one can convert expert systems to a ML platform.

The convolution neural network model for diagnosis of DR is effective for image processing, which is trained with a GPU system provided by Google Colab. This model DR has 80% accuracy. Deep learning methodologies cover all the domains in the health-care system and are more effective in image processing, risk assessment, and disease prediction. The model DR uses FastAI libraries. With the help of FastAI libraries, anyone can create a design model using fewer programming codes. This CNN model is effective for the image processing model trained with a GPU system provided by Google Colab. The pre-compiled neural network will help in getting a timely and accurate result. This model classifies images of DR and normal retina. It can assist ophthalmologists in clinical diagnosis. It is important to conduct extensive research in health-care for accurate diagnosis and prognosis of many diseases.

References

[1]   Whiting D.R., Guariguata L., Weil C., Shaw J. 'IDF diabetes atlas: global estimates of the prevalence of diabetes for 2011 and 2030'. *Diabetes Research and Clinical Practice*. 2011;**94**(3):311–21.

[2]   Sherwani S.I., Khan H.A., Ekhzaimy A., Masood A., Sakharkar M.K. 'Significance of HbA1c test in diagnosis and prognosis of diabetic patients'. *Biomarker Insights*. 2016;**11**:95–104.

[3]   Mastoli M.M., Pol U.R., Patil R.D. 'Machine learning classification algorithms for predictive analysis in health-care'. *Machine Learning*. 2019;**6**(12):1225–9.

[4]   Seuring T., Archangelidi O., Suhrcke M. 'The economic costs of type 2 diabetes: a global systematic review'. *PharmacoEconomics*. 2015;**33**(8):811–31.

[5]   International Diabetes Federation (2013) IDF Diabetes Atlas. 6th Edition, International Diabetes Federation, Brussels. 2013. Available from http://www.idf.org/diabetesatlas [Accessed Jun 2021].

[6]   Lavrac N. 'Selected techniques for data mining in medicine'. *Artificial Intelligence in Medicine*. 1999;**16**(1):3–23.

[7]   Frawley W., Piatetsky-Shapiro G., Matheus C. 'Knowledge discovery in databases: an overview' in Piatetsky-Shapiro G., Frawley W. (eds.). *Knowledge Discovery in Databases*. Menlo Park, CA: The AAAI Press; 1991.

[8]   Yang J.-J., Li J., Mulder J., *et al.* 'Emerging information technologies for enhanced healthcare'. *Computers in Industry*. 2015;**69**(3):3–11.

[9]   Wickramasinghe N., Sharma S.K., Gupta J.N.D. 'Knowledge management in healthcare'. 2005;**63**:5–18.

[10] Shortliffe E.H., Perrault L.E. (eds.). *Medical Informatics: Computer Applications in Health Care and Biomedicine*. 2nd edn. New York: Springer; 2000.

[11] Yang J.-J., Li J., Mulder J., *et al.* 'Emerging information technologies for enhanced healthcare'. *Computers in Industry*. 2015;**69**(3):3–11.

[12] Shalev-Shwartz S., Ben-David S. *Understanding Machine Learning*. United States of America: Cambridge University Press; 2014.

[13]   You W.-P., Henneberg M. 'Type 1 diabetes prevalence increasing globally and regionally: the role of natural selection and life expectancy at birth'. *BMJ Open Diabetes Research & Care*. 2016;**4**(1):e000161.

[14]   Evans J.M., Newton R.W., Ruta D.A., MacDonald T.M., Morris A.D. 'Socio-economic status, obesity and prevalence of type 1 and type 2 diabetes mellitus'. *Diabetic Medicine: A Journal of the British Diabetic Association*. 2000;**17**(6):478–80.

[15]   Bruno G., Runzo C., Cavallo-Perin P., *et al*. 'Incidence of type 1 and type 2 diabetes in adults aged 30–49 years: the population-based registry in the province of Turin, Italy'. *Diabetes Care*. 2005;**28**(11):2613–9.

[16]   Holman N., Young B., Gadsby R. 'Current prevalence of type 1 and type 2 diabetes in adults and children in the UK'. *Diabetic Medicine*. 2015;**32**(9):1119–20.

[17]   Hod M., Kapur A., Sacks D.A., *et al*. 'The international federation of gynecology and obstetrics (FIGO) initiative on gestational diabetes mellitus: a pragmatic guide for diagnosis, management, and care'. *International Journal of Gynecology & Obstetrics*. 2015;**131**(S3):S173–211.

[18]   NIH Stem Cell Information. '*In stem cell information* [online]. Bethesda, MD: National Institutes of Health'. *U.S.* 2016.

[19]   Joshi S.R., Parikh R.M. 'India – diabetes capital of the world: now heading towards hypertension'. *The Journal of the Association of Physicians of India*. 2007;**55**:323–4.

[20]   Kumar A., Goel M.K., Jain R.B., Khanna P., Chaudhary V. 'India towards diabetes control: key issues'. *The Australasian Medical Journal*. 2013;**6**(10):524–31.

[21]   Bostrom N. 'Superintelligence: paths, dangers, strategies'. *Oxford University Press*. 2014

[22]   Lee R., Wong T.Y., Sabanayagam C. 'Epidemiology of diabetic retinopathy, diabetic macular edema and related Vision loss'. *Eye and vision*. 2015;**2**:17.

[23]   Jiang F., Jiang Y., Zhi H., *et al*. 'Artificial intelligence in healthcare: past, present and future'. *Stroke and Vascular Neurology*. 2017;**2**:230–43.

[24]   Alghadyan A.A. 'Diabetic retinopathy – an update'. *Saudi Journal of Ophthalmology*. 2011;**25**(1):99–111.

[25]   Acharya R., Faust O., Kadri N.A., Suri J.S. 'Automated identification of normal and diabetes heart rate signals using online measures, comput'. *Biology and Medicine*. 2013;**43**(10):1523–9.

[26]   Mastoli M.M., Pol U.R., Patil R.D. 'AI for diabetic retinopathy'. *International Journal of Scientific Research in Computer Science and Engineering*. 2019;**7**(6):30–5.

[27]   Mastoli M.M., Pol U.R., Patil R.D. 'Machine learning model for prediction of diabetes mellitus'. *International Journal of Recent Technology and Engineering (IJRTE)*. 2020;**8**(5):2376–81.

[28]   Tanwar S. 'Fog computing for healthcare 4.0 environments: technical, societal and future implications'. *Signals and Communication Technology*. Springer International Publishing; 2020. pp. 1–430.

[29] Tanwar S. 'Fog data analytics for IoT applications – next generation process model with state-of-the-art technologies'. *Studies in Big Data*, Springer International Publishing; 2020. pp. 1–550.

[30] Tanwar S., Tyagi S., Kumar N. Security and privacy of electronics healthcare records. *Institution of Engineering and Technology*; Stevenage, United Kingdom; 2019. pp. 1–450.

[31] Kumari A., Tanwar S., Tyagi S., Kumar N. 'Fog computing for healthcare 4.0 environment: opportunities and challenges'. *Computers & Electrical Engineering*. 2018;**72**(5):1–13.

[32] Sheth K., Patel K., Shah H., Tanwar S., Gupta R., Kumar N. 'A taxonomy of AI techniques for 6G communication networks'. *Computer Communications*. 2020;**161**(5):279–303.

[33] Kumari A., Tanwar S. 'Secure data analytics for smart grid systems in a sustainable smart city: challenges, solutions, and future directions'. *Sustainable Computing: Informatics and Systems*. 2020:1–28.

[34] Gupta R., Tanwar S., Tyagi S., Kumar N. 'Tactile-internet-based telesurgery system for healthcare 4.0: an architecture, research challenges, and future directions'. *IEEE Network*. 2019;**33**(6):22–9.

[35] Gupta R., Tanwar S., Tyagi S., Kumar N. 'Machine learning models for secure data analytics: a taxonomy and threat model'. *Computer Communications*. 2020;**153**(5):406–40.

[36] Bodkhe U., Tanwar S. 'Secure data dissemination techniques for IoT applications: research challenges and opportunities'. *Software: Practice and Experience*. 2020;**15**(12):1–23.

[37] Kumari A., Gupta R., Tanwar S., Tyagi S., Kumari N. 'When Blockchain meets Smart Grid: Exploring Demand Response Management for Secure Energy Trading'. IEEE Network; 2020. pp. 1–7.

[38] Kumari A., Gupta R., Tanwar S., Kumar N. 'Blockchain and AI amalgamation for energy cloud management: challenges, solutions, and future directions'. *Journal of Parallel and Distributed Computing*. 2020;**143**:148–66.

[39] Hathaliya J., Sharma P., Tanwar S., Gupta R. 'Blockchain-based remote patient monitoring in healthcare 4.0'. *9th IEEE International Conference on Advanced Computing (IACC)*; 13–14th December, 2019. pp. 87–91.

[40] Mastoli M.M., Pol U.R., Patil R.D. 'AI for diabetic retinopathy'. *International Journal of Scientific Research in Computer Science and Engineering*. 2019;**7**(6):30–5.

[41] Onuiri Ernest E., Ndukwe Victor U., Nkechinyere I., Olise Saviour C. 'Simulation of an expert system for diabetes diagnosis'. *International Journal of Advanced Computing*. 2015;**48**(1):1614–21.

[42] Choubey D.K., Paul S., Bhattachrjee J. 'Soft computing approaches for diabetes disease diagnosis: a survey'. *International Journal of Applied Engineering Research*. 0973-4562. 2014;**9**:11715–26.

[43] Zeki T.S., Malakooti M.V., Ataeipoor Y., Tabibi T. 'An expert system for diabetes diagnosis'. *American Academic & Scholarly Research Journal*. 2012;**4**(5):1–13.

[44] Pratama A.Y., R. D.A., Senjaya R. 'Design of mobile expert system for diabetes risk diagnosis and information'. *Journal of Information System*. April 2013;9(1):32–6.

[45] Prajapati H., Jain A., Pal S.K. 'An enhance expert system for diagnosis of diabetes using fuzzy rules over PIMA dataset'. *International Journal of Advance Engineering and Research Development*. 2017;4(9):2348–6406.

Chapter 12

Analytics for data security and privacy in 5G health-care services

K Rajkumar[1] and U Hariharan[2]

The modern technological, global wearable computing devices have witnessed a selection of electronic advances, communication paradigms, and micro-controllers, including sensors and intelligent societal demand. It's providing technology progress in the digital health-care system. Nowadays, the improved variety of connected health-related units continuously gathers information. Businesses inhibit keeping medical, and compliance means adhering to the requirements for authorized people to enter. Cloud information storage space provides scalable and flexible surroundings less expensive than on-premise deployments, attractive to discussed entities. Companies checking out data analytics expect their storage space specifications to be continuously boosted when the Internet of mobile devices and Things accumulate information that has to be kept. Smart Healthcare 1.0 to 4.0 has essentially transformed how groups deal with, analyze, and influence data. Health-care information has many opportunities to enhance diligent results, anticipate outbreaks of epidemics, gain valuable insights, stay away from avoidable illnesses, cut down on the price of health-care shipping and delivery, and enhance the caliber of a living whole. Big data analytics could be utilized within large-scale gene scientific studies, public health, fitness, personalized and accurate medication, brand new medication advancement, and so on.

Nevertheless, choosing the allowable information applications while protecting protection and a person's directly to secrecy. Several obstacles can found associated with privacy and security. Smart health-care devices have particular needs when handling privacy and security problems. We explored recreation concerning authentication, access control, and de-identification through a conceptual viewpoint and concentrated primarily on essential features and features driven in electric-powered health-related methods.

[1]Department of Computer Science and Engineering, Faculty of Engineering and Technology, Jain University, India
[2]Department of AIT-Computer Science and Engineering, Chandigarh University, India

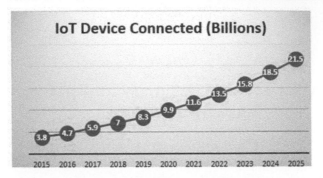

Figure 12.1   Internet of Things (IoT) active device connections installed globally from 2015 to 2025 (in billions)

12.1   Introduction

Health-care organizations are attempting to develop their IT infrastructures with increased flexibility and scalability to satisfy the increasing need for information. They are even worse by the quickly improving earth inhabitants, the issue significantly senior citizen rate increases (65 years of age and above). As per WHO, 2018 [1] massive figure on elderly citizens has increased by approximately 2 billion by 2050. Internet of Things (IoT) has, in tandem with many other emerging technologies, such as machine learning, AI, edge computing, and 5G, started to create value and also provide a naturally competitive edge to organizations in several industries ranging from production to fleet management to asset and energy control to even intelligent urban areas [2]. Figure 12.1 shows that the IoT market in India could touch 22 billion dollars by 2025 and account for nearly 6 per cent of the global market. India's IoT units could probably increase considerably, from about 200 million devices in 2016 to 4.7 billion devices by 2020. As these devices generate data, it will fuel originality in treatments highly targeted for customers, manufacturing procedures, program distribution systems, and for producing business models. It is predicted that by 2025, IoT equipment will produce 94 zettabytes of data.

The value-based rewards for increasing numbers and data analytics of connected health units that are continuously collecting information, the businesses are actually in the demand of maximum information storage space abilities that each Health Insurance Portability and Accountability Act (HIPAA) acquiescent for authorized people to access. They're opting for possibly an ideal to command IT administrators more than actual physical data centers, or maybe they're applying cloud storage and creating their IT infrastructure due to reduced maintenance cost and HIPPA compliance [3].

The worldwide medical information storage space industry is segmented on the basis of structure, deployment, kinds, storage space methods, end-users, and regional country. Based on structure, the worldwide health-care or medical information storage space market is categorized into block storage space, file storage space, and object storage space. Based on the component integration, drivetrains mainly include series, parallel, and hybrid power split designs. The marketplace is split into magnetic storage space and flash solid-state storage space based on the kinds [4]. According to storage space devices, the worldwide medical information storage space marketplace is categorized into network-attached storage space, storage area networking, and direct-attached storage space. Based chiefly on end-users, the worldwide health-care information storage space marketplace is categorized into pharma, hospital, Contract Research Organization (CRO), biotech, clinic, and research center [5]. The areas covered in that information storage space industry in Europe, Asia-Pacific the Rest, and of the world. On the country level, the marketplace is subdivided directly into the United States, Mexico, Canada, the UK, Germany, China, Japan, France, India, South-East Asia, Italy, Africa, Gulf Cooperation Council (GCC), and so on.

Thus, research came up with a solution to blockchain engineering in medical healthcare, which won't just protect information from being tampered, but guarantee that the information leakage stopped. This technology might protect information and hence guarantee reliability. And if this concept is needed and cloud computing technology, storage issues could also vanish because the cloud is reliable for storing and controlling information. Furthermore, blockchain can deal with the security problems of the cloud. Indeed, health data sharing and storing with the blockchain-based cloud can address a great deal of health data issues. This technology may also be applied in the individual's wearable device, keeping his information private. The patient's entire movement will scan for the biometric signature, and this signature is needed while scanning this wearable gadget embedded with IoT technology, in which information is saved for further analysis.

Furthermore, wireless mobile technology is developing, and Telecare Medical-related information Systems could utilize far more and more, to help monitor the individuals and the data [6, 7]. This particular place can help monitor individuals suffering from a chronic disease, infectious disease, etc. This telemedical information can additionally be manipulated or perhaps eliminated by the assailants. Once again, the blockchain comes into the picture when discussing the patients' information privacy and confidentiality while information sharing through telemedical engineering. Blockchain characteristics are shown in Table 12.1.

The blockchain has several features that make it appealing for the Internet of Medical Things (IoMT) to fix many of its issues.

The chapter, structured as follows in the second section, discusses the four-layer design of IoMT. It is used to evaluate protection risks and secrecy issues. According to the IoT structure, the third section proposed a taxonomy for IoT-dependent sensors inside the e-health-care program. The fourth section includes the taxonomy of IoT security. In the fifth section, we analyze the structure protection framework and a protection mechanism via the IoT protection requirements.

Table 12.1　Blockchain characteristics in IoMT

S. No	Characteristics	Explanation
1.	Anonymity	Legal rules to worry about sensible contracts and dispute resolution have yet to create appropriately. Some effort has been to conclude realistic contracts with smart contracts.
2.	Security	Blockchain provides much better security because there is no individual point of failure to shut down the whole community.
3.	Open Source	Blockchain technology is developing to offer open-source access to everybody connected to the network. This unique versatility entitles anyone to examine the information publicly and build different impending applications.
4.	Immutability	Constructing immutable ledgers is actually among the significant quality of blockchain. All centralized databases could be corrupted and generally requires trust in a third party to keep the information integrity. When you've agreed on a transaction and recorded it, it can certainly not be modified.
5.	Decentralization	The absence of centralized control ensures robustness and scalability by using all participating nodes' materials and eliminating many-to-one website traffic flows. In latency is decreased by turn and resolve an individual point of failure in the centralized model.

(Continues)

Table 12.1   Continued

S. No	Characteristics	Explanation
6.	Increased Capacity	Among the substantial factors about blockchain, engineering can increase the capability of a whole network. Getting a massive number of computer systems working together as an entire might have greater power than several centralized serves.

12.2   IoMT security and privacy architecture model

IoMT architecture system design comprises four levels: awareness level, middle ware level, networking level, and finally, the application level, as shown in Figure 12.2. The responsibility of the awareness level is collecting information with a wide variety of products. The network level of the wires, wireless systems and middleware, and its procedures also communicates input received by the belief level supported by a technological framework. Well-structured transport protocols boost

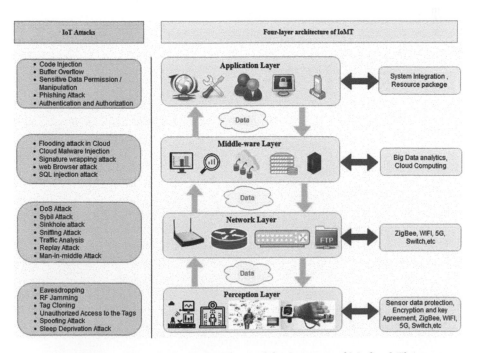

Figure 12.2   Four-layer architecture of the Internet of Medical Things

transmission effectiveness and decrease energy usage and ensure privacy and security. The application-level integrates the health, smart cities, and other information resources to offer personalized services and fulfill the ultimate user need, based on the target users' real circumstance and the service demand. IoMT layers due to the awareness of health-related methods, it's essential to handle the several thousand MTs attached above the Internet in a heterogeneous manner to ensure maximum dependability. Thus, there's a requirement to have a versatile layered structure. The IoT four-layer design discussed by Das *et al.* [8] provides a layered structure whereby every level offers specific efficiency. Each performance has unique security and privacy issues. Consequently, we catalog security and privacy problems based on their occurrence for each level as follows.

12.2.1   Awareness or perception level

Awareness level remains liable to obtaining and gathering information (e.g., heat, pulse, temperature, etc.) by utilizing essential tools like sensors before moving information on the system (i.e., community level). For instance, found overall health keeping track of methods, many sensors interconnect to make specific inpatient was administered and assist if needed quickly [9]. As shown in Figure 12.2, the primary critical solutions are radio frequency identification tags, digital cameras, receptors, wireless sensor systems Wireless Sensor Networks (WSN), and so on. The methodology of awareness (or) perception level is impacted by electrical power and computing energy. While doing so, a sensor unit could be employed , which can easily be damaged (unintentionally and intentionally).

a) Embedded devices:

These units are embedded into the human body; some of the available gadgets are:

- *Swallowable:* Envisions intestinal area of the human inside.
- *Embedded cardiac*: Records information and directs information to a surrounding ubiquitous community.

b) Surrounding devices:

These units feel human environments and keep track of exercise patterns, bathroom visits, sleep quality, and supply warnings to the family members once distinctive designs are found [10]. This kind of receptor is likely to initiate areas more ingenious and less dangerous for individuals with persistent factors. Background receptors include:

- *Motion sensors:* identify motions of individuals within an area.
- *Room climate sensors:* record the kitchen heat.
- *Pressure sensors:* computer monitor gasoline, air volume, and fluid.
- *Door sensors:* identify doorstep changes (i.e., opened, or close)

c) Motionless system:

This group contains products that are fixed and never typically together with the affected person such as:

- *Photography devices:* generate graphic illustrations of an entire body for medical intervention and clinical analysis, like X-rays, computerized tomography (CT) scanners, and magnetic resonance imaging (MRI).
- *Medical system:* tools utilized for operations or surgeries.

12.2.1.1   Some of the awareness layer attacks

Attacks on integrity and secrecy of information are affected by these devices and might result in unwanted outcomes that could be deadly. Potential awareness-level attacks include:

- **Side-channel:** Hackers can use several side-channel methods, like information action timing and strength usage evaluation, to keep track of electromagnetic pastime all-around health-care products to draw out vulnerable details [11].
- **Cloned tags:** An adversary could customize the information collected due to a prosperous side-channel encounter or even identical information in an existing label. For instance, the duplicated label might be utilized illegally to create information, such as patients' confidential information. Assailants can easily duplicate RFIDs utilizing affordable gadgets [12]. The privacy and security of cloud storage space-related data are two essential ideas. Information safety measures mean the data are preserved and transferred correctly to ensure validity. Then authenticity, together with information secrecy, implies the specifics noticed exclusively by humans, who have the authorization to be receptive and make sure it is used [13]. Much more sensible security techniques may be made based on different needs and purposes. The overall utilization of IoT items has a significantly more straightforward guarantee for people's smart health. However, it puts significant strain on information protection and secrecy.
- **Unauthorized alterations on devices:** A sensor stays concerning the body firmly that may move, and it's feasible for every enemy to unauthorized alterations with receptors toward entirely nor partially prevent nor even control their functionality. Assailants can turn on products to ruin nearly every health-care gear with a receptive USB port [14]. Assailants also unauthorized can-do alterations with products in manipulating several hardware liabilities to set up malware, allowing them to consider Hojo motor magnetic generator [15, 16].

12.2.2   Communication layer

The communication or network layer is liable to facilitate transfer, find articles, routing of information to the spot, and community handling. The media utilized by the MTs are as follows:

- *Fixed connection / Wireless connection:* IoT products utilize fixed connection or wireless connection networks to hook up to the entryway and conclusion customers/users. Products that use interaction tend to fix due to their need for dependable energy supply—this ideal for IoMT methods that need high speed.
- *Radio interaction:* Some IoT-enabled gadgets make use of technologies such as 3G, bluetooth, LTE, 4G, and also RFID to establish the communication between the gadgets. Bluetooth minimal energy (BLE) is an essential short [17].
- Range correspondence is moderately applied to most wearable mobile tele systems. A fixed bluetooth hub (beacon) inside a clinic suite links several products through the suite permitting information transmission back and forth from products. Cellular grounded (third generation of broadband cellular network technology/4G long-term evolution/LTE-A) IoT products are ideal for extended ranges.
- Mobile Tele systems could also hook up through WSNs whereby they typically use a conventional WiFi link or perhaps a reduced run wireless individual place system (6LoWPAN) to interconnect. Most strikes relevant to social networking occur in typical computer system networks or even WSNs [18].

12.2.2.1   Some communication or network layer attacks

Nevertheless, just fewer brand-new attacks come from brand new solutions, including the routing protocol for energy like conventional routing protocol for the IoT-based applications. Prospective communication-level attacks include:

- **Eavesdropping:** This is becoming among the simplest methods for assailants to gather information from a detector. Assailants find the necessary physical device and intercept it to gather information transferred by hardware systems effectively. For instance, the sufferer's vitals can become intercepted during transmission. Information hence collected illegally may be utilized to do different sorts of strikes. Although encryption can conquer the problem, effective encryption isn't necessarily sensible, particularly with lower-run units.
- **Replay:** An assailant might recycle an authenticating email, which was an earlier exchanged between genuine people. The assailant might have grabbed the idea by eavesdropping or even compromising several of the nodes. For example, the insulin pump OneTouch Ping is famous for being susceptible to this particular strike since it lacks protected correspondence systems [19].
- **Man in the middle:** The (person not having official permission) unauthorized intruders can gain access to information with a backdoor and secretly replay and modify the genuine party's communications. The IoMT products usually transmit and get information that can be changed which results in incorrect treatment (e.g., medication overdose) [20]. Lately, an equivalent vulnerability described in St. Jude cardiac products enables the man in the middle to remotely compromise the unit and eavesdrop on communications between the transmitter and the products associated with it [21].

- **Rogue access** is a particular assault. An established gateway is placed inside the wireless community assortment to enable genuine PC user entry and intercept site traffic. Based on the SANS Institute, this particular strike could be performed working with free software and can't easily be found because a forged gateway might conceal its existence [22, 23].
- **Distributed denial of service (DDoS/DoS):** This strike disturbs accessibility of medical equipment and services by flooding the d~~evi~~ ~~..iui~~ program requests. Distributed denial of ser~~vice i~~ ~~.. iui~~ more intense kind of DoS where numerous ~~nod~~ ~~..u~~ associated with the flooding, and that helps make it harder and fiercer to identify. Attackers can use automated equipment, like botnets, to use infected IoT products without having the original node. Botnets can utilize affected nodes in a beautiful community to release a broad range of distributed denial of service encounters on some other products. Throughout 2017, a huge-scale DDoS attack utilizing the IoT devices was successful because of a significant deployment of insecure IoT devices [24, 25].
- **Sinkhole:** These attacks are much more typical in a wireless sensor network. In this particular assault, a malicious node draws in visitors by guaranteeing much better website link quality (e.g., marketing phony routes). Many other strikes can be launched when the website stream of traffic is drawn to the harmful node, like selective forwarding or eavesdropping. The malicious node could separate a few nodes by shedding packets moving through them.

12.2.3 Middleware layer

The middleware level controls gathering and filtering the attained information from notion-level products (i.e., sensors), executing access and service discovery management on the equipment. Cloud computing platforms are typical in the existing IoMT locations. Based on a Hewlett Packard (HP) review on a few IoT tasks, 60 per cent of all are cloud computing connected IoT products that have cross-site demand forgery (Session & CSRF) hijacking vulnerabilities [26]. The middleware level supplies service and interfaces for the application level. Hackers can strike the program (e.g., web app services) to influence the end-user level—the attack on the database and server influences the product's information security and operational security. Strikes on the cloud primarily aim for data and virtualization, posing an enormous risk to users' privacy. The goal of the assault center is to destroy the QoS and the end-users' privacy.

12.2.3.1 Some middleware layer attacks

- **Cross-site request forgery (XSRF or CSRF):** It is a one-click attack, much more typical in RESTful-based IoT methods. The cross-site request forgery attacks the end-user into taking several activities on an invalid code without understanding. The internet user interface of the IoT level gets susceptible to CSRF strikes if they are not set up correctly [27].

- **Session hijacking:** Strike is also typical in representation state transfer and its concept, based on the IoT methods. Smart IoT products have period link to connect with the user interface amount, which is to be governed by period hijacking.
- **Cross-site scripting (XSS):** Cross-site scripting additionally exploits RESTful (Representation state transfer and its concept) based IoT uses by injecting edge scripts to avoid entry settings through pages [28]. The internet user interface of cloud computing and IoT products is susceptible to such strikes.

12.2.4 Software or application layer

The application level may be the user interface whereby consumers link with the IoMT products through a middleware coating. Since the cloud's arrival, software producers lean much more toward webpage-hosting uses in the cloud domain due to the better elasticity and suppleness.

12.2.4.1 Potential strikes in this level are as follows:

- **Structure query language injection:** It encounters a place where an assailant tries to strike the back-end repository attached to the program by inserting a malformed structured query language (SQL) declaration. This particular strike poses a tremendous threat to the IoT systems, particularly in the medical segment. A good SQL injection episode can compromise sensitive affected person information or even alter serious details [20, 29]. An SQL injection vulnerability continues to be found in a cardio management method.
- **Account hijacking:** A large number of IoT products share the data in text format in the system or have inadequate encryption of position. An assailant can complete account hijacking by intercepting the package while a client is now being authenticated [30]. Used open system interconnects with unpatched vulnerabilities have become the primary element in the rise of the assault, as discussed in several occurrences.
- **Cryptoviral extortion:** It encrypts valuable details as well as asks for an enormous ransom for restoration. This particular risk can begin with only one particular printer, spreading to the entire community [31, 32]. Attackers can encrypt susceptible details as the affected person captures and stores the decryption element in return for cash.

12.3 Suggested taxonomy for IoT-based receptors within the e-health-care system domain

The broadly classified IoT dependent e-health sensor strategies to a higher organization (Figure 12.3):

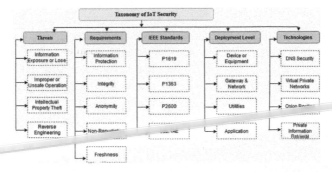

Figure 12.3   Suggested taxonomy for IoT-based receptors within the e-health-care system domain

- Disposable health and also health and fitness receptors (temperature, ingestible, invasive, strip, diagnostic, implementable, wearable, pressure, accelerator, bio-sensors, monitoring) along with therapeutics
- Embedded overall health receptors (consumer, flow sensor, embedded receptors, wearable, level sensor IoT supported detectors, patient tracking, diagnostics, treatment administration, therapy, health-care provider, hardware, individuals, than mere software)
- IoT industry cap receptors (suitable medical sensor, fitness wearable, sleep monitoring, infant overseeing, a medical quality biometric sensor, consumer/home overseeing sensor, brain sensor).

12.4   Taxonomy of IoT security

Figure 12.4 depicts the taxonomy that was invented influenced by diverse details, including IoT security risks or threats, prerequisites, IEEE standards, deployment layer, and also solutions.

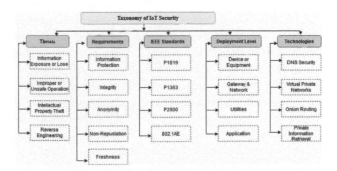

Figure 12.4   Taxonomy of IoT security

12.4.1   IoT security risk

Within the IoT prototype, many changes, such as unsuitable functioning, destructive code mitigation, bypassing functions, and tampering with information integrity, are taking place. Facts coverage, as well as the damage, can take place in IoT apps. And so, safeguarding information such as credentials, keys, and private details is essential [33]. Intellectual homes are usually jeopardized since unprotected IoMT uses, and supplements expose lodged proprietary algorithms that could effortlessly be pirated, (or) perhaps examined [34]. It is proposed to prevent new vulnerabilities, which makes it typically more challenging for online hackers to be able to overturn, exploit, analyze, and advance programming.

12.4.2   Prerequisite

System integrity is utilized to assure the accuracy and consistency of the information. Digital signatures and Hash functions are utilized to ensure the integrity of the information. Furthermore, information confidentiality should also be preserved within the IoT environment with the storage space's quantity and along the system track. The protection of information from the unauthorized access is the main issue that needs to be tackled. For instance, the IoT products should not present the sensor readings to their neighbors. Anonymity is going to be the program of concealing information solutions. This technology system aids the problems of assuring information confidentiality and secrecy [35]. Inside IoT, non-repudiation aids in creating a particular get-together on the understanding cannot refute the authenticity on their signature on recognized papers.

12.4.3   Institute of electrical and electronics engineers standards

The IEEE P1363 fundamentally identifies asymmetric encryption techniques, such as mathematical, elementary for the specific essential age group. Besides, it makes use of precisely the same mathematical bases due to the crypto analytics program [36]. The IEEE P1619 (standardization project encryption of storage data) says elements of the cryptographic framework for information safeguard on chunk-oriented storage space equipment details, strategies, algorithms, and information security schema. The mechanism supports the enhancement of valuable resources for secure and interoperable safeguard of saved information. The IEEE P2600 offers protection and the protection of devices methods, such as transcriber and publisher. The IEEE 802.1AE fundamental says the provision of connectionless computer operator information, confidentiality, frame information integrity, together with information origins authenticity by mass press entry impartial protocols and entities that run transparently to MAC clients. IEEE 802.1X allows for interoperable computer operator identification, centralized authentication, and essential managing. User-based identification is seated on a local community entry identifier that allows roaming to access public aspects through effective essential control.

12.4.4 Deployment level

Device or product security is a significant problem. In literature, different solutions exist to secure them consist of establishing the most excellent methods, lowering external unit link, disabling insecure devices/endpoints coming from immediate access into the world wide web. These make sure that the specified solutions are empowered, shielded booting (utilizing secure firmware as well as keys) utilizing merchandise authentication inside each hook-up establishment, putting on software update and patches on gadgets operating system, producing link safe listing and utilizing secure crucial interchange [33, 37]. IoT gateway protection against malware and intrusions must be protected by employing various systems, air filtering, and entry managing prospect lists (Router, hub, and gateway). Moreover, actual hardware and also community protection tasks cure relating to isolating sensitive information. The assistance provider ought to get as well as yield guarantee accreditation [34]. This process uses several methods, like by utilizing remote entry safety measures, enabling authentication for remote entry to privileged proprietors as administrators, employing upkeep specialists for signing within thoroughly coming from remote places along with the method, as well as running protected stations, such as VPN for continues associates accessing the device out of outside places. Secure is made specific by wireless marketing communications protection configurations when talking throughout WSN and IoT devices or sensors to gateways by dealing with encryption and authentication systems. Managing as well as cloud protection needs particular interest offered by IT industries. Information created by the IoT products is primarily stored in a centralized cloud storage [38]. As a result, in some of the virtual machines' security blocks may get unauthorized entry, in which there is a need to have a strong security solutions. These security solutions defense the cloud using authorized encryption algorithms, which includes effective management methods. Safeguarding of websites facing cloud situations can be guaranteed with IDS/IPS, host-based firewalls.

Moreover, logs of individuals and online resources must be verified . This will bring down the risk of program-connected strikes, halting time replay, XSS, SQLite, and a buffer. To reduce the attacks, a few of the methods that might check out as most acceptable methods include scanning/fuzz assessment of apps (dynamic, fixed, and hybrid) for vulnerabilities and snapping remedial measures to correct them. Additionally, code signing might also ensure customers' authenticity concerning all application programs and non-repudiation. Information that's vital together with scanned documents should be administered and shielded against any unauthorized alterations. For example, prospects and setup documents can be administered against deliberate or accidental unwanted alterations (i.e., integrity monitoring). Suitable solutions as integrity overseeing products need to placed to prevent or conserve the alert about the above-mentioned issue and combine with experimental modification endorsement and examine processes.

12.4.5 Technical knowledge

Virtual private networks are extranets that permit entry then companions, that they ensure to support confidential and have assured the integrity. Nevertheless, this particular idea is not apparent, creating a robust information exchange method to protect the data from outside breaches. Domain Name System SECurity (DNSSEC) utilizes asymmetric cryptography for signing supply captures to obtain origins authenticity and acquire and deliver data integrity. Onion routing technologies encrypt and combine internet guests originating from more senders. Consider, for example, information is wrapped in several encryption levels, employing the public strategies of the onion routers and the transmission tracking. The particular method can impede a corresponding internet process package to a particular source of energy. Nevertheless, onion routing raises waiting around occasions, thus leading to general performance issues [39]. Private information retrieval (PIR) techniques are accustomed to conceal consumer information curiosity. Nevertheless, issues of management that are key and scalability, and the general performance troubles, are encountered to an around the world accessible telephone system. For that reason, this process just might be impractical.

12.5 S-health framework and techniques

Smart health-care structures have carried out excellent handiness for individuals. In the procedure for collecting and monitoring information from several domains, WSN becomes commonplace and has also been popular in ITS (intelligent transport system), ad hoc networks for R-health (remote), and smart meter-employed metering gasoline usage. Collectively, these may be utilized to provide IoT uses. The primary concept of the IoT is connecting all types of items (IoT and sensors), which may easily design the lives of living things better. Existing tasks such as S-Santander considerably relied on IoT technologies. A testbed was created to monitor the website traffic status by deploying sensors in various towns and helping owners find available parking areas [40, 41] rapidly. Various data types could be collected by a metropolitan IoT process and exploited to market local governments' activities and work with their citizens. For instance, the London Oyster Card item can produce 7 million information captures daily and 160 million monthly. With a broad spectrum of information sets getting gathered up in such measurements, big data solutions could be followed to allow for many smart health-care programs, from gathering, and processing to analyzing multivariate data sets.

Figure 12.5 shows that the S-fitness and health (electronic healthcare) study might be considered the result of projecting an e-wellness plane with an intelligent society plane [42]. Both sensible well-being (movable well-being and smart health) (mobile health) might be provided as electronic health subsets. Nevertheless, smart health might not include portable applications but fixed sensors in the feeling of root infrastructures. Due to the assistance of big data analytic methods (e.g., predictive modeling, pattern recognition, and different ML algorithms), a health framework

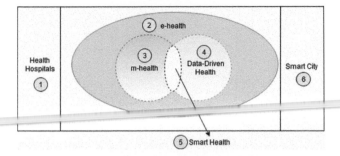

Figure 12.5   Diagram for smart health and related concepts

can be provisioned via automatic services. An extra s-health framework was created utilizing many analytic methods on health-related databases [43, 44].

As shown in Figure 12.6, a layered, scalable smart health infrastructure made of four practical PH levels for data link, data analytics, data storage, and wind up the presentation. After gathering information on products from several scenarios, the initial issue is how to process this heterogeneous data (e.g., laboratory and radiology files, records, hospital information, and prescriptions from pharmacies). At the storage layer, synthetic details might be viewed and operated flexibly through the use of cloud-based relational directories or maybe No Structured Query Language (NoSQL) storage room offerings to organize unstructured, semi-organized, along with structured information solutions. Putting this together, the analytic level can offer many functions [45]. They are based on information processing requirements. Lastly, a user-friendly dashboard can be constructed to display the analytic leads to the awareness or presentation layer. Throughout the treatment process, clinicians and researchers are competent to make much better, real-time decisions.

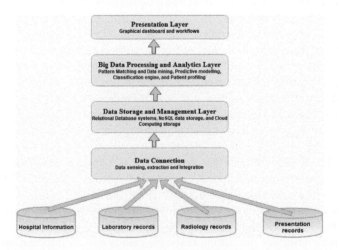

Figure 12.6   Architecture for smart health-care framework

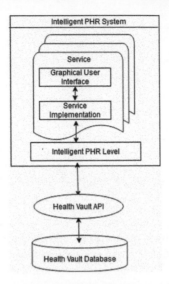

Figure 12.7   Intelligent PHR system built for health care

Data-driven platforms such as google-Health and HealthVault are used by s-health-care providers. Figure 12.5 shows that a high-level framework might underlie the bright patient health record method [46, 47]. In this style, remote suppliers delivered at the human level, information acquired through Health Vault Application programming interfaces. Thus, a lightweight sensible patient health record item might be started with absolutely no hometown storage space. A further main idea of this strategy is that people can control their information, and consequently, they are urged to get active in their treatment.

Furthermore, the suggested PHR item may benefit researchers and treatment providers by supporting mixed analytical fixes. For instance, by checking health conditions and locating hospitalization examinations advantages, treatment providers can make much better options at a minimum cost. In contrast, public health researchers are proficient at foreseeing and avoiding harmful incidents from an incredible massive public through an opportunity to get into healthcare, including laboratory information in PHR captures.

To produce maximum use of wireless remedies [48, 49], developed IoT mindful, smart homes by extending clinic treatments in the IoT group. In general, the following three components have to be incorporated into the architecture:

1. A town developed with wireless receptors for information acquisition.
2. An IoT s-gateway for authenticating local and remote (Figure 12.7) Intelligent PHR structure developed on Microsoft HealthVault [50]. Safety and secrecy ways for accessing sensitive information in smart health-care systems, the owners can log onto have the competent rights.
3. An operator interface permitting real-time results and an information management screen.

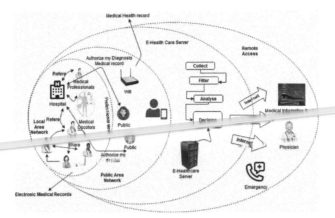

Figure 12.8   Data saved within the health-care server might be sent to remote medical hospitals

The IoT aware system could be ready to collect and provide patients' environmental factors and symptoms to an operating center, like processing information with smart algorithms and permitting careful communications mailed in crisis. According to the sensor variants in use [51], more categorized the smart health products as mobile health monitoring system (MHMS), wearable health monitoring method (WHMS), and remote-health monitoring system (RHMS). Specifically, a WHMS includes the utilization of wearable receptors while an MHMS is seated on movable products. Through pairing movable communication and wearable tracking engineering, a remote health monitoring system is to be used to transfer the confidential messages, for example, by a wellness center over the patient's house. Figure 12.7 shows that wireless body region networks could provide hardworking sign data like blood pressure, electrocardiogram, plus heartbeat through receptors placed over the human body. Working for mobile items, health-related details might be transmitted to the vicinity networking and electronic health servers to allow for treatment and data analytics—finally, the last level solutions to people able to access remotely. Figure 12.8 shows that the data saved within the e-health server might be sent to a local medical hospital.

Along with healthcare, remote access to health-related information additionally supports services that are critical [52]. To generalize the use of such a structure Lu and Sinnott [53] developed a multitiered telephone system to provide a larger group of customers, health insurance providers, medical doctors, pharmacists, and so on, located at small businesses. Through the adoption of interaction solutions, several strategies are linked to create an intelligent entry solution. Wise-health tracking methods are referred to as using better solutions to look at patients' health problems. Based on the behavioral designs extracted by checking out systems Seliem *et al.* [54] proposed a generic framework and its interaction within an intelligent, society infrastructure. As revealed in Figure 12.9, it can be utilized in numerous contexts like outdoors, hospital, and home.

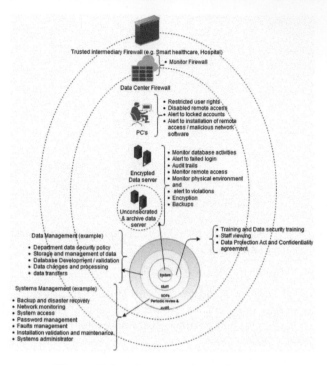

Figure 12.9   Data security and privacy

As a result of the vulnerable qualities bundled in PHRs, shield from unauthorized use (or) access is crucial. Dependent upon a systematic analysis , two main features are there in the smart health frameworks: the adoption of examining answers (e.g., movable, wearable sensors) within ubiquitous locations and the complex analytics (e.g., information integration and also machine mastering methods) on heterogeneous datasets. As a result, different safety methods are essential in a smart health framework in which various program functionalities have been constructed [55].

12.6   Identified issues and solutions

Security and privacy disputes in EHR the electronic health-care system security facets are in the investigation phase amid scholars. Security is the most significant hurdle avoiding e-Health patient information allegiance and using e-Health process incapacity that is full. It can facilitate or maybe encourage essential morals such as individual sovereignty or human individuality. Additionally, patients control their e-healthcare information handled and used by other users along with clinicians besides e-health-care. Toward people, secrecy is more important, and it's administrated to enforce the responsibility on exact methods toward making particular problem. Inside the smart health-care framework, security and privacy are connected when both are viewed as the same and are occasionally used interchangeably.

Therefore, confidentiality is viewed as saving the business's fascination and security as saving the person's autonomy; in typical e-healthcare, privacy and security are in the same aspect [56]. Also, all achievements of e-healthcare realize to mirrored in protecting the privacy of patient's information.

To protect information exchange in e-healthcare, the professional calls more often for protection actions and security requirements. Thus, the EHR methods have been used for worldwide security and also privacy. That includes worldwide morals intended for the doctor's role, patient's permission, and an explanation of review trials and records. Several leading security and privacy encounters in EHR methods are given below. They are gaining access and validation management is required to ensure adequate permission and also privacy in patient information. Saving in the cloud server, dependable, and requirements authentication styles are vital for safeguarding patient record security. In the earliest phase of user authentication, they must figure out their identity to make sure they're authorized to use the product [57]. By privacy laws, people need complete exposure to just how their health records are employed and for what purposes.

Nevertheless, this particular element hasn't been thoroughly answered by apprehensive patients and it remains prohibited. Additionally, participation in controlling their e-health data in EHR might help to project security problems. Information truthfulness ensures the integrity among the essential secrets in the EHR guarantees the process since its dependability reduces mistakes and enhances individuals' safety [58].

System availability is vital to attain the steadiness of e-healthcare to confirm the most excellent facilities. Foe example, when the system in downcast mode, the medical providers won't have the ability to use the patient's information and cannot prescribe. It measures the accessibility of connection, and information is incredibly crucial. It shouldn't deem a particular period. Usually, the doctor must build composite conclusions that cannot be done as required in a day-to-day scenario [59]. In this framework, information loss plays a significant role in confidentiality, and patient information is saved electronically; it is crucial to safeguard the information without any loss. Figure 12.9 shows data loss; it is essential to make data recovery difficult due to software program and security attacks, network errors, or hardware errors. Network security data safety also becomes essential when other critical assets also depend on network security [60]. Disruption to system performance and denial of service attacks can have a significant effect on health-care delivery. The most popular network security method is the usage of firewalls. Utilizing a firewall is a highly effective strategy to keep organizations networking and protected health information safe. On the other side, the usage of any firewall is pricey and varies based on many factors, like the work atmosphere and size of a company, and also the budget criteria.

Nevertheless, a particular patient's information could be jeopardized. Another important aspect is that using different encryption algorithms to maintain individual health-care information sensitivity needs enormous financial support, mainly when there is any change in the method we use. Some existing critical solutions for security are discussed below:

- **TTP auditing**. To guarantee the correctness of the information, a third-party auditor Trusted Third Party (TTP) can verify the integrity of the information stored in the cloud. Each time the review petition results from the prospect, the third-party auditor directs the task petition to the cloud program provider. And then, it compares the process reaction to produce personal information integrity as well as accessibility. Also, an auditor can audit the information stored over the cloud to check the life cycle of the information. Many scientists have provided auditing strategies within history seasons. For instance [59], given an evaluation demonstrating the effects of health-care auditing on clinic expenditures, they evidenced that medical auditing might do the job as a great instrument and, for that reason, reduce expenses. Thus, the third-party auditor is used for the movable user's computational help attaining cost-effectiveness to improve loyalty inside the cloud storage space server.
- **Data access management**. You can use encryption strategies, including crucial asymmetric encryption, crucial symmetric encryption, and attribute-based encryption, which might be used with entry control. Nevertheless, overall health information methods can find several disadvantages for authorization in team conferences and long-suffering wellness information specifications. Substantially the noncryptographic methods are some times inadequate to provide security and reliability for entry policy enforcement. However, the cryptographic methods are becoming expensive, complex, and restricted within indicating policies [61]. Therefore, it's given an architecture-dependent on attribute-based encryption with information worth to voice validity information of crucial element. Scientists [62] proposed a novel framework determined by attribute-based encryption methods to encrypt each person's information history to guarantee a maximum affected person secrecy. Furthermore, role-based entry managing and attribute-based gain access to care plan clouds.
- **Data search**. It is crucial to encrypt vulnerable specifics before delivering them throughout a product. Nevertheless, after the information is encrypted, it is impossible to put on plaintext key phrase online searches, which means that enabling encrypted cloud information analysis is essential. Furthermore, when the encrypted information search engine results cannot be used faster, most protection and secrecy techniques have much less meaning. Wei *et al.* [63] recommend a multi-keyword research pattern of encrypted personal S-health specifics inside a difficult multi-owner establishing support both enough grained entry managing and multi-word exploration of cloud storage space [62]. In addition, it proposed a decryptable attribute-based key phrase analysis device that might stop selected plaintext hits and selected search term strikes. This system uses the S-Health cloud , especially, for telemedicine.
- **Data encryption**. Encryption may be the regular alternative employed. Even though it supplies quick access management, it does not apply to complicated EHR methods requiring various entry demands. The main task from the protection pastime of e-Health marketing communications plays essential managing protocols. In addition, the transmission payment is significantly impacted by complicated encryption algorithms or maybe transmission protocols which

usually belong brief to complete data transmission [60], created a prototype system based on a lightweight personal homomorphism algorithm, along with an encryption algorithm substantially enhanced due to the information Encryption Standard. In addition to crucial understanding design based on the thought of DES, protected authentication might acquire secured techniques due to the technique individuals whenever they buy suggestion by Li *et al.* [64]. This particular system is a perfect for setup within the existing mobile crisis medical-related procedures.

- **Data anonymization:** The affected person is categorized into three categories: explicit identifiers (ID quantity, title, cellular phone), quasi-identifiers (age, date of birth, address), also secrecy attributes (illness, income). Information engineering can be used to solve issues such as k-anonymity self-confidence bounding [61]. But the process of wearable devices' information is depending on the k-anonymity algorithm . For instance, k-anonymity is needed in any application to process the required information from source to destination [22].

12.6.1 Summary of analyzed effort held through this particular research

To guarantee effective utilization of this innovation, privacy and security problems ought to be appropriately looked after. Table 12.2 offers a summary of the analyzed work completed within this research.

12.7 Open issues and challenges

In pharmaceutical industries, the medical-related files are converted into electronic format (stored in electronic health records) which can be accessible on the Internet using cloud computing services. How ever, there is always a scope that the attacker can breach the cloud server protection and obtain unauthorized entry on the person's health-related information. This section highlights various protection and secrecy issues in healthcare, as revealed in Figure 12.10.

- **Ethical challenges:** Some natural obstacles are confidential, information secrecy, information gain access to management, profit orientation of individuals information, possession, and the administration of the crucial components that obstruct the exchange of details between the individual and HSP. Thus, when proper care develops into a task, the total picture's entry on the affected person details.
- **User authentication:** Authorized customers are permitted to enter patient data coming from electronic health records. Nevertheless, an assailant can take the identity of the person to look at the person's information. Nevertheless, it's very hard as well as challenging to determine unauthorized entry.

Table 12.2 Survey of analyzed work carried through within this research

Approach/year published	Strength	Weakness
Lengthy Role-Based Access Control (xRBAC)/2014	Seamless information sharing	Not suitable for distributed surroundings. Additionally, it is not scalable
Delay —totally free anonymization/2015	This method does not produce precious time lag time because the stream of information is anonymized directly with bogus worth.	It doesn't check out the timing just for late validation
Transportation Layer Security (TLS)/Secure Socket Layer (SSL)/2015	It helps to prevent an alien from unauthorized access.	It's platform reliant and never scalable
Attribute Based Encryption (ABE)/2011	Privileges have been mapped directly into different functions with attribute-based encryption entry building.	Cloud storage space of e-Health data is situated in a centralized server
Decentralization of authorization server/2012	A person is allowed to enter, determined by their privileges, without disclosing their identities and attributes.	There is no area for collaborative sharing of healthcare details throughout numerous domains. It lacks interoperability
Anonymization (Statistical Disclosure Control (SDC))/2013.	It offers reliable and accurate outcomes of SDC solutions.	This particular framework can't benefit a large dataset. Likewise, the frame does the job of creating a tremendous hold off throughout the anonymization operation.
A trust-based evaluation security model/2014.	*Much better outcomes within the terminology of loyalty computation when set alongside the different current loyalty versions.*	It has mathematical variables whose values can't be evaluated.
Steganographic strategy/2015	The message is shielded to avert any kind of hit through lossless compression and asymmetric encryption algorithm.	It couldn't manage sound cancellation as well as data reduction
The privacy-preserving tactic as well as the security preserving tactic, along with catastrophe recovery/2016	The former strategy is a robust mechanism for accomplishing both secrecy and healthcare information integrity, as the latter strategy might solely be utilized for reliability.	Failure of the mechanism to work effectively if the techniques don't work out.

(Continues)

Table 12.2 Continued

Approach/year published	Strength	Weakness
Mandatory Access Control (MAC), Discretionary Access Control (DAC), and also Role-Based Access Control (RBAC)/2016	Individuals to determine as well as fixed entry privileges.	The model can't be used within a sent-out atmosphere.
DUKPT, along with a two-stage mixture of crucial encryption used/2016	It tolerates significant amounts of simultaneous authorization requests with a superb effect period.	It's restricted variety of entities, client or end-users U, a Service provider in Cloud Cd, a Secure Program er SP, and also an authentication and entry management supervisor EMS.
IBE (Identity-Based Encryption) Based Proxy Re-Encryption Schemes/2017	Freshly established Identity-Based Encryption Based Proxy Re-Encryption Scheme is efficient and better for decryption.	The performance on the unit isn't dependable as well as cost-efficient
Recommended a biometric grounded remote patient checking approach/2018	Biometric authentication, as well as ECC plan. Movable health-care atmosphere. Health vulnerable information. Movable health-care framework. Much better quality care.	Network congestion.
Created aggregation and certification much less signature pattern for WSN health-care program/2018	Electronic signature pattern. Guarantees information integrity.	Hard to determine the authorized user.
Created reliable secrecy protecting health-care products in a social networking system/2018	Sybil episode detection program trust atmosphere. Health-care program framework. Enhance loyalty among caregivers and patients.	Not a lot more efficient.
Recommended an FHIR Chain-based decentralized app for the health-care structure/2018	Health-related details. Properly discuss medical-related data.	A lot more complex.

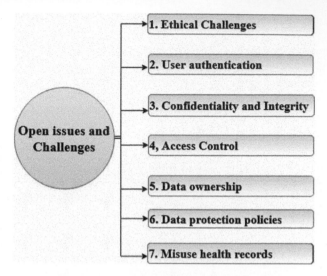

Figure 12.10   Open issues and challenges

- **Integrity and confidentiality:** Confidentiality conceals the crucial information of unauthorized people, whereas integrity guarantees information reliability. Any kind of adversary can change the saved information, which results in information inaccuracy. Protecting against the information for several protection and change strikes is a demanding problem [65].
- **Access control:** Health-care systems gather and process sensitive and usually life-critical health-care information and make profound choices based on this information. Cybercriminals targeting the vulnerabilities within these IoMT products can acquire possible entry into the hospital network and obtain unauthorized access to sensitive personal and health-care information. Attacks on these connected products may also result in significant bodily damage and life-threatening harm to the individuals.
- **Data ownership:** Data ownership means the right of the individual to their data.' Assailants can change the ownership specifics to create their ownership invalid [66]. And so, stopping the ownership information from unauthorized entry is very important to help make the device secure and secure.
- **Data protection policies:** Strict administration and security are needed for information on overall health analysis to stop it from theft or loss. A protected EHR device has to be created with various protection measures, which is a complicated issue [61].
- **Misuse of health records:** Some websites present an internet e-health records process with no-cost restricted storage space room and aren't much more worried about information secrecy. They may market the information or information to the following organization or even an advertising and marketing company. Providing protection and secrecy to the health information , the heterogeneity of the data needs to be taken into consideration.

12.8 Conclusions and open research issues in future

Incredible innovations in sensor technology have paved the way toward a new computing paradigm called the IoT. This particular research discussed the ransomware attacks and protection problems in IoMT. With improvement in mobile computing and data analytics, healthcare systems can offer much more smart and appropriate services and applications. Additionally, assisted by machine learning, data mining, artificial intelligence, and any other sophisticated methods, health-care systems may also play a similar role in healthy lifestyles, as something to help with decision-making, and as a supply of innovation in the changing health-care ecosystem. This chapter discusses security risks and privacy worries at each level of the IoMT architecture design. The security of every level on the IoT architecture needs to be used simultaneously. Significant additional analysis is necessary to develop a detailed protection mechanism for the whole IoT architecture. Conversion on a taxonomic framework of market cap internet of thing-based sensors enhances sensor-centric knowledge plus usability understanding. It offers threat analysis to help law making by assisting owners in understanding and quantifying shelter on the Internet of health-care issues and discusses privacy and security issues regarding sensor information and methods to eliminate them.

Further analysis may be done with various other characteristic selection and SEO (search engine optimization) techniques to enhance the efficacy of predictive evaluation of cardiovascular disease evaluation. The article proposed is realized employing wearable devices and technologies that are available in the market.

1. Processing an enormous volume of information concerning home amenities, visitors, overall health is concerned, along with male information, information analytical techniques must be small to provide seamless, proper period products. Concerning security and privacy, a constructive cryptographic algorithm is chosen while swapping patients' information among platforms—it's in a position to ensure confidentiality and integrity have a bit of computation expense.
2. There is a need to create a new policies to restrict the unauthorized entry into the healthcare systems. However, the attackers are investing their resources to gain access to the network. Nevertheless, the bulk of these details has personal information and sensitive attributes that may bring about serious secrecy issues in the future. Then, to anonymize private information, federal terms and conditions are to be used to establish transparency between various stakeholders so the faith on these security solutions will be developed from the stakeholders side also.
3. The establishment of wise s-health methods depends upon realizing products usually deployed inside the receptive air in which many protection consequences occur. As a result, it's crucial to get a design to evaluate and mitigate potential risks. it may acquire many people who select furnished solutions. Nevertheless, due to the heterogeneity of information gathered up by receptors, it's tough to conceptualize this as a knowledge design determining almost all

possible factors and risks relevant to the analysis. Also, creating a mechanism for mitigating every address style is not applicable. Preferably, strategies can be used jointly to protect the data and provide privacy [67].

4. People tend to be in the center of sensible urban areas. Therefore, when examining overall health information, individuals must present with the right of finding out with whom the information of theirs is talked about and precisely how it is utilized. Therefore, the initial phase of acquiring protection and secrecy treatment options is realizing individuals' protection worries regarding information exchange and providers in wise health methods. Incorporating these very subjective components on the product or service (suggested within the last point) can ensure the correctness of method formation [68].

References

[1] Kumari A., Tanwar S., Tyagi S., Kumar N. 'Fog computing for healthcare 4.0 environment: opportunities and challenges'. *Computers & Electrical Engineering.* 2018;**72**(5):1–13.

[2] Gupta R., Shukla A., Mehta P. 'VAHAK: a blockchain-based outdoor delivery scheme using UAV for healthcare 4.0 services'. *IEEE International Conference on Computer Communications (IEEE INFOCOM 2020)*; Beijing, China, 27–30 April; 2020. pp. 1–8.

[3] Cisco. *Making connected health a reality, Cisco Systems [online].* 2019. Available from www.cisco.com/c/dam/en_us/solutions/industries/docs/healthcare/connected_health_brochure.pdf [Accessed Aug 2019].

[4] CATcert. *Identity and capability management in eHealth: the CATCert approach* [online]. 2017. Available from http://www.projectliberty.org/liberty/content/download/3691/24338/file/071011%20I%20Alamillo%20CATCert%20v1r0%20case%20study.pdf [Accessed Aug 2019].

[5] CMS. *National health expenditure data, Centers for Medicare and Medicaid Services* [online]. 2019. Available from www.cms.gov/ [Accessed Aug 2019].

[6] Rachakonda L., Mohanty S.P., Kougianos E. 'iLog: an intelligent device for automatic food intake monitoring and stress detection in the IoMT'. *IEEE Transactions on Consumer Electronics.* 2020;**66**(2):115–24.

[7] Iwendi C., Khan S., Anajemba J.H., Bashir A.K., Noor F. 'Realizing an efficient IoMT-assisted patient diet recommendation system through machine learning model'. *IEEE Access.* **8**; 2020. pp. 28462–74.

[8] Das A.K., Zeadally S., He D. 'Taxonomy and analysis of security protocols for Internet of things'. *Future Generation Computer Systems.* 2018;**89**(7):110–25.

[9] Broadband Commission. *Digital health: a call for government leadership and cooperation between ICT and health* [online]. 2017. Available from www.broadbandcommission.org/Documents/publications/WorkingGroupHealthReport-2017.pdf [Accessed Aug 2019].

[10] Sakr S., Elgammal A. 'Towards a comprehensive data analytics framework for smart healthcare services'. *Big Data Research*. 2016;**4**(9):44–58.

[11] *Hackers can remotely kill hospital patients with drug pumps, IT expert discovers* [online]. Available from https://www.rt.com/news/266491-drug-pumps-hacking-hospitals/ [Accessed 11 Mar 2017].

[12] Vatsalan D., Sehili Z., Christen P., Rahm E. 'Privacy-preserving record linkage for big data: current approaches and research challenges'. *Handbook of Big Data Technologies*, Springer, Cham, 2017. pp. 851–95.

[13] Anthony S. *USB killer, yours for $50, lets you easily fry almost every device* [online]. Available from https://arstechnica.com/gadgets/2016/12/usb-killer-fries-devices/ [Accessed 09 Mar 2017].

[14] Khandelwal S. *This $10 device can clone RFID-equipped access cards easily, the hacker news*. [online]. Available from http://thehackernews.com/2015/07/hacking-rfid-access-card.html [Accessed 09 Mar 2017].

[15] Samonas S., Coss D. 'The CIA strikes back: redefining confidentiality, integrity and availability in security'. *Journal of Information System Security*. 2014;**10**(3).

[16] Fouad H., Hassanein A.S., Soliman A.M., Al-Feel H. 'Internet of medical things (iomt) assisted vertebral tumor prediction using heuristic hock transformation based gautschi model–a numerical approach'. *IEEE Access*. **8**; 2020. pp. 17299–309.

[17] Sikarndar M., Anwar W., Almogren A., Ud Din I., Guizani N. 'IoMT-based association rule mining for the prediction of human protein complexes'. *IEEE Access*. **8**; 2020. pp. 6226–37.

[18] Wang X., Gui Q., Liu B., Jin Z., Chen Y. 'Enabling smart personalized healthcare: a hybrid mobile-cloud approach for ECG telemonitoring'. *IEEE Journal of Biomedical and Health Informatics*. 2014;**18**(3):739–45.

[19] Prakash R., Ganesh A.B. 'Internet of Things (IoT) enabled wireless sensor network for physiological data acquisition'. *International Conference on Intelligent Computing and Applications*; Springer, Singapore; 2019. pp. 163–70.

[20] Zhang Y., Gravina R., Lu H., Villari M., Fortino G. 'Pea: parallel electrocardiogram-based authentication for smart healthcare systems'. *Journal of Network and Computer Applications*. 2018;**117**(3):10–16.

[21] Visvizi A., Lytras M.D., Damiani E., Mathkour H. 'Policy making for smart cities: innovation and social inclusive economic growth for sustainability'. *Journal of Science and Technology Policy Management*. 2018;**9**(2):126–33.

[22] Prakash R., Balaji Ganesh A. 'Internet of Things (IoT) enabled wireless sensor network for physiological data acquisition'. *International Conference on Intelligent Computing and Applications*; Springer, Singapore; 2019. pp. 163–70.

[23] Raj R.J.S., Shobana S.J., Pustokhina I.V., *et al.*. 'Optimal feature selection-based medical image classification using deep learning model in Internet of medical things'. *IEEE access: practical innovations, open solutions*. 2020;**8**:58006–17.

[24] Fernandes E., Jung J., Prakash A. 'Security analysis of emerging smart home applications'. *2016 IEEE Symposium on Security and Privacy (SP)*; 2016. pp. 636–54.

[25] Guo C., Zhang J., Liu Y., Xie Y., Han Z., Yu J. 'Recursion enhanced random forest with an improved linear model (RERF-ILM) for heart disease detection on the Internet of medical things platform'. *IEEE Access*. 2020;**8**:59247–56.

[26] Cho J.-S., Yeo S.-S., Kim S.K. 'Securing against brute-force attack: a hash-based RFID mutual authentication protocol using a secret value'. *Computer Communications*. 2011;**34**(3):391–7.

[27] Hossain M.M., Fotouhi M., Hasan R. 'Towards an analysis of security issues, challenges, and open problems in the internet of things'. *2015 IEEE World Congress on Services*; 2015. pp. 21–8.

[28] Papp D., Ma Z., Buttyan L. 'Embedded systems security: threats, vulnerabilities, and attack taxonomy'. *2015 13th Annual Conference on Privacy, Security and Trust (PST)*; 2015. pp. 145–52.

[29] Khoo B. 'RFID as an enabler of the internet of things: issues of security and privacy'. *2011 International Conference on Internet of Things and 4th International Conference on Cyber, Physical and Social Computing*; 2011. pp. 709–12.

[30] Ray S., Chen W., Bhadra J., Al Faruque M.A. 'Extensibility in automotive security: current practice and challenges'. *2017 54th ACM/EDAC/IEEE Design Automation Conference (DAC)*; 2017. pp. 1–6.

[31] Koscher K., Czeskis A., Roesner F., *et al.* 'Experimental security analysis of a modern automobile'. *2010 IEEE Symposium on Security and Privacy*; 2010. pp. 447–62.

[32] Qin E., Long Y., Zhang C., Huang L. 'Cloud computing and the internet of things: technology innovation in automobile service'. *International Conference on Human Interface and the Management of Information*; 2013. pp. 173–80.

[33] Bugiel S., Heuser S., Sadeghi A.-R. 'Flexible and fine-grained mandatory access control on android for diverse security and privacy policies'. *22nd {USENIX} Security Symposium {USENIX} Security 13*; 2013. pp. 131–46.

[34] Gope P., Hwang T. 'Bsn-care: a secure IOT-based modern healthcare system using body sensor network'. *IEEE Sensors Journal*. 2016;**16**(5):1368–76.

[35] Mahendran R.K., Velusamy P. 'A secure fuzzy extractor based biometric key authentication scheme for body sensor network in Internet of medical things'. *Computer Communications*. 2020;**153**(1):545–52.

[36] Lu Y., Sinnott R.O., Verspoor K., Parampalli U. 'Privacy-preserving access control in electronic health record linkage'. *2018 17th IEEE International Conference on Trust, Security and Privacy in Computing and Communications/12th IEEE International Conference on Big Data Science and Engineering (TrustCom/BigDataSE)*; 2020. pp. 1–14.

[37] Alqassem I., Svetinovic D. 'A taxonomy of security and privacy requirements for the Internet of Things (IoT)'. *2014 IEEE International Conference on Industrial Engineering and Engineering Management*; 2014. pp. 1244–8.

[38] Daghighi B., Mat Kiah M.L., Iqbal S., Rehman M.H.U., Martin K. 'Host mobility key management in dynamic secure group communication'. *Wireless Networks*. 2018;**24**(8):3009–27.

[39] Riahi A., Natalizio E., Challal Y. Mitton N. ~~. A systemic and cogni-tive approach for lot security'.~~ *Computing, Networking and Communications (ICNC), 2014 International Conference on. IEEE*; 2014. pp. 183–8.

[40] Daghighi B., Mat Kiah M.L., Shamshirband S., Rehman M.H.U, Kiah M.L.M. 'Toward secure group communication in wireless mobile environments: issues, solutions, and challenges'. *Journal of Network and Computer Applications*. 2015;**50**:1–14.

[41] Bhattacharya P., Tanwar S., Bodke U., Tyagi S., Kumar N. 'Bindaas: blockchain-based deep-learning as-a-service in healthcare 4.0 applications'. *IEEE Transactions on Network Science and Engineering*; 2019. pp. 1–14.

[42] Padhy R.P., Patra M.A., Satapathy S.C. 'Cloud computing: security issues and research challenges'. *International Journal of Computer Science and Information Technology & Security*. 2011;**1**(2):136–46.

[43] Ray S., Chen W., Bhadra J., Faruque M.A.A. 'Extensibility in automotive security: current practice and challenges'. *2017 54th ACM/EDAC/IEEE Design Automation Conference (DAC)*; 2017. pp. 1–6.

[44] Gupta R., Shukla A., Tanwar S. 'AaYusH: A Smart Contract-based Telesurgery System for Healthcare 4.0'. *IEEE Conference on Communications (IEEE ICC-2020)*; Dublin, Ireland, 07–11 June; 2020. pp. 1–6.

[45] Sakr S., Elgammal A. 'Towards a comprehensive data analytics framework for smart healthcare services'. *Big Data Research*. 2016;**4**(9):44–58.

[46] Bai X., Xing L., Zhang N., *et al.* 'Staying secure and unprepared: understanding and mitigating the security risks of apple zeroconf'. *2016 IEEE Symposium on Security and Privacy (SP)*; 2016. pp. 655–74.

[47] Gupta R., Tanwar S., Tyagi S., Kumar N., Obaidat M.S., Sadoun B. 'HaBiTs: blockchain-based telesurgery framework for healthcare 4.0'. *International Conference on Computer, Information and Telecommunication Systems (IEEE CITS-2019)*; August 28–31, 2019. pp. 6–10.

[48] Arias O., Wurm J., Hoang K., Jin Y. 'Privacy and security in Internet of things and wearable devices'. *IEEE Transactions on Multi-Scale Computing Systems*. 2015;**1**(2):99–109.

[49] Vora J., Tanwar S., Verma J.P., *et al.* 'BHEEM: a blockchain-based framework for securing electronic health records. *IEEE Global Communications Conference (IEEE GLOBECOM-2018)*; 09–13th 2018. pp. 1–6.

[50] Ray S., Yang J., Basak A., Bhunia S. 'Correctness and security at odds: post-silicon validation of modern SoC designs'. *Proceedings of the 52nd Annual Design Automation Conference*; 2015. pp. 1–6.

[51] Zhang P., White J., Schmidt D.C., Lenz G., Rosenbloom S.T., Trent Rosenbloom S. 'FHIRChain: applying blockchain to securely and scalably

share clinical data'. *Computational and Structural Biotechnology Journal.* 2018;**16**:267–78.

[52] Khan., Mobeen., Jilani M.T., Khan M.K., Bin Ahmed M. 'A security framework for wireless body area network based smart healthcare system'. *International Conference for Young Researchers in Informatics, Mathematics and Engineering (ICYRIME)*; 2017. pp. 80–5.

[53] Lu Y., Sinnott R.O. 'Semantic-based privacy protection of electronic health records for collaborative research'. *2016 IEEE Trustcom/BigDataSE/ISPA*; 2016. pp. 519–26.

[54] Seliem M., Elgazzar K. 'BIoMT: blockchain for the internet of medical things'. *2019 IEEE International Black Sea Conference on Communications and Networking (BlackSeaCom)*; 2019. pp. 1–4.

[55] Bodkhe U., Tanwar S., Ladha A., Bhattacharya P., Verma A. 'A survey on revolutionizing healthcare 4.0 applications using blockchain'. *International Conference on Computing Communications, and Cyber-Security (IC4S 2020), Lecture Notes in Networks and Systems*; 12–13 October 2019. pp. 1–16.

[56] Vora J., Italiya P., Tanwar S., *et al.* 'Ensuring privacy and security in e-health records'. *International Conference on Computer, Information and Telecommunication Systems (IEEE CITS-2018)*; 11–13 July 2018. pp. 192–6.

[57] Tanwar S. 'Fog computing for healthcare 4.0 environments: technical, societal *and Future Implications*'. *Signals and Communication Technology.* Springer International Publishing; 2020. pp. 1–430.

[58] Tanwar S., Tyagi S., Kumar N. 'Multimedia big data computing for iot applications: concepts, paradigms and solutions'. *Intelligent Systems Reference Library.* Singapore: Springer; 2019. pp. 1–425.

[59] Tanwar S., Parekh K., Evans R. 'Blockchain-based electronic healthcare record system for healthcare 4.0 applications'. *Journal of Information Security and Applications.* 2019;**50**:1–14.

[60] Hathaliya J.J., Tanwar S. 'An exhaustive survey on security and privacy issues in healthcare 4.0'. *Computer Communications.* 2020;**153**(6):311–35.

[61] *Future of blockchain technology, in connected health ecosystem* [online]. 2019. Available from https://innovationsprint.eu/wpcontent/uploads/2017/08/Briefing-Deck-Future-of Blockchain-Technology-_19th-Sept.pdf [Accessed Jun 2020].

[62] Yazdinejad A., Srivastava G., Parizi R.M., Dehghantanha A., Choo K.-K.-R., Aledhari M. 'Decentralized authentication of distributed patients in hospital networks using Blockchain'. *IEEE Journal of Biomedical and Health Informatics.* 2020;**24**(8):2146–56.

[63] Wei K., Zhang L., Guo Y., Jiang X. 'Health monitoring based on internet of medical things: architecture, enabling technologies, and applications'. *IEEE Access.* 2020;**8**:27468–78.

[64] Hathaliya J.J., Tanwar S., Evans R. 'Securing electronic healthcare records: a mobile-based biometric authentication approach'. *Journal of Information Security and Applications.* 2020;**53**(102528):2214–2126.

[65] Nguyen D.C., Pathirana P.N., Ding M., Seneviratne A. 'Blockchain for secure ehrs sharing of mobile cloud based e-health systems'. *IEEE Access.* 2019;7:66792–806.

[66] Schmidlin K., Clough-Gorr K.M., Spoerri A., SNC Study Group. 'Privacy preserving probabilistic record linkage (P3RL): a novel method for linking existing health-related data and maintaining participant confidentiality'. *BMC Medical Research Methodology.* 2015;15(1):46–54.

[67] Santagati G.E., Dave N., Melodia T. 'Design and performance evaluation of an implantable ultrasonic networking platform for the Internet of medical things'. *IEEE/ACM Transactions on Networking.* 2020;28(1):29–42.

[68] Jain P., Joshi A.M., Mohanty S.P. 'iGLU: an intelligent device for accurate noninvasive blood glucose-level monitoring in smart healthcare'. *IEEE Consumer Electronics Magazine.* 2019;9(1):35–42.

Chapter 13

Contactless attendance system: a health-care approach to prevent spreading of Covid-19

*Arvind R Yadav[1], Jayendra Kumar[2], Dr. Anumeha[3],
Ayush Kumar Agrawal[2], and Roshan Kumar[4]*

The Covid-19 pandemic is an unparalleled threat in today's environment of quick development, and we face it as a global community. Like climate change, it is challenging our resilience from environmental health, social security, and government to knowledge exchange and economic policy in all sectors of the economy and growth fields. So much as climate change, this too would require everybody to come together and take an appropriate initiative. The coronavirus outbreak has highlighted our strengths and vulnerabilities that it has influenced and enabled us to benefit from each other's accomplishments and shortcomings. The entire globe might appear small amid this state of disaster and global travel bans. However, it is a period when the concept of teamwork and looking forward were never more relevant. In the wake of Covid-19, all contact-based biometric attendance systems have been rendered practically useless. Thus, a contactless biometric attendance system is the need of the hour to prevent the spreading of Covid-19.

The present-day attendance systems are quite difficult to manage and maintain record. The attendance in classes or industries is mostly done manually, and logbooks are used to maintain records. This can be a cumbersome process as sometimes humans can make a mistake which might lead to inconsistency. This chapter proposes a completely automatic attendance system that uses contactless biometric as a health-care major in the Covid-19 pandemic. In a system using facial recognition, there are lots of challenges involved most of the time. These may include low intensity of light or face that is occluded. The You Only Look Once (YOLO) algorithm for facial detection has been used in this chapter to overcome this issue.

[1]Department of Electronics and Communication Engineering, PIET, Parul University, India
[2]Department of Electronics and Communication Engineering, NIT, India
[3]Department of Electrical and Electronics, Netaji Subhas University, India
[4]Department of Electronics and Information Technology, Miami College of Henan University, China

13.1 Introduction

This chapter discusses the prologue of the need for a contactless biometric automated attendance system. We briefly talk about the traditional attendance system first and then discuss the motivation behind this project. Later in the chapter, we present the organization of the thesis as an overview of the report.

13.1.1 Traditional attendance system

The traditional attendance system that is used nowadays in schools and colleges has many disadvantages. First of all, the faculty members take attendance on paper, which involves the unnecessary usage of paper. This practice can be avoided keeping in mind the 'Save the Earth' mission. Another disadvantage of traditional attendance taking is that teachers call out the roll numbers and hear the responses. It wastes the precious time, which could otherwise be utilized for class hours. Many times the current teacher starts taking the attendance when the teacher for the next period has arrived. This results in wastage of time for the other classes [1–4].

Another reason for the distortion of authenticity of the attendance is the proxy attendance that is marked by the fellow mates of the absentee. This could be avoided if the practice of manual attendance is replaced with an automated one. Another possible drawback of the currently used traditional attendance system is that it is highly prone to errors. An error might occur while updating the attendance in the system or while calculating the aggregate percentage of attendance. This could be avoided by using the automatic system.

Also sometimes when the faculty members take attendance on a loose sheet of paper, it might get misplaced or lost. This may increase the chances of discrepancy in the attendance data.

13.1.2 Automated attendance system

We propose an automated attendance system to overcome the error-proneness and time-consuming nature of the traditional pen and paper attendance system. This proposed system will not require any manual intervention for taking the attendance. Also, it will minimize the wastage of time and paper. It will ease the process of updating and calculating attendance accurately. This system may be used to take attendance of students, teachers, and non-teaching staff in the academic institutions and may also be used in non-academic premises for attendance of any desired set of people [5, 6].

13.1.3 Motivation

Engineering is not merely a profession. It is a quest to find new things, invent, and innovate to solve a problem. In a class of 90 students, we found our professors struggling to take attendance. This manual process was not only time consuming but also cumbersome while maintaining records.

After a lot of planning and discussions, we thought of developing an electronic attendance app that could save the trouble of maintaining and managing the attendance of a class. However, unfortunately, it still could not ease up the process completely. We found that biometrics could solve our problem, but it was quite expensive to implement. We have a few fingerprint detectors installed in our academic section, but it is available only for the Ph.D. and M.Tech. students. We needed something universal that could be less prone ~~...~~ Fingerprint biomet- ~~...~~ be deceived, and proxies could be easily planted into the system, making it inconsistent. This drawback posed a major setback.

The next best method we could think of was facial recognition. All it needs is a good quality camera installed in a class to monitor the real-time attendance of all students. However, facial recognition also has its own challenges, for example, facial orientation and distortion of images, to name a few. Therefore, currently, we focus on face detection using various algorithms such as Viola and Jones algorithm and Eigenfaces which could be taken forward for recognition using Convolutional Neural Networks (CNNs).

13.2   Literature review

According to Dixit *et al.* [1], while keeping in mind the need to increase the speed of detection in the object detection techniques, we require to cater to the needs of real-time detections. In the paper, they discussed You Only Look Once (YOLO) [2], an entirely different approach for detecting objects in a given image using CNNs. They concluded that building such a model with YOLO was easy, and the model training was also very straightforward. Furthermore, they compared YOLOv2 and YOLOv3 with YOLO. They found that YOLO generalizes the representation of objects other than models. Hence, the modern applications that demand robust object detection and speed can depend on the YOLO algorithm.

In May 2016, Nilesh D. Veer and B.F. Momin published a paper on automated attendance using a video surveillance camera [3]. In that paper, they discussed the installation of an automated attendance system. However, in that method, the major drawback was that the students needed to go in front of the camera to mark their attendance. They decided to reduce the students' efforts and thus proposed a system that could take the attendance of the students present in the classroom after some periodic interval of time. They concluded that their system was error-free until the number of students in the class was below 40. The errors went up to 3% when the system was tested for the number of students between 40 to 70.

In 2016, E. Varadharajan *et al.* presented a paper on the automatic attendance management system. In that paper, they said that out of all the biometric processes available at the time, facial recognition was the best method to use [4]. Out of the various methods available of comparing the faces for recognition, they used Eigenfaces.

In 2015, Priyanka Wagh *et al.* published a paper on how Eigenfaces and PCA algorithms could be used for face recognition. She tried to solve the major issues faced while taking attendance of the students manually. Her proposed solution was to use an automated biometric system to minimize manual efforts. She concluded that facial recognition could be the best way to perform the task and avoid any proxies. She tried some basic facial recognition algorithms, but they failed due to the lack of adequate light or head position. Hence, Viola and Jones algorithm, illumination invariant, and Principal component analysis [5], which easily eliminated these issues, came into the picture. However, there is still some scope for improvement in recognition algorithms.

In 2008, Lang Liying and Hong Yue presented a paper on the study of entrance guard and check on work attendance system based on face recognition. They worked on developing an automated attendance system for a logistic industry to keep a check on the guards and monitor their activity. They suggested dividing each captured image into sub-images to reduce the dimension and memory capacity and apply the famous Fisher method for recognition in combination with the general minimum distance classifier [6]. The stored images were picked up from the ORL database for comparison, and it was found that the efficiency of this method was more than 90%, which is quite remarkable than the older techniques.

In 2014, Ross Girshick *et al.* presented a paper at IEEE Conference on Computer Vision and Pattern Recognition on rich feature hierarchies for accurate object detection and semantic segmentation. They laid stress on the canonical PASCAL VOC dataset, a topic of vivid discussions for object detection. It is commonly found that the best performance system usually has complex methodologies that use the combination of multiple low-level image features with high-level context. They used a special technique called R-CNN [7], to increase the precision of object detection by 30%. CNNs are implemented to segment the objects with domain-specific tuning that result in significant improvement in image detection and recognition.

In 2016, Joseph Redmon *et al.* came up with a new approach for object detection in their paper on You Only Look Once: Unified, Real-Time Object Detection. They used regression analysis rather than treating object detection as a classifier problem. With the help of spatial bounding boxes and calculation of the associated class probabilities, only a single neural network was sufficient to identify an object from its image [8]. This method was found to be really fast for real-time object detection as it takes 45 frames per second and with some improvements, it could go up to 155 frames per second. Although this technique is more prone to localization errors, it reduced false predictions on the background. They concluded that YOLO outperformed R-CNN and DPM.

In 2016, Dr. P. Shanmugavadivu and Ashish Kumar published a paper on rapid face detection and annotation with loosely face geometry. In that paper, they put on a serious concern that though there have been lots of advancements and improvements in facial recognition, most of them fail in terms of different head postures or face angles. They have suggested using a face part dictionary based on Partially Occluded Face Detection (POFD) [9]. Their algorithm finds the most occluded part of the face, i.e., the nose, and keeping that as a reference, it detects the other features of the face, which are used to recognize a person.

In 2017, Mangayarkarasi Nehru and Dr. Padmavathi S. presented a paper on illumination invariant face detection using the Viola-Jones algorithm. They emphasized on the fact that it is a perennial challenge in modern science to make computers that have senses more like humans. The Viola-Jones algorithm has proved to be the most effective and efficient facial recognition technique in real-time scenario. The biggest challenge in computer vision algorithms is the illumination of the subject to further processing and recognition. However, the Viola-Jones algorithm proved to be a boon in dealing with faces under all kinds of illumination conditions. They used Haar-like features for obtaining an integral image as feature extraction. Usually, the classifiers are pretty complex, so boosting techniques such as AdaBoost, a machine learning algorithm, can create basic classifiers. Further, they used several filters for the final classification provided by Cascade Classifier [10]. It helps in classifying the facial and non-facial features.

In 2018, Smit Hapani *et al.*, at an IEEE conference on Computing Communication Control and Automation, published a paper on automated attendance system using image processing. They emphasized the significance of image processing and its ever-growing applications. Most biometric systems, such as video surveillance and teleconferencing, use various image processing techniques to achieve the desired results. However, challenges such as orientation and size of the image, clarity, and intensity prove quite cumbersome. Further, they used a training dataset to obtain a positive image by subtracting the negative background image. To obtain an automated attendance system, they used Fisher Face algorithm [11] in sync with the Viola-Jones algorithm to detect and recognize faces. These techniques were quite effective in real-time facial feature identification and recognition with a success rate of 45% to 50%. Ultimately, the goal of an independent automated attendance system is achieved with minimal human interaction. These algorithms are useful for real-time video monitoring systems, which enables the detection of faces in motion with a maximum accuracy of 50%.

In 2019, Luis Fung-Lung *et al.* published a paper on an image acquisition method for face recognition and the implementation of an automatic attendance system for events. Most image acquisition methods often fail to obtain a high-quality image that is suitable for recognition. Therefore, they proposed an image acquisition algorithm that would obtain optimal images. These images could be mapped to a Smart Even Faces Database [12]. Further, ResNet 34 [12] has been used for feature extraction. The subsequent classifiers, including K-nearest neighbors, Random Forest, Naive Bayes, AdaBoost, and SVM are also used. These methods have been compared with each other in terms of accuracy and execution of time. It was found that the SVM algorithm with K-nearest neighbors proved to the best with an accuracy of 0.96 and execution time less than 1.5 s. However, in mass face detection, the attendance system worked well with 0.94 and 0.5 s of accuracy in execution time. The algorithm was implemented on a real-time video stream.

In 2017, C.B. Yuvaraj *et al.* published a paper on an approach to maintain attendance using image processing techniques at the Tenth International Conference on Contemporary Computing (IC3). They proposed that the world is moving towards new approach to innovation and technology. The attendance has already been monitored using biometric, thumb impression, and access card. However, these systems had their limitations. Therefore, in order to ease out the process of attendance management, face recognition technique could be really useful. A four-step approach is used in face recognition, including detecting a face, labeling it, and then training the classifiers on the labeled database. Finally, the image is sent for face recognition. The database uses a combination of positive and negative images [13] in sync with the classifier to recognize faces in the real-time scenario. After the faces are recognized, attendance is marked in a pair of faces and their respective ID numbers.

Further, to avoid missing any face due to some rotational issues, a video of 60 s is taken into consideration before processing it frame by frame. They also claimed that their work could be extended to detect criminal faces with the help of CCTV footage. This would help in evicting crime through technology.

In 2019, Akbar M.S., at an IEEE conference, published a paper on face recognition and Radio Frequency Identity (RFID) [14] verified attendance system. They stressed the importance of attendance in complying with proper and quality education in any institution. To reduce the chances of fraud and to ease out the manual efforts in terms of marking attendance, they have developed this model. Simultaneously, with facial recognition, they also used radio frequency identification to count the number of times a student comes in and goes out of the class and hence mark their attendance if they are authorized to take the class. This smart attendance continuously logs in data of every authorized student, which can be used on-demand from the database. They also worked on power management and minimal electricity usage through IR devices to detect people inside a room and then only switch on the electronic.

In 2019, Shreyak Sawhney *et al.* presented a real-time smart attendance system paper using face recognition techniques at the 9th International Conference on Cloud Computing, Data Science, and Engineering (Confluence). To lessen the burden of the teachers, an automatic smart attendance management system can be useful. The only obstacle in this scenario is the authentication of students and preventing unauthorized entry into the class. A biometric system for recognition usually accompanies the smart attendance system. Out of these biometric systems, face recognition can be useful to improve the existing system. Facial recognition is already used in various CCTV surveillance systems and has been a boon in computer vision. They have developed a model that uses Eigenface values, principal component analysis [15], and further CNN to achieve face recognition. After faces are recognized, it is matched with the master database for each class to authorize a student and mark the attendance subsequently.

In 2019, Wenxian Zeng *et al.* published a paper on the design of intelligent classroom attendance system based on face recognition at IEEE, 3rd Information Technology, Networking, Electronic, and Automation Control Conference (ITNEC), 2019. To minimize the attendance cost in Chinese schools and institutions and to simplify the process of traditional attendance methods used by them, they proposed using the AlexNet [16] convolutional network. This could help to implement a facial recognition attendance system. To improve the testing and training of models, a

Web face dataset is implemented in the network. They found out that the error rate of Top5 was as low as 6.73%. Further, facial recognition was combined with RFID cards to make the system more secure, efficient, and stable.

In 2017, Nicholas Delbiaggio presented his Bachelor's thesis for degree programme in Business Information Technology at Haaga-Helia University of applied sciences. He compared various algorithms qualitatively and quantitatively for facial recognition. His purpose was to compare various algorith such as Eigenfaces, Fisherfaces Local Binary Pattern Histogram, and the commercial deep CNN algorithm OpenFace and compare for their accuracy. He concluded in his thesis that among the compared facial algorithms, the open face algorithm based on CNN had the highest accuracy to identify faces.

13.2.1   5G and Covid-19 blockchain: value and importance

In the medical service industry, with the utilization of brilliant gadgets, sensors, and the Internet of Things (IoT), an enormous measure of multi-modular and heterogeneous information is produced each day [17]. Working with Big Data (BD) requires a particular approach to deal with and measure the information. Mist computing has been embraced in medical care 4.0 for capacity and calculation of patient's information (BD) [18]. Security of the Electronic Health Records [19] is of prime significance to maintain trust between medical service experts and patients, and refute the patient's information by the reprobates. In the Covid-19 circumstance, one of the prime worries of the medical service industry has been the least human mediation. Along these lines, a blockchain-imagined programming multi-amassing Unmanned Aerial Vehicles (UAV) correspondence plot dependent on a 6G network with shrewd availability was proposed in 2020 [20] to give the framework uphold. Blockchain innovation can likewise be utilized to productively deal with the Industrial Internet of Things (IIoT) information in Industry 4.0 [21]. The unified medical services framework impediment is that it cannot give information permanence, straightforwardness, recognizability, protection, and data security highlights accommodating to find out Covid-19 related cheats, for example, those related to medical supplies, immunization accreditation, and immunizer testing [22]. The blockchain presents disseminated, decentralized, and permanent records of exchanges, which can be warehoused on a circulated organization of hubs over topographically spread spots [23]. Blockchain is an exceptionally dependable and hearty innovation that can help battling Covid-19 viably. The 5G innovation offers heterogeneous gadgets and machines with upgraded network limits, predominant framework throughput, and a high caliber of administration. Being a heterogeneous organization, security is one of the most difficult errands of the 5G network [17–23]. The amazing security parts of blockchain innovation give answers to the worries of the 5G network. As the number of Covid-19 cases are increasing step by step, the chest X-beam information produced will be humongous. Protection and security of patient's information is a difficult errand wherein blockchain innovation will assume an uncommon job. In this work, the creators have recently centered around perceiving Covid-19 patients, yet the following stage would present blockchain innovation for giving hearty arrangements in the medical service frameworks [24].

13.3   Proposed system

Attendance management has always been a cumbersome task. It is quite tedious for the teachers to maintain and record attendance through traditional ways. With the advancement in technology, better ways of maintaining attendance and recording them have come into existence.

Most institutions and industries are now using an advanced automatic attendance system that uses either biometric input or RFID cards to generate logs and further processes them to mark the attendance. However, it has been obvious that due to the outbreak of Covid-19, most of these methods, such as thumb impressions in biometric and RFID cards, would need contact. These contacts can be contagious and could lead to mass outbreaks.

Keeping these things in mind, we propose a system that can maintain and record attendance without any physical contact and has similar efficiency as RFID and thumb impression biometric systems.

We are proposing an automated attendance system with facial recognition. Facial recognition is also a certain type of biometric technique, but it does not require any human contact and smartly manages the attendance without discrepancies. Face recognition is an advanced feature of computer vision that can be achieved through deep learning models. However, the major challenge involved in this is image acquisition. The face of an individual can only be processed further if it is optimal for detection. Most devices that we have today for image acquisition fail to obtain optimal images due to environmental conditions or frame error [13].

The primary concern of any face recognition system is obtaining optimal images. Since hardware changes are very difficult and costly, we need to work on algorithms, such as AdaBoost and ResNet to obtain optimal images. After obtaining an image suitable for further processing, the background is subtracted to detect faces. Once faces are detected, they can be compared with the database for recognition. Our proposed model also has similar architecture.

In Figure 13.1, the block diagram of the proposed system is displayed. Each block is essential, and its functioning can be portrayed by visiting each block at a time.

13.3.1   Student and capture image

The first block, Student, is the first step in the automated attendance system. By student, this block aims to obtain optimal images of the students, which is one of the most important steps in facial recognition. The image acquisition occurs in the Capture block. It is challenging to obtain high-quality, adequate fit images for further processing. During this process, some of the common challenges are adverse real-life situations, such as bad lighting or improper focusing of the camera lens.

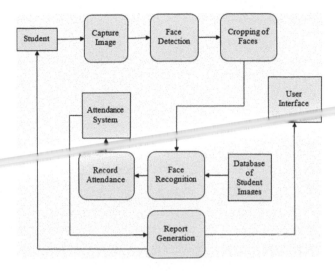

Figure 13.1   Block diagram of the proposed system

However, these shortcomings can be taken care of either by using high-end hardware, but that would be costly. Hence, better algorithms are used to obtain optimal images.

13.3.2   Face detection

Once the image is captured and processed for further operations, it is sent to the Detection block. The image background is subtracted in the detection block, and all the faces are detected using trained classifiers. Face detection involves classification of images using a convolutional neural network (ConvNet). The ConvNet gives the output as some feature vector. This helps figure out which class the images belong to if some existing class is defined for it. This is how a human face is separated from other faces. Just in case an animal, for example, a cat appears before the camera, it will still capture the image, but this image would be discarded since it does not qualify for a human face. This way, the data can also be minimized. This would make the face detection system more sound.

13.3.3   Cropping of faces

After the detection of faces in the procured image, the next step involves the cropping of faces. Cropping of faces is essential for further processing as it limits the scope to which the recognition algorithm can work and save time. It makes the entire system a bit lighter and increases the response time by decreasing the further load on the system.

13.3.4   Face recognition

The most crucial block of the system that follows after the cropping of faces is Face recognition. It has its own set of problems; one such case is One Short Learning Problem. The face recognition algorithm will be efficient only if it can detect an individual face by providing a single image as input. Here, the similarity function can be deployed in a neural network, which can calculate the difference between any two images. Considering the output, it can decide if the face is familiar or not. The large output would correspond to an unfamiliar image, whereas the small output will assure the familiar faces.

13.3.5   Database of students' images

Now, an image for comparison needs to be compared with every image in the database, but that would require a large amount of time, given that we are working on a large-scale database. Hence, it is a tedious task altogether. A simple solution for this issue would be to calculate the measurement of some facial features and then comparing only those images that have close measurements. However, this approach will still be a cumbersome task as there would be plenty of facial features to compare. To tackle such a scenario, it will be best to find out one of the most prominent features or best features out of all features in an individual image. These objectives can be achieved using Siamese Network. Further, taking into account the Triplet Loss during the model's training, this process becomes more effective [20–22].

13.3.6   Record attendance and attendance system

The recognized face can be used to mark attendance. The attendance system uses Roll No as the key to enter record on the database. The results of the recognized students would be stored under a NoSQL database with date as the main node, followed by the subject and Roll ID of the child. This would help to obtain a fast report as searching is easy in comparison to regular SQL databases. A user interface is implemented for a simpler view of daily attendance.

13.4   Face detection

For detecting faces in the input image, we use object detection techniques to detect whether the desired object, which is a human face in our case, is present in the image or not. If it is not present, then the image is skipped. If a human face is present in the image, we localize that image as to where that image is present. We put a bounding box around the face. For face detection, we use object detection techniques. The face acknowledgment cycle can be divided into three stages: plan to prepare information, train face recognizer, and expectation. Here, preparing information will include the pictures present in the dataset. They will be allocated with a whole number name of the understudy it has a place with. These pictures are then utilized to face acknowledgment. The face recognizer utilized in this framework is the Local Binary Pattern Histogram. At first, the rundown of nearby paired examples (LBP)

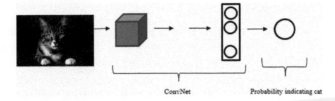

       ConvNet   Probability indicating cat

Figure 13.2   Image classification architecture

of the whole face is acquired. These LBPs are changed over into decimal numbers, and afterwards, histograms of each of those decimal quantities are made. Toward the end, one histogram will correspond to each picture in the information preparation. Afterwards, during acknowledgment, the measured histogram of the face to be perceived is determined and contrasted. The histograms generally figured out return the best-coordinated name related to it.

13.4.1   Object localization

In this phase of the detection method, an object is localized within an image. Three things are done at this stage. These include localization and detection of the image, classification with localization, and landmark detection.

13.4.2   Classification with localization

Simple classification of images is done with the help of a ConvNet. In this, we provide the input image as input to the ConvNet which in turn gives some feature vector as output that tells us which class of object this input image contains out of some predefined classes, as shown in Figure 13.2.

If we want the ConvNet to localize the detected object, we have to make the Neural Network output with four new numbers b_x, b_y, b_h, and b_w. The numbers b_x and b_y represent the position of the midpoint of the detected object. While b_h represents the height of the bounding box, and b_w represents the width of the bounding box.

Thus, our target label y becomes the vector of five features.

$$y = [p_c, b_x, b_y, b_h, b_w]^T$$

where y: target label
  p_c: probability that the picture has a human face
  b_x: x-coordinate of the midpoint of the face
  b_y: y-coordinate of the midpoint of the face
  b_h: Height of the bounding box
  b_w: width of the bounding box.

13.4.3　Landmark detection

Now that we have found the features representing the bounding box around the detected face(s), what if we want certain points on the face for face recognition based on the distance between different landmarks on the face? We shall add two more points for each landmark describing its coordinate location on the image.

If there are three landmarks on the image to be detected, we shall add six features l_{1x}, l_{1y}, l_{2x}, l_{2y}, l_{3x}, and l_{3y}, into the final feature vector. Thus y becomes:

$$y = [p_c, b_x, b_y, b_h, b_w, l_{1x}, l_{1y}, l_{2x}, l_{2y}, l_{3x}, l_{3y}]$$

13.5　Object detection

Object detection involves training set creation and training of the Neural Network's fully connected layers with the help of the sliding window technique. This sliding window technique is later implemented convolutionally to improve the accuracy and efficiency of the system.

13.5.1　Training set creation and training

We create a labeled training set (x, y) where x is the closely cropped picture of a human face and y is 1. We also include some negative examples with images not containing human faces and corresponding y as 0.

Given this labeled training set, we can now train a ConvNet, which will take an image as input and output depending on whether the image is a human face or not.

13.5.2　Sliding window technique

When we have an image to process, we start by taking a window size. We then start from the top-left corner of the image and take the part of the image of the size of the window taken. We feed this part to our ConvNet, which we had trained earlier. The ConvNet tells us whether or not this part of the image contains a human face. We then shift the box forward by a stride to determine and feed this part to ConvNet, and this goes on until we have covered the whole image.

We get the result that tells us whether any part of the image contains a human face. We determine the stride size, keeping in mind the performance bottleneck created by it. The sliding window technique becomes costlier when the stride size is reduced because then many more parts have to go through the ConvNet for checking. If we reduce the size of the stride, then the accuracy of the model reduces because there might have been a human face between two boxes.

13.5.3　Fully connected layers to convolutional layers

A lot of work in the Sliding window is duplicated. If our stride size is small, then huge computation needs to be done. The fully connected layers in the Neural Network are converted to the convolutional layers by applying an appropriate filter, as shown in

Figure 13.3   A neural network classifier

Figure 13.3. The shape of the convolutional layers is the same as that of the fully connected layers [23–28].

13.5.4   Convolution implementation of sliding windows [29]

If we implement the Sliding windows algorithm convolutionally, as shown in Figure 13.4, we can reduce the computations significantly. There are as many features available in the final layer as several strides in the corresponding stride-sized Sliding window. Thus, we get all the strides in a single pass of the ConvNet, hence reducing the computation. The size of the final output layer in the convolutional implementation increases as we decrease the stride size to deal with the increased number of searches in the corresponding sliding window algorithm.

13.5.5   Drawing bounding boxes

The problem we were facing was due to the objects of different shapes. In YOLO, we divide the image into square grids. Then we classify each of the cells by feeding them to the trained classifier. We will get (5×1) vector for each grid cell. The YOLO algorithm outputs the presence of an object in the given cell if the midpoint of the object lies within the given cell. The specification of the bounding boxes is the same as described in the subsequent section. However, there might be one drawback that it will not detect multiple objects per grid cell. We can avoid that by making the grid cell size smaller, i.e., instead of taking a 3×3 grid, we can take a 19×19 grid, thus reducing the possibility of multiple objects per grid cell.

13.5.6   Intersection over Union

Intersection over Union (IoU) is a measure of the overlap of two bounding boxes. Let us say that two bounding boxes are intersecting with each other, as shown in Figure 13.5.

Then their IoU is calculated as

$$IoU = \frac{Size\ of\ Intersection}{Size\ of\ Union}$$

(13.1)

Figure 13.4   Convolutional implementation using filters

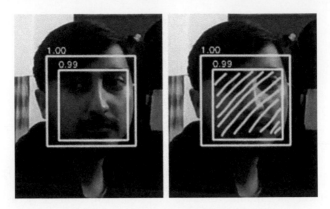

Figure 13.5   Intersection over Union

The higher is the IoU, the more accurate is our detection system.
    We consider the bounding box to be correct if the IoU > 0.5.

13.5.7   Non-max suppression

It ensures that the algorithm detects the object only once. For non-max suppression, we highlight the box with maximum probability value in the whole image. Then we calculate its IoU with all other boxes and drop all boxes with whom its IoU turns out to be greater than 0.5. We go to the box with second max probability and repeat the process until all boxes have been either marked correct or the boxes are dropped for overlap with other more probabilistic bounding boxes.

    In non-max suppression, we need to carry out this process separately for all the classes present. Since we have only one class with us, i.e., human face, we need to do non-max suppression only once.

13.5.8   Anchor boxes

We are predicting the objects with their midpoints in different grid cells. But what if two objects have the same midpoint in the same grid cell? Then comes the concept of anchor boxes. We can choose any number of shapes we want and train the ConvNet on them. Thus, when we provide an input, instead of giving out a feature vector of shape (5×1), we get a feature vector of shape $(m \times 5 \times 1)$ where m is the number of anchor boxes.

    It has some disadvantages also. The maximum number of objects detected in a grid cell is bounded by the number of anchor boxes we have taken. Also, if two objects have similar anchor boxes, then this will not be able to handle the case. However, if we use a 19×19 grid, then the chances of two or more objects of similar anchor boxes coming in the same grid cell will be reduced.

Figure 13.6   Single-face detection

13.5.9   Results

The results were observed on the image in different conditions, and they were recorded. The input images provided to the system were in different conditions. We provided different input images with single person, two persons close together, two persons farther apart from each other, images with blurred faces, tilted faces, faces against light, and faces in the crowd.

Figure 13.6 shows that an image with a single person was provided as the input to the system, and the output was generated with the bounding box around the face of the detected person. The same thing was done to an image with two persons sitting close to each other, and the system detected both the persons with high accuracy, as shown in Figure 13.7.

We provided various images to our face detection system with two people farther away from each other. The system detected both the persons present in the input image, as shown in Figure 13.8, and drew the bounding boxes around both of their faces.

13.6   Face recognition

Now, as we have completed the face detection process, in this chapter, we shall discuss in detail the process to be applied for face recognition on the detected faces in the input image. We shall discuss facial recognition problems such as the one-shot learning problems and train our CNN based on the Siamese network [30].

Figure 13.7   Two close faces

13.6.1   Introduction

In this section, we shall first discuss the basic difference between face verification and face recognition. Then we shall talk about various processes involved in face recognition.

13.6.2   Face verification vs. face recognition

First, let us discuss the two popular terms. These are face verification and face recognition.

Figure 13.8   Two farther faces

In face verification, you are given an image as input, and the work of the system is to verify whether the given person is some fixed person or not. This is a 1:1 problem that includes verifying whether the person is indeed who he claims to be.

In the face recognition problem, the system recognizes the given input image from among various people in the database. This is a 1:k problem, k being the number of people in the database. The recognition is harder than verification.

13.6.3   Processes involved in face recognition

Face recognition is the process of looking at an image and telling exactly who the person is in the image (if there is any).

This process may further be broken down into several simpler sub-processes. Let us study these sub-processes in detail. Firstly, we take the image and detect faces to confirm that there are faces in it before applying a face recognition algorithm to it. Secondly, we should identify the two faces in the image, even if they are distorted or rotated or have inadequate/excessive lighting. Thirdly, we pick out the unique features of the faces to be distinguished from one another. Lastly, we compare those picked out unique features to tell the name of the person.

Some pipeline has to be designed or built for the process where the output of one of the steps is fed as an input for the next step. The first step, i.e., the detection of the faces in the image, has been discussed and completed in the previous chapter. Now we shall continue from there.

13.6.4   One-shot learning problem

One of the many challenges involved in face recognition is that we have to tackle one-shot learning problem, which means that our system should identify any individual in an image using only one input image of his/her face. Let us understand this with an example. Suppose we have a database of 10 pictures of students in our class. If someone out of them turns up in the class, their attendance has to be recorded. Therefore, despite having only a single image of the person, our face recognition software has to recognize him/her as the same person. If it encounters someone who is not in the database, it should identify him/her as an 'unknown' person. Thus, in a one-shot learning problem, our system has to recognize the same person again by learning from a single image sample. This is required because we might not be able to fetch hundreds of images of each student to feed as input to our CNN.

To solve the one-shot problem, we have a similarity function. We require neural network to learn a function that can take two images as input and then give the difference between the two images. If two input images are of the same person, then the neural network's output should be small and if the images are of different persons, then the output should be big. During face verification, if this difference is greater than a prescribed threshold, then the images are of a different person; otherwise, the images are of the same person. This is the solution to face verification. We can extend this method for face recognition. We can take the input image and use the function which we have learned with all the other images that we had stored earlier in the database of the recognized people. Suppose the difference comes to be less than the threshold, then we take the lowest predicted value and identify the corresponding person in the database as the given person; if none of the images in the database gives the output of the learned function as less than the prescribed threshold, then we understand that the given person is not present in the database. We label the person as "unknown."

Now we shall see how we can learn the discussed function, which gives the difference in the images as its output.

13.6.5   Recognition model

In this section, we will first identify the model that will be used in our project for face recognition. After that, we shall discuss how we shall train this model using a loss function called triplet loss.

13.6.6   Identifying the model

A simple model

The simplest method to recognize a face, which we found during the detection method, involves comparing it with all the available faces we have in our database. If and when we detect a face in our database similar to the extent of the decided threshold to the face detected, we assume that the faces are of the same person and report the result.

This approach will cause a big problem in our face recognition system. If our dataset of known users is very large, we cannot loop through our database and compare each of the faces in the database to the detected faces quickly. We need to do it in a reasonable amount of time.

A better model

What we can do is, we can extract some measurements from each of our stored faces. Then measure the same features from the unknown face and compare the measurement with those in the database. This way, we can find the known face having the closest measurements with our unknown face. For example, we may measure the space between the eyes as a feature or the size of the nose or length of the ear, etc.

The best model

Now how do we decide what is the best feature to be measured in a face so that it may distinguish itself from the faces of other persons? It turns out that researchers have discovered an approach to solve this problem. The most accurate among them is to let the computer figure out what measurements are to be taken as the features and then take the measurements themselves. Research shows that deep learning does a much better job of detecting the best distinguishable features in a face than a human being.

We have to train a deep convolutional neural network for this job. In the last chapter, while we were detecting faces from images, we trained CNN to detect faces in a picture. We shall train a neural network to generate 128 measurements for each of the faces provided [31].

13.6.7 *Training the model—triplet loss [20]*

For training our deep convolutional neural network, we used the "single-triplet training method." In this method of training a CNN, one image of a person is taken, then two more images are taken, which one is of the same person, and the other is of a different person. Then, 128 measurements are taken of all three images. After comparing results, our model of neural network is adjusted to obtain different measurements of different persons and almost similar measurements of similar persons. This process is repeated on a large number of picture dataset which is labeled. The more the data in our dataset, the more accurate our convolutional neural network will be in identifying any person's unknown image. This process gives us our recognition model that is capable of generating 128 measurements of individuals uniquely. Any of their pictures generates almost similar measurements to a picture of any other individual. In the language of machine learning, the 128 measurements are called "Embedding."

Triplet loss

One good way of learning the hidden layer parameters of the CNN for better encoding (the 128-dimensional vector representing the image) is to apply the Gradient Descent algorithm to optimize the "Triplet Loss" function.

For this, we take a reference image and call it an "Anchor image." We then take a positive image and a negative image to that anchor. The positive image to the anchor is of the same person as in the anchor image. The negative image is of the person who is different than the person in the anchor image. We want the distance between the anchor image and the positive image to be very near to each other and the distance between the anchor image and the negative image to be far away from each other. This generates the "triplet loss" when we look at three images simultaneously.

Our learning objective:

$$\text{Distance}(A, P) + \alpha \leq \text{Distance}(A, N) \tag{13.2}$$

$$\|f(A) - f(P)\|^2 + \alpha \leq \|f(A) - f(N)\|^2 \tag{13.3}$$

where α is the margin chosen by us at our own discretion.

We add α to the equation so that the network does not learn to give zero as every output or any one value for all outputs, which will satisfy the equation.

$$\|f(A) - f(P)\|^2 - \|f(A) - f(N)\|^2 + \alpha \leq 0 \tag{13.4}$$

Given three images, i.e., anchor image (A), positive image (P), and negative image (N), we define our loss function as:

$$L(A, P, N) = \max(\|f(A) - f(P)\|^2 - \|f(A) - f(N)\|^2 + \alpha, 0) \tag{13.5}$$

and the cost function is:

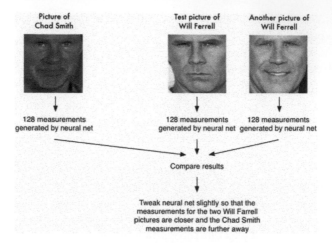

Figure 13.9   Single triplet training method

$$J = \sum_{i=1}^{m} L(A, P, N) \tag{13.6}$$

There is one important point to be kept in mind while choosing images for triplet loss training. Suppose we choose this set randomly from across our database, then probably our network will not be trained for the difficult recognition that involves differentiation of one person who is very similar to the other. To solve this issue, we should manually choose the triplet set to train the network for better comparisons [25].

To train these types of deep neural networks, we need a huge amount of data. More than tens of millions of images are often used for training purposes to give the required accuracy to the model. Some companies even use over 100 million images for training. Thus, we can use some parameters of the trained network made public by these companies.

13.6.8   Encoding faces

After the convolutional neural network model training, we then calculate embeddings (the 128 measurements) for all our images in the database and store them for future comparisons.

We do not know what part of the face is being measured for embedding, but we do not care. All that matters to us is that the model generates the same 128 measurements for different pictures of the same person, as shown in Figure 13.9.

13.6.9   Results

The results were taken on the image in different conditions, and they were recorded.

We provided the input image with a single person in the frame, and the face was recognized and marked, as shown in Figure 13.10. Figure 13.11 is the output image where the input image shows two persons sitting close to each other.

Figure 13.10   Single face

Then we tested our recognition system on the image with two persons far apart from each other, and the output, as shown in Figure 13.12, indicates that the model recognized both the faces in the image.

Figure 13.11   Two close faces

Figure 13.12   Two farther faces

13.6.10   Recording attendance

We have considered the use of two databases. One is the in-built SQLite database of python, and the other is the Excel file storage. It will be persistent in data losses due to physical dangers or system failure.

Requirements:

1.   Python
2.   SQLite.

For the attendance monitoring system, we consider three parameters to store detailed data. These three parameters are:

1.   Index or Roll
2.   Name
3.   Time of face capture.

Creating a table and establishing a connection to the database

- To communicate with the database, create a connection to the database, and then create a table as required.
- After creating the table, return the connection to the database for future use. Inserting data into a table
- This can involve two cases. First, the data to be inserted are already there in the table, or second, the data are entirely new to the table.
- When data are already there, just update the attendance column for the given data.
- When data are new, then insert data with the attendance count column set to 1.

13.7   Attendance and visitor management

13.7.1   Why change?

- They are making it more advanced so that no manual entry of the data is required at the gate.
- No biometric issue (COA)
- ~~R...~~ location of the employee and also the visitor (Android users/ IOS users)
- As the company's name is now changing, it's the right time to update ourselves with the latest trend and technology.

13.7.2   Intervention

- Android-based entry and exit of the visitor
- Android-based location and notification to the employee and the company
- Automatic door locking and unlocking system for access of a certain department
- Appointment booking and conversation platform in one application
- Automatic attendance of the employee.

13.7.3   Possible demerits

- Smartphone requirement

    - We can have a manual entry for such people (as per research, only 1 out of 50 individuals in India is not using any smartphones).

- Internet requirement

    - After Jio revolution, everybody is having an active internet pack in the phones
    - We can give access to an open Wifi at gate, which allows users to connect and use that application.

13.8   Final takeaways

In this section, we shall conclude our report by mentioning the highlights of the project. We shall discuss some future works that shall further improve the system and ponder over some other practical uses of the model discussed in this project.

13.8.1   Face detection

Till now, we have taken an image and processed it with the convolutional neural network to get the coordinates of the faces in it. We have applied various optimizations for the detection of faces, such as detecting the faces with a probability of more than 0.5. Then taking all the faces with more than 0.5, we apply the Non-Max Suppression to remove all the bounding boxes.

13.8.2   Image classification and recognition

After completing the detection phase, we worked on the recognition problem in the next phase. We created a dataset of lots of labeled images of different people and trained our model on it to classify different people with their names or IDs assigned to them. We used the Siamese Network for the recognition phase. We used the "Triplet loss" function to train the CNN.

13.8.3   Storage of the attendance date and time

When the image detects all the faces in it and classifies and recognizes the people present in it along with the IDs assigned to them, the system communicates the date and time of capturing the image and stores in the database. In this way, any individual's time spent in the classroom or any specified premise can be judged.

13.8.4   Better system with liveness detection

The automated attendance requires a facial recognition system to mark the attendance of the students. However, image acquisition techniques cannot obtain optimal images for face detection and recognition. Therefore, ResNet and AdaBoost can generate such optimal images, which can ease out the recognition process. These methods would also help in resolving the illumination issues that are often faced in real-time scenarios. Further, to encounter the rotation screen issues and to ensure that the attendance of a particular student is not skipped, a video stream of a minimum of one minute can be used and then processed frame by frame.

Till now, our system has been recognizing the images of the people. Thus, it can take the image of an image and still recognize the person in it and record attendance. One of teh solution to this problem is to i develop a liveness detection that can differentiate between any live person or any image of the person. Then, take into account the attendance made by any live person only. This can be achieved by training a model using supervised learning.

13.8.5   Practical usage of the system

Since recognition and detection are not enough to prevent frauds, RFID cards can be used as a double-check to encounter issues like authorization. It can be paired up with video surveillance to log in the details of students entering and leaving the class and only provide attendance if the student is qualifying all parameters.

These face recognition systems can be further implemented in various real-life detection schemes, such as detecting and notifying criminals trying to break into a house or stealing something, via CCTV footage. A notification system can be added to it to notify the police immediately if any such activity or unauthorized access is observed.

13.8.6   Online database and user interaction

To send push notification to the user using the android application, we need to set up an online database from where the app can get d~~..~~ ~~..~~ ~~.~~ ~~of~~ this purpose, we can use Firebase Console. The main ~~...~~ ~~...~~ of Firebase is that it supports the real-time updates of ~~...~~ ~~...~~ in Firebase, the database is arranged in the form of parent-child architecture. Apart from providing a database facility, Firebase provides many extra facilities, such as Google Cloud Messaging, Real-Time Analytics, Firebase Auth.

Apart from Firebase, we can implement Google Cloud Messaging using PHP and a Web Server named GCM_PUSH_IMPLEMENTATION.

To access Firebase database, we need:

- Python Ide with Firebase module
- Firebase database
- Android app
- Internet connection.

13.8.7   Communicating with the user

To communicate with the user, we may develop an android application to notify them about the changes. For this purpose, the database should be kept online.

- Whenever the attendance database is updated, a notification is sent to the concerned users notifying them about the attendance updates.
- When the user clicks on the notification, it takes the user to the application, where the attendance database is displayed.

The format of the displayed data remains the same as that of the local database. It has two columns:

- Roll or ID
- Name.

13.9   Conclusion

This framework plans to fabricate a powerful class participation utilizing face acknowledgment strategies. The proposed framework will have an option to stamp the participation through face ID. It will identify faces using a webcam and afterwards perceive the appearance. After the acknowledgment, it will check the participation of the perceived understudy and update the participation record.

References

[1] Dixit K.G.S., Chadaga M.G., Savalgimath S.S., Rakshith G.R., Kumar M.R.N. 'Evaluation and evolution of object detection techniques YOLO and R-CNN'. *International Journal of Recent Technology and Engineering (IJRTE)*. 2019;**8**(2S):3.

[2] Redmon J., Divvala S., Girshick R., Farhadi A. 'You only look once: unified, real-time object detection'. *IEEE Conference on Computer Vision and Pattern Recognition*; 2016.

[3] Veer N.D., Momin B.F. 'An automated attendance system using video surveillance camera'. *IEEE International Conference on Recent Trends in Electronics Information Communication Technology*; India; May 20-21, 2016.

[4] Varadharajan E., Dharani R., Jeevitha S., Kavinmathi B., Hemalatha S. 'Automatic attendance management system using face recognition'. *Online International Conference on Green Engineering and Technologies (IC-GET)*; 2016.

[5] Wagh P., Chaudhari J., Thakare R., Patil S. 'Attendance system based on face recognition using eigen face and PCA algorithms'. *International Conference on Green Computing and Internet of Things (ICGCIoT)*; 2015.

[6] Liying L., Yue H. 'The study of entrance guard & check on work attendance system based on face recognition'. *International Conference on Computer Science and Information Technology*; 2008.

[7] Girshick R., Donahue J., Darrell T., Malik J. 'Rich feature hierarchies for accurate object detection and semantic segmentation'. *IEEE Conference on Computer Vision and Pattern Recognition*; 2014.

[8] Redmon J., Divvala S., Girshick R., Farhad A. 'You only look once: unified, real-time object detection'. *IEEE Conference on Computer Vision and Pattern Recognition*; 2016.

[9] Shanmugavadivu D.P., Kumar A. 'Rapid face detection and annotation with loosely face geometry'. *2nd International Conference on Contemporary Computing and Informatics (IC3I)*; 2016.

[10] Nehru M., Padmavathi D.S. 'Illumination invariant face detection using viola jones algorithm'. *International Conference on Advanced Computing and Communication Systems (ICACCS)*; 2017.

[11] Hapani S., Parakhiya N., Prabhu N., Paghdal M. 'Automated attendance system using image processing'. *Fourth International Conference on Computing Communication Control and Automation (ICCUBEA)*; 2018.

[12] Fung-Lung L., Nycander-Barua M., Shiguihara-Juarez P. 'An image acquisition method for face recognition and implementation of an automatic attendance system for events'. *IEEE*. 2019.

[13] Yuvaraj C.B., Srikanth M., Kumar V.S., Murthy Y.V.S., Koolagudi S.G. 'An approach to maintain attendance using image processing techniques'. *Tenth International Conference on Contemporary Computing (IC3)*; 2017.

[14] Akbar M.S., Sarker P., Mansoor A.T. 'Face recognition and RFID verified attendance system'. *IEEE*. 2019.

[15] Sawhney S., Kacker K., Jain S., Singh S.N., Garg R. 'Real-time smart attendance system using face recognition technique'. *9th International Conference on Cloud Computing, Data Science & Engineering (Confluence)*; 2019.

[16] Zeng W., Meng Q., Li R. 'Design of intelligent classroom attendance system based on face recognition'. *IEEE 3rd Information Technology, Networking, Electronic and Automation Control Conference (ITNEC)*; 2019.

[17] Tanwar S. *Fog Data Analytics for IoT Applications – Next Generation Process Model with state-of-the-art Technologies, Studies in Big Data*. Springer International Publishing; 2020. pp. 1–550.

[18] Tanwar S. 'Fog computing for healthcare 4.0 environments: technical, societal and Future Implications, Signals and Communication Technology'. *Springer International Publishing*. 2020:1–430.

[19] Tanwar S., Tyagi S., Kumar N. 'Security and privacy of electronics healthcare records'. *The IET Book Series on e-Health Technologies*. Stevenage, United Kingdom; 2019. pp. 1–450.

[20] Gupta R., Kumari A., Tanwar S., Kumar N. 'Blockchain-envisioned softwarized multi-swarming UAVs to tackle COVID-19 situations'. *IEEE network*. 2020:1–8.

[21] Kumari A., Tanwar S., Tyagi S., Kumar N. 'Blockchain-based massive data dissemination handling in IIoT environment'. *IEEE Network*. 2020;**35**(1):318–25.

[22] Ahmad R.W., Salah K., Jayaraman R., Yaqoob I., Ellahham S., Omar M. 'Blockchain and COVID-19 pandemic: applications and challenges'. *TechRxiv. Preprint*. 2020:1–20.

[23] Nguyen D., Ding M., Pathirana P.N., Seneviratne A. 'Blockchain and AI-based solutions to combat coronavirus (COVID-19)-like epidemics: a survey'. *TechRxiv*. 2020.

[24] Nguyen D.C., Pathirana P.N., Ding M., Seneviratne A. 'Blockchain for 5G and beyond networks: a state of the art survey'. *Journal of Network and Computer Applications*. 2020;**166**(4):102693.

[25] Delbiaggio N. 'A comparison of facial recognition's algorithms'. *Bachelor's Thesis, Degree Programme in Business Information Technology. Haaga-Helia University of Applied Sciences*. 2017.

[26] Taigman Y., Yang M., Ranzato M., Wolf L. 'Deepface: closing the gap to human-level performance in face verification'. *Proceedings of the IEEE conference on computer vision and pattern recognition*; 2014. pp. 1701–8.

[27] Schroff F., Kalenichenko D., Philbin J. 'Facenet: a unified embedding for face recognition and clustering'. *Proceedings of the IEEE conference on computer vision and pattern recognition*; 2015. pp. 815–23.

[28]   Arampatzis T., Lygeros J., Manesis S. 'A survey of applications of wireless sensors and wireless sensor networks'. *2005 IEEE International Symposium on Intelligent Control & 13th Mediterranean Conference on Control and Automation*; Limassol, Cyprus; 2005. pp. 1-2–719-24.

[29]   Sermanet P., Eigen D., Zhang X., Mathieu M., Fergus R., LeCun Y. OverFeat: Integrated Recognition, Localization and Detection using Convolutional Networks. International Conference on Learning Representations (ICLR) (Banff), arXiv. 2014. Available from https://www.researchgate.net/publication/259441043_OverFeat_Integrated_Recognition_Localization_and_Detection_using_Convolutional_Networks.

[30]   Mirabella O., Brischetto M. 'A hybrid wired/wireless networking infrastructure for greenhouse management'. *IEEE Transactions on Instrumentation and Measurement*. 2011;**60**(2):398–407.

[31]   Liu H., Meng Z., Cui S. 'A wireless sensor network prototype for environmental monitoring in greenhouses'. *International Conference on Wireless Communications, Networking and Mobile Computing (WiCom 2007)*; Shangai, China; September 2007. pp. 21–5.

Chapter 14

Blockchain-based smart contracts for e-health care management 4.0

J S Shyam Mohan[1], Ramamoorthy S[2], Harsha Surya Abhishek Kota[3], Vedantham Hanumath Sreeman[3], and Vanam Venkata Chakradhar[3]

Secure and reliable exchange of data in the fields of finance, supply chain management, agriculture, and health care, and so on became easier with the advancements in blockchain technology. Modern health-care systems are complex and costly and moreover, data privacy is a key issue. Blockchain technology tries to improve this aspect by reforming the existing health-care systems by providing quick access to patient records with correct prescriptions, device tracking, and hospital assets, including the complete life cycle of a device within the blockchain infrastructure. This chapter discusses medical system workflows, calculating latency throughput, performance, and average execution time for surgical and clinical studies conducted on Apache JMeter by providing policies improving accessibility through solidity-based electronic health records (EHR). This chapter also tries to provide an overview of the 5G network system for Ethereum to provide tamper-proof data. Further, this chapter explores the applications of blockchain technology in health-care sectors supported by a case study that would facilitate the stakeholders involved in the health-care system to understand the system design of Ethereum for providing better health-care services to the patients. The abbreviations used in this chapter are given in Table 14.1.

14.1 Introduction

In the era of digital technology, blockchain technology has become an important part of healthcare and many different fields and sectors. Many research proposals emphasize the expected benefits of blockchain in the structure of medical

[1]Faculty of CSE, SCSVMV, India
[2]Faculty of CSE, SRM IST, India
[3]IV-B.E (CSE), SCSVMV, India

Table 14.1   Abbreviations used

EHR	Electronic Health Records
Dapps	Decentralized applications
EVM	Ethereum Virtual Machines
SEK	Symmetric Encryption Keys
GUI	Graphical User Interface
PoW	Proof of Work
IPFS	Interplanetary File System
CRUD	Create, Read, Update, and Delete
TTC	Transaction Time for Completion
TTD	Transaction Time for Deployment

services [1]. It is believed that the global blockchain market will promote the development of health-care services. The global blockchain market is expected to reach US$500 million by 2022 [2]. In recent years, blockchain technology has transformed the traditional clinical framework into a collaborative mechanical framework [3]. Blockchain technology is popular because of its decentralization, transparency, and anonymity, which is attributed to its implementation in all fields and applications [4]. Bitcoin is a use case of blockchain technology with approximately 400 million completed transactions [5]. Blockchain technology is applicable in many applications and sectors including healthcare. IBM predicts that 70 per cent of the biggest impact of blockchain technology will be used to improve clinical services, preliminary services, and regulatory compliance and will provide a decentralized system for EHRs. The growing importance of e-health-care systems varying from remote access to EHR to real-time monitoring of patient's health data and the huge amount of data being exchanged, poses significant challenges like privacy and confidentiality of the patients' data and unauthorized usage. Blockchain technology provides a scalable and interoperable solution for the e-health-care sectors [6] by continuous and identifiable monitoring of diseases and treatment through robotic therapy or robotic operations.

14.1.1   Evolution of Healthcare 1.0 to 4.0

Blockchain can simplify the process and then enable convincing correspondence between patients and health-care providers. Healthcare 1.0 states that the health structures were restricted and could not influence each other due to lack of resources, and integration of biomedical systems was difficult. Most of the prescriptions and reports were paper-based; this increased the costs and time of health-care systems. During Healthcare 2.0 (1991–2005), health and computing tools jointly created a health framework that introduced computerized surveillance and monitoring functions and provided photo frames for professionals that became popular with social media. Many health-care providers and hospitals have started working online. The community brings more people together, shares health information, and helps doctors establish contact with patients, and vice versa. They started sharing information for providers and patients, accessing reports on mobile devices, etc. [7]. There was much criticism related to confidentiality of information exchange and patient data. Medical videos are provided and clinical research is included in the clinical imaging framework; this helps doctors to enter patient information more safely and accurately.

Healthcare 3.0 is an idea borrowed from Web 3.0. The idea is how customers can personalize access and delivery of patient files. The user interface became simple for real-time monitoring of patient health. EHRs are user-friendly and easy to integrate with networks and non-operational systems including social media to facilitate data exchange [8].

The fourth industrial revolution Healthcare 4.0 adopted blockchain technology in traditional industries, sectors, and even for the health-care system. Advancements in telemedicine, remote patient monitoring, and so on were possible only with artificial intelligence (AI) and Machine Learning (ML) tools. There is a lot of evidence that Healthcare 4.0 should be regarded as a subset of Industry 4.0. Since the concept of health is of the utmost importance, safety should be regarded as a mandatory rule of the "Healthcare 4.0" supplementary plan. Mobile phones played a vital role in smart drugs; however, mobile phones had some limitations, like Bluetooth's range supported at short distances, limited battery life, and so on. Bluetooth does not meet the prerequisites of keen asthma treatment and general customized medication approaches.

Smartphone devices play an important role in the dissemination of health information and real-time chronic disease monitoring with predictive analysis functions that will have a low-cost model and will be more transparent. In both cases, mobile phones, smartphones, or tablets play a vital role in collecting video logs and reports. Smart medicines based on 5G networks and technologies such as NarrowBand-Internet of Things (NB-IoT) are close to the market and can be used for many years. A new plan to implement pharmaceutical businesses may evolve, in addition to simply assembling medicines. Auxiliary industries also have other new functions. Blockchain acts as an intermediary for all revolutionary technologies. It can even support new ecosystems in the field of health and life sciences. Customer/client or patient opposition is the main challenge for virtualized health care that can be overcome by blockchain technology. Virtualized care includes empowering patients to assume responsibility for their health, and disease, as well as improving the information and skills of health-care professionals [9].

14.1.2   Blockchain in health-care applications used for preventing diseases

There are many challenges faced by the health-care sector. Some of the challenges include the security of patient records, the lack of simplicity in the flexible drug chain, the lack of interoperability between information bases that keep tolerant health records and dispersed healthcare. Data relating to patients, medical history, or clinical reports are confidential and need to be tamper-proof. The current situation leads to problems in sharing and exchanging medical information. Blockchain technology can solve all the challenges faced in the health-care sector by ensuring safety and security of the health-care data. All the data stored in the blocks are tamper-proof.

14.1.2.1   Blockchain for drug traceability

Blockchain provides a solution for ensuring drug traceability as it is licensed after each drug until it is launched. Blockchain can be used to type data about the drug at each stage of its life cycle (e.g., creation, dissemination, etc.). On the drug data blockchain, a hash is tied to another square, and each square contains a timestamp that cannot be adjusted. Blockchain provides an effective framework for conducting meetings related to drug discovery and development, and so on. Drug buyers also have the option of verifying the authenticity of the purchase of items by checking the QR code and viewing the data of the manufacturer and other members of the blockchain.

14.1.2.2   Facilitating clinical trials and research

Blockchain technology is the future for years to come. Blockchain helps address the problems in clinical research. Misrepresentation will result in data being altered to hide the real effects of tests, drugs, or other drugs. Specialists can rely on the blockchain to ensure the safety and simplicity of clinical preparations. The final goal of the clinical research is to store the confidential data and reports securely. The reports consist of patients' medical summary, blood tests, and so on. Blockchain offers many other advantages for clinical research. It reduces verification costs and eliminates the problem of missing records.

14.1.2.3   Taxonomy of the paper

This chapter is divided into the following sections:
  Section 1: Introduction
  Section 2: Related works on blockchain technology in health-care sectors
  Section 3: Blockchain-based health-care and management applications
  Section 4: Benefits of blockchain technology in the health-care industry
  Section 5: Ethereum system design
  Section 6: 5G networks and Ethereum for the health-care sector
  Section 7: Real-time examples for Ethereum in health-care sectors
  Section 8: 5G networks and smart contracts
  Section 9: Advantages of smart contracts
  Section 10: Choosing the smart contract platform
  Section 11: Applications of smart contracts in health care
  Section 12: Case study—design and architecture
  Section 13: System implementation
  Section 14: Experimental set-up
  Section 15: Results
  Section 16: Conclusion

Table 14.2   Related works on blockchain technology in health-care sectors

Author	Year	Short description
Dimiter V Dimitrov [11]	2019	Discussed benefits and applications for health-care data management
Panesar [12]	2019	Suggested a machine learning and AI model for health care in big data for improved health outcomes
Seyednima Khezr et al. [13]	2019	Proposed blockchain technology in health care. A comprehensive review and directions for future research
Grant Carson et al. [14]	2020	Worked on a blockchain beyond the hype: What is the strategic business value
David Randall et al. [15]	2017	Discussed blockchain applications and use cases in health information technology
Nir Kshetri [16]	2018	Discussed the concepts of blockchain and electronic health-care records
Brennan Bennett [17]	2018	Proposed blockchain HIE overview and a framework for health-care interoperability
James T. Whilson et al. [18]	2018	Proposed geospatial blockchain and promises, challenges, and scenarios in health and healthcare
Skiba et al. [19]	2017	Discussed about the potential of blockchain in education and health care
Thomas Heston [20]	2017	Introduced a case study in blockchain health-care innovation

14.2   Related works on blockchain technology in health-care sectors

Conventional medical systems transmit only medical data to internal systems. In the field of healthcare, blockchain innovation is at the forefront of many new developments. Table 14.2 shows some related work on blockchain technology in the health-care field from 2017 to 2020 [10].

14.3   Blockchain-based health-care and management applications

Because of its adaptability and the secure exchange of medical data, blockchain technology is redefining real-time health applications in an unprecedented way. Blockchain-based applications in health-care systems are classified into the following layers:

a.   Data sources
b.   Blockchain technology
c.   Health-care applications
d.   Stakeholders.

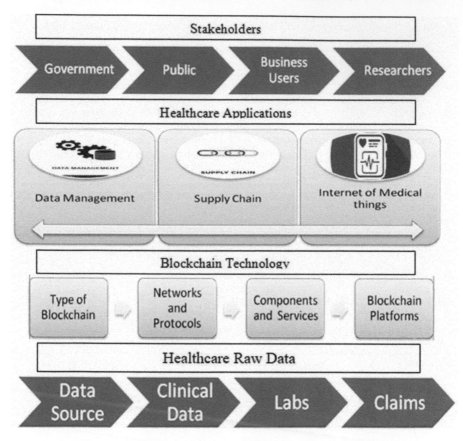

Figure 14.1   Blockchain-based health-care applications workflow

As shown in Figure 14.1, all the raw data are collected from medical devices, laboratories, and other sources (big data) which are the main components in the blockchain-based health stack. A data layer for creating a secure health-care architecture is divided into four components. The next layer is a coordination in full framework.

With blockchain, users can create and manage their transactions [11]. For example Ethereum [12], Ripple [13], and Hyperledger [14]. The main segments of blockchain are smart contracts, cryptowallets, and so on. Based on the requirements, policymakers use public, private, or federated types of services. Blockchain-based health-care applications can be divided into three classes:

1. **Data management:** includes data exchange for research and development
2. **Supply chain management:** clinical studies, and so on
3. **Data storage:** for cloud and EHR-based applications.

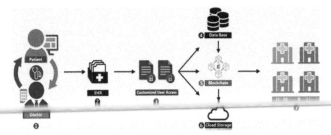

Figure 14.2   Blockchain-based health-care data management applications [16]

Advances in EHRs and cloud-based health-care data storage helped health-care employees and patients to share data directly and communicate with each other easily [15]. Blockchain technology solves the challenges in health applications such as securing, and managing and integrating data smoothly and effectively.

The steps described in Figure 14.2 are given below:

1. Patients work with doctors and specialists to generate preliminary data that consists of the patient's medical history and other information.
2. An EHR is created for each patient for the data collected in step 1.
3. Authorized access control is granted only to the rightful owner based on the request made by the patient.
4. Steps 4 and 5 form the core part of the blockchain, which forms the framework for providing privacy and security.
5. Health-care providers, clinical staff, community care centers, and hospital administration can access patient data if the owner gives permission. Patients can access it anywhere in the world with the help of a distributed ledger.

14.4   Benefits of blockchain technology in the health-care industry

Blockchain offers many benefits to medical researchers in healthcare [17]. It provides a single storage scheme for all health data and makes it easy to track and monitor patients in real time [18]. Medical researchers need access to extensive data to understand and identify diseases, tracking drug development, and design treatment plans [19]. By including the details of patients from different geographic areas, blockchain offers a wide range of data sets [20]. Blockchain provides information for longitudinal studies as it collects health data from people [21] and helps to expand to different groups of people [22] across the globe. The data shared by the blockchain help people understand the basic nature of the blockchain, making it easier for them to access their data [23]. Health-care blockchain promotes the development of smart applications that support medical research [24]. Health-care providers and patients can access and collaborate on the same information [25]. The

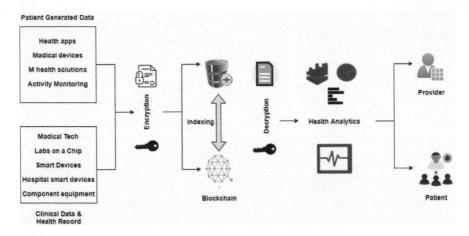

Figure 14.3   Overview of the health-care sector

health-care sector is a complex, data-driven field, where data access or authentication is a key factor. Health-care sectors must provide access to data for researchers and professionals. During the development of drugs, health-care sectors must provide assistance for conducting experiments, and in return, research institutes provide the latest tools to health-care sectors. The data source provides audibility and transparency in the EHR. The health sector has a huge demand for original data for research and development [26]. Blockchain provides attributes such as decentralization, distributed ledger, and transparent transactions for secure data to maintain trust [27]. Figure 14.3 shows the overview of the health-care sector.

14.5   Ethereum—system design

Ethereum is the second-largest digital currency of blockchain. Before Ethereum, bitcoin was used as an exchange mode for transactions. This is a form of a centralized exchange with no intermediary agency between the two parties, and no central agency to control it. Bitcoins are widely used in blockchain transactions. Every bitcoin transaction is valid and confirmed by the entire network. Therefore, the system cannot be shut down, managed, or controlled. Blockchain is built with bitcoins by combining existing technologies or methods such as encryption, proof of work (PoW), and decentralized system design to create a structure that provides choices without centralized management. Ethereum was first proposed in 2013 and rejuvenated in 2014 by Vitalik Buterin, the benefactor of *Bitcoin Magazine*. Ethereum is a milestone for decentralized projects (also known as Dapps, decentralized applications). When Ethereum was created, even the creator of Dapps could not control Dapps. Solidity is a programming language used to create smart contracts that run Dapps. Ethereum is a connection of systems that together constitutes an incredibly decentralized supercomputer. People without central authority can legally communicate with each other. Ethereum developers write conditions for launching

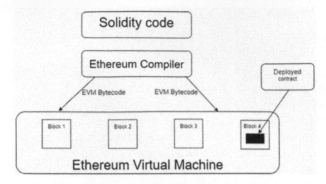

Figure 14.4   Block diagram for applications in Ethereum

Dapps. If the insidious Ethereum organization protocol is provided, it cannot be changed or adapted even by its sole initiator as it is permanent. The best way to change this protocol is to convince the entire Ethereum, which is highly difficult. It consists of reliability code, Ethereum compiler, Ethereum virtual machine (EVM), EVM bytecode, and contracts provided as core functions. Due to its extensive development and security, Ethereum is used in various fields such as microfinance, real estate, travel, auto insurance, legal procedures, education, healthcare, secure voting, and digital identity. Figures 14.4 and 14.5 show applications and design of Ethereum in health-care systems.

14.6   5G networks and Ethereum for the health-care sector

Research in the health sector is helpful to find drug discovery for new diseases, and so on. Innovations in blockchain technology and with 5G networks would provide easy accessibility and data exchange compared with 4G networks. The principal issue for scientists is that a patient's EHR is distributed across various databases [28]. By storing a patient's EHR on an Ethereum blockchain, stocks of shared information can be distributed without relying on any substance that provides or modifies the parts of the EHR. In addition, scientists, reviewers, and even pharmaceutical manufacturers can analyze the effects of their products and possible symptoms [29].

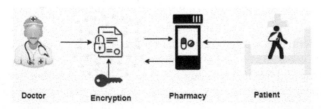

Figure 14.5   Ethereum in healthcare

14.6.1   Challenges in the health-care sector

The challenges faced by the health-care sector are as follows:

1. **Digitization:** Many patient records are only available on paper. Therefore, digitization of patient records is an important aspect [30, 31].
2. **Timelines:** In the workplace, the exchange of documents between a patient's general practitioner and a specialist is very cumbersome. This method is moderate, expensive, and unstable. Unapproved parties may be able to view the patient's clinical data during the data transfer.
3. **Ownership:** The medical record is the medical history of the patient's health. The patient must have clinical information. The doctor's office is the only supervisor.
4. **Transparency:** Because medical records are recorded on paper and sent to doctors. Workplaces and individual and institutional clients (such as clinical scientists, government agencies, and insurance agencies) can easily tamper with the data and can use the clinical data for other purposes. Blockchain can be used to advance clinical research, organize drug improvement, or formulate government health strategies.

All the above-mentioned points are some of the major health-care challenges that can be solved through Dapps.

14.7   Real-time examples of Ethereum in the health-care sector

Healthureum is a new revelation in cryptography that brings blockchain and medical services together to bring the best of both under one roof. The Healthureum phase is planned for an Ethereum-based blockchain, which in accordance uses new technologies to fundamentally improve the effectiveness and interoperability of health administrations [32]. London-based blockchain organization Medicalchain along with the Mayo Clinic US clinical center started using blockchain for storing clinical records. The MediLedger project, operated by Link Lab and Chronicled, began in 2017 and brought competing pharmaceutical manufacturers and wholesalers to a similar table. Together, they designed and implemented a process to leverage blockchain innovation to improve physician-approved drug tracking and tracking functions [33].

14.8   5G networks and smart contracts

Example scenario: Alice accesses her cryptocurrency wallet from home, a hidden city, and multiple remote systems at work. This situation is consistent with the 5G network architecture, in which multiple remote systems under development are coordinated through cloud computing and control-based computing. Alice has

different wallets and sometimes, Alice forgets the password for each wallet at some times [34].

1. At home, Alice has a universal 5G connection. While at home, Alice must deal with her elderly mother and young children. With this in mind, Alice owns a shared encrypted wallet and keeps paying attention to its importance. All the buying and spending is done by Alice at her own influence.
2. In the smart city, Alice uses a mobile phone to create quotas for daily crypto wallets to manage transportation, social security, and other daily transactions.

However, 5G technology should control the exchange of encrypted resources using smart contracts and should control the operation. After registering in the blockchain, the transactions in the blockchain will not change. Nick Szabo proposed the term "smart contract" in 1994. Although the concept of smart contracts was conceived in the mid-1990s to robotize the execution of traditional contracts, it was not updated until the introduction of bitcoins' hidden blockchain into an open system. The Byzantine fault-tolerant consensus algorithm made the execution of smart contracts conceivable in a decentralized open system. Several existing blockchain platforms support all Turing programming languages, which simplifies the necessary reasons for creating smart contracts. Since smart contracts are created and implemented on the blockchain, they are beneficial to all functions of the blockchain. None of the parties can change or alter the smart contracts in blockchain when initiated. Blockchain provides complete simplification because anyone can confirm the existence of the agreement at any time [35].

14.9 Advantages of smart contracts

1. **Faster organization and execution:** To prepare a contract the traditional way, the customer would have to put in a lot of time to prepare and do the desk work. A smart contract is just a large number of guidelines that mechanize these tasks and eliminate unnecessary work.
2. Executing smart contracts on a blockchain is more cost-effective than traditional contracts, which require input from intermediaries to prepare.
3. **Secure administration:** The main feature of blockchain is security. All contracts in a blockchain are securely monitored.
4. **Counterfeit tests:** Due to the decentralized open registration in the system, each contract is located in each node of the system and offers different reinforcements and hence, it is difficult to lose a smart contract in a blockchain system.
5. **Execution:** Smart contract agreements are made with many policies that are reliably executed on every hub on the blockchain network. This ensures that smart contracts work consistently and accurately. Due to the Byzantine fault tolerance of the blockchain, the system ignores any incorrect execution of the contract [36].

14.10 Choosing the smart contract platform

Smart contracts are self-executing that can be streamed in any blockchain application that supports running basic scripts on transactions. Most stages of the blockchain require the use of domain-specific languages, viz. the Script, a stack-based language. Although scripting is a bad language in Turing, there are only a few options for complex transactions. It can perform multi-signature transactions, payment channels, and atomic interconnection work transactions. Many blockchains have adopted the use of the explicit language of their themes to provide progressive scripting capabilities, such as Solidity by Ethereum and Plutus via Cardano. These stages have their operating state, in which the ordered smart contract will be executed. Blockchain virtual machine (VM) provides a way to run untrusted code in an open system. These VMs also protect against attacks such as denial of service (DoS) attacks, which are an important part of untrustworthy code frameworks.

Some of the blockchain platforms that have their scripts are:

1. EOS
2. Ethereum
3. Hyperledger Fabric
4. NEO
5. NXT.

Choosing a platform for creating a smart contract depends on the type of usage being created, the execution required, the language of the smart contract, and many different factors. It is important to consider all the prerequisites before choosing the scenario [37].

14.11 Applications of smart contracts in healthcare

1. **Blockchain-based framework for safe telesurgery:** It is a proprietary framework for health management that prevents the third party from establishing trust between specialists and human service associations. The widespread idea of the blockchain eliminates the need for tiered review to improve framework execution and reduces health-care transportation costs [38].
2. Dagher *et al.* [25] suggested using six smart contracts as access controls to exchange clinical records between health-care providers and insurance providers. The first contract registers the customers and mining activities, the second identifies the customers as patients, suppliers, or third parties, the third identifies the connections between customers, the fourth identifies the responsibility for the records, the fifth identifies the permissions to enter these records, and the last offers Symmetric Encryption Keys (SEKs). Patients interact with the blockchain by changing consent. SEKs are used by providers to encrypt clinical records before they are submitted or after they are accessed through an off-chain correspondence channel.

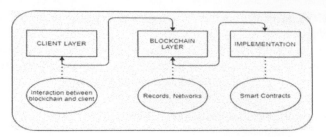

Figure 14.6   Proposed framework system design

3. Ahram *et al.* [39] used smart contracts for limited purposes. A smart contract first ensures that only one patient creates the underlying form of their clinical records during their first visit to a hospital. At this point, the smart contract guarantees updation of the clinical record by the provider [40].

14.12   Case study—design and architecture

The proposed model is shown in Figure 14.6. The proposed model contains the modules, design, and components that together form a decentralized blockchain framework. The framework consists of three modules: patients, doctors, and hospitals [41].

14.12.1   Client layer

Customers perform the following operations: create, read, update, and analyze clinical records using the Decentralized application (DApp) program that contains the Graphical User Interface (GUI) user name. The GUI contains all of the functionality that a particular customer may have. The clients can use the GUI to connect to the blockchain layer doing specific work.

14.12.2   Blockchain layer

The blockchain layer contains the code for connecting the client to the DApp. This layer contains three components:

1. **Blockchain assets:** In the Ethereum blockchain, the transaction is the process by which external clients can update the state of the registry or update data. These transactions are treated as resources by the Ethereum blockchain because they are blocks of data that clients can send to another client or simply save for future use.
2. **Administrative rules:** Blockchain technology generally adheres to some compliance rules so that the transactions can be carried out effectively. Hence, the data need to be safe and secure (tamper-proof). Ethereum blockchain uses the PoW algorithm to ensure that the management of the blockchain is reliably

maintained, with the consent of all centers believed to be connected to the blockchain network.

3. **System:** It uses the distributed system in which all nodes are connected without a node acting as a central hub that controls all elements of the system. All the assigned nodes have the same status and authorization.

The framework includes the following steps:

1. Include records that are used to convert client reports to clinical records in the DApp. DApp contains ID, name, blood group, and interplanetary file system (IPFS) hash fields. The client's essential clinical records are stored along with the IPFS hash contained in the transferred file with the client's laboratory results or other clinical records [42].
2. The updated records would update the customer's clinical records, change critical client data but not IPFS hash. The IPFS hash cannot be updated to ensure data security. Records and visualization reports can be viewed by the customer to view clinical records stored in DApp using the framework. Therefore, the framework uses the customer's open record address to ensure that only meaningful clinical records have been viewed by the customer.
3. Specialists have the option to delete the customer records in the blockchain.
4. Grant access. Customers contact specialists as they are authorized to make changes, and modify or delete the customers' record. Customers can also view their medical records. However, customers cannot modify their records.

14.13 System implementation

System implementation is discussed in the below sections.

14.13.1 Smart contracts

Smart contracts are an important part of DApps that are used to perform basic activities, viz. client records and roles. These contracts are used to grant customers access to the DApps and to carry out create, read, update, and delete (CRUD) procedures for customer records. Matching of the client's records is done to ensure that the proposed framework is effective. "Roles" is a smart contract that is predefined by the OpenZeppelin smart contract library. This library contains various contracts to define the incoming leads [43].[44]

14.13.2 Algorithm

Figures 14.7–14.10 show the working of smart contracts for customer records. The algorithm has four functions to make smart contracts more effective, including viewing, updating, and deleting records. The administrator and the various clients of the framework use these functions. The jobs defined by the algorithm are run by

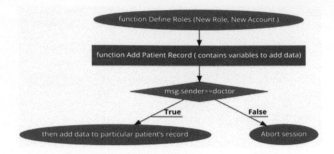

Figure 14.7   Smart contracts access and records in flow chart representation

the administrator that has two factors, new job, and new record. The client jobs can be deleted only by the administrator. "msg.Sender" is used in Solidity to track the customer's location. After the authorization checks, the specialist adds the patient records and closes the connection when the records are verified.

The second function is to review the records where the identification of the patient is passed as a variable. This is done via patient record search framework where the records are reset. This feature also includes approval for patient or specialist split jobs, as only the patient and specialist can view the transactions.

The approval process is carried out to ensure that verified customers have access to the update feature for the records that have not been saved.

For deleting the customer's record, the patient's identification and information are confirmed and the specialist performs the delete function. This work-based access would ensure that no outsiders could reach these functions, and only validated clients of the framework have access to these functions.

14.14   Experimental setup

The experimental setup of the proposed model is carried out with system specifications as following: System with Intel Core i7-8550U processor (8th generation)

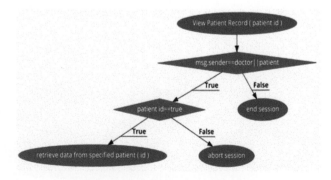

Figure 14.8   View records flow chart

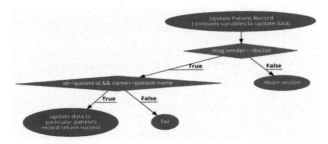

Figure 14.9   Update records flow chart

at 4.6 GHz and 16 GB of RAM, Windows 10 with the 64-bit operating system. Ethereum for writing smart contracts typed in JavaScript and Python under Solidity.

14.14.1   Performance evaluation

Performance is evaluated by considering the following factors.

14.14.1.1   Transaction data

To evaluate the performance of the proposed system, the following transaction terms are used:

1. **Transaction time to implementation (TTD)** is defined as the time at which the exchange or transaction is transmitted.
2. **Transaction time for completion (TTC)** is defined as when the exchange or transaction is completed and confirmed by the blockchain.

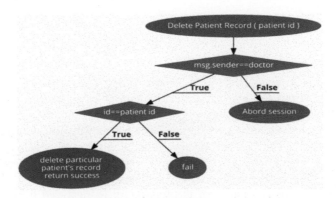

Figure 14.10   Flow chart for erase records

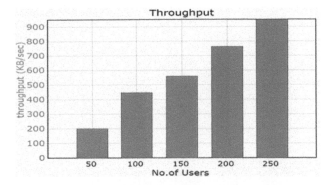

Figure 14.11   Proposed framework throughput

14.14.1.2   Evaluation of measurements

The evaluation measurements used for the assessment include the execution time, latency, and performance of the proposed framework. These are briefly explained as follows:

1. **Execution time** is defined as the difference between TTC and TTD.
2. **Throughput** is defined as data transferred from one location to another.
3. **Latency** is the waiting time for the framework to react to an activity. It is defined as the difference in time taken for deployment and the time taken for the transaction to complete.

14.15   Results

All the experiments were carried out with Apache JMeter. Apache JMeter is a workspace execution test appliance used to examine and test applications. Figure 14.11 shows the proposed framework throughput. Figure 14.12 shows the average frame latency along with the performance of the proposed model. The highest recorded latency in this test is 14 ms. Tables 14.3 and 14.4 show the throughput and average latency of the framework.

1. **Average execution time:** The execution time is calculated by the number of transactions. Transactions take place using various functions as mentioned in the above sections. For a single customer, the functions to assign roles, add patient records, and view patient records individually take approximately 20.56 seconds, 2 minutes, 13 seconds, and 44 seconds, and so on. This time would increase if 100 clients used the frame continuously.
2. **Performance:** Performance of the framework is measured using JMeter for clients ranging from 50 to 250 with data in KB/s. During the implementation,

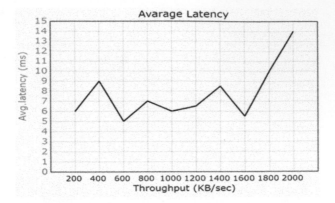

Figure 14.12   Proposed framework average latency

the number of customers is replicated according to the framework for calculating the performance.
3. The average latency is calculated by taking the difference of time between one segment of the frame sending a request to another part of the frame generating a response. The average latency is calculated using JMeter and measured in milliseconds.

14.16   Conclusion

This chapter discussed the applications of blockchain technology in the health-care sectors. Challenges faced in health-care systems can be effectively solved by using blockchain technology using Ethereum and smart contracts. This chapter suggests some of the access rules for accessing EHRs without the involvement of any third party and therefore, the confidential details of the patients cannot be altered and the details are tamper-proof. This chapter also suggests ways to implement 5G networks for Ethereum system design to provide tamper-proof data for the health-care sector. Finally, all the technical aspects like average latency time, throughput, and so on, are calculated and graphs are plotted for the proposed framework.

Table 14.3   Throughput table

Number of users	Throughput (KB/s)
50	200
100	450
150	550
200	750
250	900

Table 14.4   *Average latency of the framework*

Throughput (KB/s)	Average Latency (ms)
200	6.00
400	9.00
600	5.00
800	7.00
1 000	6.00
1 200	6.50

References

[1] Linn L.A., Koo M.B. 'Blockchain for health data and Its potential use in health IT and health care related research'. *Use of Blockchain for Healthcare and Research Workshop*; ONC/NIST: Gaithersburg, MD, USA, 2020; 2016. pp. 1–10.

[2] Frost & Sullivan. Global blockchain technology market in the healthcare industry. 2018–2022, (2019). Available from https://www.marketresearch.com/Frost-Sullivan-v383/Global-Blockchain-Technology-Healthcare-12732534/ [Accessed Jul 2020].

[3] Bryatov S.R. 'Blockchain technology in the pharmaceutical supply chain: researching a business model based on hyperledger fabric'. *International Conference on Information Technology and Nanotechnology (ITNT)*; Russia; 2019.

[4] Mettler M. 'Blockchain technology in healthcare: the revolution starts here'. *E-health Networking Applications and Services (Healthcom), IEEE*; 2016.

[5] Rifi N. 'Towards using blockchain technology for eHealth data access management'. *International Conference on Advances in Biomedical Engineering (ICABME)*; IEEE; 2017.

[6] Tanwar S., Parekh K., Evans R. 'Blockchain-based electronic healthcare record system for healthcare 4.0 applications'. *Journal of Information Security and Applications*. 2020;**50**(10):1–13.

[7] Vora J. 'Blind signatures based secured e-healthcare system'. *International conference on computer, information and telecommunication systems (CITS)*; 2018. pp. 1–5.

[8] Ingraham A., St. Clair J. 'The fourth industrial revolution of healthcare information technology: key business components to unlock the value of a blockchain-enabled solution'. *Blockchain in healthcare today*. 2020:1–4.

[9] Kumar A., Krishnamurthi R., Nayyar A., Sharma K., Grover V., Hossain E. 'A novel smart healthcare design, simulation, and implementation using healthcare 4.0 processes'. *IEEE – Special Section on Blockchain Technology: Principles and Applications*. 2020;**8**:118433–71.

[10]   Khatoon A. 'A blockchain-based smart contract system for healthcare management'. *Electronics Journals*. 2020;**9**(1):94.

[11]   Panesar A. *Machine learning and AI for healthcare: big data for improved health outcomes*. Springer; 2019.

[12]   Khezr S., Moniruzzaman M., Yassine A., Benlamri R. 'Blockchain technology in healthcare: a comprehensive review and directions for future research'. *Applied Sciences*. 2019;**9**(9):1736.

[13]   Carson B. 'A blockchain beyond the hype: what is the strategic business value'. *McKinsey.com*. 2020.

[14]   Randall D., Goel P., Abujamra R., *et al*. 'Blockchain applications and use cases in health information technology'. *Journal of Health & Medical Informatics*. 2017;**08**(03):10.4172/2157–7420.

[15]   Kshetri N. 'Blockchain and Electronic Healthcare Records [Cybertrust]'. *Computer*. 2018;**51**(12):59–63.

[16]   Bennett B. 'Blockchain HIE overview: a framework for healthcare interoperability'. *Telehealth and Medicine Today*. 2018;**2**(3).

[17]   Kamel Boulos M.N., Wilson J.T., Clauson K.A. 'Geospatial blockchain: promises, challenges, and scenarios in health and healthcare'. *International Journal of Health Geographics*. 2018;**17**(1):25.

[18]   Skiba D.J. 'The potential of blockchain in education and health care'. *Nursing Education Perspectives*. 2017;**38**(4):220–1.

[19]   Heston T. 'A case study in blockchain healthcare innovation'. *ResearchGate*. 2017:131–48.

[20]   Stawiki S.P. 'What's new in academic medicine? Blockchain technology in healthcare: bigger, better, fairer, faster, and leaner'. *ijam-web.org*. 2018:1–11.

[21]   Coiera E. '*Guide to health informatics*'. CRC Press; 2015.

[22]   Raj K. '*Foundation of blockchain*'. O'Reilly; 2019.

[23]   Kilroy K. '*Blockchain as a service*'. O'Reilly; 2019.

[24]   Gupta R. 'Habits: blockchain-based tele surgery framework for healthcare 4.0'. *IEEE*. 2019.

[25]   Dagher G.G., Mohler J., Milojkovic M., *et al*. 'Ancile: privacy-preserving framework for access control and interoperability of electronic health records using blockchain technology'. *Sustainable Cities and Society*. 2018;**39**(1):283–97.

[26]   Ahram T. 'Blockchain technology innovations'. *IEEE Technology & Engineering Management Conference*; 2017. pp. 137–41.

[27]   Shukla A., Bhattacharya P., Tanwar S., Kumar N., Guizani M. 'DwaRa: a deep learning-based dynamic toll pricing scheme for intelligent transportation systems'. *IEEE Transactions on Vehicular Technology*. 2020;**69**(11):1–11.

[28]   Mehta P., Gupta R., Tanwar S. 'Blockchain envisioned UAV networks: challenges, solutions, and comparisons'. *Computer Communications*. 2020;**151**(14):518–38.

[29]   Gupta R., Tanwar S., Al-Turjman F., Italiya P., Nauman A., Kim S.W. 'Smart contract privacy protection using AI in cyber-physical systems: tools, techniques and challenges'. *IEEE Access*. 2020;**8**:24746–72.

[30] Bodkhe U., Tanwar S., Parekh K., *et al.* 'Blockchain for industry 4.0: a comprehensive review'. *IEEE Access*. 2020;**8**:79764–800.

[31] Tanwar S., Parekh K., Evans R. 'Blockchain-based electronic healthcare record system for healthcare 4.0 applications'. *Journal of Information Security and Applications*. 2019;**50**:1–14.

[32] Hathaliya J.J., Tanwar S. 'An exhaustive survey on security and privacy issues in healthcare 4.0'. *Computer Communications*. 2020;**153**(6):311–35.

[33] Hathaliya J.J., Tanwar S., Evans R. 'Securing electronic healthcare records: a mobile-based biometric authentication approach'. *Journal of Information Security and Applications*. 2020;**53**(3):102528–14.

[34] Hathaliya J.J., Tanwar S., Tyagi S., Kumar N. 'Securing electronics healthcare records in healthcare 4.0: a biometric-based approach'. *Computers & Electrical Engineering*. 2019;**76**(4):398–410.

[35] Gupta R., Tanwar S., Tyagi S., Kumar N. 'Tactile-internet-based telesurgery system for healthcare 4.0: an architecture, research challenges, and future directions'. *IEEE Network*. 2019;**33**(6):22–9.

[36] Gupta R., Tanwar S., Kumar N., Tyagi S. 'Blockchain-based security attack resilience schemes for autonomous vehicles in industry 4.0: a systematic review'. *Computers & Electrical Engineering*. 2020;**86**(106717):1–15.

[37] Tanwar S. *Fog computing for healthcare 4.0 environments: technical, societal and Future Implications, Signals and Communication Technology*. Springer International Publishing; 2020. pp. 1–430.

[38] Tanwar S. *Fog data analytics for IOT applications – next generation process model with state-of-the-art technologies, studies in big data*. Springer International Publishing; 2020. pp. 1–550.

[39] Ahram T. 'Blockchain technology innovations'. *IEEE Technology & Engineering Management Conference*; 2017. pp. 137–41.

[40] Gupta R., Shukla A., Tanwar S. 'AaYusH: a smart contract-based telesurgery system for healthcare 4.0'. *IEEE Conference on Communications (IEEE ICC-2020)*, 07–11 Jun; 2020. pp. 1–6.

[41] Hathaliya J., Sharma P., Tanwar S. 'Blockchain-based remote patient monitoring in healthcare 4.0'. *9th IEEE International Conference on Advanced Computing (IACC)*; Tiruchirappalli, India; 13–148 December, 2019. pp. 87–91.

[42] Gupta R., Tanwar S., Tyagi S., Kumar N., Obaidat M.S., Sadoun B. 'HaBiTs: blockchain-based telesurgery framework for healthcare 4.0'. *International Conference on Computer, Information and Telecommunication Systems (IEEE CITS-2019)*; August 28–31, 2019. pp. 6–10.

[43] Kumari A., Shukla R., Gupta S., Tanwar S., Tyagi N., Kumar N. 'ET-DeaL: A P2P smart contract-based secure energy trading scheme for smart grid systems'. *IEEE International Conference on Computer Communications (IEEE INFOCOM 2020)*; Beijing, China; 27–30 April, 2020. pp. 1–8.

[44] Dimitrov D.V. 'Blockchain applications for healthcare data management'. *Healthcare Informatics Research*. 2019;**25**(1):51–6.

Chapter 15

An amalgamation of blockchain, Internet of Medical Things and 5G technologies for the Healthcare 4.0 ecosystem

Desai Karanam Sreekantha[1] and R. V. Kulkarni[2]

The term Healthcare 4.0 is derived from Industry 4.0 for the health-care industry. The philosophy of Healthcare 4.0 is to deliver patient-oriented quality services at the doorsteps of the patients. Healthcare 4.0 services are implemented by integrating disruptive technologies such as artificial intelligence (AI), blockchain, Internet of Things (IoT) and data science into existing health-care systems. Internet of Medical Things (IoMT) is a derived version of IoT technology for the health-care industry. IoMT systems integrate smart wearable medical devices into health-care information systems using high-speed fifth-generation (5G)-enabled networks. Patient data are very sensitive and valuable hence data are often stolen, misused, and sold. Providing security and integrity to this sensitive patient data is the basic ethical and statutory requirement of every health-care service provider. Blockchain technology was successfully implemented to ensure the security of data in the cryptocurrency and finance industries, so it can also be applied in the health-care industry. The authors have carried out an extensive study of literature on the applications of IoMT, 5G, and blockchain technologies in the health-care industry. The highlights and concepts from each research paper are presented in this chapter. A pie chart shows the technology-wise number of papers reviewed. A comparative analysis with specific parameters from curated papers is presented. The research issues, implementation challenges, and future directions are also illustrated. A case study on the implementation of advanced health-care solutions has been discussed. This chapter presents a holistic view of Healthcare 4.0 solutions.

[1]Department of Computer Science & Engineering, NMAM Institute of Technology, Karnataka, India
[2]Department of Computer Studies, CSIBER, Kolhapur, India

15.1   Introduction

15.1.1   Motivation and significance for the study

The Institute of Medicine review report discovered that the health-care industry is not operating efficiently. About 20–30% of total medical expenses incurred are wasted and medicines are not producing expected results. Healthcare 4.0 standards prescribe that health-care services are to be personalised based on the patient's specific hereditary, environmental, and lifestyle parameters. The health-care service industry gathers a large quantity of sensitive data on a day-to-day basis. The patient data are captured during patient registration, monitoring, interventions, managing health records, and processing medical insurance bills. Healthcare 4.0 standards enable patients to securely share their health-care data for availing efficient and high quality health-care services.

A cost-effective Healthcare 4.0 compatible system should be interoperable on mobile phones and different operating platforms. The data shall be seamlessly shareable in a secure manner among the stakeholders of the health-care ecosystem. The medical data stored in a public cloud platform are prone to cyber attacks. These cyber attacks will severely affect the security and integrity of these sensitive data. So, there is an urgent need to enforce stringent policy controls on sharing of patient data. Secure online sharing of medical data would improve the quality of services and speed up the decision-making process.

15.1.2   Market potential for the health-care industry

Globally, the health-care industry has a huge market. The health-care expenditure has increased from US$7.1 trillion to US$8.7 trillion during the period 2015–2020. The US health-care market size was US$3.55 trillion in 2017, and it is estimated to increase up to US$5.5 trillion by 2025. The estimated IoMT industry international market size is US$72.02 billion in 2021, and it is increasing at a CAGR of 26.2%. The number of people above 65 years of age is estimated to double by the year 2050. The market size for blockchain-based solutions is estimated to exceed US$500 million by 2022. The Indian health-care market is expected to reach US$372 billion by 2022.

15.1.3   Overview of blockchain, 5G and IoMT technologies

15.1.3.1   Blockchain technology

Blockchain technology is expected to revolutionize the present and future applications in various sectors. Blockchain technology provides an open, distributed, decentralized, and immutable ledger to carry out secure online transactions. The objective of blockchain technology is to create a trusted group for addressing the challenges such as security, scalability, mutual trust, and collaboration. Consensus algorithms of blockchain ensure reliability and security in sharing of data. The timestamps of transactions in blockchain network nodes prevent data infringement providing additional security. Only authorized people can access or change data by obtaining permission and consensus from all sources. These security features make blockchain technology suitable for the health-care industry. Blockchain eliminates the need for centralized control to manage peer-to-peer transactions in interconnected networks. Secure sharing of data across the health-care ecosystem enables patients to avail themselves the health-care services from different service providers. Blockchain-based IT systems leverage doctors to access the patient's historical data to carry out precise diagnoses and plan for better interventions. The various limitations of blockchain-based systems are lack of interoperability and integration with legacy systems, high cost of implementation, technology adoption barrier, regulatory compliance, and scaling of applications.

15.1.3.2 5G network communication

5G technology enables high-speed and reliable communication between billions of wearable devices, Androids, iPhones, and tablets. 5G networks enable higher bandwidth, low latency, low operational costs and manage huge network traffic with the least network congestion. 5G networks are more suitable for edge computing devices. These edge devices are used in diverse internet-based applications and they generate large network traffic. The deployment of 5G networks exponentially boosts the amount of data generated with enhanced interactions between the users and devices. 5G technology leverages IoMT systems to support patient monitoring and services in near-real-time.

15.1.3.3 Internet of Medical Things (IoMT)

IoMT is a global network of connected medical wearable devices, health-care apps and health-care IT systems. Medical wearable devices are connected to the patients in their smart homes. These IoMT systems regularly gather patient data, monitor, and alert caregivers and health-care service providers in real-time. IoMT system interactions with health-care service providers help them to discover critical health issues in patients in near-real-time. Doctors can initiate necessary medical interventions remotely through IoMT systems. IoMT systems promote self-organizing and self-healing capabilities in patients. IoMT and edge computing systems are portable, and hence can be deployed on diverse hardware platforms to process huge amounts of data locally and work on-premise. Ensuring security at the edge devices in IoMT systems is a very difficult task. Providing intelligent data processing at the edges of IoMT systems enables intelligent and cost-effective health-care services.

15.1.3.4 Integration of 5G, blockchain, and IoMT solutions

5G technology enables reliable and high-speed connectivity between billions of edge devices. IoMT system interact with smart, secure wearable medical devices and cloud-based health-care information systems connected by 5G enabled networks. The blockchain-based open distributed, decentralized, immutable ledgers of health-care systems provide high security to all transactions. The transparent nature of blockchain transactions prevents unauthorized data access, alterations, and theft.

Healthcare 4.0-enabled solutions reduce the patient's unnecessary hospital visits. Patients from their smart homes can consult doctors online. The integration of IoMT, 5G, and blockchain technologies with health-care systems offers many advantages for health-care industry stakeholders. The stakeholders of Healthcare 4.0 ecosystems are patients, doctors, physicians, health-care providers, clinical researchers, insurance companies, biomedical, and neurology experts. All these stakeholders can carry out cost-effective and secure transactions in the Healthcare 4.0 ecosystem.

15.1.3.5 Evolution of technological shift from Healthcare 1.0 to Healthcare 4.0

The major objective of Healthcare 1.0 was to computerize the day-to-day operations to reduce the manual and paper work to enhance productivity. Healthcare 2.0 focused on data processing and sharing data within the organization. Healthcare 3.0 introduced patient-oriented information systems. The objective of Healthcare 4.0 standards is to provide real-time tracking of patients' conditions and to provide on-site medical assistance. Healthcare 1.0 has advanced from the computerization of health-care data processing to real-time on-site patient healthcare, diagnostics and context-awareness using AI-based solutions. The health-care data/information sharing which was initiated within the hospitals was now extended to the cluster of health-care providers across the country.

Healthcare 4.0 promotes health-care data sharing across the globe, complying with technical and statutory standards. Healthcare 1.0 provided information technology solutions for hospital administration and advanced through technologies such as electronic data interchange (EDI), cloud computing, big data, big data analytics, fog computing, IoT, electronic medical records (EMR), wearable devices, blockchain, and AI technologies. Today the major challenges faced by Healthcare 4.0 systems are interoperability, conforming to technical standards, and ensuring privacy, security, and confidentiality to comply with the prevailing statutory framework.

15.1.4 Organization of the chapter

This chapter has been structured into five sections. Section 5.1 presents a basic introduction. Subsection 5.1.1 discusses the motivation and significance of the study. Section 5.1.2 shows international market potential, and 5.1.3 presents the overview of blockchain, 5G, and IoMT technologies. Section 5.1.4 deals with the organization of the chapter. Subsection 5.1.5 shows the author's research contribution to the existing knowledge domain. Section 5.1.6 illustrates taxonomy and acronyms. The review of recent literature is described in Section 5.2. Section 5.2 is further divided into four subsections. Each subsection presents the papers reviewed from one technology domain and tabulates the highlights and findings. Section 5.2.3 deals with a comparative analysis of curated survey papers with specific parameters. Section 5.3 shows Healthcare 4.0 ecosystem architecture. Section 5.4 discusses the research issues and challenges. Section 5.5 presents the case studies of Healthcare 4.0 solutions from the industry. Section 5.6. summarizes the findings and conclusions. Figure 15.1 shows the organization of this chapter.

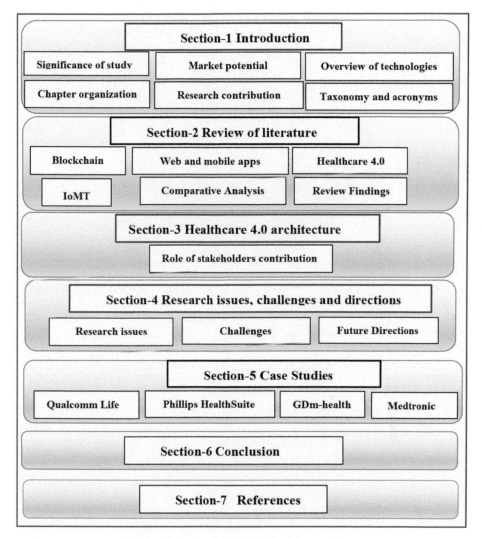

Figure 15.1   Organization of the chapter

15.1.5   Authors' research contribution

1. The authors have selected papers from highly reputed publishers such as IEEE, Elsevier, Science Direct, and Springer. Reviewed 90 papers covering blockchain, 5G, and IoMT concepts and applications. This study covered various technologies, concepts, and algorithms that are applied to Healthcare 4.0 systems across the world. These papers have been further classified technology-wise and presented as a pie chart in Figure 15.2.
2. A list of acronyms is shown in Table 15.1.
3. The enhanced quality services driven by Healthcare 4.0 are shown in Figure 15.3.

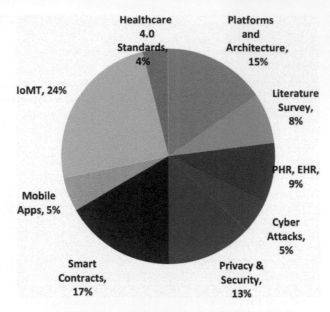

Figure 15.2   Summary of papers reviewed

4. The taxonomy of concepts applied in 5G, blockchain, and IoMT systems in health-care domain from the literature are mapped and shown in Figure 15.4.
5. Research issues, challenges, and future directions of technologies are discussed.
6. Five Healthcare 4.0 case studies implemented in the industry are discussed.
7. A comparative study curated survey papers with specific factors such as architecture, open issues and challenges, applications, taxonomy, and security is carried out to discover the research gaps, as shown in Tables 15.4 and 15.5.

15.1.6   Taxonomy and acronyms

This section shows the number of papers reviewed technology-wise in the pie chart Figure 15.2. Figure 15.4 shows the taxonomy of various concepts of IoMT technology discussed in this chapter. Table 15.1 presents a list of all the acronyms used in this chapter for easy reference.

15.2   Review of recent literature

Researchers have surveyed the literature on Healthcare 4.0, blockchain, IoMT, 5G domains from highly reputed research journals from IEEE, Elsevier, Science Direct, and Springer publications. The findings from this survey revealed the various technologies, models, and algorithms applied to health-care systems across the world. The authors have presented some highlights from these curated papers for discussion in this section.

Table 15.1   List of acronyms used in this chapter

Acronym	Description	Acronym	Description
AI	Artificial Intelligence	ABE	Attribute-Based Encryption
IoT	Internet of Things	M2M	Machine-to-Machine
IoMT	Internet of Medical Things	PDP	Provable Data Possession
P2P	Peer-to-Peer	MRI	Magnetic Resonance Images
AES	Advanced Encryption Standard	POW	Proof of Work
PHDM	Personal Health Data Management	CIoMT	Cognitive Internet of Medical Things
ICT	Information and Communication Technology	SIP	Strategic Innovation Promotion Program
OASIS	Organization for the Advancement of Structured Information Standards	CAGR	Cumulative Annual Growth Rate
MedRec	Medical Records Software tool	FV	Finger Vein
SHA	Secure Hash Algorithm	5G	Fifth Generation
DPAS	Decentralized Patients Assignment System	PRISMA	Preferred Reporting Items for Systematic Reviews and Meta-Analysis
HERMIT	HERMIT is a benchmark suite for the Internet of Medical Things.	IETF	Internet Engineering Task Force
EHR	Electronic Health Records	AMR	Advanced Medical Reviews
EMR	Electronic Medical Records	PPR	Patient Provider Relationships
PHR	Personal Health Record	VO	Virtual Organization
HAR	Human Activity Recognition	21CCA	21st Century Cures Act
ML	Machine Learning	RFID	Radio Frequency ID
RTT	Round Trip Time	NFC	Near Field Communication
RASPRO	Rapid Active Summarization for effective Prognosis	HIMS	Hospital Information Management System
CPS	Cyber Physical system	CT	Computerized Tomography
QoS	Quality of Service	DoS	Denial of Service
HIE	Hypoxic Ischemic Encephalopathy	ITU-T	International Telecommunication Union for IoT

15.2.1   Blockchain

MedRec is a blockchain-based tool with viewing, sharing, and updating features of data through a user-friendly interface. The design of MedRec satisfies the Blue Button health record competition requirements. Smart contracts are designed for secure online sharing of sensitive patient data among doctors, clinicians, hospitals, and patients [1]. The decentralized patients assignment system (DPAS) is a decentralized decision-making system used globally. DPAS was designed using integer

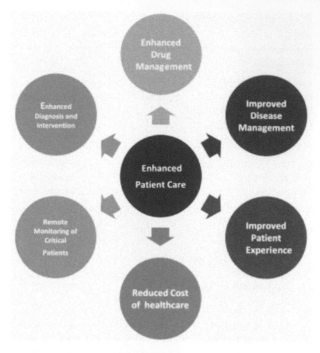

Figure 15.3　Health-care services

programming, blockchain and machine learning technologies to improve the collaboration between hospitals and patients. DPAS was implemented as an agent-based prototype using Ethereum technology. DPAS shows the significance of interoperability and smart contracts in decision-making. The results produced from DPAS system revealed that it is efficient in reducing the computing time and increased

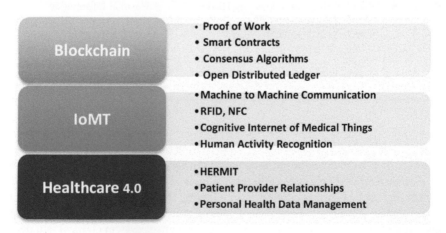

Figure 15.4　Taxonomy of concepts

the acceptance rates of patients transfer [2]. A patient-oriented health-care information management system (HIMS) based on blockchain technology was hosted in the cloud. This system ensures security and privacy in transactions. The results obtained from this system showed its efficiency [3]. Smart contracts and privacy-protecting procedures are applied in HIMS to protect magnetic resonance images (MRI) data. Each node in the blockchain network validates the MRI data to ensure data integrity before forwarding. The formal equivalence-checking technique of automata theory was applied to validate MRI data. The continuous equivalence checking ensures that final images received are not tampered by attackers [4]. Ethereum and hyper-ledger fabric platforms of blockchain technology increase the data access controls, interoperability, and data integrity in electronic health record (EHR) and personal health record (PHR) [5]. Statutory bodies enforce patient-driven interoperability by giving incentives and also charge heavy financial penalties for its non-compliance. The patient-driven interoperability features are patient engagement, privacy, security, clinical data transaction, and incentives. These features can be implemented using blockchain technologies [6]. The patient's historical data are mapped electronically to enable doctors to visualize the patient conditions for some time. These mapped electronic data can be distributed across the hospital networks. The patient data can be visualized as a single logical database in real time for better diagnosis and medication purposes. Smart contracts can be designed to record all the patient history, diagnosis details, and interventions given to the patients into a single public digital medical data store [7]. Secure medical data sharing in real time reduces the cost and time to process these data enabling faster decisions [8]. The data can be captured directly from patients through medical wearable devices attached to the patients. These data can be securely transmitted to health-care providers to deliver better quality health-care services [9]. The potential research problems and standards for implementing disruptive technologies are discussed. Smart contracts are designed use hashing and encryption algorithms to build immutable transactions to ensure trust and robustness in every transaction [10].

A blockchain-based model was developed for the implementation and evaluation of distributed PHR. This model implements interoperability standards of openEHR. The OmniPHR framework adopts a distributed and interoperable PHR. The experiments were carried out on this model using the 40 000 adult patients' dataset. The response time was less than 500 ms with 98% availability [11]. The applications of smart contracts, digital soft identities, IoMT, and AI technologies in health-care domain enable us to carry out online monitoring of patients, hospital wards, and clinics. A smart contract can be designed to automatically send instructions to the patient's health-care service provider when the patient's IoMT device detects atrial fibrillation (irregular heartbeat) in patients. This type of autonomous medical assistance is very useful for aged and differently enabled patients who need constant observation [12].

An integrated system comprising a database server, blockchain server, patients having IoMT devices, and a set of health-care apps is ideal for providing real time smart health-care services. This system is designed to exploit the explosive growth in the smartphone population for health-care apps [13]. A survey on the implementation of blockchain technologies from 2008 to 2019 in the health-care domain was conducted. This survey discovered that applications of blockchain enhances security and privacy, decreases operations costs and supports accurate diagnoses. Authors discovered the need for further research to design innovative ways to meet health-care service providers' needs and compliance with standards [14]. A scalable and multi-layered blockchain-based architecture to manage personal health records was presented. Every patient's health-care data need to be stored in digital form for quick access by the doctors in the diagnosis, intervention, and referral process. Patients should be able to share their medical data securely across the stakeholders of the health-care ecosystem. This approach has driven the reforms in the health-care services domain in China [15]. This chapter presented the disadvantages of existing blockchain-based systems in healthcare. The authors called the researchers of blockchain to conduct further research on issues such as misleading data, data breaches, tampering of data [16]. Private blockchain is more suitable for securely transmitting sensitive medical data. The various parameters for identifying the correct type of blockchain for health-care data sharing are discussed. The consensus algorithm and smart contracts have a significant role in selecting the right type of blockchain for health-care data [17].

This chapter discovered the parameters to improve the quality and methods to overcome the limitations of current health-care platforms. A comparative analysis of blockchain platforms and tools such as Docker Container, Hyper-ledger Fabric, Composer, Hyper-ledger Caliper, and Wireshark capture engine was carried out. An access control policy algorithm for secure data exchange using EHR and hyper-ledger was designed. The performance parameters such as round-trip time (RTT), latency, and throughput are optimized for improved results. The performance of this system was enhanced by 1.75 times and latency decreased by 1.5 times [18]. Research on the applications of blockchain technology in biomedical domain was explored. This research helps us to design a secure, safe, and reliable system. This system was used for manufacturing, storing, and distribution of authorized drugs by pharmaceutical companies. The applications of blockchain technology in neurology and brain studies were less explored. Blockchain can securely manage brain information which is very sensitive [19]. Blockchain helps us to conduct business operations efficiently and securely by decreasing the cost of operations. Blockchain-based systems can improve patient care, enhance legal compliance, and secure sharing of medical data. The health-care blockchain-based systems should be designed using a 'fit-for-purpose' prototype [20].

The applications of blockchain in the public health systems in South Africa are studied. This study showed how blockchain ensures transparency and accountability of transactions in the public health domain. The authors highlighted the need for implementing the standards and regulatory policies for the secure exchange of medical data [21]. The traditional health record-keeping systems are designed considering only health-care service provider's requirements. Healthcare 4.0 standards enforce the personalized and patient-oriented health-care paradigm. Healthcare 4.0 protocols can be implemented using emerging technologies such as AI, IoMT, 5G, and blockchain technologies. Blockchain enables secure global access to patient data through an open distributed, decentralized, and immutable health-care data ledger. The health-care service provider needs to upgrade their existing platform to a blockchain-enabled platform. This blockchain platform enables patients with the freedom to securely share their medical data with any other health-care service providers [22].

A survey on IT-based health-care solutions discovered many disadvantages in present systems. The authors also identified some areas for improvement in health-care IT systems. The focus areas are medical data privacy, data security, building mutual trust among patient and service provider community, promoting scalability, and interoperability. Authors have developed a blockchain-based health-care solution model using smart contracts. The source code of their solution was also shared in the GitHub repository. The global health-care sector is transforming from volume-based services to value-based services. Health-care service providers and stakeholders should securely share medical data simplifying patient care [23]. The implementation of blockchain is a multi-disciplinary field involving social sciences, information science, and management science. Blockchain will have a significant role in sustaining the development of health-care services across the world [24]. Thirty-eight vulnerabilities associated with blockchain are discovered from the survey of the literature. Only six very significant vulnerabilities are discussed. The authors assessed the impacts of these attacks and ways to mitigate them. The suggestions to decrease the potential impact of these security risks are discussed [25]. Patient medical data are very vulnerable to attacks, and it is very essential to protect this data as per legal and ethical mandates. Centralized cloud-based medical record-keeping systems are more vulnerable to cyber attacks. Blockchain-based decentralized systems can provide privacy, security, and transparency. Blockchain-based systems are computationally expensive to implement in e-healthcare domains [26].

Smart medical systems based on the blockchain can securely share sensitive data of patients, medical professionals, and other stakeholders. The seamless integration of medical and financial data related to medical fees, medicine prices, and other health-care expenses into a public immutable distributed ledger would create many cost-effective business operations [27]. Blockchain technology was implemented for supply chain operations in the pharmaceutical industry. This industry demands high safety, security, and integrity of data. Blockchain implementation promotes transparency and helps to closely monitor the human mistakes, delays, costs, and labor in the drugs supply chain. This chapter also discussed genome market opportunities of sharing genomic data with high security. This genomic data market size is in billions of dollars [28]. The blockchain applications in biomedical domain were reviewed and curated 47 research papers from August 2018. The authors found that the results of the research are in the early stages, and most of the work is limited to hypothetical and design of platforms. The authors found only one case of demonstration and implementation [29]. This chapter presented the blockchain applications in supply-chain, IoT, data privacy, business, health-care, and data management areas. The limitations and research gaps are identified to trigger the future directions for health-care data management research [30].

This chapter reviewed the applications of blockchain technology in medical goods supply chain management, patient data management, pharmaceutical research, prescription management, patient billing, claims management, data analytics, and telemedicine. The authors found that most of these use cases are confined to white papers, proof of concepts, and prototypes with limited scope. The quality and maturity of these use cases are increasing continuously. Patient-centric global health-care services can be implemented using blockchain-based decentralized trust and incentive models [31]. A secure framework for patient authentication in the blockchain network was designed. The authors proposed an algorithm for integrating radio frequency detection and finger vein (FV) biometric characteristics to increase randomness and safety in the input structure. Integration of stenographic, encryption, and blockchain was carried out to design a composite model. This model was used to transmit the data from the point of access to the nodes in the blockchain network. Particle swarm optimization, stenographic, processes and sophisticated encryption algorithms are applied to ensure privacy in data transmission. This model was tested using 106 samples selected from a large dataset of 6 000 FV sample images. The outcome of testing revealed that this network has a huge resistance and tolerance to attacks such as brute force and spoofing. This model performs 55.56% better in data communication between the enrollment node and the nodes in the database [32].

Patient medical data should be owned and controlled by the patient himself. The patient data records are timestamped. Every current block is linked to its preceding and successive blocks. So, it is almost impossible to manipulate this data by unauthorized persons. The data owner has the authority to share his data with those people whomever he is confident with. There are many challenges in successfully implementing blockchain in the health-care domain, such as health-care data sharing in cross-border jurisdictions [33]. The study of transparency in the health-care supply chain has discovered many pitfalls. These pitfalls affect the security aspects of health-care service providers, manufacturers, and suppliers. The health-care service providers are not able to track the source of medical supplies. This lack of facility to track enhances the cost of supply and reduces the quality of service in emergencies. The direct strategic partnership between suppliers, manufacturers, and health-care service providers enhances the product availability, enhances patient care, and reduces the cost of operations [34].

The authors studied the blockchain implementations in the health-care domain using permission-less bitcoin networks. These networks have disadvantages such as consuming more energy, limited scalability, and less throughput. There is a need for a highly secure, scalable, fault-resistant, private, traceable blockchain framework for the health-care industry. This framework should simplify health-care data administration, and decrease computing time and operating costs. The results from these experiments have shown that this proposed framework generates 11 times lesser traffic in the network than the bitcoin network and increases the number of blocks. The ledger updates are 1.13 times faster [35]. IoT applications use medical sensors for on-site monitoring of patient health in real time. These sensors gather a huge quantity of data from the patient and transmit it to the cloud. There is a good scope for cyber attacks to steal these sensitive data during transmission. The application of blockchain technologies integrated with fog computing can build a security layer between the sensor layer and the health-care cloud. Implementing bitcoin concepts into the health-care cloud and IoT is not so easy, since there is a need for high-end resources for efficient proof of work (POW) consensus, reduced communication delays, and decreased processing overheads [36]. This chapter reviewed the blockchain applications in healthcare. The authors discovered 16 types of solutions and classified them into two main classes. One class is dedicated to storage optimization and the second one to the re-design of blockchain.

The constraints identified for blockchain are the number of transactions, block size, large number of nodes, large volume of data, and protocol challenges. This survey has been carried out in six phases. They are designing research questions, methodology for research, curating articles, identifying keywords based on abstracts, data mining activity, and mapping activities. The authors showed the results in 48 codes and 403 compiled quotations [37]. Blockchain technology enables patients to access their private health-care records using a security key provided by health-care service providers. Authors have used blockchain technology to create trusted, secure medical data by keeping patients' identities safe. The anonymity of medical transactions is provided and patient's consent is obtained for securely sharing the medical data [38]. Blockchain can enhance healthcare through mobile apps, monitoring machines, storing, sharing EHR, data from clinical trials, and medical insurance data. The ongoing research in blockchain technology in healthcare is less, but soon the blockchain implementations will transform the health-care systems. Blockchain technology changes the health-care hierarchy so that patients can manage their data and services better. Today acquiring patient consent is a complicated process. A doctor has to obtain approval each time they wish to use the patient's medical data, and doing this iterative procedure every time is a very difficult and time-consuming task [39].

Advanced medical reviews (AMRs) ensure that autonomous medical case investigations are carried out with at most precise and suitable data accessible. Authorized reviewers have to access related, genuine, and reliable data when examining the detailed information of each case. Practically, this additional trust permits more investigations to be completed without any extra appeals that demand more time and workforce to complete. This system would promote timely decisions rooted in the best existing data and documents in each case, even under stringent turnaround time. In many cases, complete and precise patient information will avoid additional levels of appeals, as declared by AMR General Manager Megan Kaufman. The blockchain would be the key to ensure that all autonomous medical investigation components are available and quickly retrieved using highly secure permissions across heterogeneous EHR systems. Foolproof security authorization in blockchain technology would be necessary before any health-care company can completely utilize blockchain for EHR management; if this is realized, then the number of applications of blockchain would increase significantly [40]. The majority of Japan's population is undergoing health transformation. Japan has fewer birth rates. This aging population is creating new challenges to the public health-care systems in Japan. The typical problems faced in Japan's health-care systems are increased public health expenses, enhanced demand for quality health-care services, an acute shortage for old people long-term care, and shortage of health-care workers. The Japanese government and public health-care systems are exploring applications of blockchain and other advanced technologies [41].

Blockchain technology can support the pharmaceutical industry to control the growing risks of fictitious and unauthorized drugs supply. IoT devices and smart contracts can monitor drug transport. The pill containers are incorporated with GPS and series-of-custody logging for real-time tracking. MedRec health-care system empowers patients and doctors with a tamper-proof log of medical records. MedRec adopts a distinct method to pay incentives to miners by providing access to anonymous health-care data. This chapter discusses the use-cases and applications of blockchain technology in healthcare. The authors discuss the evaluation of blockchain-based systems, interoperability, a patient-centric approach, and a secure access to patient history. The implementation issues such as regulations, system evolution, data privacy, and scalability are highlighted [42]. The authors identified the research efforts and the cost involved in solving challenges faced in the e-Health domain.

The integration of diverse custom-built software systems from pharmaceutical companies, government agencies, hospitals, research institutions, and health insurance companies is a real challenge. This chapter covers issues such as usage of crypto-currency in the health-care industry, quality enhancement of health-care services, compliance with regulations, and transparency in operations [43]. The authors proposed an effective medical data exchange policy named MedChain. MedChain integrates the structured P2P network, blockchain, and digest chain techniques. MedChain architecture provides a decentralized framework with high scalability and trust. MedChain implementation results revealed the efficiency in data sharing by satisfying all security needs. MedChain implements organizational data sharing agreement between current and previous health-care service providers. Whenever a patient is shifted to a new hospital, it retrieves data from previous hospital systems. This data sharing demands compliance at both technical and regulatory levels [44]. There are many applications of blockchain in healthcare for managing EHR, clinical diagnosis, and health insurance claims. The perspective of managing medical data by healthcare providers is shifting to patient-centred health-care as proposed in Healthcare 4.0 standards [45].

This chapter presents the implementation of smart contracts for secure health-care data sharing. Smart contracts create a chain of unbreakable blocks by integrating the medical data into clinical frameworks. Smart contracts of blockchain prevent duplicate copies of patient data in the medical systems. The timestamping of patient data transactions permits access to historical data. Blockchain implementation ensures that data cannot be tampered within the pharmaceutical industry. Low-quality and counterfeit drugs are not accepted in the supply chain. This benefit is achieved by controlling all factors during manufacturing, transportation, and sales. The real-world applications of blockchain technology would be profitable to all the stakeholders in the health-care industry [46]. The integration of two novel technologies such as virtual organization (VO) and blockchain solves so many information and communication technology (ICT) issues. Virtual health-care systems engage patients and health-care service providers over virtual networks. An architecture for the authentication of patients, health-care service providers, record verification, and validation issues was proposed. This architecture was designed for health-care systems on a virtual breeding environment in VO. The authors explained the applicability of this architecture taking a health-care scenario [47].

Extensive use of mobile phones and wearable devices in day to day life boosted digitized personal health-care apps business. Sharing patient data securely is very important for the growing health-care industry. Today's health-care industry is facing many security problems. The Personal Health Data Management (PHDM) web portal enables patients to synchronize data sensed by medical wearable devices with cloud storage. Foolproof authentication methods ensure the privacy and integrity of health-care data. The authors propose U-Prove-based protocols for controlling access to data using hyper ledger fabric [48]. The authors presented a smart contracts-based methods for auditing, interoperability, and controlling medical data access. Today, the IT systems in health-care domain manage medical data in diverse text, image, and video file formats for different purposes. The digital health-care industry has opened up many new opportunities. Digital healthcare is influencing government policies across the world. The major challenge encountered by these digital health-care systems is secure data sharing between the data sources, applications, and interoperability among these heterogeneous systems. There is no universal secure data sharing standard in the health-care ecosystem. The patient is the owner of his medical data. A patient can access and share securely his data across all the stakeholders. The implementation of smart contracts provides a method to securely share PHR [49]. The authors have presented a simplified data privacy protecting technique for the health-care system. An interleaving encoder method was adapted to secure the original EMR enabling the patient's data privacy and security.

This original EMR data are saved in immutable blockchain network nodes. This mechanism ensures the higher security of data. The experimental results revealed that this method is cost-effective and robust [50]. Table 15.2 summarizes the highlights of the literature survey.

15.2.2 Survey on web portals and mobile apps literature

Today medical professionals and patients can use the services of intelligent chatbots for faster and informed decision-making. Dutch researchers have conducted controlled experiments on 200 curated adults having alcohol addiction. These adults are subjected to the online portal-based medical treatment using CBT principles and also inspirational interactions for six months. The outcome of these adults' progress assessment has shown a significant enhancement in their wellness status. This study also revealed that youngsters do not want to have personal visits to doctors for mental health services. Mobile apps-based services are attracting adults and protecting them from social embarrassment. Mental health service portals and mobile apps help adolescents and prevent them from the shame of personally visiting a

Table 15.2   *The summary of blockchain literature*

Ref No	Methodology/application	Tools used	Dataset sources	Results
1	Decentralized Patients Assignment System (DPAS)	Agent model and Ethereum	Real and simulated datasets for a three-month period	DPAS outperforms in terms of time taken for computing and rate of rejections for transferring patient data
2	A platform for preserving privacy for health-care data	Cryptographic algorithms	Patient data stored in the cloud	Satisfactory results
3	Literature review on EHR, PHR	Searching tools	High impact publications	Ethereum and Hyper-ledger fabric are widely used in this domain
4	Formal equivalence checking method	The finite automata and formal equivalence	Patient magnetic resonance images	Integrity is checked against hacker attacks
5	Mapping to patient historical medical data which are in digital format	Smart contracts	Builds an integrated public digital medical store	Simplifies data processing and updates in specialized registers
6	Applications are designed using IoT, machine vision and blockchain technologies	Hashing and encryption algorithms	Reviewed papers	Ensures immutability, trust and robustness in every transaction using smart contracts
7	Interoperability standards are fulfilled using openEHR, and OmniPHR	Distributed PHR based on blockchain techniques	Forty thousand adult patients' data	The response time was less than 500 ms on an average with 98% system availability
8	PRISMA	Structured searching model	Four databases	Blockchain prototype for implementation and analysis of efficiency in the health-care domain

(Continues)

Table 15.2 Continued

Ref No	Methodology/application	Tools used	Dataset sources	Results
9	Real-time patient monitoring in hospital wards and clinics	Smart contracts	Atrial fibrillation (irregular heartbeat) data in patients	For old age patients in critical condition who need constant monitoring
10	Survey on the implementation of blockchain technologies	Survey of literature	From high impact journals during the period 2008 to 2019	Emerging contextual requirements of health-care service providers
11	Multiple layers and scalable blockchain architecture	Integrated into digital formats	Patient data	Sharing medical data securely across the health-care ecosystem
12	Solving the issues related to security and privacy for sharing medical data	The need for further research is highlighted	Disadvantages in blockchain systems in health-care are highlighted	Misleading data, data breaches, tampering of data issues can be successfully resolved
13	Private blockchain	Consensus algorithm and smart contracts	Patient's sensitive medical data	Selecting the right type of blockchain
14	Analysed many blockchain platforms	Docker container, hyper-ledger fabric, composer, hyper-ledger calliper, and Wireshark engine	Algorithm for enhancing the data exchange among the hospitals by EHR based on hyper-ledger	The performance of this system was enhanced by 1.75 times and delay decreased by 1.5 times
15	Explored innovative ideas in biomedical domain	Investigation	Safe and reliable manufacturing, storing, and distribution of authorized drugs data	Blockchain networks can securely manage very sensitive brain information
16	Fit-for-purpose prototype based on emerging disruptive technologies	Smart contracts and consensus algorithms	Enhances legal standards compliance, better usage and sharing of medical data	Efficiently and securely sharing data by decreasing the cost of operations and improving patient care

(Continues)

Table 15.2 Continued

Ref No	Methodology/ application	Tools used	Dataset sources	Results
17	Applications of blockchain for public health in South Africa	Distributed, immutable public/ private open ledger	Secure exchange of medical data	Transparent and accountable transactions in public health
18	Basic issues in the digitization of health-care records	Presented a health-care system	Generates a big health-care databank for the authorities	Shares patient data securely with all stakeholders
19	Medical data privacy, security, and mutual trust among patients and service providers	Healthcare solution model using smart contracts	Source code is shared in the GitHub repository	Securely sharing the medical data by simplifying patient care
20	The real-world issues, innovative approaches for delivering health-care services	Cryptography, blockchain-based data structures, consensus, and smart contracts	Secured patient data	Sustaining the development of health-care services
21	Resolving predominant vulnerabilities using blockchain	Risk factors, standards, and regulations of the blockchain	Data risks	The solutions to mitigate these attacks are discussed
22	Public immutable distributed ledger	Smart medical systems	Patient medical data	To reduce the cost of intermediary agents and to create reliable transactions
23	Medical supply chain	Blockchain implementation	Data integrity, security, and authenticated access	Medical insurance claims transaction processing
24	A blockchain model for EHRs	EHR	Medical data history, diagnosis, interventions, and clinical progress	Stakeholders of the health-care domain can securely access and manage data efficiently

(Continues)

Table 15.2 Continued

Ref No	Methodology/application	Tools used	Dataset sources	Results
25	Framework for authenticating patients' access to a node in the blockchain	Integrating RF determination and FV characteristics	One hundred and six samples selected from a large dataset of 6000 FV sample images	Architecture is secured from attacks such as brute force and spoofing
26	Blockchain-based health-care data distributed ledger	Digital medical data	Storing and managing the patient's medical data	Ensuring that patient data is secure and tampering and stealing are practically not possible
27	Applications of blockchain technology in the health-care domain	Blockchain technology	The patient data are timestamped	Sharing of health-care data across the borders in different jurisdictions
28	The highly secure, scalable, fault-resistant, private, and traceable blockchain framework	Bitcoin network	Secure and private data transactions	Creates 11 times lesser traffic in the network and ledger updates are 1.13 times quicker
29	Smart health-care domain	POW consensus	Sensors gather a lot of data from the patient wearable devices	Efficient POW consensus reduces the delays in communication by decreasing processing overheads
30	Applications in health-care data storage optimization and redesign of blockchain	Data mining and mapping activities	Optimizing the data storage	Blockchain, reading, writing performance, and bi-directional transfer network
31	Creating trusted, secure medical data of patients	Access to private health-care records using a security key	Patient data	Keeping the identities of patients safe and providing anonymity of medical transactions

(Continues)

Table 15.2 Continued

Ref No	Methodology/ application	Tools used	Dataset sources	Results
32	Advanced medical reviews	Autonomous medical investigation	Access to original and reliable data when examining the detailed information in each medical case review	Blockchain is implemented for EHR management to ensure foolproof security and authorization
33	Blockchain applications in Japan's public health-care system	AI and big data solutions in health-care	Medical database with powerful security features	The feasibility of innovative blockchain and IoT technology solutions
34	Blockchain supports the pharmaceutical industry to manage the growing risks of fictitious and un-approved drugs	MedRec applied smart contracts to link patient-provider relationships (PPRs)	Tamper-proof log of medical records	Blockchain provides a possibility for interoperability in health-care systems with a decentralized ledger of medical records
35	Incorporation of blockchain technology in health-care and build use cases	Regulations, system evolution, the privacy of information, and scalability	Patient data	Patient-centric approach and secure access to patient complete history
36	Integration of diverse custom-built software systems in the e-Health domain	Cryptocurrency in the health-care industry	Patient data	Cost-effective development and implementation of third-party licensed software services
37	To achieve optimal levels of security and cost in IoT systems	Lightweight encryption algorithms	Patient data are very sensitive, so privacy and security are very important	Compared the pros and cons of different security algorithms
38	Implementation of smartcontracts in health-care	Timestamping of patient and drug data	Minor and major health-care data sharing	Low-quality or counterfeit drugs are not accepted

(Continues)

Table 15.2 Continued

Ref No	Methodology/ application	Tools used	Dataset sources	Results
39	Managing medical records by auditing, controlling the data	Smart contracts	Secured data sharing among the data sources and applications	Managing medical data security for proof-based practices and validation procedures

psychologist. About 70 per cent of adults have shown curiosity in chatbot mobiles to monitor and manage their psychiatric problems for themselves. Adults trust these chatbots and share the data securely within the health-care ecosystem. At the outset, the demand for chatbots, their utility, and trust is increasing [51]

This paper reviewed the application of mobile apps and blockchain technology in the health-care domain. Mobile apps are used to authenticate the users while purchasing specific medicines. For instance, a mobile app called Apothecary switches on automatically the mobile camera and GPS tool to read the bar-coding on medicine strips to authenticate the sale of medicine to the patient. The mobile apps are used for tracking the patient's physical activity level and give suggestions for the general well-being of the patients. About four million people in China are using mobile apps for booking personal visits to doctors. Blockchain technology empowers these mobile apps to securely share their health-care data with all stakeholders in the health-care ecosystem. Secure medical data sharing in real time reduces the cost and time to process these data to enable faster decisions [52]. Table 15.3 shows the summary of the mobile apps literature survey.

15.2.3   Healthcare 4.0 ecosystem

The summary of the literature on Healthcare 4.0 is shown in Table 15.4.

15.2.4   IoMT survey

The objective of HERMIT is to promote research on micro-architectures and enhance the performance of IoMT systems. HERMIT consists of applications such as wearable devices, ultrasound, CT scan, MRI, and other implantable heart monitors. HERMIT also covers subsidiary tools to provide security and compressing of data. The authors experimented on HERMIT on the IoT model platform to acquire in-depth knowledge of IoMT systems. The features of HERMIT are compared with MiBench, SPEC CPU2006, and PARSEC. The outcome of this study revealed the need for further research into IoMT-targeted micro-architectures [53]. A smart system for remote monitoring the patient's health conditions and uploading these data to the cloud was designed. The physical location of the patient can be identified using GPS location tracking systems. These smart systems enable the doctors to provide a quality diagnosis and prescribe intervention based on the patient's condition in remote places. The experiments conducted on this smart system revealed that good quality health-care services could be provided to the patients cost-effectively [54].

A well-organized study on the current applications of blockchain in the health-care domain was carried out. This study is based on Preferred Reporting Items for Systematic Reviews and Meta-Analysis (PRISMA). A structured search model was applied for searching four databases to download all related research papers. This study has revealed that many surveys and use cases are adopting blockchain in health-care domain. The authors found the deficiency in prototypes, analysed the efficiency of use-cases and their limitations [55]. The applications of smart contracts, digital soft identities, IoMT, and AI enable us to carry out online monitoring

Table 15.3   The summary of mobile apps survey

Ref No	Methodology/ application	Tools used	Dataset sources	Results
1	Sharing of patients' data among the doctors, clinicians, and other stakeholders in clinical decision support systems	MedRec Chatbots	Survey data of 200 adults for a six-months period where 70% of the youngsters responded positively	Won the Blue health record competition. Improved the mental health of adolescents and prevented them from social embarrassment
2	Mobile apps are used to authenticate the users while purchasing specific medicine	Apothecary mobile app	Patient personal health-care dataset	The secure sharing of medical data in real time reduces the cost and time to process the data
3	Database server, blockchain, and mobile app	Health-care apps	Patient data	Online doctor consultation
4	Healthcare 4.0 standards.	Mobile apps and wearable devices	Patient data	Remote monitoring of patients' health. Patients can be informed at any time from anywhere, and doctors can also track patients' conditions
5	Enhance health-care quality by storing and sharing of EHR	Mobile apps and monitoring machines	Data from clinical trials and medical insurance	Speeded up access, more productivity, saving costs, and creativity through novel medicine discovery

of patients, hospital wards, and clinics. A smart contract can be designed to send instructions to the patient's health-care service provider or emergency health-care services when the patient's IoMT device detects atrial fibrillation (irregular heartbeat) in patients.

This type of smart medical assistance is very useful for aged and differently enabled patients who require continuous monitoring. An integrated system consisting of a database server, blockchain server, clients based on embedded systems, and mobile apps is ideal for providing smart healthcare. This system is designed to exploit the growing trends in smartphone popularity for health-care apps. Human

Table 15.4   The summary of Healthcare 4.0 literature survey highlights

Ref. No	Methodology /application	Tools used	Dataset sources	Results
1	Enforcing patient-driven interoperability	21CCA standard	Clinical data transactions	Enhanced privacy, security, and incentives
2	Healthcare 4.0 standards for patient-centric health-care paradigm	AI, blockchain, and IoT	PHR	To reduce the cost of managing the health-care data and to provide the freedom to patients to share their medical data
3	Healthcare 4.0 standards	Mobile apps and wearable devices	Patient data	IoMT systems enable remote monitoring of patients' health. Patients can be informed at any time from anywhere, and doctors can also track patients
4	Patient-centric health-care services	White papers, proof of concepts, and prototypes	Patient data	Supply-chain management, patient data management, pharmaceutical research, prescription management, patient billing claims management, and data analytics
5	Healthcare 4.0 standards	Health-care management using EHR	Clinical diagnosis and patient health insurance claims data	Patient-centric approach
6	Personal Health Data Management (PHDM)	U-Prove based protocols to control the data access	Sharing the patients' medical data securely	The safety and integrity of health-care data are assured by foolproof authorization

(Continues)

Table 15.4   Continued

Ref. No	Methodology /application	Tools used	Dataset sources	Results
7	Managing medical data supporting auditing, interoperability, and controlling the data access	Smart contracts	Secured data sharing among the data sources and applications	Manage medical data security for foolproof practices and validation procedures
8	An innovative framework is designed using IoT, AI, and 6LoWPAN and RFID/NFC	Cryptographic SIM card and simplified MIPv6 protocol	Share the EHR data between hospital and patient's residence	Results revealed a decrease in the time taken for the handover process and enhanced security
9	IoMT-based remote health-care management	Ingestible sensor	Safety and confidentiality are real problems	Smart hospitals and enhanced chronic disease treatment

activity recognition (HAR) is a very difficult task for e-health service providers. IoMT systems enable us to capture the real-time data of people affected by mental disorders. These patient data are communicated to e-mental health service providers to know their current state and to provide the necessary assistance remotely. Ensuring the security of medical data shared between the patient IoMT systems and e-health service providers is very critical. A trusted platform can be built to solve this difficulty by using blockchain technology. The authors proposed an activity recognition and monitoring architecture using a multi-class cooperative classification algorithm. The videos of human activities are processed using an integrated fog, blockchain, and cloud computing systems. The experimental results derived from this integrated system revealed that this method was accurate and efficient for recognizing human activities [56]. A survey on the implementation of blockchain technologies in the health-care domain was conducted from the literature published in high-impact journals from 2008 to 2019. The application of blockchain enhances security and privacy, decreases the operations costs and supports accurate diagnoses. The authors discovered the need for further research in discovering innovative ways to satisfy the emerging contextual health-care service providers' needs. The multi-layered and scalable blockchain-based architecture was presented to manage personal health records. Every individual's health data records were gathered and integrated with his historical data in digital form. This digital data helps doctors to diagnose, intervene, and refer to other doctors, and enables the patients to share medical data securely across the health-care ecosystem. This approach has driven the reforms in the medical technology domain in China.

The authors have highlighted the shortfalls and disadvantages in the present Indian manual health-care service providers' services. The major parameters affecting the access to data are the patient's gender, geographic places, and socio-economic status. Today health-care data are suffering from many problems such as non-standard formats, fragmented, distributed, and paper-based records without any integration and consistency. This chapter focuses on these primary issues and promotes the digitization of health-care records. The authors explained how disruptive technologies such as IoT, blockchain, big data, and AI leverage to develop a system to facilitate real-time and quality health-care services to the public. The authors presented a health-care system that uses Aadhaar identification number as the primary key for uniquely identifying every person and managing his health history. This system enables to share patient data securely to all stakeholders in the health-care ecosystem. This system also overcomes the basic problems with distributed, inefficiently managed, and unorganized patient data. This system assures interoperability and availability of medical data. This proposed system helps us to generate a big health databank for authorities without violating the privacy norms of citizens. These patient big data gathered since several years can be utilized as a resource for research purposes to understand the insights and make predictions about contiguous disease outbreaks, and plan massive interventions and curative measures [57]. IoMT systems offer personalized and effective health-care services to the patient. The IoMT devices are subjected to cyber attacks and the number of attacks are increasing day by day. Hackers can take control of these devices and force them to malfunction. A study was conducted to discover the potential dangers of IoMT devices. The authors used the Shodan tool to capture a huge set of IP addresses screened by the Nessus tool to check whether any threats exist. The authors investigated some devices produced by original suppliers.

These devices permit the execution of the code remotely and allow us to bypass user login credentials making them vulnerable for attackers. This study has given directions for further research on the security features of IoMT systems [58]. PMDs are connected to the patient's body to monitor the patient's conditions. These PMDs interact with programmable IoMT products for different purposes such as observation, software, and configuration updates. PMDs are always connected and enable patient mobility. These PMDs are vital components of IoMT systems and hence vulnerable to cyber attacks [59]. The traditional health data record-keeping systems are designed by considering only health-care service provider's requirements. The Healthcare 4.0 standards enforce a personalized and patient-oriented health-care paradigm. Healthcare 4.0 standards can be implemented by integrating 5G, AI, IoT, and blockchain technologies into health-care IT systems. The blockchain enables secure global access to patient data through an open distributed, decentralized, and immutable health-care data ledger. The health-care service providers need to upgrade their platform to blockchain-enabled solutions to reduce the cost of managing the health-care data and to enable patients to share their medical data across the health-care ecosystem. The authors surveyed IT-based health-care solutions and discovered many disadvantages of the present systems. This chapter also suggests some areas of improvements in the health-care systems. There is a focus on medical data privacy and security, building mutual trust among patients and service providers for promoting scalability and interoperability of health-care systems. The authors also developed a smart contract-based health-care solution model. The source code is freely shared in the GitHub repository. The global health-care sector is transforming from volume-based services to value-based services. All the health-care domain stakeholders should securely share the medical data for simplifying patient care. Securing patient-sensitive medical data is not only ethical but also a legal obligation to health-care service providers. IoMT systems identify and alert the presence of critical diseases in patients through constant observation of electro-physiological body conditions.

The authors have designed a Rapid Active Summarization for effective PROgnosis (RASPRO) device that helps the physicians in detecting and warning on discovering critical conditions in patients. This mechanism is used in edge comput-ing devices to enable pervasive computing in remote places [60]. IoMT technology drives innovation and efficiency in the health-care industry. Healthcare is one of the biggest industries adopting IoT technology to meet Healthcare 4.0 standards. IoMT is going to bring about a revolution in the health-care industry. Health-care service providers and medical device manufacturing companies have to comply with indus-try standards to support the interoperability between millions of connected devices. The health-care industry is still not effectively using medical data to enhance the quality of services. This industry demands many smart integrated solutions based on emerging technologies. People are using mobile apps and wearable devices for booking visits to doctors. Mobile apps are used for knowing the variations in blood pressure and calories burnt. IoMT systems enable patient's health monitor-ing remotely. Patients can be informed at any time from anywhere. The doctors can also track the patient conditions through IoMT systems and reduce the time spent through a secured connection. IoMT systems are adopted rapidly by the people. IoMT has a huge impact on the health-care market and policies [61].

Managing patient's EHR efficiently has attracted maximum attention in recent years. An EHR comprises a patient's brief medical history, diagnosis, interventions, and clinical progress. A blockchain-based model for EHR may be viewed as a pro-tocol by which only authorized stakeholders can securely access and manage data efficiently [62]. The authors analysed the major problems in IoMT technologies. A flexible prototype model to resolve these problems was presented. This chapter introduced a trusted architecture for IoMT that addresses many problems of pri-vacy, security, and integrity associated with sensed data. Authors have applied data encryption techniques such as attribute-based encryption (ABE), advanced encryp-tion standard (AES), and provable data possession (PDP) [63].

The authors proposed an IoT and Hadoop-driven medical emergency manage-ment system. This system collects the medical data through several million sensors and processes it. These medical data are stored in a central facility. This central facility has three sections; data gathering, Hadoop processing, analysis and decision. This system is implemented using UBUNTU 14.04 LTS coreTMi5 on a 3.2 GHz processor, 4 GB memory computer with sample datasets, and a real-time network environment. The results revealed that this system works satisfactorily and processes WBAN sensory data effectively [64]. IoT applications in healthcare have potential risks, and the concerns related to security are very high. The sensors are collecting sensitive health-care data using IoMT systems and are vulnerable to threats. The authors have carried out a safety and security analysis using a standardized meta-model [65]. An innovative linguistic model for patient's e-health called k-healthcare is presented. The layered models interact with one another to form a smartphone app to gather data from patients. Today m-health and e-health services are readily accepted to prevent and diagnose diseases, for health risk evaluation, tracking patient conditions, and intervention of potential patients. Many IoT platforms have been developed for managing e-health and m-health services. k-health-care systems store the patient data in the cloud, and it can be accessed by all stakeholders of the health-care industry in the future [66]. IoMT-based patient care is provided with a context-awareness to make the old-aged patient's life comfortable. An innovative IoMT framework is designed using IoT, AI, 6LoWPAN, and RFID/NFC. The patient mobility issue is resolved using the 6LoWPAN network to ensure less energy usage [67]. This chapter presents a summary of IoMT systems driving remote healthcare, tracking ingestible sensors, smart hospitals, mobile health, and improved acute diseases care [68].

The IoMT-based e-health-care services are more flexible and convenient, so that they can substitute conventional health-care services. Security and privacy are the two major issues in IoMT devices due to their computing resources, memory, and power restrictions. These devices cannot execute heavyweight traditional cryptography methods involving more complex computations. The friendly jamming (Fri-jam) methods do not lead to additional computing overhead on sensors and assure security in IoMT systems. The outcome from these experiments shows that Fri-jam methods considerably reduce the intruder's risk without affecting the authorized communication. Innovative utilization of cognitive radio (CR) integrated with IoMT is called a CIoMT. The application of CIoMT is highly suitable during pandemic situations because every individual has to be linked and observed remotely. CIoMT uses a large network that demands effective spectrum administration. The CIoMT architecture leverages online tracing, real-time health condition tracking, diagnosing the cases, interaction tracing, grouping, examination, and policing. CIoMT also decreases the work burden on the health-care workers for taking precautions and managing the infection. The authors discussed the problems and emerging research opportunities [69].

The authors discussed IoMT technology usage in the current COVID-19 pandemic situation for treating orthopaedic patients. The sharing of data, reporting, tracking of patients, gathering information and its analysis, quality healthcare are the list of cloud-based services provided by IoMT systems. IoMT also supports quality smart health-care and mobile clinic services [70]. Bio-sensors play a very vital role in IoT-driven e-health-care services. A wide variety of sensing devices and apps are readily available in stores to enable citizens to track their health status and various smarthome-based diagnostics. These services are also accessible on smart watches. The authors surveyed current IoT-based sensor systems. A comparative analysis of the security and privacy issues of sensors is presented [71].

Today one of the fatal types of cancers is pancreatic cancer because of its prognosis is exceedingly difficult. Automated pancreatic tumour segmentation can be carried out by computer-aided screening, diagnosis, and quantitative measurement in CT and MRI images. The authors have applied deep learning-based Hierarchical Convolutional Neural Network (HCNN) for pancreatic tumour discovery. The experimental results revealed that this approach would enhance the accuracy of the classifier and decrease the cost of IoMT architecture. A fuzzy extractor integrated with the fuzzy vault method was used in securing the patient data. This is method used biometric-key authentication. A fuzzy extractor was developed to securely retrieve features like QRS, PR, and QT interval and the private key creation for authentication. The IP address of the node was used as the public key for the assessment of the bit-rate of sensors at the decoding phase. The method showed improved results, that is, a 40 per cent reduction in data loss, a 20 per cent reduction in energy intake, and decreased delay [72]. The authors proposed an intelligent platform for managing medical information so that patients are provided with safe, comfortable, and high-quality diagnosis services with minimum waiting time and at primary medical expenses. The authors have developed an integrated and distributed health-care system for sharing heterogeneous medical data. This system was implemented in advanced hospitals. The interactions and fieldwork revealed that this system performed better than the earlier system. The health-care data sharing between the stakeholders was enhanced by 79 per cent, and the quality of medical treatment was also enhanced considerably [73]comparative analysis of survey papers wi. Table 15.5 shows a summary of IoMT literature.

15.2.5   Comparative analysis of survey papers with specific parameters

The authors have selected twelve survey research papers for comparative study in health-care 4.0 domain. A list of specific feature parameters is used for analysing these papers. Table 15.6 shows the analysis of the results.

The authors have selected ten survey papers for comparative study in IoMT domain. A list of specific feature parameters is used for analysing these papers. Table 15.7 shows the analysis of the results.

15.2.6   Findings from literature survey

The authors observed that people are adapting online e-health services due to prevailing pandemic times. The people cannot visit the doctors personally and hence they use digital solutions like tele-medicine, web portals, and mobile apps for getting health-care consultancy. People are also preferring touchless technologies for interacting and interfacing with other people and machines. During this pandemic period IoMT systems are better used to gather medical data from patients remotely. These data can be accessed by doctors for diagnosis purposes. At the outset, these pandemic times have boosted the growth and adoption of IoMT devices and Healthcare 4.0 solutions.

15.3   Architecture of the Healthcare 4.0 ecosystem

The architecture ecosystem of Healthcare 4.0 is shown in Figure 15.5. The patient is the primary stakeholder of this ecosystem. The Healthcare 4.0 ecosystem promotes a patient-centric approach. The patient is staying in his/her smart home. The patient's

Table 15.5   The consolidated summary of the literature survey highlights

Ref No	Methodology/application	Tools used	Dataset sources	Results
1	Eliminate or decrease the significance of centralized third parties	Medical wearable devices	Data can be captured directly from patients through their medical wearables	Data can be securely transmitted to health-care service providers to enable high speed and quality health-care services
2	Micro-architectures and optimization for the effective performance of nascent IoMT	HERMIT	Data are captured from wearable devices, ultrasound, Computerized Tomography (CT) scan and MRI	Future research into IoMT-targeted micro-architectures
3	Cloud-based control centre	Wearables and location tracking systems	Gathering data about physiological parameters of a patient	Good quality health-care services can be provided cost-effectively
4	Human activity recognition	IoMT	IoMT enables capturing the real-time data of patients affected by mental disorders	Knowing the current state of a patient remotely and providing the necessary medical assistance
5	The attacks on these IoMT devices	Shodan tool	Captures a huge set of IP addresses that are screened to check whether any vulnerabilities exists	This study has given directions for further research for providing security in IoMT Systems
6	Assisting in patient tracks, physical processes, and medical states	Personal medical devices	Data losses or tampering of data	Primary solutions to discover the threats
7	Healthcare 4.0 standards for patient-centric health-care paradigm	AI, Blockchain, and IoT	PHR	Reducing the cost of managing health-care data and freedom to patients for sharing their medical data

(Continues)

Table 15.5 Continued

Ref No	Methodology/application	Tools used	Dataset sources	Results
8	Medical data privacy, security, mutual trust among patients and service providers	Healthcare solution model using smart contracts	Source code is shared in the GitHub repository	Securely share the medical data and simplifying patient care
9	The real-world issues and innovative approaches for providing health-care services	Cryptography, blockchain-based data structures, consensus mechanisms, and smart contracts	Securing patient data	Sustained development of health-care services
10	Significant vulnerabilities in blockchain	Risk factors, concerns associated with standards and regulations of blockchain	Data risks	The solutions to mitigate these attacks are discussed
11	Monitoring the electro-physiological body parameters	RASPRO	Multi-sensor time-series data	Edge computing, pervasive computing techniques are applied
12	Genome market opportunities	Electronic chip for storing the patient data	Genomics data	Transparently monitor human mistakes, delays, costs, and efforts in the drugs supply chain
13	Healthcare 4.0 standards	Mobile apps and wearable devices	Patient data	Patient's remote health monitoring and informing patients at any time from anywhere and track the patient's locations
14	A blockchain model for EHRs	EHR	Data of medical history, diagnosis, interventions, and clinical progress	Stakeholders of the health-care domain can securely access and manage data efficiently

(Continues)

Table 15.5 Continued

Ref No	Methodology/application	Tools used	Dataset sources	Results
15	Supply chain transparency in the health-care domain	The direct strategic partnership between suppliers and manufactures	Tracking data about the source of medical supplies and supply chain	Better product availability and enhanced patient care at reduced cost of operations
16	Analysis of IoMT technologies and major problems	Trusted architecture for IoMT	Security, privacy, and sensor data integrity problems	Enhances data availability, storage requirement, and computing power
17	IoT systems are implemented in the health-care industry	IoT and Hadoop driven medical emergency management system	Huge quantity of data in different types and formats	The system works satisfactorily and processes WBAN sensory data effectively
18	Healthcare 4.0 standards	Healthcare managing EHR	Clinical diagnosis and patient health insurance claims data	Patient-centric approach
19	Implementation of smart contracts in Healthcare	Timestamping of patient and drug data	Minor and major health-care data sharing	Low-quality or counterfeit drugs would not be accepted
20	Smart living for senior and disabled people	IoT-S2A2F for IoT-MD architecture	Sensors collecting sensitive health-care data	Data security and safety optimization
21	A semantic model for patients' e-health	k-health-care	Smartphones gather health-care data from patients	Patient medical data are stored in the cloud that can be accessed by all stakeholders of the health-care ecosystem
22	Virtual health-care systems	Virtual Breeding Environment and VO	Data collected through IoMT	Applicable in a simple health-care scenario
23	Personal Health Data Management (PHDM)	U-Prove based protocols for controlled access to data	Sharing the patient's medical data securely	The privacy and integrity of data is ensured by foolproof authentication
24	Handling medical records for interoperability, auditing, and controlling the data access	Smart contracts	Secured data sharing among the data sources and applications	Managing medical data security for proof-based practices and validation procedures

(Continues)

Table 15.5 Continued

Ref No	Methodology/application	Tools used	Dataset sources	Results
25	The innovative framework using IoT, AI, and 6LoWPAN and RFID/NFC	Cryptographic SIM card and simplified MIPv6 protocol	Share the EHR data between hospital and patient's residence	Reduction in the time taken for the handover process and enhanced security
26	IoMT drives remote health-care	Ingestible sensor	Safety and security are serious concerns	Healthcare 4.0 services for improved critical disease care
27	Privacy protection technique for blockchain-based health-care	e-EMR	EMR	The proposed scheme is very cost-effective and steady when compared to other schemes
28	The IoMT enabled e-health-care	Friendly Jamming (Fri-jam) schemes	Body sensors data	Reduced intruder risk which is enhancing the data transfer quality
29	CloMT	Online tracking, real-time health tracking, quality diagnosis	Every individual data are to be mapped and observed remotely	The decrease in the work burden on the health-care staff to take precautions and managing infection
30	IoMT technology applied to orthopaedic patients	Networked smart devices, software, Cloud and big data	Cloud-based services of IoMT	Promoting the quality of e-health-care solutions
31	Virtual e-health-care services	Bio-sensors	Enable citizens for tracking their health status in smart homes	IoT drives e-health-care services
32	Autonomous pancreatic tumour segmentation	Hierarchical Convolutional Neural Network	Diagnosis and quantitative measurement in CT and MRI images	Enhance the accuracy of the classifier and decrease the cost of IoMT architecture
33	Body Sensor Networks	Fuzzy tools developed for authentication	Easier access to patient's data with remote access	40% decreased data loss and 20% less energy consumption and decreased latency time

Table 15.6 Comparative analysis of specific features of Healthcare 4.0 survey papers

Sl. No	Authors	Year	Study objectives	Advantages	Disadvantages	1	2	3	4	5	6	7
1	Abdullah Al Omar et al. [3]	2019	A patient-oriented medical data system based on blockchain to promote data privacy	Cryptography-based functions are applied to encode medical data and to create anonymous data	Interoperability between devices and managing key distribution	√	√	X	X	X	√	√
2	Luca Brunese et al. [4]	2019	Exploiting formal equivalence checking for modelling MRI	The proposed method ensures that an attacker does not alter the received information	Evaluation of proposed architecture in the context of a real hospital network	√	X	X	√	X	X	X
3	William J. Gordon et al. [6]	2018	Patient-driven interoperability, managing data privacy and security	Facilitating the transition from institution-centric to patient-centric data sharing	Blockchain to promote clinical big data volume is a problem	√	X	X	√	√	X	X
4	Antonio CLIM et al. [52]	2019	To assess the applications of blockchain to support mobile-based health-care	Customized smartphones apps to offer patient-oriented care and to provide total control on sharing of data	Improved interoperability enhances the utilization of e-health-care services	√	√	√	X	√	X	X

(Continues)

Table 15.6 Continued

Sl. No	Authors	Year	Study objectives	Advantages	Disadvantages	1	2	3	4	5	6	7
5	Cornelius, C et al. [55]	2019	This research work technique has implemented PRISMA standards	Discussed the latest blockchain-based solutions, problems, and challenges in the health-care domain	Need for further research in health-care	√	√	√	X	√	X	X
6	Hoger Mahmud et al. [47]	2018	To solve the problems in record verification and validation for health-care services	Designed a blockchain-based framework to address the issues in VBE-based health-care	No Implementation	√	X	X	√	X	√	X
7	A.H. Mohsin et al. [31]	2019	Developing a merging procedure by combining RFID and FV attributes to enhance randomness features to enhance safety	55.56% more efficient in protecting biometric templates during data transfer		√	√	√	√	X	X	X
8	Asaph Azaria et al. [1]	2016	To provide patients with a comprehensive, unchangeable log and friendly access to patient data	MedRec supports sharing of patient data and motivates researchers to preserve the system	Contracts are encoded in the basic prototype	√	X	√	√	X	X	X

(Continues)

Table 15.6 Continued

Sl. No	Authors	Year	Study objectives	Advantages	Disadvantages	1	2	3	4	5	6	7
9	Junsong Fu et al. [68]	2020	Establishing a simple privacy-preserving technique for blockchain in health-care	This technique is the most efficient in terms of energy utilization, and storage management	The data processing operation of EMR should be made more efficient	√	√	X	√	X	X	X
10	Ahmed Farouk et al. [74]	2020	Studied the impact of IoMT and blockchain in the health-care domain	Enhanced security in health-care big data analytics	To prevent patient data leakages	√	√	√	√	√	X	X
11	Anton Hasselgrena et al. [5]	2020	Systematically reviewed the papers dealing with blockchain techniques to enhance the security of health-care data	Data integrity, access control, and interoperability are enhanced using blockchain	Designing blockchain solutions to ensure trust by controlling threats	√	√	√	√	X	X	X
12	Haider Dhia Zubaydi et al. [16]	2019	A study was carried out on recent applications of blockchain in health-care	A case study of a blockchain-based health-care platform is presented addressing the drawbacks of current designs	Not identifying the research gaps from the existing work	√	√	√	√	X	√	X

Table 15.7 *Comparative analysis of specific features of IoMT survey papers*

Sl No	Author	Year	Study objectives	Advantages	Disadvantages	1	2	3	4	5	6	7
1	Ankur Limaye et al. [53]	2018	The goal of HERMIT is to facilitate research into new micro-architectures and optimization for IoMT applications	The characteristics of HERMIT benchmarks substantially differ from those of existing benchmark suites	Optimizations for adaptable microprocessors is to be carried out	√	√	X	√	X	X	X
2	Ravi Pratap Singh et al. [69]	2020	Exploring possibilities for confronting the ongoing COVID-19 pandemic with IoMT	Remote-location health-care has also become feasible with the proposed IoMT approach	Security is a concern in cloud-connected databases. The interoperability in IoMT systems is to ensured	√	√	√	X	√	√	X
3	S. Vishnu et al. [12]	2020	Overview of IoMT-based remote health-care services	Discussed the tracking ingestible sensors, mobile health, smart hospitals for enhanced chronic disease treatment	Security and privacy are serious concerns that restrict the consumer usage of IoMT devices	√	√	X	X	√	X	X

(Continues)

Table 15.7 Continued

Sl No	Author	Year	Study objectives	Advantages	Disadvantages	1	2	3	4	5	6	7
4	Swati Swayamsiddha et al. [50]	2020	Cognitive Internet of Medical Things (CIoMT) is explored to tackle the global pandemic challenge	The CIoMT platform enables real-time tracking, remote health monitoring, rapid diagnosis of the cases, contact tracking and clustering	The privacy and security of the patient data is the prime concern	√	√	√	X	√	√	X
5	Xuran, Li et al. [50]	2020	Using Fri-jam schemes to protect the confidential medical data of patients collected by medical sensors from being eavesdropped on	The Fri-jam method will significantly decrease the eavesdropping risk while leading to no significant influence on legitimate transmission	Security performance of IoMT systems still needs to be improved	√	√	√	X	√	√	√

(Continues)

Table 15.7 Continued

Sl No	Author	Year	Study objectives	Advantages	Disadvantages	1	2	3	4	5	6	7
6	Mazhar, Rathore, M.et al. [64]	2016	Propose to deploy a real-time medical emergency response system in IoMT	Efficiently processing WBAN sensory data from millions of users to perform real-time responses in case of emergencies	Processing big data and performing real-time actions in critical situations is a challenging task	√	X	X	X	√	√	√
7	Rauscher et al. [66]	2016	The proposed model named k-Healthcare makes use of 4 layers	Provides an efficient platform for accessing patients' health data using smartphones	Investigation into the security and privacy issues of k-Healthcare is required	√	√	X	X	√		√
8	75 Tange H.J. et al. [81,[76],83] Jigna J Hathaliya et al.,[77][87]	2019	Biometric-based authentication scheme to ensure secure access of the patients EHR	The proposed scheme is superior in comparison with the traditional state-of-the-art existing schemes	To be implemented in a Tactile Internet environment	√	√	√	√	√	X	X

(Continues)

Table 15.7 Continued

Sl No	Author	Year	Study objectives	Advantages	Disadvantages	1	2	3	4	5	6	7
9	Jigna J. Hathaliya [78, 2020	2020	Explored the blockchain-based solutions to give insights to both researchers and practitioners communities	Advantages and limitations of various security and privacy techniques are explored	Blockchain-based secured decentralized architecture is to be explored	√	√	√	√	√	√	X
10	Jigna J. Hathaliyaa [79,80]]	2020	Mobile-based health-care system for Healthcare 4.0	Greater security compared to other state-of-the-art schemes		√	√	√	√	√	X	X

1. Architecture, 2. Applications, 3. Open Issues and Challenges, 4. Taxonomy, 5. Security, 6. Future Directions, 7 Case Study

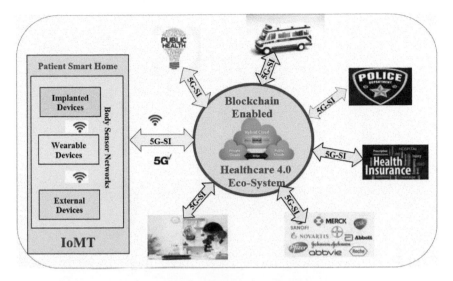

Figure 15.5   Architecture of the Healthcare 4.0 ecosystem

body may be embedded and attached with IoMT devices. The patient also has medical wearable devices like smart watch, smartphone, and so on. The smart home also has cameras, sensors, and other smart devices to observe the patient's conditions. All these smart devices have a wireless connection to the smart home network gateway. Patients need to register with an online health-care service providers to avail remote Healthcare 4.0 services. The blockchain-enabled Healthcare 4.0 service provider ensures the security and privacy of patient data. The patient securely shares his data with a hybrid cloud-based health-care system for availing smart services. There are many Healthcare 4.0 ecosystem stakeholders such as hospitals, public health departments, police, ambulance services, clinical laboratories, health insurance services, medical equipment, and pharmacy companies. All these stakeholders are integrated and share data and services. The blockchain layer enables secure and distributed sharing of data and transactions [81].

15.4   Research issues, implementation challenges, and future directions

The major issues in Healthcare 4.0 systems and applications are shown in Figure 15.6 and Section 15.4.1 discusses these issues.

15.4.1   Research issues in IoMT and Healthcare 4.0

The IoMT systems and devices are highly diverse in make, capabilities, and features. IoMT devices have heavy resource and power constraints. A survey by Hewlett Packard in 2015 revealed that about 70 per cent of IoT devices are vulnerable to attacks because of

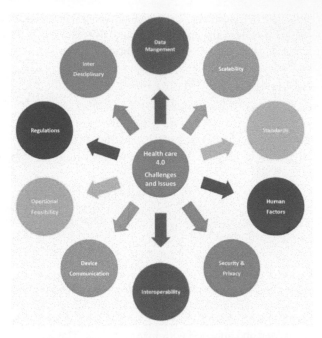

Figure 15.6   Healthcare 4.0 challenges

no transport encryption, no robust authentication, insecure web, software, and firmware interfaces [72].

15.4.1.1   Patient data management

The health-care data is captured from IoMT devices that are implanted in the patient body and also from wearable devices such as smart watch, smartphone, and so on. The physiological conditions of the patient's body are dynamic and generate a lot of data continuously. These data types are heterogeneous in nature such as text, signals, video, and images in different formats. All these devices are connected to a smart home e-health gateway. The smart e-health gateway should select a suitable routing algorithm for routing these data to a secure cloud. The e-health-care system designs and implementation require a deep knowledge of multi-disciplinary domains.

15.4.1.2   Scalability

The patients can save their time and effort by booking doctor visits online, online consultancy, and waiting time for test results. IoMT systems provide remote access to medical resources in the Healthcare 4.0 system. There are millions of connected devices in the smart-health ecosystem of a smart city. The scalability of Healthcare 4.0 e-health services is a challenge for the benefit of all citizens in a smart city. The Healthcare 4.0 ecosystem should create a trust among all the stakeholders of the ecosystem.

15.4.1.3 Standardization

The domain of Healthcare 4.0 standards is still emerging. There are no established international rules, protocols, and standards for heterogeneous devices from diverse manufacturers to interoperate, interface, and interact in the market. There are no stringent security features incorporated in these products. These devices are vulnerable to all kinds of cyber attacks.

Attackers can discover these online smart home devices connected to the internet through search engines such as Shodan. Hackers would attack these devices to steal or tamper with sensitive and valuable patient data and exploit the Healthcare 4.0 ecosystem.

15.4.1.4 Human factors in engineering and interfaces

The device manufacturers and software developers should consider the needs of all the stakeholders of the Healthcare 4.0 ecosystem. This need would enable them to understand the interoperability and ergonomic issues in the devices and software. The activity would promote the design of user-friendly and patient-oriented IoMT devices for the Healthcare 4.0 ecosystem [22]. The international standard committees such as international standard organization (ISO), American National standard institute (ANSI), institute of electrical and electronics engineers (IEEE), internet engineering task force (IETF), and other bodies should establish standards for Healthcare 4.0 ecosystem.

15.4.1.5 Security and privacy

The emergence of healthcare-related cyber attacks is a leading problem and a challenge to HIMS. According to Bloomer news, 90 per cent of HIMS have been subjected to attacks in the last two years, making them more vulnerable. These attacks discourage the stakeholders of Healthcare 4.0 from implementing HIMS. The reliability and dependability of HIMS would be seriously affected. Patients would not share their sensitive health data in the connected health-care systems. Intruders can access IoMT devices and pose a serious threat to patient data privacy. The sensors and actuators in the IoMT system are also vulnerable to attacks such as spoofing, tag cloning, cloud polling, RF jamming, and denial of service (DoS). DoS affects health-care systems and has an adverse impact on patient health-care services. Reliable security features are required for health-care solutions to build trust in stakeholders for carrying out digital health transactions.

15.4.1.6 Lack of interoperability

An international collaboration between the various nations is essential to build interoperability in digital health systems. A federated identity solution called Shibboleth promotes object authentication inside and among the organizational systems. Liberty Alliance Projects also work on integration issues between diverse platforms and protocols for inter-realm authentication into one common system. The OpenID, inames, Openliberty, World Wide Web Consortium, Organization for the Advancement of Structured Information Standards (OASIS), and Liberty Alliance Project are some examples of projects. Many international bodies such as ETSI, ITU-T, IEEE, and IETF are collaborating on enforcing standards in the IoMT domain.

15.4.1.7   Optional feasibility

Smart health-care systems are not very user-friendly to all the stakeholders of Healthcare 4.0 ecosystem. The existence of too many features would lead to system complexity for operation and demotivates health-care workers to use it. Building user-friendly health-care systems and apps is very vital for the success of e-health-care systems.

15.4.1.8   Regulations

Today the disruptive technologies are advancing very rapidly, and the regulators are not following them at the same pace. Healthcare is a highly regulated domain that is affected by the slow adoption of advanced technologies. The regulations related to granting authorization for conducting experiments with the latest technological solutions are outdated. By the time authorization is granted, technology becomes absolute. The internet connectivity is 81 per cent in developed countries while it is only 17.5 per cent in underdeveloped countries, leading to difficulties in implementing Healthcare 4.0 services.

15.4.1.9   Interdisciplinary

This customization of medicine and services to individual patient's requirements demands very efficient and near-real-time interventions. Healthcare 4.0 service implementation requires integrating IoMT devices with cyber-physical systems, software components, big data management software, IoT, 5G, AI, and blockchain tools. Personalized health-care services provide autonomy to patients to choose their treatment phase and the sharing of medical data.

15.5   A Healthcare 4.0 ecosystem platforms and tools case study

The diverse tools used in the Healthcare 4.0 ecosystem platforms are discussed in Section 15.5.1 and are shown in Figure 15.7.

15.5.1   Qualcomm Life—Capsule

Qualcomm Life is a specialist company for delivering connected health-care applications and biological solutions. A Qualcomm Life solution called Capsule gathers and analyzes the data from several hundred types of IoMT devices. These data are mapped

Figure 15.7   Healthcare 4.0 products

into the EHR of patients stored in the cloud. More than 2 200 health-care service providers are using the Capsule application to automate the gathering and transfer of critical
data to the patient EHR. This data collection work is normally carried out by nurses
manually and automation of this data collection saves at least 30 per cent of the time.
The fieldwork was carried out in one of the hospitals in France to prevent manual data
gathering and to transmit patient data into the EHR solution. This department could save
about 164 manual hours every year, permitting nurses to spend their valuable time in
patient care and enhancing patient data collection by 54 per cent. Qualcomm Life also
has a Memorandum of Understanding (MoU) with Phillips to increase IoMT interoperability with its HealthSuite platform.

15.5.2   Phillips HealthSuite

Philips corporation has developed the Phillips HealthSuite platform for the health-
care domain. This platform is an open source and provides security services. Philips
is also collaborating with many leading research centers to design innovative products for patients suffering from chronic diseases.

Phillips is working with a university medical center to develop an integrated
product using wearable device technology. This device is to be kept on the chest
of a patient with chronic obstructive pulmonary disease (COPD) after discharge
from the hospital. This device gathers data from the patient heart rate, and physical and respiratory activities. This device permits the patients and doctors to
trace the health conditions of the patient remotely. Phillips HealthSuite leverages IoMT devices to share data through open platforms that securely collect and
analyze data from diverse sources. These medical data may be retrieved online
by the doctors, patients, and caregivers using mobile or web apps to provide
real-time patient data. This open platform provides personalized, precise, predictive insights about patient conditions. The platform supports features such as
precision diagnostics, remote monitoring, genomics analytics, and telemedicine.

At present, the Phillips HealthSuite platform manages over 15 petabytes of data collected from several hundred million medical records, imaging studies, and patient data [82, 83].

Philips has declared HealthSuite Insights, an industry-first service that offers specific tools and technologies for healthcare to cater to the complete process of development, maintenance, deployment, and scaling of AI products.

15.5.3　GDm-Health system for gestational diabetes mellitus

The Oxford Academic Health Science Network (O-AHSN) contributed significantly for designing the proof of concept, identifying a business leader for testing, designing, and marketing GDm-Healthcare products. About ten per cent of pregnant women are suffering from gestational diabetes mellitus (GDm). Every year about one hundred thousand women are affected in England. The patient's conditions are monitored for maintaining blood glucose at safe levels. O-AHSN promotes the utilization of GDm-health™—a mobile app to monitor online, manage, and interact with pregnant women suffering from gestational diabetes. About 2 000 women have participated in a local pilot testing project. The outcome of this study revealed that 25 per cent of unnecessary hospital visits were reduced. Patients have shown an improved control of glucose levels by March 2017. The GDm-healthcare app was integrated with a blood glucose meter which sends online blood glucose levels of patients and their remarks to the dashboard of healthcare information system (HIS) web portal. The doctor's team can monitor patients' conditions. The portal's dashboard helps the doctors to prioritize health-care to those women who need immediate attention and inform the patients online by sending messages. Patients and doctors can also interact with nursing staff in the care team. This app enables patients to get advice from the care team to manage their glucose levels and to correct the diet or medication patterns. This product was implemented in different hospitals as per the planned research for a 5-year strategic agreement between Drayson Health, the University of Oxford, and Oxford University Hospitals NHS Foundation Trust starting from July 2017.

15.5.4　Medtronic insulin pump

Medtronic is a company manufacturing insulin pump systems. Medtronic collaborates with two leading US health insurance organizations that are using Medtronic's insulin pumps for diabetic patients. The recordings from these pumps are used for insurance bill reimbursements. MiniMedTM 670G is a hybrid closed-loop insulin pump model that monitors glucose levels in patients.

These insulin pumps constantly monitor the glucose levels using sensors and controls the pumps automatically to inject insulin into the patient. This insulin pump reimbursement model is based on outcomes that operate on sharing risk basis for manufacturers and the payers to map the reimbursement of these insulin pumps to enhance glycated hemoglobin levels in the patient.

15.5.5 Medtronic CareLink

The Medtronic CareLink Network service has developed IoMT devices which are implantable cardiac products. This company is a web-based patient monitoring system compatible with all Medtronic devices. These implantable cardiac products enable remote monitoring of patient conditions in real time by medical professionals. Medical data are gathered from these cardiac devices implanted in the patient body and are transmitted to the cloud of the Medtronic CareLink Clinician portal.

This portal offers secure access to medical data collected from cardioverter implantable defibrillators, pacemakers, implantable cardiac resynchronization therapy with pacing devices, defibrillator devices, and implantable loop recorders. The clinicians can also access CareAlert messages. These messages are created as a result of clinical events to discover the possible device malfunction issues before they become more critical. The CareLink Network service may decrease the necessity for the patient to visit their doctors in person. The results from these operations of CareLink in patients with heart failure indicate that it reduces the time from the identification of a clinical event to a clinical decision. These alerts decrease the number of emergency visits by patients having heart problems.

15.6 Conclusion

The authors are motivated by the market potential and industry interests in the implementation of IoMT technology and Healthcare 4.0 standards as a future game changer. An extensive study of literature on IoMT and Healthcare 4.0 ecosystems was carried out. Intelligent and autonomous health-care systems are designed using AI, IoMT, 5G, and blockchain technologies. All the reviewed papers are classified into blockchain, mobile apps, Healthcare 4.0, and IoMT sections. A section-wise summary table highlighting the methodology, results, and applications from each paper is presented. A taxonomy of concepts of IoMT, 5G, and blockchain is presented. A comparative analysis of selected survey papers with specific parameters is also presented.

The current prevailing Corona pandemic across the world is forcing people to stay at home and to avoid touching things. In these times people prefer using web portals, digital e-health solutions, IoMT devices, and mobile apps to avail healthcare services and consult doctors. These days people prefer touchless interactions with other people and things. Hence these pandemic times boost the growth and adoption of Healthcare 4.0 solutions. The architecture of the Healthcare 4.0 ecosystem is also illustrated. The research challenges and future directions in this domain are discussed. A case study of five leading international Healthcare 4.0 products implemented was discussed. At the outset, the authors realized that blockchain, 5G, and IoMT are empowering the implementation of the Healthcare 4.0 ecosystem. The Healthcare 4.0 system should leverage trust, security, flexibility, and efficiency in operations.

The authors have tried to provide a holistic view of IoMT and Healthcare 4.0 applications and presented a review of algorithms, techniques, and methods applied in the e-healthcare domain. The authors conclude that Healthcare 4.0 services enhance the quality and efficiency of personalized patient services and reduce operations costs. A pie chart showing the number of concepts illustrated from each paper in the study of 87 papers has been shown. Healthcare 4.0 services and products would revolutionize the health-care industry in the near future.

References

[1] Asaph A., Ariel E., Thiago V., Andrew L. *Medrec: using blockchain for medical data access and permission management* [online]. *2nd international conference on open and big data*. 2016. Available from https://people.cs.pitt.edu/~babay/courses/cs3551/papers/MedRec.pdf [Accessed 16 Oct 2020].

[2] Adrien B., Shima M., Leili S. 'Secure decentralized decisions to enhance co-ordination in consolidated hospital systems'. *IISE Transactions on Healthcare Systems Engineering*. 2020;**10**(2):99–112.

[3] Abdullah A., Omar. M., Zakirul. A., *et al.* 'A privacy-friendly platform for healthcare data in cloud-based on blockchain environment'. *Future Generation Computer Systems*. 2019;**95**:511–21.

[4] Luca B., Francesco M., Alfonso R., Santone A. 'A Blockchain-based proposal for protecting healthcare systems through formal methods'. *Procedia Computer Science*. 2019;**159**:1787–94.

[5] Hasselgren A., Kralevska K., Gligoroski D., Pedersen S.A., Faxvaag A. 'Blockchain in healthcare and health sciences – a scoping review'. *International journal of medical informatics*. 2019;**134**:1–20.

[6] Gordon W.J., Catalini C., William J., Christian. 'Blockchain technology for healthcare: facilitating the transition to patient-driven interoperability'. *Computational and Structural Biotechnology Journal*. 2018;**16**:224–30.

[7] Koshechkin K.A., Klimenko G.S., Ryabkov I.V., Kozhin P.B. 'Scope for the application of blockchain in the public healthcare of the Russian Federation'. *International Conference on Knowledge–Based and Intelligent Information and Engineering, Systems, KES2018, 3-5 September 2018*; Belgrade, Serbia; 2018. pp. 1323–8.

[8] Mohamad K., Joanna D., Tarek M., Giuseppe D., Valdemar V., Graciano N. 'Investigating quality requirements for blockchain-based healthcare systems'. *IEEE/ACM 2nd International Workshop on Emerging Trends in Software Engineering for Blockchain (WETSEB)*; 2019. pp. 52–5.

[9] Devrim U., Mohammad H., Mehmet, Sabir K. 'Policy specification and verification for blockchain and smart contracts in 5G networks'. *IoT Express*. 2020;**6**:43–7.

[10] Taylor P.J. *A systematic literature review of blockchain cybersecurity, digital communications and networks* [online]. 2019. Available from https://doi.org/10.1016/j.dcan.2019.01.005 [Accessed 16 Oct 2020].

[11]   Alex R., Cristiano A., Da Costa. R., *et al.* 'Analysing the performance of a blockchain-based personal health record implementation'. *Journal of Biomedical Informatics.* 2019;**92**:1–10.

[12]   Vishnu, Ramson S.R.J., Jegan R. 'Internet of Medical Things (IoMT) – an overview'. *5th International Conference on Devices, Circuits and Systems (ICDCS)*; Coimbatore, India; 2020. pp. 101–4.

[13]   Minglin S., Zhang J. 'Research on the application of blockchain big data platform in the construction of a new smart city for low carbon emission and green environment'. *Computer Communications*;2020(149):332–42.

[14]   Maria P., Maria P. 'Blockchain in healthcare'. *Australasian Journal of Information Systems.* 2019;**23**:1–23.

[15]   Yan Y., Zhao. W., Ze L., Tian G. 'A multi-layered blockchain network for individual-oriented health-care records storage and management'. *ICBTA 2019: Proceedings of the 2019 2nd International Conference on Blockchain Technology and Applications*; 2019. pp. 64–9.

[16]   Zubaydi H.D., Chong Y.-W., Ko K., Hanshi S.M., Karuppayah S. 'A review on the role of Blockchain technology in the healthcare domain'. *Electronics.* 2019;**8**(6):679–98.

[17]   Hölbl M., Kompara M., Kamišalić A., Nemec Zlatolas L. 'A systematic review of the use of Blockchain in healthcare'. *Symmetry.* 2018;**10**(10):470–85.

[18]   Sudeep T., Karan P., Richard E. 'Blockchain-based electronic healthcare record system for healthcare 4.0 applications'. *Journal of Information Security and Applications.* 2020;**50**:1–12.

[19]   Chen H.S., Jarrell J.T., Carpenter K.A., Cohen D.S., Huang X. 'Blockchain in healthcare: a patient-centered model'. *Biomedical Journal of Scientific & Technical Research.* 2019;**20**(3):15017–22.

[20]   Mackey T.K., Kuo T.-T., Gummadi B., *et al.* ''Fit-for- challenges and opportunities for applications of blockchain technology in the future of healthcare'. *BMC Medicine.* 2019;**17**(1):68–79.

[21]   Ndayizigamiye P., Dube S. 'Potential adoption of blockchain technology to enhance transparency and accountability in the public healthcare system in South Africa'. *International Multidisciplinary Information Technology and Engineering Conference (IMITEC)*; Vanderbijlpark, South Africa; 2019. pp. 1–5.

[22]   Thomas F.H. *Introductory chapter: blockchain technology and smart healthcare, smart healthcare* [online]. 2020. Available from http://dx.doi.org/10.5772/Intechopen.90633 [Accessed 16 Oct 2020].

[23]   Nghia, Duong T., Ha, Xuan S., Hai, Trieu L., Tan, Tai P. *Smart care: integrating blockchain technology into the design of patient-centred healthcare systems* [online]. 2020. Available from https://doi.org/10.1145/3377644.3377667 [Accessed 16 Oct 2020].

[24]   Sami U., Aslam, S H., Arjomand N. *Blockchain in healthcare and medicine: a contemporary research of applications, challenges, and future perspectives.* 2020. Available from http://dx.doi.org/10.5772/Intechopen.90633 [Accessed 16 Oct 2020].

[25]   Efpraxia Z., Ying H., Matthew P. On the security risks of the blockchain. *Journal of Computer Information Systems*. 2018. Available from https://doi. org/ 10.1080/08874417.2018.1538709 [Accessed 16 Oct 2020].

[26]   Sebahattin D., Irem D., Andrew M. 'Blockchain technology in the future of business, cybersecurity and accounting'. *Journal of Management Analytic*. 2020;**7**(2):189–208.

[27]   Kurt Y., Michael M., Jonathan R., Anthony C. 'Emerging blockchain technology solutions for modern healthcare infrastructure'. *Journal of Scientific Innovation in Medicine*. 2019;**2**(1):1–5.

[28]   Marques L., Marina M., Cláudia A. *The healthcare supply network: current state of the literature and research opportunities* [online]. 2019. Available from https://doi.org/10.1080/09537287.2019.1663451 [Accessed 16 Oct 2020].

[29]   Drosatos G., Kaldoudi E., George D., Eleni K. 'Blockchain applications in the biomedical domain: a scoping review'. *Computational and Structural Biotechnology Journal*. 2019;**17**:229–40.

[30]   Fran C., Thomas K., Dasaklisb, Constantinos P. 'A systematic literature review of blockchain-based applications: current status, classification and open issues'. *Telematics and Informatics*. 2019;**36**:55–81.

[31]   Ali H., Mohsin. A., Zaidan. A.Z., Bahaabila B., I A., Mohammed K. I. 'Based on blockchain-PSO-AES techniques in finger vein biometrics: a novel verification secure framework for patient authentication'. *Computer Standards & Interfaces*. 2019:1–22.

[32]   Yong, Sauk H., Jae, Min L., Jaechan P., Min, Cheol C. 'Medical doctor's and patient's attitudes toward the use of blockchain technology in the management of medical information: a study based on expectancy theory'. *Journal of Medical Internet Research*. 2019;**21**(12):e15870.

[33]   Khezr S., Moniruzzaman M., Yassine A., Benlamri R. 'Blockchain technology in healthcare: a comprehensive review and directions for future research'. *Applied Sciences*. 1736;**9**(9):1736–48.

[34]   *Blockchain: A healthcare industry review, Capgemini report* [online]. 2016. Available from https://www.capgemini.com/wp-content/uploads/2017/07/ blockchain-a_healthcare_industry_view_2017_web.pdf [Accessed 16 Oct 2020].

[35]   Citustech. *Blockchain for healthcare an opportunity to address many complex challenges in healthcare* [online]. 2018. Available from https://www.citiustech.com/uploads/knowledgehub/pdf/blockchain-for-healthcare-341.pdf [Accessed 16 Oct 2020].

[36]   Sobia Y., Muhammad M., Khan. R., *et al.* 'Use of blockchain in healthcare: a systematic literature review'. *International Journal of Advanced Computer Science and Applications*. 2019;**10**(5):1–17.

[37]   Laure A., Linn, Martha B., Koo M.D. *Blockchain for health data and its potential use in health and healthcare-related research* [online]. 2017. Available from https://www.healthit.gov/sites/default/files/11-74-ablockchainforhealthcare.pdf [Accessed 16 Oct 2020].

[38] Jn A.-K., Al-Karakiamjad., Gawanmehmeryeme A., Ayacheashraf M., Ashraf M. 'DASS-CARE: a decentralized, accessible, scalable, and secure healthcare framework using Blockchain'. *15th International Wireless Communications and Mobile Computing Conference*. 2019.

[39] Randhir K., Marchangrakesh T. 'Distributed off-chain storage of patient diagnostic reports in the healthcare system using IPFS and blockchain'. *International Conference on Communication Systems & Networks (COMSNETS)*; 2020.

[40] Constantinos L., Dimka K., Christos, N S. Measuring the impact of blockchain on healthcare applications. *In Proceedings of the 2nd International Conference on Applications of Intelligent Systems (APPIS '19). Association for Computing Machinery*; New York, NY, USA; 2019. pp. 1–5.

[41] Mackey T., Bekki H., Matsuzaki T., Mizushima H. 'Examining the potential of blockchain technology to meet the needs of 21st-century Japanese healthcare: viewpoint on use cases and policy'. *Journal of medical Internet research*. 2020;**22**(1):e13649.

[42] Peng Z., Douglas, C S., Jules W. *Blockchain technology use cases in healthcare* [online] Vanderbilt University, Nashville, TN Gunther Lenz, Varian Medical Systems, Palo Alto, CA. 2018. Available from https://www.dre.vanderbilt.edu/~schmidt/PDF/blockchain-bookchapter-2018.pdf [Accessed Jan 2021].

[43] Erikson J., De A., Bruno S.F., Bhaskar K., Jó U. 'A survey of blockchain-based strategies for healthcare'. *ACM computing surveys*;53(2):1–27.

[44] Daraghmi E.-Y., Daraghmi Y.-A., Yuan S.-M. 'MedChain: a design of a blockchain-based system for medical records access and permissions management'. *IEEE Access*. 2019;7:164595–613.

[45] Jing J., Gail-Joon A., Hongxin. H., Hongxin. H., Xinwen Z., Xinwen Z. 'Patient-centric authorization framework for sharing electronic health records'. *SACMAT 2009, 14th ACM Symposium on Access Control Models and Technologies*; Stresa, Italy; June 3–5, 2009.

[46] Ik-Whan K., Sung-Ho K. 'Framework for successful supply chain implementation in the healthcare area from the provider's perspective'. *Asia Pacific Journal of Innovation and Entrepreneurship*. 2018;**12**(2):135–45.

[47] Hoger M., Joan L., Qiang X. 'A blockchain-based service provider validation and verification framework for the healthcare virtual organization'. *UHD Journal of Science and Technology*. 2018:24–31.

[48] Gary L., Cunningham J., Ainsworth J. 'A ledger of me: personalizing healthcare using blockchain technology'. 2019;**6**:162–71.

[49] Asma K. 'A blockchain-based smart contract system for healthcare management'. *Electronics*. 2020;**9**(94):1–23.

[50] Li X., Dai H.-N., Wang Q., Imran M., Li D., Imran M.A. 'Securing internet of medical things with friendly-jamming schemes'. *Computer Communications*. 2020;**160**(1):431–42.

[51] Paul C., John H. *Innovations in mHealth, Part 1: The role of blockchain, conversational interfaces, and chat-bots*, The Transformative Power of Mobile

Medicine: Leveraging Innovation, Seizing Opportunities and Overcoming Obstacles. Available from https://doi.org/10.1016/B978-0-12-814923-2. 00001-5 [Accessed 16 Oct 2020].

[52] Antonio C., Răzvan, Daniel Z., Radu C. 'Data exchanges based on block-chain in m-health applications'. *9th International Conference on Current and Future Trends of Information and Communication Technologies in Healthcare (ICTH 2019)*; Coimbra, Portugal; November 4–7, 2019. pp. 281–8.

[53] Limaye A., Adegbija T. 'Hermit: a benchmark suite for the Internet of medical things'. *IEEE Internet of Things Journal*. 2018;**5**(5):4212–22.

[54] Hongju L. 'Remote intelligent medical monitoring system based on the Internet of things'. *International Conference on Smart Grid and Electrical Automation*; 2016.

[55] Cornelius C.A., Qusay, Mahmoud H.J., Mikael E. 'Blockchain technology in healthcare: a systematic review'. *Healthcare*. 2019;**7**(56).

[56] Naveed I., Yasir F., Ikram U., *et al.* 'A blockchain-based fog computing framework for activity recognition as an application to e-healthcare services'. *Future Generation Computer Systems*;100:569–78.

[57] Devendra D., Mohit G., Sarma P.R.S., Abhijit C. 'Big data and blockchain supported conceptual model for enhanced healthcare coverage'. *The Indian Context, Business Process Management Journal*. 2019;**25**(7):1612–32.

[58] McMahon, R W., Samtani M.E, S., Patton, Chen M, H. 'Assessing medical de-vice vulnerabilities on the internet of things'. *IEEE International Conference on Intelligence and Security Informatics (ISI)*; 2017. pp. 176–8.

[59] Mohan A. 'Cybersecurity for personal medical devices and internet of things'. *IEEE International Conference on Distributed Computing in Sensor Systems*; 2014. pp. 372–4.

[60] Pathinarupothi K. 'Clinically aware data summarization at the edge for the internet of medical things'. *IEEE International Conference on Pervasive Computing and Communications Workshops (PerCom Workshops)*; 2019. pp. 437–8.

[61] Dharmin D., Shalin P., Reema P., Nishant D. 'A survey on blockchain technol-ogy and its proposed solutions'. *Procedia Computer Science*. **160**. Coimbra, Portugal; *November 4–7, 2019*. pp. 740–5.

[62] Natsuki K. 'Application of blockchain to supply chain: flexible blockchain technology'. *Procedia Computer Science*. 2019;**164**:143–8.

[63] Rathnayake R., Karunarathne M.S. *Adaptive solution for key challenges on the internet of medical things*. Available from http://ir.kdu.ac.lk/handle/345/2503 [Accessed Dec 2020].

[64] Rathore M.M., Ahmad A., Paul A., Wan J., Zhang D. 'Real-time medical emergency response system: exploiting IoT and big data for public health'. *Journal of Medical Systems*. 2016;**40**(12):283.

[65] Premalatha V., Sreedevi E., Sivakumar S. 'Contemplate on the internet of things transforming as medical devices – the internet of medical things (IoMT)'. *International Conference on Intelligent Sustainable Systems (ICISS)*; Palladam, Tamilnadu, India; 2019. pp. 276–81.

[66] Rauscher., Bauer B. 'Safety and security architecture analyses framework for the internet of things of medical devices'. *IEEE 20th International Conference on e-Health Networking, Applications and Services (Healthcom)*; Ostrava; 2018. pp. 1–3.

[67] Valera A.J.J., Zamora M.A., Skarmeta A.F.G. 'An architecture based on internet of things to support mobility and security in medical environments'. *7th IEEE Consumer Communications and Networking Conference*; Las Vegas, NV; 2010. pp. 1–5.

[68] Junsong F., Na W., Yuanyuan C. 'Privacy-preserving in healthcare blockchain systems, based on lightweight message sharing, sensors';**20**(7):1–19.

[69] Ravi P., Singh M., Javaid A., Haleem R., Vaishya R., Ali S. 'Internet of medical things (IoMT) for orthopaedic in COVID-19 pandemic: roles, challenges, and applications'. *Journal of Clinical Orthopaedics Trauma*. 2020;**11**(4):113–717.

[70] Ray P.P., Dash D., Salah K., Kumar N. 'Blockchain for IoT-based healthcare: background, consensus, platforms, and use cases'. *IEEE Systems Journal*. 2020;**15**(1):85–94.

[71] Wei X., Guangqiang Y. 'Detection and diagnosis of the pancreatic tumour using deep learning-based hierarchical convolutional neural network on the Internet of medical things platform'. *Future Generation Computer Systems*. 2020;**111**:132–42.

[72] Xin Z., Xiaob W., Lu W., *et al.* 'Intelligent city intelligent medical sharing technology based on internet of things technology'. *Future Generation Computer Systems*. 2020;**111**:226–33.

[73] Choudhary D., Kumar R., Gupat N. 'Biomedical signal processing through wireless system for body sensor networks'. *Journal of Signal Processing Theory and Applications*. 2012;**2**(1):1–8.

[74] Ahmed F., Amal A., Shohini G., Atefeh M. 'Blockchain platform for industrial healthcare: vision and future opportunities'. *Computer Communications*. 2020;**154**:223–35.

[75] Häyrinen K., Saranto K., Nykänen P. 'Definition, structure, content, use and impacts of electronic health records: a review of the research literature'. *International Journal of Medical Informatics*. 2008;**77**(5):291–304.

[76] International Organisation for Standardisation. *Health informatics – electronic health record – definition, scope, and context (ISO/DTR 20514)*. 2014. Available from https://standards.globalspec.com/std/776539/iso-tr-20514 [Accessed Jul 2021].

[77] Tange H.J., Hasman A., de Vries Robbé P.F., Schouten H.C. 'Medical narratives in electronic medical records'. *International Journal of Medical Informatics*. 1997;**46**(1):7–29.

[78] Hathaliya J.J., Tanwar S., Tyagi S., Kumar N. 'Securing electronics healthcare records in healthcare 4.0 : a biometric-based approach'. *Computers & Electrical Engineering*. 2019;**76**(4):398–410.

[79] Hathaliya J.J., Tanwar S., Evans R., Sudeep T., Richard E. 'Securing electronic healthcare records: a mobile-based biometric authentication approach'. *Journal of Information Security and Applications*. 2020;**53**(3):102528.

[80]   Jigna J., Hathaliya., Sudeep T. 'An exhaustive survey on security and privacy issues in healthcare 4.0'. *Computer Communications*. 2020;**153**:311–35.

[81]   Desai K., Sreekantha. S., Shetty., Nithin K. *Fog computing application for biometric-based secure access to healthcare data, pages 355-383, fog computing for healthcare 4.0 environments technical, societal, and future implications*. Available from https://www.springer.com/gp/book/9783030461966 [Accessed 16 Oct 2020].

[82]   Ehnfors M., Florin J., Ehrenberg A. 'Applicability of the international classification of nursing practice (ICNP) in the areas of nutrition and skin care'. *International Journal of Nursing Terminologies and Classifications*. 2003;**14**(1):5–18.

[83]   Kovner C., Schuchman L., Mallard C. 'The application of pen-based computer technology to home health care'. *Computers in Nursing*. 1997;**15**(5):237–44.

Chapter 16

Detection of COVID-19 and its symptoms using chest X-rays for healthcare

Jayendra Kumar[1], Arvind R. Yadav[2], Anumeha[3], Shivam Kumar[1], and Anukul Gaurav[1]

In this chapter, an application of computer vision and deep learning approach for detecting an outbreak of the influenza virus 2019-nCov caused by the novel coronavirus has been discussed. The deadly and fatal virus that originated in November 2019 has been adversely felt worldwide and declared as a pandemic by the World Health Organization (WHO). COVID-19 is increasing rapidly across the world, and as of November 12, 2020, India has reported more than 86.8 lakh cases, and around the globe, the number has crossed 524 lakh cases in the absence of any effective vaccine for it. Due to the limited number of rapid test kits and the Indian Council of Medical Research (ICMR) labs, more and more people are getting infected by COVID-19 with each passing day. Therefore, the chest X-ray modality has been investigated to detect COVID-19 infected person(s) and understand its impact on a human chest and respiratory system. Further, the convolutional neural network (CNN), a deep learning technique has been used to comprehend the correlation of coronavirus on the human respiratory system using the chest X-ray data of patients. The proposed model has reported a COVID-19 detection accuracy of 99.59% with attention and 99.92% without attention.

16.1 Introduction

Necessity is the mother of inventions, a saying we have all heard since our school days but never realized on a global scale. No one could believe that the beginning of this decade will show us the weakness and imperfections of humanity to prepare itself for uncertainties and the challenges. This present decade marked the beginning of one of the most challenging times for humanity leading to an unprecedented loss

[1]Department of Electronics and Communication Engineering, NIT Jamshedpur, India
[2]Department of Electronics and Communication Engineering, Parul Institute of Engineering & Technology, Parul University, India
[3]School of Engineering and Technology, Netaji Subhas University, India

of lives and livelihood. The entire world was brought to a standstill, and the public economy crashed. Everyone was forced to stay within their corridors due to an invisible enemy, a virus, Coronavirus. In December 2019, the first cases of the disease were reported from Wuhan in China's Hubei province. The cases started to multiply without information of the disease, its symptoms, and causes. On the initial screening, the Chinese health system and government concluded that the disease had been caused due to a Novel Coronavirus, a series of Coronaviruses that has long been known to affect animals. It was believed that the source of this virus was bats and the virus spread because of the seafood market in Wuhan [1, 2]. The spread of this virus was exponential and new for humanity, and there is no vaccine for it till today. The virus and COVID-19 disease quickly spread from China to all parts of the globe, and now, confirmed positive cases had been found in over 215 countries all around the globe with USA and Europe the most affected places due to the virus. The situation reminds me of a chat room conversation on a global platform, Ted Talks, in 2015, where Mr. Bill Gates, co-founder of Microsoft, mentioned that the world is monotonously moving in the direction of exploration and exploitation and is not prepared for the next outbreak which could be more challenging than Ebola. The biggest challenge for this outbreak is the lack of vaccines, information, and kits that the healthcare system is facing. We are in a war-like situation in front of an invisible enemy. COVID-19 has already been declared a pandemic by the WHO in early 2020, and all the governments have issued certain precautionary measures and advisories. More than 475.68 lakh COVID-19-positive cases have already been confirmed, with more than 12.14 lakh deaths as of March 11, 2020 [3]. USA is the most severely affected by this pandemic with over 95.79 lakh positive cases and 2.37 lakh deaths, with the global economy shrinking by around 3 percent, the steepest since 1930. Figure 16.1 illustrates (a) Country-wise case distribution, (b) Cumulative number of cases by the number of days since 10 000 cases, (c) Cumulative numbers of cases by the number of days since 100 deaths, and (d) Daily new cases.

The exponential increase of COVID-19 cases is the biggest challenge for the government and health workers. The lack of testing kits, personal protective equipment (PPE) kits, testing time, and lack of knowing the systems are some of the major challenges that cannot be neglected. Hence, this work is based on integrating medical sciences, artificial intelligence (AI), and deep learning. Even in India, various developments and technologies are being employed to combat or further strengthen ourselves in this fight against COVID-19. Recently in China, an AI-based helmet was designed to detect the body temperature of human beings from a distance of 5 meters. The use of chest X-ray images in the detection of COVID-19 is already being used in underdeveloped nations like Turkey as it is a cheaper form of detection. The situation in India has also become uncontrollable with the relaxation in lockdown norms, and the numbers of cases has crossed over 83.10 lakhs till March 11, 2020.

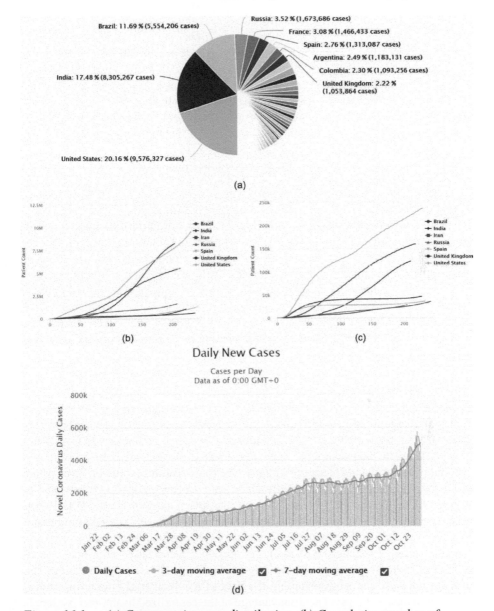

Figure 16.1   (a) Country-wise case distribution, (b) Cumulative number of
cases, by number of days since 10 000 cases, (c) Cumulative
numbers of cases, by number of days since 100 deaths, and
(d) Daily new cases [3].

Table 16.1   Cost of current COVID-19 testing kits in India

Sr. No.	Cost in INR	Description
1	2 000–3 000	Cost of these new testing kits depending on their availability and supply.
2	4 500	Cap put by the government for COVID-19 test, under the existing PCR test in private labs.
3	1 500	For a screening test for suspect cases and an additional Rs. 3 000 as confirmation test charges.

16.1.1   Motivation

Since the COVID-19 outbreak in India (March 2020), one of the difficulties has been an accurate diagnosis of COVID-19-affected people. Though the testing kits were made available by ICMR, the diagnosis cost was not affordable by a large mass of the population in India. The cost of current COVID-19 testing kits in India is listed in Table 16.1. Due to the nationwide lockdown for almost the entire two months, thousands of daily wage workers lost their bread and butter. With the aim of effective diagnosis, the authors have employed the chest X-ray modality, the cheapest one among the available modalities, and deep learning technique for accurate detection of COVID-19.

16.1.2   Importance of blockchain in 5G and COVID-19

In the health-care industry, with smart devices, sensors, and the Internet of Things (IoT), a huge amount of multi-modal and heterogeneous data are generated every day [4]. Working with big data (BD) requires a specific methodology to handle and process the data. Fog computing has been adopted in Healthcare 4.0 to store and compute patient data [5]. Security of the electronic health records [6] is of prime importance to keep the trust between health-care professionals and patients and to negate the misuse of the patient's data by the miscreants. In the COVID-19 situation, one of the prime concerns of the health-care industry has been minimum human intervention. Therefore, a blockchain-envisioned software multi-swarming unmanned aerial vehicles (UAV) communication scheme based on a 6G network with intelligent connectivity was proposed in 2020 [7]. Blockchain technology can also be used for efficiently handling the data of the Industrial Internet of Things (IIoT) in Industry 4.0 [8]. The disadvantage of the centralized health-care system is that it is unable to provide data immutability, transparency, traceability, privacy, and information security features helpful to ascertain COVID-19-associated frauds such as medical supplies, vaccination certification, and antibody testing [9].

Blockchain presents a distributed, decentralized, and immutable account of transactions that can be warehoused on a distributed network of nodes over geographically spread places [10]. Blockchain is a highly secure and robust technology and can assist in fighting COVID-19 effectively. 5G technology offers interconnectivity of heterogeneous devices and machines with enhanced network capacity, superior system throughput, and high quality of service. Being a heterogeneous network, security is one of the challenging tasks of the 5G network [6, 8, 11]. The excellent security aspects of blockchain technology provide a solution to the concerns of the 5G network. As the numbers of COVID-19 cases increase day by day, the chest X-ray data generated will be humongous. Maintaining patient data privacy and security is a challenging task in which blockchain technology plays an exceptional role. In this work, the authors have just focused on recognizing the COVID-19 patients, but the next step would be introducing blockchain technology for providing robust solutions in the health-care system [7].

16.1.3   Research contributions

The key contributions of this chapter are as follows:

1. Highlighting the impact of COVID-19 pandemic across the globe.
2. Providing brief information about the tools and techniques useful for carrying out research work in detecting COVID-19 by using a data science approach.
3. Exploring and enhancing the CNN-based deep learning approach to detect COVID-19 virus disease using the chest X-ray modality.
4. Providing a background of the blockchain platform, its components, advantages and disadvantages, and highlighting the open issues and challenges in using blockchain technology for applications in 5G networks and services and COVID-19.

16.1.4   Organization of the chapter

The remaining sections of the manuscript are structured as follows: Section 16.2 gives objectives, and the relevant literature review work is presented in Section 16.3. Section 16.4 outlines the theoretical background. The experimental analysis is discussed in Section 16.5. Section 16.6 outlines the results and discussion, followed by a case study on blockchain technology and open research challenges in Section 16.7. Research opportunities and open issues are presented in Section 16.8, followed by the conclusion given in Section 16.9.

16.2   Objective

The practice of integrating deep learning and AI into medical sciences is of the most recent and significant advancements of technology. Deep learning and computer vision have shown tremendous progress in various medical practices like cancer detection, skin problems, and blood pressure problems. Even in this time of COVID-19 crisis, various research institutions, technological colleges, and IT companies have worked significantly toward progress in the fight against corona. They have had successful progress in some of the fields. Thus, the idea to use chest X-rays for COVID-19 detection came to the minds of various researchers owing to its cheap and straightforward procedure [12]. COVID-19 is a new disease with very little information and non-availability of a vaccine. The only preventive measures taken are physical/social distancing, washing and cleaning of hands, use of sanitizers, nationwide lockdowns, and setting up of a large number of services. There has been a lot of confusion about the symptoms of the virus. This is a significant reason why the virus is spreading at such an alarming and exponential rate since we have not been able to filter out the patients suffering from the COVID-19 disease or whether we are at a higher chance of being affected. If we can make ourselves reach such a position where we can conduct many tests, we can prepare ourselves better.

India ranks second in the list of the world's most populous countries with a population of over 130 crores with a very high variation in lifestyles and living standards of the citizens. To cope with this pandemic, our medical system which ranks over 100 on a global scale is not prepared enough if the situation goes way beyond control, as it happened with countries like Italy and Spain. The traditional methodology of using testing kits that are both expensive and less in number is not feasible if we have to increase our testing rate significantly. We need to use automated detection systems to reduce the burden on our health-care system and on the government. The production line has moved backwards owing to stricter lockdown laws, and we had to rely heavily on Chinese kits, which have been under scrutiny for being false. Thus, in this environment of limited resources, the use of chest X-rays for COVID-19 detection can be a major progress if shown to have the required results. This shall enhance the testing rate for human beings by making the tests affordable, faster, and at various locations. We have a minimal number of ICMR-verified hospitals and laboratories in India, which forces the citizens to form long queues to get tested. Another boost will be that the less probable and asymptotic patients can be tested using this mechanism, reducing the burden on our stressed health-care workers. We can detect the patients at earlier stages using deep learning and image processing and increasing our testing rates. Those who are shown to have more chances of Coronavirus can be marked out, isolated, or put into quarantine. This will be beneficial in preventing the further spread of the virus.

16.3   Literature review

COVID-19 is known to occur from a novel coronavirus. Coronaviruses are a series of influenza viruses that have long been known to infect animals. However, no vaccines are available. This is the reason that doctors and health-care workers all around the globe have stressed the need for preventive measures rather than curing them.

16.3.1   Current methodology

The chest X-ray images of COVID-19 patients may help to diagnose or triage COVID-19 disease [13]. People showing the disease symptoms are currently tested at ICMR-certified hospitals, and their samples are tested using real-time reverse transcription polymerase chain reaction (RT-PCR) [14]. This diagnostic tool is currently the most preferred and accurate methodology. The symptoms of the COVID-19

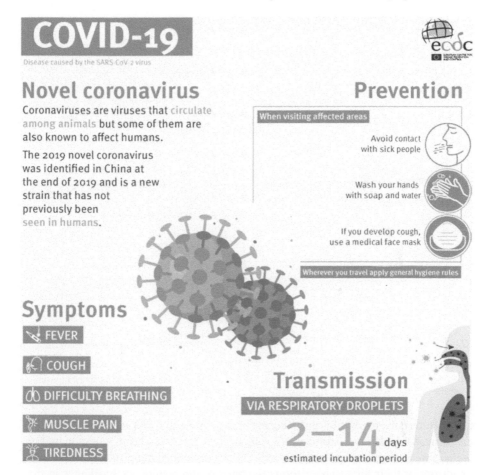

Figure 16.2   Symptoms and precautionary measures for COVID-19 [15]

disease include fever, cough, running nose, chills, breathing problems, pain in the body, loss of taste, and other respiratory blockages, as illustrated in Figure 16.2 [15].

Different nations have established different testing mechanisms and procedures for the battle against this global outbreak. Figure 16.3 [16] depicts the procedure of the current methodology of testing. Their health-care system has adopted those procedures after the analysis of their testing capabilities, demographics of their population, stages of the outbreak they are in, and various other resources available. However, there are molecular RT-PCR and serological treatment methods that are mostly being followed. These two are a different testing mechanism that operates at the different history of patients. It has been found that the novel coronavirus is different from the previous SARS and MERS viruses of the same family that wreaked havoc in the past decade. This new normal coronavirus is a spherical-shaped microorganism that is high in protein. Their proteins are studied through the spine-like protruded structures in its nuclei, as reported by Dr. Jason's laboratory

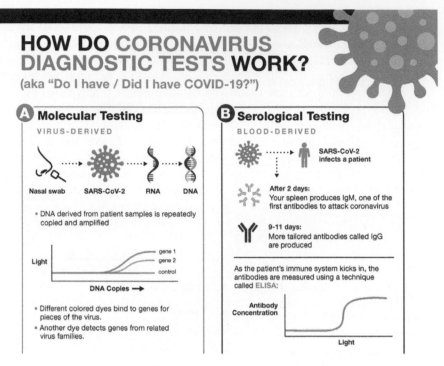

Figure 16.3   *Procedure of the current methodology of testing [16]*

at the University of Austin and Vaccine Research Centre at Texas. It consists of long stretches and single-stranded RNA molecules. It has very high mutation ability because its genes can penetrate the cells of human beings and produce more similar viruses of their kind, which forms the basis of the respiratory blockages in the patients and further contributes towards spreading and transmission to other human beings. To trace the presence of this virus, the PCR and serological or antibody tests investigate the presence of these proteins in the human body.

The molecular RT-PCR test is for the patients showing or having the possibility of being infected due to being in transmission range or contact with the other infected patients. During the initial screening, these patients may not show the antibodies in the blood as the virus may not have reached the blood circulation of the body; hence, samples of nasal swabs and throat swabs are collected for testing the serological tests. While the person who is already showing the symptoms of the disease or has been previously diagnosed with the same undergoes the serological antibody test as the bodies' immune system may have generated the antibodies to combat the normal coronavirus. In this test, the blood samples of the patients are collected and tested for the presence of these RNA proteins. The antibody or serological testing is more time-saving and is also known to be rapid testing kits. However, these tests are currently being conducted at fewer ICMR-certified hospitals and laboratories in India. In India, we have only 175 such ICMR-approved government testing facilities for over 1.3 billion people, and most of them are located in big cities of the states. These tests are further sent to the National Institute of Virology, Pune, for confirmation. Thus, although these testing methods are more reliable and accurate in their results, these traditional testing methods may not be sufficient to win the battle between humanity and COVID-19 successfully. While the testing is being carried out, various governments have issued various advisories and preventive measures for their citizens. The preventive measures include social distancing, lockdowns, self-isolation, quarantine, avoiding unnecessary travel, wearing face masks, and washing hands and frequently used clothes. They may help slow the transmission rate from one patient to another, but cannot give any conclusive solutions. As signified by the WHO, all these precautionary approaches of governments, organizations and the changed lifestyle of human beings are insufficient to do away with the normal coronavirus completely. WHO has given the mantra of test, test, test as the only true solution for this war while the doctors and the researchers are inventing the vaccines and other curing facilities.

The testing rate of COVID-19 in India cannot be significantly increased by following the traditional testing procedure of antigen analysis. Also, there are a very high number of asymptomatic patients suffering from the coronavirus. Thus to conduct the tests on an even larger scale, especially in the villages at a reasonable cost and less time, COVID-19 detection using chest X-ray analysis could be an optimum solution. This detection method can be a big boost for the health-care system. It will increase the testing centers, reduce queues in the hospitals, and make the tests more affordable. The result can also be generated in a few minutes without any human contact between the patients and the health workers. It will also allow us to test those who are currently not showing any virus symptoms, and contact tracking could be increased.

16.3.2   Related work

Coronaviruses is a new type of virus that affects the respiratory system of human beings, just like the influenza A and influenza B viruses. The way in which the virus affects an individual draws the attention of medical researchers to implant similar technologies-affiliated using influenza and pneumonia.

Various research scientists and technological universities decided to explore the possibility of radiography on COVID-19. The various Chinese and Japanese scientists analyzed the chest X-rays of infected patients and came to several conclusions. Yoon *et al.* [17], Chinese experts, found single nodular opacities in the lower lung region. These irregularities are used extensively in the analysis of X-rays. Fu *et al.* [18] have proposed using the ResNet-50 model for the classification of computed tomography (CT) scans into five categories: COVID-19, non-COVID-19, normal, pulmonary tuberculosis, and bacterial pneumonia. Jaiswal *et al.* [19] proposed COVIDPEN (a transfer learning on pruned EfficientNet-B0-based model for COVID-19) for the detection of COVID-19 cases. The effectiveness of the proposed model had demonstrated its efficacy on two systematic datasets of chest radiographs and CT scans and is on par and confers clinically explicable instances. Ozturk *et al.* [20]

proposed the use of deep neural networks for automated detection of COVID-19 by X-ray images. They had used the DarkNet model, which produced a classification accuracy of 98.08% for binary classes and 87.02% for multi-class cases. Using the ResNet50 model has produced an accuracy of 98% COVID-19 detection accuracy using chest X-ray images [21].

Sethy *et al.* [22] applied a support vector machine (SVM) model to the radiographs of the patients, and the prediction was found to be 80% correct in their results. This research formed the basis of analyzing various human organs and identifying whether they correlate with the COVID-19 disease. Their study showed various distinguishing features used in the models to classify and separate normal human beings and those suffering from the COVID-19 disease. Kaggle [12], the world's biggest data science and machine learning community, collaborated with WHO, governments of various countries and health departments like the US Centers for Disease Control (CDC), and private data acquiring companies like Cohen JP and collected a large set of datasets for the coronavirus outbreak including the chest X-rays of the testing persons. This brought a significant number of research teams to try to build an automated testing and diagnosis tool. If these models can yield satisfactory results, then they can be approved by the health-care departments.

16.4   Theoretical background

Various programming languages can build and train our model, like MATLAB®, R, Python, and so on. However, we chose Python as the coding software due to the list of libraries and in-built functions embedded into its systems. We have used the dataset from Kaggle and preferred implementation using the CNN algorithm.

16.4.1   Technologies used

16.4.1.1   Python

This work has been coded using Python, a high-level programming language that is a general-purpose interpreter-based language. The code in Python software is straightforward and easy to code and performs logic operations. It follows an object-oriented approach that aims to break the overall functioning of the program into smaller blocks. It is a dynamically coded software that supports the functionality of multiple paradigms of programming. There are various versions of Python, like python2 and python3. This work has been built using python3 and its libraries.

16.4.1.2   OpenCV

OpenCV stands for open-source computer vision library, one of the most commonly used libraries of the programming language in computer vision. This library and its functionality are mostly cross-platform and open source. It is accessible on the license and has been used by machine learning engineers and researchers for many applications. OpenCV is used for 2D and 3D feature toolkits, object detection and recognition face detection systems, stereopsis with vision, structure from motion drowsiness detection system, motion understanding, and robotics. OpenCV became most prominent by its use in augmented reality and human–computer interaction. The OpenCV library performs the following operations owing to its inbuilt statistical machine learning libraries like decision tree making, SVM, deep learning, gradient boosting, and random forest algorithms. It runs on various platforms and operating systems like Windows, Linux, OpenBSD, Android, and Mac OS. An important functionality of OpenCV is that it is handy to work with GitHub so that various people can work simultaneously and the code can be easily documented.

16.4.1.3 Keras

Keras is a compelling python library that is an open-source neural-network-based algorithm. It is built over TensorFlow 2.0 and Microsoft cognitive toolkit, and other machine learning algorithms. It was designed for very fast experimentation with neural networks and deep learning applications on computer vision. It is an API that is designed to perform like the human brain and not machines. This application programming interface (API) is used in addition to TensorFlow to build various machine learning and deep learning models. It reduces a significant cognitive load, thereby increasing the speed of the execution of training of the model. Its clear and simple interface makes it more preferable in image processing over other similar tools. It makes the way for very fast prototyping, and the graph of layers for the models is assembled by it to provide an efficient learned model with better accuracy.

16.4.1.4 TensorFlow

TensorFlow is a Python library coded on Jupiter notebooks (text editor for Python) and runs directly. It is an open source software whose license is free to use. TensorFlow is widely used for deep learning applications, as illustrated in Figure 16.4. One can use it in the code for data flow and other machine learning applications. It is a compelling mathematical library that performs various mathematics and transformations

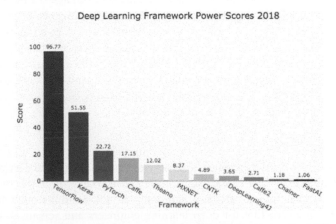

Figure 16.4   Power scores for different frameworks [23]

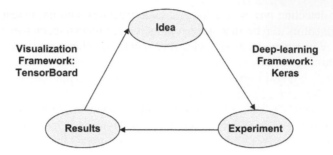

Figure 16.5   Flow chart between classes of TensorFlow and Keras

of image processing. It uses a vast range of data flow graphs and then assembles them to form a neural network model. In almost all the computer vision and image processing functionality, one needs to use the TensorFlow library for detection, classification, prediction, and processing needs. We have used TensorFlow 2.0 and its repositories uploaded on GitHub by the developers of TensorFlow and Python. Figure 16.5 shows the flow chart between the classes of TensorFlow and Keras.

16.4.1.5   Scikit-learn

Scikit-learn is a powerful Python library used for traditional machine learning algorithms to train the model using the given training data. It implements the various regression, classification, and clustering algorithms and estimates of predicted future outputs. It is included in a deep learning code because of its fast learning efficiency curve.

16.4.1.6   Scikit-image

Scikit-image is a similar library to scikit-learn. While scikit-learn is based more on the traditional machine learning functionalities, the scikit-image is a library containing the list of inbuilt algorithms for image processing. It is also an open source and free-to-use licensed library. It generally uses NumPy arrays as an input for image objects. It is widely used in every computer vision project and has a pre-included working interface with NumPy, SciPy, and matplotlib. It has various algorithms such as feature detection, filtering, transformational analysis, and segmentation. Various repositories of scikit-image are available on GitHub to be used as and when in any computer vision-trained deep learning projects.

16.4.1.7   Dlib

Dlib or davisking library is a general-purpose multi-platform library written in C++ language. However, it can be easily installed and worked within the Python code for facial and other image detection and analysis. Like various other libraries, it is also an open source tool for deep learning engineers and scientists. It contains inbuilt support and functionality for a list of networks like networking and threads.

It has high-handling power with graphs, data structures, and linear algebra. In our case, we have used dlib for machine learning, image processing, data extracting, and optimization purposes. Its repositories are available on github.com/davisking/dlib.

16.4.1.8   MXNet

MXNet is an open source Python library designed exclusively for deep learning and computer vision. It has a powerful framework specially designed to train the system on deep learning neural networks. It is widely used for its fast execution speed in training the model.

16.4.1.9   imutils

imutils is a powerful library included in Python to perform basic image processing operations. It contains various inbuilt functions relating to image processing applications like a translation of the image, rotation of the image, restructuring and resizing the image, performing scaling operations, and skeletonization. It also comes in handy with the OpenCV library in displaying the Matplotlib images quickly. It converts the input images feature set into a useful data source by filtering images, sorting the contours, and removing the edges of the image.

16.4.1.10   Kaggle

Kaggle is a subsidiary company owned by Google, which is branded to be the world's largest data engineer community for data sciences and analysis. It has the highest number of trained and aspiring data scientists and machine learning professions. It is the house of the world's most significant number of datasets. It acts as a platform to construct and publish various works on various datasets. The works are shared with millions of other practitioners and can build better and more efficient models by continuing the research done before. Thus, it acts as a cloud-based learning class form for machine learning, deep learning, computer vision, and AI. The datasets used have been collected from Kaggle. The dataset used is the Kaggle chest X-ray dataset and COVID-19 chest X-ray dataset.

16.4.1.11   GitHub

GitHub is a global USA-based platform that acts as a hosting platform for various software and programming development using Git. It is a company owned by Microsoft and is most widely used in all team projects because every update or modification in any development can be easily shared and communicated. Above all, once the final project is ready, it can be easily formed and used by everyone who wants to make use of it. We have also hoisted our work on GitHub for further development and modifications if anyone wants. Git has been extensively used to install various repositories of Python libraries. Flask is a web hosting tool integrated with Python. It has the inbuilt capability to convert a deep learning code in Python to a web app and upload it on Kaggle.

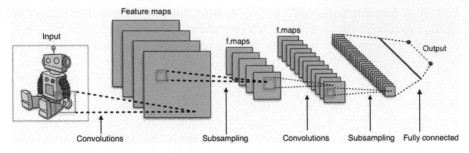

Figure 16.6   Working of convolutional neural networks [25]

16.4.1.12   Convolutional neural networks

The CNNs [24] are an important class of neural networks in deep learning and AI. They are mostly used in visual imagination and image analysis in computer vision-related projects. They have much-shared weight architecture which has translation invariance attributes. They are generally also called space-invariant artificial neural networks (ANNs). This algorithm works to duplicate the human brain. They work on various layers of the graph, and then these layers are assembled to yield a trained model. Various regularization techniques are used to prevent the overfitting of data. CNNs have an advantage over other ANNs because they require very little and straightforward pre-processing for different image classification algorithms. This algorithm is convolutional because of the series of convolutional operations of mathematics that the entire network employs. It is a linear operation and there is no use of matrix multiplication. Various convolutional layers in CNN form the core block of this algorithm. They are widely used for image recognition and object detection purposes. The working principle of CNN is shown in Figure 16.6.

16.4.1.13   Conceptual model

Integrating deep learning and AI with medical sciences is the latest advancement in health and technology. This is achieved by collecting a large set of information and organizing it into datasets with rows and columns or images and outputs. The dataset is constructed such that we have a set of input or independent variables and specific output or dependent variables. The variables or the columns in the datasets can be numerical, alphabetical, or an image. In this work, we have used datasets integrated from three different sources. The dataset which is available on a public platform has been used. It was compiled by Kaggle [12], Cohen JP [26], and Andrian Xu [27]. The dataset has four different sets of chest X-ray images classified into their respective categories.

1.   Normal patients (79 images)
2.   COVID-19-infected patients (69 images)
3.   Pneumonia caused due to bacteria (79 images)
4.   Pneumonia caused due to virus (79 images).

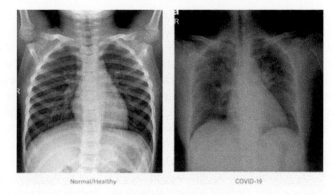

Figure 16.7   Selected input images

For illustration purposes, the normal/healthy and COVID-19 input images are shown in Figure 16.7. The dataset needs to be filtered and pre-processed. Various deep learning AI models are available to train the dataset, but we have used ANNs. Within the ANN, we selected k-nearest neighbor (KNN), CNN, and eXtreme Gradient (XG) boosting [28]. However, we have used CNN [29] on our datasets and built a real-time feature detection system. As we know, a CNN consists of various layers. Similarly, we have chosen to make 19 layers in our model and assembled them to create a model, as shown in Table 16.2. These layers are time-pooling layers.

Table 16.2   Linearizing of the model with each layer

Number of Layer	Layer type	Output shape	Number of trainable parameters
1	Conv2d	[8,256,256]	216
2	Conv2d	[16,128,128]	1 152
3	Conv2d	[32,64,64]	4 608
4	Conv2d	[16,66,66]	512
5	Conv2d	[32,66,66]	4 608
6	Conv2d	[64,33,33]	18 432
7	Conv2d	[32,35,35]	2 048
8	Conv2d	[64,35,35]	18 432
9	Conv2d	[128,17,17]	73 728
10	Conv2d	[64,19,19]	8 192
11	Conv2d	[128,19,19]	73 728
12	Conv2d	[256,9,9]	294 912
13	Conv2d	[128,11,11]	32 768
14	Conv2d	[256,11,11]	294 912
15	Conv2d	[128,13,13]	256
16	Conv2d	[256,13,13]	294 912
17	Conv2d	[2,13,13]	4 608
18	Conv2d	[338]	0
19	Conv2d	[2]	678

With each layer, certain features from the images are extracted and re-scaled as per the requirements, and the model is trained with each pooling layer. The number of convolutional layers is chosen, keeping in mind that the model is sufficiently trained to analyze the results. At the same time, care has been taken not to outfit the data on our training data. As convolution is a linear mathematical operator, the process is relatively more straightforward and faster in execution. With each layer, a convolution operation is performed, and we use a rectifier unit to linearize the output. For the visualization of the images, certain modifications in the image are carried through hard and soft attention. While the images are cropped to remove the unnecessary pixels in hard attention, we smoothen the images. After the algorithm is trained, the proposed CNN architecture model would be tested using precision, accuracy, specificity, and sensitivity. Only if a certain threshold limit is passed we can conclude that the model has effectively predicted the COVID-19 disease. The following parameters would be calculated in percentage, and we will be building the algorithm and keep training the layers till these parameters exceed the threshold value of 0.85. After the execution of the code, the model would be ready to be used and applied to various datasets. Once the model is trained and tested, the final objective is to host it over the server as a web app. This is where we use Flask API, whose documentation and functionality come in handy within Python. Flask is a web framework that does not possess any database management system, so we will have to integrate it with Python. The integration of Python and Flask is illustrated in Figure 16.8.

16.5   Experimental analysis

The deep learning and CNN codes are written in Python. In any model building, the first step is to import the dataset from various sources and include them within the source code so that various data extraction, data mining, pre-processing, model building, and output prediction can be done.

16.5.1   Importing the dataset

In our code, we have made use of datasets from two different sources. The first one is the Kaggle chest X-ray dataset, extracted from the official website of Kaggle, and the second one is the COVID-19 chest X-ray dataset compiled by Cohen JP [26], University of Montreal, Canada. The dataset [12] has 306 input chest X-ray images of human beings divided into four different categories.

1. Normal/healthy person
2. COVID-19-tested positive
3. Pneumonia due to virus
4. Pneumonia due to bacteria.

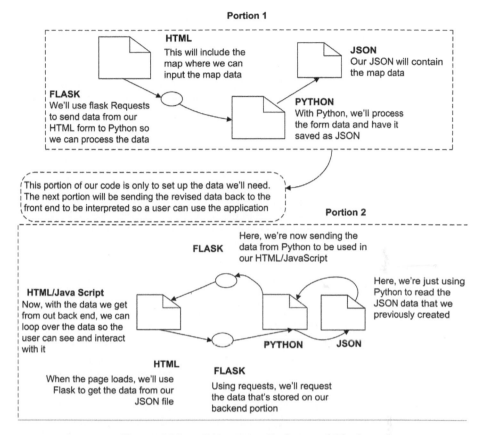

Figure 16.8   Integrating Python and Flask

16.5.2   Pre-processing of the data

After completing the first step, that is the extraction of the dataset from the various sources in our source code, we need to pre-process the data. The steps involved in pre-processing are depicted in Figure 16.9.

Pre-processing means to filter the unnecessary contents from the data and make it more meaningful and appropriate for our model building. Data pre-processing involves a specific list of operations and processes carried out to prepare the data for model building. There are various constraints in our dataset that force pre-processing; otherwise, the accuracy of the model would be severely compromised. The biggest constraint in our dataset is a low sample size. This will cause overfitting or underfitting of the data if we apply the CNN directly on this dataset. Some of the other data corruptions in the dataset could be the presence of the unoptimized weights of the images that can assign certain priorities within the model, which will reduce the efficiency of the model. One significant outlier in the image datasets is the presence of background noise in the input variables. The background noise refers to the unwanted or unnecessary pixels present in the image not being studied. There are

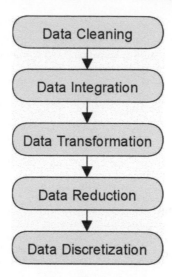

Figure 16.9   Steps involved in pre-processing

certain methods and operations executed to remove these distractions. To remove overfitting of the data due to fewer input data sources, we have augmented the data. Data augmentation is a deep learning process that is implied to expand the dataset by creating a large number of similar datasets on their own based on the fewer number of input data sources. This is done to prevent the overfitting of the data and to have a certain number of input training data for our model building. The Keras library in Python is designed to support the process of data augmentation due to the presence of a special class called ImageDataGenerator [30, 31] inbuilt within them. Data segmentation is done to filter out the unnecessary contents from the image. In this process, the input image is segmented or divided into a large set of pixels, selecting the pixels with important information and ignoring the unwanted feature set. Data segmentation is accompanied by data feature extraction. We classify the important features based on which we have to distinguish the input sources with feature extraction. Python libraries are considered to be one of the most powerful among other software. The Keras library also contains a certain number of classes for various data transformations, which magnifies the usefulness of the dataset. These include re-scaling, translating, flipping, zoom, and shear-based transformations. In the process of re-scaling, we change the size of the image to match the standard sizes. Translating the image leads to the geometrical transformation of the image. In zooming and shearing transformation, we change the contrast and viewing size of the image. The Keras library is not the only library being used to pre-process the data; we have used the TensorFlow library in Python to perform various transformations and randomizations. The brightness and contrast of the image are adjusted using TensorFlow by the brightness and contrast randomization process. Hue randomization is done to adjust the image colour. Finally, the transfer learning is done to nullify the problems of overfitting the data by normalizing the weights of the image. After all these operations, our dataset is converted to its best possible form with meaningful information. Different convolutional algorithms can be applied to it which can be trained using training datasets. After the model is trained, we can test the efficiency of the model on test datasets.

16.5.3   Splitting the training and test data

After the pre-processing of the data, we need to split the data source into two different categories; one is the training dataset while the other is the test dataset. As we have four classes of input images, namely, the human beings that are normal and not suffering from any disease; the COVID-19-tested positive patients, and the patients suffering from pneumonia whether due to bacteria or virus. All these four data categories are split into training and test datasets. The datasets are divided as follows.

1.   Healthy/normal person: 70 training images, 9 test images
2.   COVID-19 positive: 60 training images, 9 test images
3.   Pneumonia due to bacteria: 70 training images, 9 test images
4.   Pneumonia due to virus: 70 training images, 9 test images.

16.5.4   Architecture of CNN

CNN is a variant of neural networks having various architectural models like the VGG16 [32] model, ResNet-50 [33], DarkNet [20, 34], ImageNet [35], and so on. The CNN is a supervised learning method that takes input images, extracts features, and performs gradient boosting to train the model. The VGG16 architecture model has been used to fully automate the model building using callbacks. It operates in two blocks. The first block is also called AlexNet [32], and it is the core of the entire architecture of this algorithm. It works to extract the features from the input images and their modified versions with every passing convolutional layer. With each feature extraction from the convolutional layer, the model becomes more and more learned.

To achieve this extraction, the convolution operation matches the extracted input features with the same feature of templates, and necessary filtering is done within it. The feature maps are compared with the convolutional maps and the learning of the model occurs. To speed up the execution of the process, certain normalized and activation functions are applied in linear combination with the kernel. The process has been changed a few times again so that the model can learn the entire parameters of the training data. The second block of the architecture is not a unique or typical characteristic of the CNN model. Rather, it is attributed to the neural networks in deep learning itself. This is the block from where the internal mathematics and predictions start taking place. In the previous block, feature extraction was carried out. With this feature extraction and its combination with the activation function, a new vector of outputs is formed based on the probability calculations. The sum of the probabilities is unity, and these probabilities form the basis of classification

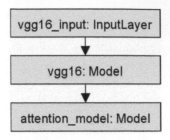

Figure 16.10   Final model architecture

predictions. The output is a binary class, and the logistic function optimizes the cross-entropy.

The two blocks of the convolutional network are built over four significant layers. They are the convolutional, pooling, correction, and connected layers. As the name suggests, the convolution layer performs the convolution operation on the input images with kernels and activation function, which is provided to increase the execution speed of the model building. Figure 16.10 illustrates the final model architecture, and the attention model architecture is depicted in Figure 16.11.

In this layer, feature extraction and normalizing of the weights take place due to the gradient descent. The pooling layer is the next layer of operation in which image scaling, segmentation, and transformation operations occur. In this layer, the input images are segmented into a large number of smaller cells used for feature mapping with better results. The segmentation of the image reduces the parameters, thereby simplifying and speeding up the model-building process. The correction layer consists of the rectifier linear unit, which is done to linearize the operation, which was non-linearized due to the activation functions.

This layer converts the negative values to zero, which forms the basis of mathematical calculations. Finally, there is a fully connected layer; this layer concatenates a column into the output vector, which is the probability of the occurrence of the classifiers and normalizing it with their weights and facilitates the process of back propagation.

16.5.5   Callbacks

Once the building of the model is done and the CNN algorithm starts, it is essential to adjust the stopping time of the model's training. Care must be taken of both the factors. The model should not stop training even before a certain level of accuracy is achieved, and at the same time, the model should not be allowed to keep operating as this will lead to overfitting of the data. The process of callbacks does this. Callbacks contain a set of inbuilt functions which takes care of specific parameters such as accuracy, learning rate, and other statistical constraints. There are certain classes in Keras library like ModelCheckpoint [36] and EarlyStopping [36], in which there are specific matrices like accuracy and learning rate which adjust the training of the model.

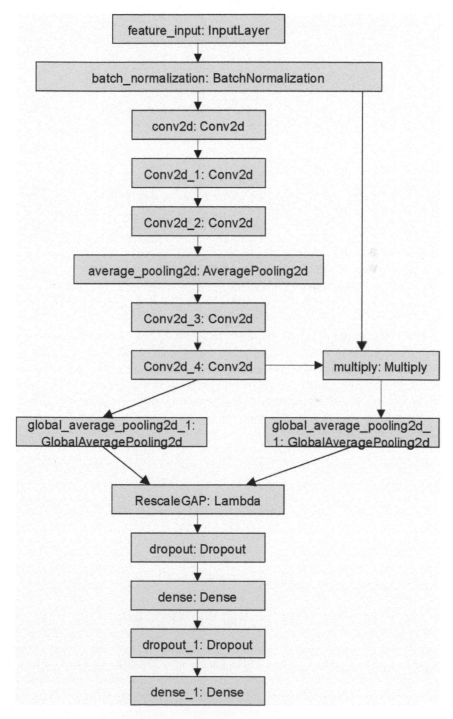

Figure 16.11   Attention model architecture

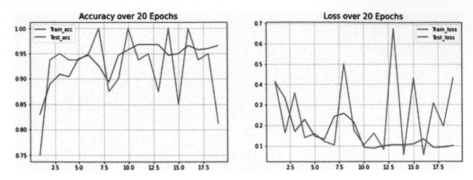

Figure 16.12   Accuracy and loss function in binary case

16.5.6   Fitting model

After the architecture is constructed, the next step in the model building is the fitting of the model. After fitting the model, our CNN model is ready to predict the future classification and process the results.

16.5.7   Graphical plot of accuracy and loss function

After the fitting of data, it is important to know the accuracy and loss function of the entire model before concluding the model's effectiveness. The three graphs shown in Figures 16.12–16.14 are the graphical representations of the gradual increase in inaccuracy of the model during the overall model building. The first graph is for the binary case where the model predicts whether the person is healthy or not. The other graphs are after taking into consideration the classification of patients with pneumonia and COVID-19.

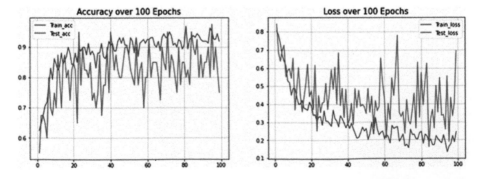

Figure 16.13   Accuracy and loss function in three-class case

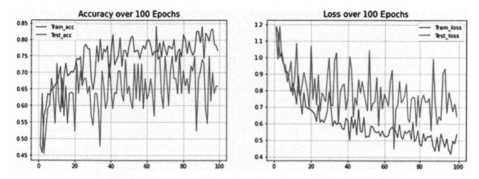

Figure 16.14   Accuracy and loss function in four-class case

16.6   Results and discussion

The accuracy and loss function plot with the classifiers gave a positive quantitative result that the model's accuracy has kept increasing during model building. However, quantitative results cannot form the decisive outcome for a model. Thus, we have analyzed the quantitative measure of the three significant parameters in classification deep learning model. These three parameters are accuracy, sensitivity, and specificity. Sensitivity is the measure of the ability of the model to predict the category correctly; in this model, that category is COVID-19. Specificity is the efficiency with which the model can process the outer parameter, while accuracy is the measure with which both the categories are correctly measured. The performance matrix of the model is presented in Table 16.3.

The analysis of the F1 scores and three parameters clearly shows that validation test score of the model is over 85%, suggesting that the model is showing a positive correlation with the actual values. Now we have analyzed the model further for two different cases. In the first one, we classified COVID-19 and pneumonia patients together and tested the model and its ability to predict whether the person is healthy or not. The result of this classification is shown to have very accurate predictions.

Table 16.3   Performance matrices of the model

Folds			Performance		
			Metrics (%)		
	Sensitivity	Specificity	Precision	F1-Score	Accuracy
Fold-1	88.17	93.66	90.97	89.44	89.33
Fold-2	84.57	90.61	89.38	86.63	84.89
Fold-3	84.13	91.14	89.88	86.54	85.78
Fold-4	83.66	92.29	90.61	86.42	87.11
Fold-5	85.83	92.75	89.71	87.57	88.00
Average	85.35	92.18	89.96	87.37	87.02

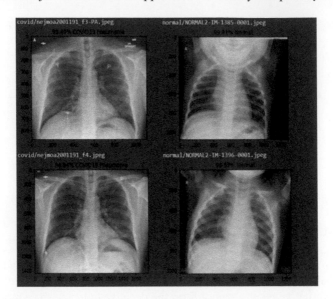

Figure 16.15   Accuracy in classifying healthy and ill patients

The correct prediction of a normal person with and without projections is over 95%. The infected patients can also be detected with an accuracy of over 85%, which can be seen in the given figure.

It can be concluded that the proposed model works sufficiently well in detecting and classifying whether the person is healthy or is suffering from any disease affecting the respiratory system. In the last phase, we have checked with all the classifiers and tried to predict the correctness with which the model classified the X-rays with pneumonia, COVID-19, and healthy persons.

The accuracy with which the model predicts and classifies the different categories is very striking and optimum. The model has an accuracy of over 85% with and without attention. COVID-19 has been classified correctly with over 99.59% with attention and 99.92% without attention. The accuracy in classifying healthy and ill patients is depicted in Figure 16.15, whereas Figure 16.16 illustrates accuracy in classifying the images as normal, COVID-19, or pneumonia. However, the accuracy would still be sufficient enough to separate or isolate patients based on its results. The model will have a positive outcome with other datasets. Thus, our model is trained well and is ready to predict the outcomes with high accuracy. The result obtained by the proposed model is compared with other similar approaches and is listed in Table 16.4. It is evident from Table 16.4 that the proposed model has produced better classification accuracy for detection of COVID-19 using chest X-ray images.

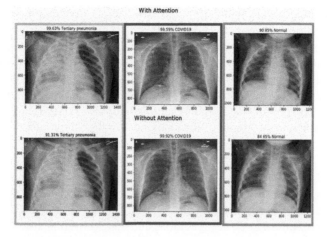

Figure 16.16   *Accuracy in classifying the images as normal, COVID-19, or pneumonia*

16.7   Blockchain for integration with 5G networks and handling COVID-19

Blockchain can be effectively deployed to monitor distribution of relief material, donation, supply chain management, track the spread of the COVID-19 virus, tracing of COVID-19 patients/clusters, vaccination planning, and so on, in a translucent manner without violating the norms of user data. Further, cases of the spread of the virus by use of traditional currency were also reported. The blockchain platform's security and transparency features support the need for digital payment/transaction and other online platforms. The key characteristics of blockchain are security, privacy, transparency, auditability, decentralization, persistence, and immutability, making it effectively address the challenges of 5G and COVID-19. Some of the challenges faced during the COVID-19 pandemic are as follows: social distancing, fake infodemic, continuation of vital governmental facilities, dissemination of funding and charity, proficient supply of medicines and health-care equipment, online

Table 16.4   *Comparison with other similar approaches*

Sr. No.	Method	Accuracy (%)
1	Resnet50 [37]	95.38
2	COVID-CAPS without pre-training [36]	95.70
3	Pre-trained COVID-CAPS [38]	98.30
4	ResNet50 with 5 and 10 folds cross validation [39]	97.28
5	VGG network [40]	98.52
6	Proposed model (with attention)	99.59
7	Proposed model (without attention)	99.92

education and exam [41], real-time data sharing, food distribution, migration of the workers, and transportation of necessary goods. The characteristics of blockchain that can help in taming the COVID-19 pandemic are as follows; decentralization, consensus mechanism, digital currency and minting, distributed ledgers, enhanced security, tamper-proof database and immutability, smart contracts. The advantages of blockchain are decentralization, provenances, non-repudiation, anonymity, immutability, availability, auditability, automation, lower operating cost, and confidentiality. Following are some of the challenges in the integration of blockchain in existing 5G networks [6]:

- **Lack of infrastructure:** Most of the existing prevalent networks that use 5G services, namely smart city, supply chain, and smart health are not having decentralized network architecture.
- **Standardization:** Lack of regulations and standardization also hamper the efficient integration of 5G and blockchain technology.

Blockchain offers enormous potential to handle the COVID-19 pandemic, however, following are the challenges [42] that need to be addressed for reaping the fruits of the blockchain platform:

- Legal dispute
- Privacy requirement
- Security issues
- Latency
- Throughput and scalability
- Resource utilization.

16.8 Research opportunities and open issues

Some of the open issues and challenges of blockchain technology are as follows [43]:

- Development of an efficient algorithm to handle the security of the private key,
- To handle the issue of 51% vulnerability,
- Issues in the blockchain network due to double spending,
- Prevention of privacy leakage in the transaction,
- To prevent the increase in criminal activities in the blockchain network,
- Securing the blockchain network from malicious users and attackers,
- Need of standardization protocols for interacting users with different network,
- High operational cost to run and maintain the blockchain network for reaping its advantage,
- High energy consumption, and
- Slow and cumbersome network.

16.9 Conclusion and future scope

COVID-19 has brought the entire world to a standstill, with all the major cities of the globe entering into a state of lockdown. Looking to the efforts of scientists, researchers, and doctors, it was initially believed that vaccination could be developed at the earliest. However, it has been realized that the fight is long and preventive measures and numerous testing are the only potential solutions to curb the spread of the virus. While different social distancing exercises are being followed, there is a need to increase the testing capabilities. The current mechanism of testing is costly, limited, and unaffordable for all. Thus, COVID-19 detection using chest X-ray images has been used to predict infection with COVID-19, and patients can be isolated on this basis. This will reduce further spread of the virus and make it more affordable for individuals. The centers for X-ray scans can be found in large numbers near homes, which will reduce long queues for testing at a limited number of ICMR-verified laboratories in the country. This will render the health workers less exposable to the patients, and the result of the test can also be procured in less than five minutes. Our proposed model has produced classification accuracy of 99.59% with attention and 99.92% without attention. Thus, a large number of X-ray images should be tested over it, and the accuracy of the model should be analyzed. And after the necessary advancements, the process can be employed in the health-care system for testing the patients. Taking the cue from the idea, several other organs could be scanned, like the throat, to be integrated with this model to have more exact results. This methodology of integrating medical sciences with deep learning and AI should be used on a large scale, much like China deploying an AI-based temperature sensing device from five meters in all public places. Countries with not so robust economies like Turkey have adopted this mechanism. Thus, this work can be made much more helpful by first testing it over a large scale of X-ray images of individuals whose data are not available on public platforms. The model can be instrumental in speeding any country's testing rate and capabilities at an affordable cost.

References

[1] Huang C., Wang Y., Li X., *et al.* 'Clinical features of patients infected with 2019 novel coronavirus in Wuhan, China'. *The Lancet.* 2020;**395**(10223):497–506.

[2] Wu Z., McGoogan J.M. 'Characteristics of and important lessons from the coronavirus disease 2019 (COVID-19) outbreak in china: summary of a report of 72 314 cases from the Chinese Center for Disease Control and Prevention'. *JAMA.* 2020;**323**(12):1239–42.

[3] *COVID-19 coronavirus pandemic* [online]. Available from https://www.worldometers.info/coronavirus/ [Accessed 19 Sep 2020].

[4] Tanwar S. *Fog Data Analytics for IoT Applications – Next Generation Process Model with State-of-the-Art Technologies, Studies in Big Data.* Springer International Publishing; 2020. pp. 1–550.

[5]   Tanwar S. *Fog Computing for Healthcare 4.0 Environments: Technical, Societal and Future Implications, Signals and Communication Technology.* Springer International Publishing; 2020. pp. 1–430.

[6]   Tanwar S., Tyagi S., Kumar N. 'Security and privacy of electronics healthcare records'. *The IET Book Series on e-Health Technologies, Institution of Engineering and Technology.* Stevenage: UK; 2019. pp. 1–450.

[7]   Gupta R., Kumari A., Tanwar S., Kumar N. 'Blockchain-envisioned softwarized multi-swarming UAVs to tackle COVID-19 situations'. *IEEE Network.* 2020:1–8.

[8]   Kumari A.T., Tyagi, S S., Kumar N. 'Blockchain-based massive data dissemination handling in IIoT environment'. *IEEE Networks.* 2020:1–8.

[9]   Ahmad R.W., Salah K., Jayaraman R., Yaqoob I., Ellahham S., Omar M. 'Blockchain and COVID-19 pandemic: applications and challenges'. *TechRxiv.* 2020:1–20.

[10] Nguyen D., Ding M., Pathirana P.N., Seneviratne A. 'Blockchain and AI-based solutions to combat coronavirus (COVID-19)- like epidemics: a survey'. *TechRxiv.* 2020.

[11] Nguyen D.C., Pathirana P.N., Ding M., Seneviratne A. 'Blockchain for 5G and beyond networks: a state of the art survey'. *Journal of Network and Computer Applications.* 2020;**166**(4):102693.

[12] *Kaggle-Chest X-ray and pneumonia andrei dataset* [online]. 2020. Available from https://www.kaggle.com/paultimothymooney/chest-xray-pneumonia/ [Accessed 5 Apr 2020].

[13] Sarkodie B.D., Osei-Poku K., Brakohiapa E. 'Diagnosing COVID-19 from chest X-ray in resource limited environment-case report'. *Medical Case Report.* 2020;**6**(2):1–3.

[14] Emery S.L., Erdman D.D., Bowen M.D., *et al.* 'Real-time reverse transcription-polymerase chain reaction assay for SARS-associated coronavirus'. *Emerging Infectious Diseases.* 2004;**10**(2):311–6.

[15] *Inforgraphics:CoVID-19* [online]. 2020. Available from https://www.ecdc.europa.eu/en/publications-data/infographic-covid-19 [Accessed 28 Mar 2020].

[16] *Inforgraphics: How do coronavirus diagnostic tests work?* [online]. 2020. Available from https://www.technologynetworks.com/diagnostics/infographics/how-do-coronavirus-diagnostic-tests-work-333798 [Accessed 15 May 2020].

[17] Yoon S.H., Lee K.H., Kim J.Y., *et al.* 'Chest radiographic and CT findings of the 2019 novel coronavirus disease (COVID-19): analysis of nine patients treated in Korea'. *Korean Journal of Radiology.* 2020;**21**(4):494–500.

[18] Fu M., Yi S.L., Zeng Y., *et al.* 'Deep learning-based recognizing COVID-19 and other common infectious diseases of the lung by chest CT scan images'. *MedRxiv : The Preprint Server for Health Sciences.* 2020.

[19] Jaiswal A.K., Tiwari P., Rathi V.K., Qian J., Pandey H.M., Albuquerque V.H.C. 'COVIDPEN: a novel COVID-19 detection model using chest X-rays and CT scans'. *MedRxiv : The Preprint Server for Health Sciences.* 2020:1–23.

[20] Ozturk T., Talo M., Yildirim E.A., Baloglu U.B., Yildirim O., Acharya U.R. 'Automated detection of COVID-19 cases using deep neural networks with X-ray images'. *Computers in Biology and Medicine*. 2020;**101**:1–11.

[21] Narin A., Kaya C., Pamuk Z. 'Automatic detection of coronavirus disease (COVID-19) using X-ray images and deep convolutional neural networks'. *arXiv preprint 2020; arXiv:2003.10849*:1–31.

[22] Sethy P.K., Behera S.K., Ratha P.K., Biswas P. 'Detection of coronavirus disease (COVID-19) based on deep features and support vector machine'. *International Journal of Mathematical, Engineering and Management Sciences*. 2020;**5**(4):643–51.

[23] Hale J. *Deep learning framework power scores 2018* [online]. 2020. Available from https://www.kdnuggets.com/2018/09/deep-learning-framework-power-scores-2018.html [Accessed 15 May 2020].

[24] Liao Y., Kodagoda S., Wang Y., Shi L., Liu Y. 'Understand scene categories by objects: a semantic regularized scene classifier using convolutional neural networks'. *Proceeding of IEEE international conference on robotics and automation (ICRA)*; Stockholm, Sweden, 16-21 May; 2016. pp. 2318–25.

[25] Dataflair team. *Convolutional neural networks tutorial – Learn how machines interpret images* [online]. 2020. Available from https://data-flair.training/blogs/convolutional-neural-networks-tutorial/ [Accessed 20 Sep 2020].

[26] Cohen J.P., Morrison P., Dao L. COVID-19 image data collection. arXiv preprint 2020; arXiv:2003.11597. 2021. Available from https://github.com/ieee8023/covid-chestxray-dataset.

[27] Xu A.Y. *Detecting COVID-19 induced pneumonia from chest X-rays with transfer learning: An implementation in tensorflow and keras* [online]. 2020. Available from https://towardsdatascience.com/detecting-covid-19-induced-pneumonia-from-chest-x-rays-with-transfer-learning-an- implementation-311484e6afc1 [Accessed 19 Sep 2020].

[28] Browniee J. *A gentle introduction to XGBoost for applied machine learning* [online]. 2016. Available from https://machinelearningmastery.com/gentle-introduction- xgboost-applied-machine-learning/ [Accessed 19 Sep 2020].

[29] Apostolopoulos I.D., Mpesiana T.A. 'Covid-19: automatic detection from X-ray images utilizing transfer learning with convolutional neural networks'. *Physical and Engineering Sciences in Medicine*. 2020;**4343**(2):635–40.

[30] Keras [online]. 2020. Available from https://keras.io/ [Accessed 08 Aug 2020].

[31] Shorten C., Khoshgoftaar T.M. 'A survey on image data augmentation for deep learning'. *Journal of big data*. 2019;**6**(6):1–48.

[32] Simonyan K., Zisserman A. 'Very deep convolutional networks for large-scale image recognition'. *arXiv preprint arXiv:1409.1556v6*. 2014:1–14.

[33] He K., Zhang X., Ren S., Sun J. 'Deep residual learning for image recognition'. *Proceedings of the conference on computer vision and pattern recognition*, Las Vegas, NV, June 2016; USA: IEEE; 2016. pp. 770–8.

[34] Redmon J., Farhadi A. 'Yolov3: an incremental improvement'. *arXiv preprint arXiv:1804.02767*. 2018:1–6.

[35]   Krizhevsky A., Sutskever I., Hinton G.E. 'Imagenet classification with deep convolutional neural networks'. *Proceedings of the 25th International Conference on Advances in neural information processing systems*; 2012. pp. 1097–105.

[36]   Dwivedi R. *Beginners guide to keras call backs, mode l check point and early stopping in deep learning* [online]. 2020. Available from https://analyticsin-diamag.com/tutorial-on-keras-callbacks-modelcheckpoint-and-earlystop-ping-in-deep-learning/ [Accessed 15 Aug 2020].

[37]   Sethy P.K., Behera S.K. *Detection of Coronavirus Disease (COVID-19) Based on Deep Features. Preprints*; 2020. p. 2020030300.

[38]   Afshar P., Heidarian S., Naderkhani F., Oikonomou A., Plataniotis K.N., Mohammadi A. 'COVID-CAPS: a capsule network-based framework for identification of COVID-19 cases from X-ray images'. *Pattern Recognition Letters*. 2020;**138**:638-643.

[39]   Abdulmunem A.A., Abutiheen Z.A., Aleqabie H.J. 'Recognition of corona virus disease (COVID-19) using deep learning network'. *International Journal of Electrical and Computer Engineering*. 2021;**11**(1):365–74.

[40]   Al-Bawi A., Al-Kaabi K.A., Jeryo M., Al-Fatlawi A. *CCBlock based on deep learning for diagnosis COVID-19 in chest x-ray image*; 2020. pp. 1–12.

[41]   Kalla A., Hewa T., Mishra R.A., Ylianttila M., Liyanage M. 'The role of Blockchain to fight against COVID-19'. *IEEE Engineering Management Review*. 2020;**48**(3):85–96.

[42]   Yadav A.R., Talati K.N., Gurjwar R.K. 'Leveraging technology platform for timely conducting online university-level examinations amid covid-19 pandemic: An experiential narrative by engineering faculty from western india'. *Proceedings of the Research Technologies of Pandemic Coronavirus Impact (RTCOV 2020) Yekaterinburg*, Russia, Oct 2020. Atlantis Press; 2020. pp. 533–8.

[43]   Namasudra S., Deka G.C., Johri P., Hosseinpour M., Gandomi A.H. 'The revolution of blockchain: state-of-the-art and research challenges'. *Archives of Computational Methods in Engineering*. 2021;**28**(3):1497–515.

Chapter 17

Security and privacy control in 5G-enabled healthcare using blockchain

Rima Patel¹, Amit Ganatra², and Khushi Patel²

Smart healthcare (SH) is growing with the support of various technologies to offer a wide range of remote health-care services such as remote tele surgeries and diagnosis, a special type of diagnosis, remote consultation, and intrahospital monitoring. SH connects billions of sensors and smart devices through different communication technologies which generates and exchanges data on a regular basis. The evolution of the fifth-generation (5G) networks with the Internet of Things (IoT) for healthcare will meet the current demand in SH in terms of faster file download capacity, faster data transmission, remote monitoring of smart devices, resource utilization, quality of service (QoS), energy efficiency, mobility, reliability, and so on. Security and privacy of sensitive data are still an open issue which needs to be focused as it is a legal requirement to protect a patient's medical data from unauthorized access. It is challenging to integrate complex security solutions with resource-constrained IoT devices, but blockchain fulfills the requirement of 5G and SH in terms of decentralization, data sharing, data access, authentication, immutability, and so on. This chapter focuses on the issues and challenges of 5G-enabled SH. Also, the security and privacy concerns of 5G-enabled SH are analyzed. Moreover, comparative analysis with various blockchain-enabled health-care solutions with 5G is covered along with open challenges and issues.

17.1 Introduction

SH is the most promising area of the IoT nowadays. With the help of various technology-equipped devices, wearables, and sensors, the patient's health can be

¹Department of Computer Science & Engineering, Devang Patel Institute of Advance Technology and Research (DEPSTAR), Faculty of Technology & Engineering (FTE), Charotar University of Science and Technology (CHARUSAT), India
²Department of Computer Engineering, Devang Patel Institute of Advance Technology and Research (DEPSTAR), Faculty of Technology & Engineering (FTE), Charotar University of Science and Technology (CHARUSAT), India

monitored remotely. Moreover, telesurgery and remote surgeries with the help of artificial intelligence (AI)-assisted robots are also possible using various communication technologies like 4G, LTE, Wi-Fi, and so on. Still, these communication technologies face issues related to latency and bandwidth rate while working in real time. During telesurgery, latency issues can have a significant impact on the patient's health. SH also demands higher bandwidth to send the data from medical sensors to the server for real-time data processing and diagnosis. The health records generated by various sensors are in different formats which need to be managed by a third-party server. The server utilizes network capacity for communication, which demands network infrastructure to handle large amounts of heterogeneous data communication between medical equipment. 5G is the fifth-generation communication technology that can solve SH's current issue related to communication technology by offering ultra-low latency, higher bandwidth, and fault-tolerance. 5G offers lower latency with a higher frequency range and device-to-device massive communication support that fulfills SH requirements to some extent. Still, the security and privacy of the patients' health records are the central issues nowadays.

Since decades, healthcare has become a problem-oriented area for storing and managing extensive data. Dealing with a large amount of data in consideration of security, privacy, and confidentiality is crucial for the health-care service providers. Data management also takes editing, accessing, and trusting data into account. The various operations that can be performed on the data of the medical field can be categorized into saving the data, analyzing the data, making a clinical decision, and evaluating the health-care data. In this scenario, achieving the desired health outcome is a challenging task as it depends on the interdisciplinary team of data management on which the medical sector relies. In any sector, whenever there is an involvement of a third party, there is a trust issue. Cost and quality are two other factors, along with the trust that needs to be handled by the health-care staff. When new technologies enter the market, it becomes challenging to integrate them to improve the QoS. Patient's medical data are susceptible and hence regulation, security, and transaction management of those data are some other challenges that need to be addressed. It is very promising for any technology to initiate digital transformation and help the industry to solve the issues associated with excessive operation cost and efficiency where blockchain is not an exception. Due to its key features like a decentralized, distributed, and immutable public ledger, blockchain technology can improve and achieve a high level of interaction, information transferring, data integrity, and access control.

Despite its immutability and security features, blockchain has become a trending technology because of its capability of eliminating the need for trusted third parties. Solve.Care is one of the most prominent examples which has adopted the technology in the field. Arizona Care Network's blockchain is another example similar to Solve.Care, where the patients are allowed to access their data they deserve as their requirement.

Using blockchain technology, Solve.Care has developed a comprehensive health-care platform. Following are the key components of the platform:

1. Care.Wallet: It is a personalized health-care administrator for individuals and providers.
2. Care.Coin: It is an intelligent programmable token that is used to pay the service providers.
3. Care.Cards: It stores the user's specific needs.
4. Care.Protocol: It is responsible for connecting and synchronizing wallets, cards, and coins between users.
5. Care.Vault: A secure organizer for data that manages the data access.

Following are the five major areas where blockchain technology can be helpful in the health-care industry:

1. Data confidentiality: Cryptography plays a vital role while talking about blockchain technology. Cryptography and blockchain together make it impossible for someone who tries to steal or edit data.
2. Reduction in duplication of data: Blockchain allows multiple users to come together and join the network. In such cases, different hospitals, staff, patients, and insurance companies can be the part of the network. This kind of solution will lead the system to be non-redundant and helps to improve the work productivity of employees.
3. Cost management: All the data that can be stored in the blockchain are permanent and immutable. Also, data redundancy is avoided, so the system becomes cost-effective.
4. Innovation: The utilization of blockchain in the clinical field is simpler to extend and create, and development is intended for improvement [1].
5. Risk mitigation: Blockchain in healthcare reduces transaction processing risk between two parties by avoiding compliance violations.

Thus, the integration of 5G and blockchain with SH can revolutionize the current scenario of healthcare in terms of quality and security by adopting the higher bandwidth of 5G and immutability with transparency of blockchain technology, as shown in Figure 17.1.

Figure 17.1   Blockchain in healthcare [1]

17.1.1   Motivation

Many researchers are currently working on integrating 5G with blockchain to make the system transparent and secure. Nonetheless, the detailed discussion and review of the latest survey of 5G networks, like 5G technology, blockchain for 5G, and the IoT with 5G is not available. Motivated by this constraint, we present in this paper the mixture between blockchain and 5G with detailed discussions on different aspects of 5G. 5G offers numerous benefits in terms of speed and reliability, whereas blockchain offers immutability and integrity. These features of 5G and blockchain can be integrated with the IoT network to provide security, privacy, and higher bandwidth in health care. The integration of 5G-enabled IoT with blockchain can revolutionize the current scenario of health-care services by building trust among customers and healthcare providers to offer the various health-care services remotely with higher bandwidth.

17.1.2   Contribution

In this chapter, we have provided

- The survey for how to integrate blockchain with 5G for the medical domain. The basics of blockchain technology, types of blockchain technology, evolution of the blockchain, basics of 5G technology, and 5G-enabled healthcare are covered in detail.
- The security and privacy issues and challenges related to 5G technology in healthcare are also discussed.
- The comparison analysis of the existing blockchain-based solutions used in the health-care domain and 5G is also discussed.

17.1.3   Organization

The structure of the chapter is shown in Figure 17.2. Section 2 represents the background theory that covers the current smart health-care scenario, how 5G is suitable for SH and blockchain technology, the evolution of blockchain technology, and blockchain applications in 5G-enabled SH. Section 3 covers the issues and challenges in 5G-enabled healthcare. Section 4 depicts the security and privacy concerns in 5G-enabled healthcare. The following section discusses the existing blockchain-based security solutions and a comparative study of existing solutions for SH with challenges and open issues. Section 5 represents the relative comparison and analysis. Section 6 concludes the chapter.

17.2   Background theory

SH is one of the vertices of the IoT which uses various sensor-based technologies to collect health-care information from the patient and communicate with health-care professionals. To understand the role of blockchain and 5G for the security and

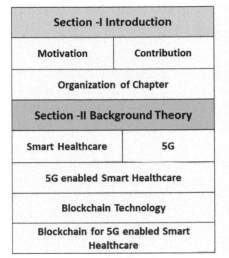
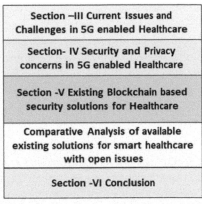

Figure 17.2   Organization of the chapter

quality enhancement in healthcare, the basics of blockchain technology, 5G, and SH are essential which are covered in this section.

17.2.1   Smart healthcare

With the increasing demand for various technologies such as big data analytics, cloud computing, IoT, AI, blockchain technology, 5G, and so on, the concept of SH is also in momentum to facilitate the patients by providing a happier and healthier lifestyle. The advances in various technologies boost the transformation of the health-care approach from a traditional centralized approach to a distributed patient-centric approach.

Health-care organizations facilitate patients by delivering the facilities such as medical services, insurance, medical equipment, and so on [2]. Traditional health care doesn't have sufficient resources to meet up the demand of the current population. Moreover, the traditional health-care system also suffers from other challenges like the increasing burden of lifestyle-related diseases, unavailability of patient-centric models, scalability, lack of human resources, heavy medical services, and so on [3]. To fulfill the demand for health-care services, intelligent, efficient, and sustainable medical services are required for managing the increased population of the world [4].

Currently, SH is one of the most trending areas of IoT in which various sensors, wearables, and intelligent devices collect data from the human body and send it to the health-care service providers or professionals for evaluation through communication technologies [5]. In order to provide various services remotely, health-care providers use different communication technologies for connecting with their patients and devices. Still, they demand low latency and high-speed networking technology to diagnose and offer efficient treatment in real time.

With the increasing rate of globally connected devices with the internet, 5G and IoT are also changing the scope of SH. To establish communication between servers and IoT sensors, various communication technologies with different range support such as short-range- supported technologies Wi-Fi, Bluetooth, and so on, and long-range-supported technologies, such as General Package Radio Service (GPRS), Global System for Mobile Communication (GSM), Long Term Evolution (LTE), and so on, play important roles [6]. The increasing demand for IoT also increases the complexity of the systems, which leads to certain issues which are described below [7, 8]:

1. Interoperability: The number of connected devices is increasing day by day which increases the requirement of hardware and software support. The connected devices face the problem of interconnection and communication due to compatibility issues. Moreover, data generated by these devices will be different in nature and format which leads to interoperability issues. The issues related to differences in data formats lead to semantic interoperability, and issues related to differences in communication technologies and software supports fall under technical interoperability.
2. Standardization: The lack of standardization leads to many issues such as privacy of data, interoperability of network resources, and so on, that increase security risks. Many industries are manufacturing sensors, actuators, and other devices with their own needs at low rates without considering any standards or quality which are susceptible to many security threats.
3. Security and privacy: Data integrity and privacy are the most sensitive part of IoT systems. The data stored at various sensors, RFID tags, and so on are required to be protected from threats. Moreover, IoT devices and sensors are resource-constrained devices, the data collected by these sensors/devices need to be transferred to some server or third-party storage for processing and analysis. During the communication, the data must be protected from unauthorized modification and alteration.
4. Scalability: The connected IoT devices differ in terms of a protocol stack, architecture, processing power, and so on, which leads to interoperability issues. The scaling of IoT networks by keeping in mind the heterogeneous nature of various devices and seamless connectivity is the biggest challenge today.

5G solves the issues related to latency and connects SH devices, patients, and health-care professionals. In remote telesurgery, 5G offers higher speed to connect hospitals with telesurgery robots operated by any expert surgeon anywhere in the world. Medical professionals and patients can communicate seamlessly with 5G to exchange the parameters related to health through the SH platform. The patient can be observed remotely by using various sensors, wearables, personal devices, and so on, which bridges the gap between the physical world and the digital world [5]. Sensors and medical devices monitor the health parameters like blood pressure, sugar level, heart rate, and so on of the patient and store it in some remote system at cloud infrastructure where intelligent systems can process data. The data stored in the cloud infrastructure are available to medical professionals' end systems through high-speed 5G technology.

17.2.2 5G

5G is the fifth generation of mobile communication technology. The first generation (1G) of mobile communication technology was introduced in the 1980s based on the analog signal. The next-generation mobile communication system, the second generation (2G), based on digital signals, was introduced in the 1990s, which gave a better user experience by personal mobile communications. The evolution of the third-generation mobile networks (3G) has changed the scenario of mobile networks by providing a faster Internet experience after 2000 [9].

With the advancement of technologies, the number of devices connected with the Internet increases drastically. As the number of devices increase, network traffic also increases. This situation is expected to continue with respect to current scenarios that demands low latency communication technology and improved network capacity. According to research, it is predicted that the mobile data traffic will increase 20,000 times from 2010 to 2030 [3]. The fifth-generation communication technology (5G) connects heterogeneous devices and machines [2]. Cisco's annual Internet report (2018–2023) shows that the number of Internet users in 2018 was 3.9 billion, that is 51% of the total population. It will be around 5.3 billion, 66% of the global population, in 2023 [10].

5G, the next generation of 3G and 4G, fulfills the current requirements of resource-constrained devices to migrate computational activities on distributed environments by solving the issue related to bandwidth. By 2023, the speed of 5G will be 13 times higher than the average mobile connection [10]. To fulfill the demand of traffic generated by billions of connected devices from the diverse applications, the combination of various technologies such as edge computing, network functions virtualization, network slicing, device-to-device communication, and millimeter-wave communication can be used to provide flexible network deployment, operation and resource optimization that increases the overall performance by enabling high-speed and low-latency network connection [2]. It also opens doors for various IoT-based applications such as smart city, smart grid, SH, vehicular network, and so on. The computational requirements of latency applications running with resource-constrained systems can be fulfilled by offloading computational activities on the remote distributed infrastructure using 5G [11]. Currently, SH is one of the promising areas which demands 5G for various applications like remote telesurgery, remote patient monitoring, virtual consultancy, and so on.

17.2.3 5G-enabled SH

Integration of 5G with SH can offer higher efficiency and performance in terms of delay. Many latency-sensitive health-care use cases such as wireless telesurgery, service robots, and so on, work in real time, which requires data transmission between sensors or machines and medical professionals without delay. This can be achieved

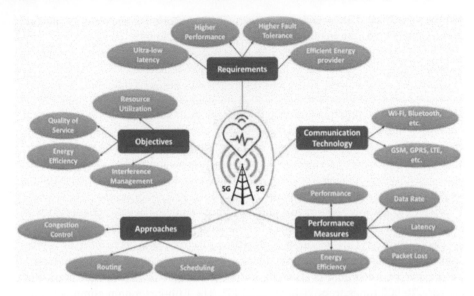

Figure 17.3   Requirement of 5G-enabled healthcare [6]

with the help of 5G but at the same time security and privacy of the data must be focused upon.

Figure 17.3 depicts the requirements, objectives, approaches, and performance measures for 5G-enabled health-care systems.

The rapid deployment of 5G technology in various fields also increases the opportunities for attackers. It poses new security challenges such as data integrity, privacy, fault tolerance, and so on, that must be resolved before the wide expansion of 5G.

The variant nature of sensors and data generated by those sensors lead to a complex system that complicates the identification of various threats [7].

However, IoT and 5G offer numerous benefits to the health-care sector. While taking the health-care sector into account, some security and privacy requirements need to be considered on high priority. The availability of patient medical records is the most crucial part of the SH system to provide remote medical services in real time with higher accuracy and lower error rate [5]. Moreover, any patient's medical records are the most sensitive information that must be secure during every stage of SH such as collection, transmission, processing, and storage. The security of IoT applications must be ensured in every layer of the IoT architecture. Application layer, middleware layer, network layer, and perception layer are the four layers of the IoT architecture. The efficient authentication and access control mechanisms must be applied at every stage of SH to prevent unauthorized access to various data at the respective layers [7].

The security of the patient's health-care records requires a unique security service which fulfills the legal requirement of medical health records. Authentication, interoperability, data sharing, and security during transmission are the special requirements of medical records [12].

Many times sensitive information can be targeted by intruders during the computational offloading process, leading to data integrity issues.

Moreover, 5G connects billions of devices across different domains to provide various opportunities to global industries and business stockholders in cloud computing, edge computing, IoT, vehicular network, smart grid, and so on. The number of machine-to-machine connections, also known as IoT connections, will be 14.7 billion by 2023, 50% of globally connected devices, from which 48% of devices are from home applications [10]. To increase the aerial capacity, energy efficiency, and data rate with lower latency of the current network, 5G uses the ultra-dense network (UDN), which introduces trust and interoperability in sub-networks. The 5G network works upon a new service delivery model that also demands security requirements in terms of transparency and immutability. To fulfill the security requirements of the 5G network in terms of reliability, to establish trust among connected devices from diverse fields and to provide immutability, traditional centralized security solutions are not suitable as the new service model desires a decentralized environment. The highly dynamic nature of 5 G-enabled IoT devices' communication environment in complex networks and ubiquitous services makes it crucial to solve security and privacy issues [2].

17.2.4 Blockchain technology

Blockchain is picking up footing and is one of the wide-spreading themes these days in the digital world. Blockchain became famous because of bitcoin, a remarkable cryptographic achievement. Bitcoin is a cryptocurrency created by Satoshi Nakamoto in 2008, a purely peer-to-peer version of electronic cash that would allow online payments to be sent directly from one party to another without going through a financial institution [13]. Bitcoin was the first application that runs with underlying technology called a blockchain. The primary function of the blockchain was the registration of transactions of the bitcoin cryptocurrency as a peer-to-peer ledger [14]. However, blockchain is not bitcoin. It's a technology that runs bitcoin. Apart from cryptocurrency [15], blockchain can be used as keeping the logs of events in the ledger. Blockchain, by definition, is a decentralized, distributed, digital public ledger that is used to record the transaction across many nodes in the network. It works without the need for a trusted third party.

Blockchain is a linked list-like data structure in which all the blocks are connected cryptographically. Each block in the chain is connected to another block cryptographically. The idea behind the connection of blocks is to provide security. The address of the block is a hash value. It will impact safety in the context of blockchain. Hashing makes the blockchain more secure. Hashing is the process which results in a fixed length of output regardless of the input size. Bitcoin uses SHA-256 for generating the hash value. The block in blockchain stores the transactions. Apart from hash addresses, blocks contain the following fields as shown in Figure 17.4.

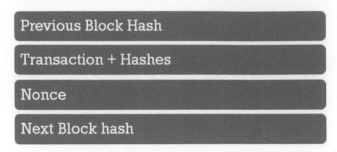

Figure 17.4   Contents of the block

1. Previous Block Hash: This field contains the address of the previous block of the chain. Each block in the chain will include the address of the previous block of the chain.
2. Transaction + Hashes: The transactions occurring between the nodes are being stored in this field with their hashes.
3. Nonce: Nonce is the number that is generated only once. Using the nonce and other block data, miners can create the hash for the particular block they want to mine.
4. Next Block Hash: This field contains the address of the next block in the chain.

Mentioned above are the main fields of the block. Figure 17.5 depicts the structure of blocks where blocks are connected via cryptographic algorithms. Additional fields in the blocks are timestamps and Merkel root. The timestamp contains the time at which the block has been created. A Merkle tree is a data structure that is used in computer science applications [16]. Merkle trees serve to encode blockchain data more efficiently and securely [16].

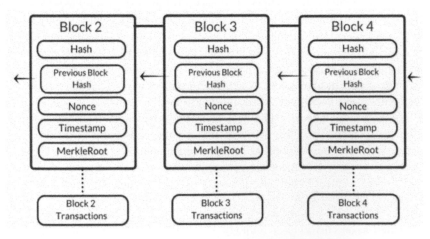

Figure 17.5   Structure of the blocks in blockchain

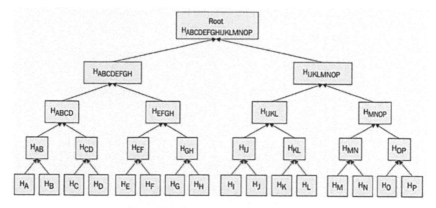

Figure 17.6   Merkle tree [17]

A Merkle tree allows users to verify the particular transaction. In this case, users do not need to download the whole blockchain. A block transaction runs from the algorithm to generate the hash [16]. The hash is used to verify that the transaction data are the same as the original set. But this does not allow the user to obtain the initial stage of the transaction. The transaction processing rate in the case of bitcoin is 10 minutes through one function at a time. So, it would be a great idea if the pair of transactions can be hashed together instead of a single transaction. A Merkle tree works on the same idea in which the transactions at leaf nodes can be combined and hashed together. The new combined hash can again be hashed with another leaf node and generate the following hash function. The process will go on till the root. The root node is known as the Merkel root. A Merkle root is one of the essential fields in the block structure. Figure 17.6 represents the working of a Merkle tree.

The concept of the Merkle tree was introduced by Ralph Merkle [17]. A diagram of the Merkle tree is shown in Figure 17.6. Merkle trees enable secure and efficient verification of large datasets [17]. As shown in the Figure 17.6, the Merkle tree is a binary tree. It takes input at the lowest level, that is, child node or leaf node. These leaf nodes will be hashed to generate a parent node. Apart from the concepts like hashing, Merkle tree, and block structure, blockchain is supported with other important ideas that make blockchain more capable and secure. Blockchain has a wide range of applicability in different sectors like e-governance, education, finance and banking, healthcare, and many more. Blockchain is supported by various ideas, as shown in the Figure 17.7. Peer-to-peer network, consensus mechanism, e-cash schemes, state machine replication, and computational puzzles are the parts which supports blockchain to achieve the goal.

17.2.5   Evolution of blockchain

Blockchain is an emerging technology, starting with Bitcoin, which has emerged from Blockchain 1.0 to Blockchain 4.0. All the versions have their specifications

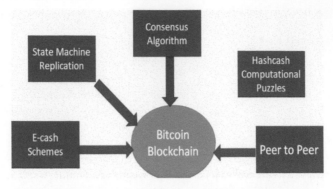

Figure 17.7   Supporting concepts [17]

and usefulness. Figure 17.8 represents the evolution of the blockchain technology. Blockchain has three types:

1. Permissionless Blockchain: Permissionless Blockchain is also known as a public blockchain. In this type of blockchain, anyone can join the network, read and perform the transaction, and participate in consensus mechanisms. It eliminates the need for the middle man. Bitcoin is the first application that runs under blockchain technology and which is an example of a public blockchain. It is fully transparent, so every node in the network can observe the transaction between any party in the network. Ethereum Blockchain is another example of a public blockchain.
2. Permissioned Blockchain: Permissioned Blockchain is also known as the private blockchain. In this type of blockchain, authorized users can be part of the network and can perform the transaction. It is partially decentralized. There will be the intervention of a third party. The in-charge will decide who will be the part of the consensus and who will not be the part of the mining process.
3. Federated Blockchain: This kind of blockchain removes the sole autonomy of a single authorized user. Unlike the private blockchain, there will be a group of

Figure 17.8   Evolution of blockchain technology

authorized users. Hence there will be more than one in-charge who will decide what is beneficial to the network.

Figure 17.8 represents the growth of blockchain technology from Blockchain 1.0 to Blockchain 4.0.

As shown in Figure 17.8, Blockchain 1.0 had only the exchange of value in bitcoin cryptocurrency. There is no programmable software involved. Blockchain 2.0 has ether as a cryptocurrency that includes more sophisticated transactions. In addition to cryptocurrency, Blockchian 2.0 includes smart contracts. Smart contracts are the agreements that run automatically on the occurrence of certain events or conditions. The deal is between the two parties that wish to communicate with each other. A large volume of microtransactions cannot be supported by the current technology, as smart contracts are growing every day.

Although Ethereum improved the exchange rate to 15 tps over bitcoin which is 7 tps, it still is not adequate to help the present economy [18]. Blockchain is currently moving towards a decentralized web. It will incorporate information stockpiling, correspondence networks, smart contracts, and open principle platforms [18]. Thus, there is a requirement for decentralized applications.

DApp in the background has a blockchain network, and the front end may use any programming language that supports blockchain as a functionality. Blockchain is now adopted by huge industries, where they demand a high degree of trust and privacy of the data. To fulfill the requirement of the industry, a more scalable blockchain network is required. This is where Blockchain 4.0 comes into the picture. DApp allows different industries to come together and access the platform to work as a single unit and fulfill the industry's requirements and demands.

As blockchain is a fast-growing technology because of its tremendous potential and benefits, future projects from different industries will adopt the technology to solve their business problem. The chart shown in Figure 17.9 highlights that while the technology is relatively young, it is now transitioning from early adoption into the early phases of growth [19].

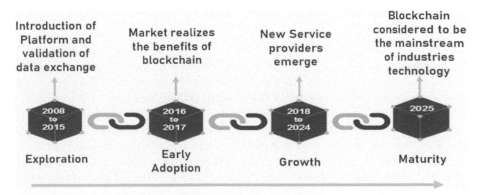

Figure 17.9   Projected blockchain adoption [19]

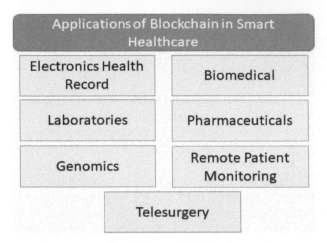

Figure 17.10   Applications of blockchain technology in 5G-enabled healthcare [20]

Blockchain, outside the cryptocurrency, can be adaptable in many sectors like IoT-based applications, 5G technology, citizen identification, post-trade settlement, health financial crime prevention, media, insurance, and so on. The following sections discuss the 5G technology and SH where blockchain can be applied to fulfill the requirements of the particular sector for secure and confidential data transfer.

As shown in Figure 17.10, this is an era in which many industries are adopting blockchain technology that is also known as Blockchain 4.0, to resolve the trust issues among unknown peers. The decentralized nature of blockchain technology completely matches the requirements of SH providers in terms of trust-building among patients and health-care professionals to offer various medical services remotely.

In SH, blockchain can be integrated with different electronic health records [21], biomedical applications, laboratories, supply chain management in pharmaceuticals, genomics, remote patient monitoring, telesurgery, and so on.

17.2.6   Blockchain for 5G-enabled healthcare

5G connects billions of IoT devices in various scenarios such as smart cities, SH, smart grid, and so on, which continuously generates large amounts of heterogeneous data. It is challenging to observe the thousands of activities and to identify malicious ones among them. Many centralized solutions are available to detect malicious activities in IoT networks. 5G supports a new service model that offers the dynamic mobile environment with complex network architecture and ubiquitous services that demand decentralized solutions due to latency and privacy issues in the presence of third-party solutions [15]. Moreover, health-care data of the patients are essential and sensitive to provide quick and efficient treatment to improve the health scenario. SH requires a low latency communication network to facilitate the nurses and

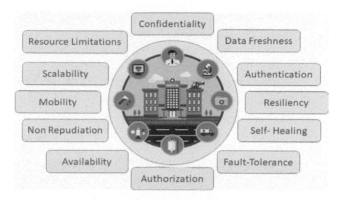

Figure 17.11   Open security issues with smart healthcare [5]

doctors to observe the patients' activities remotely to make real-time decisions for providing treatment [17].

Currently, SH uses 4G and other communication technologies, which many times leads to latency and speed issues, but 5G can be deployed to solve the same. To offer proper treatment to the patient with efficiency, the patients' health records must be secured during transmission from sensors to medical profession-als and at the storage. As shown in Figure 17.11, the open security issues with SH are confidentiality, integrity, availability, access control, privacy, user authenti-cation, data ownership, and misuse of private data by offering free storage [22]. 5G also suffers from security issues that can be addressed by decentralized, trusted, and immutable distributed blockchain technology.

Health-care networks connect multiple hospital groups to offer all types of med-ical services to the patients. To manage the activities of patients, the medicine sup-ply chain for patients, data storage and data sharing, decentralized and distributed systems are suitable which offer trust among unknown parties. In healthcare, record management, access control policies, secure data sharing, identity management, immutable data storage, scalability, interoperability, and so on can be achieved by adopting blockchain for the health-care network [23].

The traditional security solutions and public key infrastructures are not suit-able for IoT devices due to resource constraints. Many security solutions based on cryptography [24–27] have been proposed. Still, cryptographic encryption-based approaches provide security against confidentiality as many of these solutions can-not solve issues related to side-channel security attacks.

Blockchain offers the below-mentioned attractive features [2, 4, 28], which makes it possible to be adopted as a security solution in diverse environments.

• Decentralization: Blockchain supports peer-to-peer communication by avoid-ing centralized/third-party authority for transaction and ledger management. Some special nodes called miners will validate and verify the transactions based on the previous entries in the distributed ledger.

- Pseudonymity: Users are assigned the address to communicate with others based on their public-private key pairs. The actual identity of the users will be hidden in the network, which keeps the owners of the transactions secret from others.
- Transparency: Blockchain supports the concept of a distributed ledger. The copy of all the transactions is maintained at every node. Every transaction occurring on the blockchain network is known to all the nodes that make a transparent and secure environment.
- Democracy: The new block is added into the chain only after validation of every transaction. This can be possible by executing the consensus algorithms at all the nodes on the network and allows to involve all the nodes in the decision-making process of the block inclusion in the blockchain.
- Security: The decentralized environment of blockchain solves the problem of availability. Usage of asymmetric key cryptography offers integrity, authentication, and non-repudiation. The smart contracts, introduced in Blockchain 2.0, provide privacy by providing efficient access control policies.
- Immutability: The blockchain uses the digital signature for signing every transaction carried out by any node, decreasing the chances of non-repudiation. Moreover, once the block is added to the blockchain network, it is impossible to make changes to the transaction details of that block due to the hash of the block being included in the upcoming block in the network. Hence, to make unauthorized changes to any block, users need to make changes in every block of the network at every copy of the block into the ledger to get accepted, which depicts the concept of an immutable distributed ledger.
- Persistence: The changes can be detected easily by using hash chain concepts, making the whole network persistent. Every block gets verified by the particular nodes called miners by solving the cryptographic puzzle, and after validation, it will be added to the network.
- Auditability: Blockchain includes timestamping to provide better accountability and auditability. Any node of the blockchain network can easily audit the transactions at any time in the network.

17.3   Current issues and challenges in 5G-enabled healthcare

Challenges are an immanent part of any developing technology, and 5G is not an exception. The journey from 1G technology to 5G is only 40 years. The challenges faced in 5G technology are categorized into technological and common challenges.

17.3.1   Technological challenges

1. Inter-cell interference: This is one of the significant technical issues that need to be solved. The size variation in traditional and concurrent cells leads the technology towards interference.

2. Efficient medium access control: In circumstances where the deployment of access points and user terminals is on different geographical locations, throughput will be low, and latency will be high. In this kind of situation, hotspots will not be proficient in cellular technology to provide high throughput.
3. Traffic management: In contrast with the customary human-to-human traffic in cell arrangements, an incredible number of machine-to-machine (M2M) gadgets in a cell may cause genuine framework challenges, for example, radio access network (RAN) challenges, which will cause overburden and congestion [29].

17.3.2 Common challenges

1. Multiple services: Unlike the radio signal service, 5G has to fulfill the different technologies, heterogeneous networks, and devices situated and operating in various geo-locations. Here the challenge is to provide user-centric and data-rich wireless services to the consumers.
2. Infrastructure: As 5G is concerned with the high accessibility of data, the infrastructure of the technology is one of the most significant issues for researchers.
3. Communication and sensing: 5G will help to process a large amount of data coming from different and distinct sources across the world. This also requires more extensive infrastructure support.
4. Security: The new service models introduced with 5G open up the doors for a new set of security threats to compromise the integrity and confidentiality of the data during the communication process.

The medical sector in this era faces several obstacles. Many of the problems can be solved by investing time and funding. But the rest of the issues requires the support of technology. This section highlights the common problems related to 5G-enabled healthcare.

1. Slow dissemination of medical knowledge: As it is a sensitive industry of society, any technology adoption in this field takes a long time. According to Balas, only 14% of new scientific discoveries make their way into daily clinical practice [30]. The one who adopts the technology takes 17 years of an extended period.
2. Good care costs less: It's an era where there is a revolution in the health-care industry. For example, earlier, patients were paying fees for service, but in the competitive world, now the payment modules have changed by adopting pay as per performance [30].
3. Access to health-care service: The patient's needs should be fulfilled with respect to every prospect. Patients require access not only to the physician but also to their data. Whenever data accessibility is concerned, the data's security, privacy, and confidentiality play a considerable role. The health-care industry must adopt the technology that provides good QoS.

4. Virtual care visit: On the digital front, it has been predicted by numerous surveys that virtual care visits will have tremendous growth in upcoming years. In virtual care visits, patients can be virtually connected to the doctors via text, video call, or another platform. This requires high-speed data and a platform to transfer the data between communication parties securely.

5. Costs and transparency: The patients are the consumers of the service, and hence the service provider has to be transparent to their consumers in the context of cost and data. This in turn will lead to QoS.

6. Interoperability: Integrating and improving the exchange of data of service provider, consumer, payer, and patient in real time is a challenging task. The health-care industry works with various types of machines and sensors, which generate data in different formats and stores them at some centralized data server that leads to the issues of interoperability [12].

7. Security: Due to the highly confidential patient information collected by the health-care sector, it has become a highly prime suspect for malicious users and attackers. The cybercriminal can steal the data, and the industry has to compromise the patient's information. The health-care industry also has to compromise its regulation policy and standards if there is a cyber attack to the system.

   The medical records stored in databases and data collected from the human body using various sensors can be vulnerable to tampering and copying, which must be secured from unauthorized access and change by applying efficient authorization and access control policies [12].

8. Mobility: The usage of smart devices, wearables, and sensors in SH systems is common now, and data transmission from these devices in real time is the most important service of SH. The mobility of the devices is connected with mobile healthcare, wireless devices, and IoT sensors. Mobile health-care devices such as wearables have potential security threats which can be exploited to perform various attacks like disclosure of information, unauthorized access, and alteration of data.

17.4   Security and privacy concerns in 5G-enabled healthcare

Confidentiality, integrity, and availability are the three primary security goals of information security. The medical devices and sensors generate billions of health-care records of the patients with different formats and communicate the same with the server in real time. These data must be secured from unauthorized access. Also the integrity and consistency of the information and availability of health records for providing treatment in a timely manner need to be ensured [5]. The heterogeneous nature of data coming from various IoT sensors and equipment makes systems complex and harder to manage [7]. Unauthorized access, routing attacks, data disclosure, data modification, man-in-the-middle attack, replying attacks, node hijacking, denial of services attack, flooding, Sybil attacks, and so on are the latest security threats [5]. Figure 17.8 shows the primary security goals that need to be focused upon for implementing smart and secure healthcare.

Confidentiality: SH offers various medical services with the support of cloud service providers to process the data in real time. Confidentiality is the primary concern due to third-party involvement in the health-care system. Moreover, the usage of various kinds of sensors makes it more difficult to find out the ideal security solutions which can be applied to all types of sensors and communication technologies. In some cases, confidentiality breaches of patient data may affect the personal safety of patients.

Data freshness: The health-care data must be updated at the health-care professional's end periodically to offer efficient services. The old data may lead to wrong diagnosis, which can affect the patient's health. It is a more significant challenge to decide the interval of data updation as a delay in updating problematic status may put patients' lives in danger. Moreover, frequent data update calls may increase network traffic.

Authentication: Due to the standardization issues of sensors and communication technologies, it is difficult to adopt all the sensor types to secure health-care data. The authentication of the sensors is the most important parameter to facilitate the patient with efficient services on time. It is mandatory to verify the authorization of sensors submitting the data.

Resiliency and self-healing: Due to the lower capacity of sensors in memory and computation power, some of the sensors cannot have a backup. The ability to recover from failure with lesser delay must be ensured with sensors and storage devices to avoid emergencies. The link failures and issues related to the hardware must be recognized and resolved automatically. The variety in the types of sensors and lack of standardization is the open issue that needs to be addressed to design ideal solutions for security and resiliency.

Authorization: Due to the distributed and decentralized nature of 5G and SH systems, it is important to design and implement fine-grained control systems to access health-care data. The health-care data should be accessible only by authorized users or sensors.

Availability: The patients' health-related data should be available remotely and should be accessible from anywhere. This must be ensured to offer medical facilities on time. The various breaches on availability may harm the patient by breaking the connection between patients and health-care professionals.

Non-repudiation: Due to the resource-constrained nature of various sensors, it isn't easy to apply the exact security mechanisms on all the sensors to ensure non-repudiation. Currently, a digital signature is the best option to provide non-repudiation, but spoofing attacks can be used to fool the authentication system, which may lead to repudiation.

Mobility: Generally, health-care devices are attached to the patient's body to monitor the various parameters which can frequently move with the patient. Due to the continuous mobility of wireless devices with patients, it may hinder transmission.

Scalability: As continuous usage of remote services increases, the number of connected devices in the network also increases which leads to scalability issues.

The use of the 5G network for healthcare improves performance, but the management of devices and data security is an open challenge.

Resource limitations: The wireless sensors for healthcare are resource-constrained devices that need to be changed frequently due to the computation. Moreover, the size of the sensors is small, which leads to memory issues. To maintain the energy level and physical size, low computation power and memory are not enough to implement the security mechanisms on the devices.

17.5   Existing blockchain-based security solutions for healthcare

Many blockchain frameworks like hyperledger, Corda, Ethereum, and so on are being used on different projects for deploying SH on blockchain for secure data sharing, data storage, medicine supply chain, telemedicine facilities, and so on. Kitchen, MELLODDY Project, MyClinic.com are verified and well-known projects of Hyperledger [31]. They work on the health-care domain with blockchain technology to provide a secure and trustworthy health-care network, clinical supply chain, secure data sharing, telemedicine consultancy, and secure digital identity network, respectively [31]. IBM blockchain and IOTA are the other platforms that provide blockchain-based solutions for healthcare [32]. Corda offers use cases in healthcare for pharmaceutical supply chain management, claim management, and health record exchange [33].

The favorable characteristics of blockchain technology such as decentralization, immutability, transparency, persistence, auditability, security, and privacy attract many 5G-enabled IoT applications to adopt blockchain infrastructure to offer a transparent and distributed trust model which provides authentication and access control to ensure data privacy [2].

Saravanan *et al.* [34] propose a blockchain-based health-care solution for continuous monitoring of diabetic patients, and doctors can observe the patient's insulin level remotely. The wearables are used to monitor the various parameters of the human body and also to monitor the diabetes of the patient. Moreover, the medicine dosage required based on the predicted value of diabetics will be suggested to the users by sending an alert to take medicine on time. For emergencies, the model is configured to send notifications to the caretakers via a mobile network.

Xia *et al.* [35] have proposed blockchain-based architecture to share the health data among multiple parties through a cloud environment. The system architecture is divided into three layers. The user layer is the topmost layer that handles the different types of user activities. The system layer takes record verification and block generation by using its consensus algorithm. The lower layer is the storage layer that handles the data storage environment. The top layer of the system is implemented, but still, the system is not tested for security and performance concerns.

Nguyen *et al.* [2] covered a rigorous survey on the impact of blockchain integration with various applications using 5G as a communication technology. Blockchain offers opportunities such as security enhancement, performance improvement, and network simplification, which helps manage complex and heterogeneous health-care data. The authors have also discussed the open issues while integrating blockchain technology with 5G communication. Currently, 5G offers numerous benefits while integrating with blockchain in terms of security and performance. However, standardization, infrastructure, security and privacy, scalability, QoSs, and blockchain performance are the still open areas that need to be focused on. Blockchain with 5G can be integrated with Big Data and machine learning is another research direction for enthusiastic researchers.

Ahad *et al.* [6] have focused on the issues while adopting 5G as a communication technology for health-care networks. The authors have mentioned that connectivity, interoperability, security, and Big Data are currently the emerging challenges required to be solved. The authors have also given weightage to security and privacy concerns while using 5G for health-care data that need to be secured from internal and external threats, and some mechanism that needs to be designed to detect and prevent the threats at the network as a device layer.

The Table 17.1 shows some more solutions that includes the integration of 5G with SH or SH with blockchain technology and open issues.

17.5.1   Challenges of blockchain with 5G-enabled SH

The blockchain offers immutability with a transparent environment to the 5G-enabled SH applications for health record management, telesurgery, and supply chain management in pharma industries, and so on, but still there are some open issues that needs to be solved [2] .

1. Scalability in throughput, storage, and networking is the major challenge in the blockchain ecosystem with 5G-enabled SH.
2. However, blockchain solves many security concerns of SH. Recent statistics state that 51% of attacks, privacy leakage, and smart contract logic modification are still open issues for blockchain with 5G.
3. The integration of blockchain with 5G introduces a new level of challenges related to the QoS, which affects the overall system's throughput. Table 17.1 depicts the open challenges that need to be focused on for integrating 5G with blockchain [2].
4. No standard architecture of blockchain or 5G is available. Those which are available and compatible with each other, lead to interoperability and infrastructure issues.

17.6   Conclusion

Blockchain is capable of transforming the health-care industry to bring about a revolution in the health-care field. The decentralized and distributed nature and the immutability of blockchain data will place the patient at the center of the system and yet provide increasing security, privacy, and interoperability of the data. The

Table 17.1 Comparative analysis of various security solutions and open issues

Reference	Year	Approach used	Remarks	Open issues discussed
[36]	2014	A cryptographic algorithm is used; describes the privacy and security issues in Wireless Body Area Network (WBAN)	The advantage of the approach was that it had a better message delivery	Loss of data was a significant issue
[20]	2020	Machine Learning (ML)-based security schemes, security and privacy-based schemes, Internet of Things (IoT)-based security schemes are compared. ZigBee mesh Protocol, Aggregate Message Authentication Codes (MAC) and Bloom filter hashing, Radio Frequency Identification (RFID) Security, Elliptic Curve Cryptography (ECC), and RSA (Rivest–Shamir–Adleman) Algorithm	Different techniques are compared in the context of security and privacy in the health-care domain	Security, privacy in blockchain
[2]	2020	Blockchain for 5G and IoT	The advantages of blockchain with 5G-enabled IoT in various industries are discussed	Applications and services of the blockchain for 5G should be considered
[37]	2019	Blockchain Distributed Ledger Technology (DLT) technology	5G infrastructure sharing, spectrum sharing, network slicing are discussed. Various areas in which blockchain can be integrated are discussed, along with challenges	Applications and services of the blockchain for 5G should be considered, and integration can be considered

(Continues)

Table 17.1 Continued

Reference	Year	Approach used	Remarks	Open issues discussed
[38]	2020	Hyperledger caliper framework for blockchain, smart healthcare	A blockchain-based patient-centered data sharing system is proposed, implemented on a hyperledger caliper framework, and optimized in terms of performance, security and scalability	Scalability, latency, privacy, interoperability
[20]	2019	Blockchain and machine learning for competent healthcare	The blockchain-based patient monitoring system is proposed, using a machine learning approach for real-time decision-making about diseases	Latency, scalability, interoperability, security, and privacy
[6]	2016	5G with smart healthcare	The survey paper covered the advantages of integrating 5G with smart healthcare and the open research issues while integrating 5G with smart healthcare	Connectivity, interoperability, communication cost, security, data management
[39]	2019	5G, smart healthcare for telesurgery	An efficient and reliable telesurgery architecture based on 5G is proposed. Recent robots technology by various industries for telesurgery are compared	Ultra-low latency, reliability, security and privacy, communication cost

health-care ecosystem with 5G as communication technology is created by the decentralized nature of the technology, making a system in which patient data can be efficiently and quickly accessible by the hospitals, staff members of hospitals, doctors, and pharmacists. The integration of blockchain and 5G in healthcare will lead to faster diagnosis and personalized health-care plans. The medical fraternity will be boosted and will be at the next higher level by using 5G technology. This includes the patient's comfort where they can stay at home and wear remote medical sensors and is also beneficial to medics to manage the patients' treatment plans, screen the various vitals of patients, and conduct a discussion or even intervention over webcam. In this chapter, the security and privacy controls in 5G-enabled healthcare have been enlightening. The current issues in blockchain and 5G technology and the medical field's challenges to adopt the technology are of significant concern. Despite technical and other challenges, the impact of both technologies in healthcare will bring innovation in the next generation.

References

[1]   Goryunov M. *Blockchain and healthcare. Transforming medicine through innovations* [online]. 2020. Available from https://3commas.io/blog/block-chain-and-healthcare-transforming-medicine-through-innovations [Accessed 2020].

[2]   Nguyen D.C., Pathirana P.N., Ding M., Seneviratne A. 'Blockchain for 5G and beyond networks: a state of the art survey'. *arXiv preprint arXiv:1912.* 2019;**05062**.

[3]   Latif S., Qadir J., Farooq S., Imran M. 'How 5G wireless (and concomitant technologies) will revolutionize healthcare?' *Future Internet*. 2017;**9**(4):93.

[4]   Xie J., Tang H., Huang T., *et al.* 'A survey of blockchain technology applied to smart cities: research issues and challenges'. *IEEE Communications Surveys & Tutorials*. 2019;**21**(3):2794–830.

[5]   Algarni A. 'A survey and classification of security and privacy research in smart healthcare systems'. *IEEE Access*. 2019;**7**:101879–94.

[6]   Ahad A., Tahir M., Yau K.-L.A. '5G-based smart healthcare network: architecture, taxonomy, challenges and future research directions'. *IEEE Access*. 2019;**7**:100747–62.

[7]   Patel K., Vyas S, V. 'Pandya and others, IoT: leading challenges, issues and explication using latest technologies Pandya and others, IoT: Leading Challenges, Issues and Explication Using Latest Technologies'. *2019 3rd International Conference on Electronics, Communication and Aerospace Technology (ICECA)*; 2019.

[8]   Mistry I., Tanwar S., Tyagi S., Kumar N. 'Blockchain for 5G-enabled IoT for industrial automation: a systematic review, solutions, and challenges'. *Mechanical Systems and Signal Processing*. 2020;**135**(5):106382.

[9]   Liu G., Jiang D. '5G: vision and requirements for mobile communication system towards year 2020'. *Chinese Journal of Engineering*. 2016;**2016**:1–8.

[10] Cisco annual Internet report (2018–2023) white paper. Cisco; 2020. Available from https://www.cisco.com/c/en/us/solutions/collateral/executive-perspectives/annual-internet-report/white-paper-c11-741490.html [Accessed 09 Mar 2020].

[11] Xu X., Chen Y., Zhang X., Liu Q., Liu X., Qi L. 'A blockchain-based computation offloading method for edge computing in 5G networks'. *Software: Practice and Experience.* 2019;**18**(3):1–18.

[12] McGhin T., Choo K.-K.R., Liu C.Z., He D. 'Blockchain in healthcare applications: research challenges and opportunities'. *Journal of Network and Computer Applications.* 2019;**135**(1):62–75.

[13] Nakamoto S. *Bitcoin: A Peer-to-Peer Electronic Cash System*; 2019. pp. 1–9.

[14] Malibari N.A. 'A survey on blockchain-based applications in education'. *7th International Conference on Computing for Sustainable Global Development (INDIACom)*; 2020.

[15] Aras S.T., Kulkarni V. 'Blockchain and its applications–a detailed survey'. *International Journal of Computer Applications.* 2017;**180**:29–35.

[16] Frankenfield J. *"Merkle tree,"investopedia* [online]. 2020. Available from https://www.investopedia.com/terms/m/merkle-tree.asp [Accessed 18 Feb 2020].

[17] Bashir I. *Mastering Blockchain: Distributed Ledger Technology, Decentralization, and Smart Contracts Explained.* Packt Publishing Ltd; 2018.

[18] Srivastava A., Bhattacharya P., Singh A., Mathur A. 'A systematic review on evolution of blockchain generations'. *International Journal of Information Technology and Electrical Engineering.* 2018;**7**(6):1–8.

[19] *Harvest Portfolios Group Inc. Blockchain evolution* [Online]. 2020. Available from https://harvestportfolios.com/wp-content/uploads/2018/02/Blockchain_Evolution.pdf. [Accessed 2 Aug 2018].

[20] Hathaliya J., Sharma P., Tanwar S., Gupta R. 'Blockchain-based remote patient monitoring in healthcare 4.0'. *IEEE 9th International Conference on Advanced Computing (IACC)*; 2019.

[21] Zhang X., Poslad S. 'Blockchain support for flexible queries with granular access control to electronic medical records (EMR)'. *IEEE International Conference on Communications (ICC)*; 2018.

[22] Hathaliya J.J., Tanwar S. 'An exhaustive survey on security and privacy issues in healthcare 4.0'. *Computer Communications.* 2020;**153**(6):311–35.

[23] Aggarwal S., Chaudhary R., Aujla G.S., Kumar N., Choo K.-K.R., Zomaya A.Y. 'Blockchain for smart communities: applications, challenges and opportunities'. *Journal of Network and Computer Applications.* 2019;**144**(5):13–48.

[24] Chaudhary R., Aujla G.S., Kumar N., Zeadally S. 'Lattice-based public key cryptosystem for internet of things environment: challenges and solutions'. *IEEE Internet of Things Journal.* 2018;**6**(3):4897–909.

[25] Aledhari M., Marhoon A., Hamad A., Saeed F. 'A new cryptography algorithm to protect cloud-based healthcare services'. *2017 IEEE/ACM International Conference on Connected Health: Applications, Systems and Engineering Technologies (CHASE)*; 2017.

[26]   Chatterjee U., Sadhukhan D., Ray S. 'An improved authentication and key agreement protocol for smart healthcare system in the context of internet of things using elliptic curve cryptography'. *Proceedings of International Conference on IoT Inclusive Life (ICIIL 2019)*; NITTTR Chandigarh: India; 2020.

[27]   He D., Zeadally S. 'An analysis of RFID authentication schemes for Internet of things in healthcare environment using elliptic curve cryptography'. *IEEE Internet of Things Journal*. 2014;**2**(1):72–83.

[28]   Mettler M. 'Blockchain technology in healthcare: the revolution starts here'. *2016 IEEE 18th International Conference on E-Health Networking, Applications and Services (Healthcom)*; 2016.

[29]   5G – Challenges [online]. 2020. Available from https://www.tutorialspoint.com/5g/5g_challenges.htm.

[30]   Australia E. *What are the 4 biggest challenges facing the healthcare sector?* [online]. 2020. Available from https://www.elsevier.com/en-au/connect/what-are-the-4-biggest-challenges-facing-the-healthcare-sector   [Accessed Sep 2020].

[31]   Hyperledger. *Five healthcare projects powered by hyperledger you may not know about* [online]. 2020. Available from https://www.hyperledger.org/blog/2020/01/29/five-healthcare-projects-powered-by-hyperledger-you-may-not-know-about.

[32]   *Enabling privacy and control of healthcare data, IOTA* [online]. 2020. Available from https://www.iota.org/solutions/ehealth [Accessed 2020].

[33]   *Corda for healthcare, corda, 2 oct 2018.* [online]. 2020. Available from https://www.corda.net/blog/corda-for-healthcare/ [Accessed 2020].

[34]   Saravanan M., Shubha R., Marks A.M., Iyer V. 'SMEAD: a secured mobile enabled assisting device for diabetics monitoring'. *IEEE International Conference on Advanced Networks and Telecommunications Systems (ANTS)*; 2017.

[35]   Xia Q., Sifah E., Smahi A., Amofa S., Zhang X. 'BBDS: blockchain-based data sharing for electronic medical records in cloud environments'. *Information*. 2017;**8**(2):44.

[36]   Kumar M. 'Security issues and privacy concerns in the implementation of wireless body area network'. *International Conference on Information Technology*; 2014.

[37]   Chaer A., Salah K., Lima C., Ray P.P., Sheltami T. 'Blockchain for 5G: opportunities and challenges'. *IEEE Globecom Workshops (GC Wkshps)*. 2019.

[38]   Tanwar S., Parekh K., Evans R. 'Blockchain-based electronic healthcare record system for healthcare 4.0 applications'. *Journal of Information Security and Applications*. 2020;**50**(10):102407.

[39]   Gupta R., Tanwar S., Tyagi S., Kumar N. 'Tactile-internet-based telesurgery system for healthcare 4.0: an architecture, research challenges, and future directions'. *IEEE Network*. 2019;**33**(6):22–9.

Chapter 18

M2M for healthcare with blockchain security aspects

Kiran Ahuja[1], Indu Bala[2], Anand Nayyar[3,4], and Bandana Mahapatra[5]

The e-healthcare management system is currently the most vulnerable system due to a variety of security threats associated with it. Such systems demand huge bandwidth and secure and reliable internet connections all the time. Machine-to-machine (M2M), Internet of Things, and 5G wireless networks are few examples of the recent telecommunication technologies that have the potential to connect multiple heterogeneous computing devices and facilitate interaction and knowledge sharing in a wireless mode. These networks are reliable and fast and have good coverage with enhanced security features. More specifically, the 5G wireless networks are designed for high data rates with the ability to scale up to thousands of subscribers, improved coverage area, and low latency due to the efficient use of signal processing. In this chapter, an overview of 5G-based M2M communication technology and its use in the health-care industry with the amalgamation of other fast-growing technologies like the blockchain is presented.

18.1 Introduction

With the increasing number of wireless subscribers, telecom technologies are accelerating at a fast pace to offer the best possible services to the end users. However, the problem with the existing network standards is the lack of bandwidth due to overuse or inefficient use of the existing spectrum. To meet the unprecedented demand for bandwidth to satiate mobile traffic, telecom companies are looking toward 5G networks as a game changer [1]. The upcoming 5G technologies have the potential to offer information transmission speed of 10 Gb over the air, latency in the order

[1]DAV Institute of Engineering and Technology, India
[2]Lovely Professional University, India
[3]Graduate School, Duy Tan University, Vietnam
[4]Faculty of Information Technology, Duy Tan University, Vietnam
[5]Symbiosis Skills and Professional University, India

Parameter	LTE-evolution; LTE-M Rel.13	Narrowband NB-IoT	Next-generation 5G
Range (outdoor)	<11 km	<15 km	<15 km
MCL	156 dB	164 dB	164 dB
Spectrum	Licensed (7–900 MHz)	Licensed (7–900 MHz)	Licensed (7–900 MHz)
Bandwidth	1.4 MHz or shared	200 kHz or shared	Shared
Data rate	<1 Mbps	<150 Kbps	<1 Mbps
Battery life	>10 years	>10 years	>10 years
Availability	2016	2016	2025

Figure 18.1   Communication channels for the M2M network

of 1 ms, and Internet of Things (IoT) devices that can run on batteries for up to 10 years [2].

The emerging communication systems/applications like car–satellite connectivity, home automation, health security remote control, smart cities, and mobile point on sale (POS), require full automated communication with no human intervention. This novel way to communicate between devices is referred to as machine-to-machine (M2M) communications. The M2M envisages a scenario in which the equipment on both sides has tens, hundreds, or thousands of antennas, allowing for higher data rates for users while conserving electricity and bandwidth. The feasibility of this intelligent communication between devices is the main reason behind the evolution of "IoT" and applications like "Smart City" [3]. M2M communication has opened up new horizons for faster and easier communication while consuming the least power. Figure 18.1 shows the performance comparison between various communication channels for the M2M network.

The M2M communication allows direct communication between the users/devices without involving the core network by exploiting physical proximities between devices. The technology provides the extra degree of freedom by connecting multiple machine-type devices (MTDs) anytime, anywhere without using additional devices. Figure 18.2 describes the ways devices can be configured for M2M communication [4].

A. Cases for M2M connectivity

The various cases for M2M connectivity are as follows:

i.   Basic M2M connectivity
ii. M2M in which a single application shares information with a group of similar devices
iii. M2M communication using the gateway device.

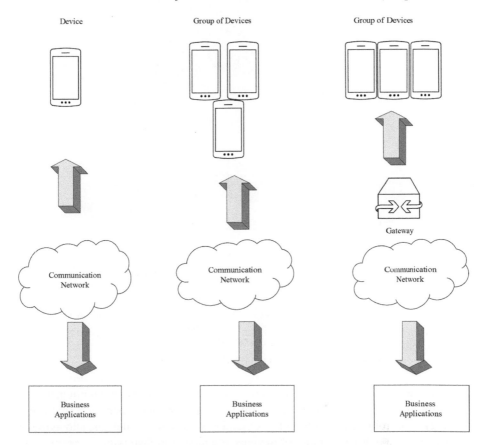

Figure 18.2   Various cases for M2M connectivity

With the different cases of M2M connectivity, new applications with worldwide services are mushrooming by connecting various types of IoT-enabled machines/gadgets to generate huge revenues. The IoT and M2M collaboratively link various networks for applications like remote industrial control systems, security metering tracking of transportation, third-party video streaming, and gaming content, voice signaling, e-health-care emergency tracking, and metering, and home and industrial automation [5]. Figure 18.3 shows the diverse applications of M2M networking.

The real-time applications using this technology require ubiquitous coverage of M2M communications due to the massive evaluations and high service requests. Though satellite connections are capable of providing ubiquitous access at prohibitive prices, they pose serious concern when utilized in confined areas. Under such circumstances, radio technologies like M2M are capable of providing broad coverage areas with low power consumption and reduced cost. Since such well-structured networks cannot replace existing cellular networks overnight, the MTC (Machine)-Type Communication) devices must be integrated with the services of the existing communication networks.

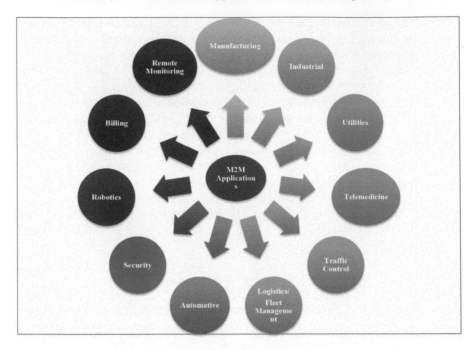

Figure 18.3   M2M communications in diverse areas

To meet the end user's expectations these days, a widespread mobile network is required that supports M2M communication and provides increased efficiency, security, and robustness. The current standards, which are designed to provide connectivity to a small number of devices, are unable to deal with the predictable increase in traffic in M2M communication networks, posing a major challenge for the 5G networks. On this basis, the main emphasis is on enforcing M2M services, which include a myriad of devices that generate efficient periodic transmissions of short data in future 5G networks.

The current generation of technology has immensely contributed to the shrinking of the huge world into a virtual ball wherein users can be connected through various devices irrespective of their geographic location. The e-health-care system in the near future is seen on the edge of undergoing significant improvements due to the widespread use of mobile devices with ever-increasing connectivity among them. The rapid advancement in technology in many fields, such as the networking and communication sector, has resulted in the introduction of new goods and services in the market. Such progress has paved the way for new business opportunities and acceptance to the previously unknown models, such as M2M communication.

According to a very recent study, approximately 10 billion IoT units were connected in 2013. An estimated 50 billion devices will be connected by the end of 2020. These devices include medical equipment, electric cars, smart lighting system, and household consumer electronic stuff, such as TVs, washing machines, refrigerators, ACs, and heaters. The related data, services, user interfaces, various platforms, and frameworks are also emerging with the rapid acceptance of these devices in our everyday lives. The data collection and communication processes of these connected machines are reliable, precise, and well-structured, allowing for the development of stable and secure applications. IoT technology has also reshaped the health-care industry by reinventing existing health-care equipment.

The chapter discusses the main challenges posed to the wireless cellular network standards to support secured massive M2M services, its applications in the e-health-care system. Section 2 highlights the state of the art, providing current standards for enabling secured M2M services in the health-care industry. Section 3 provides integration of blockchain to secure M2M communication technology with a case study/used cases. Section 4 covers the various challenging issues that need to be addressed while integrating secured blockchain to the current health-care system. Section 5 focuses on M2M implementation in the health-care industry followed by the conclusion and future research directions in Section 6.

18.2   State of the art: blockchain and M2M

The current M2M physical network system is susceptible to multiple threats and vulnerabilities. The issue has been addressed by various researchers to design some robust security mechanisms for the considered M2M/IoT network that connects multiple heterogeneous devices at the same time. The section briefly covers the M2M technology and blockchain security designed for such networks.

18.2.1   Background of the M2M network

The M2M technology aims to provide seamless connectivity to the various devices with the ability to stay connected all the time irrespective of their underlying architecture or platform. M2M can be defined as the direct communication existing among various heterogeneous devices designed using wired/wireless communication channels. M2M solutions focus on data sharing without a human interface or interaction. It includes serial connection, powerline connection, and wireless communications among IoT devices. The M2M network is quite promising while implementing the concept of IoT/5G networks that can scale up to almost millions of devices ranging from vending machines to medical equipment building vehicles. With the huge popularity of M2M among organizations and people, even hackers are keen at over-exploring the technology.

18.2.2   Background of blockchain

The concept of blockchain denotes a chain of digital blocks carrying records of transactions carried over. The data structure of blockchains is a linear link list, in which every block is attached to its next and previous blocks. This arrangement renders the blockchain content difficult to tamper with and almost immutable because a hacker may have to change the block content containing the record which once linked to it to prevent its detection.

The concept of blockchain also has certain inherent character sticks that make it much more reliable. The principle of cryptography has been used to encrypt the blockchain content data. The network participants have their private keys associated with the transactions that work as the personal digital signature. The attached signature becomes immediately invalid informing the peer network about them being hampered as soon as these records are altered in some way. The process of early notification prevents further damage to the contents and the records. Moreover, blockchains have certain desirable features that facilitate the security feature of the recorded transactional data. Although inherent security aspects are evident in the blockchain, they are quite vulnerable with regard to the infrastructures that are susceptible to manipulation.

The few main features of blockchain are as follows:

i.　It uses P2P (Peer to peer) networking along with a consensus mechanism, which helps in establishing the first among the nodes forming a decentralized system.

ii.　It uses an asymmetric encryption mechanism to protect records/ transaction data.

iii.　All the data in the transactions are possible due to the blockchain structure.

18.2.3　Integration of blockchain and M2M

The concept of a cyber-physical system (CPS) can be defined as a complex system consisting of computation and networks along with the physical world. The CPS is capable of digitalizing the physical world keeping intact the unity of the information world with the help of 3Cs, namely, computation, communication, and control technologies. The concept of the cyber-physical world can be segregated into two parts:

i.　Physical world

ii.　Information world/digital world.

The CPS constantly keeps track of the action of the entities in the physical world to mine and analyze the data from the information world and take actions to change their behavior to make entities work efficiently. Given the current volatile nature, the industrial IoT carries the physical and virtual bodies that have their own identities and properties. The current security protocol supported by M2M lacks the capabilities of resolving problems related to the intercommunication between the heterogeneous devices involved in the CPS. Hence, the blockchain as a security system seems to be quite a promising proposition for integration with the current M2M communication system.

18.2.4 Literature survey/related work

Researchers have predicted that more than a billion devices would connect with the M2M communications through mobile networks by 2020 [5]. Statistics disclose that worldwide versatile traffic will encounter development around 70% in which 26% PDAs (Personal Digital Assistants) are accountable for 88% of complete traffic. The present 4G cell frameworks failed to help this immense size of information utilization because they were designed to first hold up to 600 RCC (Resident Computer Consultant) associated clients for every cell [6]. M2M interchanges and the IoTs require to support a huge number of associated gadgets in a single cell. This situation makes it essential to support the standards to enable M2M communications.

Laya *et al.* [7] stated to differentiate the M2M communications from mobile human to human-based communication (H2H) because the H2H traffic (browsing, file transfer, and video streaming) cannot be directly applied to the M2M [8]. The M2M traffic direction is an uplink, whereas the H2H traffic direction works as a downlink. The M2M applications are duty-cycled with a short connection and promise fast access to the M2M network. These applications resolve the major traffic problems in M2M communications.

Wireless communications cannot refrain from facing the novel challenges of radio spectral congestion due to increased H2H and M2M traffic. BatoolTalha [9] was surveyed to provide a complete analysis of the M2M fading channels in cooperative and coordinated networks under the propagation conditions of the line of sight (LOS) and non-LOS. The survey evaluated the act of dual-hope-relay-systems with equivalent gain combination, which improved the overall system recital of the LOS components in the transmitting links [9]. Apart from the radio spectral congestion, current research studies defined the problems determined by M2M gadgets (utilizing radio advancements), for example, channel quality variances and noise presenting coordination ambiguities in the medium access [10], making the communication unreliable. Lu *et al.* [11] explained that this unreliable processing and transmissions in the communication medium lead to data loss, causing a major M2M failure. Thus, reliability is an unresolved challenge for the M2M standards.

A notable increase in the concurrent accesses can be observed with the rapid increase in the number of wireless users, making simultaneous access to increase more packet collisions due to interference resulting in data loss. Subsequently, augmenting the uplink channel and streamlining the radio asset assignment improved with proficient quality of service (QoS). Alongside dependable QoS, M2M gadgets are designed to ensure that they are commonly reasonable and small in size with vitality, transmission capacity, and other storage requirements for communication. The networks on which these M2M gadgets work offer wide inclusion zones with high information rates and diminished idleness; despite the assured benefits, many more challenges to the M2M networks have been specified in the paper by Hattangady [12]. Marwat *et al.* [13] testified the M2M traffic in the presence of 4G traffic, which is not to be considered negligible; accordingly, the performance of the 4G networks in terms of QoS degraded. Thus, the operation of M2M should be seamless (i.e., without human intervention preventing occasional physical attacks) [14].

This plausible success of the M2M applications overcoming all these challenges can promise to increment the variety and number of the gadgets to be associated and the traffic in the upcoming years. The current studies are focused on improving the performance and the usefulness of the framework, as far as power utilization, proficiency, or delay are concerned.

Moreover, further improvements supporting M2M communications have been analyzed using sensor-to-gateway communications in terms of delay and energy efficiency in wireless M2M introducing contention-based MAC (Media Access Control) protocols [15]. The study defined the use of gateways in the wireless M2M network driving a large number of devices that regularly wake their radio interfaces to the gateway carrying out high data rates with low latency. This use of gateways is supposed to reduce the number of devices to be accessed, thereby making the transmission less complex and reducing interference with increased efficiency.

The idea of clone-to-clone to solve the issues obstructing the development of the next-generation applications by reducing the traffic, recovering overall network performances, and mitigating the power consumption of the devices had been explained by Aucinas *et al.* [16]. Prasad and Kumar [17] also mentioned the principle of energy efficiency and reliability and the use of green allocation with zone algorithm to achieve overall power and energy efficiency for a reliable M2M communication.

With the sudden advancements in user-supported communication, including e-health, security, and surveillance, industrial and energy, which are among the crucial areas in need of the M2M devices communication, are the intelligent transportation systems (ITS). The key component of ITS is the Vehicular Ad Hoc Network, which is created and connected by the mobile and adhoc networks for data sharing among the wireless networks. Emphasis on the same has been made to define the M2M vehicular networking with the standardization of communication interfaces as a major challenge with high mobility and variability of components [18]. Lo *et al.* [19] characterized the data aggregation methods that can be presented for channel access improvements in M2M communication for cell networks that express the utilization of delay to increase uplink transmission efficiency. The worldwide delay would diminish with the expanded number of M2M gadgets. The transmission scheduling procedure is an additional plan to lessen delay or accomplish higher power and energy utilization efficiency [20]. The previously existing planned carriers as transfers between ground gadgets and satellites offering another M2M framework have been reviewed by Plass *et al.* [21].

M2M communication is not reliable if the portability, delay patterns, and explicit energy efficiency are not satisfied. This rule prevails during the utilization of radio advancements for communications because of the lower accessible data transfer capacity, higher connection disappointment, and higher energy utilization. Lastly, future studies could most certainly look at completely different procedures (transmission scheduling plans, data aggregation, and gateways) to reduce the measure of fundamental information to be submitted. Managing security and privacy in such a vivid network (M2M) requires good attention, making M2M communications more efficient.

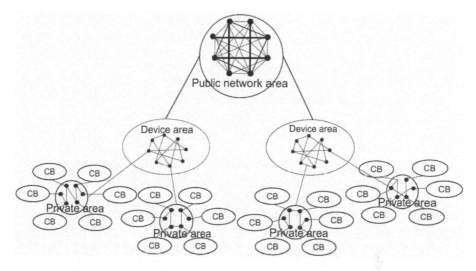

Figure 18.4   Blockchain design in the cyber-physical system

The current M2M standards that have supported the M2M communications are summarized. Then, the next section testifies the challenges that need to be overcome along with their proposed solutions.

18.3   Blockchain for M2M-enabling technologies

The data disseminators are expected to send actual, permissible, and consistent data to incorporate many features like practicality, consistency, and controllability, and so on, for attaining validity of data and ensuring data throughput and extensibility. The data communication can be encrypted, recorded, questionable, and perceptible. The receivers can obtain the data sent on behalf of the senders that may not be possibly forwarded. The data-receiving procedures can be recorded and examined. In an M2M transmission system of CPS, the blockchain design consists of three sections, as shown in Figure 18.4.

A. *Public network area* The public area network is built upon the industrial IoTs, and it typically builds the machine communication platforms. This network establishes normal communication involving different machines, registration verification of machines, machine authentication to establish connection and communication among them, and amalgamation of data formats and related communication protocols. Moreover, the network preserves various blocks of the public network area and related queries based on the communication records.

B. *Device area* It represents the communication channel established between the public network area with the private area. This channel handles the queries received from the public network area and yields results to the private area.

C. *Private area* The private area establishes and records various blocks of communication among machines. This area keeps several formatted statistics related to

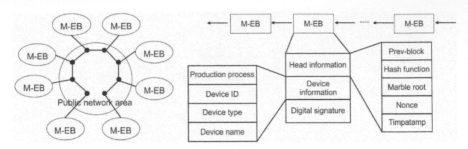

Figure 18.5   Structure of machine–equipment blockchain (M–EB)

the communication process, handles external queries, and retrieves external data while processing the query. Machines are connected to the production line through registration. To do so, every new device generates a private key by using a randomly generated number with the help of certain algorithms, such as SHA256 [22]. Later, a different algorithm, such as the Secp256K1 algorithm [23], is used to generate a public key. After a key pair is generated, a new device/machine transmits the digital certificate for the registration and approval process. The public network adds the generated public key after registration as a new blockchain into the machine–equipment blockchain (M–EB).

Figure 18.5 shows the structure of the M–EB. Once the public area accepts and registers the new device, the M–EB confirms the device identity after verification of its encrypted digital certificate.

18.3.1   Communication blockchain design in the public network area

The communication blockchain maintains records of different activities among the devices. Every communication is considered a block and connected to the blockchain. The individual block has a communication ID, information on data type, information about data size, and the type of encryption mode stored in the block. Figure 18.6 shows a query generated by a device M1 for its communication record with device M2. The device sends a query packet onto the public network area. When the query is successfully handled, M2 transmits the packet containing information related to the query raised by M1 through the public network area. Otherwise, a failure message is returned.

18.3.2   Communication blockchain design in the private network area

A typical private sector deals with recording communications between blocks, data storage, and query handling, and information retrieval. Each block as part of the blockchains (BCs) comprises the information header and data. A typical header contains a hash value that links the current block to the previous block, a target hash, a nonce, a Merkle root, a timestamp, and some other components. Communication

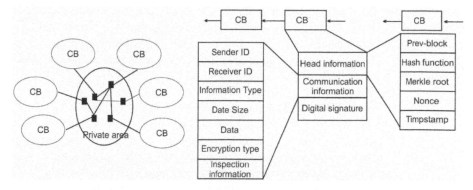

Figure 18.6   Query packet search in a public network

data contain sender's ID, recipient ID, data type to distinguish between uploading or downloading data, information size, number of byte information in the data, information about the encryption type, and verification data to check the accuracy of the transmission.

18.4   Challenges and proposed solutions of M2M

Many tech companies are jumping on board with devices spanning from wearable to beacon modules with the advancement of M2M and IoT applications. Many concerns need to be addressed for the successful deployment of M2M and IoT technologies. Thus, the challenges and resistance from each aspect varying from cost and power to the long-term product life cycle of the M2M devices must be studied. The challenges to enable the M2M communications include small-sized data transmissions supported by the larger value of devices after regular and irregular intervals, high reliability, low latency, and low energy-consuming mobile profiles assuring that regular H2H traffic is not disturbed by the M2M traffic.

18.4.1   Physical random access channel (PRACH) overload problem

The random access channel (RACH) process is one of the key challenges [24] for M2M. This difficulty is attributed to the traffic load caused by a rapid rush of myriad M2M devices trying to simultaneously access the base station. According to the latest M2M traffic survey, approximately 3.2 billion M2M cellular-based devices are estimated to join the network in 2024, making QoS provisioning an important challenge for M2M communications.

The contention to access PRACH resources is suspected to debase the M2M services. The enormous access calls by M2M devices burden the PRACH, resulting in access delay and failure rate. This traffic load can be reduced by multiplying the number of access devices scheduled per frame; however, it further introduces a new challenge of diminished capacity for the devices. Schemes must be deduced to overcome this overload problem. Holma *et al.* forwarded various methods, which include the isolation of the M2M and H2H services by simply splitting the two or making the two services share the same resource, providing them a combined name of hybrid schemes. Various other approaches have also been proposed to offset PRACH overload [25].

i.   ***Pull-based scheme***: This mechanism is a central scheme that permits the MTDs to access the PRACH paged by the eNode (eNB) [25] keeping an account of the network load conditions to prevent overloading problems. With this approach, the network channels can be managed to have regular traffic patterns by using a single server. However, the scheme cannot deal with the unexpected flow of MTD access requests because it is managed by a single M2M server.

ii. ***Resource separation***: This scheme provides the easiest and instant approach to shield H2H gadgets from the risk of crashes because of various MTC demands by allotting symmetrical PRACH assets to H2H and M2M gadgets. The separation of resources can be performed either by parting the H2H and MTC gadgets into groups or by basically allocating them diverse RA time/recurrence openings [25]. Coupling with a mechanism that progressively moves the assets among the two classes in agreement with the necessary access demand rates is required to improve impact.

iii. ***Back-off tuning***: Another scheme to effectively clear the congestion caused by the traffic of requests is by assigning the back-off intervals to the MTDs that fail the transmission in RACH procedures [25]. Although the collisions between the H2H and the M2M devices can be efficiently improved, this scheme is not effective when dealing with stationary MTD massive access due to instability issues initialized by the ALOHA (Additive Links On-Line Hawaii Area)-like mechanisms.

iv. ***Access class barring (ACB)***: The above-stated back-off tuning mechanism is a generalization of the ACB method. The ACB scheme has each class allotted with an access probability with a barrier time [25] making it probable to define several access classes with dissimilar access probabilities. The access of the device is debarred; accordingly, the device will have to wait for a random back-off time when the message transmitted in the RA slot is larger than that of the access probability factor. Another scheme, namely, extended access barring (EAB), was projected to withstand longer access delays, hence barring the device without the need for any new access class. This technique allows the MTD to mitigate the massive access issue by simply labeling it as an EAB device. Thus, ACB can help prevent the overload problem, but only during longer access delays for the MTDs. However, ACB fails in the case of contention-based access events, such as fire alarms due to power failures, or any other unexpected event that requires short-time intervals.

v. ***Self-optimizing overload control (SOOC)***: A complex scheme (i.e., SOOC) to offset PRACH overload by simply merging the pull-based, back-off, ACB, including the resource separation scheme, has been discussed. The essential element of this plan is the usage of the control circle to gather data for overburden analysis at each RA cycle. The gadget enters the overburden control mode, and the old-style p-persistent system is applied for the guideline of RA (Random Access) cycles when it cannot receive an access grant at the primary endeavor. Two access classes, namely, low-priority access need and high-priority access, have been added in this scheme for the M2M devices to separate between time-lenient and time-delicate MTDs. Although handling high traffic loads can be attained using this scheme, enough evidence relating to the performance of this scheme has not been provided.

vi. ***Bulk MTC signaling scheme***: Another scheme mentioned by Lo *et al.* [26] provided a further solution to overload problems by enabling bulk MTC signal handling stating lack of mechanisms while handling overheads generated from collective MTDs. This overhead can be reduced at the base station by using bulk processing (collecting signal data coming from MTDs before accelerating them to the core network). A representation for this plan is as follows: consider a group of MTDs that are triggered to send tracking area update (TAU), where the base station needs to wait for a default timeout or anticipate the time it has accumulated enough data to advance a message toward the mobility management entity (MME). Given that the MTDs are connected to the equivalent MME, the TAU messages will be diverse on the MME temporary mobile subscriber identity (M-TMSI). In a situation with a normal of 20 TAU msg/s with a time of 10 s, 200 TAU messages can be consolidated in a single 1211 bytes/msg; by contrast, an individual message would acquire up to 4500 bytes of space. Hence, the approach in this scheme can reduce the intensity of traffic produced by large channel access.

18.4.2   Inefficient radio resource utilization and allocation

The existing cellular standards are not capable of handling a large number of devices with small-sized payloads leading to network congestion. Given this situation, existing mobile networks must be amended to support diverse M2M devices in ensuring efficient allocation and utilization of the radio resources. Accordingly, novel methods are introduced to manage the radio access network overload issue (e.g.,

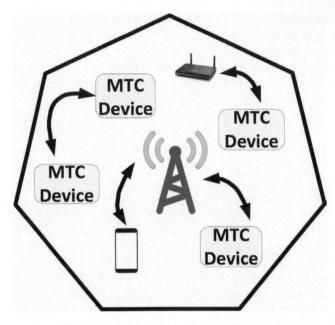

Figure 18.7   Radio resource allocation criteria in the existing mobile standards

M2M prioritization and back-off adjustment) and express those current networks that must be modified to help different M2M gadgets to be associated in the future. Cellular radio resources are significant assets that are barely open. Hence, the effective activity of such radio assets for M2M should be ensured. This effective use of the restricted radio assets must be practiced; otherwise, the performance of M2M will probably deteriorate. This concern must be addressed to minimize congestion issues in the M2M benefits. Figure 18.7 shows the resource portion in the current versatile guidelines that are neither proposed to effectively control the small data nor can simultaneously deal with myriad devices [27].

The primary challenge when assorted traffic occurs is the administration of obstruction that needs a complicated resource segregating mechanism. Segregation permits an organized radio resource division among different gadgets, thereby diminishing the congestion issues. A few scheduling calculations have been proposed to assess the performance to have real control of throughput and uniformity between the end clients [22, 23, 28, 29]. Figure 18.8 shows the resource allocation supporting M2M communication.

18.4.3   Clustering techniques

Various clustering techniques making allowance for priorities and delay restrictions to handle massive access have been introduced for supporting the maximum number of devices to be connected in the M2M network. Figure 18.9 illustrates an example of the clustering technique in the M2M networks.

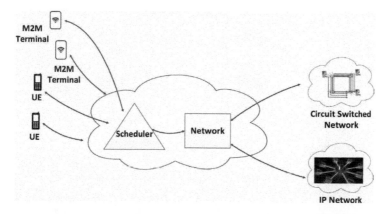

Figure 18.8   Resource scheduling supporting M2M

i.   ***PRACH-based clustering mechanism in M2M devices:*** In the clustering mechanism, all devices in a network are associated with one or more groups based on their geographical location in the QoS requirements [29]. The clustering scheme is beneficial in minimizing the energy consumption for MTDs [23], which reduces the risk of network collisions. Another scheme that has been proposed is the vigorous radio resource allocation in which an eNB assigns PRACH assets between the MTDs based on the PRACH stream of traffic capacity in that specific network [30], hence enabling this clustering mechanism.

ii. ***Energy-efficient clustering of MTDs:*** MTDs are powered with batteries that have limited energy; thus, the energy consumption

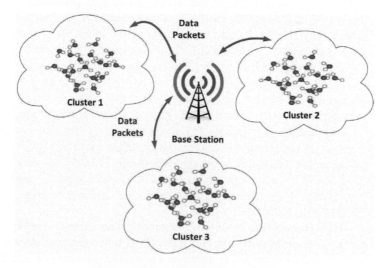

Figure 18.9   Clustering mechanism

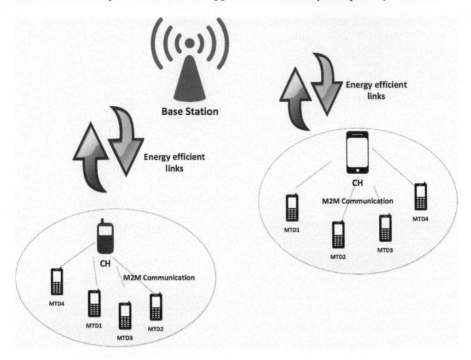

Figure 18.10   Energy-efficient clustering of MTDs

cannot be ignored in real-time networks, especially in the case of M2M communications. To enhance the MTDs' lifetime, energy efficiency has been deliberated as a significant factor due to the energy consumption during the access phase and computation. The energy consumption during data computation is also considered, which is either due to calculations at the local MTD or by the coordinator or offloaded MEC (Multi-Access Edge Computing) server. The network cognition can be controlled by appointing nodes to the base station known as cluster heads, which can limit the number of requests at the base station. The risk of cognition due to massive access could also be reduced by selecting the coordinators that can help in reducing power and energy consumption. More schemes for this massive access management and power efficiency are combined in the paper by Andres-Maldonado *et al.* [23], where the idea is to forward N MTDs, which are employed in a single cell centered at the base station maximizing the energy efficiency of the MTDs (Figure 18.10).

iii.   ***QoS-based clustering technique:*** Clustering is an effective remedy for the vast assignment of a large number of MTDs having small transmission and distinct QoS requirements to a radio resource [29, 31]. In this technique, the devices are grouped depending on their arrival rates, which helps in forming clusters of the devices having similar QoS requirements to provide efficient power and energy consumption.

18.4.4 *QoS provisioning for M2M device communication*

QoS provisioning is the most important requirement of the telecommunication system. This condition is an arrangement of service-linked chores related to the facility supplier to provide desirable service to the consumer [32]. Table 18.1 provides information related to the class types of QoS for M2M communications [33, 34].

18.4.5 *Cheap price and low power requirements for devices*

In addition to the technical complexities summarized in the paper by Mehmood *et al.* [35], a vagueness that administrators the need to deliver is on the most proficient method to charge the client for the M2M services. An essential M2M gadget requests low cost and low power utilization. The gadgets that go about as transfers for different clients utilize certain resources, such as a battery, information storage, and data transmission, which affect the price model of these gadgets to take an interest in such communication. M2M equipment/gadgets will be eventually used for a lengthier timeframe, which will become a difficult task for part networks and service providers. Moreover, devices waste most of the time in their idle state due to long inter-arrival time. This idle state is a low-powered sleep state to save battery, and the device wakes up periodically to check system information updates [36]. Therefore, the key concept is to mend the battery epoch to moderate the activity of the slothful mode which can be easily sustained using the paging cycles which should not be regular. Thus, the devices must be in active mode during data transmission only. Table 18.2 provides us an idea about the various efforts on the cost and power optimization efforts for efficient M2M communication. These devised mechanisms result in low power devices that help in reducing the cost of the services [35, 37].

18.4.6 *Security and privacy*

With the diverse heterogeneous networks, M2M communications require addressing all the threats while communicating with different network-based communication criteria [38]. We cannot imagine M2M without new threats. These threats are prone to intensify the existing ones within the M2M environment, and they will also cause financial losses and threats to human lives indirectly. M2M devices are mainly deployed in user-friendly environments and may work for prolonged periods. Therefore, numerous physical attacks will coexist with devices. Figure 18.11 illustrates the major categories of attacks in the case of M2M, and their probable solutions are shown in Figure 18.12.

A desired feature of any communication system is the non-disclosure of personal information. Otherwise, divulgence of data can create huge losses either in terms of personal assets or corporate ones. In M2M, secrecy must be observed due to the existence of smart things, which indirectly create a threat when the technology

Table 18.1   QoS class types for M2M devices' communication

Parameters	Type 0	Type 1	Type 2	Type 3	Type 4
Purpose	Health security, remote control, and maintenance	IP multimedia subsystem and wireless point on sale (POS)	Video Streaming	Home Automation	Security Metering Tracking
Features	High reliability and access priority	High security and privacy	Access priority and low latency	Increased Security	Low error rate
Traffic type	Random Real-time	Random Real-time	Random	Random	Regular
Priority	High	Low	Low	Low	Low
Mobility	Low	Low	Low	No	Low

Table 18.2   Optimization of low-cost and low-power M2M devices

Parameters	Category-0	Category-1	Category-4	Ref-13
Release	Release 12	Release 8	Release 8	Release 13
Downlink peak rate (Mbps)	1	10	15	~200
Uplink peak rate (Mbps)	1	5	50	~200
Bandwidth (MHz)	20	20	20	1.4
Mode	Half duplex	Full duplex	Full duplex	Half duplex
Complexity (%)	50	100	125	25
Transmitting power rate (dBm)	23	23	23	~20

is mishandled. A massive number of smart things create a huge challenge in preserving the seclusion of private data. One of the criteria is to launch a third-party reliable security association, which will be liable for endorsement distribution. If a huge number of M2M devices have different applications, then this scheme is expensive to be applied. Given this constraint, a lightweight cryptographic technique is preferred in M2M communications. Asymmetric and symmetric key authentication can also be applicable in a variety of deployment situations of M2M communications.

18.5   M2M implementation in healthcare—a future direction

M2M communications have a significant impact on the clinical gadget field because associated clinical gadgets can undergo progressive changes. This situation can add an entirely different measurement to understanding consideration, doctor connection, clinical gadget ease of use, and support. Umpteen roads in administrations, advancement, and business can be opened up. A couple of such use cases have been itemized below [39].

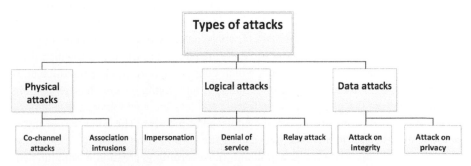

Figure 18.11   Diverse types of attacks that may occur during M2M communication

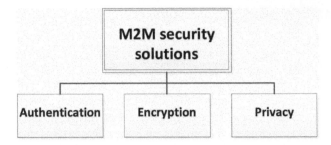

Figure 18.12   Probable solutions for the M2M security issues

18.5.1   Predictive maintenance of medical devices by employing M2M

The clinical gadgets that are utilized to treat or analyze perilous conditions are complex and costly. These gadgets should be worked by profoundly skilled faculty and should be in the best of conditions consistently to provide optimal outcomes. Mistake resilience in such gadgets is close to zero. This goal is difficult to achieve given the mileage in question. Proactive support is an ideal approach to do this task, and M2M is the best that innovation brings to the table for this reason. Associated clinical gadgets can persistently stream information for their use, which can be stored on a safe cloud. Observing and gathering utilization information should be non-stop as much as possible and can be continuously dissected to check the requirement for booked upkeep. In light of the continuous examination, future flaws or disappointments can be anticipated and mitigated, and the necessary parts or extras that are exhausted or harmed can be found and replaced. Accordingly, the maintenance costs for emergency clinics or gadget proprietors will be significantly reduced.

18.5.2   Intelligent manufacturing by M2M

Envision a situation wherein all the clinical gadgets are associated, and M2M information is progressively accessible. Gadget utilization measurements can be examined to build up use patterns and can be coordinated with the assembling division of a clinical gadget's organization, giving it the bits of knowledge into which parts are getting now and again exhausted, which ones need more stock, and which ones require less. Bits of knowledge can be brought into configuration changes that are required to make the gadgets more effective and less inclined toward mistake or to be fixed by the prolonged and chronicled usage of patterns. These sources of information are received in advance because of the combination of M2M information with the ERP (Enterprise resource planning). Accordingly, creation is smoothened, and stock expenses are diminished, thereby empowering the association to keep up a lean, spry, and flexible chain.

18.5.3   M2M creates smart hospitals

In the current situation, clinics are the sole administrators and proprietors of clinical gadgets. These gadgets act as an information generators and recorders which can be used in an emergent situation. Medical clinics can pass on a portion of the weight of observing and keeping up the gadgets to their makers or outsider associations doled out for this reason. Emergency hospitals or clinical experts can worry about just utilizing these gadgets instead of investing important energy in their support. More progressions can even prompt clinical gadgets to be offered as assistance as opposed to being sold as a gadget. In this situation, clinics or clinical experts will not own the gadget; however, just compensation for its utilization will be provided, while the gadget would be claimed by its producer or item seller. This situation can introduce fast changes in developing nations attributable to financial feasibilities.

18.5.4   M2M provisions automatic alerting systems

Smart medication allocators can record the time and date when the medicine is taken and can caution the patient when she/he neglects to take it. GPS-empowered, shrewd clinical gadgets can be worn like a watch and provide non-stop area subtleties to patients experiencing certain illnesses, such as Alzheimer's disease, rest strolling, and epilepsy. These gadgets can send cautions or alerts to the concerned clinical expert or guardian at whatever point the patient moves out of the security limits or when seen as suspiciously fixed.

18.5.5   Emergency medical services possible via M2M

If crises occur even before patients show up at the medical clinic, then their data can be sent from afar to the emergency clinic; thus, it may be prepared with the funda-mental equipment for starting treatment.

18.5.6   Remote vital sign monitoring from a hospital environment through M2M

Remotely empowered miniature gadgets can be inserted into patients with chronic illnesses, such as diabetes and hypertension; accordingly, their fundamental signs can be checked from afar by doctors without the patients visiting the clinic. This situation can be made conceivable with the ceaseless information stream that is communicated by these remote implanted gadgets that can be worked by a wide number of remote conventions accessible to date, for example, ZigBee and Z-Wave.

18.5.7   Post-marketing surveillance of medical devices

The gadgets can be checked for their security and adequacy after they are approved for usage. The information produced and streamed by the installed contributes to these gadgets is more precise and solid than information provided manually. Aside from the above-mentioned situations, a few different territories exist, for example, clinical imaging, image-guided medical procedures, working room co-ordinations, and smart ICUs in emergency clinics that can exploit this wave to obtain better planning, more productivity, and differentiated assistance.

18.5.8   Security and interoperability in healthcare

Physical frameworks, which are regarded as the center of intelligent manufacturing, have genuine security issues, particularly for the correspondence security of their terminal M2M communications. Blockchain innovation is acquainted with an address, such as a security issue of correspondences between various types of machines. The M2M, as a communication framework, comprises open system regions, gadget regions, and private territories, and a modern blockchain structure is needed between the open territory and the private region. Blockchain innovation can adequately comprehend the security of the development of machines in the creation procedure, and the correspondence information between the machines cannot be tampered with. Blockchain is used in medicinal services because of the need for security and interoperability in healthcare. A substantial amount of clinical information is recorded and moved each day with the development of IoT and the plenitude of health-care gadgets and versatile health insurance applications. This information traffic needs the board for protection and security. Blockchain innovation can provide an answer that not only assists with ensuring chronicle and sharing of clinical records but also guarantees the security of every patient's information by giving the patients their clinical information proprietorship. Apart from the benefits of blockchain for medicinal services, the difficulties of the board must be addressed ahead of time. When the supplier has the patient's information, it could have it forever by some other methods, even though the patient may not need it; this is one of the disadvantages of employing blockchain techniques in healthcare. Patients are not aware of this innovation. Disarray on where the information would be put away and who can approach this information would emerge [40]. Figure 18.13 shows the model of interaction seen in various health-care industries concerning different major fields of IT.

To date, electronic health records (EHRs) were never kept by hospitals as a lifetime record to diagnose future illnesses. Thus, new creative methods are required to maintain patient EHRs, which urges patients to take part in their latest and historical authenticated health-care information. Numerous researchers have raised blockchain innovation in keeping up the EHRs.

Figure 18.14 shows the various features that make the concept of blockchain highly applicable in various fields of the industry. Data security and privacy are the most promising and challenging features of the blockchain. Blockchain-based implementation eliminates the dependence on third-party authentication to carry out any transaction [41]. The blockchain mechanism allows the entire network to affirm the records in a blockchain plan rather than a single third party [42–44]. Accordingly, the data are skewed against possible assurance and security risks. Data accuracy will not be ensured because all nodes can be sent by a single node. The absence of a third-party endorsement requires the patient to choose at least one agent to obtain his clinical history in case of emergency. Under such

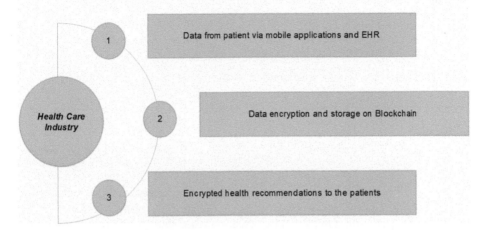

Figure 18.13   Electronic health record (EHR) interaction with other health applications, technology, and preventative care

circumstances, the agent can allow multiple people to have access to the patient records.

The data flow is restricted from one block to another to add high-security components to the information. Accordingly, the receivers will obtain restricted or fragmented information. Blockchain-based systems are inclined toward the security penetration known as 51% attack [45, 46]. This attack allows a group of miners to own 50% of the blocks in a blockchain arrangement and authorizes them to have access to the system to initiate new exchanges without obtaining consent. In CoinDesk [47], five cryptographic forms of money have been a casualty of this attack recently. A patient record may have sensitive information that is inadmissible to be on the blockchain.

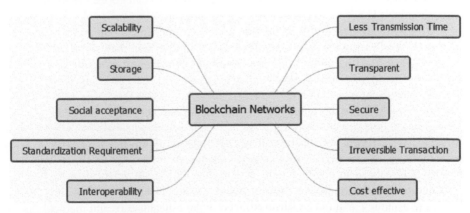

Figure 18.14   Various opportunities and challenges of blockchain technology in healthcare

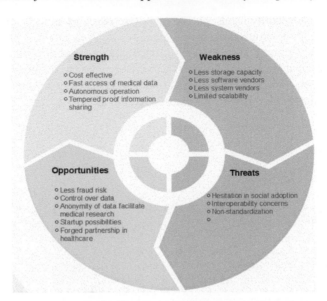

Figure 18.15   SWOT analysis for the blockchain in the health-care system

Comprehensive investigations of SWOT (Strengths, Weaknesses, Opportunities, Threats) analysis have been presented in Figure 18.15 as a reference for future researchers to additionally comprehend, inspect, and recognize the strengths, shortcomings, openings, and threats experienced during blockchain innovation in the health-care area.

18.5.9   Use cases of blockchain-based M2M-enabled health-care applications

Blockchain in healthcare can be roughly divided into three categories [48–51]:

i.   Medical records and patient data storage: the current implementation level in the case of medical records and patient data storage is low. Hence, blockchain-based solutions can offer a better alternative for the storage and exchange of medical records along with patients' data

ii.   Issues faced while transmitting data from one hospital to the other [52–58]

iii. High cost of transaction involved while gaining access over any historical record in case urgently needed.

Many researchers have greatly focused on blockchain-based medical IoT devices to remove technical constraints faced in the e-health-care and medical systems. This initiative aims to resolve few major challenges due to certain inherent features of the system, such as [59–71]:

i. Data security levels: can be mainly resolved by blockchain-based M2M communication
ii. Lack of control over patients: data-blockchain restricts the access of data related to personal health records into chosen ones
iii. Unused undervalued information: the blockchain-based integrated data storage system provides storage and access to the collected data.

18.6 Conclusion

The current cellular systems are not capable of exploiting the full potential of M2M communication. However, these systems meet the current demands and the user approaches for the M2M services to some extent. The popularity of the M2M applications in the future is more likely to rely upon a combination of proprietary technologies intended for MTD connectivity. Considering that the M2M devices and applications remain equipped for a long time with minimum intervention and maintenance, the M2M architecture is most likely to last for many years and will be ultimately absorbed by 5G. This architecture will concentrate more on dominating non-cellular technologies that are purely recommended for future M2M services. Finally, the above-stated challenges need to be worked upon, including the challenges right from the regulation of organizations, companies of network tools and consumer devices, and network operatives to the application sources, for efficient, optimized, and reliable communication. The capacity to trade information safely is significant with the goal that new borderless incorporated medicinal services administrations can be given to patients via M2M successfully. Blockchain innovation is a truly necessary move toward incorporated human services because of its decentralized nature, giving new experiences and tending to a portion of the primary difficulties of numerous health-care regions. Blockchain permits human service suppliers to record and oversee shared exchanges through a system without focal power while communicating through M2M.

References

[1] Chin W., Fan Z., Haines R. 'Emerging technologies and research challenges for 5G wireless networks'. *IEEE Wireless Communications*. 2014;**21**(2):106–12.

[2] Intelligence G.S.M.A. 'Understanding 5G: perspectives on future technological advancements in mobile'. *White Paper*. 2014:1–26.

[3] Bala I., Singh G. 'Green Communication for Cognitive Cities' in Ahuja K., Khosla A. (eds.). *Driving the Development, Management, and Sustainability of Cognitive Cities*. IGI Global.; 2019. pp. 87–110.

[4]   Aschenbrenner D. Human-robot interaction concepts for human supervisory control and telemaintenance applications in an industry 4.0 environment.[Thesis]; 2017/06/20.

[5]   Bala I., Bhamrah M.S., Singh G. 'Rate and power optimization under received-power constraints for opportunistic spectrum-sharing communication'. *Wireless Personal Communications*. 2017;**96**(4):5667–85.

[6]   Holma H., Toskala A., Reunanen J. *LTE Small Cell Optimization: 3GPP Evolution to Release 13*. John Wiley & Sons Ltd; 2015.

[7]   Laya A., Alonso L., Alonso-Zarate J. 'Is the random access channel of LTE and LTE–a suitable for M2M communications? A survey of alternatives'. *IEEE Communications Surveys & Tutorials*. 2014;**16**(1):4–16.

[8]   Lien S.-Y., Chen K.-C., Lin Y. 'Toward ubiquitous massive accesses in 3GPP machine-to-machine communications'. *IEEE Communications Magazine*. 2011;**49**(4):66–74.

[9]   Batool Talha. *Mobile-to-Mobile Cooperative Communication Systems: Channel Modelling and System Performance Analysis*. LAP Lambert Academic Publishing; 2011.

[10] Zhang Y., Yu R., Xie S., Yao W., Xiao Y., Guizani M. 'Home M2M networks: architectures, Standards, and QoS improvement'. *IEEE communications magazine*. 2011;**49**(4):44–52.

[11] Lu R., Li X., Liang X., Shen X., Lin X.G.R.S. 'The green, reliability, and security of emerging machine to machine communications'. *IEEE Communications Magazine*. 2011;**49**:28–35.

[12] Hattangady S. *Wireless M2M the opportunity is here! (Part 1)*. Cellular Whitepaper Part 1. pdf; 2009.

[13] Marwat., Khan S.N., Pötsch T., Zaki Y., Weerawardane T., Görg C. 'Addressing the challenges of E-healthcare in future mobile networks'. *Meeting of the European Network of Universities and Companies in Information and Communication Engineering*. Berlin, Heidelberg: Springer; 2013. pp. 90–9.

[14] Booysen M., Gilmore J., Zeadally S., Rooyen G. 'Machine-to-machine (M2M) communications in vehicular networks'. *KSII Transactions on Internet and Information Systems*. 2012;**6**:529–46.

[15] Gallego F.V., Alonso-Zarate J., Alonso L. 'Energy and delay analysis of contention resolution mechanisms for machine-to-machine networks based on low-power WiFi'. IEEE International Conference on Communications (ICC); 2013. pp. 2235–40.

[16] Aucinas A., Crowcroft J., Hui P. 'Energy efficient mobile M2M communications'. *Proceedings of ExtremeCom*; Zürich, Switzerland, March 10-14; 2012. pp. 1–6.

[17] Prasad S.S., Kumar C. 'A methodology for an efficient and reliable M2M communication'. *International Journal of Soft Computing and Engineering (IJSCE)*. 2013;**3**(5):2231–307.

[18] Booysen M.J., Gilmore J.S., Zeadally S.R., Rooyen G. 'Machine-to-Machine (M2M) communications in vehicular networks'. *KSII Transactions on Internet and Information Systems*. 2012;**6**(2):529–46.

[19] Lo A., Law Y., Jacobsson M. 'A cellular-centric service architecture for machine-to-machine (M2M) communications'. *IEEE Wireless Communications*. 2013;**20**(5):143–51.

[20] Yunoki S., Takada M., Liu C. 'Experimental results of remote energy monitoring system via cellular network in China'. *Proceedings of the SICE Annual Conference (SICE)*; Akita, Japan, August; 2012. pp. 948–54.

[21] Plass S., Berioli M., Hermenier R. 'Concept for an M2M communications infrastructure via airliners'. *Proceedings of the 2012 Future Network Mobile Summit (FutureNetw)*; Berlin, Germany; 2012. pp. 1–8.

[22] Safdar H., Fisal N., Ullah R., *et al.* 'Resource allocation for uplink M2M communication: a game theory approach'. *IEEE Symposium on Wireless Technology and Applications (ISWTA)*; IEEE, Kuching, Malaysia; 2013. pp. 48–52.

[23] Andres-Maldonado P., Ameigeiras P., Prados-Garzon J., Ramos-Munoz J.J., Lopez-Soler J.M. 'Reduced M2M signaling communications in 3GPP LTE and future 5G cellular networks'. *Wireless Days (WD), Toulouse*. 2016:1–3.

[24] Taleb T., Kunz A. 'Machine type communications in 3GPP networks: potential, challenges, and solutions'. *IEEE Communications Magazine*. 2012;**50**(3):178–84.

[25] 3GPP. 'Study on RAN improvements for machine-type communications'. *Technical Report, 3GPP TR 37.868 V11.0.0*; 2011.

[26] Lo A., Law Y.W., Jacobsson M., Kucharzak M. 'Enhanced LTE-advanced random-access mechanism for massive machine-to-machine (M2M) communications'. *27th World Wireless Research Forum (WWRF) Meeting*; Dusseldorf, Germany Dusseldorf; 2011.

[27] Rana V. 'Resource allocation models for cognitive radio networks : a study'. 2014;**91**(12):51–5.

[28] Bala I., Bhamrah M.S., Singh G. 'Capacity in fading environment based on soft sensing information under spectrum sharing constraints'. *Wireless Networks*. 2017;**23**(2):519–31.

[29] Bala I., Bhamrah M.S., Singh G. 'Investigation on outage capacity of spectrum sharing system using CSI and SSI under received power constraints'. *Wireless Networks*. 2019;**25**(3):1047–56.

[30] Hasan M., Hossain E., Niyato D. 'Random access for machine-to-machine communication in LTE-advanced networks: issues and approaches'. *IEEE Communications Magazine*. 2013;**51**(6):86–93.

[31] Lien S.Y., Chen K.C. 'Massive access management for QoS guarantees in 3GPP machine-to-machine communications'. *IEEE Communications Letters*. 2012;**23**(09):1752–61.

[32] Rubeena R., Bala I. 'Throughput enhancement of cognitive radio networks through improved frame structure'. *International Journal of Computer Applications*. 2015;**109**(14):40–3.

[33] Liu R., Wu W., Zhu H., Yang D. 'M2M-oriented QoS categorization in cellular network'. *Proceedings of 7th IEEE International Conference on Networking and Mobile Computing (WiCOM)*; Beijing, China; 2011. pp. 1–5.

[34] Machine to Machine (M2M) Evaluation. 'Methodology document (EMD) broadband wireless access Working group'. 2010.

[35] Mehmood Y., Görg C., Muehleisen M., Timm-Giel A. 'Mobile M2M communication architectures, upcoming challenges, applications, and future directions'. *EURASIP Journal on Wireless Communications and Networking*. 2015;**2015**(250).

[36] Le N.T., Hossain M.A., Islam A., Kim D.-yun., Choi Y.-J., Jang Y.M. 'Survey of promising technologies for 5G networks'. *Mobile Information Systems*. 2016:25.

[37] Dighriri M. 'Data traffic model in machine to machine communications over 5G network slicing'. *IEEE 9th International Conference on Developments in eSystems Engineering (DeSE)*; 2016. pp. 239–44.

[38] Tran D.-D., Ha D.-B., Nayyar A. 'A wireless power transfer under secure communication with multiple antennas and eavesdroppers'. *Proceedings of International Conference on Industrial Networks and Intelligent Systems*; Cham, August; 2018. pp. 208–20.

[39] Peterson K., Deeduvanu R., Kanjamala P., Boles K. 'A blockchain-based approach to health information exchange networks'. *Proceedings of NIST Workshop Blockchain Healthcare*; 2016. pp. 1–10.

[40] Zhang P., Walker M.A., White J., Schmidt D.C., Lenz G. 'Metrics for assessing blockchain-based healthcare decentralized apps'. *IEEE 19th International Conference on e-Health Networking, Applications and Services (Healthcom)*; 2017. pp. 1–4.

[41] Alhadhrami Z., Alghfeli S., Alghfeli M., Abedlla J.A., Shuaib K. 'Introducing blockchains for healthcare'. *Proceedings of the IEEE International Conference on Electrical and Computing Technologies and Applications (ICECTA)*; Ras Al Khaimah, UAE, November; 2017. pp. 21–3.

[42] Fernández-Caramés T.M., Fraga-Lamas P. 'A review on the use of blockchain for the Internet of things'. *IEEE Access*. 2018;**6**:32979–3001.

[43] Kuo T.-T., Hsu C.-N., Ohno-Machado L. 'ModelChain: decentralized privacy-preserving healthcare predictive modeling framework on private blockchain networks'. *arXiv 2016, arXiv:1802*. 2018;**01746**.

[44] Tanwar S., Tyagi S., Kumar N. *Security and Privacy of Electronics Healthcare Records The IET Book Series on E-health Technologies, Institution of Engineering and Technology*. Stevenage: United Kingdom; 2019. pp. 1–450.

[45] Hathaliya J.J., Tanwar S. 'An exhaustive survey on security and privacy issues in healthcare 4.0'. *Computer Communications*. 2020;**153**(6):311–35.

[46] Zheng Z., Xie S., Dai H., Chen X., Wang H. 'An overview of blockchain technology: architecture, consensus, and future trends'. *proceedings of the 2017 IEEE International Congress on Big Data (BigData Congress)*; Honolulu, HI, USA, June; 2017.

[47] Kamel Boulos M.N., Wilson J.T., Clauson K.A. 'Geospatial blockchain: promises, challenges, and scenarios in health and healthcare'. *International Journal of Health Geographics*. 2018;**17**(1):25.

[48] Hertig A. *Blockchain's once-feared 51 percent attack is now becoming regular* [online]. 2018. Available from https://www.coindesk.com/blockchains-feared-51-attack-now-becoming-regular/ [Accessed 18 Aug 2020].

[49] Linn L.A., Koo M.B. 'Blockchain for health data and its potential use in health it and health care related research'. *ONC/NIST Use of Blockchain for Healthcare and Research Workshop*; ONC/NIST: Gaithersburg, MD, USA; 2016.

[50] Hathaliya J.J., Tanwar S., Evans R. 'Securing electronic healthcare records: a mobile-based biometric authentication approach'. *Journal of Information Security and Applications*. 2020;**53**(3):102528–14.

[51] Gupta R., Tanwar S., Tyagi S., Kumar N. 'Tactile Internet and its applications in 5G era: a comprehensive review'. *International Journal of Communication Systems*. 2019;**32**(14):e3981–49.

[52] Tanwar S. *Fog Computing for Healthcare 4.0 Environments: Technical, Societal and Future Implications, Signals and Communication Technology*. Springer International Publishing; 2020. pp. 1–430.

[53] Tanwar S. *Fog Data Analytics for IoT Applications – Next Generation Process Model with State-of-the-Art Technologies, Studies in Big Data*. Springer International Publishing; 2020. pp. 1–550.

[54] Mehta P., Gupta R., Tanwar S. 'Blockchain envisioned UAV networks: challenges, solutions, and comparisons'. *Computer Communications*. 2020;**151**(14):518–38.

[55] Tanwar S., Bhatia Q., Patel P., Kumari A., Singh P.K., Hong W.-C. 'Machine learning adoption in blockchain-based smart applications: the challenges, and a way forward'. *IEEE Access*. 2020;**8**:474–88.

[56] Mistry I., Tanwar S., Tyagi S., Kumar N. 'Blockchain for 5G-enabled IoT for industrial automation: a systematic review, solutions, and challenges'. *Mechanical Systems and Signal Processing*. 2020;**135**(5):106382–19.

[57] Kabra N., Bhattacharya P., Tanwar S., Tyagi S. 'MudraChain: blockchain-based framework for automated cheque clearance in financial institutions'. *Future Generation Computer Systems*. 2020;**102**(4):574–87.

[58] Bodkhe U., Tanwar S., Parekh K., *et al.* 'Blockchain for industry 4.0: a comprehensive review'. *IEEE Access*. 2020;**8**:79764–800.

[59] Tanwar S., Parekh K., Evans R. 'Blockchain-based electronic healthcare record system for healthcare 4.0 applications'. *Journal of Information Security and Applications*. 2019;**50**:1–14.

[60] Kumari A., Gupta R., Tanwar S., Kumar N. 'A taxonomy of blockchain-enabled softwarization for secure UAV network'. *Computer Communications*. 2020;**161**(12):304–23.

[61] Bodkhe U., Tanwar S. 'A taxonomy of secure data dissemination techniques in IoT environment'. *IET Software*. 2020:1–10.

[62]   Gupta R., Kumari A., Tanwar S., Kumar N. 'Blockchain-envisioned softwarized multi-swarming UAVs to tackle COVID-19 situations'. *IEEE Network.* 2020:1–7.

[63]   Kumari A., Tanwar S., Tyagi S., Kumar N. 'Blockchain-based massive data dissemination handling in IIoT environment'. *IEEE Network.* 2020;**35**(1):318–25.

[64]   Gupta R., Kumari A., Tanwar S. 'A taxonomy of blockchain envisioned edge-as-a-connected autonomous vehicles: risk assessment and framework'. *Transactions on Emerging Telecommunications Technologies.* 2020:1–23.

[65]   Bodkhe U., Tanwar S., Bhattacharyaa P., Kumar N. 'Blockchain for precision irrigation: a systematic review'. *Transactions on Emerging Telecommunications Technologies.* 2020:1–33.

[66]   Kumari A., Gupta R., Tanwar S., Tyagi S., Kumari N. 'When blockchain meets smart grid: exploring demand response management for secure energy trading'. *IEEE Network.* 2020:1–7.

[67]   Kumari A., Gupta R., Tanwar S., Kumar N. 'Blockchain and AI amalgamation for energy cloud management: challenges, solutions, and future directions'. *Journal of Parallel and Distributed Computing.* 2020;**143**(11):148–66.

[68]   Gupta R., Tanwar S., Kumar N., Tyagi S. 'Blockchain-based security attack resilience schemes for autonomous vehicles in industry 4.0: a systematic review'. *Computers & Electrical Engineering.* 2020;**86**(2):106717–15.

[69]   Aggarwal S., Kumar N., Tanwar S. 'Blockchain-envisioned UAV communication using 6G networks: open issues, use cases, and future directions'. *IEEE Internet of Things Journal.* 2020.;**8**(7):5416–41.

[70]   Akram S.V., Malik P.K., Singh R., Anita G., Tanwar S. 'Adoption of blockchain technology in various realms: opportunities and challenges'. *Security and Privacy Journal, Wiley.* 2020:1–17.

[71]   Bhattacharya P., Tanwar S., Bodke U., Tyagi S., Kumar N. 'BinDaaS: blockchain-based deep-learning as-a-service in healthcare 4.0 applications'. *IEEE Transactions on Network Science and Engineering.* 2019:1–14.

Index